Old Ways New Roads

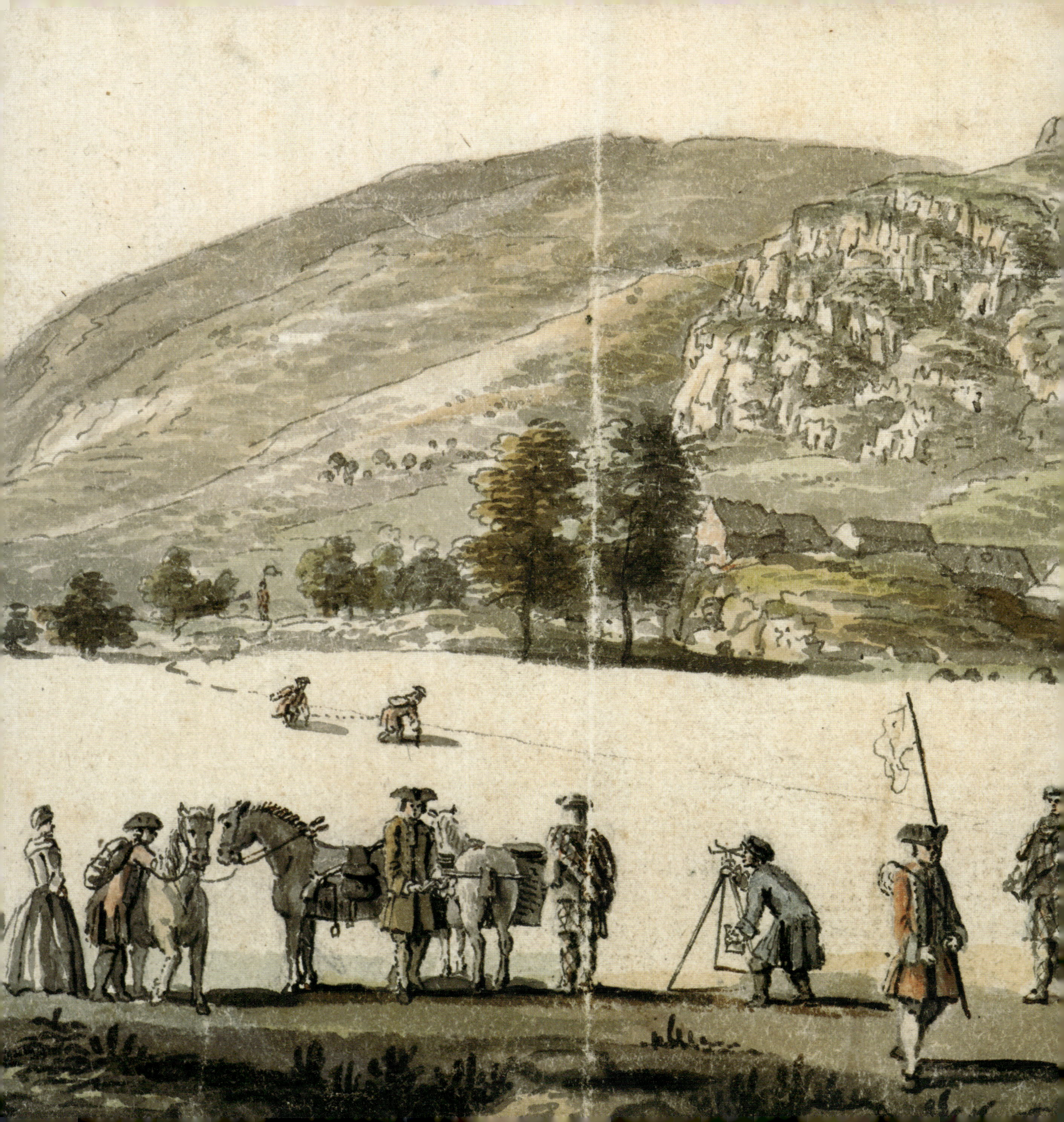

Old Ways New Roads

TRAVELS IN SCOTLAND 1720–1832

EDITED BY

John Bonehill, Anne Dulau Beveridge and Nigel Leask

Birlinn
in association with The Hunterian

Previous spread. Paul Sandby, *Surveying Party by Kinloch (Loch) Rannoch* (detail), 1748, watercolour, pen and ink (BL K.Top 50.83.2)

First published in Great Britain in 2021 by
Birlinn Ltd

West Newington House
10 Newington Road
Edinburgh
EH9 1QS

www.birlinn.co.uk

ISBN: 978 1 78027 667 0

British Library Cataloguing-in-Publication Data
A catalogue record for this book is available on request from the British Library

Typeset and designed by Mark Blackadder

Printed and bound in Latvia by PNB

CONTENTS

FOREWORD

Mungo Campbell,
Deputy-Director, The Hunterian

Over the past couple of decades, through a sustained programme of research and exhibition-making, The Hunterian has devoted particular institutional energy to a thorough re-evaluation of its eighteenth-century origins. While its founder William Hunter's intellectual roots drew deeply on his Scottish Enlightenment upbringing and education, his collecting activities were mainly centred around London's auction houses and book dealers and more widely across Europe. Having left Scotland in the early 1740s, Hunter rarely ventured far from London. He never made a European Grand Tour and he probably only returned to Scotland on a couple of occasions before his death in 1782.

Only one Scottish landscape painting is known to have entered Hunter's collection. While The Hunterian's subsequent benefactors have helped ensure that later nineteenth- and twentieth-century holdings of Scottish art are particularly strong, pre-Victorian representations of Scotland, by visitors to Scotland or Scots themselves, were long notable by their absence. Although significant acquisitions have been made to fill some of these gaps in the collections over the last twenty years, the proposal to develop the exhibition *Old Ways New Roads* was particularly welcome, making accessible as it does significant new research in this field undertaken among our wider academic community at the University of Glasgow. Much of this work has harnessed the rich resources held by Special Collections in the University Library. Their collaboration and enthusiasm for this project has, as always, been essential to its success.

The exhibition and publication appear just over forty years after the groundbreaking investigation of the subject undertaken by James Holloway and Lindsay Errington in the 1978 exhibition (*The Discovery of Scotland*) at the National Gallery of Scotland. As John Bonehill, The Hunterian's Anne Dulau Beveridge and Nigel Leask have demonstrated repeatedly during the development of this project, while the nature of research around Scotland, and its landscape from the 1720s onwards, has been transformed over the intervening decades, nobody can venture into this field without acknowledging a significant debt of gratitude to their predecessors.

In assembling a variety of eighteenth- and early nineteenth-century materials from an exceptionally wide and generous group of lenders, *Old Ways New Roads* offers a new and deeply compelling narrative about the Scottish landscape as it is experienced by the twenty-first-century visitor. Other projects, notably *Guga: Exploring Gaelic Identities* staged at The Hunterian in 2019, have sought to examine linguistic and material aspects of Scottish identity though strong collaboration with colleagues in the College of Arts at the University of Glasgow, and future projects will continue to challenge traditional material and museological approaches to these aspects of our collections. Rooted as deeply as possible in our historic collections, The Hunterian continues to ask important questions about contemporary Scotland.

NOTES ON CONTRIBUTORS

John Bonehill is Lecturer in Art History at the University of Glasgow, and has published widely on various aspects of eighteenth-century British art and culture.

Mary-Ann Constantine is Reader at the University of Wales Centre of Advanced Welsh and Celtic Studies based at Aberystwyth. She has published widely on travel writing and the cultural history of eighteenth-century Wales.

Hugh Cheape is Professor at Sabhal Mòr Ostaig, University of the Highlands and Islands, and was formerly Principal Curator in the National Museums Scotland.

Viccy Coltman is Professor of eighteenth-century History of Art at the University of Edinburgh, who specialises in visual and material culture, with a special focus on Scotland.

Christopher Dingwall is an independent landscape historian with a special interest in garden history. He is a trustee and Vice Chairman of Scotland's Garden and Landscape Heritage.

Anne Dulau Beveridge is Curator at The Hunterian, University of Glasgow, with a strong focus on eighteenth-century British and French art.

Fredrik Albritton Jonsson is Associate Professor of British History at the University of Chicago, and an expert on political economy, history of science and environmental history.

Nigel Leask is Regius Professor of English Language and Literature, University of Glasgow, and an expert on Romanticism, empire and travel writing.

Finola O'Kane is Professor in the School of Architecture, Planning and Environmental Policy at University College, Dublin. She is an expert on the designed landscape history of Ireland and of the Atlantic world.

Christina Young is Professor of Conservation and Technical Art History at the University of Glasgow, and is a specialist in the history of painted canvas and theatrical scenery.

ACKNOWLEDGEMENTS

Research

The first debt to acknowledge is to the contributors to the publication: Fredrik Albritton Jonsson, Hugh Cheape, Viccy Coltman, Mary-Ann Constantine, Christopher Dingwall, Finola O'Kane and Christina Young. They have liberally shared their expert knowledge, and their respective chapters throw new light on many of the themes at the heart of this book. We are also very grateful to them for delivering their texts on time despite the usual constraints of tight schedules and other commitments.

Many colleagues in Glasgow and elsewhere have helped in various ways with research and enquiries, including Neil Clark, Jesper Ericsson, John Faithfull, Nicky Reeves and Joseph Sharples at The Hunterian; Julie Gardham, Robert Maclean, Kirsteen McCue, Sally Tuckett and Rhona Brown at the University of Glasgow; the Duke of Fife; Alison Diamond at Argyll Estates; Rory Powell and Scott MacDonald at Buccleuch Estates; Charlotte Rostek at Mount Stuart; Joannah Meacock at Glasgow Life; Keren Guthrie at Blair Atholl Estate; Patricia Allerston, Helen Smailes, Charlotte Topsfield and Hannah Brocklehurst at the National Galleries of Scotland; Kim Sloan at the British Museum; Michael Allan, Julie Gibb and Emily Taylor at the National Museums of Scotland; Charles Wemyss; Patricia Andrews and Iain Gordon Brown; Felicity Myrone, Alexandra Ault, Laura Walker, Barbara O'Connor and Tom Harper at the British Library; Paula Williams and Chris Fleet at the National Library of Scotland; Mary Miers; Charles Withers at Edinburgh University; Robin Rodger at the Royal Scottish Academy; Ailsa Hutton; Lorna Mitchell and Henry Noltie at the Royal Botanic Garden of Edinburgh; Diana Simpson; William Murray; Julieann Koch, Stephen Daniels, and last but not least James Holloway.

Particular thanks are due to William Zachs and Sir Robert Clerk of Penicuik for their support to the project, for generously facilitating access to their collections and for sharing their knowledge.

We also wish to acknowledge Mairi Sutherland at Birlinn for her skilful editing.

Substantial help in reading and commenting on drafts was received from Mungo Campbell. Thank you.

Support

In 2018 and 2019 two workshops, gathering contributors to the publication and researchers from different fields, were organised thanks to a grant from the Centre for Scottish and Celtic Studies; thanks are due to Catriona Macdonald for her enthusiasm towards the project.

The Paul Mellon Centre for Studies in British Art provided much appreciated help towards the cost of illustrations through its publication grant scheme.

The publication was made possible by a grant from the Gordon Fraser Charitable Trust, whose continuous generous support of The Hunterian's publishing ventures has proved invaluable over the last two decades.

Photography

The most important groups of images reproduced in this publication are from William Zachs's collection, the British Library, the British Museum, Glasgow Life, the University of Glasgow Collections, the National Galleries of Scotland and the Royal Botanic Garden, Edinburgh. A number of private collectors have been very generous in allowing access to their home for the commissioning of photography of works rarely, if ever, published before. Colleagues in Archives and Special Collections, University of Glasgow, have been equally accommodating when facilitating and organising new photography for works in our collections. Margaret Wilson, of National Museums Scotland, was generous in accommodating use of images at a late stage.

We would like to record our thanks to all institutions and individuals who have efficiently and promptly assisted us in gathering the 200 or so colour images reproduced in the publication, particularly considering the exceptional circumstances during which they had to be compiled.

Special thanks are due to Alicia Hughes, ex-curatorial assistant at The Hunterian, who has tirelessly and cheerfully worked against many odds to gather illustrations, and to Antonia Reeve, for carrying out the photography of private collections despite the many challenges associated with the current circumstances.

Details regarding specific photographic credits are at the end of this publication.

Loans

A number of individuals and institutions who have provided images for this publication have also kindly agreed to lend objects to the exhibition it accompanies. The exhibition will take place from 29 January to 9 May 2021 at The Hunterian Art Gallery, University of Glasgow.

The Hunterian would like to take this opportunity to thank Atholl Estate, the British Library, the British Museum, the Buccleuch Collections, Ian Gordon Brown and Patricia Andrew, Sir Robert Clerk of Penicuik, Glasgow Museums, the University of Glasgow Archives and Special Collections, the Fife Collection, the Fitzwilliam Museum, Nigel Leask, Mount Stuart Trust, the National Galleries of Scotland, the National Library of Scotland, National Museums Scotland, the Royal Botanic Garden Edinburgh and William Zachs for their generosity.

John Bonehill, Anne Dulau Beveridge and Nigel Leask

INTRODUCTION

In 1725 General George Wade, the newly appointed Commander- in-Chief of His Majesty's Forces in North Britain, was tasked with overseeing a massive road- and bridge-building programme that would transform the Scottish landscape, connecting the 'chain of forts' constructed by the Williamite and Hanoverian monarchs in order to pacify the Highlands and tame any recurrent Jacobite military threat like that unleashed in 1715 and in 1719 (Fig. 0.1). Among other factors, government control had been severely stymied by Scotland's 'old ways'; the lack of a modern transport infrastructure over intractable terrain made many areas all but inaccessible and frustrated the movement of troops. Writing in the 1720s and 1730s, Edmund Burt, an English rent collector stationed at Inverness in the uneasy period between the two major Jacobite wars, complained that 'the old Ways (for Roads I shall not call them) consisted chiefly of stony Moors, Bogs, rugged, rapid Fords, Declivity of Hills, entangling Woods, and giddy Precipices' (Burt 1998, 282). Burt's punning 'old Ways' also played on the link between archaic travel and Scotland's traditional culture, both of which were being rapidly changed by the forces of enlightened, modern progress.[1]

In his *Letters from the North of Scotland*, eventually published in 1754, Burt weighed up some of the problems facing the topographer seeking to understand and master the mountainous crags of the Highlands, arguing: 'if it had been possible for me to procure a Landskip (I should say Heath-skip or Rock-skip) of any one tremendous view among the Mountains, it would be satisfactory and informing at one single Cast of the Eye' (Burt 1998, 154). However, the Highlands refused any such pictorialist control, 'compose'd [as they are] of Hills . . . piled one upon another, till the Complication rises and swells to Mountains, of which the Heads are frequently above the Clouds' (Burt 1998, 155: Macleod 2012, 22–23). They baffled the eye and put up obstacles against its smooth passage. Being composed of a palette of 'a dismal gloomy Brown, drawing upon a dirty Purple', there was only a sense of dreary monotony (Burt 1998, 157). So disorientating was the experience that the traveller unfamiliar with the 'old ways' was forced to 'creep slowly on, between the Hills in rocky Ways, sometimes over those Eminencies, and often on their Declivity, continually hoping the next Ridge before you will be the Summit of the highest, and so often deceiv'd in that Hope, as almost to despair of ever reaching the Top' (Burt 1998, 160). For Burt, this barren, inhospitable wilderness was an appropriate backdrop for the scenes of dirt, poverty, barbarity and superstition he claimed to witness among its peoples. It was as bleak and dull as their lives. What promised to alleviate their situation, economies and ways of life, as well as the 'tedious passages' of travellers in Scotland, was the construction of Wade's military road network described and praised by Burt. In his final letter, he claimed that 'the Roads on these Moors are [now] . . . as smooth as Constitution Hill, and I have galloped

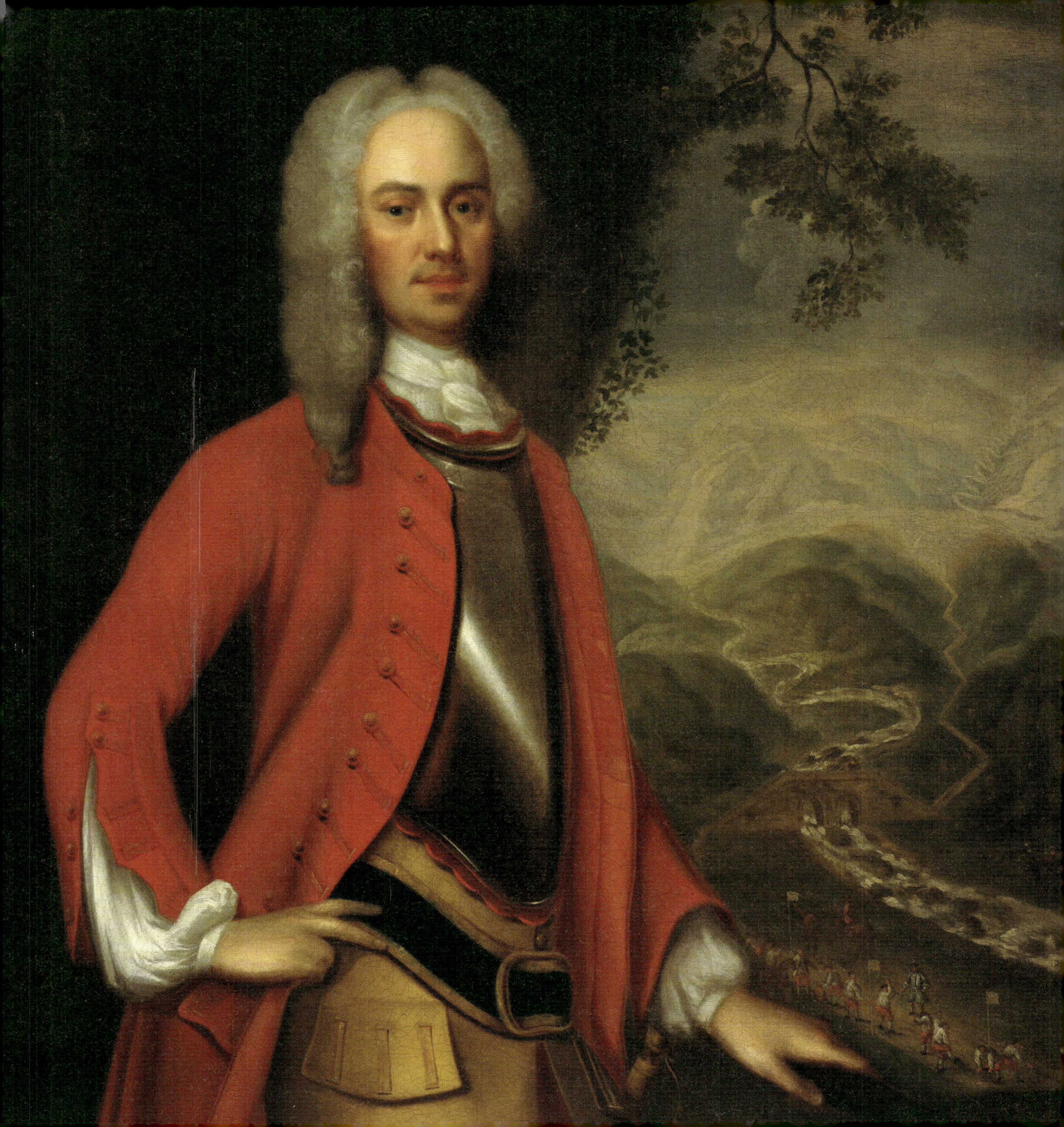

on some of them for Miles together in great Tranquillity' (Burt 1998, 282–283).

Over the next half century or more, the laying out of the new roads opened up Scotland not only to the forces of British militarism but also to commerce and trade, as well as to philosophical and scenic tourism, as a recent theatre of war became imbued with aesthetic and topographical significance. Sites and places, ancient and modern, ruinous and thriving, were brought into view by travelling along Wade's roads, as well as those constructed by his successor Major William Caulfeild, and later (after the Parliamentary Roads Act of 1803) by the Scottish engineer Thomas Telford, not to mention the new canals and steamboat routes that further opened up Scotland's most scenic regions and coasts in the early decades of the nineteenth century (Haldane 1952, 1962; Taylor 1976; Guldi 2012). Ironically, however, although travel writers routinely described the new roads and bridges, these seemed to hold little attraction for artists, and drawings and paintings are relatively scarce (George Heriot's painting of Telford's bridge at Dunkeld is, however, discussed in Chapter 5; see Fig. C5.15). Scotland's 'improvement' saw investments in agriculture, mining and industry on large, powerful landed estates, and claimed a stake in urban developments, in the growth of coastal ports and 'polite' townscapes. For enlightenment improvers, such measures had a series of overlapping associations and benefits. Variously economic, moral and social, as well as aesthetic, they were held to better the lot of those who lived in, worked or viewed the landscape. The progress of improvement was uneven, however, often put into question and made the subject of anxious debate: in the Highlands especially, the difficulty of extracting income from such a harsh environment, burdened with a growing and often starving population, raised the spectre of the limits of economic growth, which has returned to haunt the twenty-first century (Jonsson 2013).

Above all, the forces of improvement targeted places of Jacobite support, which (despite developing commercial links with the Lowlands) had proved resistant to the influence of state formation, the expansion of Presbyterianism, and the English language (Youngson 1973; Devine 1994a; Macinnes 1996; Clyde 1998). Not everyone shared the Whig enthusiasm for a progressively 'modern' world, as Hugh Cheape demonstrates in Chapter 2: although the isolation of Highland society has been exaggerated by historians, it remains true that large areas were beyond the reach of Hanoverian rule until the 1750s, even after the vigorous repression of clan society following the battle of Culloden in 1746. Some places continued to be bypassed and left behind, or resisted the improving impulse; others were subsequently emptied of population and converted into sheep walks in the notorious clearances (Richards 2002; Devine 2018). But sites and places, old and modern, sometimes seen in instructive or troubling juxtaposition, were brought into view by travel along Scotland's new transport arteries. Travellers' encounters with local scenes in Scotland would evoke comparison with other places, and raise questions about the place of the past in a modernising present, or indeed the place of Scotland and Scottishness in newly minted and contested ideas of British identity (Leask 2020).

The development of the Scottish tour coincided with a rising interest in domestic tourism in the second half of the eighteenth century: some of the parallels with contemporary developments in the other 'Celtic peripheries' of Wales and Ireland are addressed by Mary-Ann Constantine and Finola O'Kane in Chapter 8. The British 'home tour' was also coterminous with two other dominant modes of travel, the European grand tour and global navigation, but was more within the reach of private individuals among the newly affluent middle classes with limited time and resources. (Viccy Coltman opens Chapter 6 with a description of John Elliot's cabin on the long voyage out to India in order to highlight these connections.) There was a considerable overlap between the different forms of travel in the period – for example, Thomas Pennant's 1772 *Tour in Scotland* was dedicated to the Pacific explorer Joseph Banks, who made his own tour of the Western Isles in the same year (Pennant 1998, xxvii–xxviii). Each modality spawned a huge number of publications, often lavishly illustrated with engravings and maps, so that travel literature became one of the most popular reading genres of the age: an interest in natural history, antiquarianism, 'primitive' lifestyles and landscape aesthetics was a feature of domestic as well as exotic and colonial travel writing.

Some forty years or so ago, *The Discovery of Scotland*, a pioneering, landmark exhibition curated in the National Gallery of Scotland by James Holloway and Lindsay Errington, explored 'the appreciation of Scottish scenery', principally through painting and largely over what might be termed the culture of 'Balmorality'

Fig. 0.1
Opposite. Attributed to Johan Van Diest, *Field-Marshall George Wade*, c. 1731, oil on canvas (NGS PG 2416)

Wade was appointed Commander-in-Chief of North Britain in 1724 and sent to the Highlands in the same year. He spent the next eleven years supervising the building of over 250 miles of roads and forty bridges to open up the most inaccessible parts of the country. This portrait of Wade includes in the background soldiers building the military road between Dalwhinnie and Fort Augustus. Crossing the Corrieyairack Pass, the road included no fewer than eighteen traverses, a considerable engineering feat.

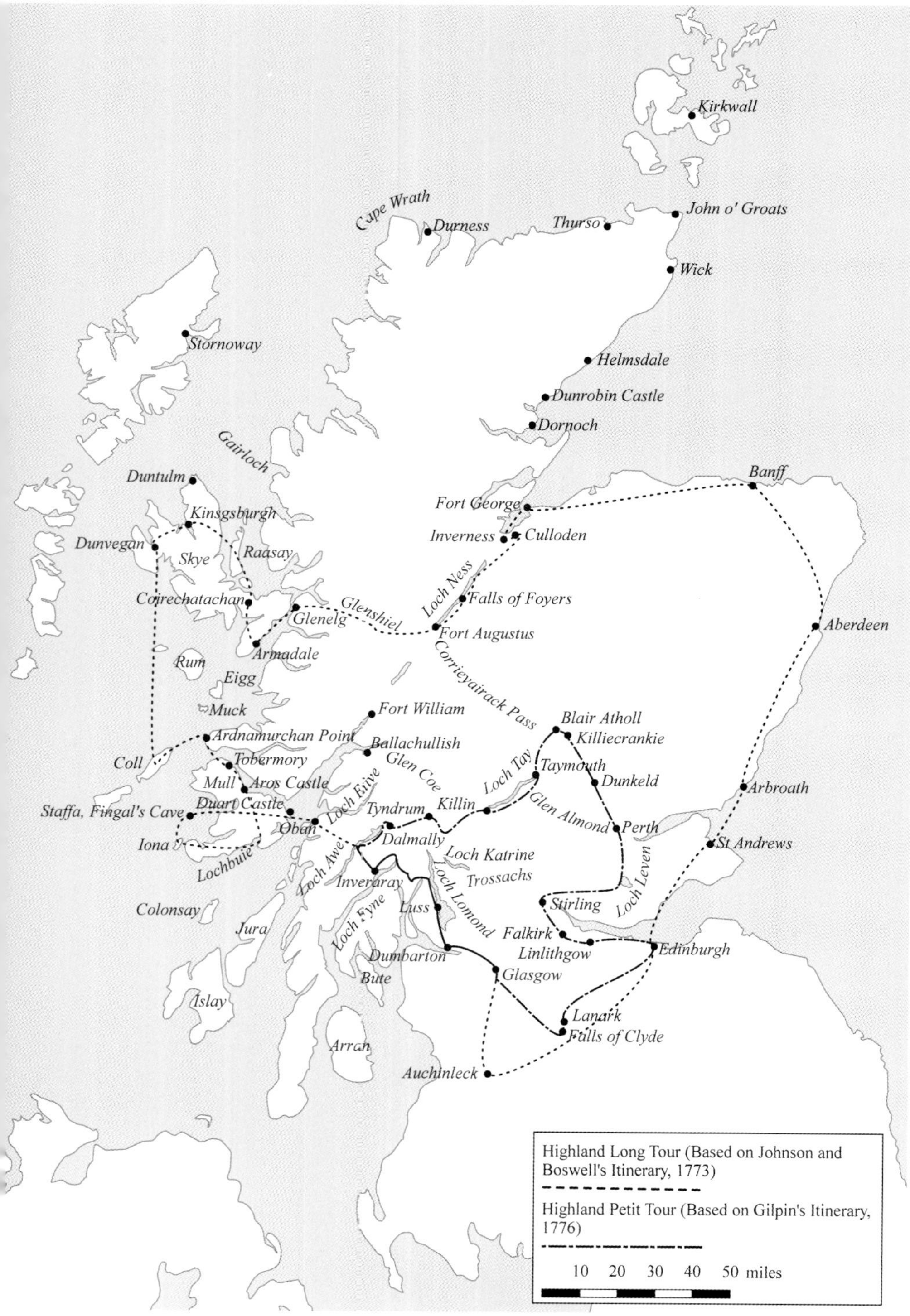

(Holloway and Errington 1978). Though it extended the chronology either side to look at important precedents and the later legacy, its dependence on views of the Scottish landscape in oil paint which only became common in the mid nineteenth century meant that the focus somewhat inevitably fell heavily on the Victorian era. The present book and exhibition seek to retrace some of the steps first taken by *The Discovery of Scotland*, while also breaking new ground. Shifting the chronological focus back over the 'long eighteenth century', we seek to open up a range of different perspectives and priorities in the depiction of Scottish landscape by focusing on the connections between military occupation and the beginnings of modern tourism enabled by the new roads. By exploring these varied though often overlapping fields of knowledge and practice, we seek to demonstrate how the appreciation of the Scottish landscape was not a narrowly aesthetic matter. It was also a terrain of historical, philosophical and scientific enquiry, being remade by a potent mix of commercial, landed, military and political interests. Taken together, the literary and pictorial traces left by this dynamic activity projected a rich and complex range of variously complementary and competing visions of eighteenth-century Scottish land and life.

Old Ways New Roads traces how some of these dramatic changes in the Scottish landscape were variously documented in word and image, evaluated, planned and imagined, and more especially 'framed up' in terms of the experience of travel. The eight chapters specially commissioned for this volume, which is published in association with The Hunterian exhibition *Old Ways New Roads: Travels in Scotland 1720–1832* (29 January to 9 May 2021), bring cross-disciplinary expertise to bear on many of the issues arising from this revolutionary transformation of Scotland's infrastructure. From the 1760s, tourists began to follow in the footsteps of pioneers like Thomas Pennant, Dr Samuel Johnson and Joseph Banks in search of Scotland's natural history, antiquities and 'local manners', explored here by Nigel Leask in Chapter 1, 'Writing the Scottish Tour'. If, in earlier decades, the road-users were mainly soldiers, agriculturalists and businessmen, naturalists and mineralogists, after mid century these were joined by that broad range of society that identified themselves as polite, taking in the sedate scenic pleasures of the so-called *petit tour* or the wilder reaches of the Highlands on the 'long tour' (Fig. 0.2). Pennant seems to have been the first to coin the term *petit tour* to describe the shorter circuit of the Highlands (exemplified by Gilpin's tour of 1776, shown in Fig. 0.2), which could be made in a fortnight by chaise travelling along the military roads, showcasing the 'improved' landscapes and plantations of the Atholl, Breadalbane and Argyll estates, which he described as 'a tract unparalleled, for the variety and frequency of fine and magnificent scenery' (Pennant 1979, 91). The long tour (represented here by Johnson and Boswell's tour) offered a more ambitious itinerary for travellers with more time, money and endurance: it took in Inverness, the Great Glen, the Isle of Skye, and some of the other Western Isles including Mull, Iona, and Staffa, and involved hiring horses, boats and ferries. The majority of Scottish tours took place between spring and autumn, with August and September being the most popular months, for obvious reasons given the challenges of the climate.

Fredrik Albritton Jonsson's chapter on 'Natural History' examines the overriding concern with natural history on the Scottish tour (matched only by a concern for antiquities), from the circuits made by 'economic botanists' in search of new plant species, through an obsession with tree planting, and the researches of mineralogists and geologists in the early nineteenth century, to the travels of enthusiastic amateur naturalists in later decades (Fig. 0.3). After 1780, the proliferation of lavishly illustrated published tours meant that Scottish sites might be enjoyed without leaving the armchair. But nothing could beat experiencing the topography first-hand: artists and travel writers, as well as general readers, were inspired after 1760 by the sublime associations afforded to Scotland's often barren landscapes by James Macpherson's *Poems of Ossian*, the poetry and song of Robert Burns (himself a celebrated Highland tourist) and, latterly, Walter Scott's best-selling verse romances and novels. The international currency of *Ossian* and the works of Scott inspired tourists from France, Germany, Poland and Italy, many of whom enriched the travel literature of their own cultures with published tours of Scotland. (Faujas de Saint-Fond, Alexandre de La Rochefoucauld, Johanna Schopenhauer and Princess Izabela Czartoryska are referred to in the chapters that follow.) However, more work requires to be done on foreign tourists in Scotland in this period.[2] In the earlier decades, publication of tours tended to be the preserve of male travellers (Pococke, Pennant, Boswell and Johnson) but in the wake of William Gilpin's *petit tour* of 1776, eventually published after some delay in 1789, travellers from both sexes sought out sublime and picturesque scenery to complement their interest in antiquities and natural history, sketchbooks in hand, paving the way for the romantic appropriation of Scotland. Although only four British women published Scottish tours in this period, dozens of lively manuscript accounts survive in libraries and archives, and others were subsequently published, such as Dorothy Wordsworth's magnificent *Recollections of a Tour Made in Scotland, 1803* (Walker 1997).[3] Given that the largest number of tourists were from south of the Tweed, it may well have been the case that 'Scotland was formulated and re-formulated in response to English needs' during a period of 'consolidating Britishness'. But it is also true that 'Scots were active participants in tourism, both as sightseers and promoters, and in so doing put forward their own variously complementary or competing definitions of Scotland' (Glendening 1997, 10; Grenier 2005, 29). This was as true of the inhabitants of the Highlands as of the Lowlands, as Hugh Cheape reminds us in Chapter 2, underlining the extent to which Gaels were often themselves active agents, as well as passive objects of an anglo-centric tourist gaze.

Travellers engaged with urban as well as rural scenes, reached along and off the coast, and took in the fertile lowlands as well as Scotland's mountainous uplands and islands. They headed for sites of antiquity, natural wonders like mountains and water-

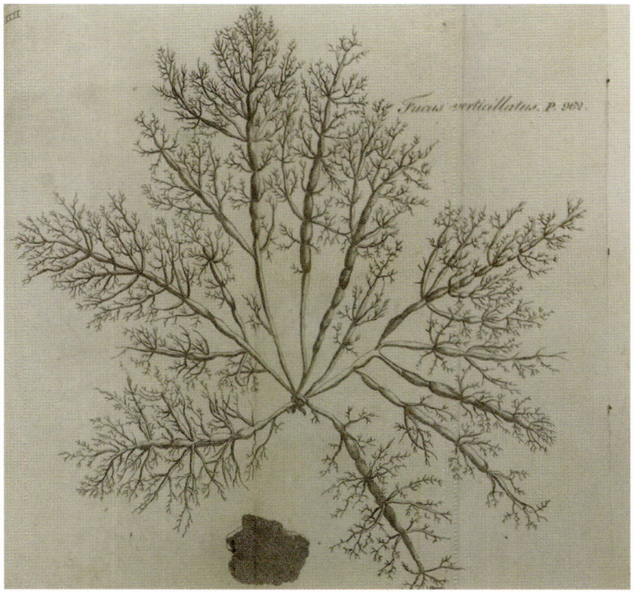

Fig. 0.2
Opposite. Alex Deans, Map of Petit and Long Tours, in Nigel Leask, *Stepping Westward: Writing the Highland Tour, c. 1720–1830* (Oxford, 2020), p. 15

Fig. 0.3
Below. Peter Mazell, *Fucus verticillatus*, engraving in John Lightfoot, *Flora Scotica: Or A Systematic Arrangement, in the Linnaean Method, of the Native Plants of Scotland and the Hebrides* (London, 1792), pl. XXXI opposite p. 962 (GLA ASC Mu53-d.29)

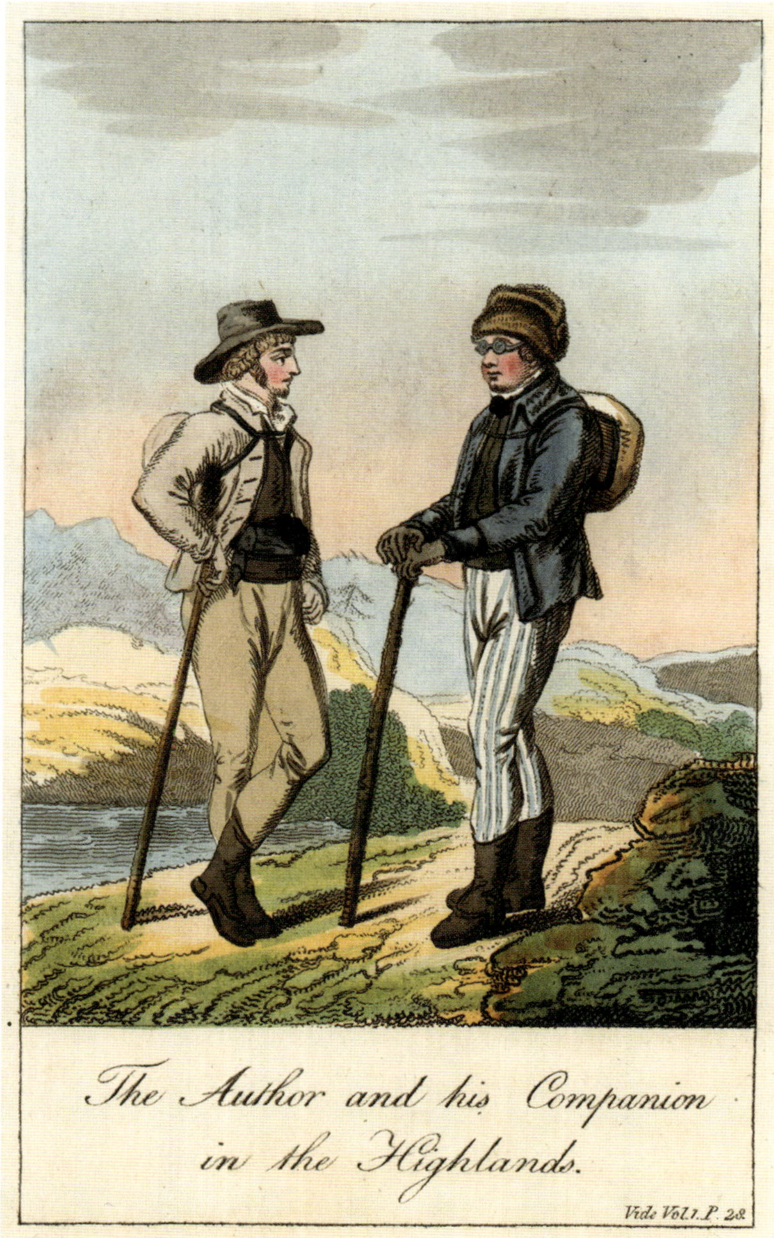

falls, as well as modern designed landscapes that in places employed such features to theatrical effect. Artists and writers, as discussed by John Bonehill in Chapter 5, would fashion their experience or the country's myths and histories into highly imaginative narratives staged in these landscapes, exploiting the aesthetic conventions of the beautiful, the sublime and the picturesque. Although the romantic taste for the sublime has been linked to the devastating effect of clearances and the introduction of sheep faming in many areas of Scotland, travellers were often vocal in condemning economic policies that resulted in emigration and environmental degradation (Womack 1989). Of particular interest is the way in which the work of tour writers and artists was shaped by these places, as well as itself shaping subsequent descriptions and views of them. To this end, a number of pivotal sites are discussed in the essays collected here, notably Edinburgh, Dunkeld ('Ossian's Hall'), Staffa ('Fingal's Cave') and the Falls of Clyde (Cora Linn; see Fig. S4.6), as well as Loch Katrine and the Trossachs, a relative latecomer to the tourist circuit, but one immortalised in Scott's verse romance *The Lady of the Lake* (1810) (see Fig. S4.2). The relationship between estate management, layouts and tourism is addressed by Christopher Dingwall in Chapter 4, underlining the role played by powerful landowners in promoting tourism, especially the Dukes of Atholl and Argyll, and the Earls of Breadalbane, whose improved and landscaped policies (the areas immediately surrounding a house) were showcased on the *petit tour*.

At the heart of this book lies the 'tourist paradox' that the romantic fascination with the 'old ways' of the Scottish Highlands and Lowlands was made possible only by the modern infrastructure of the 'new roads', and later by bridges, canals, inns and steamboats. While pedestrian tourism appealed to those with a Rousseauvian taste for humble life, prepared to wander off the beaten track, the transport revolution meant that the Scottish tour became increasingly commodified from the early decades of the nineteenth century (Fig. 0.4). As the geologist John Macculloch observed haughtily in 1824,

> the mystic portal has been thrown open, and the mob has rushed in, dispersing all these fairy visions, and polluting everything with its unhallowed touch. Barouches and gigs, cocknies and fishermen and poets, Glasgow weavers and travelling haberdashers, now swarm in every resting place, and meet us at every avenue. (Macculloch 1824, I, 195)

In Chapter 6, Viccy Coltman explores 'knick-knack tourism', the material manifestations of just such an emerging cultural practice, immediately prior to the age of railway travel, Victorian Balmoral, and the publication of Black's and Murray's travel guides. At the same time, as Christina Young demonstrates in Chapter 7, painted scenery for theatre and the new fashion for panoramas brought shows of Scottish scenery to an urban public. Loch Lomond could be experienced in a rotunda on Queen Street in Glasgow or the Mound in Edinburgh, or at the Theatres Royal in Glasgow, Edinburgh and London; the metropolitan public was now immersed in the hills and romantic myths of Scotland.

Since *The Discovery of Scotland*, the study of eighteenth-century culture has been subject to radical revision. Landscape, as a material terrain and a mode of representation, has been of central concern to that re-evaluation, not least because the complex issues at play necessarily involve dialogue between art historians, literary scholars, historical geographers and environmental historians. Of late, for instance, there has been a growing interdisciplinary interest with matters of topography, as a field of knowledge and enquiry (Myrone 2009; Barrell 2013).[4] This has seen the genre reassessed as a way of knowing that combined observation and imagination, as well as movement and narrative, often as concerned with a proposed world as with a recorded world. Topography as a genre addressed the relation of people and places in manifold textual as well as visual ways. Especially relevant to our project is new research on the rise of the 'home tour' in eighteenth-century Wales and Ireland, which invites comparison with the case of Scotland, notably in its crossing of linguistic and cultural borders, as discussed by Mary-Ann Constantine and Finola O'Kane in Chapter 8.

Old Ways New Roads seeks to bring this re-evaluation of the Scottish landscape, whether observed, imagined, recorded or experienced, to a wider audience through an accessible and innovative mix of engaging texts and compelling imagery. This book is organised into four thematic, roughly chronological sections, exploring Scotland as 'The Theatre of War', as well as a place of enquiries into 'Antiquities', 'Custom and Improvement' and the staging of 'Picturesque Prospects and Literary Landscapes', with the eight chapters commenting on specific developments within those larger fields of interest.To this end, the sections juxtapose drawings, paintings and prints in various genres, together with maps, travel accounts and examples of the paraphernalia of travel. This material, which is either rarely seen or has not previously been exhibited publicly or published, is drawn principally from Scottish collections, both public and private, and supplemented by a few key loans and images from English and Welsh institutions.[5] Aeneas Macmaster, protagonist of Neil Munro's *The New Road* (1914), ruminates at one point in the novel, expressing his ambivalence regarding General Wade's road: 'It means the end of many things, I doubt, not to be despised, – the last stand of Scotland, and she destroyed. And yet – and yet, this New Road will some day be the Old Road, too, with ghosts on it and memories' (Munro 1994, 281). It is hoped that this book will raise some of these ghosts and memories, in order better to understand the appreciation of Scotland's topography on the cusp of the modern era, and its legacy today in an era of mass tourism, environmental crisis and the urgent quest for a sustainable Highland economy.

John Bonehill, Anne Dulau Beveridge and Nigel Leask

Fig. 0.4
Opposite. Anon., 'The Author and his Companion in the Highlands', frontispiece in John Bristed, *Anthroplanomenos, or, A Pedestrian Tour through Part of the Highlands of Scotland, in 1801* (London, 1803) (GLA ASC Mu11-e.28)

NOTES

1 Robert Macfarlane (2012) also plays on the connection between 'tracks, holloways, drove roads and sea paths' and a 'lost British world' in his best-selling *The Old Ways: A Journey on Foot*.

2 See Alexandre de La Rochefoucauld and Maximilien de Lazowski, *To the Highlands in 1786: The Inquisitive Journey of a Young French Aristocrat*, ed. Norman Scarfe (Suffolk: Boydell & Brewer, 2001). Alison Hiley, '"Scotland's Name is Poetry to our Ears": German Travellers in Scotland c. 1800–1860', *Scottish Archives*, 2 (1996), 24–38; Mona Macleod (ed.), *From Charlotte's Square to Fingal's Cave: Reminiscences of a Journey through Scotland, 1820–24, by Krystyn Lach-Szyrma* (Edinburgh: John Donald, 2004); Allison Lockwood, *Passionate Pilgrims: The American Traveller in Great Britain, 1800–1914* (Associated University Presses Inc., 1981); John Hollier and Anita Hollier, 'French and German Views of Scotland in 1821: Charles Nodier's *Promenade de Dieppe aux montagnes d'Ecosse*, and Louis-Alber Necker's *Voyage en Ecosse et aux Iles Hebrides*', *Studies in Travel Writing*, 23:2 (2019), 99–118.

3 Although surprisingly there is still no modern scholarly edition of *Recollections* (Kinsley 2008; Hagglund 2010). See also the edited tours written by women published on *Curious Travellers* website: https://editions.curioustravellers.ac.uk/pages/tours.html.

4 See also the essays collected as *Picturing Places*, as part of the British Library project *Transforming Topography*: https://www.bl.uk/picturing-places.

5 The exhibition is linked to the AHRC-funded *Curious Travellers: Thomas Pennant and the Welsh and Scottish Tour 1760–1820* (Co-investigator Leask, Principal Investigator Constantine, University of Wales) (http://curioustravellers.ac.uk/en/).

CHAPTER ONE

Writing the Scottish Tour 1720–1830

Nigel Leask

Just as the new military roads, and their accompanying infrastructure of bridges, fords and inns, transformed the 'old ways' of Highland Scotland, they also created the material conditions for the new domestic tourism that emerged in the decades after 1760. There is no doubt that the old ways had deterred visitors: when Thomas Pennant made his first tour of Scotland in 1769, he wrote that Scotland 'was almost as little known to its southern brethren as *Kamtschatka*' (in fact, as Hume Brown demonstrated back in 1891, this 'terra incognita' had featured in travellers' narratives since the late Middle Ages) (Pennant 1793, 11; Brown 1973; Rackwitz 2007). Four years later, another pioneer of the Scottish tour, Dr Johnson, noted of the Wade road from Inverness to Fort Augustus that 'we went upon a surface so hard and level, that we had little care to hold the bridle, and were therefore at full leisure for contemplation' (Black 2007, 80). Although Johnson's *A Journey to the Western Islands of Scotland* hardly anticipated romanticism, his narrative suggested a link between the new roads and a new interiority, allowing visitors to cultivate an aesthetic response to the unfolding landscape, while travelling at an accelerated pace between dedicated inns and staging posts, rather than scrutinising their next footfall, wary of stumbling into bogs, holes and other obstructions.

Much of the novelty and interest of eighteenth-century travel writing about Scotland lies in its descriptive empiricism, partly motivated by English curiosity about its northern neighbour half a century after the 1707 Act of Union, and following the defeat of Jacobitism in 1746; it was a curiosity shared by many Lowland Scots regarding the previously inaccessible Highlands, and later in the period by European and other foreign visitors (Kinsley 2008; Colbert 2012). This essay explores some of these themes in Scottish tour literature c. 1720–1830, which made an important contribution to the modern literature of place, providing a catalyst for thinking about landscape, history and ecology, as well as debating Scottish and British identities in a manner that still resonates today.

The Englishman Edmund Burt was part of General Wade's circle, employed as a government rent collector for the forfeited Jacobite estates between the two Jacobite wars of 1715 and 1745 (see Fig. 0.1). His urbane, *Spectator*-style spotlight on Highland manners, and his pioneering attempts to describe Highland travel and topography, mark a departure from earlier written accounts of Scotland by topographers, antiquarians and travel writers like William Camden, Martin Martin, John Mackie and Daniel Defoe. Burt's egotistical style and novelistic attention to 'the commerce of everyday life' distinguish *Letters from a Gentleman in the North of Scotland* (Burt 1998 [1754]) from earlier travel accounts, with their interest in great houses, antiquarian monuments, natural curiosities or economic improvement. Although offering a fascinating description of traditional clan society on the eve of its demise, the tone of *Letters* is waspishly anglocentric, everywhere seeking (quite literally) to 'do the dirt' on Scotland: thus Burt's Highland huts look like 'Heaps of Dirt', and their inhabitants are 'as black as Chimney-Sweepers' (Burt 1998 [1754], 201–202, 207); see Fig. C1.1. As discussed in the introduction to the present book, even the topography looked abject, without betraying a hint of the new taste for the sublime: 'huge naked Rocks, being just above the Heath, produce the disagreeable appearances of a scabbed Head . . . [mountains] of a dismal gloomy Brown, drawing upon a dirty Purple; and most of all disagreeable when the Heath is in Bloom' (Burt 1998, 155, 157). Burt's account of two Highland excursions travelling on the 'old ways', and his final letter's valuable description of Wade's road-building programme in the 1720s and 1730s, offered his own John Bullish solution to the problem of Highland 'backwardness'.

Burt's prejudiced portrait of the Highlands may explain why subsequent travel writers during the period of 'reconciliation' after 1760, when Gaels were being recruited wholesale into the military service of Britain's empire, failed even to mention his book. It was, however, rediscovered in the Romantic period by Sir Walter Scott, who drew heavily on its ethnographic information for the Highland settings of his best-selling verse romances and his novel *Waverley*. Despite its publication date, *Letters from a Gentleman in the North of Scotland* really belongs to the propaganda literature of the previous decade, works like Michael Hughes's *Narrative or Journal of the Late Rebellion* (1746) and *Journey through Parts of England and Scotland with the Army under . . . the Duke of Cumberland* (1747), attributed to 'A Volunteer', or, from the Jacobite side, Captain John Maclean of Kingairloch's 'Journal of the Forty-Five by a Jacobite officer' (Brown and Cheape 2010). The Duke of Cumberland's campaign of terror following Culloden was followed by a whole set of pacifying and 'improving' measures, including William Roy's 'Great Map' commission, involving Paul Sandby and other artists employed by the Board of Ordnance (discussed in Section 1 'The Theatre of War'), all of them important harbingers of romantic tourism and topographical art.

Roy's employment on the post-Culloden military survey provided an opportunity to develop his antiquarian interest in Roman Britain, which he called 'the lucubrations of [my] leisure hours' (Fleet, Wilkes and Withers 2012, 88); see Fig. S1.7. In 1755 Roy had surveyed and mapped the Antonine Wall; after

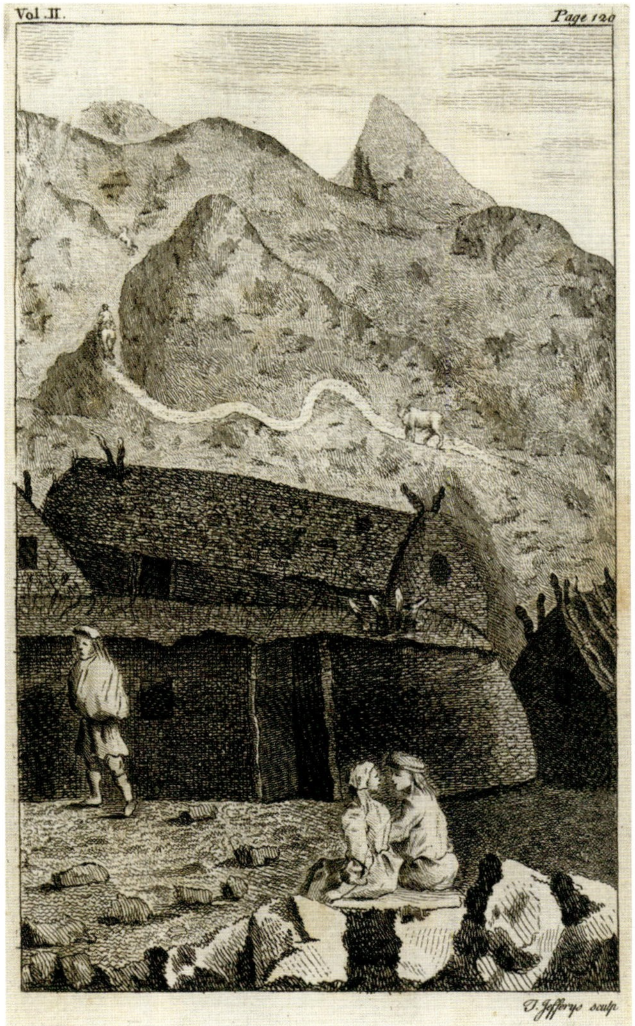

Fig. C1.1
J. Jefferys, 'Highland Township', etching and engraving in Edmund Burt, *Letters from a Gentleman in the North of Scotland* (London, 1759), Vol. II, opposite p. 121 (GLA ASC BG52-d.20)

his death, in 1793 the Society of Antiquaries of London published his *Military Antiquities*, a lavish volume in grand folio with fine maps and engravings of Roman forts and other related antiquities (see Fig. S2.1). But the mood was changing with the removal of the Jacobite threat: after the publication of James Macpherson's epical 'translations' of the Gaelic *Poems of Ossian* in the early 1760s, 'Agricolamania' or identification with Roman conquest of Scotland was complemented by a new sympathy for the defeated 'Caledonians', inspiring a series of hallmark sites for tourists in quest of sublime Ossianic topography. (This is further discussed in Section 2 'Antiquities'.) Although Macpherson was

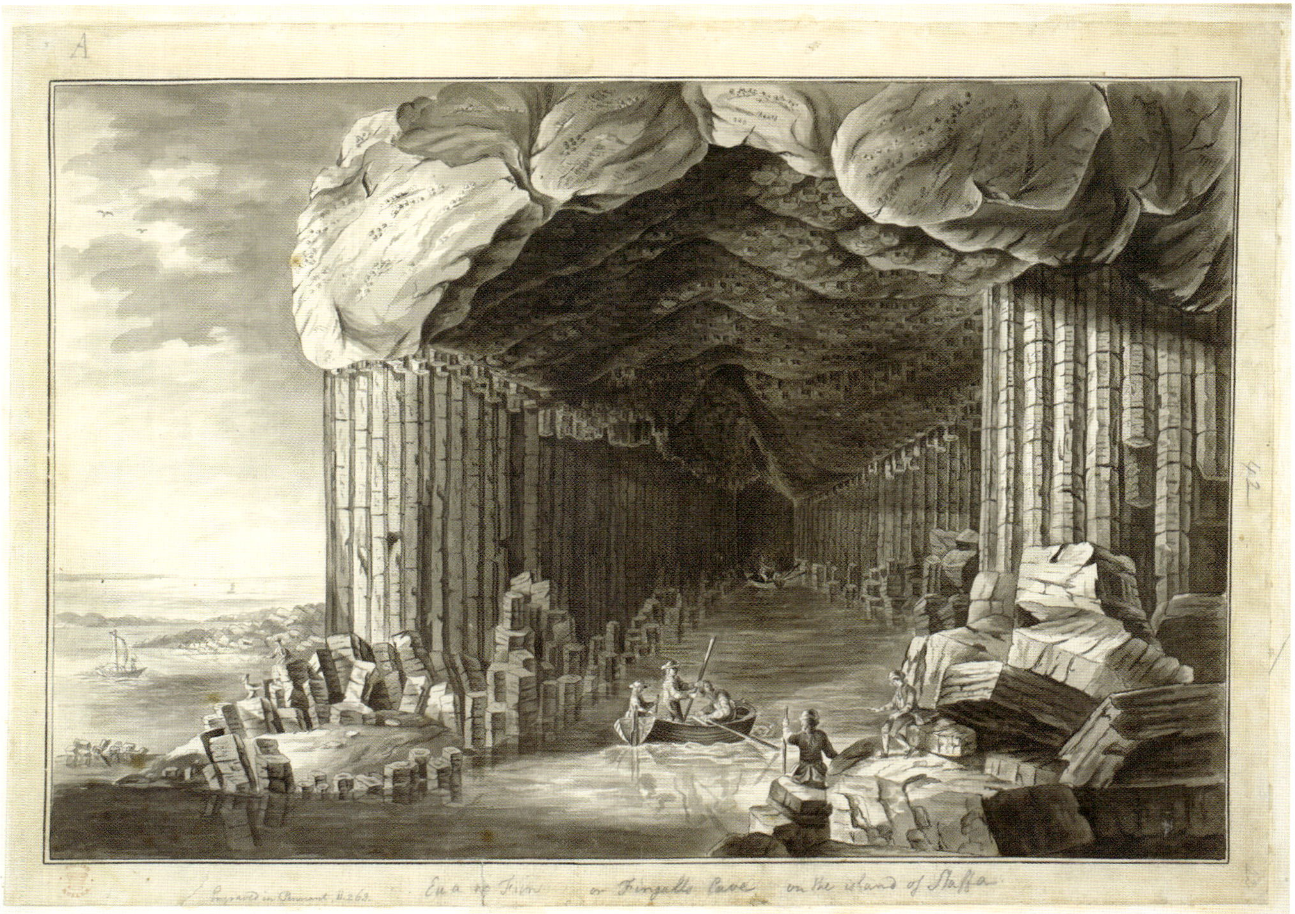

Fig. C1.2
John Cleveley the Younger, *Eua na Fion or Fingalls Cave, on the Island of Staffa*, 1772, ink drawing (BL Add MS 15 510, f. 43)

accused of having confected his Gaelic sources, the young Joseph Banks, 'discovering' Fingal's Cave on the basaltic Hebridean island of Staffa in 1772, enthused 'Compared to this what are the cathedrals or the palaces built by men! . . . How fortunate that in this cave we should meet with the remembrance of that chief, whose existence, as well as that of the whole *Epic* poem is almost doubted in England' (Pennant 1998, 257–258); see Fig. C1.2.

Despite the new roads, Scottish travel in the 1750s and 1760s was still physically challenging, and early travellers tended to be professional surveyor–naturalists like Dr John Walker and James Robertson, who sought out the prospects for 'economic botany' in the Highlands sponsored by the Board for Forfeited Jacobite Estates, or hardy gentlemen virtuosi like the English antiquarians William Burrell and Bishop Richard Pococke (Jonsson 2013, 28). Although such men travelled widely and described some of the remotest parts of Scotland, their journals remained in manuscript: it was the Welsh naturalist and antiquarian Thomas Pennant who seized the commercial opportunity by publishing his two Scottish Tours of 1769 and 1772. Pennant boasted that he had 'brought home a favourable account of the land . . . shewing that it might be visited with safety, [and] it has ever since been *inondé* with southern visitants' (Pennant 1793, 11). He was also the first traveller writer to publish an adequate visual documentation of Scotland, despite the copious sketches produced by Paul Sandby discussed by John Bonehill in Chapter 5: to this end, the 1772 *Tour in Scotland* contains ninety-one engraved plates, many of them the work of his 'artist servant' Moses Griffith, greatly surpassing the handful of crude plates published in Burt's *Letters*.

Pennant combined the personal authority of the informed traveller's eye with the encyclopaedic protocols of enlightenment knowledge, gleaned from correspondence and pre-circulated questionnaires to Highland ministers, gentlemen and naturalists. He coined the term *petit tour* to describe the circuit of the southern Highlands, travelling the new military roads through Perthshire and Argyll, which he described as 'a tract unparaleled, for the variety and frequency of fine and magnificent scenery' (Pennant 1979, 91); see Fig. 0.2. Manageable by chaise in a couple of weeks from Edinburgh or Glasgow, the *petit tour* showcased the recently improved Highland estates of the Dukes of Atholl, Argyll and the Earl of Breadalbane (described by Christopher Dingwall in Chapter 4), who had all actively invested in tourism, building roads, ferries, inns and viewing stations such as the 'Hermitages' at Dunkeld (see Fig. S2.21) and Acharn, or the gothic folly at Dun na Cuaiche overlooking Loch Fyne. Pennant's eye for scenery and his set-piece descriptions of Highland landscapes (like the views from Beinn na Caillich on Skye or Dundonald in Wester Ross, both illustrated by engravings from Griffith) did much to promote their aesthetic value in the eyes of his contemporaries (Smethurst 2012, 13–30, 27). But for all his praise of the rapid pace of improvement in Scotland, the Welsh traveller could also strike a more critical note, as in his 'vision at Ardmaddie' at the end of the 1772 *Voyage to the Hebrides*, when he criticised rapacious Highland landlords for abandoning their duties of social trusteeship in pursuit of personal profit.

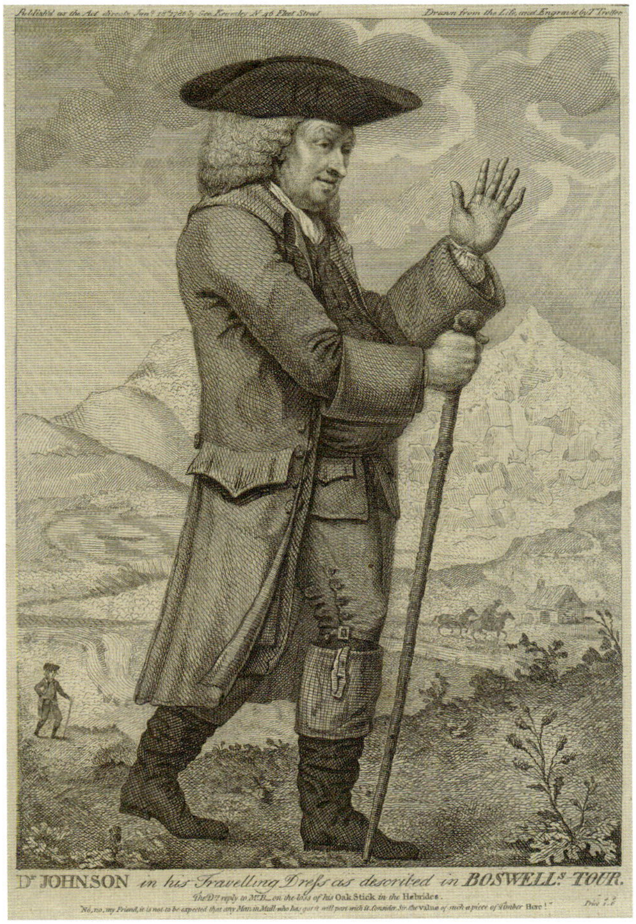

Fig. C1.3
Thomas Trotter, *Dr Johnson in his Travelling Dress*, c. 1750–1803, engraving (YCBA 52865 – B1995.9.12)

The positive Scottish reception of Pennant's *Tours* contrasts markedly with the furore that greeted the 1775 publication of Dr Samuel Johnson's *Journey to the Western Islands*, which described his own Scottish and Hebridean 'long tour' with James Boswell in 1773 (Fig. C1.3). Johnson regretted that 'we came thither too late to see what we expected, a people of peculiar appearance, and a system of antiquated life . . . Of what [the clans] had before the late conquest of their country, there remain only their language and their poverty. Their language is attacked on every side' (Black 2007, 124). But despite his acute reflections on the change in Scottish manners and the threats facing Gaelic culture in the wake of Culloden, Scottish readers resented Johnson's anglocentric perspective, his description of Highland landscape as a 'wide extent of hopeless sterility' (Black 2007, 88) and his denial of the authenticity of *Ossian* and the cultural nationalism that underpinned it. To this extent, his book threatened to undermine Pennant's success in effecting an 'act of union' between 'North' and 'South Britain'. Johnson's *Journey* is, deservedly, the best-known Scottish tour ever written, but it perhaps hasn't been sufficiently realised that the publishing success of Pennant's tours was a major, albeit unacknowledged, stimulus for Johnson, despite being widely commented on by contemporary reviewers. In a reversal of modern judgements, in January 1775 the *Monthly Review* announced that 'Mr Pennant has led the way; Dr Johnson has followed', reading the *Journey* as 'a valuable supplement to Mr Pennant's two accounts of his northern expeditions . . . Dr Johnson [is] . . . the moralist and observer of men and manners . . . [while] the ingenious Cambrian delights in painting sublime

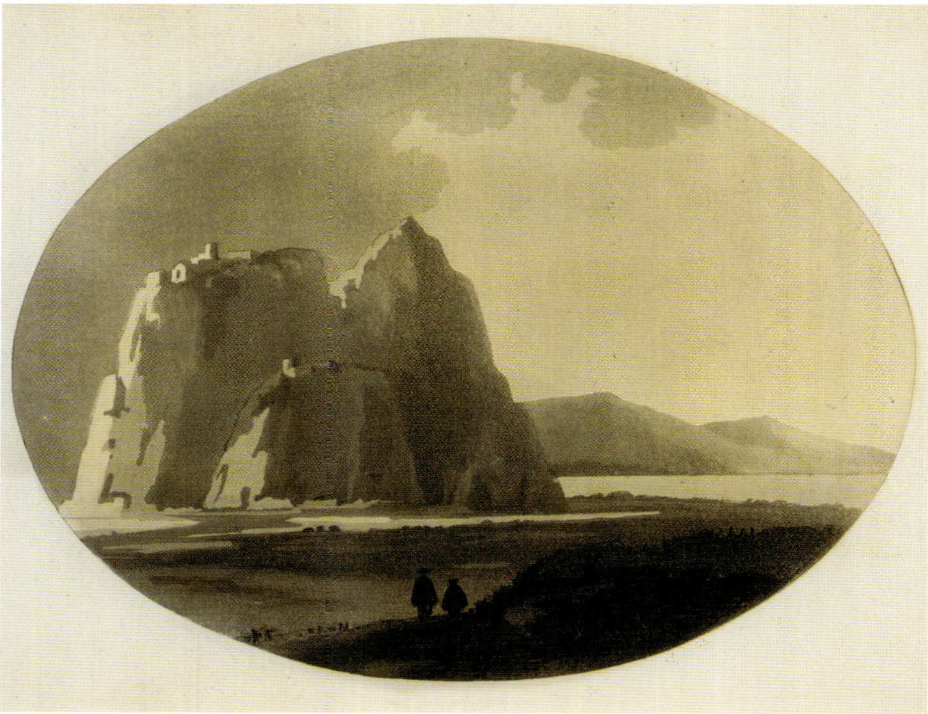

Fig. C1.4
William Gilpin, 'Dumbarton Rock', aquatint in *Observations on Several Parts of Great Britain, Particularly the High-lands of Scotland, Relative Chiefly to Picturesque Beauty, Made in the Year 1776* (London, 1808), pl. 6, between pp. 44 and 45 (GLA ASC q190)

scenes, and pleasing pictures' (*Monthly Review* 1775, 57–65, 57; Jenkins 1972, 445–462).

In the summer of 1776, just three years after Johnson and Boswell's Scottish tour, the Rev. William Gilpin embarked on a two-week *petit tour* of the Highlands in search of 'picturesque beauty', taking issue with Dr Johnson's 'picture of Scottish landscape, painted, I am sorry to say, by the hand of peevishness' (Gilpin 1789b, II, 119). If Pennant and Johnson had opened the floodgates, the decades of the 1780s and 1790s, especially following the 1789 publication of Gilpin's *Observations, Relative Chiefly to Picturesque Beauty . . . Particularly [on] the High-Lands of Scotland*, saw a peak in the outpouring of published Highland tours, many inspired by a quest for picturesque scenery (Fig. C1.4); these are discussed in more detail in Section 4 'Picturesque Prospects and Literary Landscapes'. Gilpin's books targeted the new leisure tourists who set about exploring the peripheries of Britain in these decades, especially the English Lakes, Wales and Scotland. Kim Ian Michasiw distinguishes the middle-class rural vicar Gilpin from later picturesque theorists like Sir Uvedale Price and Richard Payne Knight in terms of 'the difference between the disempowered traveller and the improving landlord' (Michasiw 1992, 82). If Pennant and earlier tourists had extolled the estate improvements of Scotland's nobility and gentry, Gilpin tended to be highly critical: for example, he dismissed the Duke of Atholl's policies at Dunkeld as 'deformed' with 'cascades, and slopes, and other puerilities', and found the red and green glass panels of the Hermitage, framing a sublime view of the Falls of Braan, as 'tricks below the dignity of scenes like this' (Gilpin 1789b, I, 114, 123). Breadalbane's Taymouth policies (discussed in Chapter 4) were censured for their 'formal and ill-contrived walks', the whole failing to take advantage of the picturesque setting at the foot of Loch Tay, the 'noble distance' seen from the house (Gilpin 1789b, I, 158–159). But, in common with other eighteenth-century travel writers, picturesque tourists like Gilpin were also interested in recording history, local traditions and agricultural improvements, and his book wasn't without a note of social critique that went beyond the old-fashioned aesthetic tastes of the rich and powerful.

Although picturesque travellers in the romantic decades generally condoned Gilpin's criticism of the 'Capability Brown' style of landscape design, they also increasingly found fault with Gilpin's pictorialism. Radical pedestrians like the Wordsworths and Coleridge, or John Bristed and his friend William Cowan (disguised as American sailors to better gauge the true condition of the common people of Scotland), challenged the aesthetic focus of the picturesque, preferring to enquire into the real conditions of life encountered on Scotland's highways and byways (Bristed 1803; Leask 2019); see Fig. 0.4. (The case of Rev. James Plumptre, discussed in Chapter 6, reminds us, however, that not all pedestrians shared a radical agenda.) John Stoddart, also travelling as a pedestrian through Scotland in 1799–1800, with the artist John Claude Nattes, reproved Gilpin for his 'frigid praise' of the magnificent prospect from Stirling Castle: bound by his 'narrowness of system', he had complained of a 'confusion of land and water'. The difficulty of representing the Forth at Stirling, Stoddart suggests, is only because 'the pencil is unable to convey its rich and brilliant effect. To make painting the standard of those pleasures which landscape can afford, is, however, to set Art above Nature, the handmaid above her mistress' (Stoddart 1801, II, 226–228); see Fig. C1.5. Stoddart was here close to his friends the romantic poets Wordsworth and Coleridge: among his book's most ambitious features are a Wordsworthian

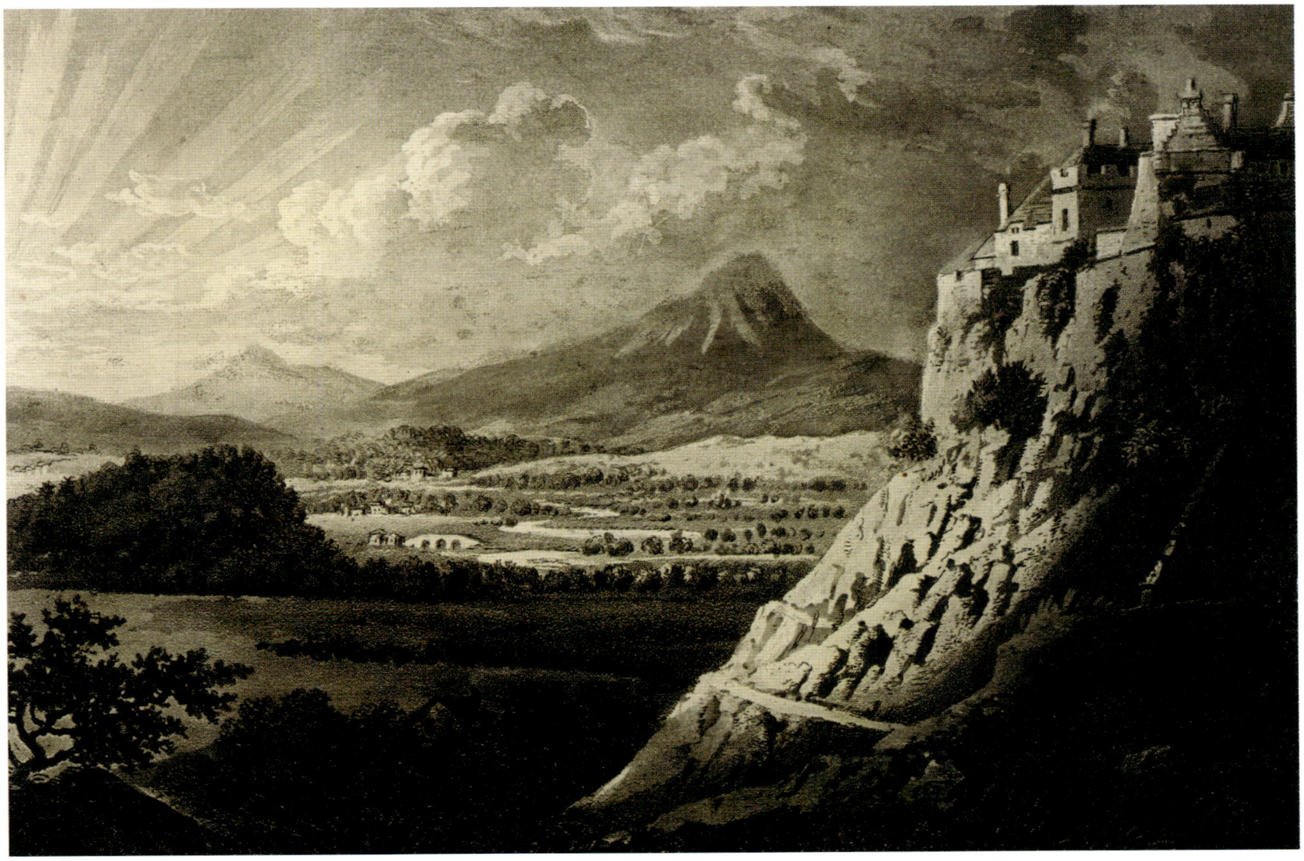

Fig. C1.5
John Stoddart, 'View from Stirling Castle', aquatint in John Stoddart, *Remarks on Local Scenery and Manners of Scotland During the Years 1799 and 1800* (London, 1801), Vol. II, facing p. 45 (PC)

attempt to evoke 'images which disdain the pencil' and a bid to purge the Pennantian travel account of its miscellaneous quality, its discursive promiscuity, by 'melting and mixing of all our thoughts, moods, knowledges, fancies, senses, feelings, into one living nature . . . that subtile, cementing, subterraneous unity' (Stoddart 1801, II, 327).

Gilpin's picturesque also offered a 'rational amusement' for middle-class women tourists lacking the erudition of a Pennant or a Johnson, but for whom skill at *pleine air* sketching was an expected accomplishment, and for whom touring offered a welcome escape from domestic drudgery. For women writers like Sarah Murray (Aust) and Dorothy Wordsworth (in a literary genre traditionally associated with men), the appreciation of natural scenery became as important as the quest for antiquarian information had been for earlier male travellers. There is a patrician *sprezzatura* to Sarah Murray's *Companion and Useful Guide to the Beauties of Scotland* (one of the few published Scottish tours by a woman in this period), with its hortatory instructions for tourists: 'provide yourself with a strong roomy carriage, and have the springs well corded', discussed in more detail in Viccy Coltman's essay (Chapter 6). Murray boasted that she had 'seen Scotland, and its natural beauties, more completely than any other individual', as well as claiming to have 'discovered' the Trossachs (Murray 1799, 39, 42; see also Hagglund 2010). The indomitable Mrs Murray's style often reveals an undiscriminating parade of picturesque language that would have made Gilpin blush: describing the views from the military road between Fort Augustus and Fort William, she enthused 'I was on the whole way in constant exclamation; – here is another; oh, how fine! How beautiful! How dashing!' (Murray 1799, 253).

As one of the literary masterpieces of romantic travel writing, Dorothy Wordsworth's *Recollections of a Tour Made in Scotland*

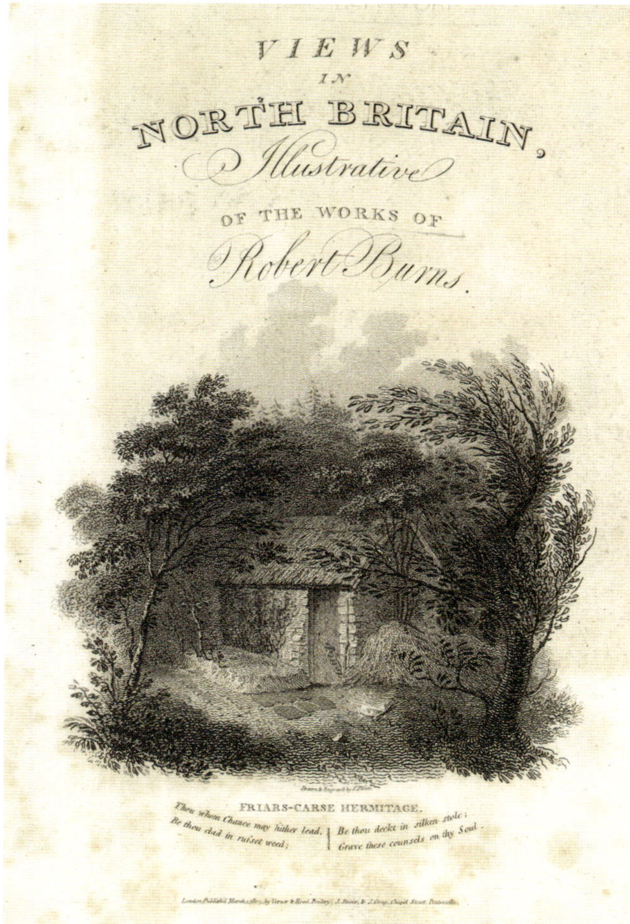

Fig. C1.6
Title page with vignette of Friars-Carse Hermitage in James Storer and John Greig, *Views in North Britain, Illustrative of the Works of Robert Burns: Accompanied with Descriptions, and a Sketch of the Poet's Life* (London, 1805) (GLA LRA HQ 00825)

made a decisive break with the Pennantian tradition, developing instead a gendered version of her brother William's poetics of 'emotion recollected in tranquillity' (Walker 1997). By studiously erasing the presence of previous travellers and guidebooks, Dorothy's tour employs memory and imagination to evoke lived experience, in a way that no other Scottish travel writer had done before. Her superb gift for natural description is nonetheless linked to the Gilpinian picturesque tradition, although Dorothy, just like her friend Coleridge (in his remarkable notebook account of his eight-day, 263-mile pedestrian tour through the Highlands, after 'breaking away' from the Wordsworths on 29 August 1803), developed the picturesque in her own way and for her own purposes (Walker 1997; Walker 2002). Read in tandem with her less ambitious second Highland tour of 1822, *Recollections* also presents a lively and sympathetic account of a traditional Gaelic world in a moment of historical crisis. Notably, Dorothy Wordsworth interpreted landscape as an indicator of Scotland's uneven level of 'improvement': 'a struggle to overcome the natural barrenness, and the end not attained, an appearance of something doing or imperfectly done, a passing with labour from one state of society into another' (Walker 1997, 177; Wordsworth 1952, II, 337–398).

Dorothy Wordsworth endorsed Gilpin's criticisms of the commercialisation of landscape viewing sites, writing 'I was grieved to hear that the Falls of the Clyde were shut up in a gentleman's grounds, and to be viewed only by means of lock and key' (Walker 1997, 59). Although the Wordsworths were uninspired by *Ossian*, much of their Scottish tour was a homage to the recently deceased Ayrshire poet Robert Burns, who had made his own Highland Tour in 1787 (Leask 2014, xx); see Fig. C1.6. In his sparse tour journal, Burns shared Gilpin's distaste for the Duke of Atholl's policies, noting on 31 August 1787 'visit[ed] the scenes round Blair – fine but spoilt with bad taste – Tilt & Gairie rivers – falls on the Tilt – heather seat' (Leask 2014, x). His critique was more tactfully expressed in his poem 'The Humble Petition of Bruar Water to the Noble Duke of Athole', in which the river beseeched the Duke to plant trees around the waterfall:

> Let lofty firs, and ashes cool,
> My lowly banks o'erspread,
> And view, deep-bending in the pool,
> Their shadows' wat'ry bed:
> Let fragrant birks, in woodbines drest,
> My craggy cliffs adorn.
> (Kinsley 1968, II, xx, lines 73–78)

According to Dorothy, the Wordsworths only visited the Falls of Bruar, on the Atholl estate, 'for the sake of Burns', whose poem had ventriloquised the waterfall's request to the landowner to plant trees to hide its nakedness, although (as Christopher Dingwall mentions in Chapter 4) she regretted that the Duke hadn't planted more native trees around the waterfall. (Walker 1997, 167–168).The Wordsworths' Highland tour was book-ended by two visits to the recently discovered tourist site of the

Trossachs, memorably described by Dorothy: 'no thoughts of dreariness or desolation found entrance here . . . nothing was to be seen but water, wood, rocks, and heather, and bare mountains above . . . near objects were not concealed from us, but softened by being seen through the mists . . . the place was all eye, and completely satisfied the sense and the heart' (Walker 1997, 102, 104).

If *Ossian* and the poetry of Robert Burns rendered the Scottish tour a profoundly literary experience, the consummate literary construction of Scotland (and especially the Highlands) as 'the faery ground for Romance and Poetry' was the achievement of Sir Walter Scott (Womack 1989; Withers 1982, 143–156; Clyde 1998, 116–149). In February 1809, Scott published a devastating anonymous review of the latest Scottish tour in the Thomas Pennant mould, Sir John Carr's *Caledonian Sketches*: 'it would, perhaps, be somewhat difficult to bring us news from Scotland . . . the information which they seek in person may be found in a hundred volumes'; Carr's book, Scott complained, was a 'hackneyed subject' treated in 'a most hackneyed manner' (Scott 1809, 178–193, 182). But at the very moment that he proclaimed the exhaustion of 'miscellaneous' travel writing, he was busy inventing the literary conditions for the next wave of Highland tourism, based on the massive success of his verse romances *The Lady of the Lake* (1810) and *The Lord of the Isles* (1815), and his novels *Waverley* (1814) and *Rob Roy* (1817).

Partly inspired by his own leisure tourism in the Trossachs and West Highlands, as well as his 1814 cruise round Scotland's coasts on board the *Pharos* lighthouse clipper, Scott's romances and novels endowed the contemporary tourist itinerary with a new imaginative resonance. As poet and novelist, Scott skilfully capitalised on the fashion for the sublime and picturesque engendered by Gilpin and his progeny: one reviewer admiringly noted how he 'sees everything with a painter's eye . . . whatever he represents is drawn with an accuracy and minuteness of discrimination which we are not accustomed to expect from verbal description' (*Quarterly Review* 1810, 512). This is exemplified by Scott's poetic description of the Trossachs, as first seen by Fitzjames, royal protagonist of *The Lady of the Lake*:

> Loch Katrine lay beneath him roll'd;
> In all her length far winding lay,
> With promontory, creek and bay,
> And islands that, empurpled bright,
> Floated amid the livelier light . . .
> High on the south, huge Benvenue
> Down to the lake in masses threw
> Crags, knolls, and mounds, confusedly hurl'd,
> The fragments of an earlier world.
> (Scott 1913, I, 211, stanza xiv)

Published by Ballantyne in 1810, *The Lady of the Lake* was a massive success, 30,000 copies being sold in the first year; it anticipated Scott's later poems and novels in being adapted for the popular theatre, opera and even as a wallpaper design. The quiet Trossachs admired by Dorothy and William Wordsworth in 1803 were transformed forever: if in 1806 six or seven tourist carriages visited daily during the season, after the publication of Scott's poem the number rose to fifty, and in the summer of 1810 Elizabeth Spence estimated that over 500 carriages had already come through to this '*far-famed* spot' (Spence 1811, I, 187). In 1818 an angry boatman on Loch Lomond was heard complaining that 'ever since [Scott] wrote "The Lady of the Lake" . . . everybody goes to that filthy hole Loch Catrine, than comes round by Luss, and I have only had two gentlemen to guide this blessed season . . . The devil confound his ladies and his lakes, say I!' (quoted in Jamieson 1818, I, 203). Conversely, the scenic centrepiece of *The Lord of the Isles* (1816) was Scott's description of Loch Coruisk in Skye (its forbidding sublimity contrasting with the picturesque delights of Loch Katrine described in *The Lady of the Lake*): 'A scene so rude, so wild as this, / Yet so sublime in barrenness, / Ne'er did my wandering footsteps press, / Where'er I happ'd to roam' (Scott 1913, 432, stanza xiii); Fig. C1.7. Scott's description of Loch Coruisk (as well as Fingal's Cave) as backdrops for Robert the Bruce's attempt to reconquer his kingdom would inspire artists like William Daniell and Turner, as well as a plethora of nineteenth-century tourists, for whom the new age of steamboat travel was opening up even the more inaccessible islands of the Hebrides to the outsider.

Although a native of the Scottish Borders, Scott played a significant role in the development of nineteenth-century 'Highlandism', defined by Allan Macinnes as 'the association of tartan with military prowess and imperial service, a peculiar weave that came in the course of the 19th century to represent Scot-

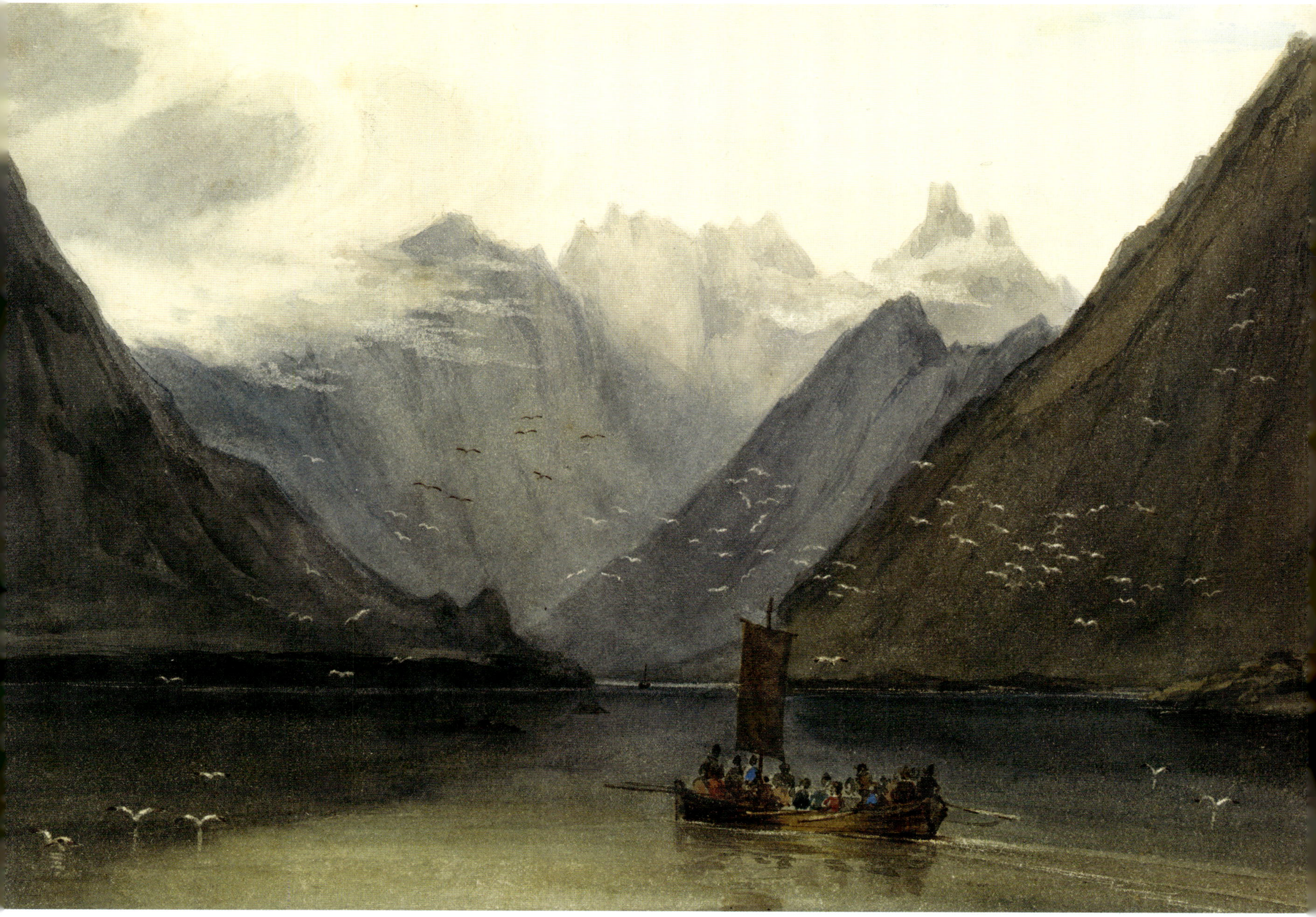

Fig. C1.7
William Daniell, *Loch Coruisk, near Loch Scavaig*, c. 1815, watercolour (GMC PR.1956.11.n)

land's distinctive presence within the British Empire' (Macinnes 2015, 1–21; see also McNeil 2007). The phenomenal success of Scott's *Waverley* novels depended in part on their fictional realisation of his view that 'the most picturesque period of history [was] that when the ancient rough and wild manners of a barbarous age [were] just becoming innovated upon' (Scott 1829–33, XXVI, vi) even when (as Scott was all too aware), in the case of the Highlands, 'innovation' often meant rack-renting, sheep clearance and forced emigration. Although Scott's novel did much to promote 'sentimental Jacobitism', the whiggish and unionist conclusion of *Waverley* (1814) is epitomised by a set-piece description of the restored estate of Tully-Veolan (formerly the property of the Jacobite Baron Bradwardine) under the English Colonel Talbot's new and 'improving' proprietorship. The publication of Scott's novel coincided with public controversy about sheep clearances on the Sutherland estates and elsewhere, but with characteristic caution he refused to be drawn into the political fray. However, in an 1816 review of *Forbes's Culloden Papers*, Scott appeared to have suffered a change of heart, as he began to attempt salvaging an ideal of 'neo-clanship', criticising the 'unrelenting avarice' on the part of improving Highland landowners who had purged the glens not just of 'their superfluity of population, but of the whole mass of the inhabitants' (Scott 1816, 333). It was a romantic social vision that Scott tried to put into practice when he wrapped Edinburgh in tartan for 'the King's Jaunt' (George IV's visit to Edinburgh in August 1822), proclaiming 'We are the clan, and our King is the chief' (Prebble 2000, 100). Scott created a potent national symbolism, albeit in the service of safeguarding and promoting Scottish identity within Britain, which would have enduring power both in Scotland and abroad. Its spirit of sublime illusion is perfectly captured in J.W. Turner's *Edinburgh Castle: The March of the Highlanders*.

In the years after Waterloo, 'Scott tourism', was furthered by a new geological interest in Scotland's 'rocks', and a second transport revolution associated with Thomas Telford (whose new Dunkeld Bridge is discussed by John Bonehill in Chapter 5), the Parliamentary Roads Act, and steamboat tourism (see Fig. S4.11). This coincided with mounting social and economic pressures associated with the post-war depression, and the collapse of the fishing and kelping industries on the west coast. As tourists poured in, hungry Gaels poured out, cleared from inland glens or fleeing from congested coastal settlements, seeking employment in Lowland cities or cheap passage across the Atlantic.

The third volume of William Daniell's magnificent and expensive *Voyage Around Great Britain* (published in 1818) was fulsomely dedicated to the author of *The Lord of the Isles* (Daniell 2006, I, xxvi). Daniell's letterpress description of key sites on the coastal itinerary reads at times like a series of footnotes to Scott's poetry. The fourth volume (1820) was dedicated to the Marchioness of Stafford, prime mover of the Sutherland clearances: here Daniell hoped that the sheep grazing the hills around Loch Duich would 'produce a favourable change on the heath-covered highlands, and will gradually render them green and fertile . . . rescu[ing] large tracts from the stern empire of desolation': he rapidly glossed over the tragic human consequences, taking refuge in the jargon of political economy (Daniell 2006, I, 148). Of the many literary tourists who flocked into the Highlands, only John Keats seems to have resisted Scott's spell during his walking tour in 1818 by giving the Trossachs a wide berth, although he visited Staffa, where his enthusiasm was dampened by the 'taint' of modern tourism: ''Tis now free to stupid face, / To cutters and to fashion boats, / To cravats and to petticoats' (Walker 1992, 200). This didn't, however, deter J.M.W. Turner from creating the consummate image of Staffa with a tourist steamboat following his visit to the island on board *The Maid of Morvern* in 1831 (Fig. C1.8).

I'll conclude this brief overview of Scottish tour literature 1720–1830 with a discussion of John Macculloch's massive, but now relatively unknown, *Highlands and Western Isles of Scotland . . . in Letters addressed to Sir Walter Scott* (1824), in which Scott's name was severely compromised (Macculloch 1824; Furniss 2018, 232). The book was based on the Guernsey-born geologist's experience of annual field trips made between 1814 and 1820, covering about 38,000 miles on foot and horseback through the region; if not travel writing in the usual sense of the term, to the extent that it strenuously avoided personal narrative and lacked any illustrations or maps, it is in part dedicated to mocking the whole tradition of Scottish travel writing discussed in this essay. (In contrast, Macculloch's more analytical *Description of the Western Islands of Scotland*, published in 1819, did contain plates and geological maps; see C3.16 (Furniss 2018, 229–264).) Macculloch's real polemical target in 1824 was the romantic 'Highlandism' with which Scott's name was deeply implicated; he diagnosed the new mass tourism as the nemesis of Scottian romance: 'the mystic portal has been thrown open, and the mob has rushed in, dispersing all these fairy visions, and polluting everything with its unhallowed touch . . . The green-coated fairies have packed up their alls and quitted the premises, and the Uriskins only caper now in your verse' (Macculloch 1824, I, 195). Macculloch here picks up on a well-worked vein of satire targeting 'Scotch tourists', especially associated with the (anonymous) *Tour of Doctor Prosody: in Search of the Antique and Picturesque*

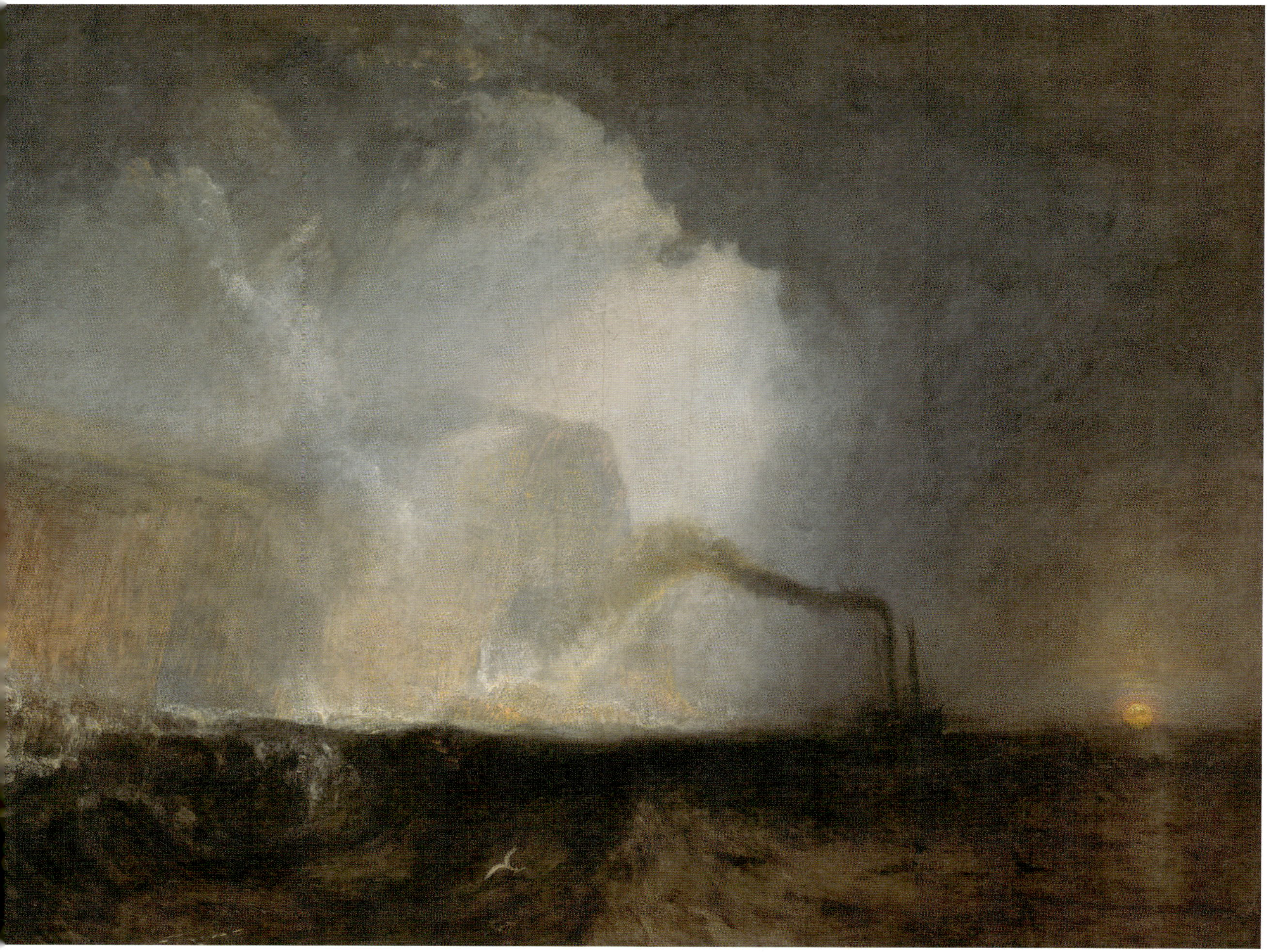

Fig. C1.8
Joseph Mallord William Turner, *Staffa, Fingal's Cave*, c. 1831–1832, oil on canvas (YCBA B1978.43.14)

through Scotland, the Hebrides, the Orkney and Shetland Isles (1820), discussed in Section 4 (Fig. C1.9).

Striking a darker tone, Macculloch's disturbing racial and colonialist views of the Gaels remind us how travel writing in this period was as preoccupied with social attitudes as with landscape aesthetics. He insisted that 'the Gothic race was ordained [for the conquest of the Celts] . . . nothing short of extermination was applicable to the correction of a people who, even yet, are resisting the improvements that surround them' (Macculloch 1824, IV, 296). As a former president of the Geological Society

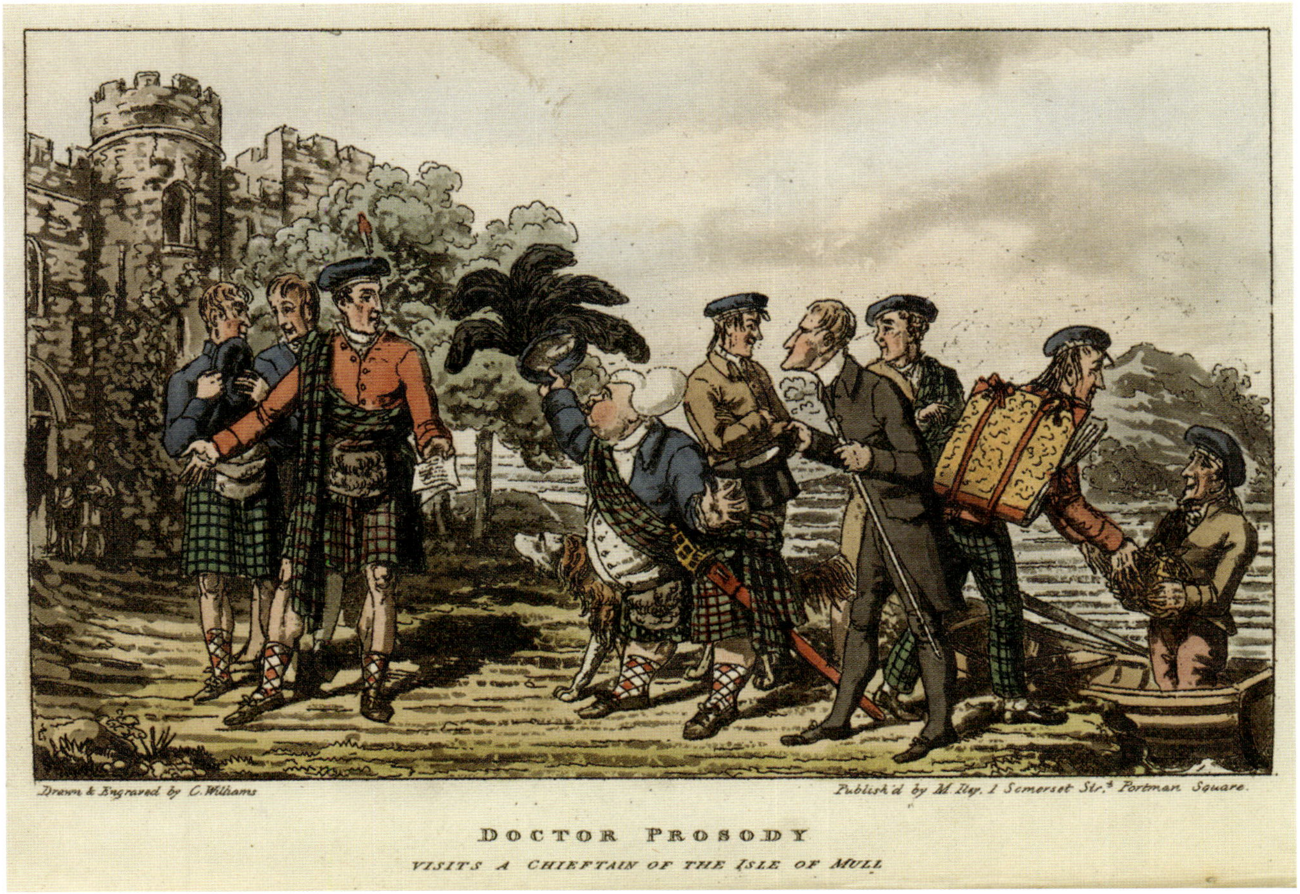

Fig. C1.9
Charles Williams, 'Dr Prosody Visits a Chieftain on the Isle of Mull', hand-coloured etching and aquatint in *The Tour of Doctor Prosody: In Search of the Antique and Picturesque, through Scotland, the Hebrides, the Orkney and Shetland Isles* (London, 1821), pl. 12, opposite p. 153 (GLA ASC RQ 1264)

of London, Macculloch's scientific reputation gave heft to his craven defence of racially motivated clearance against the strictures of 'romantic gentlemen', as he proposed converting the Gaels into a mobile proletariate obliged to sell their labour at the best market, whether at home or (better) abroad in North America. Unsurprisingly, Macculloch's book caused a storm in the Scottish press and was pugnaciously answered by Dr James Browne (Browne 1825). Scott never deigned to respond to the geologist's challenge, although it is unlikely that he endorsed many of his more extreme views. As the culmination of a century of writing about the Highlands, Macculloch's *Highlands and Western Isles* reveals a darker 'colonial' side to the romantic Highlands consummated in the 'Balmorality' of the region during the Victorian period. In exposing the paradoxical agency of tourism to disenchant and commodify the object of its romantic quest, it is prescient of many of the issues raised by tourism in twenty-first century Scotland, and elsewhere. Yet it also brings us back full circle to Edmund Burt's prejudiced analysis of the 'Old Ways', anticipating the tragic decades of Highland clearance and famine that lay ahead.

ACKNOWLEDGEMENTS

This essay is based on some of the arguments of my book *Stepping Westward: Writing the Highland Tour, c. 1720–1830* (Oxford University Press, 2020).

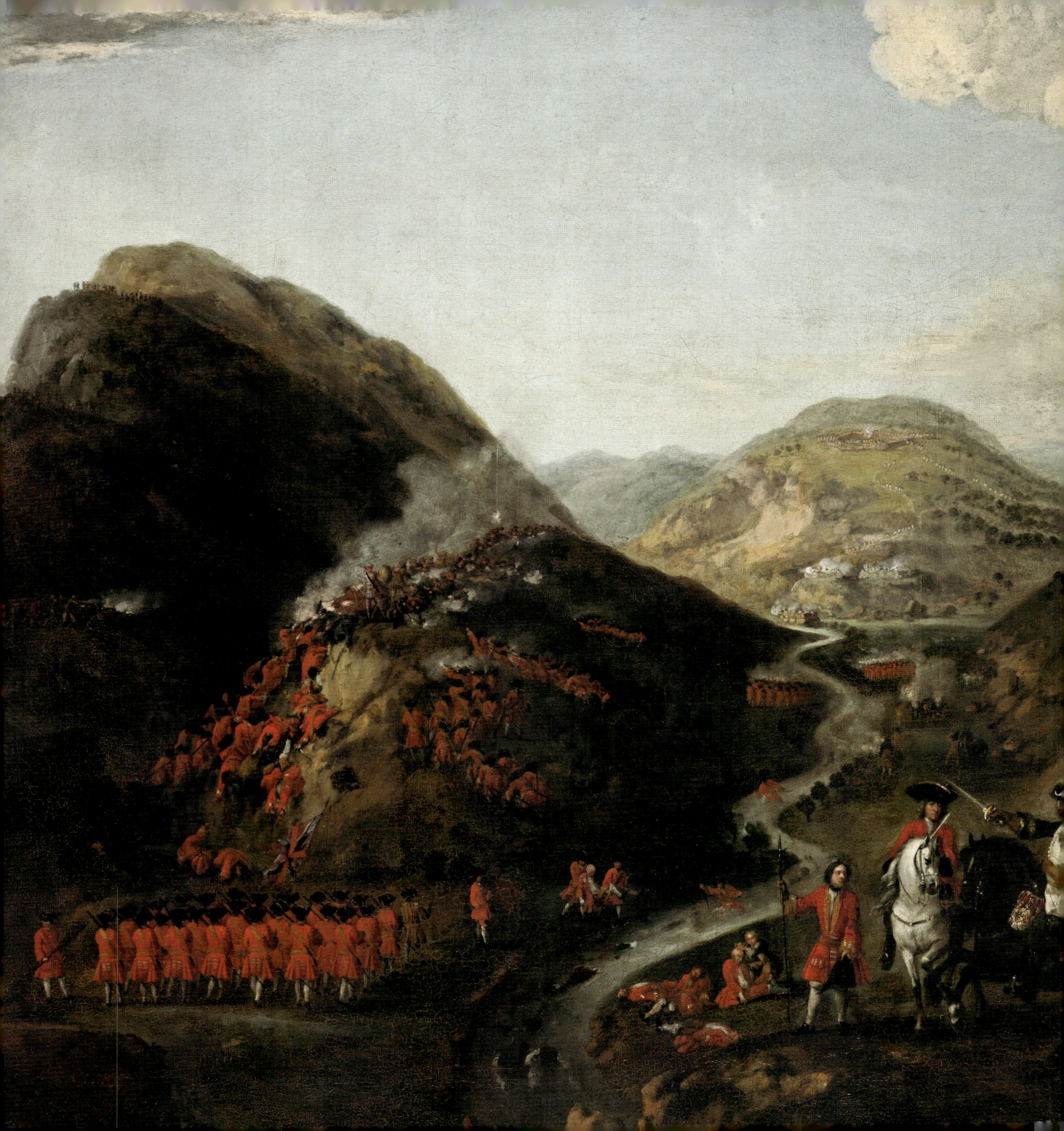

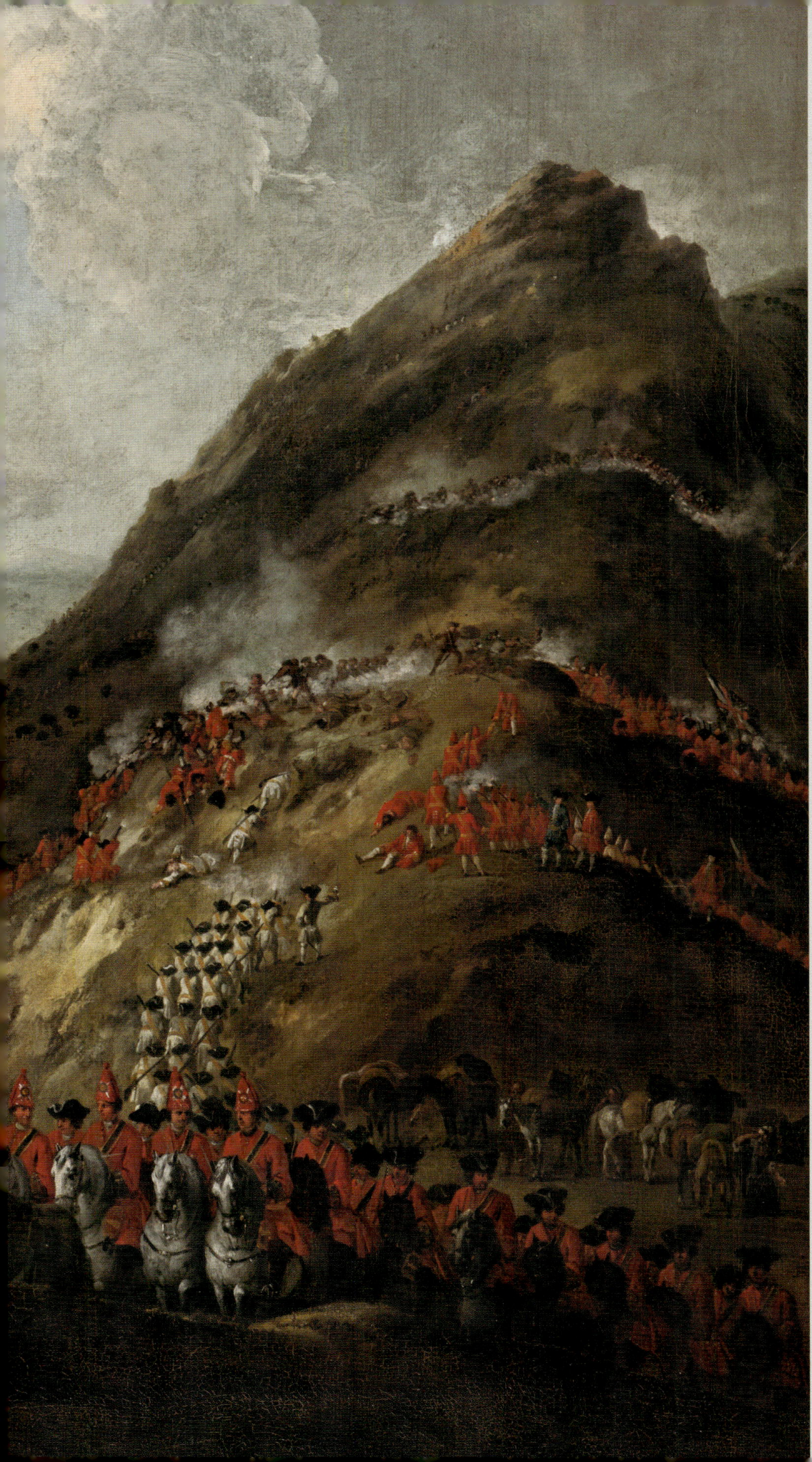

SECTION ONE

The Theatre of War

John Bonehill

Fig. S1.1
Peter Tillemans, *The Battle of Glenshiel*, 1719, oil on canvas (NGS PG2635)

Peter Tillemans' picture commemorates General Joseph Wightman's defeat of Jacobite forces on the slopes of Glen Shiel on 10 June 1719. Overlooked on the foreground rise by a mounted Wightman, who flourishes his sword as if to cue the action, the redcoats below embark on the decisive final assault, scrambling up towards the enemy (including white-coated Spanish troops) entrenched in the knolls and spurs of the hillsides above. Founded on a tradition of courtly battle painting of seventeenth-century origin, the power of such pictures largely depended on the precision with which the artist delineated the action and setting. When working on his representation of the Battle of Glenshiel, Tillemans compensated for his lack of first-hand knowledge of the terrain by drawing on a combination of eye-witness accounts and a series of highly detailed battle plans drawn up by John Henry Bastide. The resulting painting is one of the few extant oils of the Highland landscape from the first half of the eighteenth century.

Writing of the prospects out from Stirling castle, the Rev. William Gilpin counted 'not fewer . . . than a dozen fields of battle' within sight. 'In fact you can hardly ascend any elevated ground, without throwing your eye over the scene of some memorable action', he was to observe. Battles fought to defend against historic incursions from the Romans and seafaring northern nations, or between feuding clans, as well as 'constant quarrels' with the English, 'to which several have been added by rebellions, since the union', had made Scotland 'a fertile scene of military events', one vast theatre of war and memory (Gilpin 1789b, I, 84–85). With visitors heading for Culloden, Falkirk Muir and other former sites of battle, what had been a war zone just thirty years or so earlier was now opening up to polite scenic tourism. Sites of conflict and rebellion excited Gilpin, as they did other travellers of a philosophical turn of mind, where 'the rough and picturesque scenery' of Highland rivers and glens served as natural memorials, activating the historical imagination and encouraging reflections on national liberties or the country's progress. Looking to scenes of 'memorable action' associated with the Jacobite risings of the first half of the eighteenth century, this section explores the making and commemoration of the militarised landscapes of the period across a broad range of literary and visual forms, as they lay the ground for the forces of polite culture, and its representatives such as Gilpin, that were to spread throughout Scotland in the decades that followed.

When taking to the military roads in search of the picturesque, the chief advocate of such tours was following in his father's footsteps. Stationed at Fort William and Stirling, as well as on the Isle of Skye, during the 1720s and 1730s, Captain John Bernard Gilpin had been witness to the project of strengthening the garrisons of the north and opening up the most inaccessible parts of the country to the passage of troops. Under General Wade's direction, between 1725 and 1740, some 500 'Highwaymen', as he called the soldiers in his command, began work on a massive programme of road and bridge building as well as the maintenance and repair, or design and construction, of barracks and forts. Probably commissioned to mark the completion of the military road through the Corrieyairack Pass, *A Description of the Highlands of Scotland*, a map of 1731 drawn up by the French draughtsman Clement Lemprière, accords the country a degree of classical symmetry, an impression reinforced by the inclusion of the Antonine Wall and the Roman camp at Ardoch alongside the chain of new fortifications and roads linking them (Fig. S1.2). Allusions to the country's Roman antiquity also suffuse another commemorative token of the first stages of Wade's efforts to link the new upland network of fortified barracks: the portrait of the Commander-in-Chief of North Britain attributed to the Anglo-Dutch artist Johan van Diest (see Fig. 0.1). Shown as if directing work on the ground, a prospect of the construction process opening up before him, probably over the Corrieyairack Pass, Wade's relaxed, unruffled ease is an expression of the self-possession demanded by contemporary ideals of masculine power and influence founded on antique precedents. He who was in charge of himself was by extension best able to exert control over others. With the military roads and presence now extended beyond even 'the utmost Bounds of the *Roman* Empire', it was only appropriate that the artist cast Wade in an attitude that recalled classical models of authority and statesmanship (Defoe 1724–27, III, 175). Yet, while drawing parallels with the antique past, such imagery celebrated distinctly modern, enlightened British military practice as showcased in the building of Wade's roads.

Responsibility for much of this work fell under the remit of the Board of Ordnance, whose role extended far beyond the supply of munitions and equipment. Part of their task was also to improve knowledge of the geography of these northern areas of the kingdom, though the maps of the period produced by the Board's draughtsmen and surveyors at times afforded only the most schematic sense of the landscape. For all the fine quality of Lemprière's map, its outlines simply retraced those of the country delineated in the *Atlas Novus* compiled by the Dutch mapmaker Joan Blaeu back in the 1650s, and displayed scant knowledge of the wider country beyond the immediate environs of major settlements (Fleet, Wilkes and Withers 2012, 51, 83). Still, as the plan of Fort William drawn up by its overseer Robert Johnson demonstrates, however rudimentary his depiction of 'the Country ajasent' may now appear, the drawings and plans that formed the paper landscapes of the period were able to convey with striking immediacy the challenges that the rugged Highland terrain posed for military strategists (Fig. S1.3). Occupying a commanding position at the far southern end of the Great Glen, near the head of Loch Linnhe, Fort William was of decisive importance if the looming mountains of Johnson's sketch-plan suggest the insecurities of its situation deep in fiercely Jacobite Lochaber. Going forward, the need for a better and more precise understanding of Scotland's geography would see it mapped in ever greater detail and with considerable graphic sophistication.

In the wake of the Jacobite rising of 1745, and in a continuation of the work done by Wade, Colonel David Watson proposed the first extensive regional mapping project in Britain (Skelton 1967; Roy 2007 [1747–55]). Twelve months or so after the defeat of the Jacobite cause on the field of Culloden, under the direction of Watson and his assistant William Roy, the Military Survey of North Britain began. In an early progress report, Watson emphasised 'the Benefit [which] must arise from protecting the Highlands by the Regular Troops' and the need 'to acquire a perfect knowledge of the Country' (Watson 1747). Map-making, based on new surveys and expressed in skilled draughtsmanship, was central to the modern reform of military strategy that Watson and others envisioned, enabling the planning of operations in the field and increasing the mobility of tactics over a range of terrains. Under Watson's guidance, the Military Survey, as executed by Roy and others, incorporated drawing skills from various quarters – engineering, architecture, estate surveying and fine art – resulting in a range of both official and off-duty imagery displaying the lay of the land and the extent of its physical and social progress through loyally British governance. These works also expressed, sometimes self-consciously, a striking degree of expertise and virtuosity in image-making, whether on the ground in sketching and surveying, in finished drawings and engravings, or in copying and adapting existing maps and views.

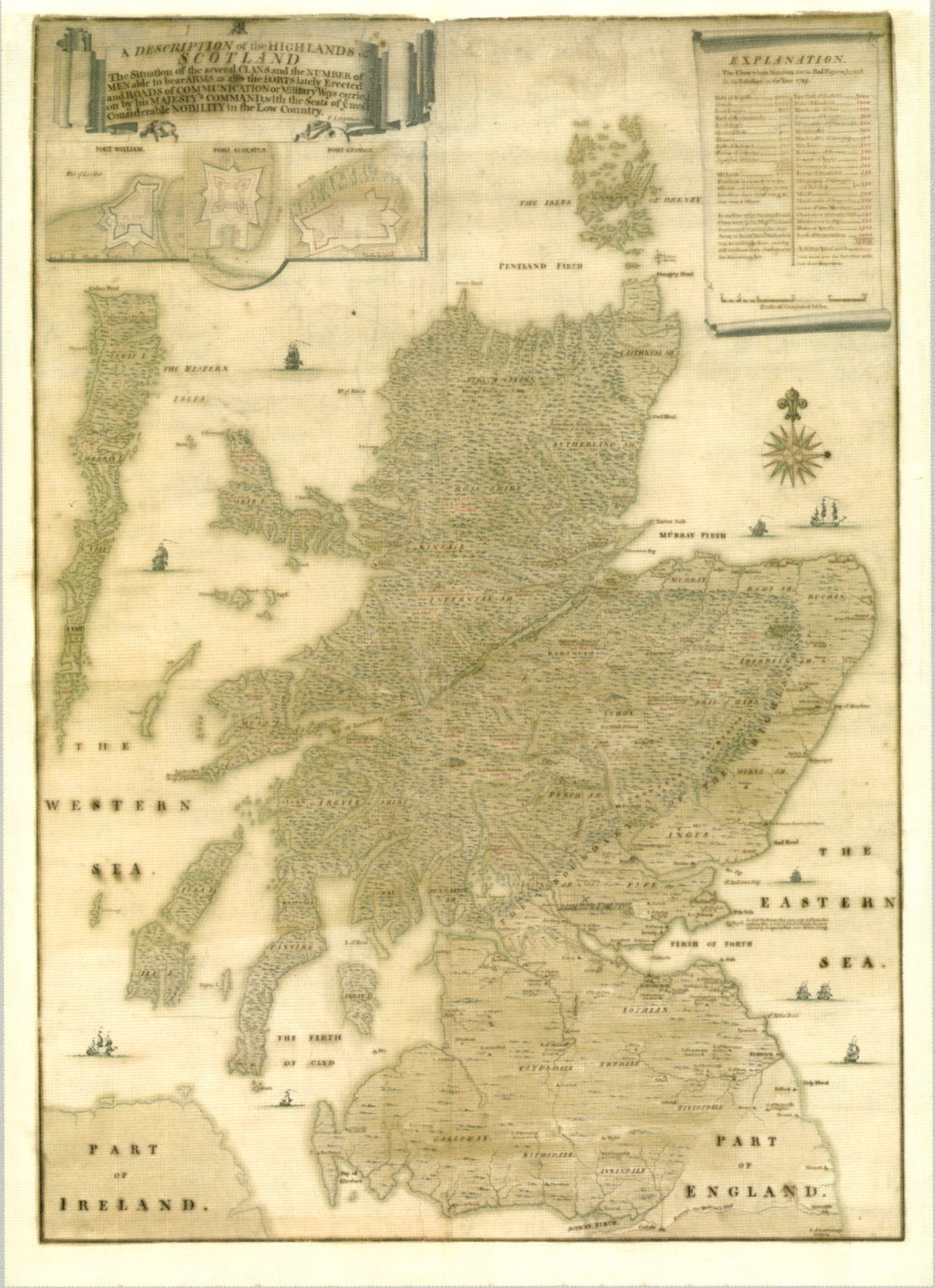

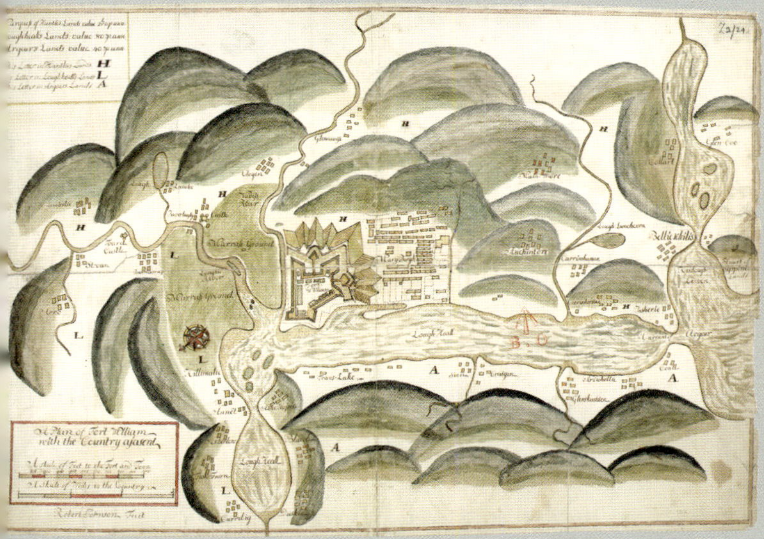

Fig. S1.2
Above. Clement Lemprière, *A Description of the Highlands*, 1731 (NLS Acc.11104 Map.Rol.a.42)

Fig. S1.3
Left. Robert Johnson, *A Plan of Fort William with the Country Ajasent*, 1710, drawing (NLS MS.1646 Z.02/24a)

Drawn up after Culloden by the Ordnance engineer John Elphinstone, *A New Map of North Britain* is a near demonstration piece for the new levels of competence in the graphic arts that would be so central to Watson's grand project (Fig. S1.4). Based on Lemprière's earlier map of the new military roads, Elphinstone's sheet makes a number of striking additions, with the margins now including perspective views of key fortresses as well as of the route carved through Glen Shiel alongside a plan of battle for Culloden. In a form of commentary on the wider significance of the recent conflict that the map commemorates, Elphinstone also incorporated a variety of allegorical elements of a placatory nature. To the right, the wall plaque lists the clans who were loyal and rebellious. Chained to the pedestal below are flanking Jacobite figures, exhibiting contrasting responses to their recent defeat: one, the leering likeness of the imprisoned Lord Lovat, was lifted directly from a famous print by William Hogarth, in the character of notorious criminals; and the other is a noble-looking kilted Highlander, contemplating his imprisonment. At bottom left, the title cartouche and elaborate scale bar take the form of a war monument, a chest tomb surmounted with an assemblage of surveying instruments and weaponry, before which a kilted soldier mourns the body of a classically styled fallen comrade (Fig. S1.4 inset). Strategically placed within the northern coast of Ireland, and resting on the border with England, this memorial has the effect of containing the defended or reconquered territory, especially its Highland and island geography. Showing scenes before and after the rebellion, the impression made by the map was of restoration rather than conquest, continuity not change (Bonehill and Daniels 2017). Made by a Lowland Scot, the map's reflective, even mournful imagery may be interpreted as a plea for clemency on behalf of Elphinstone's misguided fellow countryman, though if that was the intention the call went unheeded by William, Duke of Cumberland, and his successors.

Elphinstone copied his plan of Culloden from one made by the Ordnance draughtsman Thomas Sandby. Serving in the Ordnance Drawing Room from the early 1740s, Sandby was a key figure in raising standards. While earlier artists working for the military had done little more than delineate objects, Sandby's extraordinary large-scale watercolours of the barracks and encampment at Fort Augustus, on the southern banks of Loch Ness, exhibit considerable refinement, with their delicate tonal washes and minuteness of touch establishing a sense of atmospheric breadth married with fine detail previously unseen in Ordnance work (Figs S1.5 and S1.6). On one hand, the drawings are richly informative about the rises and falls of this militarised landscape, contrasting cultivated fields with rugged hillsides as well as picking out areas of refuge, hazard and fields of fire of strategic value. On the other hand, however, such finely wrought drawings would not have been for use in the field (Charlesworth 1996, 255–256; Bonehill and Daniels 2009, 78–79). Rather, their

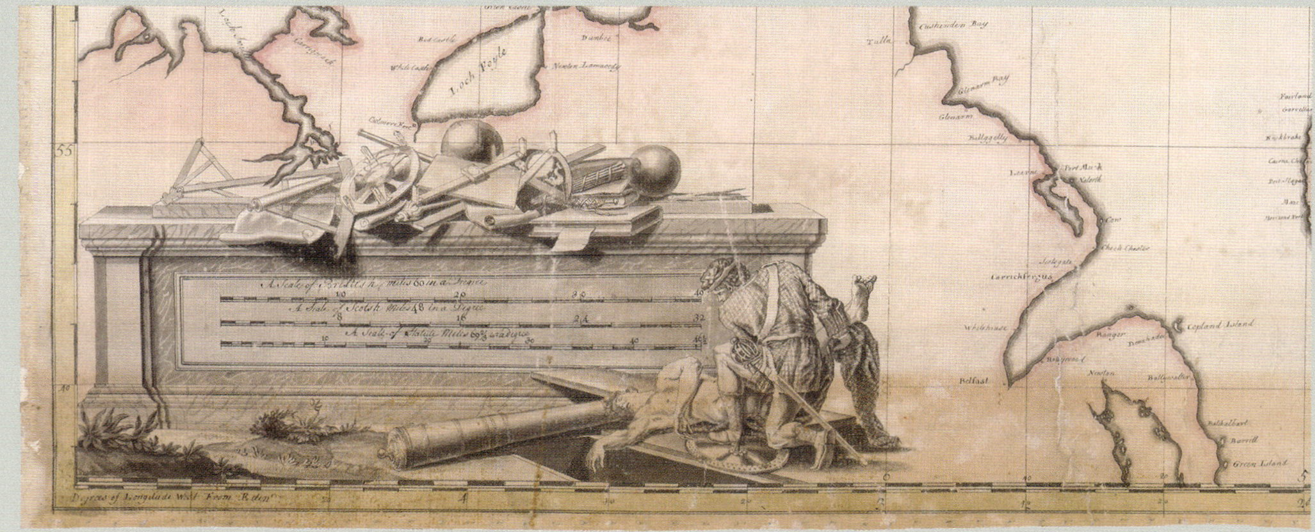

Fig. S1.4
Opposite. John Elphinstone, *A New Map of North Britain done by order of the Right Honourable the Lord of Albemarle, Commander-in-Chief of His Majesty's Forces in Scotland*, 1746, pen, wash and watercolour (BL Maps K.Top 48.22)

Right. Detail of inset bottom left: Monument with dead Highlander

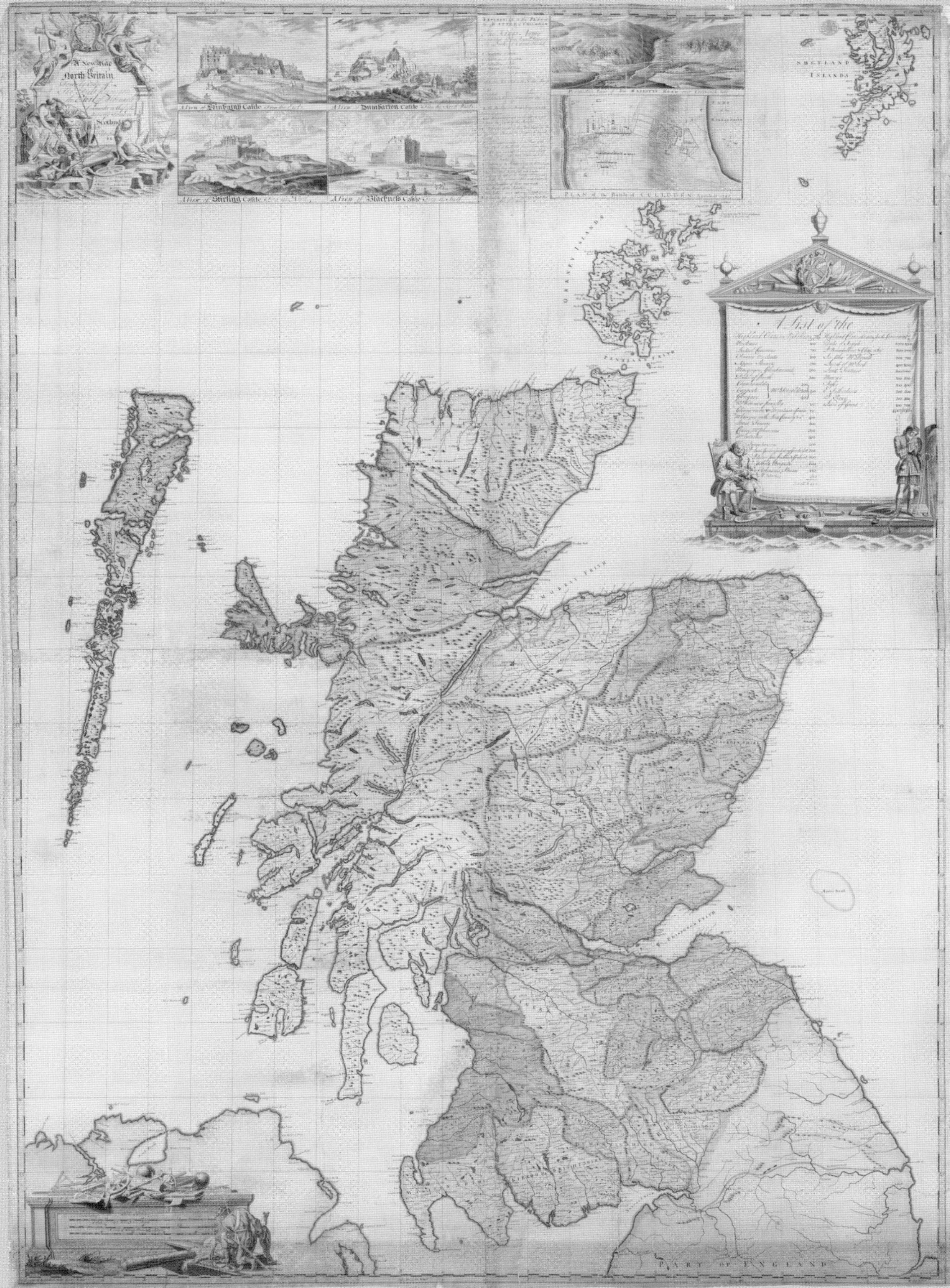

North Britain
SHETLAND
ISLANDS
A List of the
PART OF ENGLAND

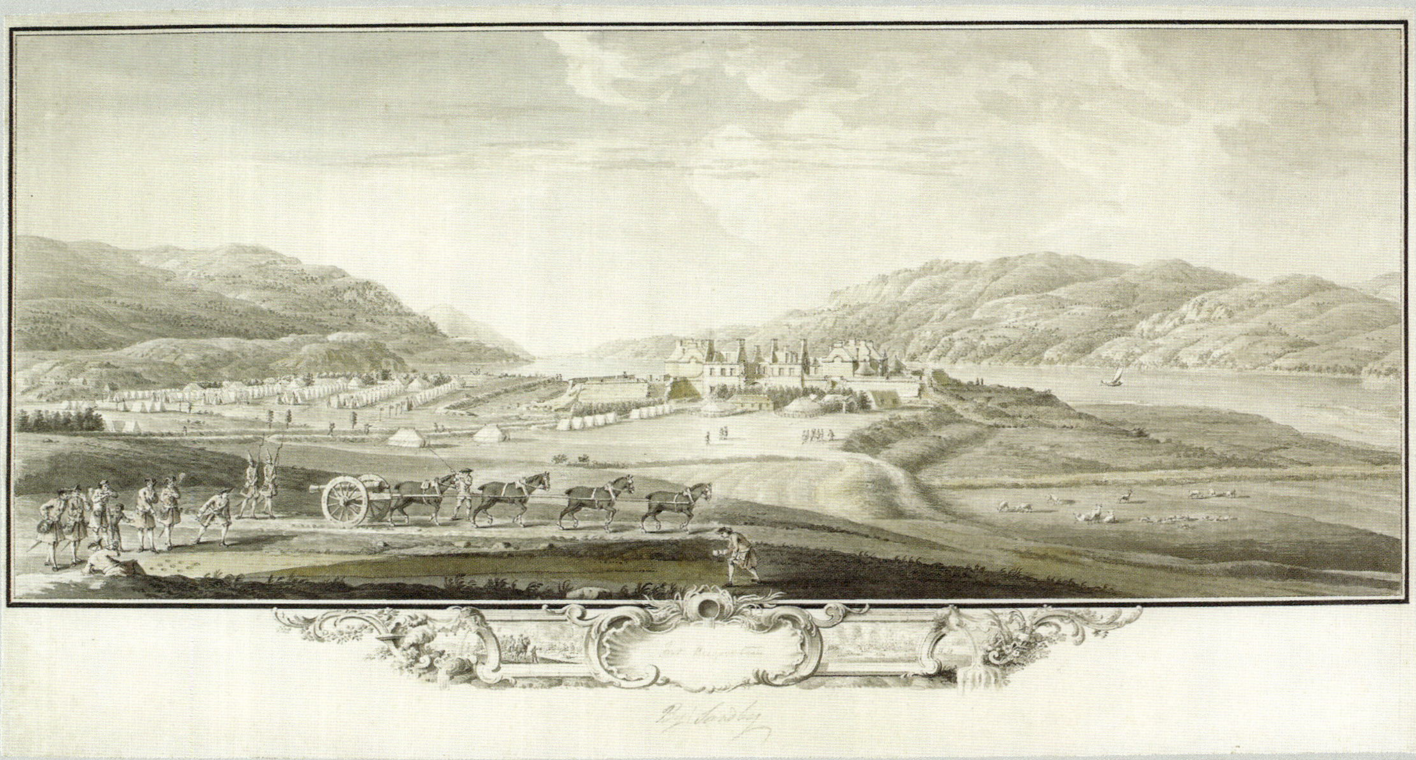

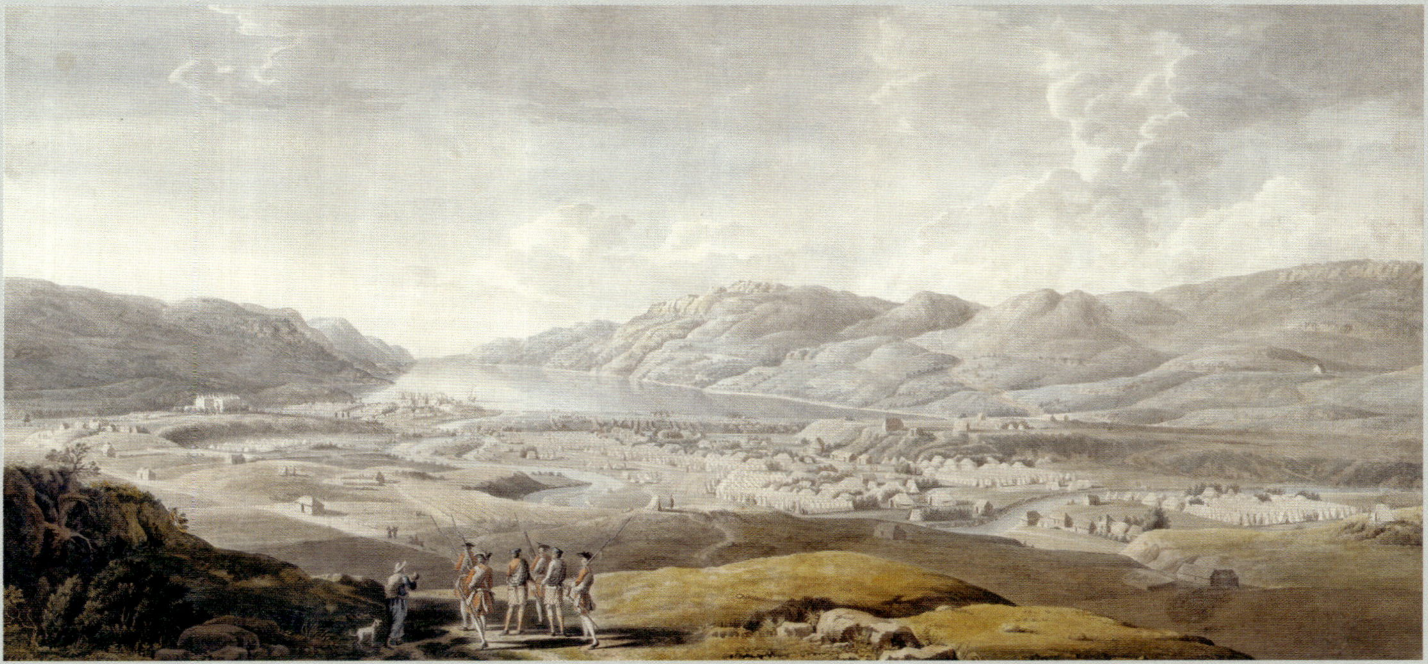

function was probably commemorative, celebrating the values of discipline and order that were widely seen as instrumental in securing victory in the Highlands. It may be that the intention was to have them engraved to capitalise on the patriotic fervour of the post-Culloden moment in England, a point reinforced by the inclusion of the pointed narrative incident of the foregrounds. In one, a group of soldiers relax with a game of 'nine holes', explaining the rules of this simple, skittles-like game to a puzzled-looking local. In the other, manacled Jacobite prisoners are being escorted to the barracks down the slope. Much like the two figures posed below the wall plaque in Elphinstone's map, one is comic, the other rather poignant. Indeed, unlike the wild and scrawny figures so often portrayed in the graphic culture of the period, the kilted prisoners of this second picture display an elegance and refinement that confers a certain dignity in defeat. In this instance, the foreground vignette was almost certainly an addition made by Thomas Sandby's younger brother, Paul, a figure who was to take forward the advances his sibling had made on joining the Military Survey of North Britain.

Over the summer months, the survey teams compiled sightings and notes out in the field, before returning to the Ordnance Drawing Room in Edinburgh every winter, so they might '[protract] on royal paper their several surveys' (Chalmers 1807, II, 63). Drawing up the original protractions or 'manuscript maps', and then collating them into a 'fair' or presentation copy, was a small team of talented draughtsmen (Fig. S1.7). While Roy was probably responsible for the often-fine detail of the so-called 'Great Map', the distinctive, highly painterly and decorative relief work was done by the 'chief Draftsman of the fair Plan', Paul Sandby (Arrowsmith 1809, 8). Probably developed in conjunction with Roy, this free interpretation of contemporary military cartographic technique was to indicate the direction of slopes through a series of closely aligned brushstrokes, with graduations of tone expressive of differences in height and steepness. A curious hybrid of 'bird's-eye' and perspectival views, the depiction of relief shown here in a section of the map covering the southern Highlands was indicative of the problems of translating the surveyors' observations, which were pictorial as well as mathematical, into cartographic form. Writing nearly forty years later, Roy was to think the survey more in the nature of a 'magnificent military sketch, than a very accurate map of the country'; as he observed: 'no geometrical exactness is to be expected, the sole object in view being, to shew remarkable things, or such as constitute the great outlines of the Country' (Roy 1785, 387).

Mapping and picturing, or what had been thought of traditionally as the arts of the compass and the palette (in the way they were brought together in the cartouche of Elphinstone's map), were closely connected in these works (Christian 1990; Bermingham 2000, 78–80; Bonehill and Daniels 2009, 74–93). In the assembled plans and views of castles Duart and Tioram, drawn up by the 'chief Draftsman of the fair Plan' to accompany a survey of their strategic value and state of repair made by Watson, for instance, the different modes of depiction employed provide multiple perspectives on matters of design and situation (Fig. S1.8). In the view of Tioram, situated on a rocky, tidal isle at the entrance to Loch Moidart, Sandby's use of hatched shading and serrated edges etched in pen in the depiction of relief is strongly reminiscent of the techniques being pioneered in the making of 'the Great Map'. These methods are also evident in the same artist's *View near Loch Rannoch* (Fig. S1.9), which shares a similarly muted palette to the fair copies.

Showing a military survey party at work, this small, unfinished drawing may well have been produced as a design for a decorative cartouche or intended to accompany reduced-scale presentation copies of 'the Great Map' rather than as a visual record of actual practice (Bonehill and Daniels 2017). The party, who are lined up in a highly formal, symmetrical way, appears to be something other than a functional unit engaged in rapid reconnaissance, taking hasty measurements and sightings in an area that had seen a great deal of fighting. Accompanying the surveyor at the theodolite and escorting redcoats are two Highlanders, local guides or interpreters perhaps, though their demeanour and dress may suggest otherwise. Striking a standard pose of gentlemanly ease and refinement, one foot forward, hand on hip, the Highlander at far right would seem to have stepped out of a contemporary conversation piece, only one in which a theodolite takes the place of the usual telescope on a terrace overlooking fine parkland. That the group as a whole might be best understood in emblematic terms perhaps, as representative of the grander civilising, modernising post-rebellion project of which the Military Survey formed part, offers an explanation for the otherwise strangely incongruous sight of the no less elegant female figure, in full formal gown to the far left. In this sense, it is striking that the

Fig. S1.5
Opposite top. Thomas Sandby, *Fort Augustus*, c. 1746, pen and grey wash and watercolour (RCT RCIN 914724)

Fig. S1.6
Opposite bottom. Thomas Sandby, *Fort Augustus*, c. 1746, pen and ink and watercolour (RCT RCIN 914725)

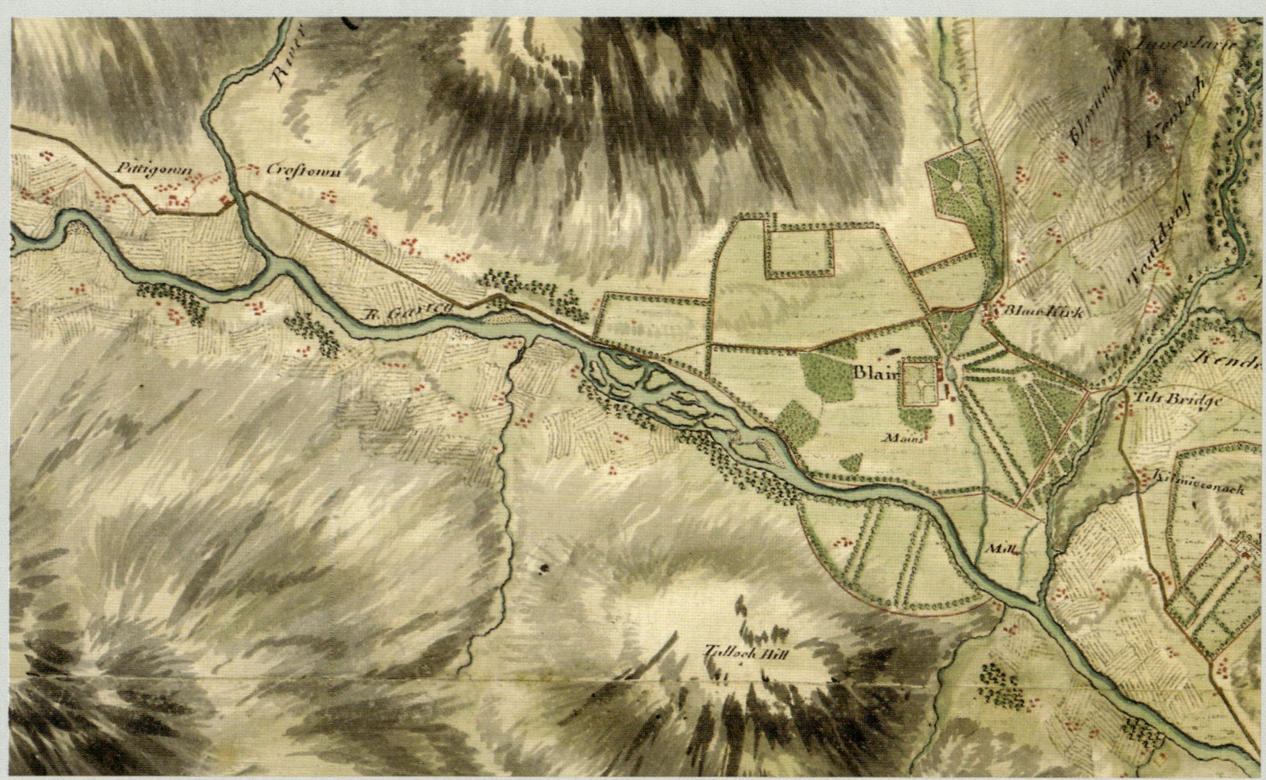

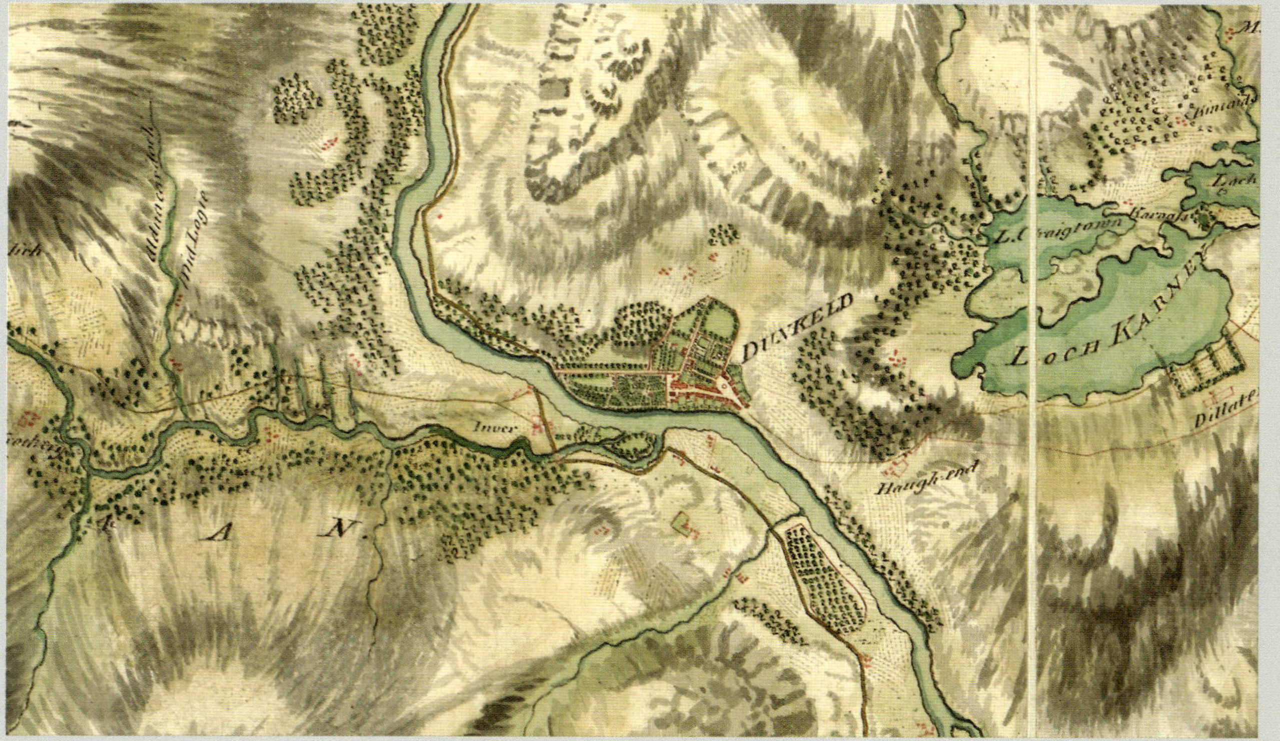

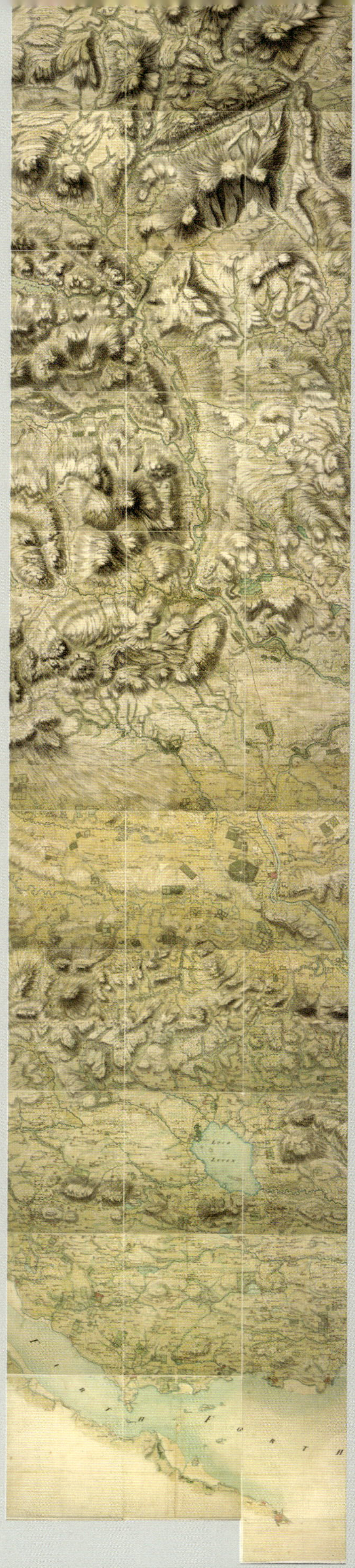

Fig. S1.7
Above. Board of Ordnance, details of the areas around Blair Castle and Dunkeld, from *A Sheet of the Fair Copy of the Military Survey of the North of Scotland*, c. 1750 (BL CC.5.a.44)

Right. Board of Ordnance, *A Sheet of the Fair Copy of the Military Survey of the North of Scotland*, c. 1750 (BL CC.5.a.44)

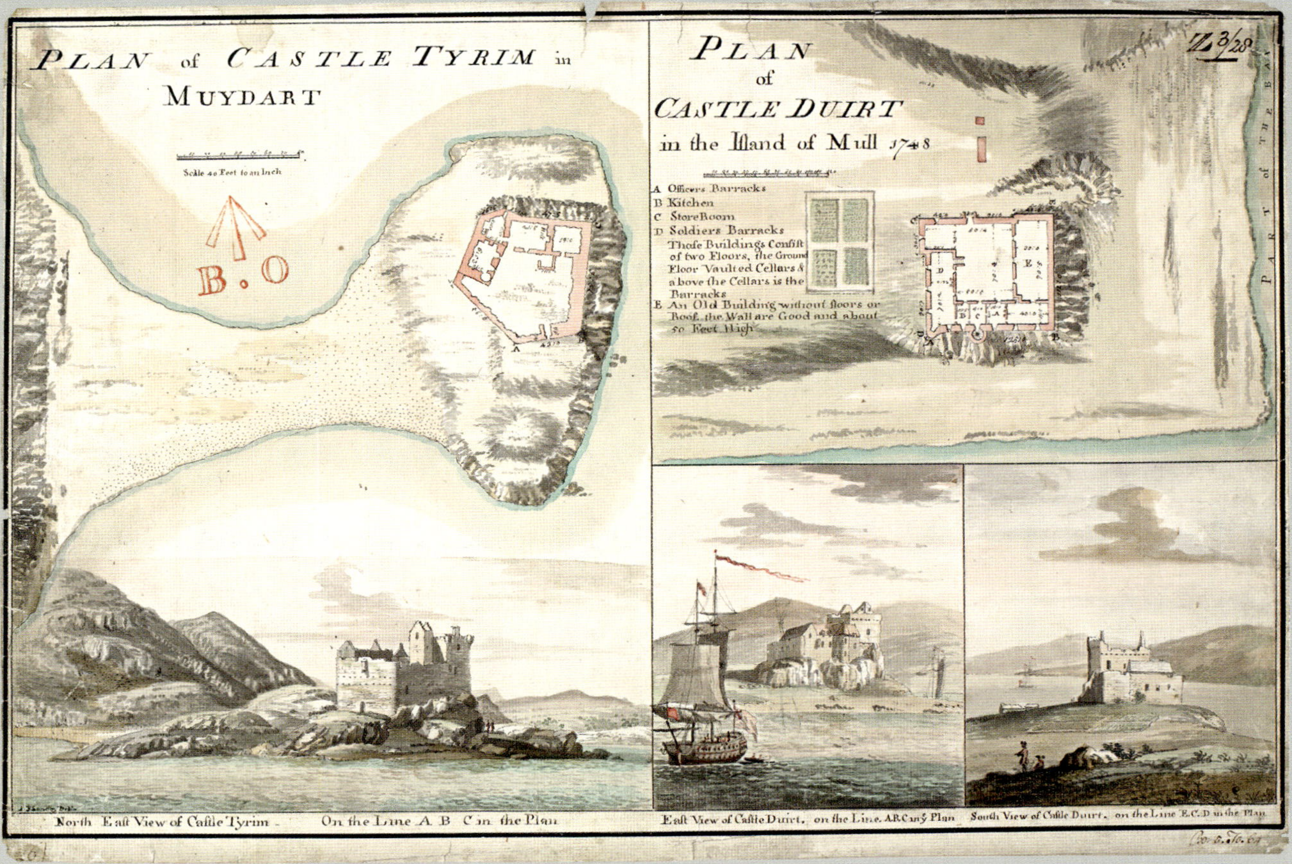

Fig. S1.8
Paul Sandby, *Plan of Castle Tyrim in Muydart; Plan of Castle Duirt in the Island of Mull*, 1748, manuscript map
(NLS MS.1648 Z.03/28e)

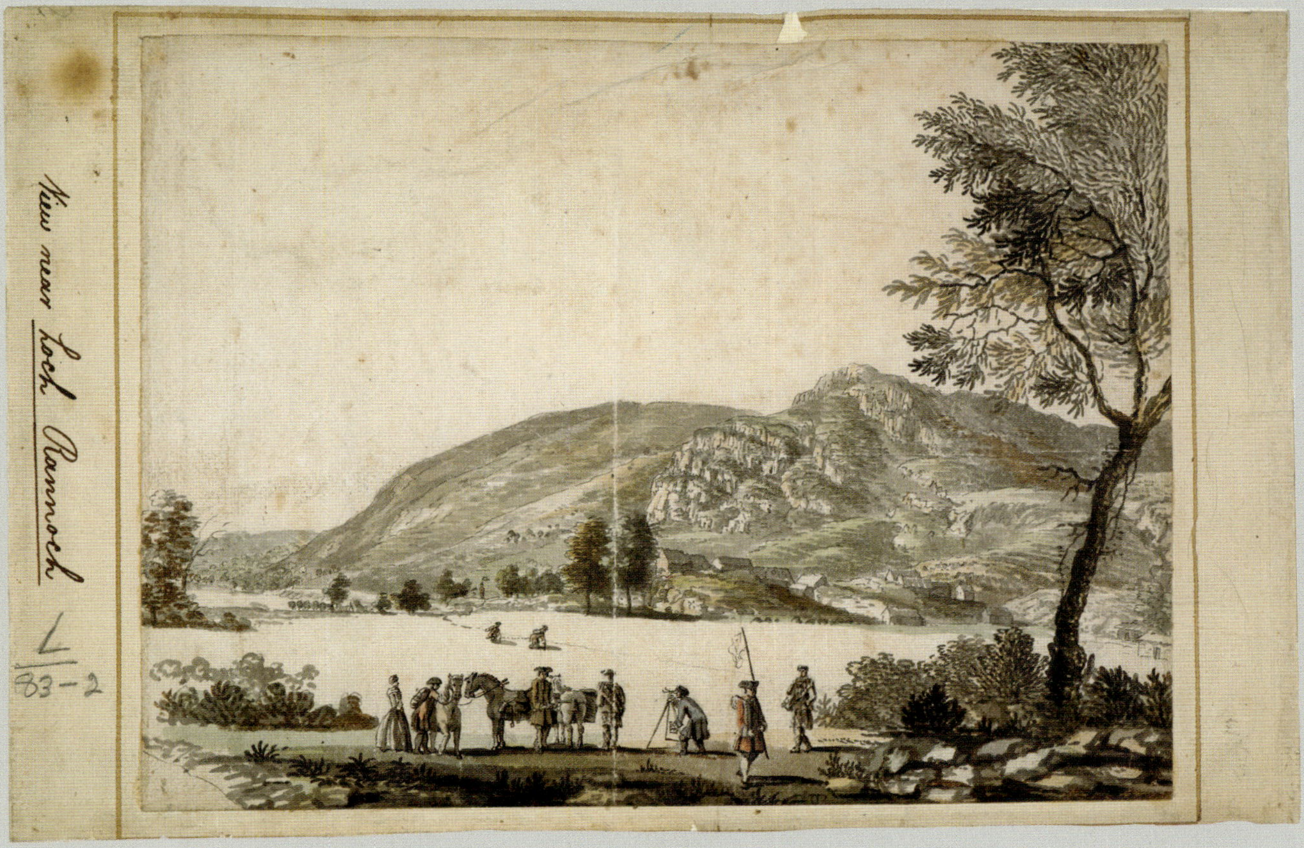

Fig. S1.9
Paul Sandby, *Surveying Party by Kinloch (Loch) Rannoch*, 1748, watercolour, pen and ink
(BL K.Top 50.83.2)

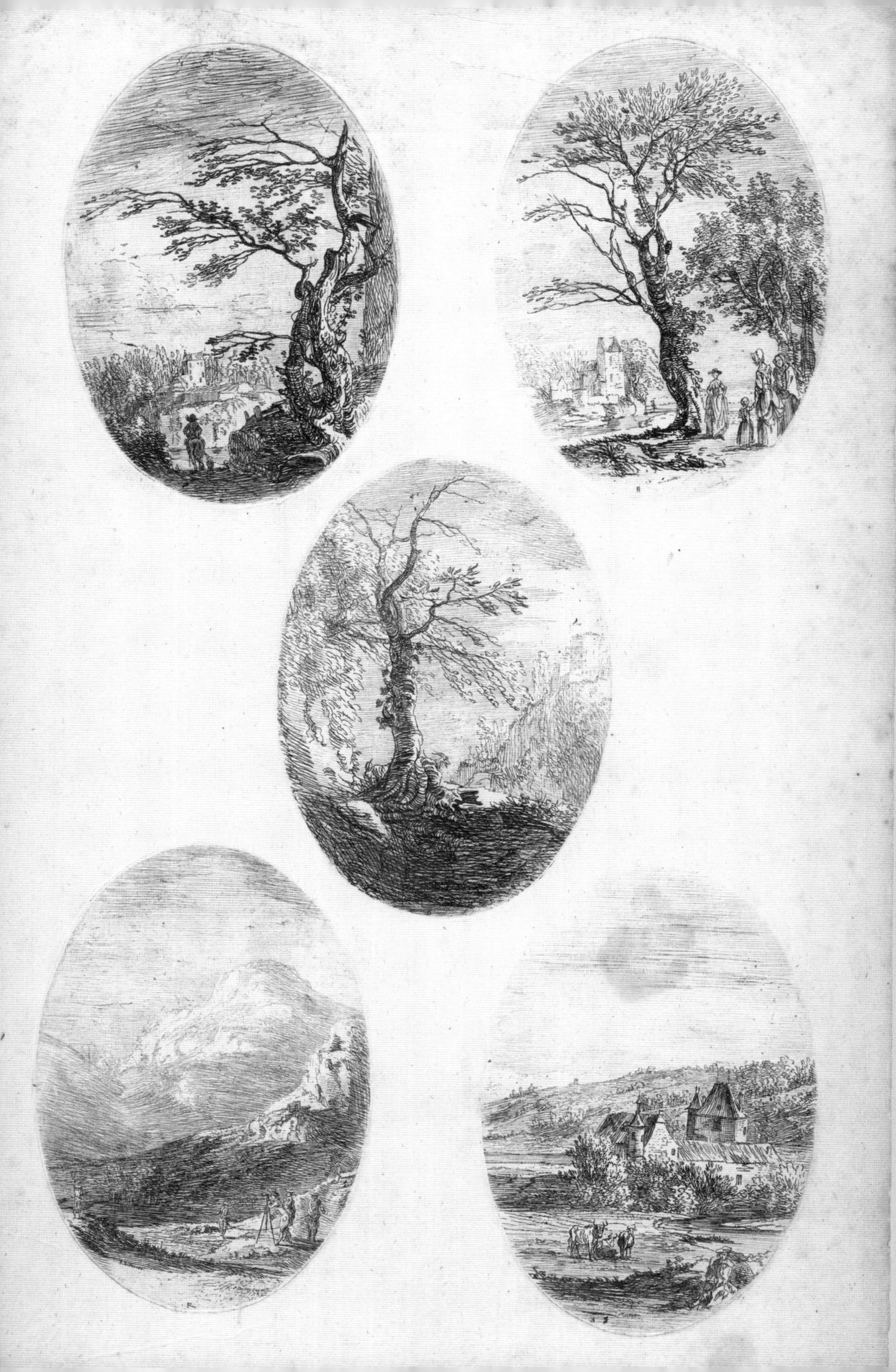

Fig. S1.10
Paul Sandby, five oval Scottish landscapes, etching, from *A Collection of Etchings* (London, 1765), p. 41 (GLAHA:57302))

measuring chain being dragged by the two figures across the ground are silhouetted against blank paper, in a reminder of the sheets on which the new view of the land being projected was to be inscribed. Lying on lands confiscated from the Jacobite Robertsons of Struan, Kinloch Rannoch was now under the control of the Westminster-appointed Board of Annexed Estates, whose progressive plans for reshaping the economy and society, as part of the broader project of pacifying the Highlands, were to see draining, planting and road building as well as the establishment of a model settlement for discharged soldiers and displaced crofters built on this spot. Surveys and remapping played a key role in these plans, so it is striking that another scene by Sandby, of a party turning a theodolite to bear on the Highlands, an etching published as part of a series of Scottish scenes, was sometimes printed up alongside views of flourishing local scenery, again connecting the mapping of this landscape with its improvement (Fig. S1.10).

Only seventeen when he travelled north to work on the survey, in a post almost certainly secured for him by his elder brother, who was by then part of Cumberland's retinue, Paul Sandby already had his eye on a subsequent professional career. He produced a broad range of off-duty studies, etched as well as drawn, taking inspiration from local scenery, sketching its antiquities and modern improvement, its 'old ways' and new roads (Fig. S1.11). He broke new ground, making studies of people and places in the midst of dramatic change, for which there were few precedents in British art. In some instances, the younger Sandby took up projects his brother had presumably left for him, adding figural incident he had observed on the streets of Edinburgh to the stretching prospect of Fort Augustus, for instance (Figs S1.5 and S1.16b). In another example of their collaboration, the younger brother worked-up a companion scene for Thomas Sandby's fine but unfinished view of the dukes of Argyll's west-coast seat of Inveraray begun when he was stationed there during the 'Forty-Five' (Figs S1.12 and S1.13). Dealing with matters of situation and its role in the design and management of a landscape, they document the changes wrought by the laying out of the military roads. With plans to replace the ruinous old castle at Inveraray already in motion, Archibald Campbell, 3rd Duke of Argyll, was also looking to improve its communications and outlook when the Sandbys took to sketching the town. Using his leverage with the Ordnance, Argyll ensured work began on a projected but until this point unrealised military road from Dumbarton, while simultaneously laying the ground for a new, or rather relocated, settlement. Gazing out across, or set along, the path of this new road, and taken from and then directed towards the headland where the town was to be resettled, respectively, the Sandby brothers' drawings reflected on this moment of dramatic transformation. They address the staging of the landscape, its scenic claims and its practical form, its sightlines and route-ways. Being attentive to such issues, especially at times of radical change, the Sandbys had a keen eye for the past management and use of the landscape as well as its modernising present. Drawing was a way of taking the measure of things, of understanding and getting to know a landscape. It had a communicative and instructive power that was not lost on others in their circle.

On sketching trips with the likes of Robert Adam and John Clerk of Eldin, probably giving instruction in drawing, Paul Sandby and party were to take note of signs of the changes taking place in the landscapes they travelled and at times the conflict and tensions that these wrought. Sketched in a way that was both summative yet informative, in one remarkable instance of this practice, Clerk's drawing of the narrows of Ballachulish, at the mouth of Loch Leven in northern Argyllshire, centres on the arresting image of a hanged man, the body that of James Stewart, sent to the scaffold (despite evidence to the contrary) for the

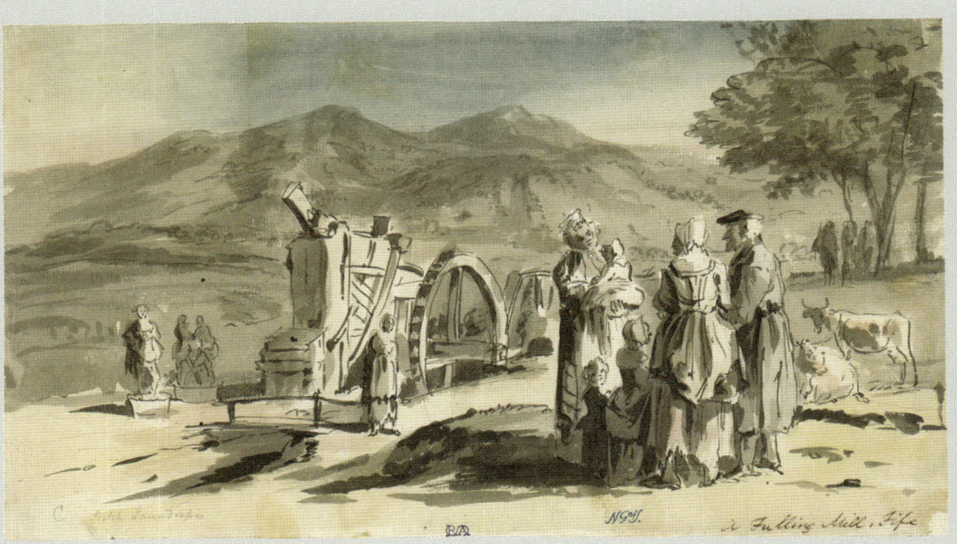

Fig. S1.11
Paul Sandby, *Fulling Mill, Fife*, c. 1750, watercolour (NGS D136)

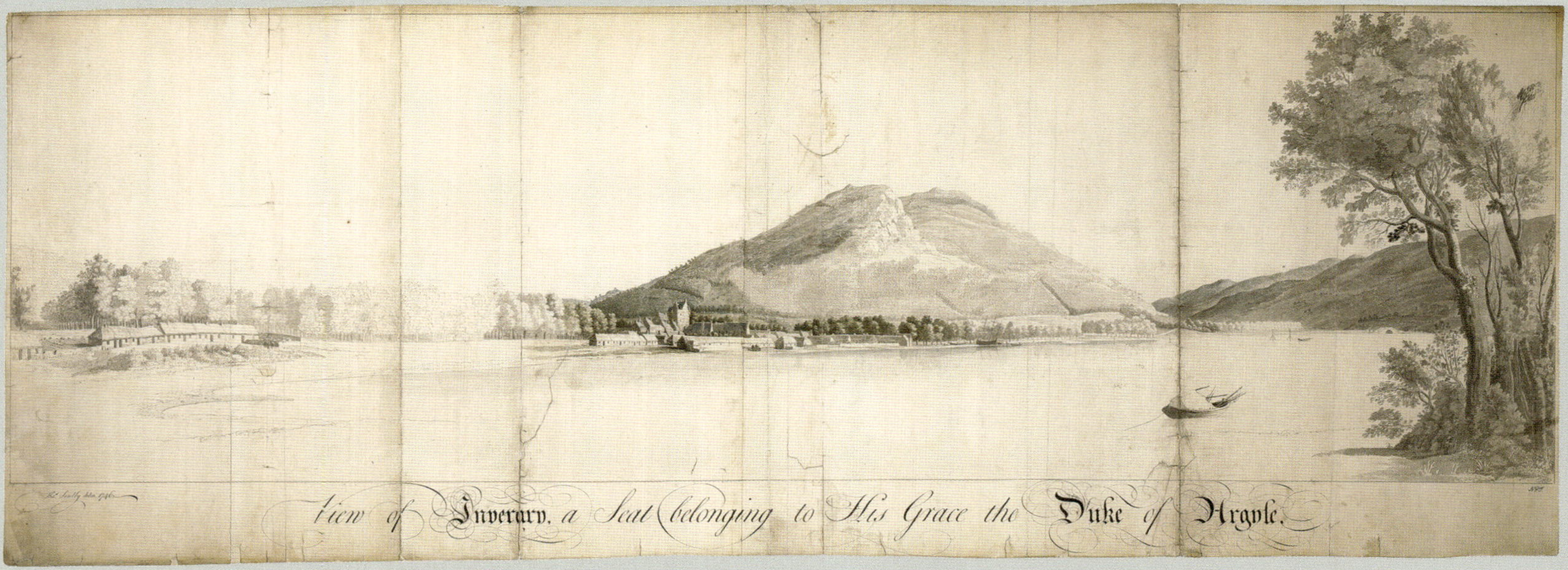

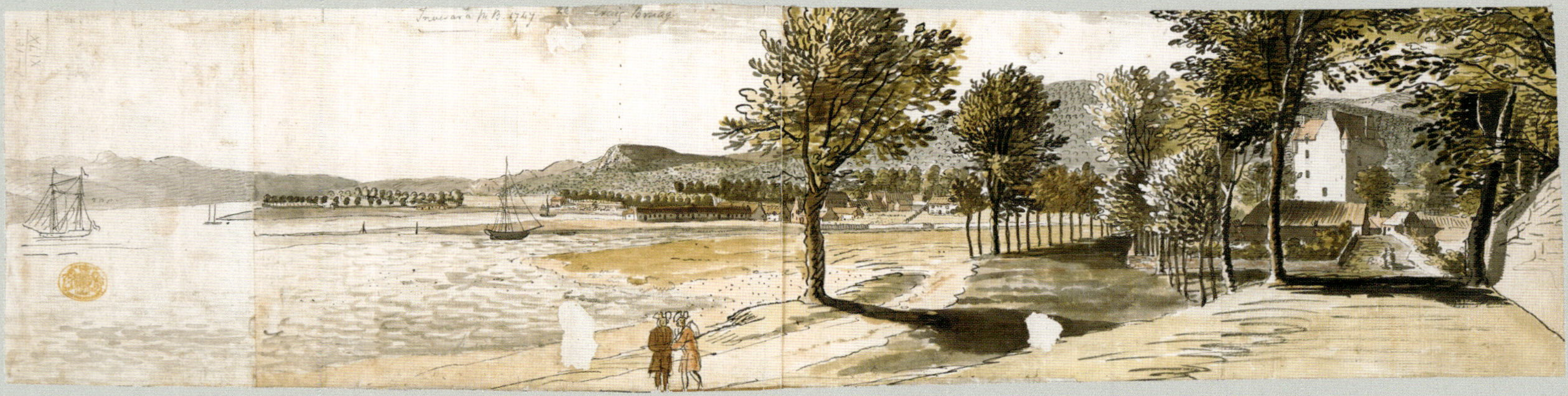

Fig. S1.12
Top. Thomas Sandby, *View of Inverary, a Seat belonging to His Grace the Duke of Argyle*, 1746, pen and wash (NGS D76)

Fig. S1.13
Above. Paul Sandby, *View of Inveraray*, 1747, pen and wash (BL Maps K.Top 49.31.1a)

murder of the 'Red Fox', the government-appointed factor of the forfeited estates of the Jacobite Stewarts of Appin (Fig. S1.14). It is a drawing that displays a well-honed eye for local detail and topicality, a quality also evident in Sandby's sketches of land and life in the aftermath of the 'Forty-Five', and something his instruction was clearly designed to nurture. Later in life, with drawings and maps being increasingly touted as critical instruments of war, Sandby would be appointed Chief Drawing Master at the Royal Military Academy, based at Woolwich, probably on the basis of his early work for the Ordnance, where students were taught to sharpen their vision with a sketchbook. Sketching the landscape, according to one of the course guides, brought 'the eye to the knowledge of it' (Jones 1851, 46). No doubt the social prestige of drawing as a polite accomplishment appealed to Adam, Clerk or his military pupils, as it was in keeping with their gentlemanly self-image, but this idea of the art as a practical means to interrogate and better understand the distinctive character of a terrain was not lost on them either. In sketchbooks from the time of the Military Survey, which show signs of being guided by Sandby's tuition, the recruits can be seen working their way through these methods of observation and depiction (Fig. S1.15a, b). They experiment and familiarise

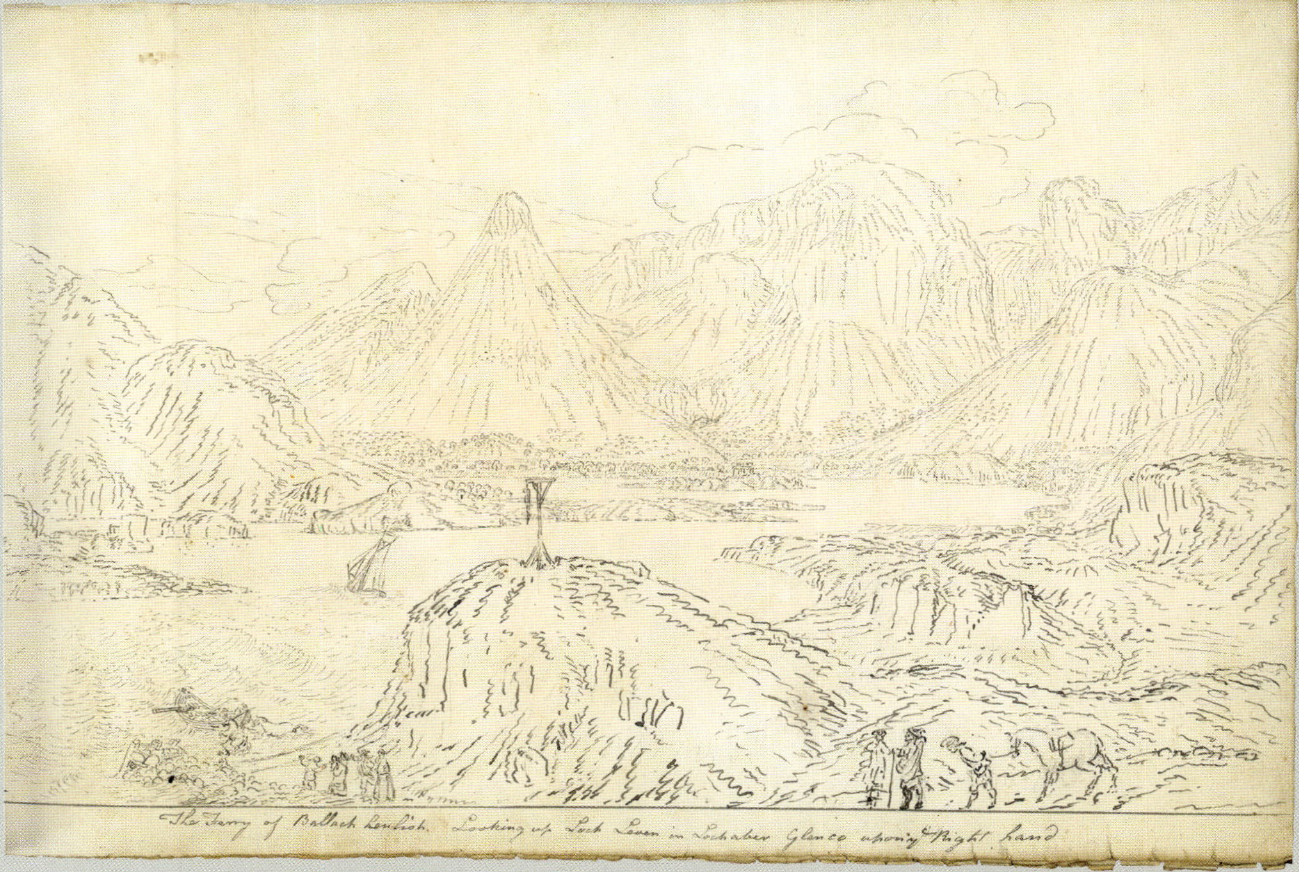

Fig. S1.14
John Clerk of Eldin, *The Ferry of Ballach houlish. Looking up Loch Leven in Lochaber Glenco*, 1752, graphite, from an album of drawings by John Clerk of Eldin (PC)

themselves with various forms of picture-making and media, producing hesitant pencil sketches of the landscape and measured plans of fortifications as well as fine watercolours of soldiers resting or sketching and a sharply observed image of a Highland 'Gillie wet feit or Errand Runner' that is reminiscent of their tutor's studies of local characters and customs.

When he was stationed in Edinburgh, the city's streets provided Sandby with a broad range of subjects, from its down-and-out to its most fashionable and polite denizens. Part of a well-established literary and visual tradition of street Cries, addressing the very nature of urban experience, he made 'many drawings of figures, in the costume, and of the habits and employments of the inhabitants of Edinburgh' (Sandby 1811, 458). Transients passing through are as much a focus of these drawings as residents, however. Beggars, hawkers and street traders, sailors, soldiers and prisoners all feature (Fig. S1.16a–c). With a series of urban backdrops of eateries, taverns, executions and fairs acting like a stage set, there is a satirical edge to many of these scenes 'done from the life'. Skewering the pretensions of the capital's polite sort or having fun at the expense of the lot of the lower orders, the artist exposed the economic and political tensions of the post-rebellion city. Street vendors protect their pitches from raggedy, itinerant peddlers touting their wares to passers-by. Scarlet-clad soldiers question a crowd or lead captured Jacobites off in chains. Some of these figures reappear in fully worked-up scenes from the period. In these, the characters Sandby observed on his rambles about the city rubbed shoulders with ones he had encountered in contemporary prints. This blurring of fact and fiction is apparent in a view of a horse fair set on the broad, open expanse of Bruntsfield Links, where the performance of an elegant, dancing couple – sampled from a design by the fashionable London-based French artist Louis-Philippe Boitard – makes for a comically incongruent

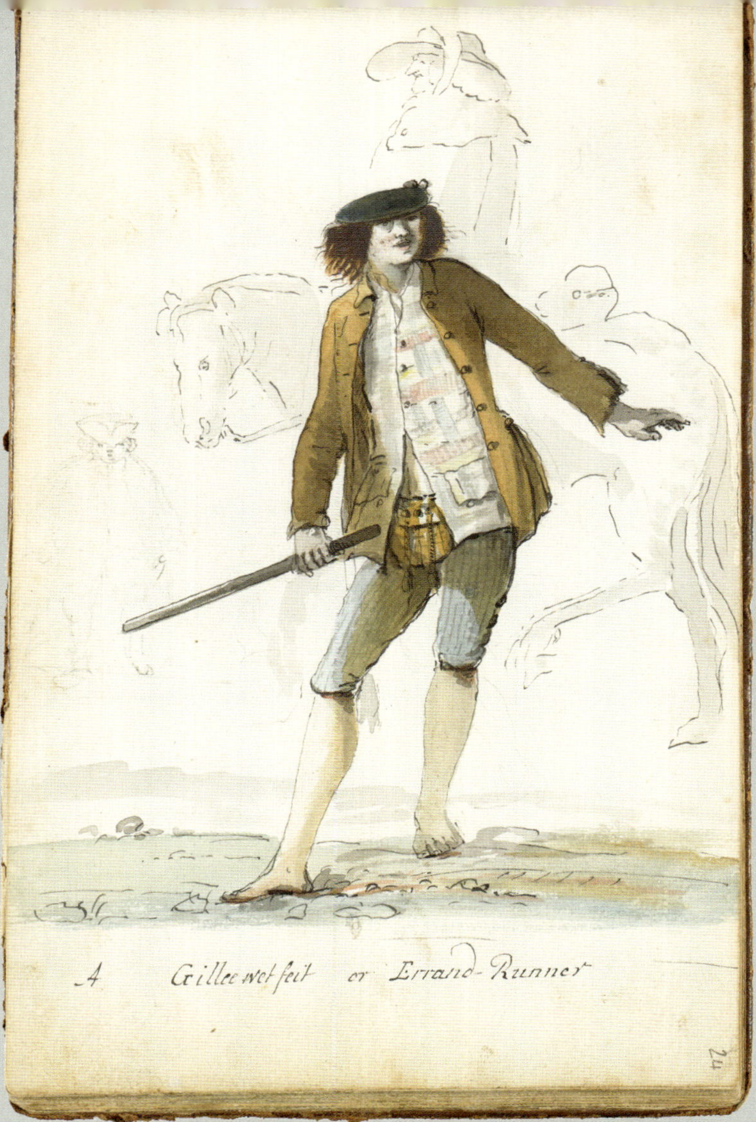

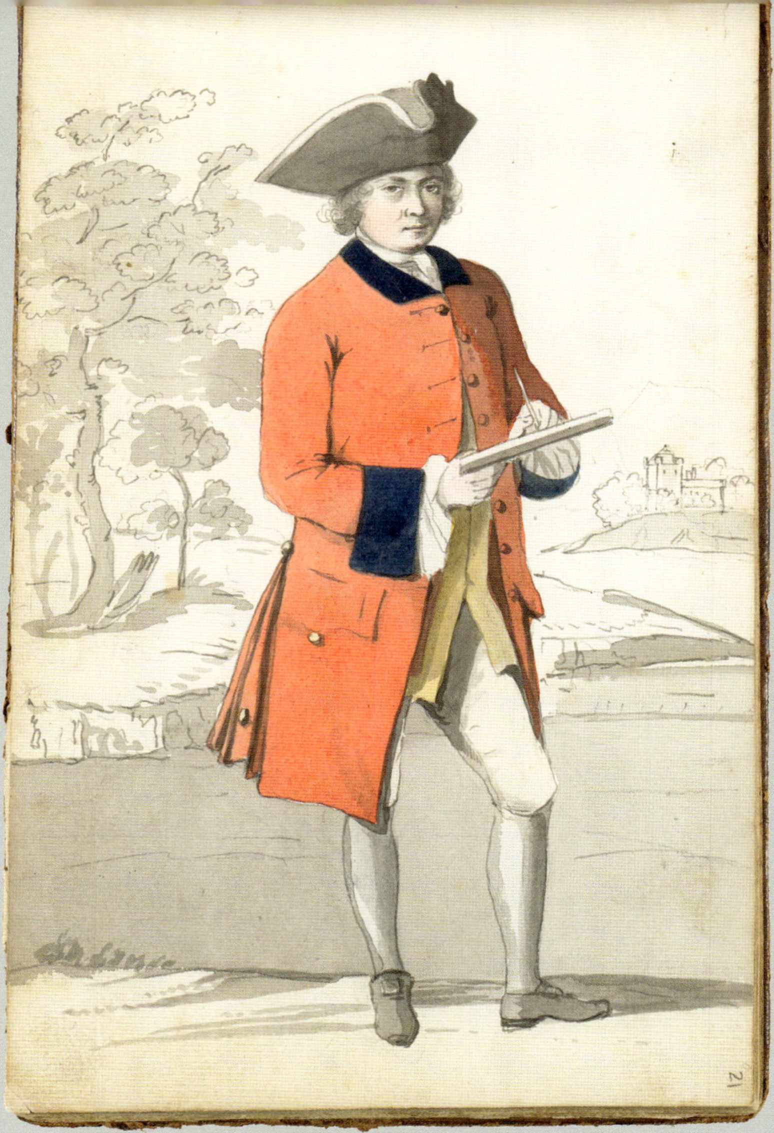

Fig. S1.15a
Above left. Circle of Paul Sandby, 'A Gillee Wet Feit', ink and watercolour over pencil, in *Sketchbook of Drawings made in the Highlands*, c. 1749 (NGS D 5339 A.24)

Fig. S1.15b
Above right. Circle of Paul Sandby, 'Portrait of a Draughtsman', ink and watercolour, in *Sketchbook of Drawings made in the Highlands*, c. 1749 (NGS D 5339 A.21)

sight amidst the noisy mayhem and drunken, slapstick antics of the motley crowd (Fig. S1.17). Such fairs were a traditional aspect of the city's economy, serving as hiring grounds, market-places and social venues, if the cattle and horse trading is relegated to the margins in Sandby's scene by the entertainments afforded by the makeshift eateries and dram shops. There is comedy, but there are unsettling elements too: a fight breaks out among the alcohol-fuelled crowd in the background; and plaid-clothed Highlanders mix with English redcoats.

That the anxieties of the period provoked such a curious mix of absurdity and fear is also apparent in the remarkable series of hasty sketches known as the 'Penicuik Drawings', which feature Jacobite troops and loyalist militia serving in and around the Clerk of Penicuik estate, on the banks of the River Esk to the south of the capital, at the time of the 'Forty-Five' (Brown and Cheape 1996) (Fig. S1.18). Although the artist has not been identified, their highly economic, pictorial calligraphy of blots, washes and scratches of the pen is certainly effective. The artist also had a sharp sense of the ridiculousness of military decorum in the face of the horrors of armed conflict. Taking in the bumbling, ludicrous clowning of both sides, the drawings include a series of portraits of named individuals, both real and imagined, as well as rank-and-file clansmen, militia and Hessian mercenaries. Some are shown in isolated studies, but others take part in staged tableaux, of comic altercations with camp sutlers, cavalry and infantry meeting in pitched battle, and the drink-filled amputation of the wounded. Much as with Sandby's observations of the awkward, tense encounters of civilian and military culture on the streets of

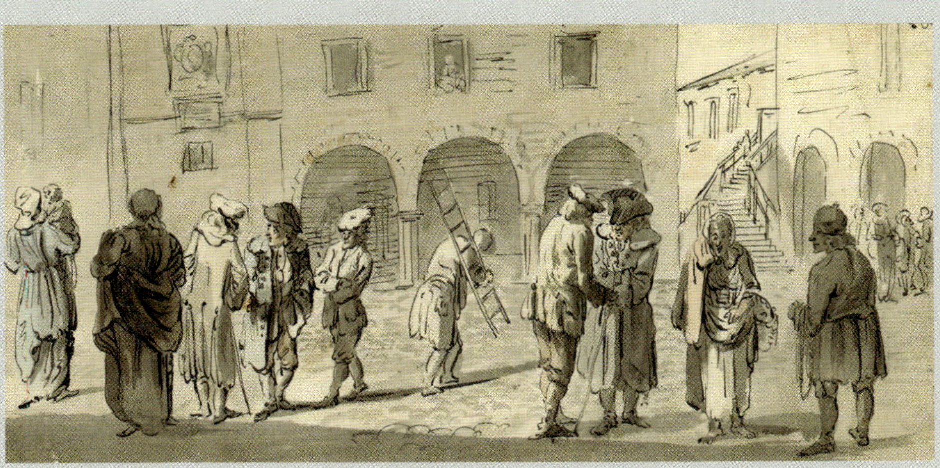

Fig. S1.16a
Paul Sandby, *Street Scene, Edinburgh*, c. 1747–1751, watercolour
(BM 1904,0819.71)

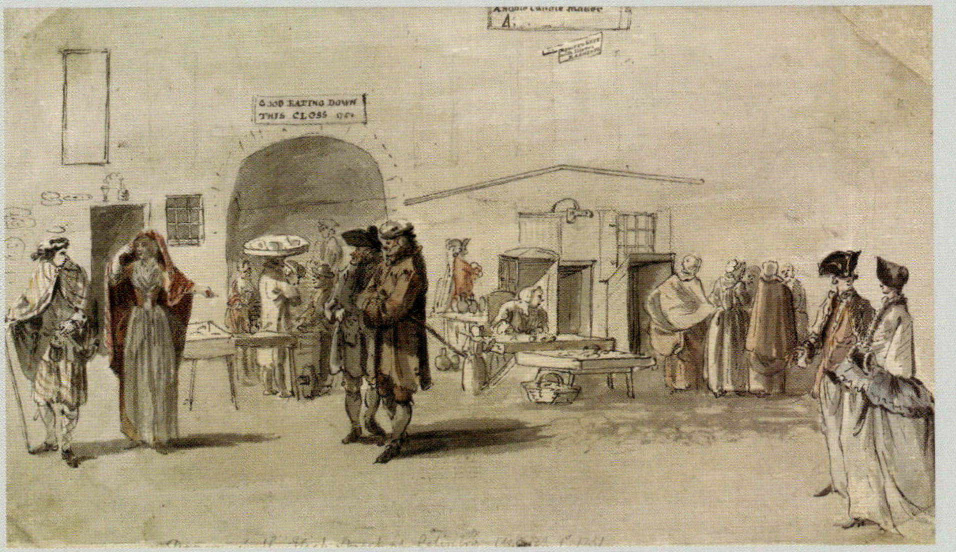

Fig. S1.16b
Paul Sandby, *A Scene in the High Street, Edinburgh*, c. 1747, watercolour
(BM Nn. 6-45-40-67)

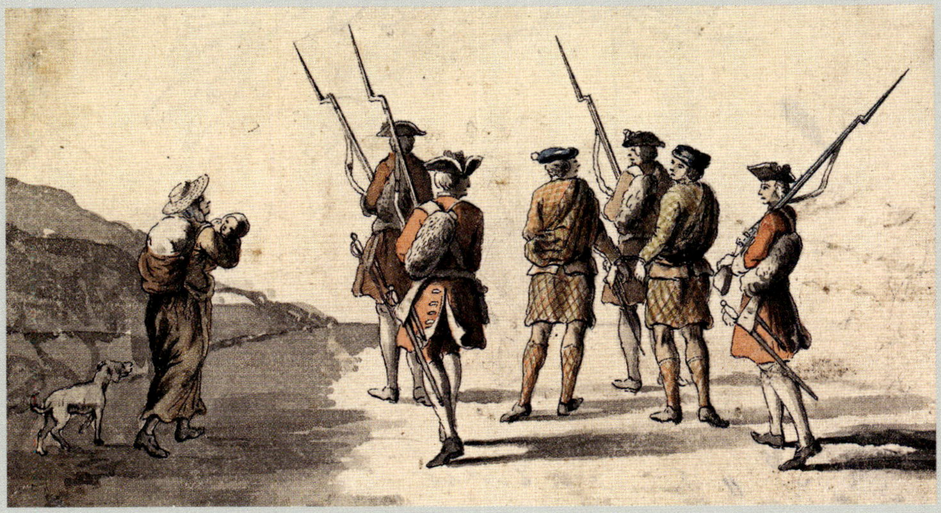

Fig. S1.16c
Paul Sandby, *The Taking of Jacobite Prisoners*, c. 1747–1751, watercolour
(BM Nn. 6-47-34-37)

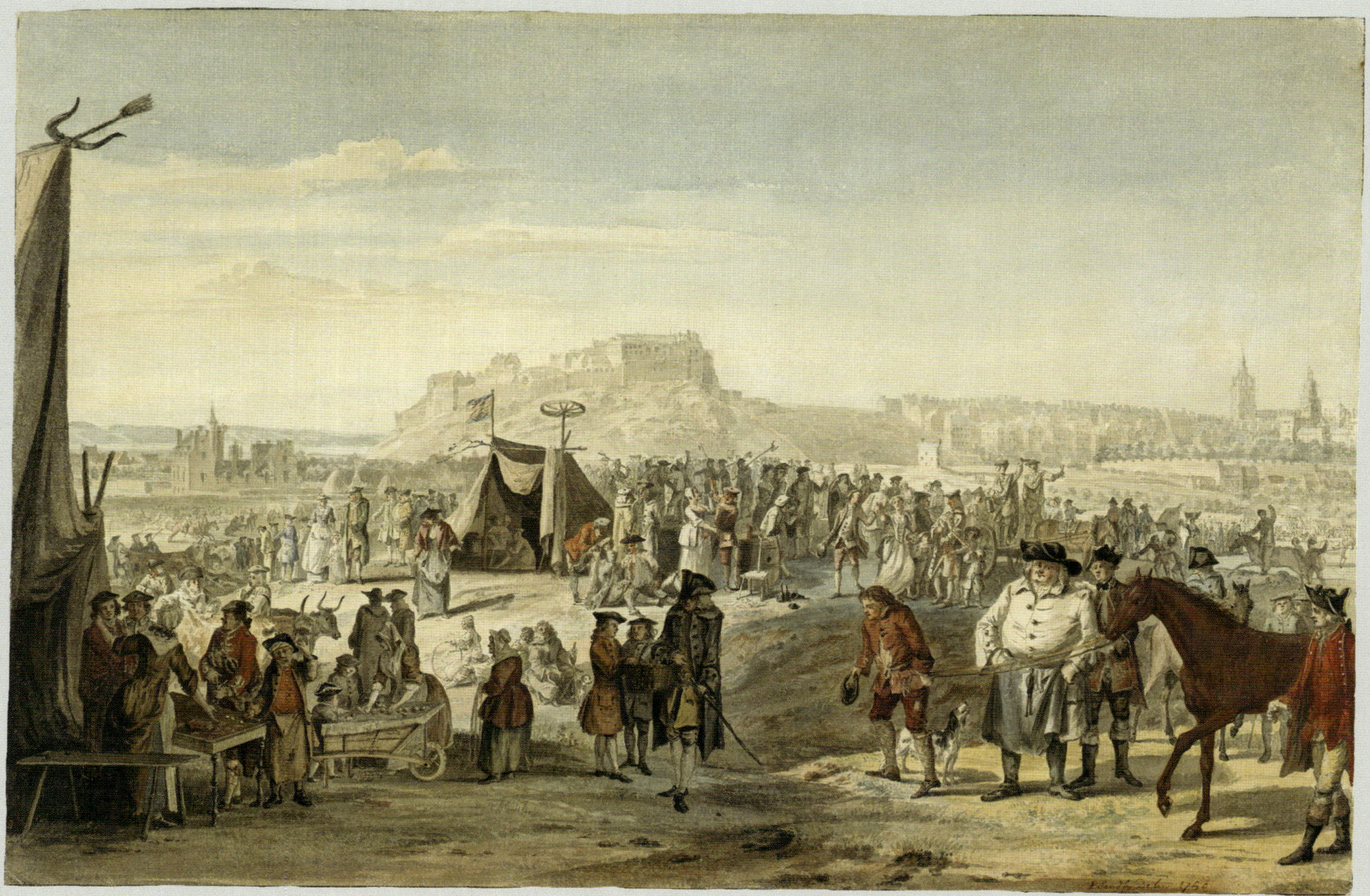

Fig. S1.17
Above. Paul Sandby, *Horse Fair on Bruntsfield Links, Edinburgh*, 1750, watercolour (NGS D 5184)

Fig. S1.18
Opposite and overleaf. Anon., a selection of the 'Penicuik Drawings', c. 1745, mixed media (PH)

Edinburgh after the rising, there is something at once playful and disturbing about these drawings, as if recognition of the absurdity and grotesqueness of war was the only sane response to the uncertainties of the day.

On the surface of things, those images of Edinburgh street life that Sandby was producing would seem far removed from the work of the Board of Ordnance. But, as the collage of allegory and satire, battle plans and views that Elphinstone was to assemble for *A New Map of North Britain* illustrates, the official commemorative productions of the Ordnance Drawing Room would readily shift across and combine a range of visual registers and sources too. Documentation and invention went hand-in-hand. In the words of Thomas Paul Sandby, writing shortly after the turn of the century, his father's years working on the mapping of Scotland were 'the source of his eminence as a landscape painter', not least as regards 'the formation of his particular style', 'though he there saw nature in her wildest form, the necessity under which he lay of attending to particular accuracy in filling up the plans, may be supposed to have formed in him that correct and faithful habit, with which he after viewed and delineated her' (Sandby 1811, 457).

The defence of Edinburgh

A maidservant shoulders a Volunteer's musket.

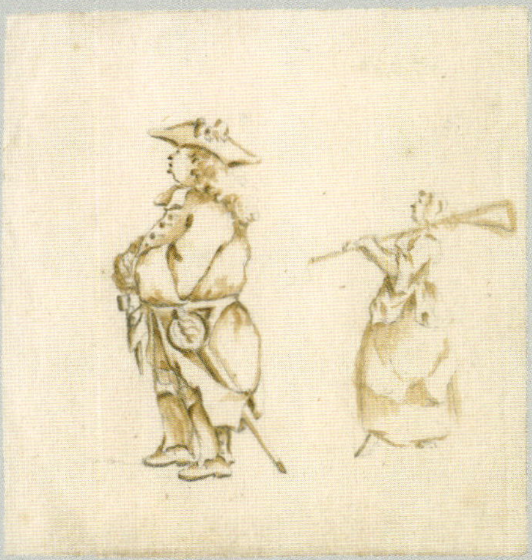

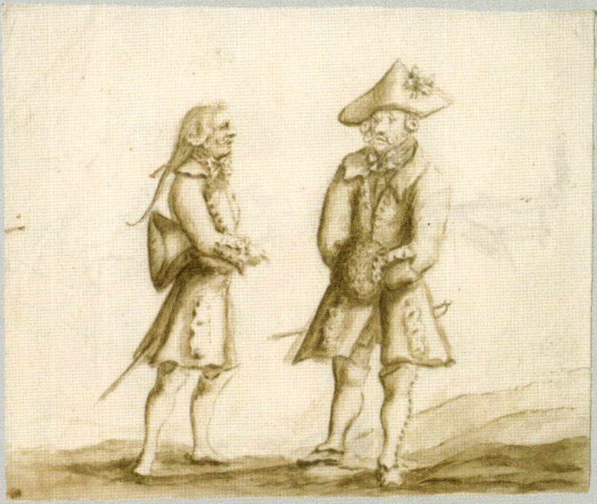

Hessian officers in the Government service.

Politics upset the tea table.

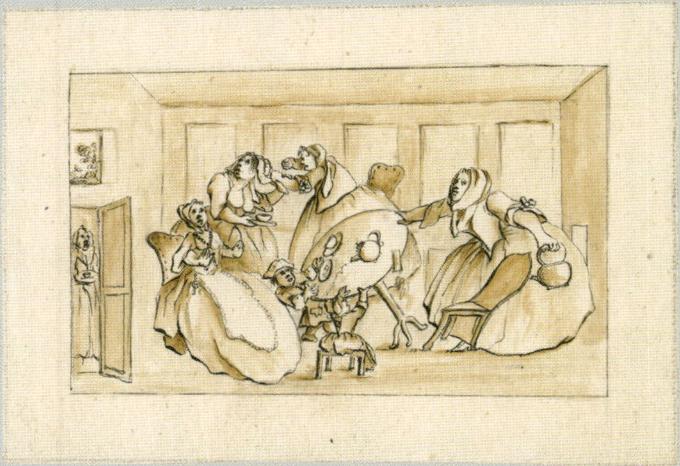

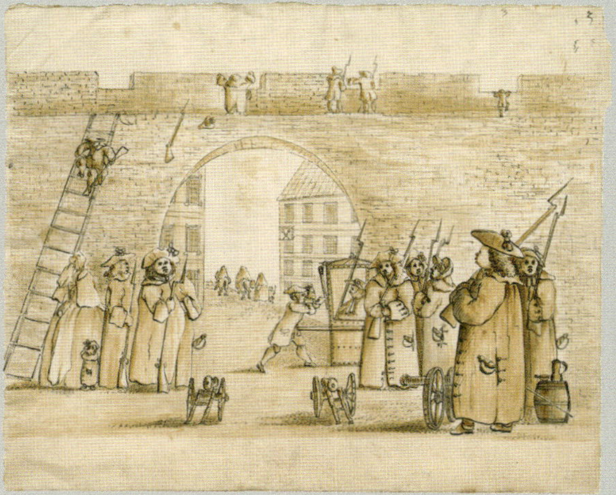

A Volunteer picket at one of the city gates.

War widow or Hanoverian spy?

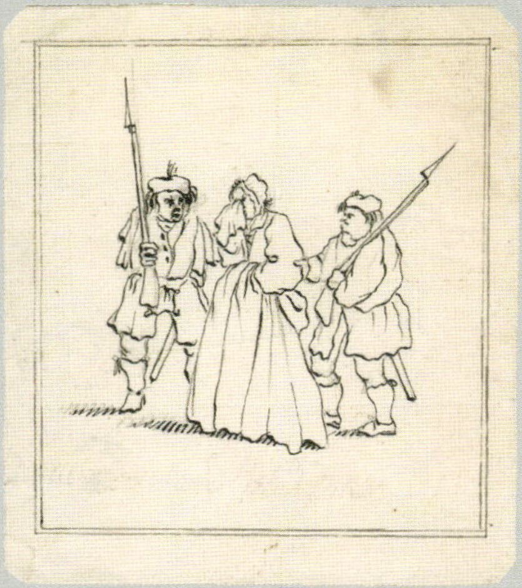

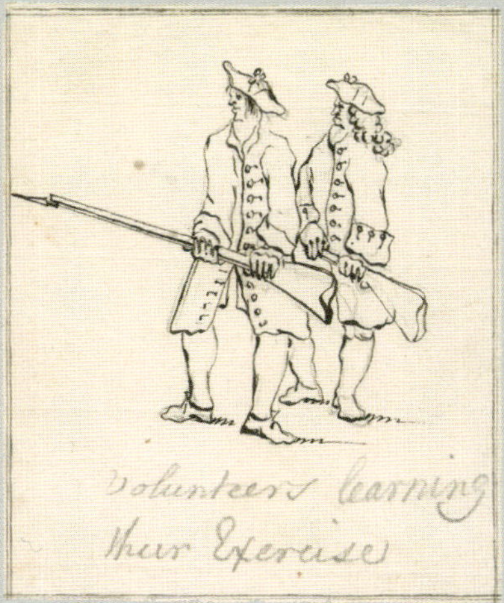

Edinburgh 'Volunteers learning their Exercises'.

The Jacobite camp

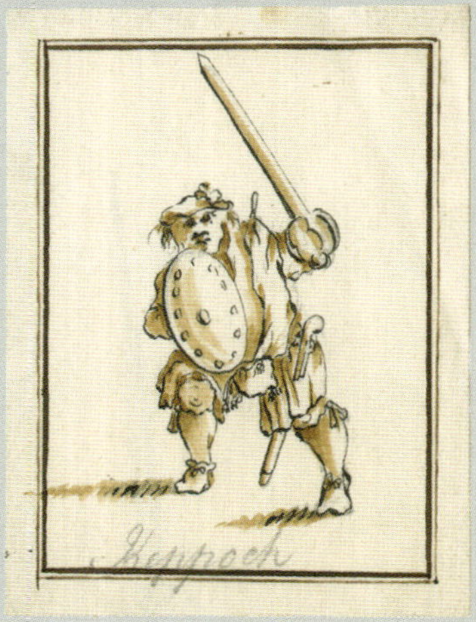

Alexander Macdonnell of Keppoch, later killed at Culloden.

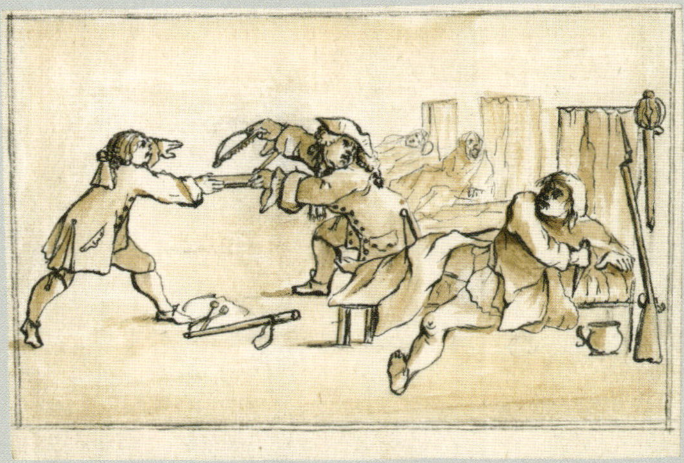

A defiant amputee reaches for his dirk.

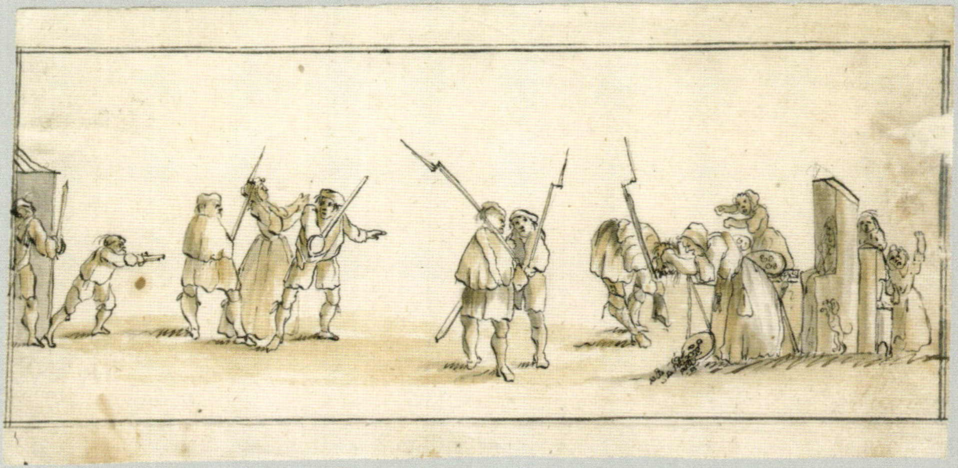

A soldier being deloused.

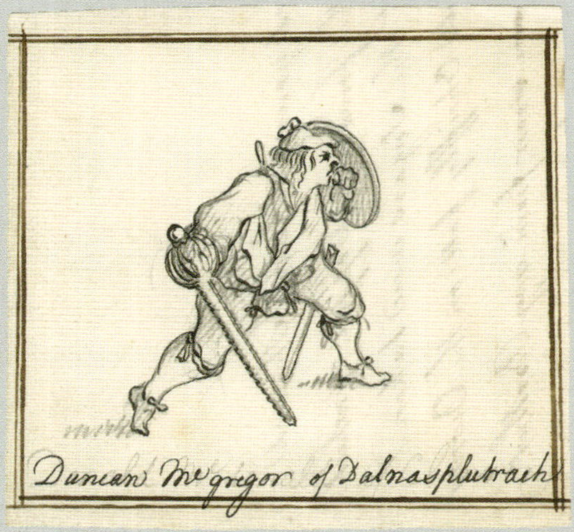

'Duncan McGregor of Dalnasplutrach': Highland braggadocio burlesqued.

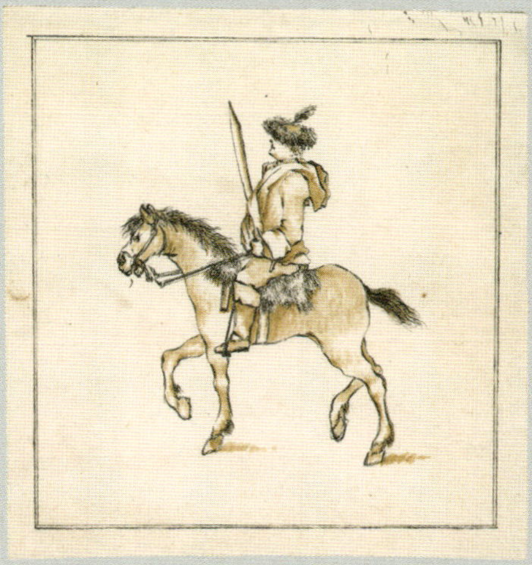

A fur-capped Jacobite hussar.

By the time T. P. Sandby was writing, his father's early Scottish views had become highly collectable, valued by figures like Thomas Pennant for their historical worth as well as their aesthetic merit, as images of a landscape in transition, which otherwise barely featured in mid century art (Fig. S1.19). From the late 1770s, these views had also begun to appear as engravings, with the artist recycling studies from his time on the Military Survey for the print-publisher George Kearsley's *The Virtuosi's Museum* (Kennedy 2003; Bonehill and Daniels 2009, 187) (Fig. S1.20). War with France and the ongoing threat of invasion throughout the period of publication gave this project a certain poignancy, reinforcing the patriotic claim made in the publisher's preface that the aim was to add to the growing 'national taste' for 'innocent and refined amusements' and all 'for less than the value of a masquerade ticket!'. Over the course of the 108 engraved plates that were eventually issued, surveying sites in England, Scotland, Wales and Ireland, and the first such enterprise to cover all three kingdoms, *The Virtuosi's Museum* projected an image of British territories united by a shared past and a commitment in the present to the values of improvement. For the Scottish scenes, Sandby edited and reworked the drawings he had produced as a young man to conform with an expectation for ruggedness and to show changes to a landscape now pacified by improvement. So a *View of Ben-Lomond near Dunbarton* now portrayed a much-reduced military encampment from that which spread across the open expanse of the foreground in the original sketch, the scene presided over by a soldier and Highlander-guide performing their own act of union.

Letterpress accompanying most of the Scottish scenes in *The Virtuosi's Museum* either quoted or paraphrased from Thomas Pennant's famous *Tours*, which portrayed the kingdom as occupying the moral centre rather than the periphery of the nation, offering a robust reproach to a metropolitan England softened by commerce and luxury. Based on travels made in 1769 and written up over the next two years, Pennant's first *Tour* was very much a response to the effects of the imperial expansion of the Seven Years' War. With some irony, it had been the defeat of the rebellion and the consolidation of the Union that had laid much of the ground for the nation's newfound imperial prowess. Large-scale diplomatic and military recruitment in the Highlands had begun at the start of the Seven Years' War, the involvement of the people from there heightening the perception of this as a war fought for and by Britons. Empire was a shared project that helped integrate the peoples of Britain, in the colonies or port cities of the Clyde, the corridors of power and fields of battle. Such were the military contributions of the newly founded Highland regiments that the region came to be seen and fostered from that point on as a nursery of martial virtue that had to be carefully cultivated, if it was to be protected from the pressures of a modern commercial society. By the time that the final plates of *The Virtuosi's Museum* were issued in the early 1780s, the loyalty of the Highlands was indeed no longer in doubt, a development symbolised by the lifting of a proscription on Highland dress and the de-annexation of forfeited estates. Some of those plates showed Highland troops at the gates of Windsor Castle, now defending the Hanoverian Crown rather than threatening it. Indeed, the tartan-clad Highlander became a prominent figure in the visual arts of the 1780s, in grand scenes of heroic action in the fight for empire and in images of the domestic security they safeguard, becoming sensible men of feeling even, in works by David Allan, for instance (Fig. S1.21).

It was Highlanders' embodiment of ancient Caledonian liberty, now assimilated into a history of British valour surviving only in remoter mountainous areas, that lit Gilpin's enthusiastic anticipation of modern 'battlefield tourism'. While Gilpin uncritically accepted Hanoverian power and the benefits of the Union, he admired the spirit of bravery and loyalty he saw as fostered by the clan system; just being in the vicinity of Glencoe led him to lament the 'horrid cruelty and treachery' of the events of 1691, while extoling the virtues of those chiefs who had delayed swearing allegiance to the Crown. Though Glencoe was too far off the beaten track for Gilpin actually to visit, he had heard that it was 'hung with rock, and wood; and abounding with beauties of the romantic kind'. Such rugged 'wild scenes' were of a kind with ungoverned independence of its warlike peoples (Gilpin 1789b, I, 160, 166). In Gilpin's mind's eye, at least, the glen was a natural memory theatre: a monument to the dead made of air, earth, wood, stone and water. The beauty and tranquility of such sites only served to cast the barbarism of the past into still greater relief. It was not just those places where conflict had left physical traces (the vestiges of the Roman occupation or the historic fortresses that attracted the antiquaries and historical tourists, the focus of Section 2) that prompted reflections on the aesthetic, moral and political significance of 'a scene of memorable action'.

Visiting the history-marked landscapes and remains of

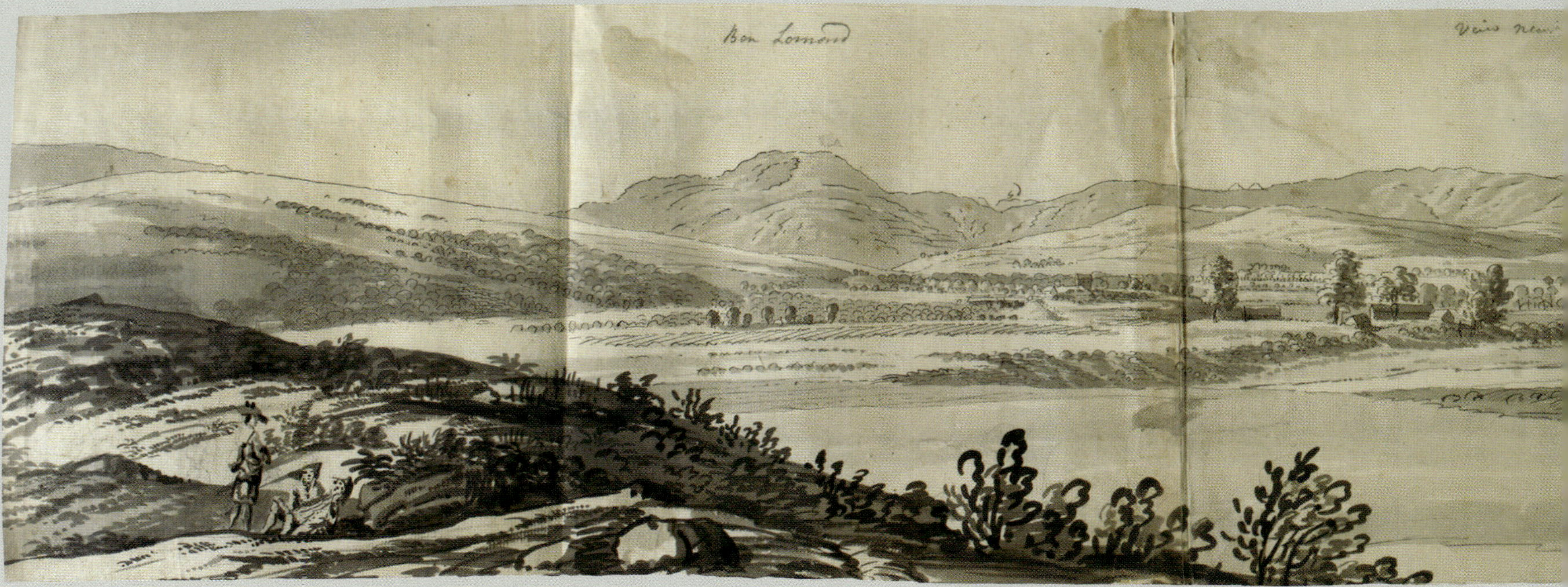

Fig. S1.19
Above. Paul Sandby, *Ben Lomond, View near Dumbarton*, c. 1747, pen, ink and wash over graphite, pasted in Thomas Pennant's own extra-illustrated copy of his *Tour of Scotland 1769–1772*, Vol. 1, part 2, facing p. 249 (NLW W6)

Fig. S1.20
Right. William Walker and William Angus after Paul Sandby, *View of Ben-Lomond near Dunbarton*, engraving in *The Virtuosi's Museum; Containing Select Views, in England, Scotland and Ireland*, 1778 (NCM 1987-1032)

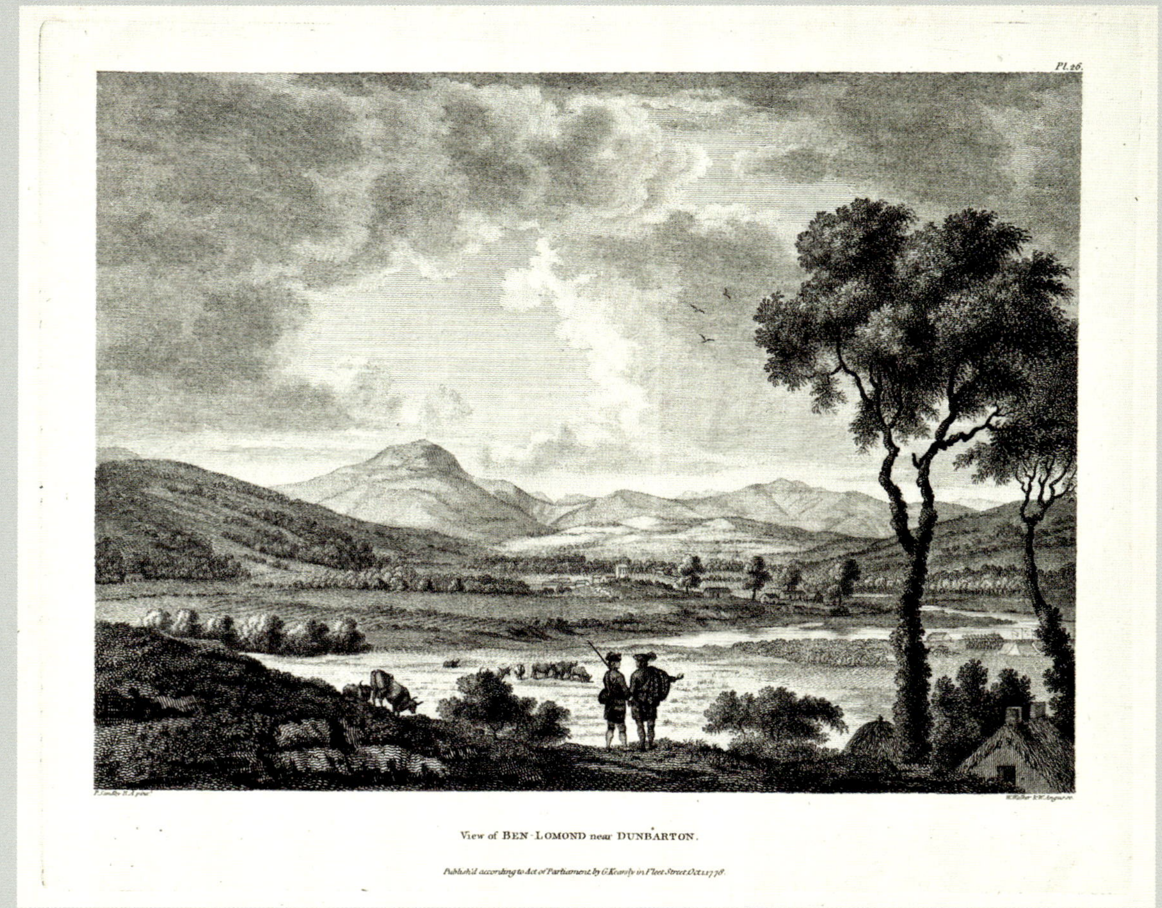

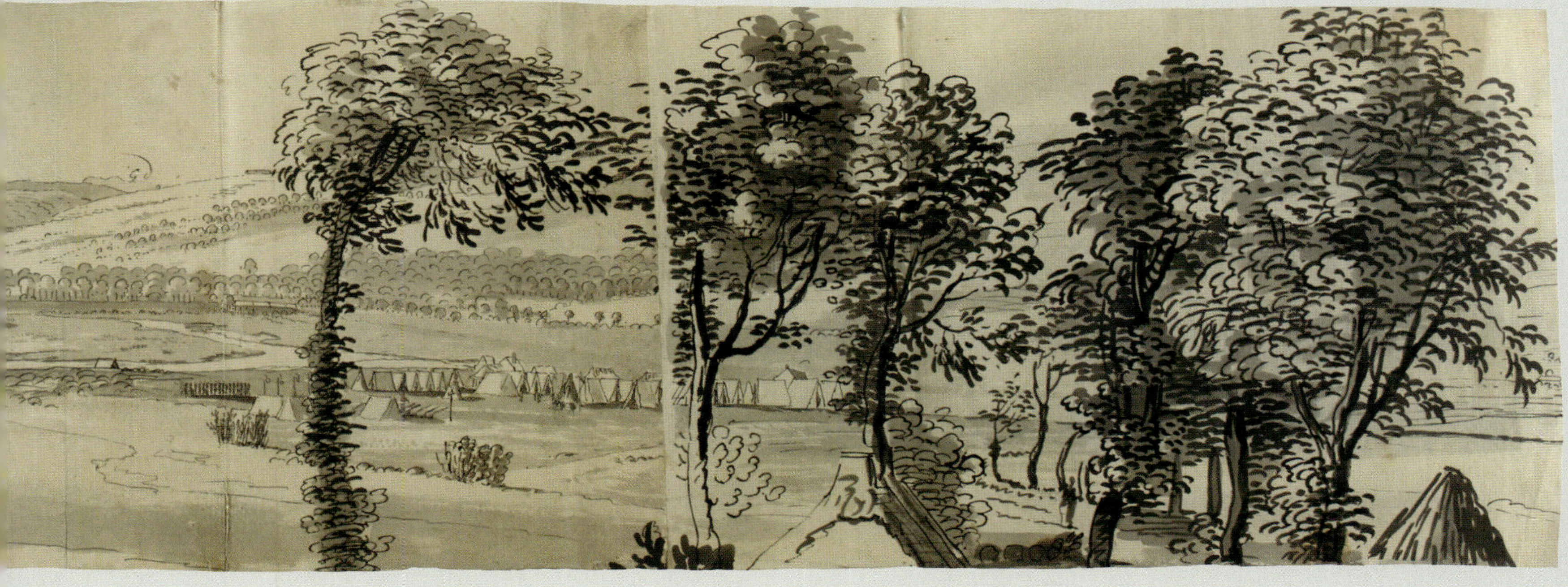

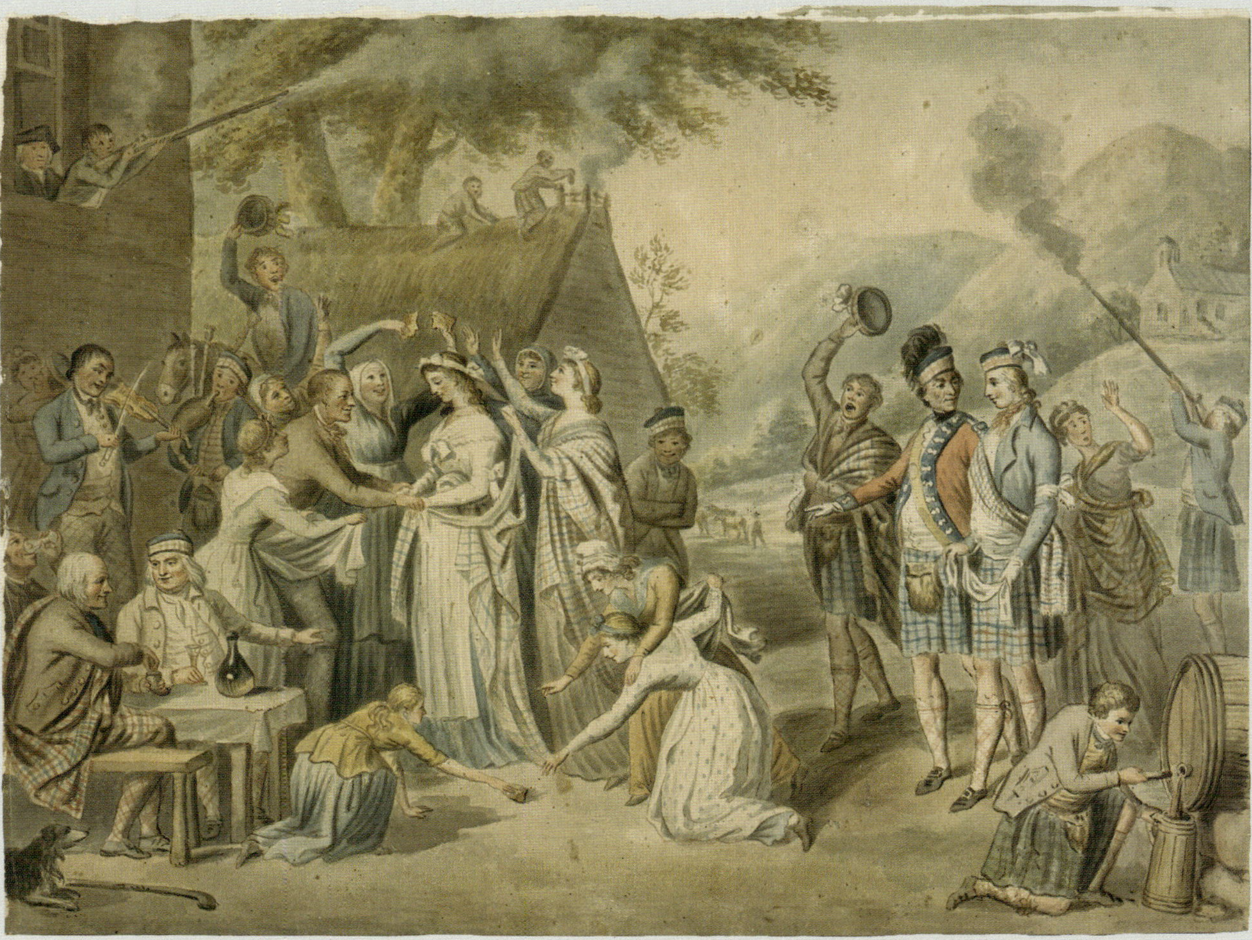

Fig. S1.21
Left. David Allan, *A Highland Wedding*, c. 1790, watercolour (NGS D4411)

Scotland's bloody past offered a means of communing with the long-since dead, or perhaps a way to make sense of terrible violence still in living memory. On surveying Culloden Moor, Pennant, whose travel itinerary was heavily inclined to places of battle, wrote of it as 'the place that *North Britain* owes its present prosperity to, by the victory of *April* 16, 1746'. For him, Scotland's very entry into the modern world was founded on the events that took place there on that day. Of 'Butcher' Cumberland's reprisals in the aftermath of the battle, however, Pennant thought it best to 'let a veil be flung over a few excesses consequential of a day, productive of so much benefit to the united kingdoms' (Pennant 1774b, 151). In this the battleground was as much if not more a place for forgetting rather than remembering (Pittock 2016, 138). Despite the many encounters with the aftermath of those days that litter his *Tours*, in the form of a continued military presence as well as the very roads he travelled or the sight of ruins in the landscape, Pennant was anxious to consign the event to history in the name of Scotland's progress. It belonged to the past in the same way as Culloden's historical antecedent, Agricola's defeat of the Caledonians at Mons Graupius. Such a Whiggish take on the battle and the days that followed it did not go unchallenged; the author Robert Riddell scrawled his disagreement with Pennant's attempt to draw a 'veil' over the Butcher's 'shameful' reprisals in the margins of his copy of the *Tour* (Hutton and Leask 2017, 134–135). Though now more likely to be carried out in words, those 'fertile scene[s] of military events' were still being fought over. Even as these sites were now being sought out by antiquaries or leisure tourists, the meanings and memory of the military landscapes that took shape on the ground as well as on paper in the early decades of the eighteenth century were still contested. Scotland remained a theatre of war.

Fig. S1.22
Opposite top. Georg Hautsch, Attempted Invasion of Scotland, medal, 1708, silver (GLAHM: 38594)

Fig. S1.23
Opposite bottom. Martin Holtzhey, Battle of Culloden, medal, 1746, silver (GLAHM: 38768)

In 1726, Joseph Addison praised medals for allowing 'you [to] see with one cast of an eye the substance of above a hundred pages' (Addison 1726, 20). Struck to mark the frustration of a plan to kindle a Jacobite rising with the landing of French troops, the reverse of the German medalist Georg Hautsch's 1708 medal shows the invasion force being intercepted by an English fleet off the north-east coast of Scotland. Mixing landscape imagery with allegory, Martin Holtzhey depicts William, Duke of Cumberland, as a Roman general being crowned by victory, rising over the vanquished Jacobites, against a prospect of the town of Inverness. Such commemorative tokens made a direct connection between contemporary events and the classical past, combining terse epigrams with pictorial and tactile qualities.

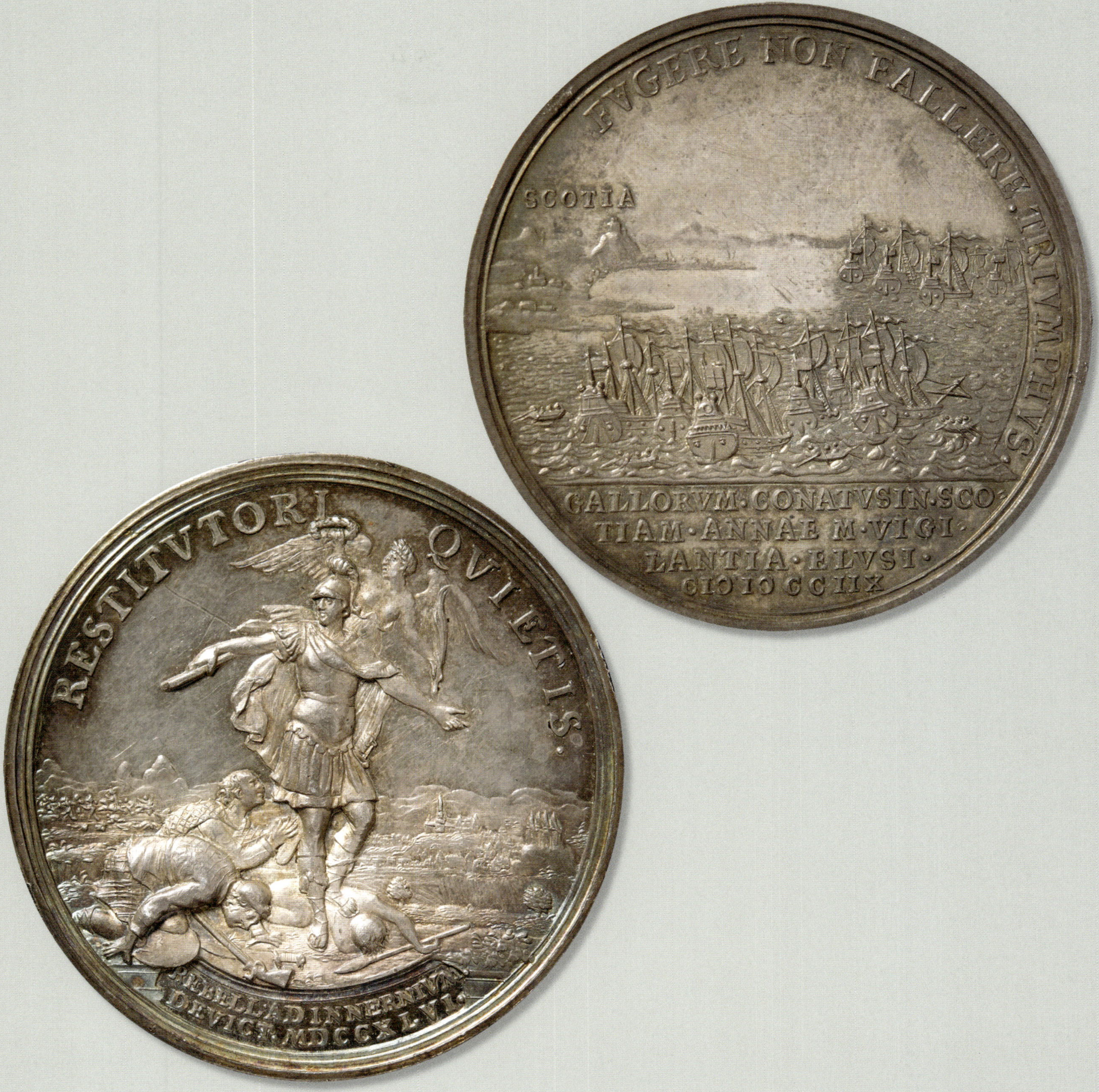
FUGERE NON FALLERE TRIUMPHUS
SCOTIA
GALLORUM·CONATUS IN SCO
TIAM·ANNAE M·VIGI
LANTIA·ELUSI·
CIƆIƆCCIIX
RESTITUTORI QUIETIS.
REBELL·AD INNERNIUM
DEVICT·MDCCXLVI·

CHAPTER TWO

The Ethnology of the 'Old Ways' in Gaelic Scotland

'There's Another Road Near the Highway'

Hugh Cheape

As the Gaelic proverb *Tha rathad làimh ris an rathad mhòr* implies, 'there's another road near the highway': there are roads beyond our ken, and we need not be constrained by the high road of authority (Nicolson 1881, 361). A modern historiography of roads is shaped by the roads that exist today, and the ways we observe and use them. But creating and building roads is a dynamic process: attending to their history (and pre-history) casts new light on our own movements through the landscape. The 'old ways' that precede the 'new roads' often seem to fade into insignificance in the historical record, as travel and transport in the eras and zones of foot traffic and pack animals are marginalised. Narrating the history of road infrastructure is usually prefaced with the concept *a priori* that there were no roads before 'these ones', no roads as we would understand them today.

Tracks, 'old ways' and 'roads' of course existed in abundance in Scotland but are neglected where they no longer exist in recognisable form. Versions might survive in our imagination: 'The Road to the Isles', a popular song written just over a century ago to an earlier pipe tune, nurses a vision of moorland tracks and a 'road' somehow embedded in the national psyche. Its author, Rev. Dr Kenneth MacLeod (1871–1955), collaborated with Marjory Kennedy-Fraser in the immensely popular art-song collections in her *Songs of the Hebrides* (1909–1921), but MacLeod was a Gaelic scholar, folklore and song collector in his own right (Murchison 1988, iii). His evocative lines take the traveller by 'heather tracks' from Tummel and Loch Rannoch and into Lochaber and then on to the coast in Morar. The assumption has been that the romanticised traveller followed, not the present-day road pattern from the Perthshire Highlands to the west coast, but the former droving route of Làirig nan Leacan through the hills and into Glen Spean (Kennedy-Fraser and MacLeod 1917, 240–241; see also Robertson 1941, 18–19).

The narrative of road creation in Gaelic Scotland has grown out of the system of military roads rather than the statute labour roads which preceded them and offered a few major lines of communication. The military focus is on primary links from Perth and Stirling to Inverness and Fort William and a strategic link along the Great Glen between the Forts George, Augustus and William. The preamble to more or less any description of Highland roads (including the present volume) draws on Burt's *Letters from a Gentleman in the North of Scotland* with his comments on the impossibility of moving round the country and the inference that a structure of communications was being created *ex nihilo* with its impact on travel, nascent tourism and topographical description. Another morsel served up in this picture is Lord Lovat's experience in 1740 on a journey from Inverness to Edinburgh, typically quoted with gusto; writing to Charles Fraser of Inverallochy, Lovat described in detail how a presumed five-day coach journey had taken twelve days, though the state of

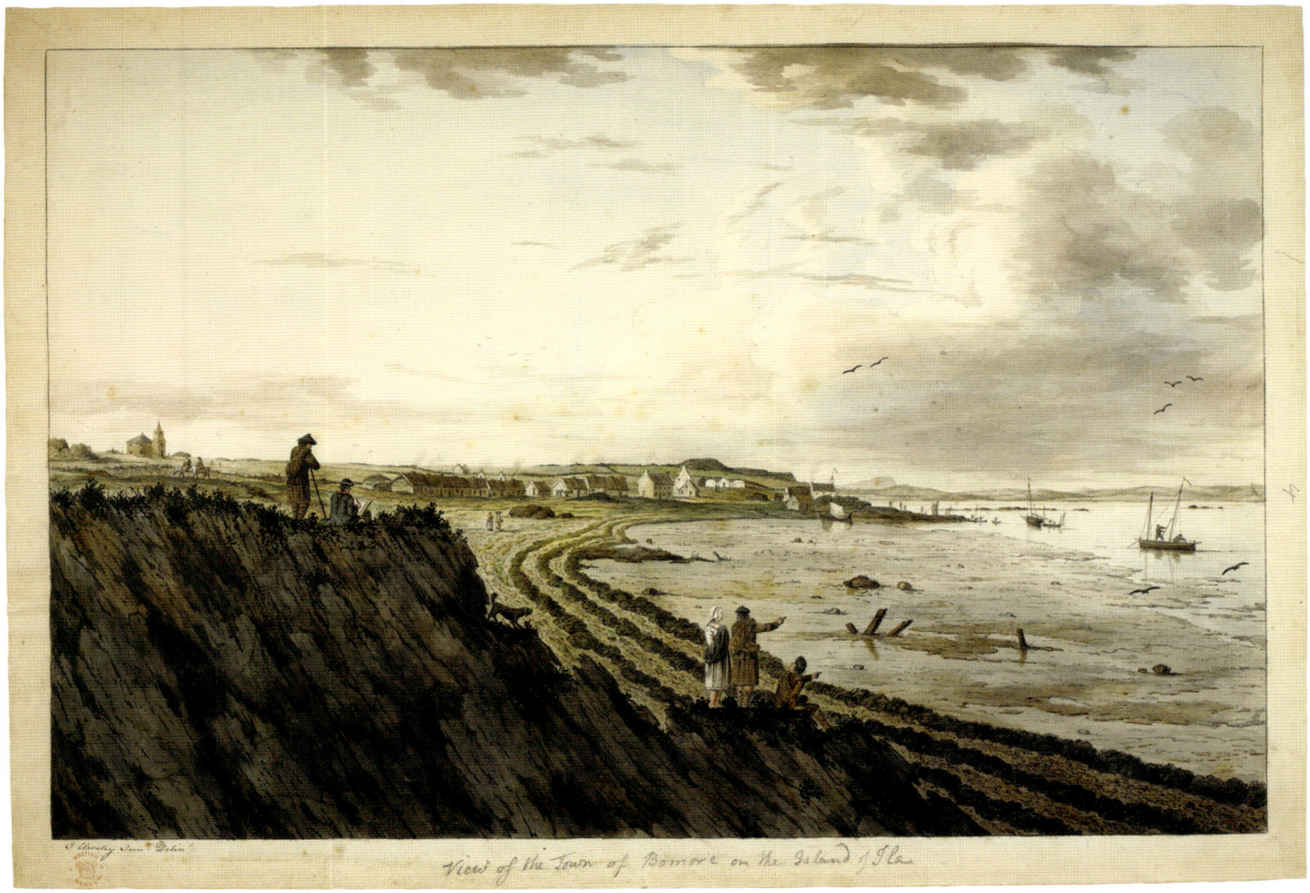

Fig. C2.1
John Cleveley, *View of the Town of Bomore on the Island of Ila*, 1772, watercolour
(BL Add MS 15509 f. 4)

Cleveley's drawing captures an 'old way', marked by a linear settlement of houses, leading inland.

his Lordship's coach might have been worse than the state of the roads, and he had not heeded the omens: 'if I was as much an observer of freits as I used to be, I would not have taken the journey' (*Spalding Miscellany I* 1842, 4). A further failed coach trip was the return home of the 77-year-old poet–chief Alexander Robertson of Struan in Sir John Cope's carriage captured by the Jacobites after the battle of Prestonpans, when it had to be carried on the shoulders of his clansmen (Chambers 1934, 137).

Our espousal of Burt distracts us from earlier sources such as the survey work of Timothy Pont c. 1583–1596 and the impressions of the *Atlas Novus* of 1654 with insights into landscape and settlement patterns in late sixteenth- and early seventeenth-century Scotland (Stone 1989; Stone 1991). We know that 'roads' pre-existed, and the literature, in terms of routes customarily followed or 'old ways', speaks of routes followed by travellers and traders, 'traditional' routes of pilgrimage or 'coffin roads', routes taken by raiders and armies and, of course, the waterways and sea-ways. The significance of the sea cannot be overstated, and Scottish Gaelic is rich in litanies of names in oral tradition of features that marked voyages; Mary Macpherson's 'Ath-urachadh m' Eolais' ('Renewing my Acquaintance') paints a word-picture with place-names to mark a voyage home to Skye from the Clyde in the 1870s (Nic a' Phearsoin 1891, 192–196).

Highlanders of old were highly mobile with a pragmatic attitude to travel, whether at home or overseas: this was never a sedentary society. A well-known proverb sums it up: *Am fear a bhios fad' aig an aiseag, gheibh e thairis uaireigin* ('He who waits long at the ferry will get over some time') (Nicolson 1881, 11). This might have spurred on the heroic builder of 'Calum's Road' in Raasay, Calum Macleod, whose patience outran the Highland

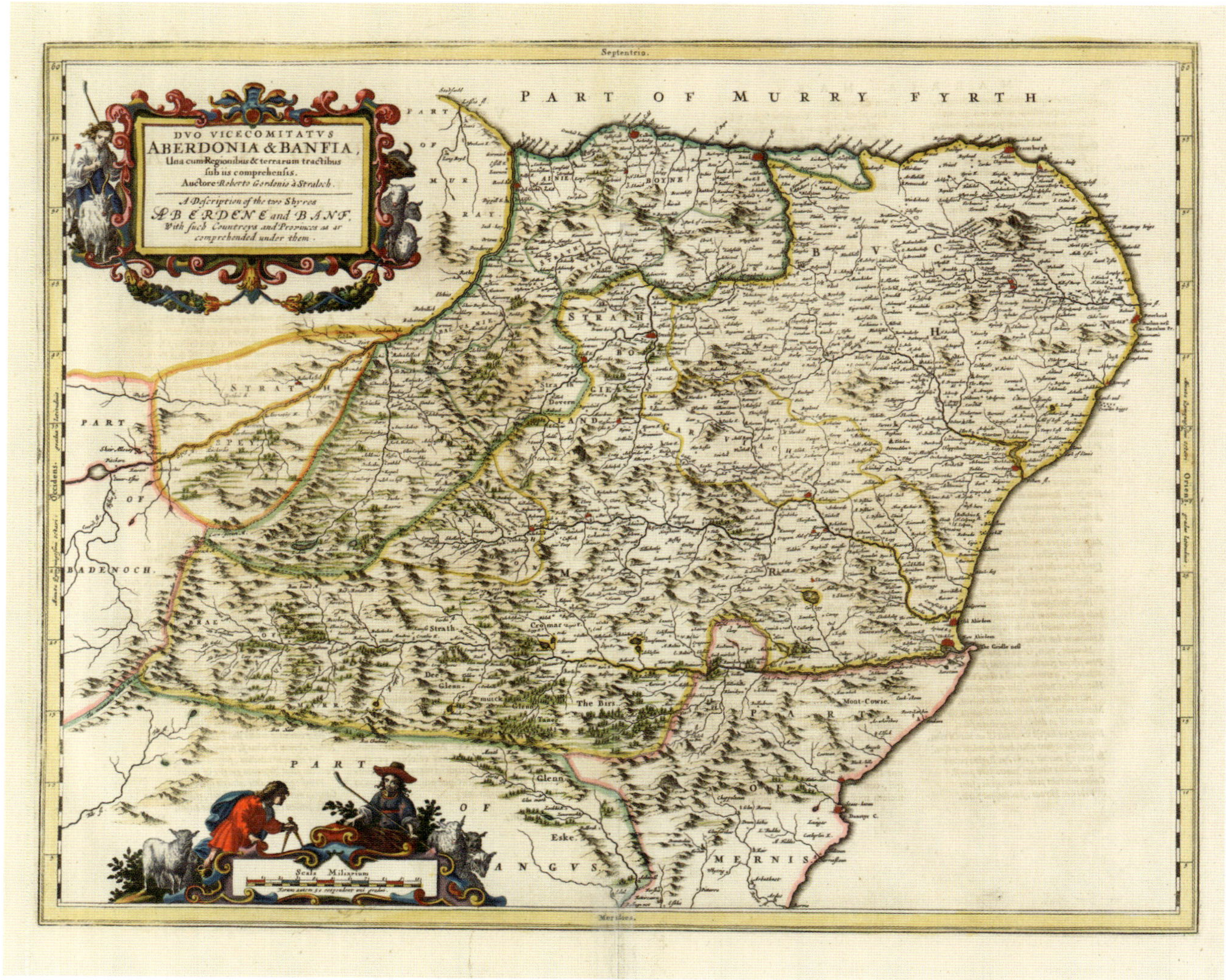

Fig. C2.2
Robert Gordon and Joan Blaeu, 'Duo Vicecomitatus Aberdonia & Banfia, una cum Regionibus & terrarum tractibus sub iis comprehensis / Auctore Roberto Gordonio à Straloch. Description of the two Shyres Aberdene and Banf, with such Countreys and Provinces as ar comprehended un', in *Atlas Novus*, Vol. 5 (Amsterdam, 1654) (NLS EMW.X.015)

This map of Strathspey from *Atlas Novus* draws on the possible first-hand knowledge of Timothy Pont and Robert Gordon and shows a dense pattern of township, settlement names and axis of movement following the River Spey.

Council (Hutchinson 2006). We must now challenge the stereotype of the *Gaidhealtachd* as a tribal and kin-based society behind the mountains. Highland society was neither wholly patriarchal nor wholly commercial, although it was both those things. The Highlander was well travelled, with education on the Continent for the social elite and a healthy acquaintance with Scandinavia, Germany, France, Spain and Mediterranean lands such as Turkey and the Near East. At home, a vignette from a still-famous song, 'Bothan Àirigh am Braigh Raithneach', goes over the 'shopping-list' of the girl in the shieling in Rannoch around 1600, and the expectation that her lover would readily access a cosmopolitan selection of high-fashion and costly commodities (Watson 1959, 192–194). An anglophone literature ignores such insights in favour of 'trackless wastes', a region remote and unknown, and a people self-absorbed and sunk in ignorance. As Dr Johnson commented:

> To the southern inhabitants of Scotland, the state of the mountains and the islands is equally unknown with that of Borneo or Sumatra. Of both they have only heard a little, and guess the rest. They are strangers to the language and the manners, to the

> advantages and wants of the people, whose life they would model, and whose evils they would remedy. (Chapman 1939, 79)

What were the 'old ways' and how were they used? What were the views of Highlanders on the *status quo ante* and the changes then emerging? Dr Johnson's and Burt's views are very familiar and seem to elide any need for response. Reasoned or extended responses to such critiques, such as Rev. Donald McNicol's *Remarks on Dr Samuel Johnson's Journey to the Hebrides* (1779), are rare. Offence prompted scathing but discreet ripostes which deserve to be better known. A vivid song in the MacLagan Manuscripts 'On Samuel Johnson Englishman when He Wrote Against Scotland', castigates him for being a 'slovenly peasant without breeding' and much more (Kennedy 1898, 177–178). A glimpse from Trotternish in the north of Skye offers a view that is perhaps more amusing than profound and assumes that Johnson's *Dictionary of the English Language* had already made his reputation: a young John MacDonald asked Rev. Dr Donald MacQueen, minister of Kilmuir, who the strange-looking gentleman was in their midst, and the minister replied: '*Sin agad, Iain, an Sassunach Mòr a rinn a' Bheurla*' ('That, John, is the big Englishman who made the English'). '*Thuirt mi fhèin, ma-tà, a Mhinisteir, bha glè bheag aige ri dheanamh*' ('I replied and said, "Well, Minister, he had precious little to do!"') (MacGregor 1878, 465).

Old ways are not immediately apparent from modern maps or in a Highland countryside and landscape currently scrutinised through an environmental or 'wilderness' lens. Tracks linking townships with local resources such as timber and fuel – 'peat-roads' – were and are still known; those linking townships with springs, wells and sources of water are largely forgotten. Bridges and place-names such as Kindrochid (for Cinn-drochaid – colloquially 'bridge-end') mark the all-important fording or crossing points of waterways where old ways converged, rather than the line of roads. A significant category of old ways is rooted in transhumance or the seasonal movement of livestock to and from high pastures (Fig. C2.3). Almost every township in the Highlands and Islands was a pivotal point for tracks leading to the high ground and to the shielings. Place-names with the element *airigh* (towards the west) or *ruighe* (towards the east) are common markers of former shieling sites and can be seen in clusters at certain 'remote' points on maps. As intriguing are place-names marking the route between winter-town and shieling, such as Bealach na h-Imriche, 'The Pass of the Flitting', the term *imrich* for 'flitting' implying a summer-time move across country in procession with animals and chattels. Cattle-breeding husbandry that was central to the Highland economy depended for its success on the system of summer shielings and the regular seasonal movement going and returning.

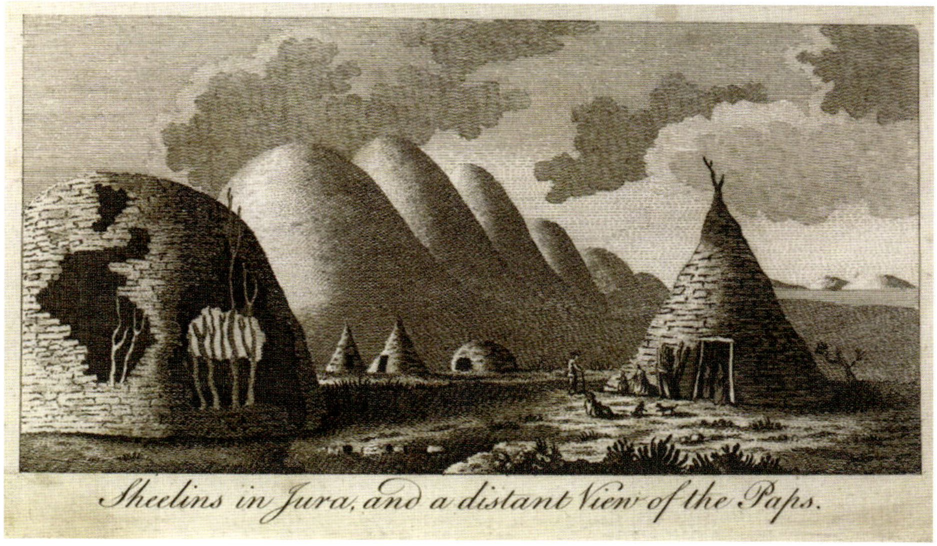

Fig. C2.3
Moses Griffith, 'Sheelins [Shieling Huts] in Jura, and a distant View of the Paps', engraving in Thomas Pennant, *A Tour in Scotland and Voyage to the Hebrides, Part 1* (Chester, 1774), pl. XV, Vol. 1, p. 246 (GLA ASC Hunterian Mu6-d.2)

Old ways in the hills have a habit of being subsumed in the modern mind into the category of 'drove roads'. Following Haldane's seminal account of the drove roads of Scotland published in 1952, we have been taught to recognise what seems to be a pre-existing and extensive network of tracks (Haldane 1997, 3–4). More recent research has expanded this towards an understanding of continuity and change, the growth of commercial practices and the impact of market forces, and a more pragmatic and varying system of roads and associated structures such as cattle stances, enclosures, bothies and inns (see Adamson 2014). Local views may differ on the history and utility of traditional routes: for example, contradicting the notion that Thomas Telford's road down Glengarry was a fixed drove route, Lachlan Fletcher of Arnisdale took a drove of beasts to the market in Fort William about 1930 and maintained that the route from Kinloch Hourn to Spean Bridge went further south, by way of the west end of Loch Quoich, Glen Kingie and Loch Arkaig. The assumption that droves followed drove roads has been questioned; instead it has been suggested that each drove took a different route, avoiding the hard surfaces of made-up roads or the muddied tracks of previous droves, and taking advantage of wayside grazing:

> He [the drover] prefers, when a choice offers, the grassy pathways which are more agreeable to the hoofs of the animals entrusted to his care and at the same time afford them a mouthful of food. Hence he usually chooses the by-roads as the hard and dusty highways are injurious to the hoofs of the cattle and afford little nourishment. (Keay 1984, 120)

The pattern of old ways in the North-West Highlands, between the Great Glen and the north coast, is more dense and complex than a modern road map might suggest. A significant facet of a changed landscape, for example, is the former status of Poolewe as the port that received and distributed all the seaborne traffic from Lewis and other parts of the Hebrides. This was the staging-post for the onward movement of people and goods towards the east and south, and Fèill Iùdha, the 'Poolewe Fair', was an important seasonal trading event for this nodal point (Pochin Mould 1950, 10–13). The memory of this was lost with the rise of Ullapool as a British Fishery Society designed settlement after 1788 and its modern function as a ferry terminal. As a development of the post-1745 phase of road building, a 'military road' was built west from Contin to Poolewe as the west-coast port and it is evident that there were many different routes going east and south. The Gairloch to Poolewe road was built as a relief measure during the potato famine. A 'military road' was not necessarily suitable for wheeled traffic, as numerous eighteenth- and ninetheeth-century tourists complained. An anecdote recounted how, at the end of the eighteenth century, Lady Seaforth's coach, bound from Contin to Poolewe for shipping to Lewis, was wrecked by the time she reached Loch Achanault before the halfway point (Pochin Mould 1950, 25). For the locals, road traffic implied travelling on foot or on a pony with goods in a pair of creels.

Other old ways in the region were the route east from Loch Maree by Loch Monar through Glens Strathfarrar, Cannich and Affric, and another route east from Craig in Strathcarron to Tomich at the head of Strathglass (Fig. C2.4). To the south of this, a well-recognised route led east from Kintail to Glen Affric and Strathglass. This was associated with the eponymous Cinntàile nam Bò ('Kintail of the Cattle') and the reputation of their cattle for properties, not of size, but of 'shape and figure', and 'a choice pile, weight, and short legs', a view retailed from drovers in 1793 by the parish minister (Morison 1793, 247; see also Cheape 2011, 141–144). The route started at the farm of Morvich and went up over Bealach an Sgairne, a feature with the alternative name of Cadha Dhubhthaich, 'St Duthac's Pass', suggesting that this was the route by which the Columban Saint travelled from Easter Ross to Loch Duich (Watson 1904, 176–177). In 1793, the minister of Kintail appealed for the conversion of old way to new road: 'But of all the roads leading to this place, none calls more for public attention than that of Affric or Belloch. This road is 13 computed miles from Kilduich in Kintail to Knockfin in Strathglass. It is allowed to be the nearest communication between the East and West seas' (Morison 1793, 244–245).

Feeding into the modern route eastwards from Skye through Glen Shiel is the way from Glenelg (and a military road built after the 1745 Rising) to link the Isle of Skye and the Bernera Barracks to Fort Augustus; it was followed by Dr Johnson and Boswell in 1773 en route to Skye. But 'traditional' traffic followed other ways. Glenelg was a ferry point receiving about 2,000 cattle per year from the islands crossing at Kylerhea in Skye, according to the parish minister in 1795 (Maciver 1795, 270). Most of this traffic followed an older way south to Arnisdale and Kinloch Hourn by the Bealach Aoidhdailean at 1,550 ft between Beinn nan Caorach and Sgurr na Laire Brice, east to Loch Quioch and Glengarry to pick up on the Lochaber drove route south at the significantly named Ach' Uaine or 'Greenfield' and the 'Greenfield Ford' (Pochin Mould 1950, 70–74). Two main routes were then followed: by Meall an Tagraidh to Loch Arkaig passing the House of Feadan, or by the east flank of Beinn Tee and Lochan na Diota to Kilfinnan. Given the traditional and historical regard for this St Finnan dedication, the latter route was a well-used 'coffin road'.

Coffin roads take their significance and frequency of use from the sanctity of the destination. With desuetude, such old ways seem to disappear rapidly from the public memory and imagination. A coffin road leading from Glen Garry to Glen Moriston, within the modern road system, is marked at the

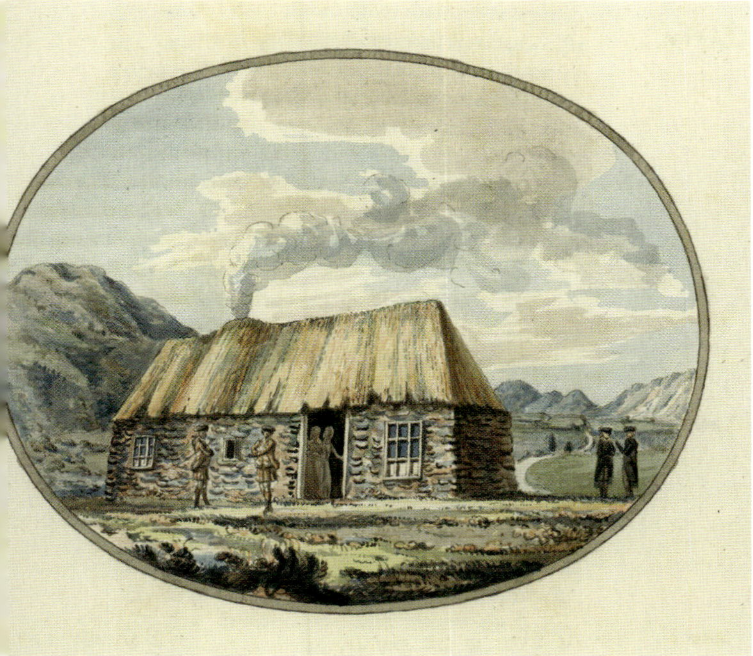

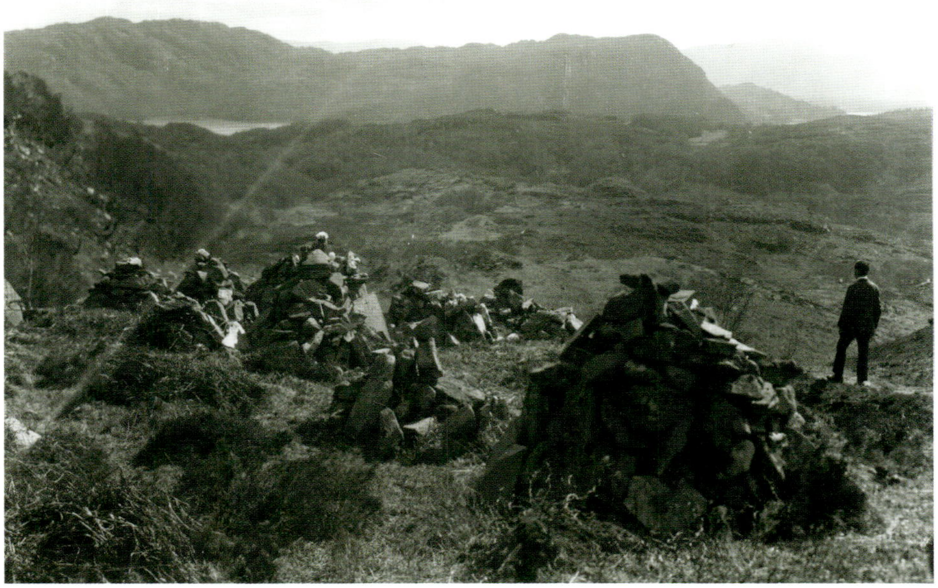

head of the pass by 'resting cairns' but otherwise is obscure (Robertson 1941, 12). St Finnan's Isle on Loch Shiel, a dedication of the seventh or eighth century, has tracks leading to it from the south and north, some of which are marked with groups of small cairns. This network includes Rathad nam Marbh ('The Road of the Dead'), between Kinlochmoidart and Glenuig, which is marked with cairns at one or two points (Fig. C2.5). Cille Choireil in the Braes of Lochaber is similarly distinguished (Mitchell 1880, 90–91). Dr John Mackenzie described in detail the traditional procedure for taking the deceased from dwelling to interment in the case of the burial of his sister-in-law, who had died in childbirth in 1834, aged 23. Her coffin, in which she lay with her baby, was carried over 70 miles from Gairloch to Beauly over three days by relays of 125 men arranged in four 'companies':

> Some distance east of Achnasheen, we halted to give the men a little rest and have some food. . . . Before we moved away again, every man had put a stone to the cairn on the spot where the coffin had rested. . . . Our next halt was at the west entrance to Tarvie Wood, opposite to Rogie Island, where another cairn still tells where the coffin rested while the bearers had some food. (Byam Shaw 1989, 209)

Further routes criss-crossing the Highlands are recalled in accounts of cattle-raiding and the lifting of spoil or 'spuilyie', an activity carrying no moral slur but rather fulfilling an admired rite of passage for young men. The value set on this rapid cross-country tactical movement is reflected in the variety of terms in Scottish Gaelic for booty and plunder – *faobh*, *creich*, *creach*, *feudail* (also 'cattle'), *meirle*, *reubainn*, *togail*. The perpetrators of 'spuilyie' were referred to as 'reivers' or 'caterans' in Anglo-Scots, meaning approximately 'robbers from the Highlands', the latter term possibly deriving from Gaelic *ceathairneach*, which unambiguously means 'soldier' or 'hero' (Grant 1941, 55, *sv* cateran). Local knowledge of cross-country tracks was the key to Montrose's dramatic mid-winter victory over the Covenanting forces at Inverlochy in 1645 (Grant 1931, 181–185). (Continuing official ignorance of the lie of the land prompted the commissioning of Roy's 'Great Military Map' after Culloden, discussed in Section 1 'The Theatre of War'.) A small selection of such

Fig. C2.4
Above left. Moses Griffith, 'Whisky House at Loch Maree', watercolour pasted in Thomas Pennant's own extra-illustrated copy of *A Tour in Scotland and Voyage to the Hebrides in 1772*, Part 1, facing p. 380 (NLW W6)

Fig. C2.5
Above right. Mary Ethel Muir Donaldson, *'Resting Cairns' on Rathad nam Marbh*, photograph, M.E.M. Donaldson Collection (IMAG neg. no. 958.20.181)

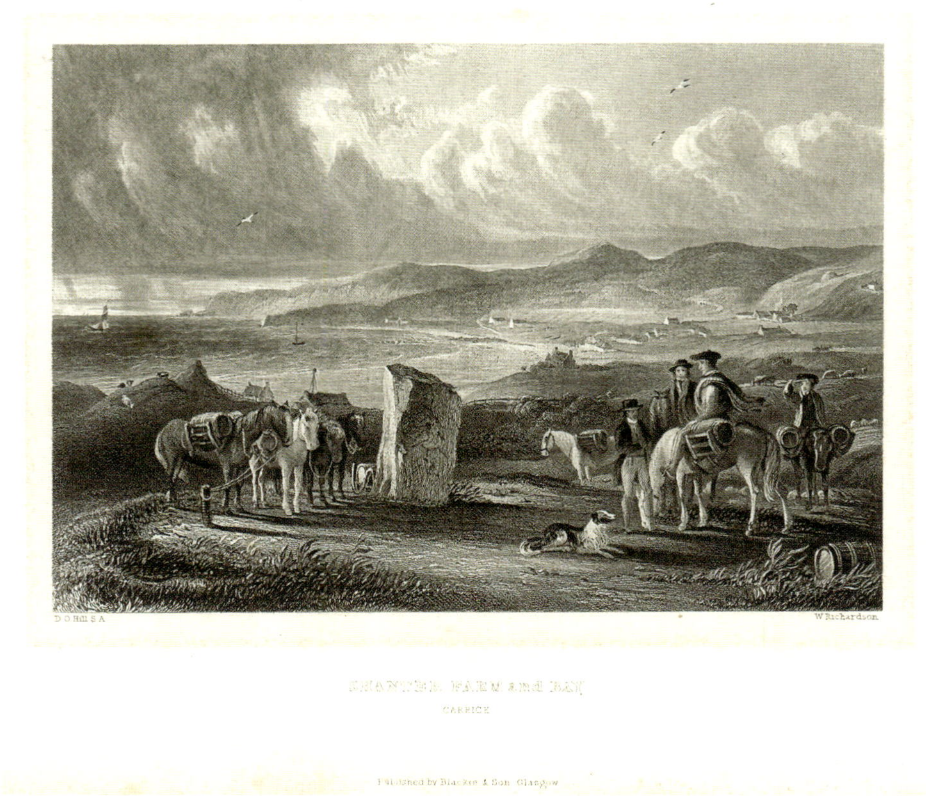

Fig. C2.6
William Richardson after David Octavius Hill, *Shanter Farm and Bay*, 1841, steel engraving (PC)

The print includes pack ponies with kegs of smuggled spirits. Old ways might carry traditional names such as 'The Priests' Road' or the 'Smugglers' Road'.

routes in the south-east Highlands has been captured for today's public access with the identification of a 'Cateran Trail' in a network of footpaths to the north of Blairgowrie, linking Strathardle, Glenshee and Glen Isla, and marking tracks used by cattle raiders, sometimes from as far west as the Braes of Lochaber, descending through the Perthshire and Angus glens to raid the low country (http://spns.org.uk/the-cateran-trail).

Rathad nam Meirleach, 'The Thieves' Road', was reputed to stretch from Lochaber to the east coast and formed a network of foot traffic – since the caterans made it a rule to return by a different way from the one they that would have come by. Rev. William Forsyth (1825–1907), minister of Abernethy and a good Gaelic folklorist, described the route of Rathad nam Meirleach in his own district: 'In this parish it hugs the hills. Entering from the heights of Rothiemurchus, it skirts the south side of Loch Morlich, passes out at the Green Loch, then by the Sleighich, the Eag-mhòr and the Crasg, into the lowlands of Banff and of Moray' (Forsyth 1900, 212–213). This network of tracks came under the scrutiny of the army of occupation after Culloden, and soldiers were stationed to arrest the foot traffic on the hill passes. Similar practices to those at Rathad nam Meirleach extended over great reaches of the Highlands, and a command-post at Tarland was designed to cover the eastern Lowlands:

> from the Depredations of the Thieves of Rannoch, Lochaber and Glengarry [who] in driving Cattle from the Counties of Angus, Mearns, Aberdeen and Banff, usually take the following Routes. Those who rob from the two first Counties drive their plunder through the Glens of Clova, all along the Mountains South side of the River Dee, and must pass near Glenclunie or Glenshee, so as to fall into the Hills of Athole or the Forest of Guiley, and in either of these Routes must afterwards cross the Chain betwixt Dalwhinnie and Dalnacardoch, unless alarmed and driven Northward towards Ruthven.
> (Allardyce 1896, 495; see also 490)

These routes crossed great swathes of country but if we narrow the focus to a single district, a dense pattern of old ways emerges from the landscape. In Sleat in the south of the Isle of Skye, John Blackadder's 'Survey and Valuation of Lord Macdonald's Estates' carried out in 1799–1800 recommended road improvement, and some new roads were being built between about 1805 and 1815 (Clan Donald Lands Trust). In the spirit of improvement, Blackadder is vague about pre-existing roads but there were 'roads' or routes which can be teased out of the landscape. They may not draw the eye because we are accustomed to different axes of movement or destinations. The main road through the Sleat peninsula runs on the east side between Broadford and Armadale and has superseded older routes on different axes and also coastal navigation. Routes radiated out, typically, from the Sleat parish church at Kilmore (a possible Columban foundation site) to townships such as Tarskavaig on the west side of the peninsula. Logically, the old way held to the higher ground, linking five townships and the hill grazings before passing through the Bealach and on down to the sea at Achnacloich and the townships beyond. The drastic clearance of the

Sleat townships in 1822 destroyed this axis of movement and it has melted away into the landscape.

Other routes in Sleat are recalled in oral tradition. An old route from the ferry point at Kylerhea to Kilmore contradicts the present road pattern and addresses the needs of a pre-existing settlement pattern. The old way hugged the coast of the Sound of Sleat and took cattle one way and coffins the other. The well-marked deserted township of Leitir Fura on Loch na Dail and the other townships sold cattle at the market stances. Faing an Alaire, a little to the north of Leitir Fura, commemorated the spot where coffins were rested and refreshment taken, *alar* being an old term for a funeral and funeral food and drink (MacLeòid 2019). An earlier sacred topography can reveal extraordinary detail for a better understanding of old ways and their culture. The approach from the north to the old ecclesiastical site of Kilmore in Sleat – A' Chille Mhòr – is marked by Bealach an t-Sleuchd, where worshippers halted to perform an act of veneration; the place-name, which does not appear on maps, has survived in oral tradition from eras before the Reformation.

As the 'age of improvement' advanced, the view spread that the military roads were of little economic use and were falling into disrepair. Arteries of communication to carry trade and merchandise were considered to be lacking; the situation is recalled in a winning phrase delivered in 1795 by the arch-improver George Dempster of Skibo and Dunnichen when he commented with a keen ear for assonance that 'a great part of this immense country is accessible only to goats and garrons' (Haldane 1962, 64). But scarcity of made roads and wheeled vehicles need not be an indicator of backwardness where terrain dictates accessibility for the most part. A long-familiar form of transport in Gaelic Scotland was the 'slide-car' or *càrn-slaodaidh* (Dwelly 1967, 169, *sv* càrn). The ethnologist Sir Arthur Mitchell referred to seeing these in Strathglass, Kintail and elsewhere in the early 1860s, as 'carts in use without wheels, exactly of the kind which Burt figures in his celebrated Letters' being used for carrying peat, bracken and hay down very steep hills (Mitchell 1880, 96); see Fig. C2.7. Osgood Mackenzie (1842–1922) described in detail the making of 'sledge-carts' in Wester Ross, 'there being no need of wheels in a roadless country'. Two shafts of birch shaped with an adze were topped with two wooden cross-members, which were bored with an auger to fit hazel-rod rungs that kept the load in place. A box would be added for carrying

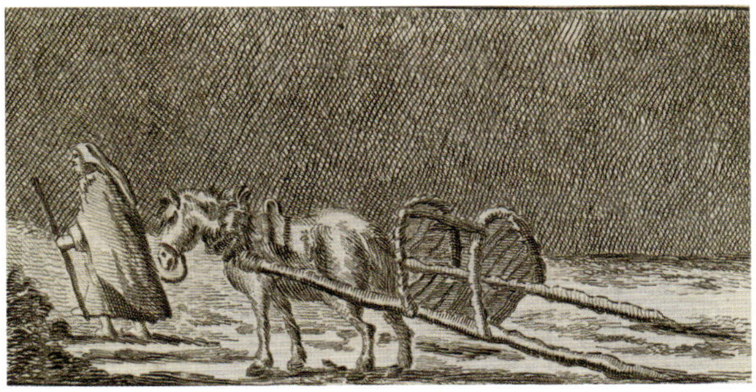

Fig. C2.7
F. Garden, *Càrn-slaodaidh* or Slide-car, engraving in Edmund Burt, *Letters from a Gentleman in the North of Scotland to his friend in London . . .* (London, 1759), vol. II, p. 86 (GLA ASC BG52-d.20)

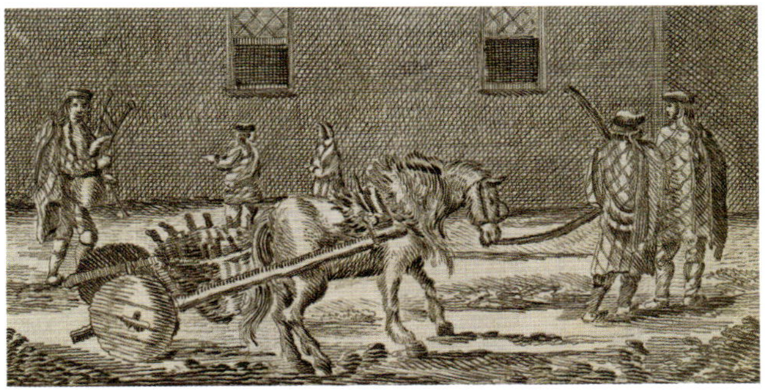

Fig. C2.8
F. Garden, Light cart or *lòpan*, engraving in Edmund Burt, *Letters from a Gentleman in the North of Scotland to his friend in London . . .* (London, 1759), vol. II, p. 86 (GLA ASC BG52-d.20)

fish, lime and manure, and 'the sledges could slide where wheeled carts could not venture, and carried corn and hay etc. famously' (Mackenzie 1922, 31–32). Other forms of transport were the *lòpan*, a type of cart with bodywork of wattle in the form of a large creel, and the *ceallach* or sledge, also with a creel body (see Figs C2.8 and C2.9). The Inverness architect Alexander Ross surveyed 'Old Highland Roads' in a paper presented to the Gaelic Society of Inverness in 1888:

> For hill travelling the sleigh was more useful, and this contrivance is still in use for peat carriage and agricultural purposes. You are all familiar with the luipen [*lòpan*] or conical basket placed in a frame between two trams, and drawn by the garron along the hillside. Though now disused, I have often seen them in use for peats in the suburbs of this town, and when on wheels in the streets. (Ross 1888, 184)

If transport on foot and on horseback was the norm, how much of this culture is recoverable? What survives in the traditions

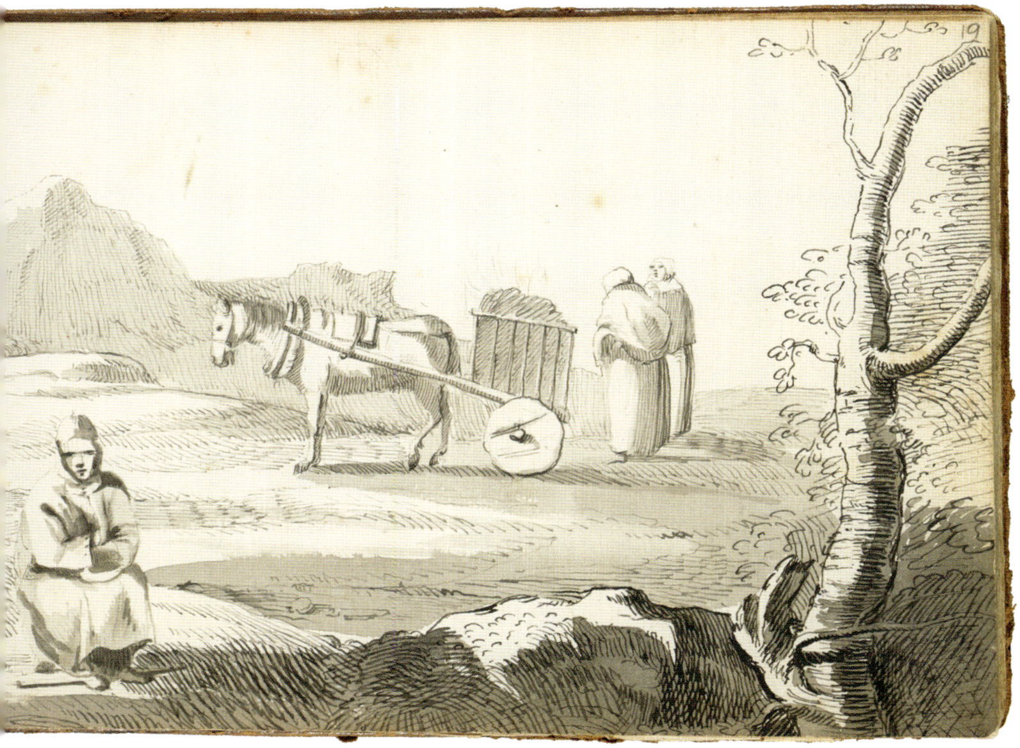

of Gaelic Scotland reveals a rich material culture. Everyone was expected to take their share of carrying food and fuel, and anyone who felt that they were above this physical work might attract the wry comment: *'Nach ann aice tha an druim airson a' chleibh'* ('Isn't it herself that has the back for the creel!') (Mackay 1919, 288); see Figs C2.10–C2.11. Basketwork creels and creel-making survive, although the burden of work has eased. Transport on horseback is recalled in items in museum collections and also in a rich glossary of terms. Rev. Duncan MacInnes of Oban, conscious of the disappearance of working practices towards the end of the nineteenth century, noted terminology that might fade from the collective memory:

> *Srathair* – creel saddle, composed of two flat boards surmounted by a bent ridge of wood called 'A' Chairb'. On the top of the ridge are formed two horns, to which the creels are slung by a rope of twisted withes called 'An Iris'.
>
> *An Èiseach* – a rope of twisted twigs connecting the saddle with the tail of the horse by a piece of wood that goes under the tail, and is called 'Maide-ton-eich'. (MacInnes 1894, 216)

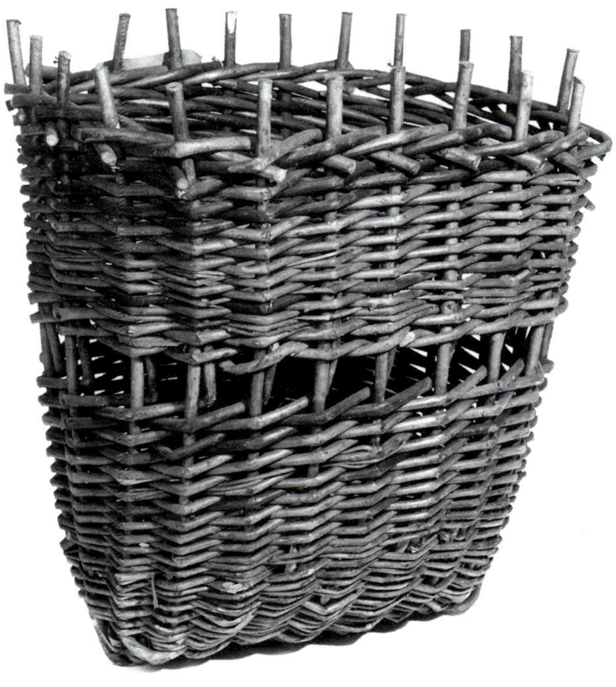

In the view of Highlanders, the 'old ways' represent a *status quo ante* of very long duration. Old ways and tracks were constantly evolving and moving but the modern historian, presupposing that comparable change had not previously taken place, has found it easier to characterise the Highlander as resistant to change in the era of 'improvement'. With old ways giving way to new roads, change was an imposed process; but was there resentment or resistance to it? Angus Campbell's 'Eulogising Duncan Taylor for his Ingenuity in Devising a Highway on the

Fig. C2.9
Top left. Circle of Paul Sandby, 'A Horse, Cart and Figures in a Landscape', ink and wash drawing in *Sketchbook of Drawings made in the Highlands*, c. 1749, (NGS D 5339 A.19)

Wheeled 'rung cart', probably in the vicinity of Inverness.

Fig. C2.10
Left. Anon., *Peat Creel*, photograph (NMS W.QP 47; copy neg. 4954)

Glen Lochay Track' welcomed such a change, and elaborated his praise into heroic lay:

> *Thilg thu 'n uchdaich anns na slochdaibh,*
> *'S tha gach cnoc a bh' ann air chall,*
> *Dh'fhàg thu sochdrach an ceum dochdrach,*
> *Chor 's nach bi ar coiseachd mall,*
> *Chuir thu guitear anns gach fèithe,*
> *Drochaid rèidh dhuinn air gach ault,*
> *Causair cloiche air gach rumaich,*
> *Ceart co-grinn 's a tha 'n Luinin thall.*
> (Caimbeul 1785, 108–109)

> You cast the rises into the hollows,
> And every hillock that was there has gone,
> You made the hard path an easy one
> So that our walking would not be slowed,
> You put a drain in every ditch,
> A level bridge for us on every burn,
> Stone paving on each marsh,
> Every bit as neat as is down there in London.

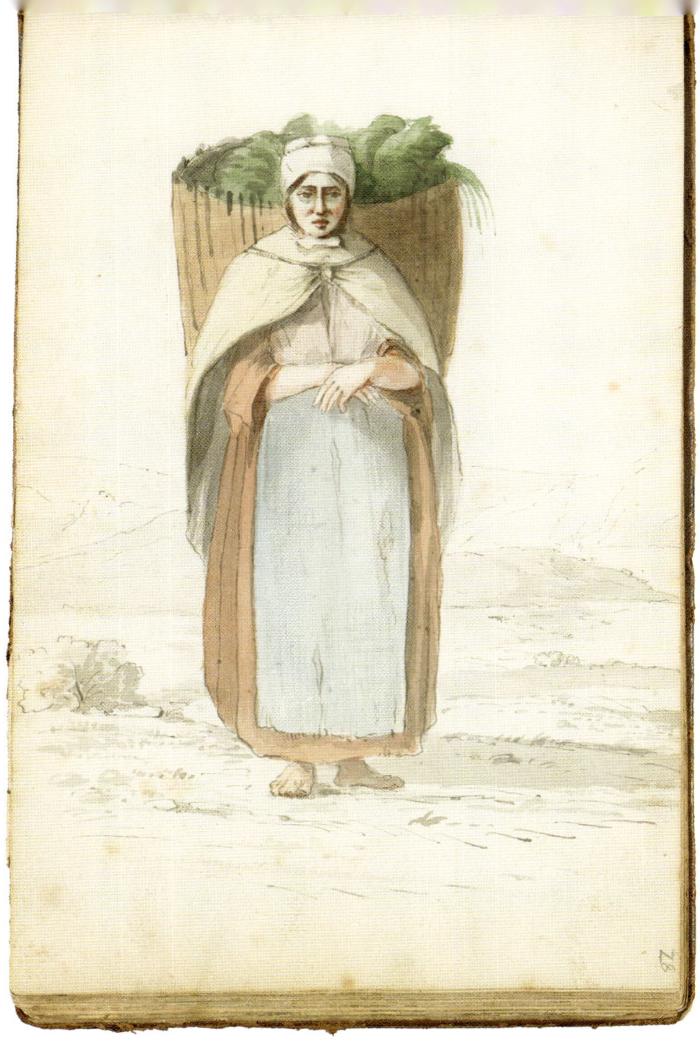

Fig. C2.11
Circle of Paul Sandby, 'A Woman Carrying a Heavy Load', ink and wash drawing in *Sketchbook of Drawings made in the Highlands*, c. 1749 (NGS D 5339 A.28)

Woman carrying creel with a load of fodder or bracken for bedding.

The process of 'improvement' accelerated through the eighteenth century, and reaction to it in terms of support or opposition was inevitable. Opposition was not necessarily resistance to change but probably something more profound. The parish minister Rev. Roderick Morison suggested: 'Till of late, the people of Kintail, as well as other Highlanders, had a strong aversion to roads. The more inaccessible, the more secure, was their maxim' (Morison 1793, 244). Given the cultural differences between Lowlands and Highlands, a view robustly stated to the south of the Highland line since the medieval period, Highlanders had little room to manoeuvre and had to begin to assimilate themselves to an alien language and values (Newton 2006, 46). They were effectively disenfranchised following the Jacobite wars and political repression, a state exacerbated by the gradual loss of their traditional leaders. For many Highlanders, the age of improvement was an age of cultural conquest; General Stewart of Garth commented that his countrymen's feelings were hurt 'when they see men without birth or education placed over them' (Stewart 1822, 155). Other aspects of resentment may be simpler for a modern mindset. Ailean Dall MacDougall's rousing 'Song on the Lowland Shepherds' warned about the environmental effects of the introduction of huge herds of sheep and of the destruction of pasture in the 1790s; and the sense of cultural conquest is in no doubt when he adds destruction of conversation and song, and then offence to all the senses, of sight, sound and smell, arising from the incomers (Cheape 1995, 96–98; Meek 1995, 47–50).

With such tangible evidence for the 'new roads', this area of past geographies is worthy of fresh summary and synthesis to add the enriching though less tangible evidence of the 'old ways'. Paucity of information or source material would customarily be pleaded for a neglect of this by earlier generations of historians, but such an excuse should no longer be proffered. Language and tradition can offer an extra dimension, and an informed awareness even suggests an editorial note to 'The Road to the Isles': the 'heather tracks' go unequivocally from east to west, although a Gaelic perception of the 'old ways' generally takes the 'road' in the other direction.

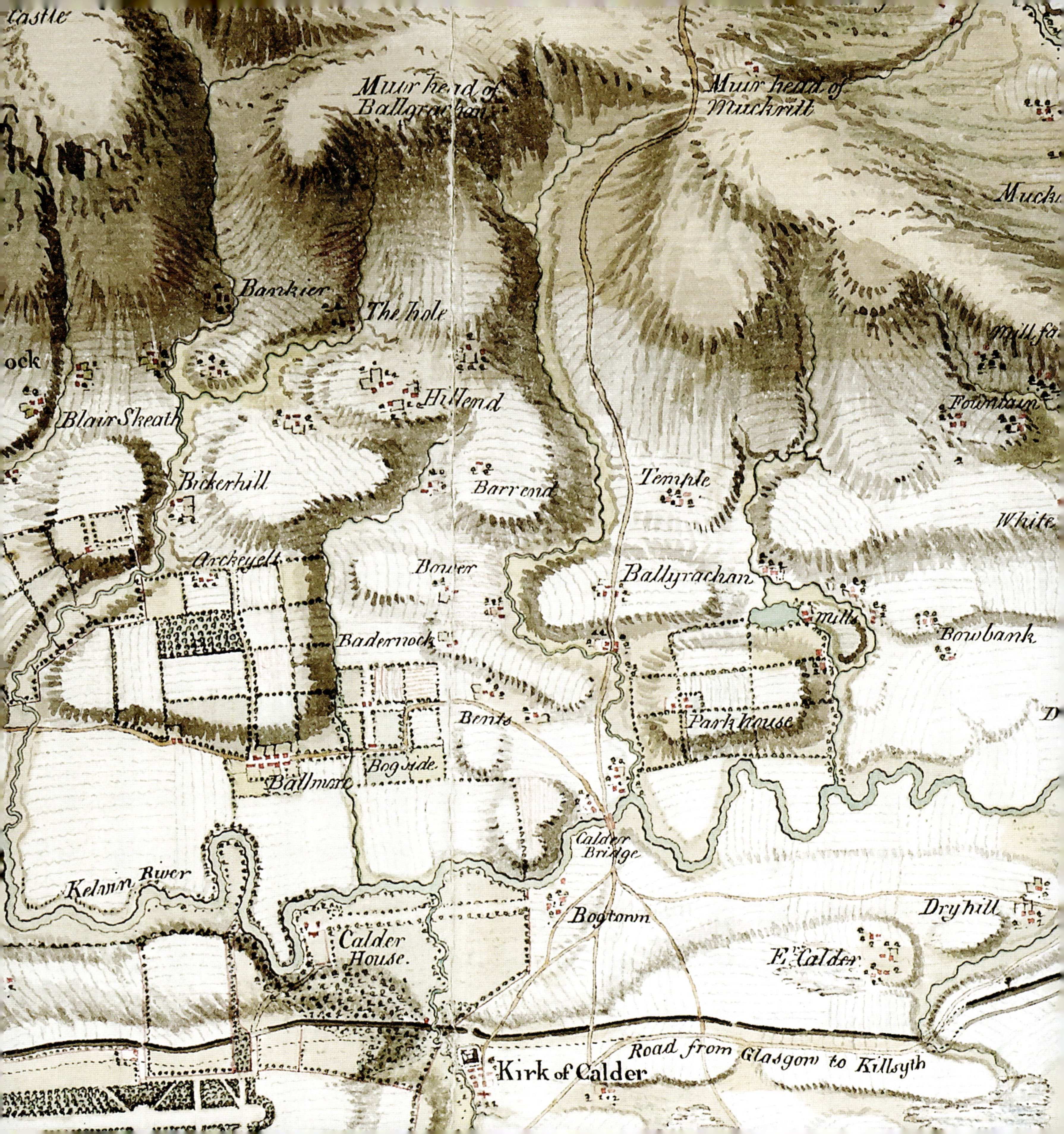

Muir head of Ballgrachan
Muir head of Muckrill
Bankier
The hole
Blair Skeath
Hillend
Bickerhill
Barrend
Temple
Bower
Ballyrachan
Fountain
mill
Bowbank
Badernock
Bents
Park house
Ballmore
Bogside
Calder Bridge
Kelvin River
Calder House
Bogtown
Dryhill
E. Calder
Road from Glasgow to Killsyth
Kirk of Calder

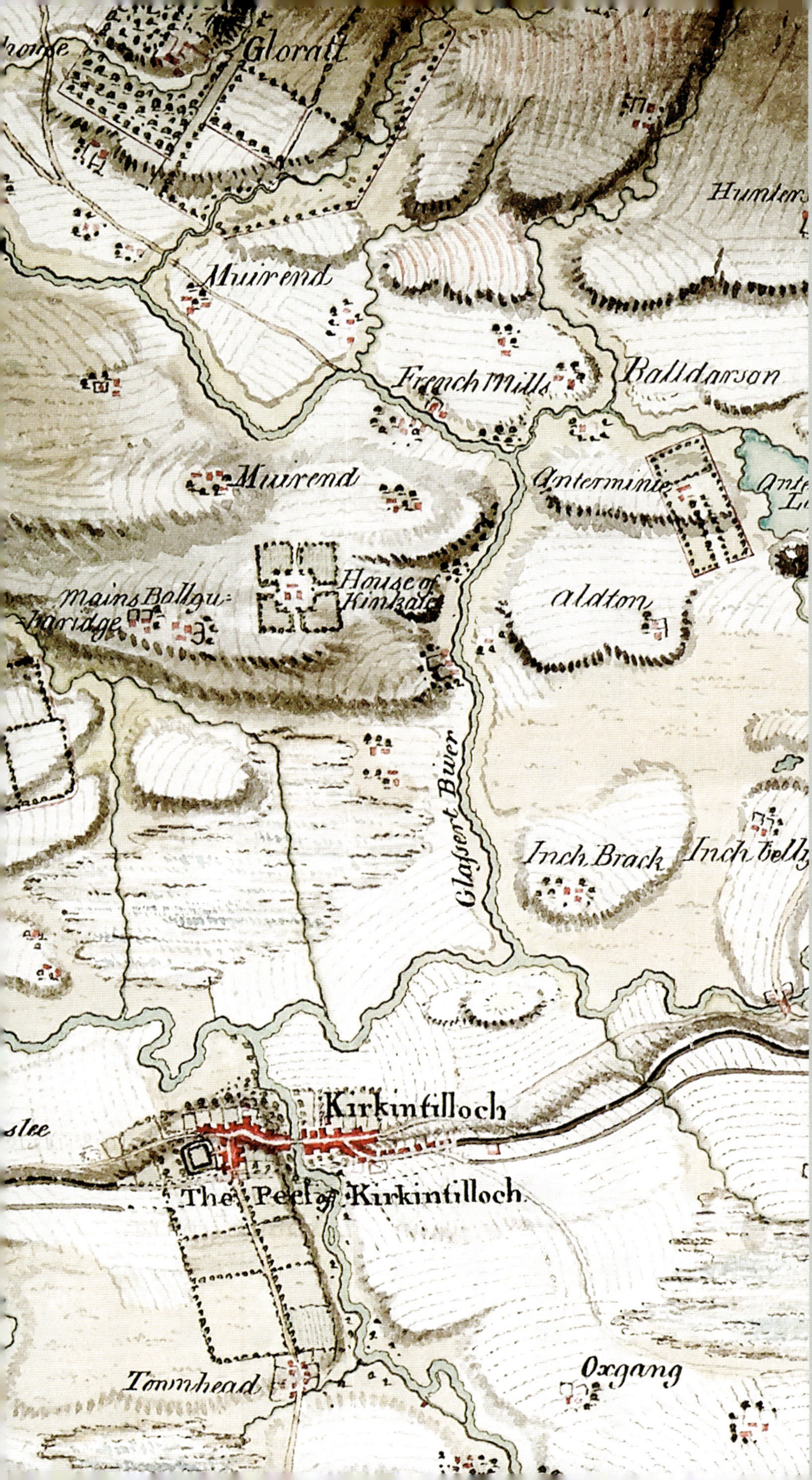

SECTION TWO
Antiquities

Nigel Leask

Fig. S2.1
(detail this page, full image overleaf) William Roy, drawing of 'Plan shewing the Course of the Roman Wall called Grime's Dyke raised along the Isthmus, between the Forth and the Clyde, in the Reign of Antoninus Pius', watercolour, title plate of *The Military Antiquities of the Romans in North Britain*, Vol II, 1793 (BL Kings MS 248)

For William Roy, 'military men' were naturally 'led to compare present things with the past; and being thus insensibly carried back to former ages, they place themselves among the ancients, and do, as it were, converse with the people of those remote times' (Roy 1793, i). Struck by the parallels between the tactics adopted by Roman generals in controlling a hostile population on the empire's northernmost frontier and contemporary military strategy, Roy first developed a fascination with the geography of ancient Scotland during the latter Lowland stages of the Military Survey of North Britain. Published posthumously at the end of the century, Roy's enquiries broke new ground, bringing the standards and techniques of the Military Survey to the production of an authoritative map of Roman Scotland as well as a survey of the Antonine Wall. Surveyed in 1755, but only drawn up in 1773, William Roy's delicately coloured and finely delineated map shows the entire course of the wall, together with plans and sections of several of its associated forts. It is richly informative about the use Roman forces made of the local terrain, tracing the distribution and character of marching camps and other temporary fortifications. Roy accorded such visual forms of knowledge particular value, thinking 'a general plan of this kind, topographically expressed', afforded 'a much truer notion . . . than what, without such assistance, could possibly be conveyed in many words' (Roy 1793, 155–156).

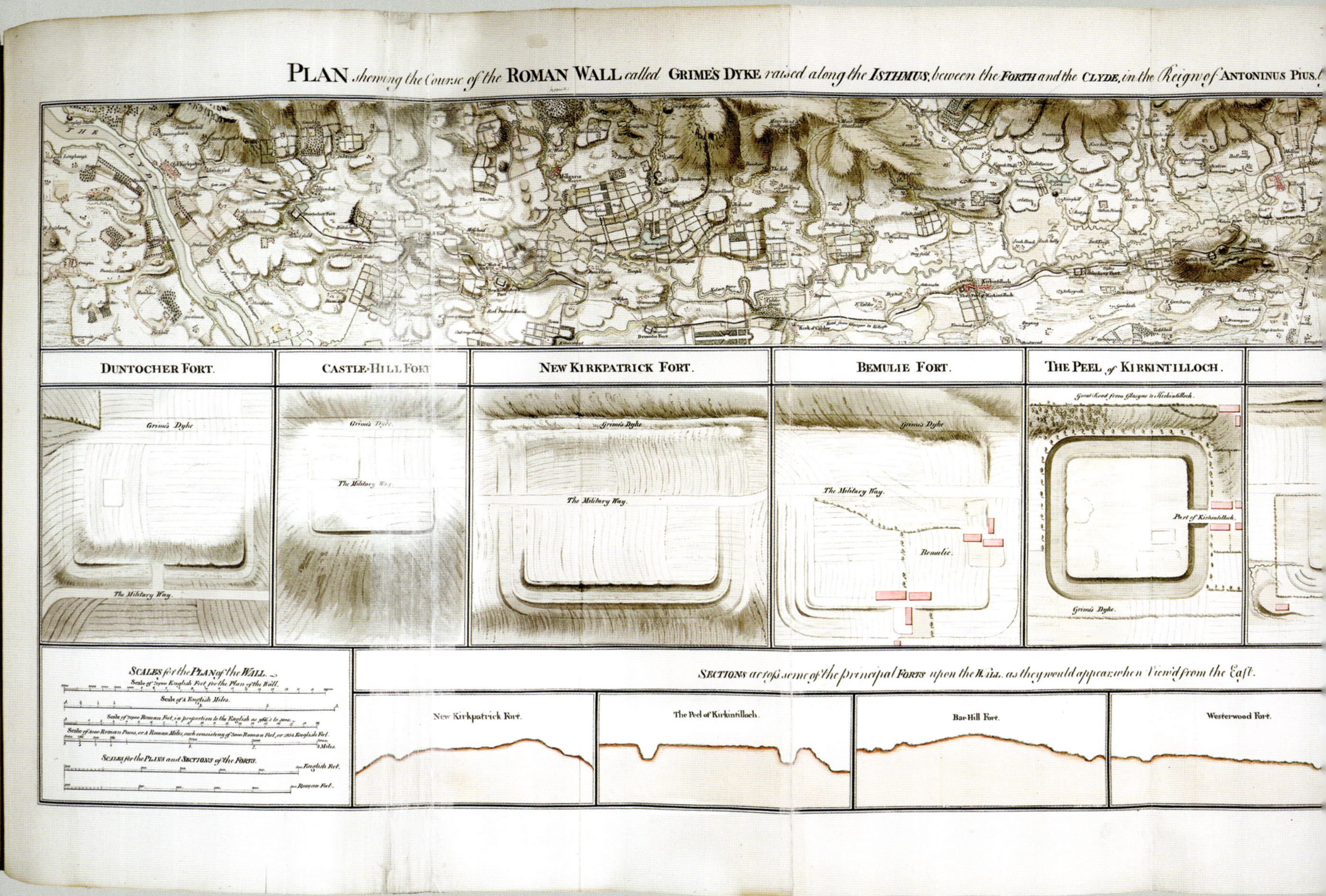

The enduring image of Scottish antiquarianism is Sir Walter Scott's portrait, in his 1816 novel *The Antiquary,* of the random clutter of Jonathan Oldbuck's '*sanctum sanctorum*': 'a chaos of maps, engravings, scraps of parchment, bundles of papers, pieces of old armour, swords, dirks, helmets, and Highland targets' (Scott 1999, 21) (Fig. S2.2). According to Scott's gently satirical image, 'the antiquary's dwelling . . . was the image of his mind' (Brown 1980, 20), but there was certainly an element of self-parody here as well, evidenced by the topsy-turvy interior of his own castellated mansion at Abbotsford. Scott followed in a venerable tradition of satirising obsessively homosocial antiquarians ('antic-queer-ones', in Francis Grose's telling phrase: Grose 1791, 51) for their passionate and unsystematic desire to scrutinise and collect the material relics of the past. The striking seventeenth-century Highland target presented to The Hunterian Museum, and the mysterious prehistoric 'stone balls' bequeathed by William Hunter, remind us that institutional collections such as that of the university were already vying in importance with those of private antiquaries like Scott's Oldbuck, which was allegedly based on the antiquarian cabinet of Sir John Clerk of Eldin, further discussed below (Brown 1980, 7, 13) (Figs S2.3 and S2.4).

Despite its uneasy relationship with the emerging academic discipline of history, antiquarianism was a major influence on eighteenth-century culture, especially travel and travel writing, and

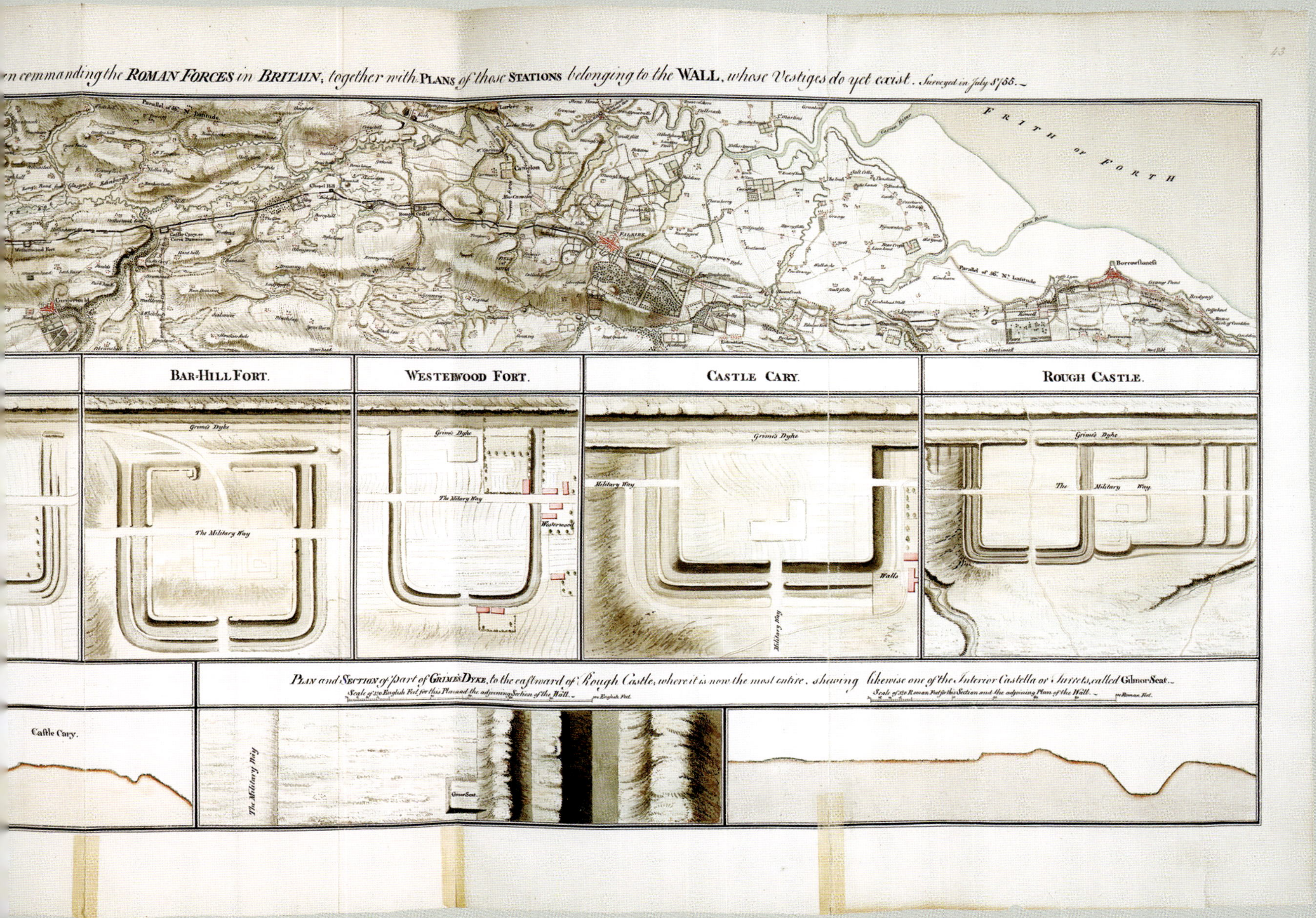

nowhere more than in Scotland. The medieval ruins of Iona Abbey had been a high point on Dr Johnson's 1773 Scottish tour, which he praised as 'the luminary of the *Caledonian* regions, whence savage clans and roving barbarians derived the benefits of knowledge, and the blessings of religion' (Black 2007, 380). James Miller's 1772 watercolour *A View of the Church of Columb Kill, on the Isle of Iona* (Fig. S2.5) juxtaposes the ruined ecclesiastical structures with the impoverished vernacular architecture of the contemporary Highland blackhouse in the right foreground: 'room for improvement' is the message here. Views and descriptions of ruined pre-reformation churches and 'gothic' castles preoccupied eighteenth-century antiquarians in Scotland, much as they did in England, Ireland and other parts of Europe. Travel writers and artists also devoted a great deal of time to describing the often fast-changing contemporary urban landscape, juxtaposing the old and the new, just like Miller on distant Iona: this was a theme that would also preoccupy nineteenth-century painters. Runciman's etching of the Netherbow Port preserves this historic Edinburgh landmark in paper form just as it was being demolished (Fig. S2.6). Once the principal gateway into the city, controlling the flow of trade and standing at the meeting point of three major arteries, it was being cleared away in the interests of better circulation. Significantly, as it was part of the capital's defensive wall, its demise was also symbolic of warlike times still well within living memory

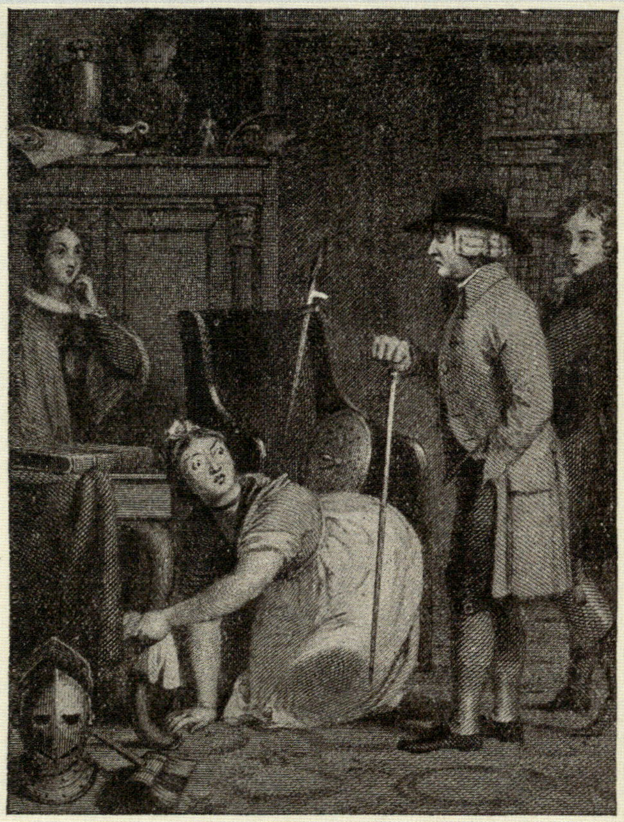

Fig. S2.2
Right. Edward Portbury after Charles Robert Leslie, 'The Intrusion of the Sanctum Sanctorum', first published in Sir Walter Scott, *The Antiquary*, 1823 (PC)

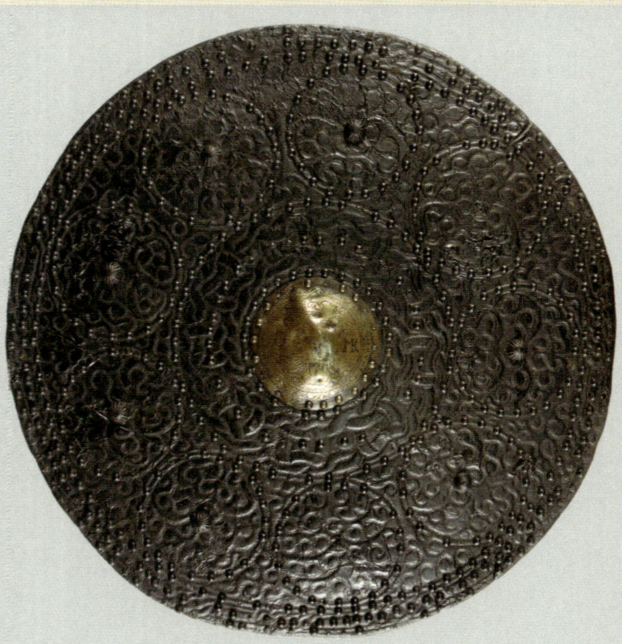

Fig. S2.3
Right. Highland targe: brass boss engraved with the date 1623 and initials DMK, Sir Donald MacKay (GLAHM:C.72)

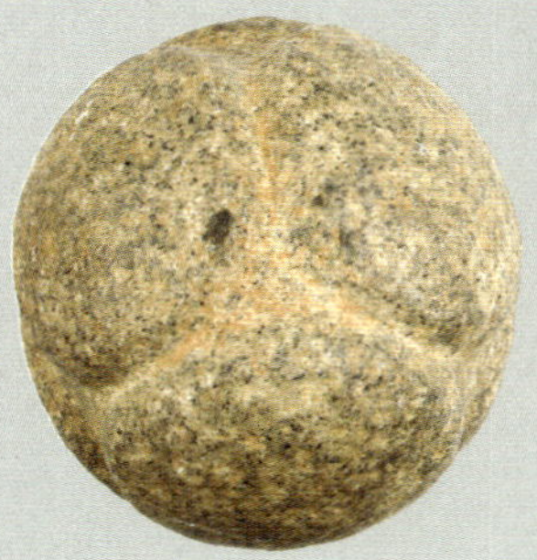

Fig. S2.4
Below. Neolithic stone ball (GLAHM:a.143)

being consigned firmly to the past. That the city's defences were now rendered obsolete was also reflected in the remaking of its citadel as a site of polite touristic interest. Made on a summer tour of 1788, Joseph Farington's prospect of Edinburgh Castle views it from the decrepit-looking buildings of the Grassmarket. The artist takes considerable delight in capturing the picturesque decay and squalor of the foreground street. Moreover, in what was a conventional conjunction, placing a scene of humble everyday life against a backdrop of epic, historic architecture made for an affective contrast (Fig. S2.7).

Yet travellers in Scotland during this period were also fascinated by visiting remoter and more archaic sites, such as Roman fortifications and battlefields, cromlechs, brochs, 'druid circles', etc., directly facilitated by the Hanoveran military occupation and the subsequent creation of the new road and transport networks. Artists often represented antiquaries at work or tourists at leisure among these relics of the past: for example, Miller's watercolour of a *Cloyster in Oronsay Abbey* shows antiquarians scrutinising memorial inscriptions in the medieval Hebridean ruin (Fig. S2.8), while John Cleveley depicts polite visitors in the remoter islands of Orkney admiring the spectacular Neolithic standing stones at Stennes, their height exaggerated by the low viewpoint (Fig. S2.9). Here enthusiasm for the past is no longer the preserve of the 'antic-queer-ones', but of polite tourists, well-dressed men and women. Cleveley and Miller were among the artists who accompanied Joseph Banks on his voyage up the west coast of Scotland to Iceland in 1772, just a year or so after he had returned from the Pacific on board Captain Cook's *Endeavour*, an important factor in opening up comparison of Scotland's antiquities with those of further-flung cultures, a foundation stone for the development of comparative anthropology.

The rise of antiquarianism in Britain was coterminous with the publication of William Camden's Latin *Britannia* (1586), the principal aim of which had been to 'describe Britain as a province of the Roman Empire': later eighteenth-century revisions of *Britannia* opened up this 'Romano-centric' picture to Danish, Anglo-Saxon and Celtic antiquities, casting a more equivocal light upon Roman conquest (Parry 1995, 23). Neither William Stukeley's *Itinerarium Curiosum* (1724) nor Alexander Gordon's *Itinerarium Septentrionale* (1726) – the first archaelogical investigation of Roman ruins in Scotland, discussed further below – are travel

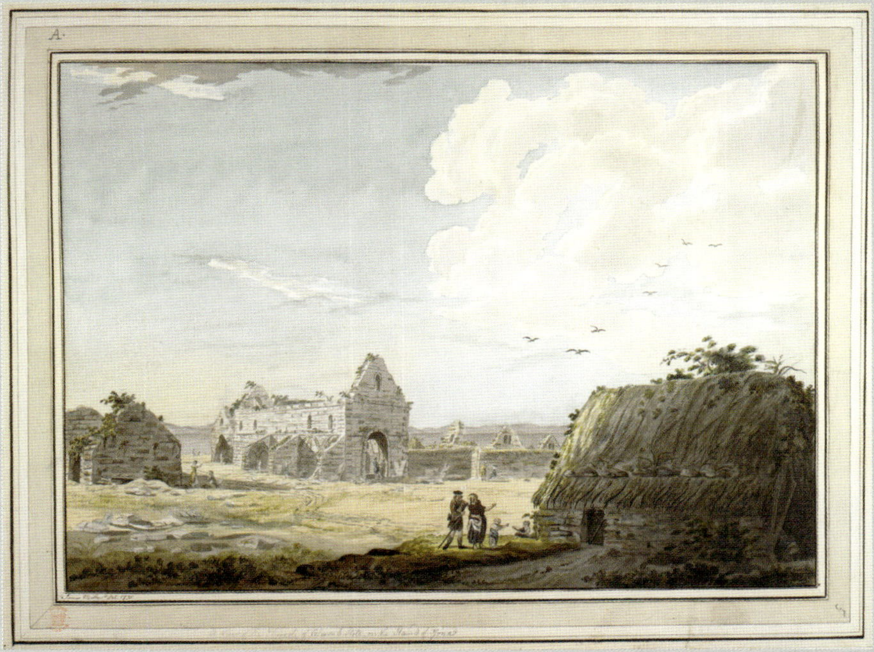

Fig. S2.5
Left. James Miller, *A View of the Church of Columb Kill, on the Island of Iona*, 1775, watercolour (BL Add MS 15510 f. 5)

Fig. S2.6
Below left. John Runciman, *Taking Down the Netherbow*, 1764, etching (GLAHA:51438)

Fig. S2.7
Below right. Joseph Farington, *Edinburgh Castle from the Grassmarket*, dated 28 June 1788, pen and watercolour (NGS D 4510)

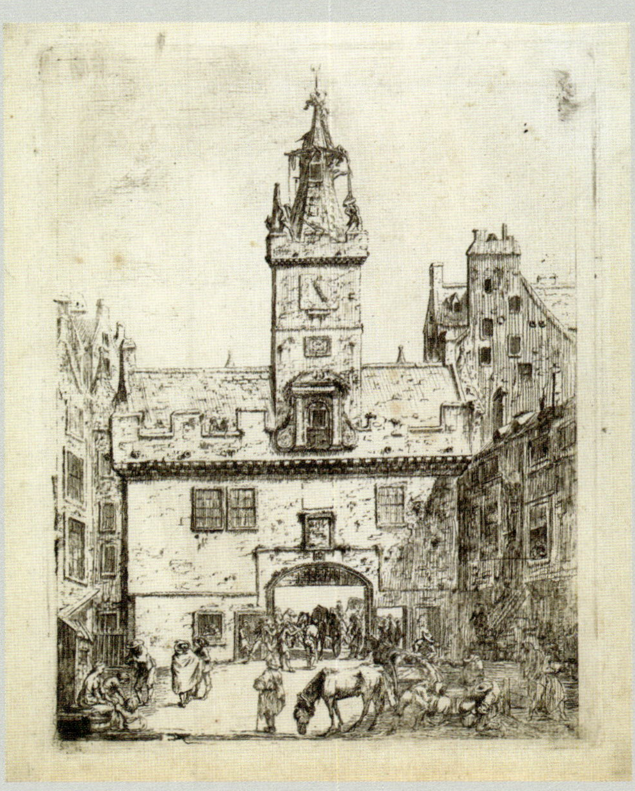

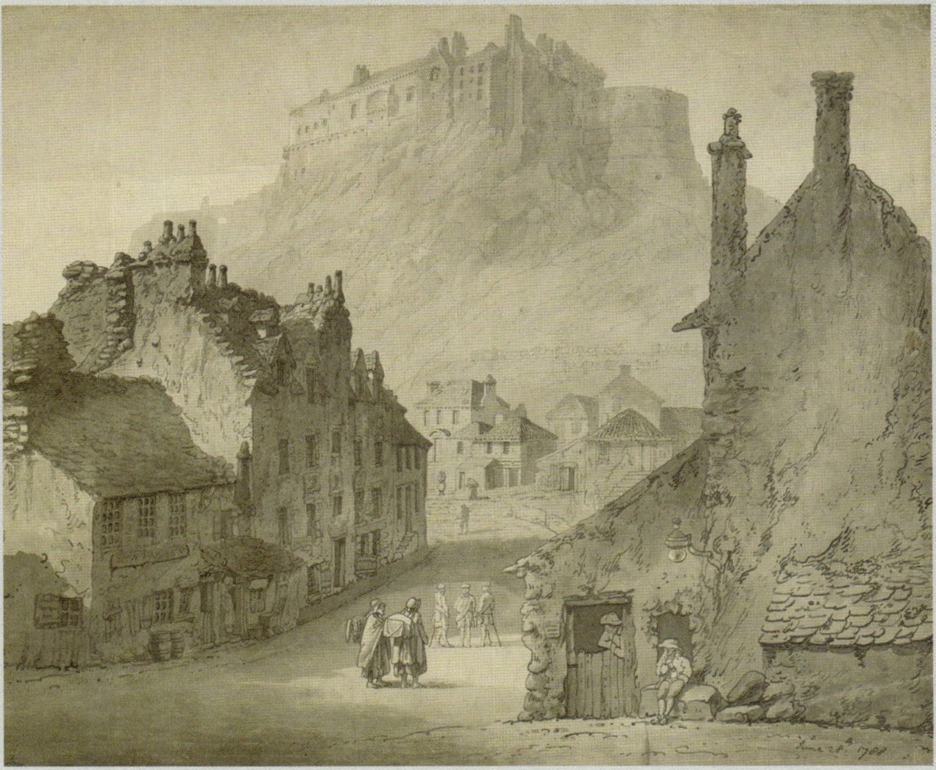

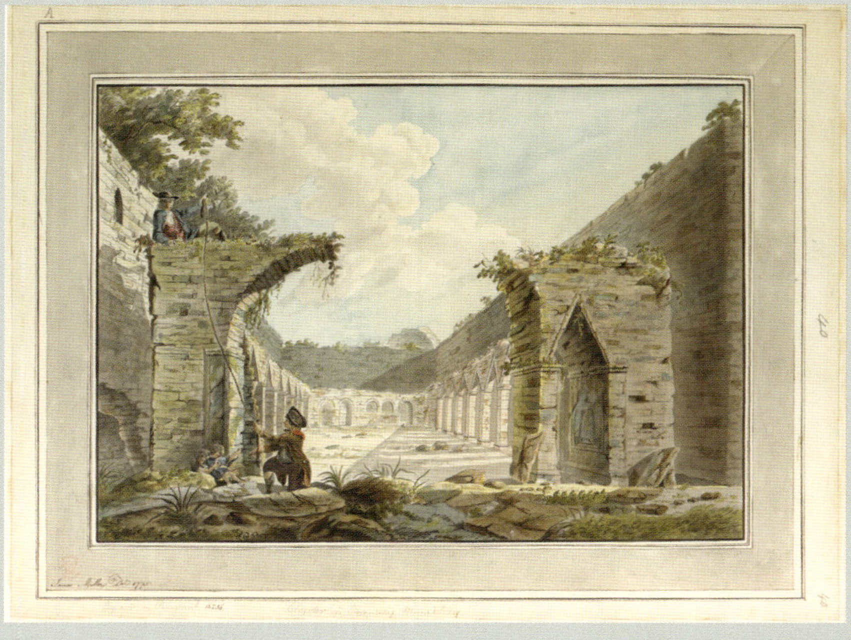

Fig. S2.8.
James Miller, *Cloyster in Oronsay Monastry*, 1775, watercolour (BL Add MS 15509 f. 40)

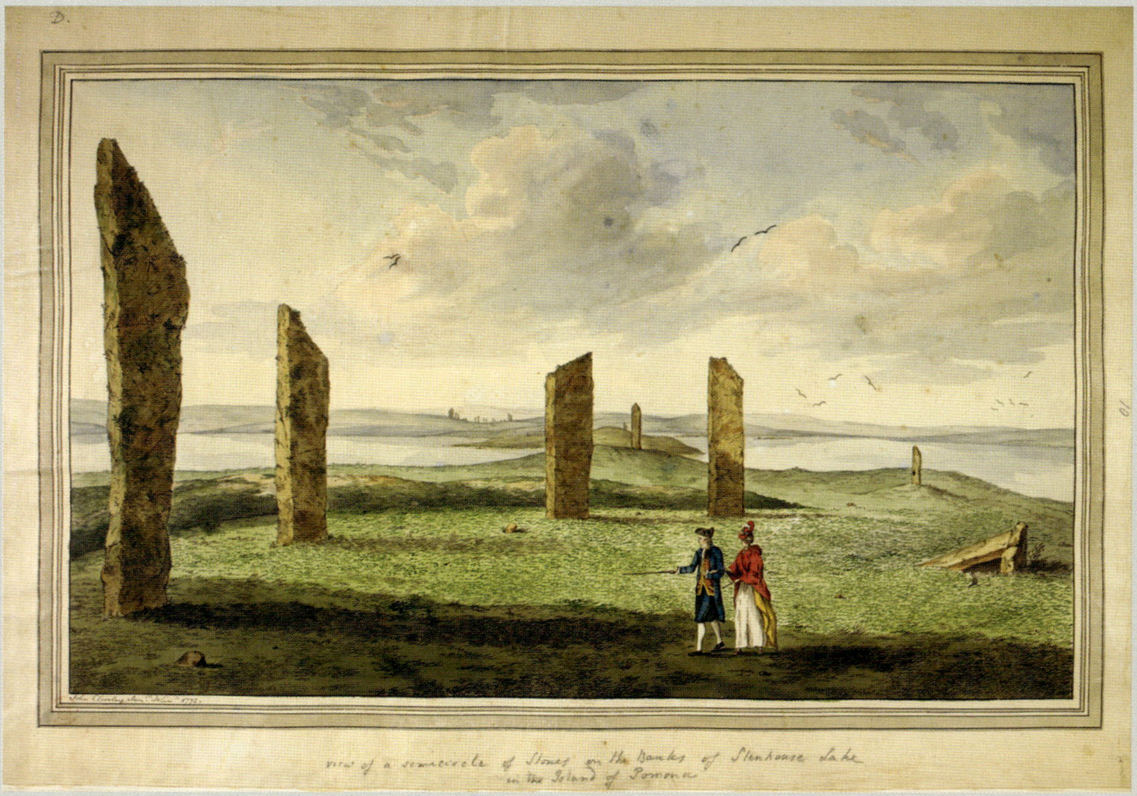

Fig. S2.9
John Cleveley, *View of a Semicircle of Stones on the Banks of Stenhouse Lake in the Island of Pomona*, 1772, watercolour (BL Add MS 15511 f. 10)

accounts properly speaking. But their legacy survives in the antiquarian tour narratives of pioneers such as Sir William Burrell, Richard Pococke and Thomas Pennant in the 1750s, 1760s and 1770s. Fieldwork and eye-witness evidence was an essential requirement for antiquarian knowledge-making: as Smart Lethieullier scoffed, 'I see evidence with my own eyes how much Antiquarys who write in theyr studies are mistaken as to matters of fact' (Brown 1980, 28–29). Painstakingly 'curious' descriptions of monuments and sites, achieved by both pen and pencil, adhered to 'the belief that the things words stand for are to be located out there, in the world' (Smiles 2000, 17).

This is exemplified by illustrations of Roman sculpture (distance slabs) from the Antonine Wall, which had formed part of the collection of Glasgow University since the late seventeenth century, admiringly described by scores of visitors in the period. Visiting in 1772, Thomas Pennant wrote 'many of the sculptures were engraven at the expense of the university; whose principal did me the honour of presenting me with a set'; this was printed by the Foulis Press, which also produced the views of Glasgow discussed in Section 3 (see Figs S3.20–S3.22). The set he was given, based on a collection of twenty prints commissioned in 1767, would later be published as part of the *Monumenta Romani Imperii*, including twelve new illustrations printed on ten sheets (1792) (Fig. S2.10). This highlights the importance of Glasgow University in the eighteenth-century recovery of Scotland's Roman heritage and antiquities, and especially the printing press (and 'Academy of Arts') instituted by the university's printers Robert and Andrew Foulis, which had produced the *Monumenta*. Pennant described Plate III, a Roman distance slab from Summerston, showing Victory crowning 'a Roman horseman armed with a spear and a shield. Beneath him are two Caledonian captives, naked, and bound, with their little daggers, like the modern dirks, by them' (Pennant 1998, 134). Visual documentation of antiquarian objects, ruins and sites played an important part in the proliferation of lavishly illustrated travel books about Scotland that flooded from the press in the aftermath of Pennant's pioneering publications in the 1770s, exemplified by Charles Cordiner's *Romantic Ruins, and Romantic Prospects of North Britain* (1781–795) (commissioned and published by his patron Pennant) and Adam de Cardonnel's *Picturesque Antiquities of Scotland* (1788–1793) (Figs S2.11 and S2.12). Cordiner, an episcopalian clergyman from the north of Scotland who had studied at Glasgow's Foulis

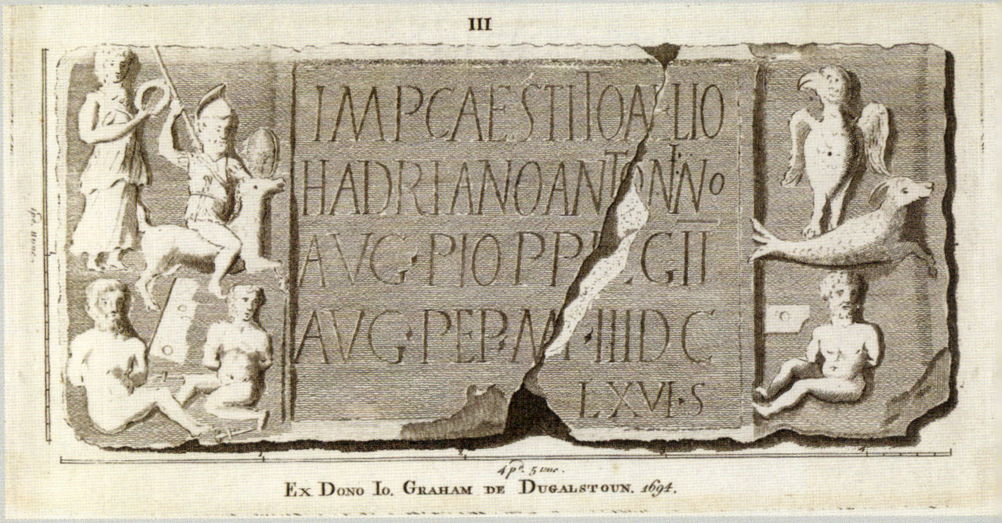

Fig. S2.10
Above. Anon., Roman distance slab from Summerston, engraving, from *Monumenta Romani Imperii, in Scotia* (Glasgow: Foulis Press, 1792), plate III (GLA ASC Hunterian.H.7.32)

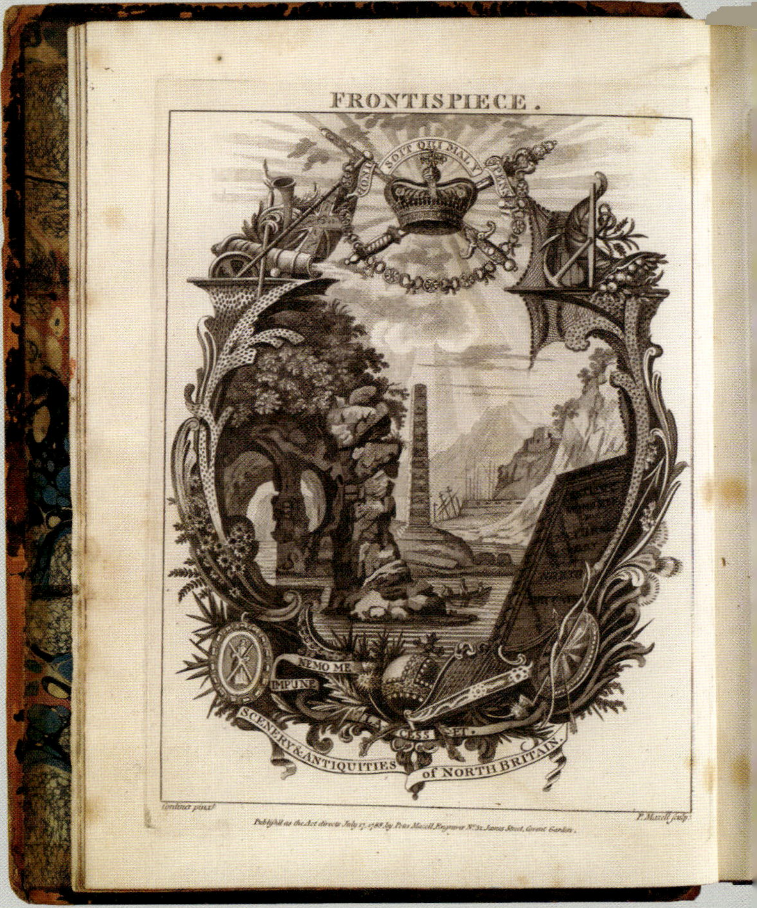

Fig. S2.11
Right. Peter Mazell, engraving, frontispiece to Charles Cordiner, *Remarkable Ruins, and Romantic Prospects of North Britain: With Ancient Monuments, and Singular Subjects of Natural History* (London, 1788–95) (GLA ASC BD5-d13)

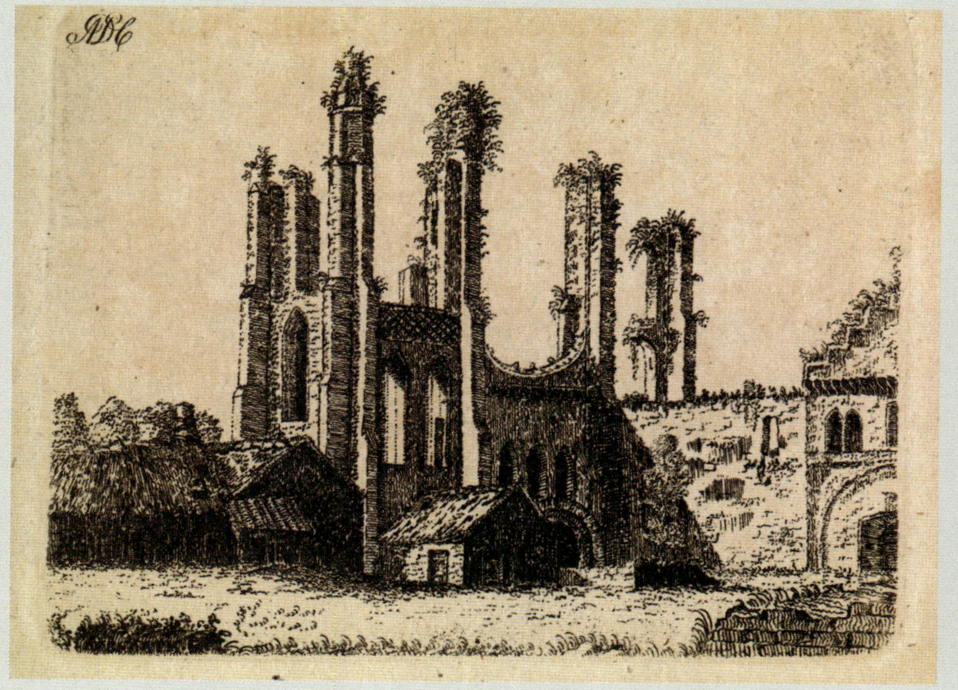

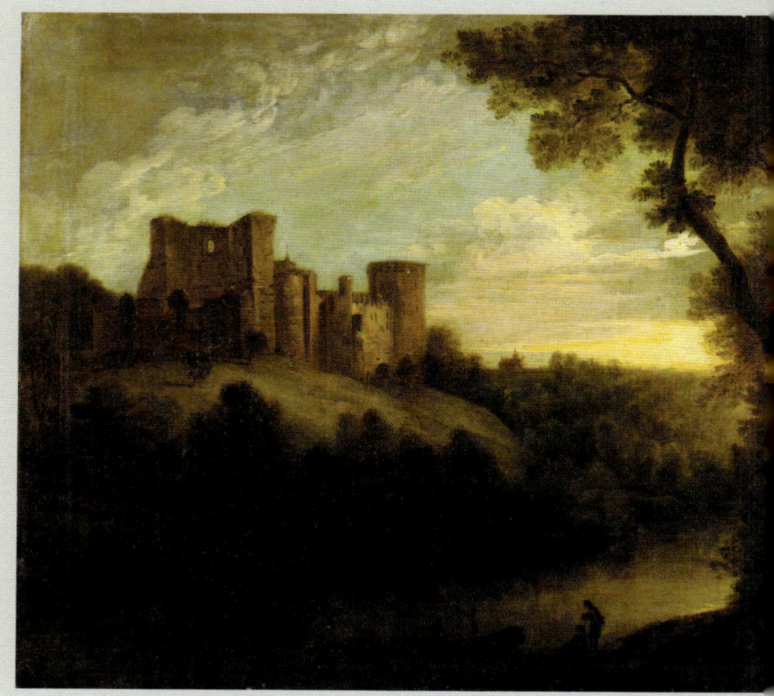

Fig. S2.12
Above left. Adam de Cardonnel, 'Aberbrothock', etching, in *Picturesque Antiquities of Scotland*, new edn (London, 1802), part III, plate 1 (PC)

Fig. S2.13
Above right. Charles Cordiner, *View of Bothwell Castle*, 1765, oil on canvas (GLAHA:43439)

Academy of Arts, was innovative in combining topographical representations of prehistoric monuments with wild scenery and providing Scotland's ruins with the 'romantic' resonance highlighted in his book's title (Fig. S2.13), as can also be seen in his album of drawings (see Fig. S2.29) (Macleod 2012, 53–54).

There was after all a close affinity between the collection and description of 'artificial' and 'natural' curiosities, as described by Fredrik Jonsson in Chapter 3: Horace Walpole described how Pennant's Scottish tours represented 'a round jump from ornithology to antiquity', given that at the time of travelling the Welshman was the author of a pioneering *British Zoology* (Evans 2017, 15–40). Pennant's 'servant–artist' Moses Griffith was responsible for many of the plates that made his publications best-sellers: his illustration of a roebuck and white hare, published as plate 14 in *Tour in Scotland in 1769* (Fig. S2.14), illustrates that similar conventions governed the visual depictions of antiquarian and zoological specimens, but, in confirmation of Walpole's judgement, all the natural history had been replaced by antiquarian plates in Pennant's third edition of 1774.

As befitted denizens of a more contemporary 'theatre of war', eighteenth-century Scottish antiquarians were possessed by the spirit of 'Agricolamania', referring to Agricola's attempted Roman conquest of Scotland in 80 CE, as described in Tacitus's *Agricola*, culminating in his spectacular defeat of the Caledonians under their leader Calgacus at the battle of Mons Graupius (84 CE). In the late seventeenth century, Scotland's Geographer Royal Sir Robert Sibbald had traced the archeological relics of the Roman conquest, as well as supporting the work of Skye-born Martin Martin, whose *Description of the Western Isles of Scotland* (1703) pioneered the study of Scotland's *Gaidhealtachd* beyond the pale of the Roman occupation, and whose account of local beliefs, apparently descended from Druid worship, inspired a new interest in domestic antiquities. Sibbald's work on Roman Scotland was taken up by Sir John Clerk of Penicuik, the great 'Maecenas' of Scottish antiquarians, and his protégé Alexander Gordon, author of the aforementioned *Itinerarium Septentrionale*. Much of Gordon's book was dedicated to relatively accessible Roman antiquities in central Scotland and Perthshire, but the construction of the new Hanoverian barracks at Bernera encouraged him to visit the spectacular Glenelg Brochs in Lochalsh. Gordon rejected claims that the brochs were either Druidic or Roman temples, preferring to see them as indigenous constructions dating from

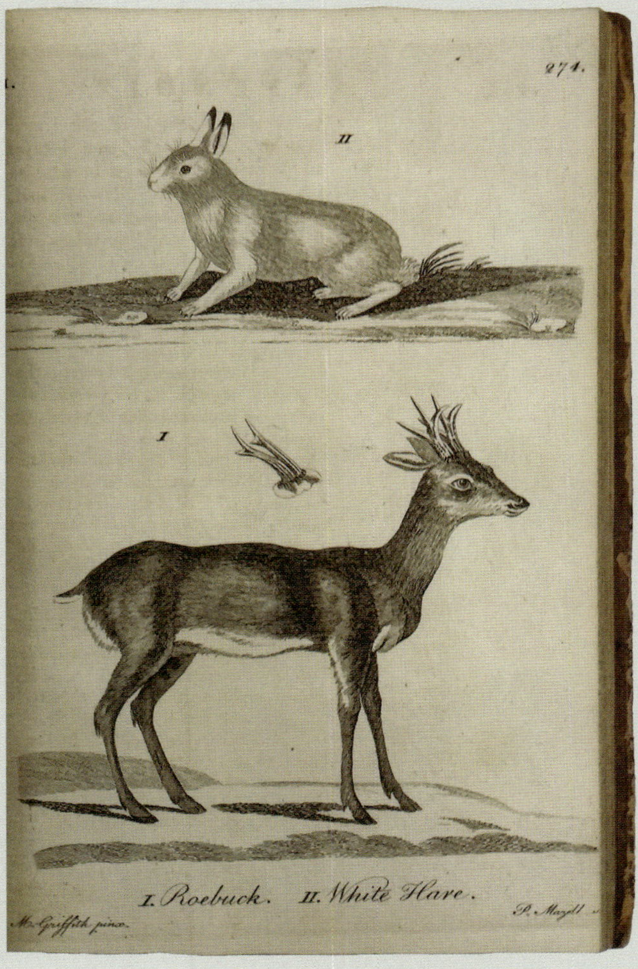

Fig. S2.14
Left. Peter Mazell after Moses Griffith, 'A Roebuck and a White Hare', engraving in Thomas Pennant, *Tour of Scotland 1769* (Chester, 1771), p. 274

Fig. S2.15
Right. 'Castle Troddan', engraving in Alexander Gordon, *Itinerarium Septentrionale; or, A Journey thro' most of the Counties of Scotland, and those in the North of England; in Two Parts . . .* (London, 1726), pl. 65
(GLA ASC Mu7-y.7)

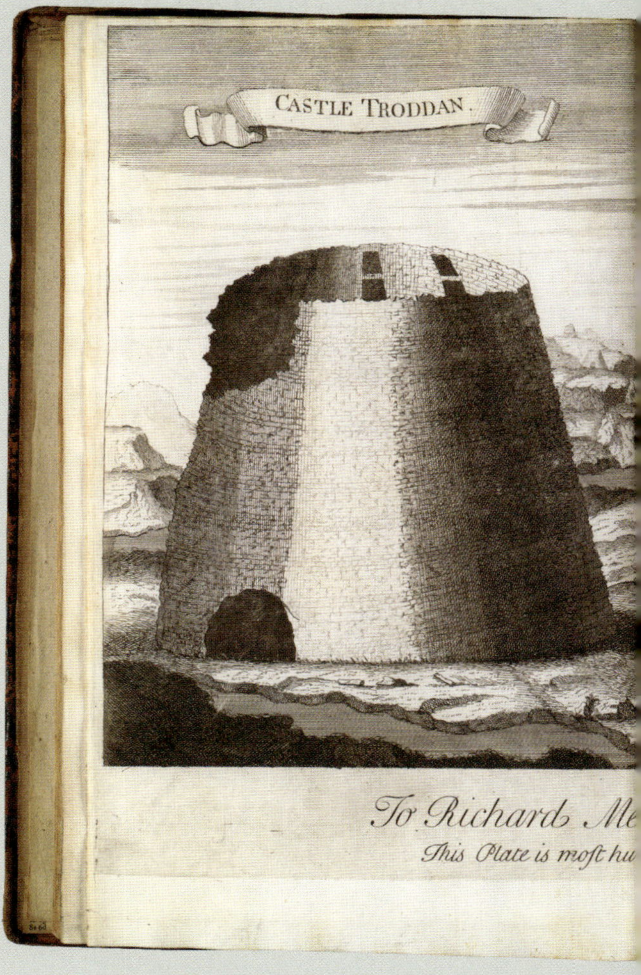

early times, which didn't, however, prevent Pennant, thirty-five years later, confidently describing them as 'Danish edifices' (Figs S2.15 and S2.16) (Macleod 2012, 50–52).

Clerk of Penicuik's second son, John Clerk of Eldin, is today best remembered for his marvellous drawings of geological strata reproduced as illustrations in Hutton's *Theory of the Earth*, discussed in Chapter 3. But he is also renowned for his etched views of Scotland, imitating Sandby's experiments in the same medium (as mentioned above, it was probably Clerk of Eldin's cluttered study that provided the model for Scott's 'sanctum sanctorum' in *The Antiquary*) (Macleod 2012, 32). Clerk was especially interested in representing Scottish castles situated around the coasts, part of a defensive wall against foreign invasion and to quell internal lawlessness; many of these, like Eilean Donan, Castle Stalker and Duart Castle in the west, or Blackness Castle on the east coast, had been refortified as Hanoverian garrisons during the Jacobite wars (Figs S2.17 and S2.18).

Sir John Clerk's patriotic mantle was assumed by David Erskine, 11th Earl of Buchan (like Clerk, an alumnus of Glasgow University), who in 1780 founded the Society of Antiquaries of Scotland to distinguish it from the older London Society founded in 1707. In an apposite metaphor, he likened his native country to 'a rude medallion of antient sculpture which ought not to be defaced or forgotten in the Cabinet of Nations' (Brown 1980, 45). While a student at Glasgow in 1762–3, Buchan had also attended the university's Foulis Academy of Arts: his drawing of Iona Abbey

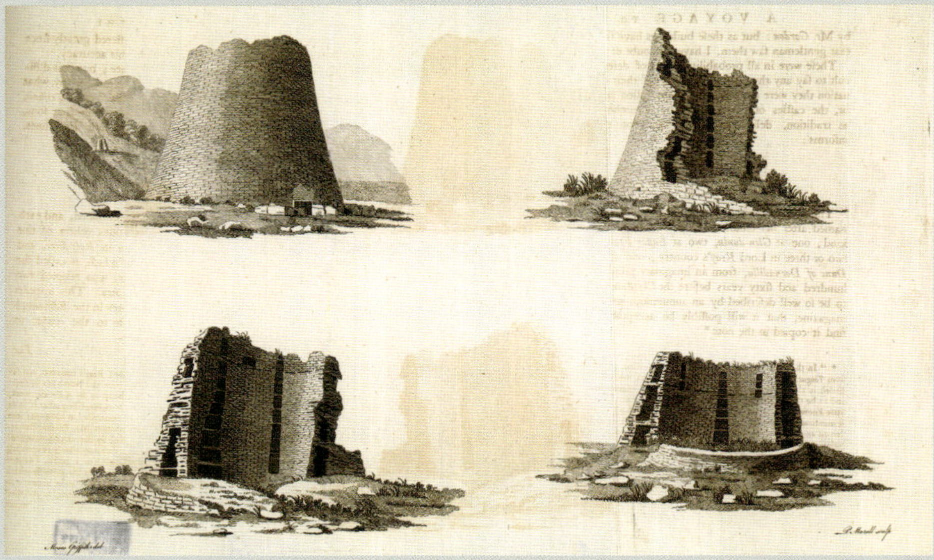

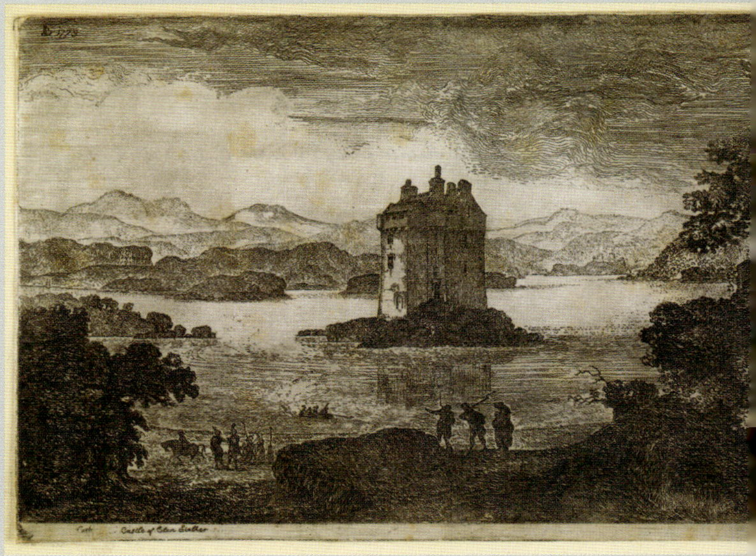

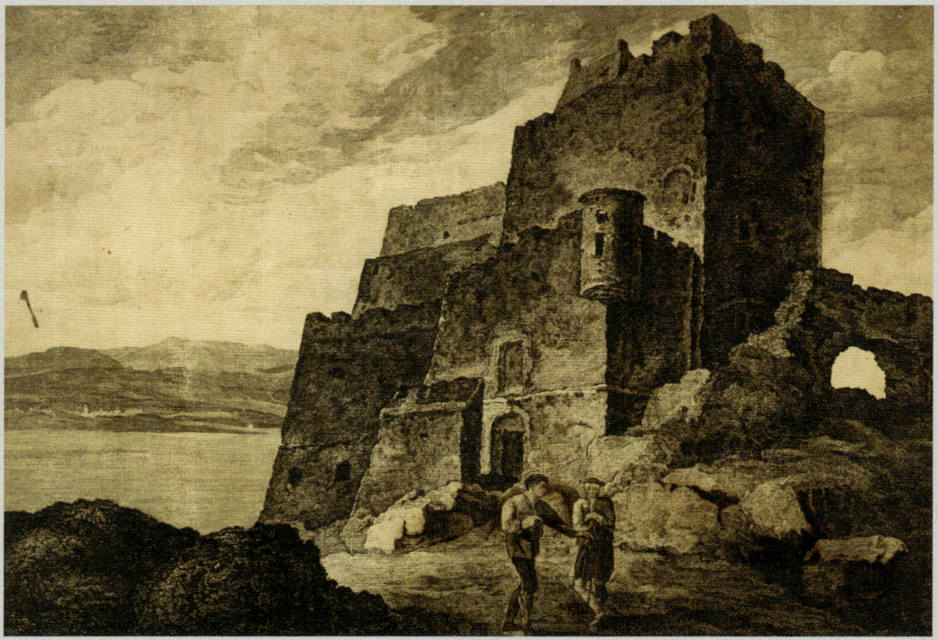

Fig. S2.16
Top left. Peter Mazell after Moses Griffith, 'Danish Edifices in Glen-Elg', engraving in Thomas Pennant, *Tour in Scotland and Voyage to the Hebrides, 1772* (Chester, 1774), Vol. 1, plate XLI, p. 392 (GLA ASC Mu6-d.2)

Fig. S2.17
Top right. John Clerk of Eldin, *Castle of Elan Stalker*, 1773, etching (GLAHA:47150)

Fig. S2.18
Above. Alexander Runciman, *Blackness Castle*, c. 1760s, etching (NGS P 6551)

(one of the fruits of his extensive Highland Tour in 1761) was published in the first volume of the *Transactions of the Society of Antiquities of Scotland*. It is one of the earliest drawings of the abbey, preceding James Miller's by over a decade (Cant 1981, 4; Christian and Stiller 2000, 9–11). Unfortunately, Buchan's radical Whig agenda alienated Edinburgh's establishment, and resigning his membership in disgust he retreated to his estate at Dryburgh Abbey in the Borders, where he rode his antiquarian hobby-horse under the pseudonym of 'the Hermit of the Tweed', established a 'Temple of Caledonian Fame', and offered patronising advice to the Ayrshire poet Robert Burns.

Agricola's conquest of Caledonia provided an historical analogy for the assertion of Hanoverian authority over Scotland in the aftermath of the 1715 and 1745 uprisings: if loyal Hanoverians mined the parallels between 'our military countrymen' and Agricola's legionaries, Jacobites and patriots often preferred to identify with the heroic resistance of Calgacus and the Caledonians, as evoked by Tacitus himself (Brown 1987, 45–46). As a member of William Stukeley's 'Society of Roman Knights', Alexander Gordon stated his patriotic allegiances by taking the name 'Galcacus', while his patron Sir John Clerk preferred the role of 'Agricola', more appropriate for a Whig Baron of Exchequer (Sweet 2004, 164; Brown 1987, 38). In 1743 Clerk was outraged to hear of the destruction of 'Arthur's O'on', a Roman monument near Falkirk lauded in Gordon's *Itinerarium*, by the local landowner Sir

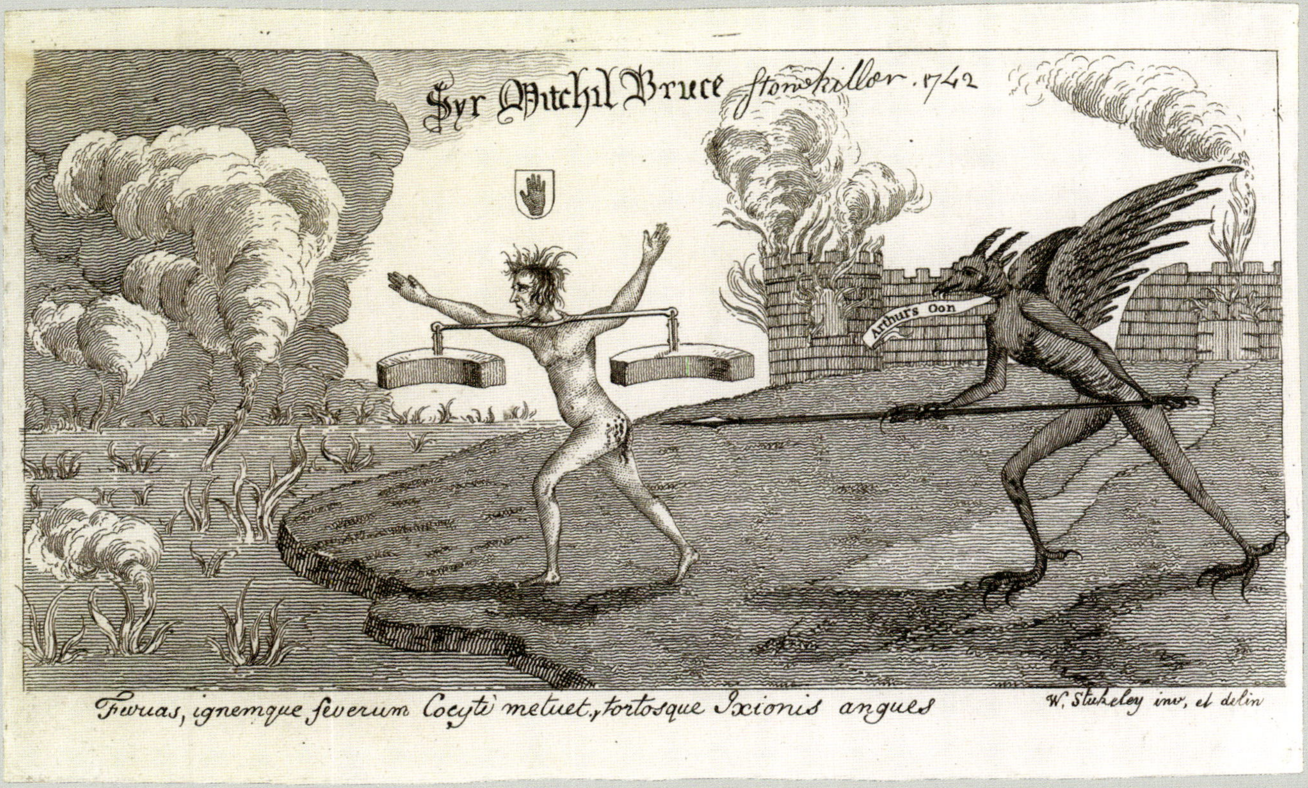

Fig. S2.19
William Stukeley, *Syr Mitchil Bruce Stonekiller*, etching, 1742 (GLAHA:52753)

Michael Bruce, whom he vilified as 'this Gothick knight' (Brown 1980, 32). William Stukeley's graphic satire *Syr Mitchil Bruce, Stonekiller* imagined a fit punishment for the vandal, shown being prodded into a sea of boiling bitumen by the devil, who is invoking the words 'Arthur's O'on' (Fig. S2.19). Clerk's son and heir Sir James would build a scale replica of 'Arthur's O'on' onto the stable block at Penicuik House, exemplifying the common incorporation of Roman architectural features into eighteenth-century buildings, most often associated with the great Scottish architect Robert Adam.

Appropriately enough, the historical analogy between Roman and Hanoverian conquest was supported by the fact that a great number of Roman remains were unearthed during the construction of eighteenth-century military roads, canals and forts, including the Roman distance slabs from the Antonine Wall, now held in Glasgow University, discussed above. This provided a basis for Lanarkshire-born William Roy's learned study of Roman military antiquities in Scotland, conducted as what he called 'the lucubrations of [my] leisure hours' (Roy 1793) when he was surveyor for the 'Great Military Map' under the command of the Duke of Cumberland in 1747–1755 (Roy 2007 [1747–55]; Hodson 2011, 117–132). In 1755 Roy surveyed and mapped the Antonine Wall, finding that 'there seemed to be much room for improvement' in previous descriptions by Gordon and John Horsely, work which earned him membership of the London Society of Antiquaries in 1776 (Roy 1793, vi). *Military Antiquities of the Romans in Britain,* a lavish volume in grand folio with fine maps and engravings of Roman forts and other related sites, was published posthumously in 1793, having circulated in manuscript from the 1770s (Fig. S2.20). A parallel is evident between the techniques employed in these images and the Great Map, not least in the delicate colouring and the use of hatching to represent relief, indicating a similar level of accomplishment and sophistication. Roy cast new light on Agricola's campaign in Scotland, drawing on his expert knowledge of the lie of the land, and the 'castramentation' of Roman forts. Although unable to

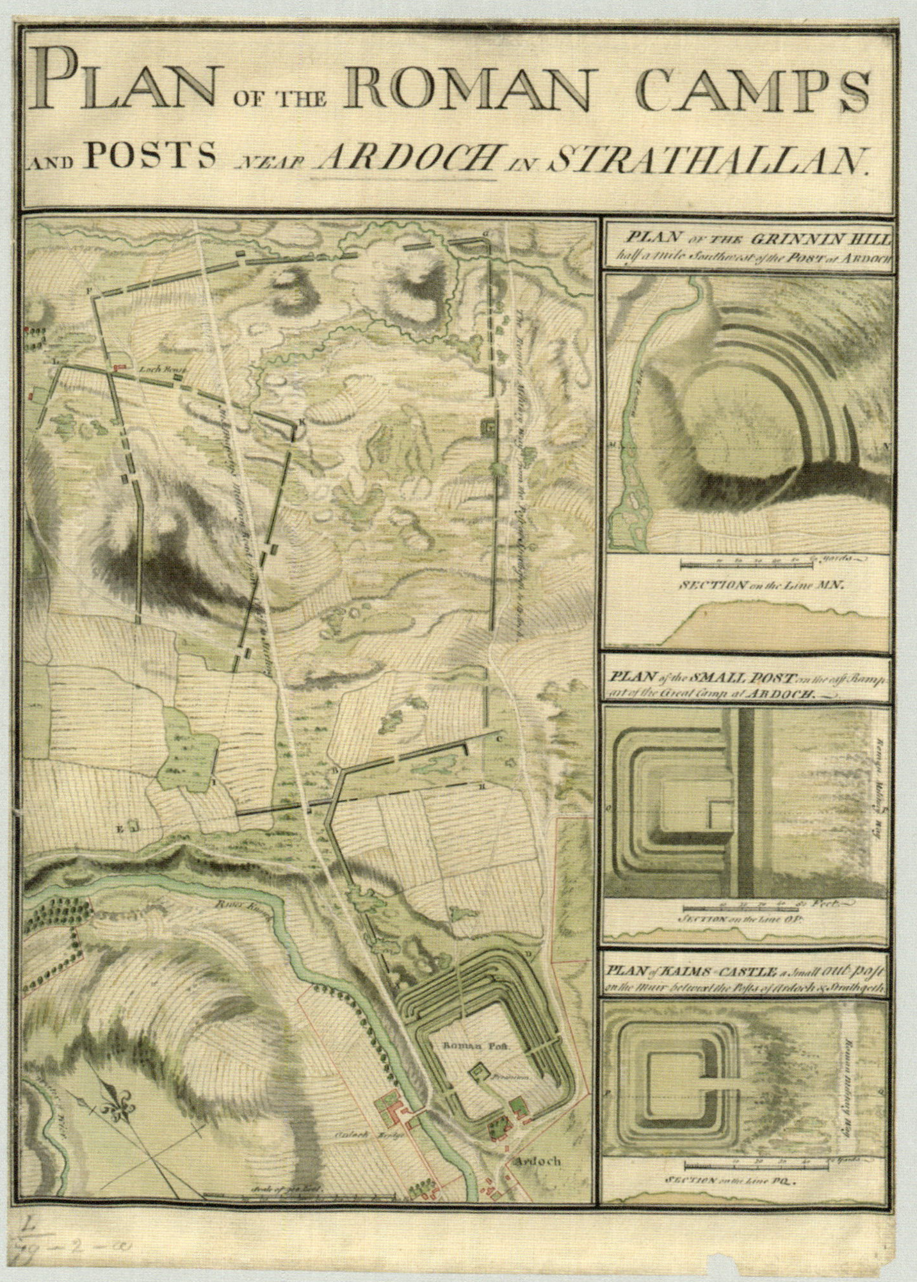

Fig. S2.20
Above. William Roy, *Plan of the Roman Camps and Posts near Ardoch in Strathallan*, July 1755, watercolour (BL K.Top.50.79.2.a)

locate the much-debated site of Mons Graupius with precision, he provided evidence to support his theory that Ardoch fort near Braco in Perthshire was the base camp of the Roman army before the battle, thereby eliminating several rival theories, which located it further north (Roy 1793, 18). Unlike Gordon, the Whig Roy displayed little sympathy for the defeated Caledonians, whose 'small bucklers, and huge unwieldy swords, blunt at the point . . . [were] unfit for a close encounter', leading to the slaughter of over 10,000 of their ranks, evoking contemporary accounts of the defeated Jacobite clansmen at Culloden (Roy 1793, 19; see also Pennant 1998, 290). This is similar to the analogy between the 'little daggers' of ancient Caledonians and and the 'short dirks' of modern Highlanders in Pennant's description of Glasgow University's Roman distance slab from Summerston discussed above, inviting comparisions between Tacitus's account of Mons Graupius and the description of Culloden by Whig propagandists in the eighteenth-century mindset.

The publication of James Macpherson's *Poems of Ossian* in the early 1760s challenged 'Agricolamania' by providing an alternative Ossianic antiquity and eliciting sentimental sympathy for the defeated Caledonians, despite the fact that many readers (especially in England) may have doubted the poems' authenticity (Trumpener 1997; Leask 2016, 183–196).

> By the side of a rock on the hill, beneath the aged trees, old Oscian sat on the moss; the last of the race of Fingal. Sightless are his aged eyes; his beard is waving in the wind. Dull through the leafless trees he heard the voice of the north. Sorrow revived in his soul: he began and lamented the dead. (Macpherson 1996, 18)

Joseph Banks, sailing up the Sound of Mull in 1772 en route for Iceland, enthused over the sight of 'Morven the land of heroes once the seat of the exploits of Fingal the mother of the romantick scenery of Ossion. I could not even sail past it without a touch of enthusiasm sweet affection of the mind': a few days later, he was delighted to learn that the dramatic basaltic grotto on the isle of Staffa was named 'Fingal's Cave' (Rauschenberg 1973, 186–226, 205; Pennant 1998, 258). The most famous Ossianic site on the *petit tour* was the Dunkeld Hermitage (discussed in Chapter 4), a pavilion for viewing the Falls of Braan, rebranded as 'Ossian's Hall' in 1783 by the 4th Duke of Atholl after the installation

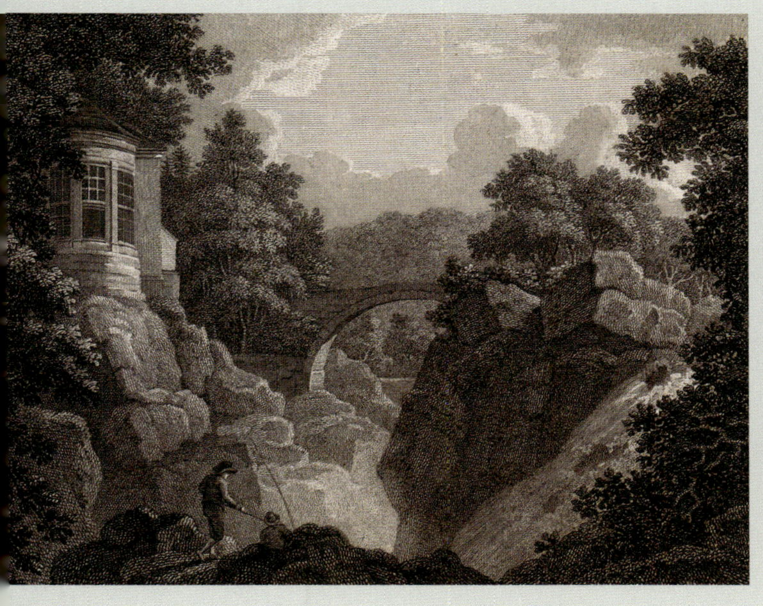

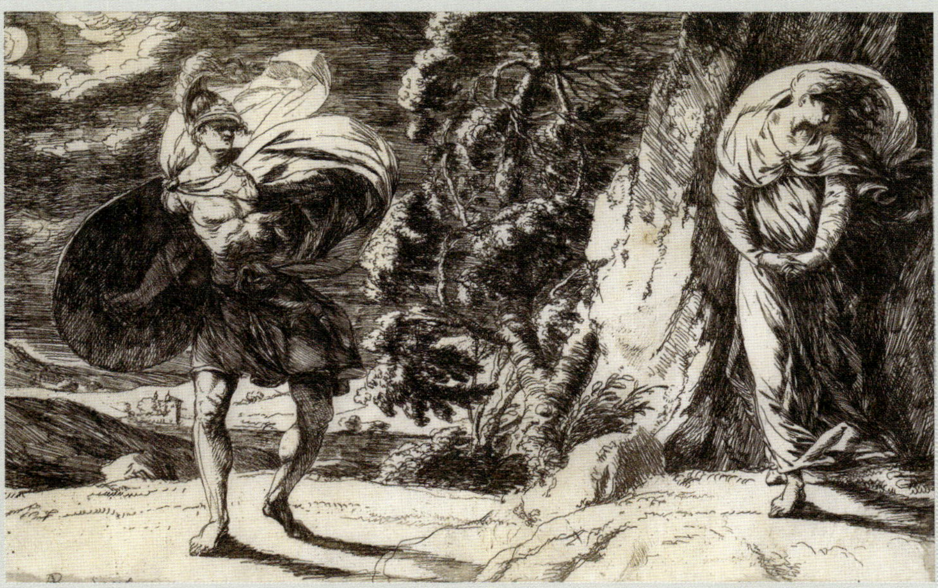

of a portrait of the blind bard, which slid open to reveal the viewing chamber (Fig. S2.21) (Dingwall 1997, 62–70). The 'Ossianification' of Highland topography is well exemplified by the fate of a 'Roman burial' under a boulder in the Sma' Glen of Glenalmond discovered by Wade's military road builders in the 1730s, redesignated as 'Clach Ossian' (or 'Ossian's Tomb') after 1760, later inspiring a tour poem by Wordsworth (Leask 2020, 58–59).

Ossian coincided in pictorial terms with the emergence of more overtly imaginative reconstructions of the relics of the national past, albeit co-existing with supposedly more 'accurate' forms of visual documentation. The historical resonance of the Scottish landscape, and the material relics of its past, were accordingly opened up to revision. Alexander Runciman's *Fingal and Conban-Cargla* (Fig. S2.22), inspired by one of his designs for Sir James Clerk's 'Ossian's Hall' at Penicuik House, adapts the visual idiom of the Italian renaissance to indigenous heroic subjects, representing a primitive world 'in which human nature shoots wild and free, though unfit for other improvements' (Hugh Blair, in Macpherson 1996, 345). The search for the 'Gaelic originals' of Macpherson's *Ossian* poems inspired a generation of tourists to scour the Highlands and Islands in search of Gaelic tradition-bearers such as the family of the celebrated Alexander McNab, blacksmith of Dalmallie (Fig. S2.23). In fact, while the defeat of the Jacobite clans at Culloden had witnessed a stepping up of the campaign led by the Scottish Society for Prompoting Christian Knowledge (SSPCK) and others to extirpate the Gaelic language, the second half of the eighteenth century saw an astonishing refloresence of Gaelic poetry by bards such as Alasdair Mac Mhaighstir Alasdair, Duncan Ban MacIntyre (Donnchadh Bàn Mac an t-Saoir) and Rob Donn: Alasdair's *Ais-eiridh na Sean Chánoin Albannaich* ('Resurrection of the Ancient Scottish Language'), published in 1751, was the first secular book to be published in Scottish Gaelic, but on account of its defiant Jacobite politics and bawdy tone was allegedly burned by the public hangman in Edinburgh (Fig. S2.24). Although Pennant's travelling companion the Rev. John Stuart was involved in the printing of Duncan Ban MacIntyre's poetry (as well as completing his father's translation of the Bible into Scottish Gaelic), unfortunately most travellers and tourists in the period were unable (or unwilling) 'to distinguish between Gaelic song of any description, and Macpherson's *Ossian*' (Baines 1997, 53).

As an appendix to his edition of the 'Gaelic originals' of Macpherson's *Ossian* translations, Sir John Sinclair excerpted ministers' reports from the *Statistical Account of Scotland* (his own major project of national description, including copious details of parochial antiquities) identifying Ossianic sites in their own parishes around Argyll and Lorne, fuelling the desire of tourists to

Fig. S2.21
Above left. William Byrne after George Walker, 'Ossian's Hall', engraving (detail) in James Cririe, *Scottish Scenery: or, Sketches in Verse, Descriptive of Scenes Chiefly in the Highlands of Scotland* (London, 1803), p. 49 (GLA ASC Hepburn q35)

Fig. S2.22
Above right. Alexander Runciman, *Fingal and Conban-Cargla*, 1773, etching (GLAHA:20528)

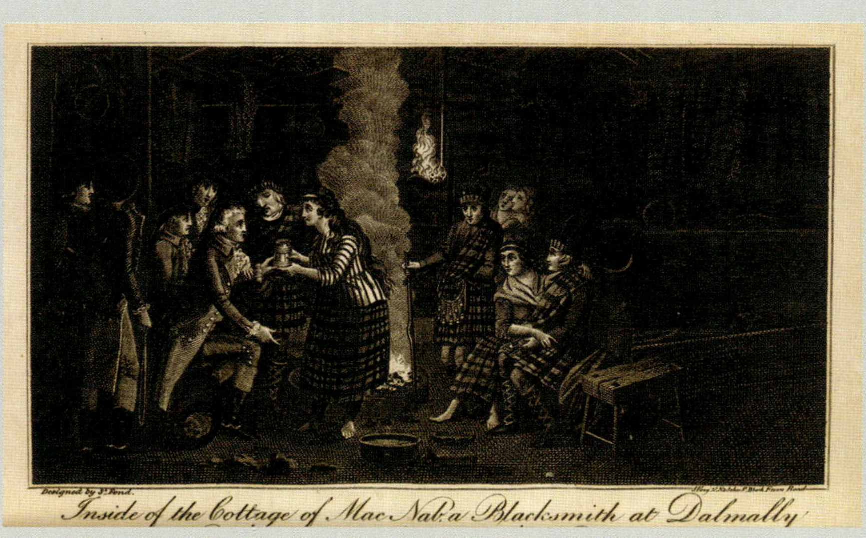

footstep the sublime and melancholy 'tales of other times' (Sinclair 1807, III, 511) (Fig S2.25). Such Ossianic traces in the Highland landscape were embraced by the greatest painter–tourist of the period, J.M.W. Turner, whose 'Scottish pencil' drawings record his tour of 1801. Although the recently identified title of Turner's painting *Ben Lomond Mountains, Scotland: The Traveller – Vide Ossian's 'War of Caros'* alludes to a specific episode in *Ossian* (see Fig. S4.5), it rather seeks to capture the artist's response to the poem's epical resonance in a sublime mountain landcape. Such understated allusion to *Ossian* also powerfully underlies one of Turner's greatest paintings, *Staffa, Fingal's Cave* (1832) (see Fig. C1.8) in which the sea mist veiling the basaltic colums of the cave is punctuated by a plume of black smoke from the funnel of the steam packet, rendering 'Ossian's capacity to speak both to the deep time of geological history and to the rapid temporal shifts of

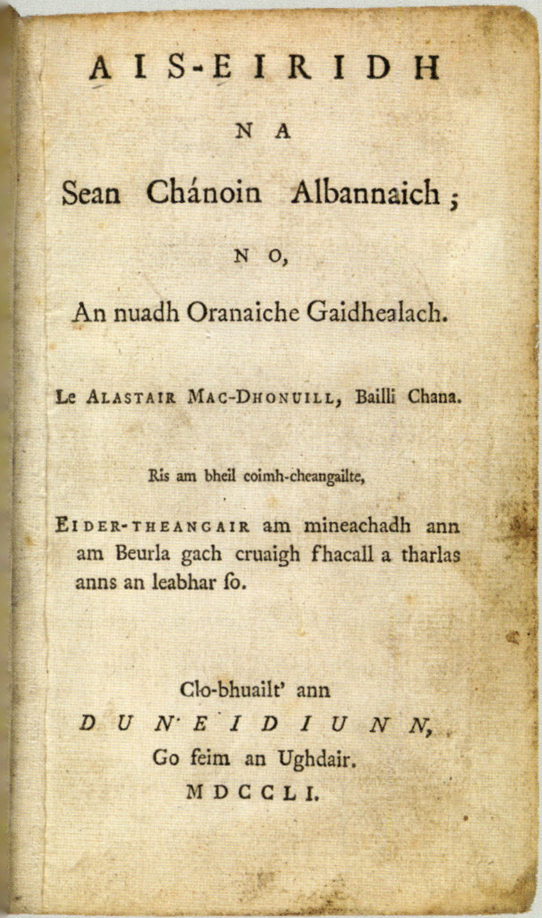
AIS-EIRIDH

NA

Sean Chánoin Albannaich;

NO,

An nuadh Oranaiche Gaidhealach.

Le ALASTAIR MAC-DHONUILL, Bailli Chana.

Ris am bheil coimh-cheangailte,

EIDER-THEANGAIR am mineachadh ann am Beurla gach cruaigh fhacall a tharlas anns an leabhar ſo.

Clo-bhuailt' ann
DUN'EIDIUNN,
Go feim an Ughdair.
MDCCLI.

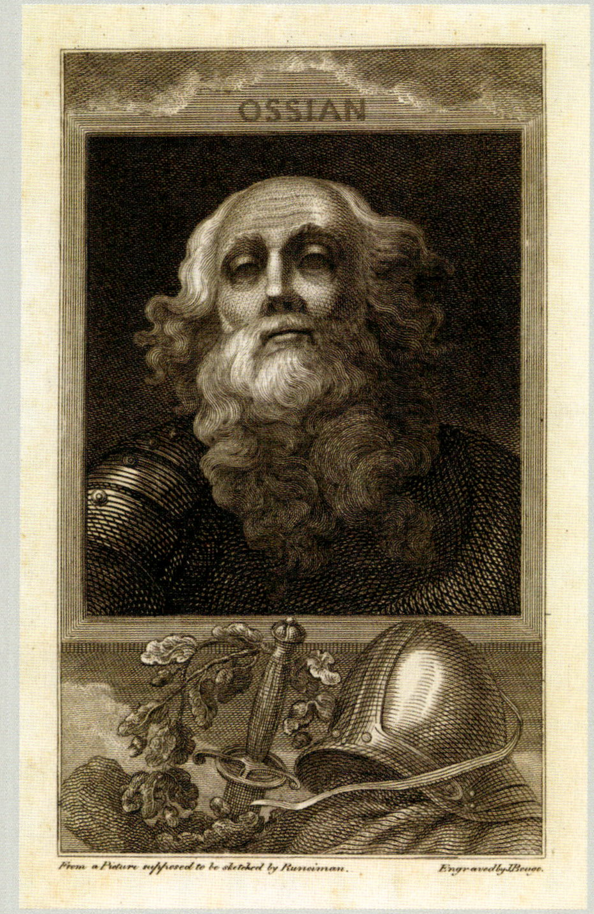

Fig. S2.23
Above. Anon., *Inside the Cottage of MacNab, a Highland Blacksmith at Dalmally, Who Possesses Several Fragments of Ossian's Poems*, engraving in Barthélemy Faujas de Saint-Fond, *Travels in England, Scotland, and the Hebrides*, Vol. I (London, 1799), opposite p. 301 (GLA ASC Mu8-g.3)

Fig. S2.24
Far left. Alasdair Mac Mhaighstir Alasdair (Alexander MacDonald), *Ais-eiridh na Sean Chánoin Albannaich; no, An nuadh Oranaiche Gaidhealach* (Edinburgh, 1751) (GLA ASC RB 3025)

Fig. S2.25
Left. John Beugo after Alexander Runciman, 'Ossian', frontispiece to Sir John Sinclair, *The Poems of Ossian, in the Original Gaelic, with a Literal Translation into Latin, by the Late Robert McFarlan. Together with a Dissertation on the Authenticity of the Poems, by Sir John Sinclair, Esq.*, Vol. 1 (London, 1803) (GLA ASC RQ 516)

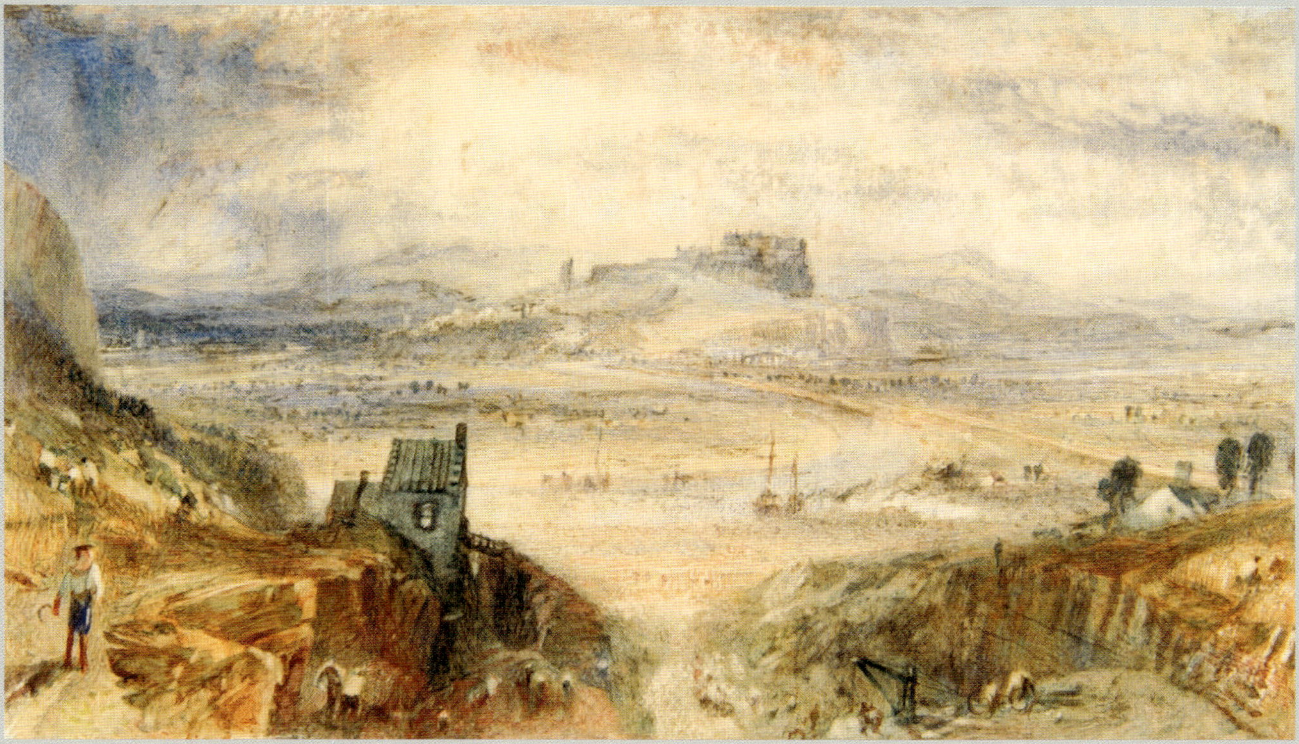

Fig. S2.26
Joseph Mallord William Turner, *Stirling*, c. 1834–5, watercolour (LWL PR.1980.22)

the industrial age' (Gidal 2015, 9). Turner's interest in the visual relationship between antiquity and the modern age is also evident in his watercolour of Stirling Castle, seen from a distance and viewed over a contemporary stone quarry (Fig. S2.26).

For the artist William Daniell in the early 1820s, referring to the ruined Hanoverian barracks at Glenelg (a landscape largely cleared of its human population in favour of sheep), antiquarian ruins were vestiges of a corrupt, violent and superstitious history, conquered by modern improvement and reason:

> Let this tranquillity be permanent and prosperous, and the military establishment of Bernera may be left to decay, and thus share the common doom of the tumuli, the duns, the druidical circles, the idolatrous altars consecrated by barbarism, as as well as of all the feudal fortifications of the empire, monuments too frequently of tyranny and oppression, and interesting only as ruins. (Daniell 2006, I, 149)

At stake here is the range of possible meanings to which the material remains of history were susceptible: as a 'useable past' for Hanoverian modernisers or Jacobite patriots; as a goad to encourage further improvement; or as a dark shadowy dreamworld, subverting modern certainties.

Although the passage from Scott's *Antiquary* quoted at the start of this section casts a rich retrospective light on the great age of Scottish antiquarianism, Robert Burns's response is perhaps more deeply lodged in the nation's imagination. Introduced in 1789 to the corpulent 'British Antiquarian' Captain Francis Grose (Fig. S2.27) by his Dumfriesshire patron Robert Riddell of Glenriddell (himself an active member of both the London and Edinburgh Antiquarian Societies), Burns was commissioned to provide a supernatural tale to gloss Grose's spare engraving of the ruined Kirkalloway in his *Antiquities of Scotland* (1789–91). This was delivered up in the form of a narrative poem in octasyllabic couplets entitled 'Tam o'Shanter. A Tale', published as a double-column footnote over three pages of Grose's volume. Amidst the

Fig. S2.27
Right. John Kay, *The British Antiquarian*, 1789, etching (GMC)

Fig. S2.28
Below. Toad stone, or witches' stone, brown and white worn glass marble, set in a silver ban (GLAHM:C.103)

This witches' charm from Renfrewshire captures the extent to which superstitious beliefs still permeated eighteenth-century Scotland.

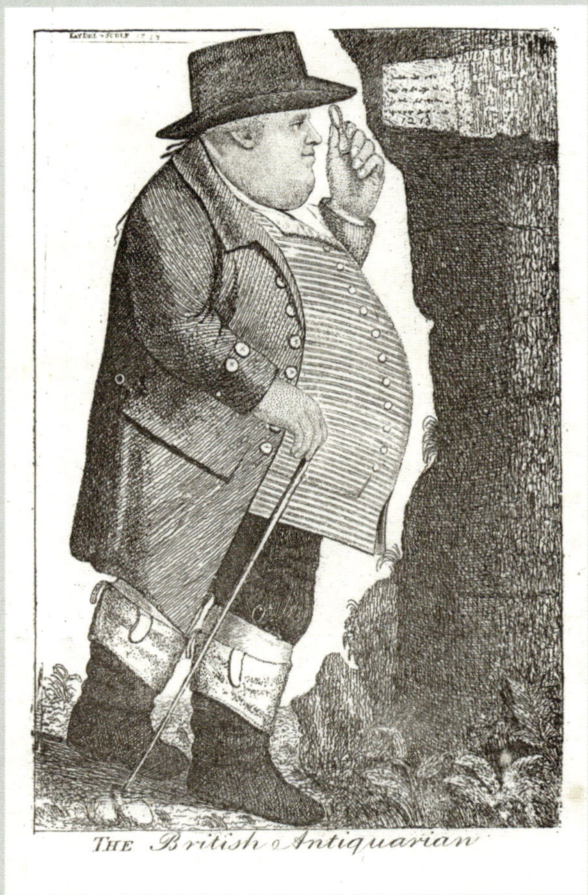

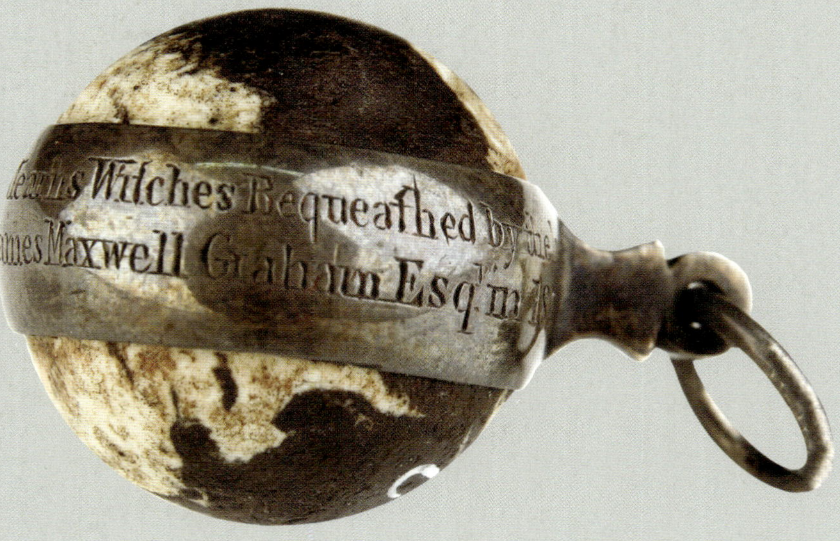

'bleeze' illuminating the remains of the medieval kirk, Tam, the inebriated night-rider, witnesses an uncanny spectacle:

> And vow! Tam saw an unco sight!
> Warlocks and witches in a dance;
> Nae cotillion brent new frae France,
> But hornpipes, jigs, strathspeys, and reels,
> Put life and mettle in their heels.
> (lines 114–118; Kinsley 1968, III, 560)

Saturated with a tipsy, bawdy irony, Burns's poem captured a subversive spirit of *popular* antiquarianism quite distinct from either 'Agricolamania' or Ossianic melancholy, exposing a 'hidden Scotland' of witches' sabbaths and hellish legions, set among the nocturnal ruins of the past (Leask 2010, 265–275) (Fig. S2.28). 'Tam o'Shanter' rightly counts as Scotland's national tale par excellence: less often remembered are Burns's superb lines evocative of the travelling antiquarian who inspired it in the first place, 'On the Late Captain Grose's Peregrinations Thro' Scotland Collecting the Antiquities of that Kingdom':

> Hear, Land o' Cakes, and brither Scots,
> Frae Maidenkirk to Johny Groats! –
> If there's a hole in a' your coats,
> I rede you tent it:
> A chield's amang you, taking notes,
> And faith, he'll prent it . . .
>
> By some auld, houlet-haunted, biggin,
> Or kirk deserted by its riggin,
> It's ten to ane ye'll find him snug in
> Some eldritch part,
> Wi' deils, they say, Lord safe's us! colleaguin
> At some black art . . . .
>
> He has a fouth o' auld nick-nackets:
> Rusty airn caps and jinglin jackets,
> Wad haud the Lothians three in tackets,
> A towmont gude;
> And parritch-pats, and auld saut-backets,
> Before the Flood.
> (lines 1–6, 13–18, 31–36; Kinsley 1968, I, 494–496)

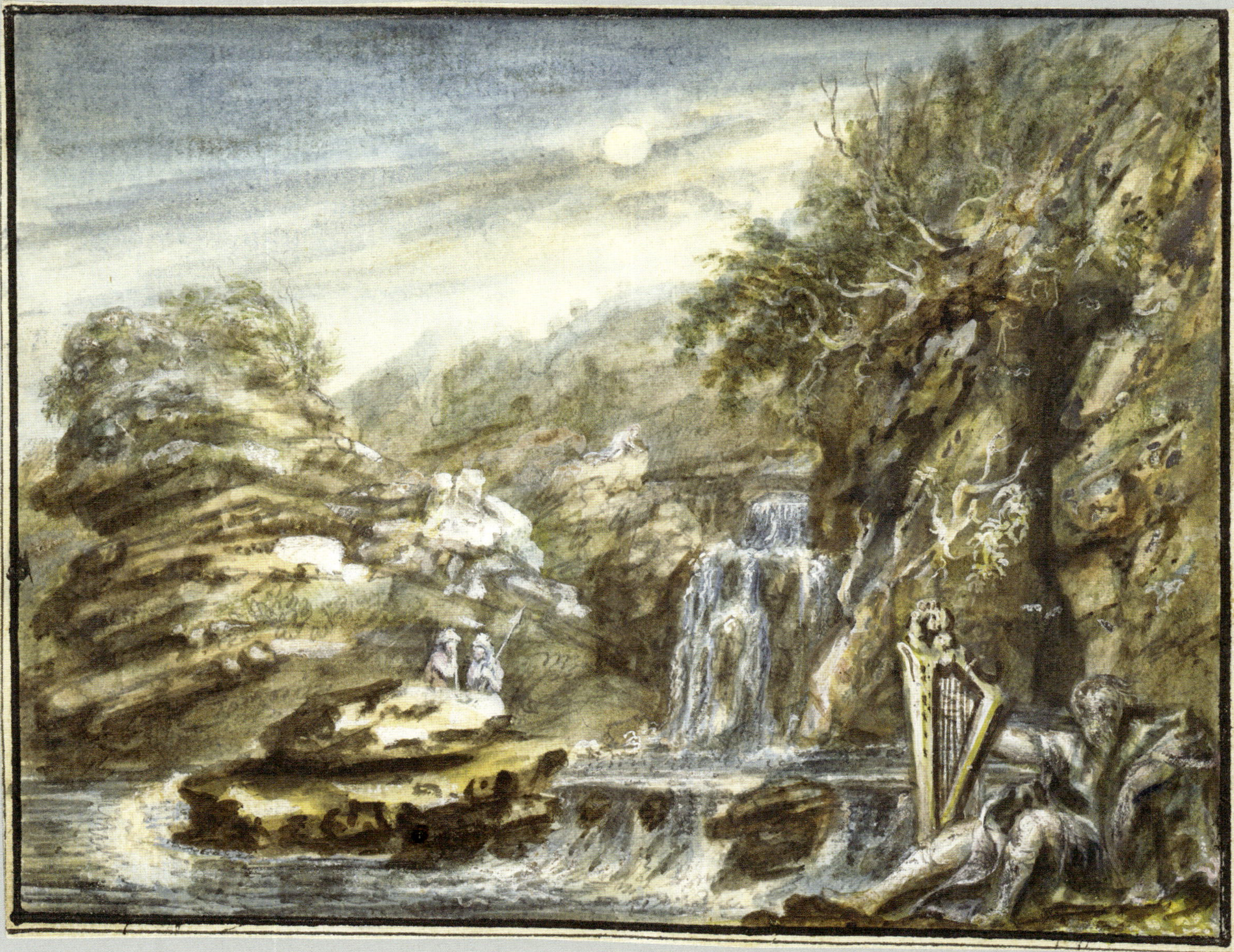

Fig. S2.29
Charles Cordiner, 'Cascade near Carril', pen and wash in 'Cordiner's drawings' album, c. 1769–77 (BM 1943,0707.1-133)

On travelling the remote, rugged landscapes of Sutherland, in the far north of the country, Charles Cordiner was thrilled to learn of a local crag that shared a name with the grey-haired bard of *Fingal*, Carril. Its wonders included a dramatic rush of water issuing from 'a cleft in the middle of the hill . . . which passing under a natural bridge of rock, dashes down the precipice, and forms a wild and beautiful cascade in its fall: the noise of the torrent echoing in a lofty and deep cavern; the cavern shagged with shrubs and aged trees, among which the wild-fowl make their nests; the rivulet murmering round insulated piles of rock; and the distant prospect of these halls and monuments of antient heroes, forcibly recall to mind the images of the *Ossian* song' (Cordiner 1788, 76–77). When preparing the illustration that would accompany these words in his account of the *Remarkable Ruins, and Romantic Prospects, of North Britain*, Cordiner accentuated the tragic, ghostly Ossianic associations of the scene, adding the blind bard, treating the crag as if it were a derelict tower and setting it at twilight.

CHAPTER THREE

Natural History

Fredrik Albritton Jonsson

A SCIENCE FOR THE NORTH

The Enlightenment flourished in many places beyond the cities and towns of Lowland Scotland, touching even the most remote landscapes of the far north and west. During the second half of the eighteenth century, the Highlands and Hebrides beckoned as an internal frontier for scientific investigation and schemes of practical improvement. In a letter written in 1764 from Stornoway on Lewis, the clergyman–naturalist John Walker (later professor of Natural History at Edinburgh University) reported that on the course of his 3,000-mile tour by land and sea he had discovered a 'New World', filled with natural wealth and economic potential, just as bountiful as the most distant islands in the South Seas:

> I have seen the most fertile Lands I ever saw in my Life, without Cultivation; a People, by nature, the most acute & industrious perfectly idle; the most valuable Fisheries, without Lines or Nets; & in every Corner, one of the finest Harbours that Nature has ever formed, a beautiful tho' useless Void, as inanimate & unfrequented as any in the Terra australis. (Withers 1995, 137)

Natural history took pride of place as a tool of exploration for enlightened travellers like the Rev. John Walker, who was commissioned (and partially funded) by the Board of the Annexed Estates and the Church of Scotland to investigate the economic and social conditions of the Highlands and Islands. In the eighteenth century, the Swedish scientist Carl von Linné – Carolus Linnaeus – pioneered a new simplified system of classification based on binomial nomenclature and sexual identification in plants. The binomial system ranked organisms in five principal groups according to class, order, genus, species and variety. Sexual classification took reproductive structure as the key to identification. The number, size, shape and placement of stamen and pistils determined the genus. Linnaeus introduced his system of sexual classification in the first edition of *Systema Naturae* published in 1735 (Koerner 1999).

For Linnaeus and his disciples, the study of plants, minerals and animals was both pious and useful. Natural history revealed the workings of providence and the divine design of all things on earth. In his infinite mercy, God had fashioned the world in such a way that every place contained hidden blessings. The trained gaze of the natural historian could discover these sources of wealth and make them public knowledge. To know the natural advantages of the territory in this way would have seemed especially important in an age before industrialisation when manufacture and agriculture depended to a very great degree on photosynthetic processes for energy and raw materials. Linnaeus also hoped to acclimatise important crops from Asia and the New World by habituating them to the Swedish climate. Such plans for import substitution appeared to create a shortcut to profits otherwise only available to nations with overseas colonies (Koerner 1999).

The new method spread quickly across polite society in Britain during the second half of the eighteenth century. For the well-connected Lincolnshire landowner Sir Joseph Banks, natural history offered a powerful instrument to improve imperial trade and colonial revenues. Banks made a name for himself as the gentleman naturalist accompanying James Cook on the expedition of the *Endeavour* between 1768 and 1771. Ostensibly, this was a scientific expedition to observe the transit of Venus across the Sun, but Cook also carried secret instructions from the Admiralty to explore and annex new lands – the 'Terra australis' referred to in Walker's letter – in the South Pacific. His orders were to examine the features of natural flora, fauna and geology, collecting useful seeds and minerals. For Banks, this voyage set in motion a new imperial agenda. Upon his return to Britain, he went about making the Botanic Gardens at Kew the hub of a global network. The aim was to introduce new crops like Tahitian breadfruit and Chinese tea to the British colonies to support subsistence needs and increase plantation profits (Gascoigne 2003).

Similar schemes of ecological exchange were launched in many European countries at the time. In Scotland, the Regius Keeper of the Edinburgh Botanic Garden, Professor John Hope, harboured dreams of diversifying the Scottish economy with cash crop transplants from distant countries (Figs C3.1, C3.2). He attempted to introduce the Chinese tea bush and also cultivated medicinal plants such as Chinese rhubarb (*Rheum palmatum*, Fig. C3.3) and Asafoetida (*Ferula foetida*, used as a digestive aid and spice). Many landlords and farmers took part in acclimatisation trials around Scotland: the Duke of Atholl established rhubarb and larch plantations on his Perthshire estate, and in the Southern Uplands a group of improvers grew tobacco on hundreds of acres during the American War of Independence (Jonsson 2016).

The fashion for Linnaean method, grafted onto the 'improving' imperative in the decades after Culloden, stimulated a burst of scientific travel in northern Scotland. John Hope sent his student-gardener James Robertson on five journeys to the Highlands between 1767 and 1771. The Rev. John Walker scoured the Hebrides in the same decades: while indebted to native authorities such as John Ray and Sir Robert Sibbald, Walker's report was also shaped by Linnaeus's binomial nomenclature and sexual classification, as well as 'problems of acclimatization and the effects of climate, the link between climate and native virtue, and the expectation of divine riches in the form of indigenous plants' (Jonsson 2013, 64). While the travel journals of Robertson and Walker were published only in the twentieth century, contemporary audiences gained a first taste of northern natural history through Thomas Pennant's accounts from 1769 and 1772 (published 1771 and 1774, respectively). To the chagrin of native naturalists, it was Pennant's English travel companion John Lightfoot who published the first *Flora Scotica* in 1777. Urging the development of a west-coast fishing industry, Pennant described the migration of herring into Highland sea lochs as

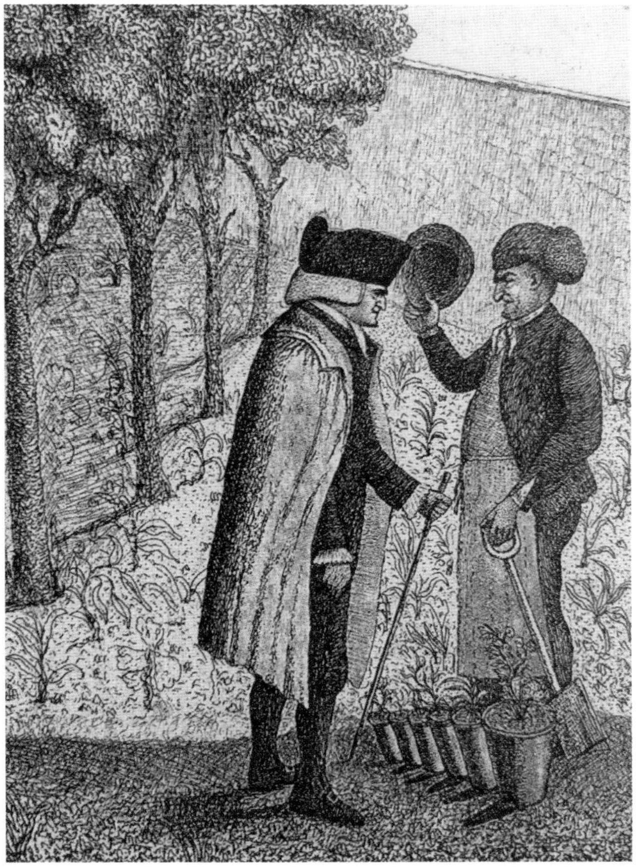

Fig. C3.1
John Kay, *Dr John Hope, Professor of Botany, University of Edinburgh*, etching, No. CXLI in *A Series of Original Portraits and Caricature Etchings: With Biographical Sketches and Illustrative Anecdotes*, Vol. 2, Part II (Hugh Paton, 1838) (RBGE)

The only known likeness of Hope depicts him in the Leith Walk Botanic Garden with his head gardener, Malcolm McCoig, or perhaps McCoig's predecessor John Williamson. The garden, with its pioneering plant collection, hinted at by the flowers dotted among the trees, was a leading teaching institution in the second half of the eighteenth century. Its pioneering informal design with winding walks through Hope's 'Sylva Botanica' was unusual for the time.

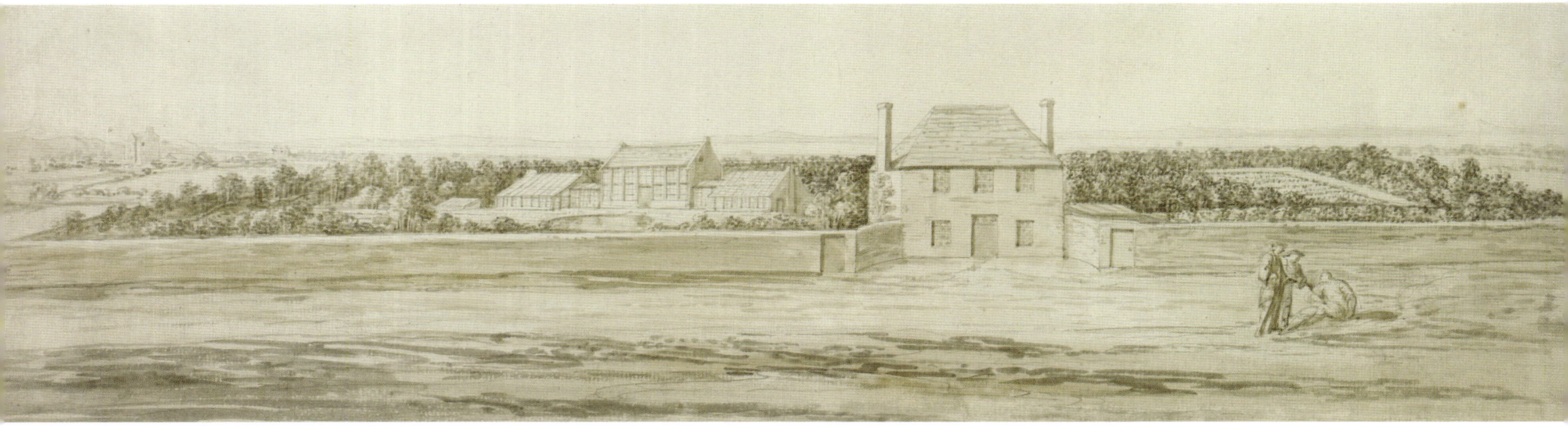

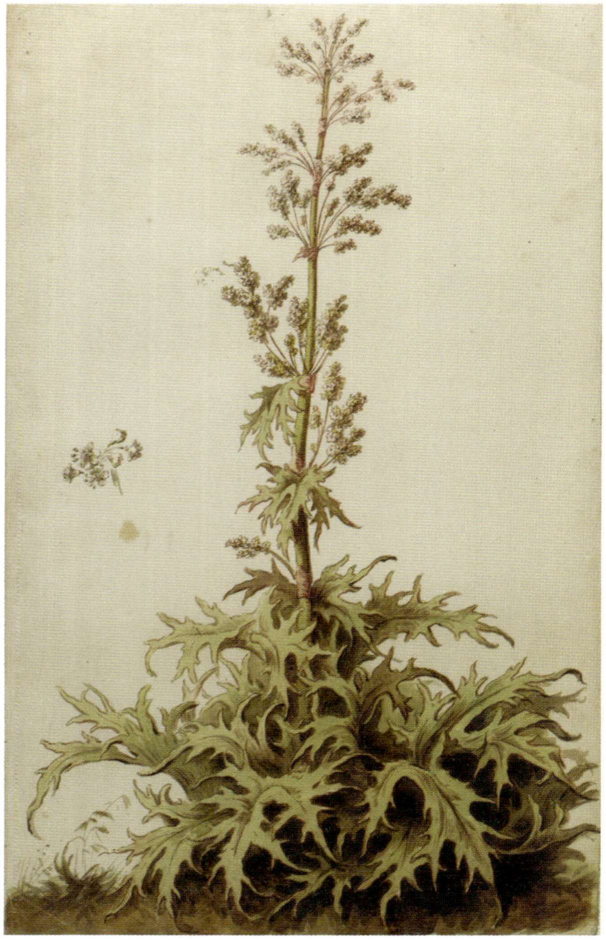

Fig. C3.2
Above. Jacob More, *Perspective View of the Leith Walk Botanic Garden with 'Good Samaritan figures'*, 1771, watercolour (RBGE D33)

In late 1771, John Hope commissioned two fine watercolours of the Leith Walk Botanic Garden from a young Jacob More, marking the recent completion of the relocation and reconstruction of the Botanic Cottage. Designed by John Adam, the building was to serve as both a residence for the head gardener and a lecture space. Taking up an elevated viewpoint, and looking to estate portraiture of the kind discussed elsewhere in this book, in this drawing, More locates the elegant new structure alongside a suite of surrounding conservatories and gardens. The 'Good Samaritan' of the foreground, a physician treating a stricken traveller, acts as a reminder that botany formed part of the medical syllabus.

Fig. C3.3
Left. William Delacour, *Rhubarb Plant* (*Rheum palmatum*), c. 1765, watercolour (RBGE B29)

Hope obtained seeds of the medical rhubarb plant in 1763. After successfully growing the plant in Leith Walk, the botanist distributed seeds around Scotland as an import substitute: the Duke of Atholl was particularly enthusiastic and planted huge quantities of rhubarb on his Perthshire estates, much commented on by travellers. This red chalk drawing was commissioned by Hope from William Delacour, the first drawing master at the Trustees Academy, Edinburgh, to illustrate an article on rhubarb (*Philosophical Transactions*, vol. 32, 1 January 1765).

a 'stupendous gift of Providence', while the traveller and economic projector John Knox 'revived the old argument that herring was of greater value "than the mines of Mexico and Peru"' (Jonsson 2012, 43); see Fig. C3.4. So strong was the lure of the north that Sir Joseph Banks embarked on a journey to the Hebrides and Iceland in the summer of 1772, having withdrawn from Cook's second voyage to the Pacific after a disagreement with the Admiralty. His travel diary contained notes on local features of all kinds: the manner of fishing; the method of burning kelp; the use of seaweed as food for cattle. Banks also contributed the first scientific account of the basalt formations on the island of Staffa to Pennant's *Tour of Scotland in 1772*. After encountering the Staffa columns at dawn, he could barely contain his wonder and joy: 'Compared to this what are the cathedrals or the palaces built by man?' (see Fig. C1.2).

Many other scientific travellers and surveyors followed after Banks and Pennant, including John Williams, John Knox, John Anderson, James Hutton, Barthélemy Faujas Saint-Fond and Thomas Telford, many of them commissioned by the Board for the Annexed Estates, at least until its dissolution in 1784, when much of its work was continued across the whole of Scotland by voluntary associations such as the Highland Society of Edinburgh (1784), the British Fisheries Society (1786) and the British Wool Society (1791) (Smith 1982). The efforts to chart Highland natural history reached a pinnacle in the collaborative project of *The Statistical Account of Scotland* edited by Sir John Sinclair; see Fig. C3.5. This parish-by-parish description of the nation, published in twenty-one volumes between 1791 and 1799, provided the most detailed account of the Scottish environment in the Enlightenment (Jonsson 2013, 51–54; Rauschenberg 1973, 207). One of Sinclair's many practical schemes was to improve native breeds of sheep to stimulate the Scottish wool industry, preferring the Cheviot to the coarse-woolled Blackface. Later, in 1812, he boasted that he had championed the spread of sheep farming across the Highlands, with 6,000 Cheviots on his own Caithness estate, and another 20,000 on those of neighbouring landowners in Sutherland and Reay (Jonsson 2013, 211–212); see Fig. C3.6. But, despite Sinclair's best hopes, sheep and a large Gaelic population were not compatible: the Countess of Sutherland had already begun the rapid clearance of tenants from the inland glens of her enormous estates, attempting to resettle them on poor coastal land. But popular resistance was growing among the tenants of Assynt, Kildonan and Strathnaver, leading to the most notorious episode in the 'Highland Clearances', culminating in the trial for manslaughter of the Sutherland's sub-factor Patrick Sellar (Richards 2002; Hunter 2016; Devine 2018). These traumatic events, still resonant in Scottish memory, remind us of the intimate link between natural history, improvement and social change in the period.

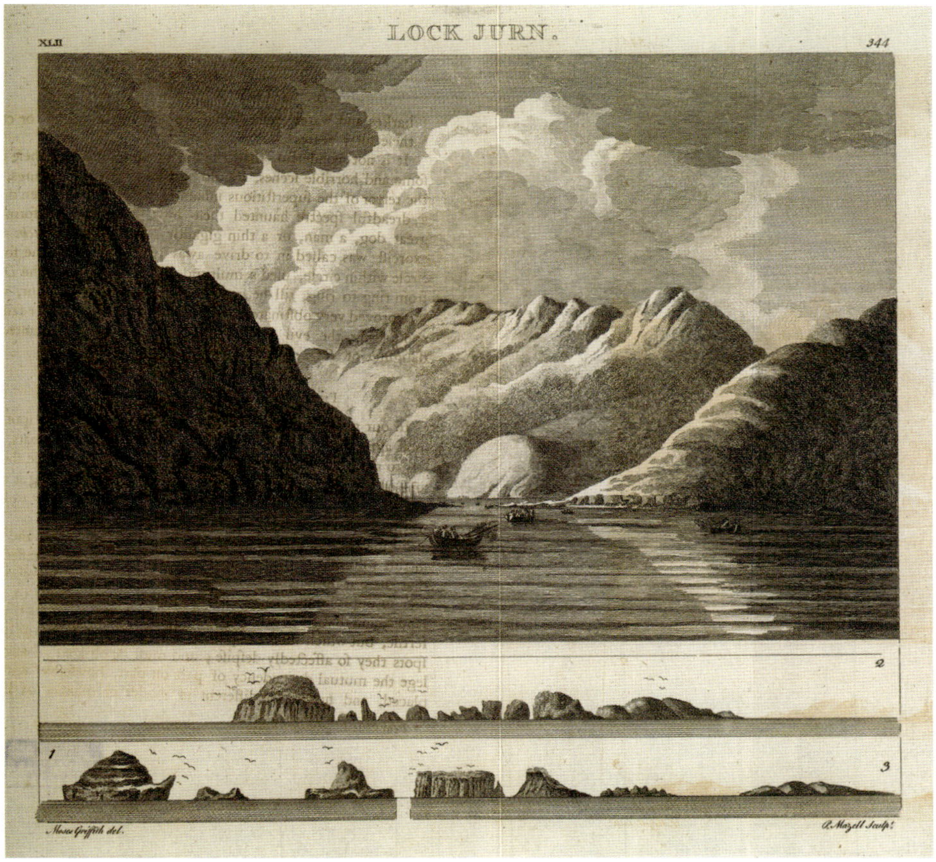

Fig. C3.4
Peter Mazell after Moses Griffith, 'Loch Jurn', engraving in Thomas Pennant, *A Tour in Scotland and Voyage to the Hebrides 1772* (Chester, 1774), Vol. 1, pl. XLII, p. 396 (GLA ASC Mu6-d.2)

Moving back several decades, a memorial (memorandum) by John Hope from 1769 summarised the principal objectives of the naturalist:

> 1. Accurate descriptions of whatever plant animal or mineral shall come in his way. 2. A distinct account of the soils & of the state of gardening & agriculture in those places he shall visit & some useful hints in relation to the fishing upon the coasts & rivers. 3. An

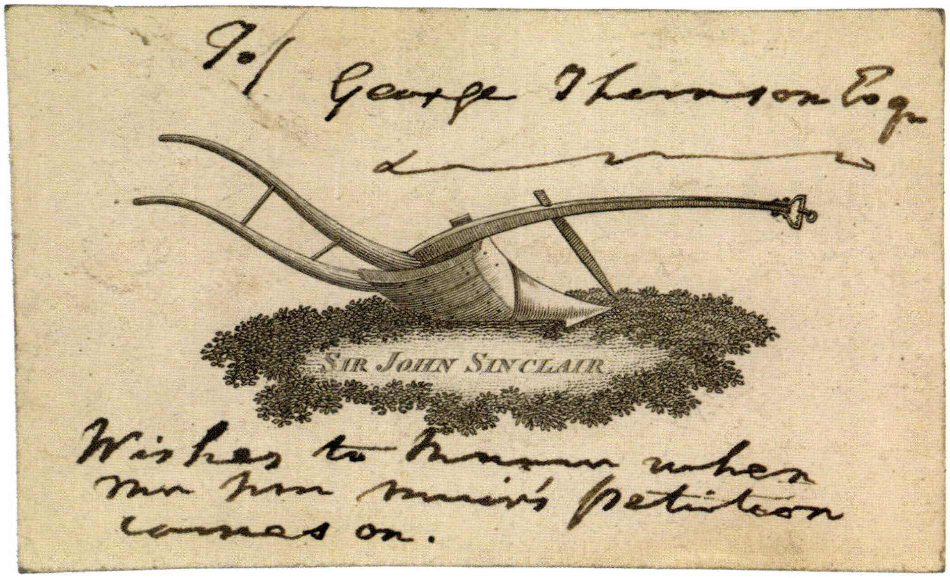

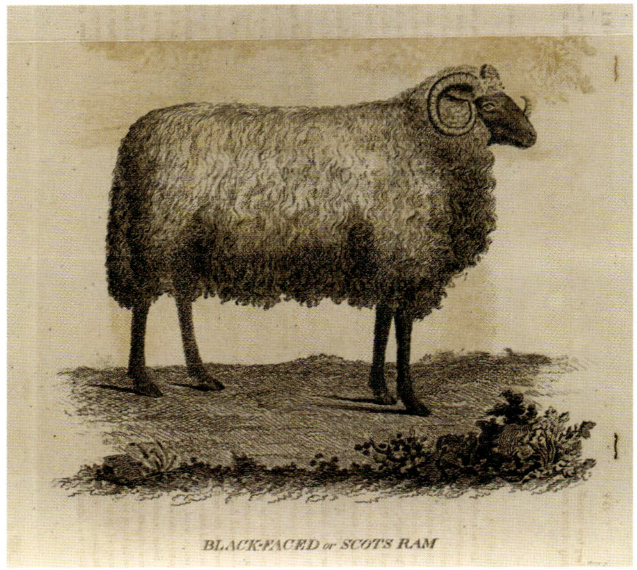

Fig. C3.5
Above left. Sir John Sinclair, visiting card (PC)

Fig. C3.6
Above right. Anon., *Black Faced or Scots Ram*, engraving in Robert Douglas, *General View of the Agriculture in the Counties of Roxburgh and Selkirk* (Edinburgh, 1798), pl. II, opposite p. 301 (GLA ASC Mu53-e.8)

> account of the appearances of Lead and other metals.
> 4. That the Museum in the college of Edinburgh may be speedily increased with the natural productions of this country by the materials he shall bring home . . .

Natural historians chronicled their work in travel diaries that recounted noteworthy geographic features and economic facts, particularly descriptions of native plants, animals, minerals, customs and industries. Information was collected from local informants, usually clergymen or members of the landowning class. Naturalists sometimes gleaned knowledge directly from local people as well, though the names of plebeian informants were usually not recorded. Drawing presented another crucial tool in the field. Images supplemented textual description in making taxonomic identifications of species or identifying other typical and useful properties of a plant. These pictures ranged from simple sketches *en plain air* to complex formal collaboration between naturalists, draftsmen and engravers (Jonsson 2013, 47–48; Nickelsen 2018). As Thomas Falconer wrote in a 1768 letter to Joseph Banks, regarding the latter's northern journey:

> you take a designer with you, & it would be easy to sketch out some of these views . . . The appearance of Nature is varied in every Climate, an Alpine scene is differ. from a Derbyshire landscape, & if yr designer would stain his drawing, it would point out the colour of the Soil & verdure, with the nature of the Rocks, & would enable us here to have a full idea of ye Country, wch no description possibly can. (quoted in Bonehill 2014, 9)

The northern explorers saw their voyages as a form of time travel. By journeying to the outskirts of the nation, they thought they were moving backwards in time, towards a more primitive stage of history. John Walker reported to his government patrons that the inhabitants of the Hebrides were 'in almost the same Situation as in the Days of Oscian [sic]' (MacKay 1980, 35). Local people below the level of the elite were depicted as rustic natives with simple customs and habits, unsullied by modern luxury and ignorant of urban civilisation (Withers 1995, 138). James Robertson's depiction of the Orkney diet argued that primitive food bred endurance and courage (Fig. C3.8):

> Oat-meal, barley, milk, Potatoes & cabbages form the chief articles of Diet, to which the inhabitants of the shores add Fish hung in the sun till they become sour, shell-fish, the flesh & Eggs of Sea-Fowl, the flesh of Seals, Navel Lavers commonly called Slake (*Ulva*

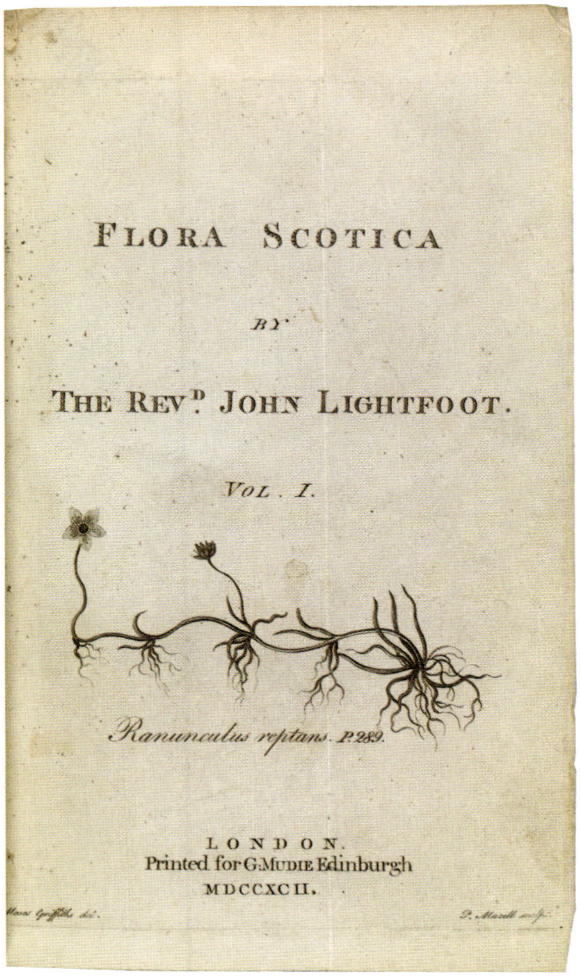
FLORA SCOTICA
BY
THE REV.D JOHN LIGHTFOOT.
VOL. I.
Ranunculus reptans. P.289.
LONDON.
Printed for G.MUDIE Edinburgh
MDCCXCII.

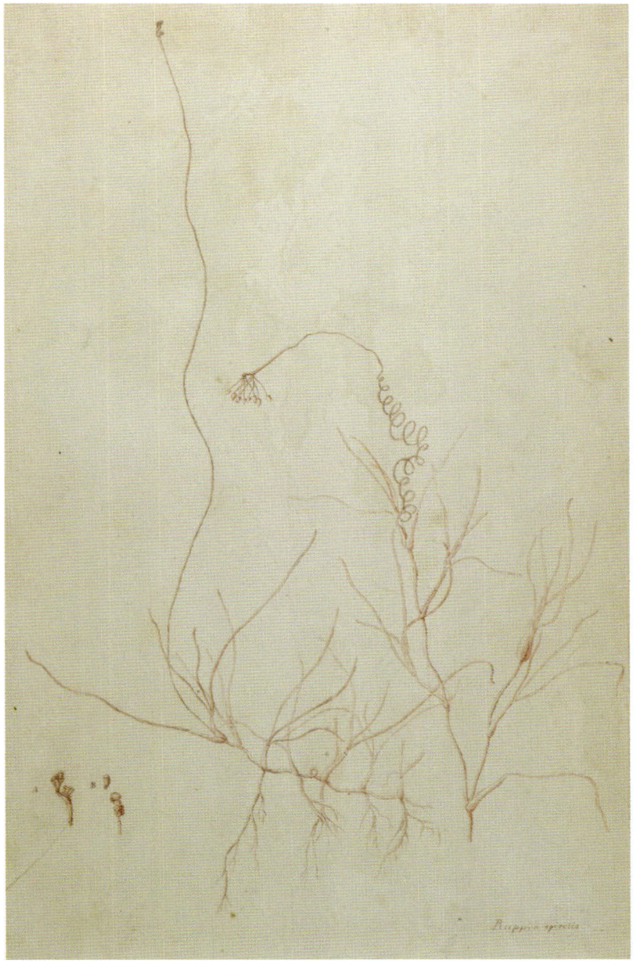

Fig. C3.7
Far left. Peter Mazell after Moses Griffith, title page illustration to John Lightfoot, *Flora Scotica: Or A Systematic Arrangement, in the Linnaean Method, of the Native Plants of Scotland and the Hebrides* (London, 1792) (GLA ASC Mu53-d.28)

Fig. C3.8
Left. James Robertson, *Ruppia spiralis [Ruppia cirrhosa]*, c. 1770, red chalk (RBGE C22)

This is one of the few surviving drawings by Robertson representing the spiral tassleweed that he discovered in the northern islands and Hebrides during his botanical tours. It is therefore of great significance for the present publication.

> *umbilicalis*) boiled to the consistency of a jelly, & broth made of the Hand Fucus or Dulse (*Fucus palmatus*) with Oat-meal. The simple food however nourishes a race of men deterred by no hardships, appalled by no danger. (Henderson and Dickson 1994, 129)

By charting the uses of local flora, naturalists painted a dual picture of northern Scotland: on the one hand, they praised the self-sufficiency and simplicity of the lower orders; on the other hand, they wooed landlords with a variety of new commercial prospects. A strong element of primitivism runs through much of Lightfoot's *Flora Scotica*: fishermen on Skye made their ropes and nets from purple melic grass (*Melica caerulea*); a 'fine red Dye' could be extracted from lady's bedstraw (*Galium verum*). *Flora Scotica* listed no fewer than seven traditional uses for fine-leaved heath (today bell heather, *Erica cinerea*): to make thatch for houses, to twist into ropes, to bind thatch in lattice shapes, to dye yarn yellow, to tan leather, to brew a 'kind of ale' and to make beds 'not quite so soft and luxurious as beds of down [but] . . . altogether as refreshing . . . and perhaps more healthy'. We see here the two worlds of self-sufficiency and improvement side by side. Heather bedding was appropriate for the lower orders whereas gentlemen and natural historians slept best on down (Jonsson 2013, 98).

Lightfoot's entry for common sea wrack (bladderwrack) in *Flora Scotica* offers another vivid picture of one of the most lucrative forms of local plant use (Fig. C3.9).

> *FUCUS, vesiculosus*
> Bladder Fucus, or Common Sea Wrack
> Sea-ware, Scotis
> *Feamainn*, Gaulis
>
> Upon the sea rocks about low-water mark abundantly, producing its fructifications in July and August. . . . The *F. vesiculosus* is applied to various uses in oeconomy and medicine. It is well known to be an excellent manure for land, to which purpose it is often applied, in the maritime parts of Scotland and other countries. . . . In the islands of Jura and Skye it frequently serves as a winter-food for cattle, which regularly come down to the shores at the recess of the tides to seek for it. And sometimes even the stags have been observed, after a storm, to descend from the mountains to the sea-sides, to feed upon this plant.
>
> Linnaeus informs us, that the inhabitants of Gothland [sic], in Sweden, boil this Fucus in water, and mixing therewith a little coarse meal or flour, feed their hogs with it; for which reason they call the plant Swintang. And in Scania, he says, the poor people cover cottages with it, and sometimes use it for fuel.
>
> In Jura, and some other of the Hebrides, the inhabitants dry their cheeses without salt, by covering them with the ashes of this plant; which abounds with such quantity of salts, that from five ounces of the ashes may be procured two ounces and a half of fixed alkaline salts, that is half of their whole weight. (Lightfoot 1789, 906)

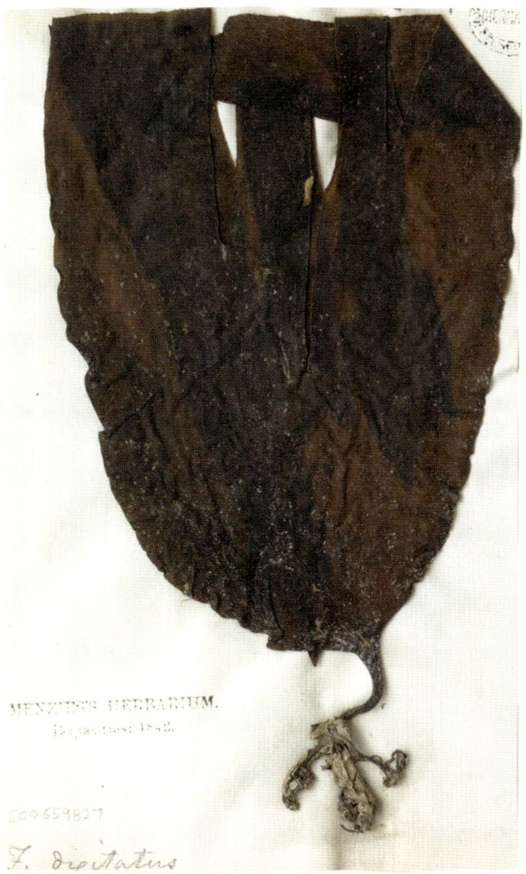

Fig. C3.9
Dried kelp or sea wrack, *Laminaria digitata [Fucus digitatus]*, from Menzies album (RBGE Mull 500659827)

Side by side with such plant lore, Lightfoot's description of sea wrack also shows us an early glimpse of the emerging kelping economy. He continued:

> [T]he most beneficial use to which the *F. vesiculosus* is applied, in the way of oeconomy, is in making pot-ash or kelp, a work much practised in the western isles. – The manner of doing it is this: The plant is collected and dried carefully upon the shore in small heaps. When thoroughly dry, a pit is dug in sandy ground, about seven feet wide, and three deep, lined with stones. In this pit a fire is kindled with small sticks, and the dried Fucus is laid upon it by little and little, and burnt. When a sufficient quantity is consumed for the purpose, and burnt to a certain degree, it appears in the pit like red-hot ashes. The operator then (to prevent its being reduced entirely to ashes) with an iron rake stirs about briskly this hot matter from one side of the pit to the other, mixing it well together, till at length it begins to congeal, and vitrify. The salts being now all melted, the matter is left to cool in the bottom of the pit, where, as in a mould, it concretes into a solid mass, call'd Kelp, which, when cold, is

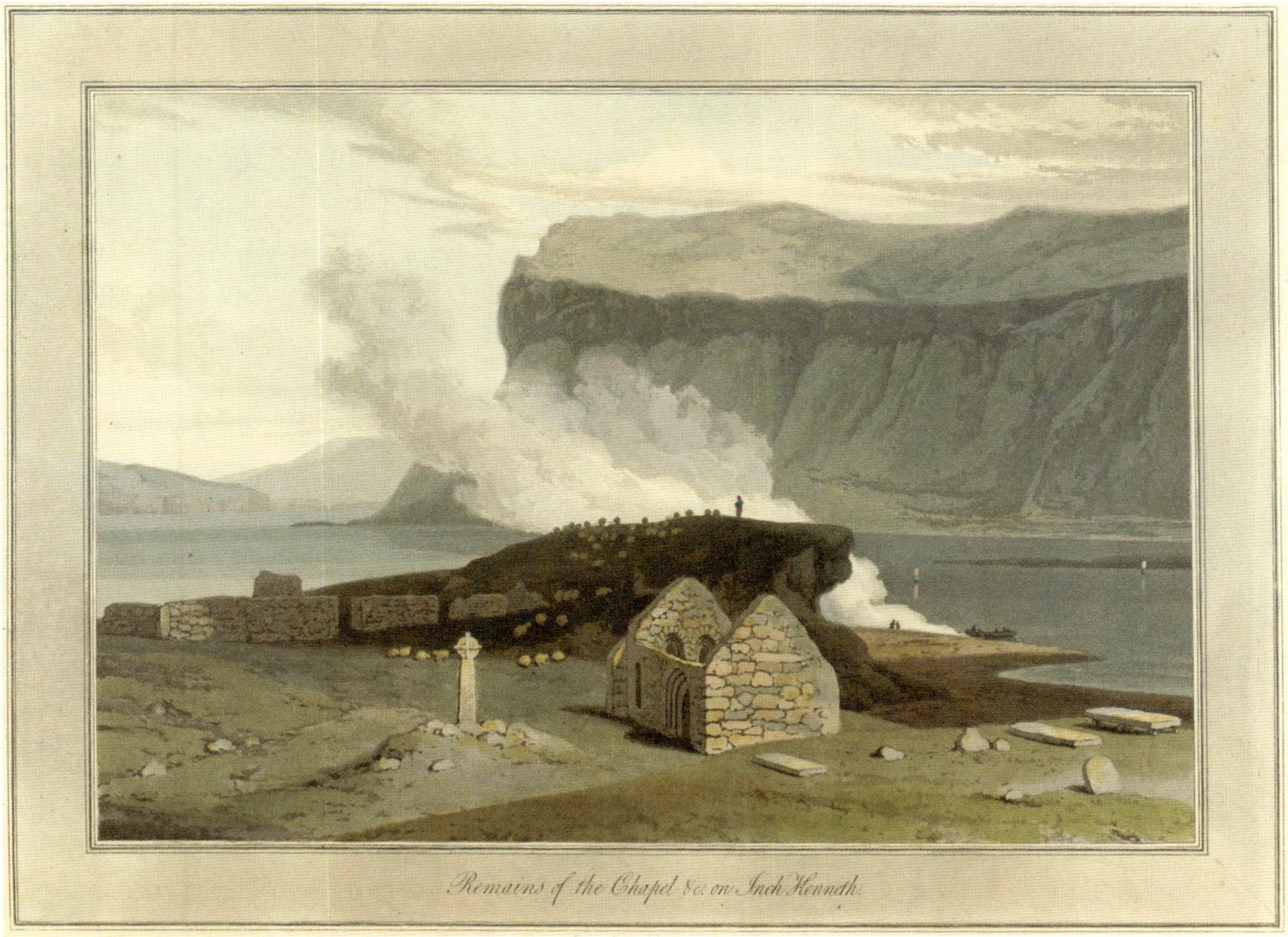

Fig. C3.10
William Daniell, *Remains of the Chapel & c. on Inch Kenneth*, aquatint in *A Voyage Round the North and North West Coast of Scotland, and the Adjacent Islands* [1820], pl. x (Al R54YF7)

broken out of the pit, and carried to market for the use of the soap and glass-makers. There is great difference in the goodness and price of this commodity, and much care and skill required in properly making it. That is esteemed the best which is hardest, finest grain'd, and free from sand or earth. – The price of Kelp in Jura is £.3. 10 s. per ton, and about forty or fifty tons are exported annually from that island. So great a value is set upon this Fucus by the inhabitants of that place, that they have sometimes thought it worth their while to roll fragments of rocks and huge stones into the sea, in order to invite the growth of it. (Lightfoot 1789, 906)

Lightfoot here describes how local workers harvested seaweed – an exhausting and intensive form of labour – and burnt it to produce alkaline ashes for English soap and glass production. The artist William Daniell, travelling throughout the Hebrides in 1815–1816, described how the smoke arising from kelp burning 'spreading along the rocks and acclivities, softens the ruggedness of their forms, and provides a very picturesque effect in certain points of view' (Daniell 2006, I, 95); see Fig. C3.10.

Landlords reaped increasing profits from this new staple crop in the closing decades of the eighteenth century, lobbying to prevent emigration to North America in order to retain the necessary labour force. But the market for Scottish kelp collapsed with the return of foreign imports of barilla (soda ash) at the end of the Napoleonic Wars, and workers on the kelping estates on the Outer Isles, Skye, Tiree, Jura and Mull, as well as Ardnamurchan and Morvern on the mainland, were cleared off the land, often to be replaced by sheep.

The enthusiasm for Linnaean natural history had not occurred in a political vacuum. After the last Jacobite war of 1745–1746, the Scottish ruling elite in alliance with the British government embarked on a venture of internal conquest and assimilation to pacify the north. In the 1760s, the government frequently employed scientific experts to guide policy: as we have seen, the Board for the Annexed Estates hired naturalists such as John Walker and James Robertson to make a natural and economic inventory of the region. But this use of natural history signalled a genuine uncertainty about the future development of northern Scotland. While we now associate the late-eighteenth-century history of the Highlands with sheep farms, kelping and clearances, at the time, none of this was a fate foretold. The surveyors and naturalists suggested a wide range of possible economic advantages in the region, from fisheries and hemp cultivation to dye plants and naval timber. The uncertainty about the future was fuelled by disagreements among the eighteenth-century natural historians about the character of the Scottish environment. Fertilisers and soil amendments like limestone, peat moss and marl promised to transform barren soils into fertile pasture or arable. Even the climate itself seemed malleable and subject to improvement (Jonsson 2013, 47–48).

THE CALEDONIAN FOREST

In the eighteenth century, the Scottish elite discovered the problem of deforestation. This was something of a belated revelation, given that Scotland had lost most of its woodlands in prehistoric times. But Scottish natural historians and agricultural writers mistook the slow rhythms of climate change and prehistoric clearing for a moral narrative about invasion and neglect. They imagined that the destruction of the great ancient forest of Scotland had made the land cold and wet. Schemes of afforestation were acts of restoration.

When Samuel Johnson and James Boswell made their famous tour of the Scottish Highlands in 1773, they were travelling through one of the least forested regions in Europe. General Roy's military survey (1747 to 1755) indicated that no more than 4 per cent of the total land surface of Scotland was covered by woodland. The Englishman Johnson sneered that 'Few regions have been denuded like this, where many centuries must have passed in waste without the least thought of future supply' (Johnson and Boswell 1984, 39; Smout 2000). The true number for the period was probably closer to 8 per cent. Scottish landowners and sylviculturists had already begun to take an interest in afforestation by the early decades of the eighteenth century. Among the more spectacular initiatives was that of Archibald Grant of Monymusk, whose men planted as many as 2 million trees before 1754 in north-east Scotland, and the Dukes of Atholl, who between 1730 and 1830 succeeded in planting over 21 million trees on their estate in the central Highlands (Smout, Macdonald and Watson 2005).

The mission to plant new forests was cast as a peculiarly aristocratic responsibility. Great landowners like the Earl of Haddington regarded tree planting as an act of paternalist foresight that would increase the value of one's patrimony while serving the wider public. In a similar spirit, the economist James Anderson encouraged the gentry to embrace forestry as a slow, but particularly secure, form of investment in his 1771 newspaper campaign. Afforestation here represented a practical version of conservative ideology, which combined an orientation towards landed investment with an ideal of long-term organic growth. Over the period 1760 to 1815, a host of Scottish naturalists and agricultural improvers amassed a speculative history of the Scottish woodlands to prove this point. They drew on a wide range of sources, including ancient history, oral tradition and botanical surveys: for example, the Finhaven chestnut in Angus, destroyed by frost in 1740, was reputed to have been the largest tree in Scotland and over 500 years old, although some accounts held that it grew from a chestnut discarded by a Roman soldier (Fig. C3.11). A recurring claim in these reports was that buried roots, stumps and sometimes entire trees submerged in the peat bogs of the Highlands and Hebrides constituted remnants of a vast pine forest. In reality, these stumps were over four thousand years old, but the eighteenth-century naturalists tended to date them as Roman or more recent in origin. Perhaps the most significant and spurious evidence offered in favour of a primeval Scottish forest came in the form of the epic poetry of James Macpherson. His so-called translations from obscure manuscripts

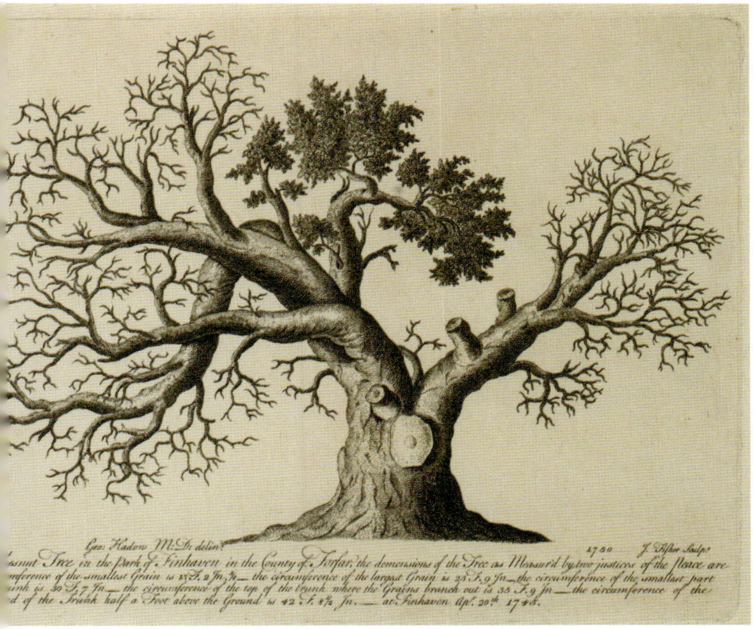

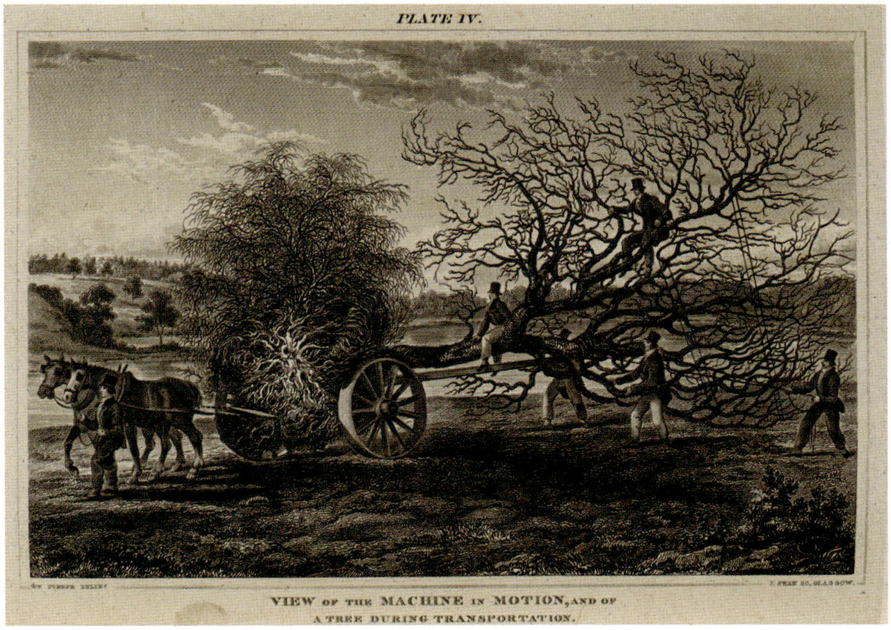

Fig. C3.11
Above left. J. Fisher after George Haddon, *Finhaven Chestnut*, 1750, engraving (RBGE A51)

Fig. C3.12
Above right. J. Swan after W. Turner, 'View of the Machine in Motion, and of a Tree During the Transportation', engraving in Sir Henry Steuart, *The Planter's Guide: A Practical Essay on the Best Method of Giving Immediate Effect to Wood, by the Removal of Large Trees and Underwood, . . . Chiefly Intended for the Climate of Scotland* (Edinburgh and London, 1828), plate IV, opposite p. 230 (WZC)

of doubtful authenticity depicted a world of Gaelic warriors of the third century AD. Macpherson's settings were often dense and gloomy woodland that seemed to cover much of his imaginary *Gaidhealtachd*. Thanks to the immense popularity of his poetry, this mythical image may well have taken root among a wide circle of readers (Macpherson 1762; Jonsson 2013, 148).

The conjectural history of forest clearance contained a theory of climate change. William Boutcher's 1775 treatise on forestry presupposed the power of trees to affect ground temperatures. In the preface to the work, Boutcher proposed that 'Making plantations of Forest trees . . . [offered] . . . the most solid foundation for promoting all the different branches of husbandry and gardening' (Boutcher 1775, viii). Woodlands provided shelter from winds and cold air, making the land more hospitable to both native and foreign crops. A good improver of land should always begin by planting trees to prepare the way for other schemes of agriculture and horticulture. Through large-scale schemes of planting, patriotic landowners could ameliorate the climate of Scotland as a whole (Fig. C3.12). Boutcher was drawing here on an ancient tradition of medical thought, which linked forests to climate change. But he was also reversing the received notion that forest clearance could make a cold climate more temperate. Whereas natural historians of colonial peripheries tended to see deforestation as a necessary step towards establishing European agriculture and a healthy, temperate atmosphere conducive to settlement, Boutcher's book pointed in the other direction and opened the door to a critique of anthropogenic cooling caused by deforestation. The myth of the primeval Scottish forest assumed a world susceptible to violent ecological swings, natural disasters and fundamental alterations, still alive today in debates about 'the Great Wood of Caledon'. It also dictated that state and civil society must be mobilised to counteract these movements when necessary. Last but not least, the myth gave natural historians a central role to play in guiding the work of restoration (Boutcher 1775, viii–ix; Glacken 1967; Golinski 2007).

THE TIME OF SOIL AND ROCKS

For most of the eighteenth century, natural history and mineralogy remained detached from 'geotheory' or speculations about the origins of the earth: 'the goal was [rather] to produce natural histories of particular regions and to construct a general system

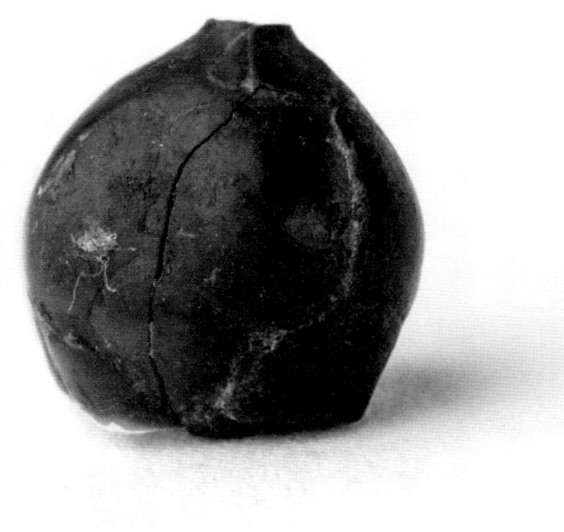

Fig. C3.13
Ureocrinus bockschii, crinoid cup (GLAHM:114911)

This specimen from The Hunterian Collection comes from the collection of David Ure (1749–1798), best known for his pioneering role in the early development of palaeontology in Scotland. A student at the University of Glasgow from 1770 to 1776, he developed a friendship with John Anderson, professor of natural philosophy, and an interest in the natural sciences. But it was not until Ure was appointed assistant minister in the Parish of East Kilbride in 1783 that he started to gather a collection of local fossil specimens while travelling between the different settlements under his care. This led him to publish in 1793 his classic work, *The History of Rutherglen and East-Kilbride*, and with it the first scientific description in words and in images of a number of fossil organisms.

of classification' (Furniss 2018, 64–5, 99). This empirical emphasis is exemplified in a request published by Thomas Pennant in the *Scots Magazine* in April 1772, in preparation for his extensive summer tour of the same year, in which the Welsh naturalist asked his correspondents: 'please to observe and collect against my coming, specimens of all sorts of earths, clays, stones, marbles, pebbles, sands, asbestus, minerals, and ores; also bituminous fossils, petrified shells, wood, fossil-wood, in short, fossils of all denominations' (quoted in Furniss 2018, 103); Fig. C3.13. As with the pursuit of 'economic botany', mineralogists were dedicated to the quest for lucrative ores, coal seams or other mineral deposits, such as those being extracted from profitable coal seams worked by landowners in Fife and the Central Belt, or the lead mines worked by the Earl of Hopetoun at Leadhills and Alexander Murray of Stanhope at Strontian (Fig. C3.14a–c refer to Figs S3.15–S3.16).

In the 1760s and 1770s the Welsh mining engineer and naturalist John Williams was dispatched by the Board of Annexed Estates on a series of extensive expeditions to search for coal in the Highlands; its absence posed a major problem for regional development, given the taxes on imported coal that was needed for burning lime, the major agent in improving the acidic soils of the region. After an abortive attempt to mine coal at Brora (which turned out to be self-combusting), Williams surveyed Perthshire, Cromarty, Moray, Kinlochmoydart and other districts. Although encouraged by successful slate extraction from quarries at Ardshiel and Ballachulish, by 1775 disappointing results led to a recommendation that the Board should be 'at no further Expense at making Mineral Trials on the Estate of Perth, or indeed . . . upon any of the Annexed Estates'. In his *Natural History of the Mineral Kingdom* (1789), Williams was one of the first to warn of the economic and social consequences of coal exhaustion (Jonsson 2013, 171, 168). The high stakes attached to mineral prospecting attracted adventurers like the German Rudolf Raspe (better known as the author of *Baron Munchausen*) who 'salted' mineral deposits on the Caithness estate of Sir John Sinclair before absconding to Ireland, providing a model for the egregious character of Dousterswivel in Sir Walter Scott's novel *The Antiquary* (1816); Fig. C3.15a, b.

Eighteenth-century mineralogists might have largely eschewed theorising about earth formation in favour of careful collection, description and classification, but orthodox opinion generally favoured the biblically sanctioned 'Neptunist' belief that most minerals were formed by sedimentation on primeval ocean beds, and that volcanic activity was largely an aberration, especially in Scotland. Increasingly, however, travelling naturalists like Thomas Pennant and (more forcefully) the French traveller Faujas Saint-Fond presented a convincing case for the importance of volcanic action in shaping Scotland's geomorphology Although the Neptunist position was maintained well into the nineteenth century by Professor Robert Jameson, John Walker's pupil and successor to Edinburgh's Chair of Natural Philosophy, it came under serious challenge from James Hutton (1726–1797), often claimed as the founder of modern geology (Fig. C3.16). Hutton 'revolutionized the interpretation and representation of Scotland's landscapes . . . arguing that rocks and landforms are continually being eroded by weathering agents, carried by streams and rivers to the bottom of the oceans, consolidated or transformed by subterraneous heat and pressure and then uplifted by those forces to become new land masses' (Furniss 2018, 156). For Hutton, the rocks themselves participated in the great drama of natural history.

At harvest time in 1785, Hutton and his companion John Clerk of Eldin found themselves scrambling over stone and heather in the steep valley of Glen Tilt, just north-east of Blair Atholl in upland Perthshire. An account of the trip to Glen Tilt

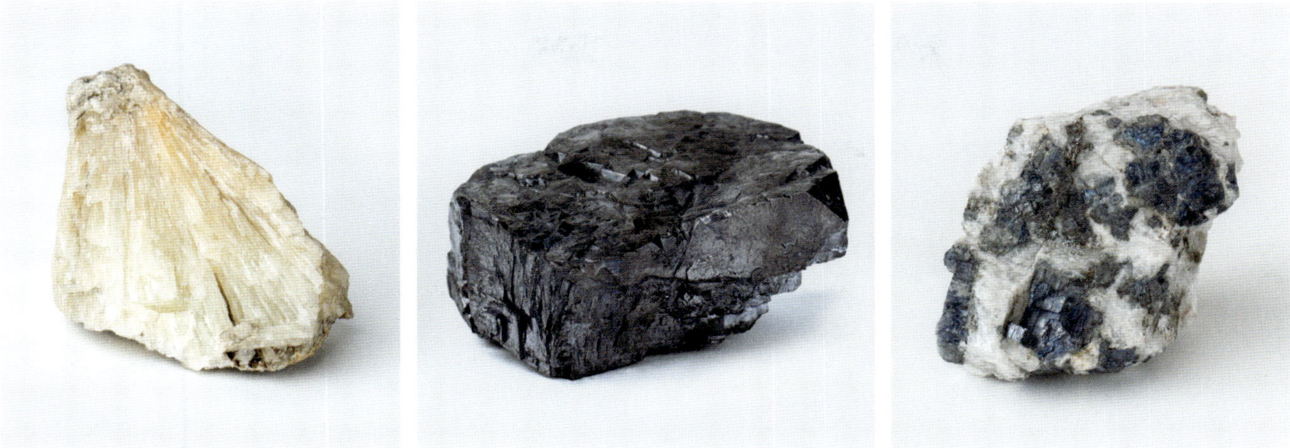

Fig. C3.14a–c
A selection of minerals from the eighteenth- and early nineteenth-century mine workings at Leadhills–Wanlockhead, Tyndrum and Strontian.

(a)
Pale brown strontianite, from the lead mines at Strontian (GLAHM 100346)

This mineral, and the element strontium, were first described by Irish chemist Crawford Adair in 1790, and named after the place. Strontian is an anglicisation of the Gaelic *Sròn an t-Sìthein*, meaning 'nose-like hillside of the fairy mound'. Strontium is thus the only element with a Gaelic-derived name. In 1729, Edmund Burt, author of *Letters from the North of Scotland* (1754), was appointed manager of the Strontian lead mines, in which his patron General Wade was a major investor.

(b)
Crystals of galena, the main ore of lead from the mines at Leadhills (GLAHM 100281)

As well as producing very large quantities of lead for industry, these mines were a significant source of specimens for scientific investigation from the late eighteenth century.

(c)
Galena (lead ore), in quartz-rich vein material, from the dumps of the eighteenth-century lead mines (GLAHM 164274)

The mines were discovered by Sir Robert Clifton at Tyndrum around 1730, and then worked periodically until the early twentieth century.

was published in Hutton's magnum opus *The Theory of the Earth* in 1795. Hutton and Clerk stayed as the guests of the 4th Duke of Atholl in his hunting lodge. After exploring the valley in the immediate vicinity of the lodge, Hutton and Clerk followed the Duke on a deer hunting party into the wilderness at Fealar. Hutton was struck by the great solitude of the location: 'the most removed . . . of any in Britain from the habitations of men'. Hutton had just presented his new theory of geological change to the Royal Society of Edinburgh in March and April that year (Fig. C3.17). To explain the appearance of marine fossils on mountaintops, Hutton proposed a perpetual cycle of uplift and erosion, which had shaped the rise and fall of land: 'We find no vestige of a beginning, – no prospect of an end.' His model of geological processes thus openly challenged the conventional biblical chronology of a young earth. While moderate views of religion were commonplace in enlightenment Edinburgh, Hutton's vision of deep time was difficult to swallow for many members of the Scottish establishment. The expedition to Glen Tilt was meant to bolster his theory by confirming it with fieldwork. Hutton wanted to disprove the idea that granite comprised a 'primary' stratum preceding all others in formation. By mapping the distribution of granite at Glen Tilt, he sought evidence of jumbled strata that would support his idea of never-ending cycles (Hutton 1899, I, 16; Leneman 1986, 34).

Near the hunting lodge, Hutton found veins of red granite injected into the 'black micaceous' rock of 'alpine schistus'. This layering of strata was exactly what Hutton had hoped to encounter. The mixture of granite and schistus at Glen Tilt suggested that the history of geology must be understood on a temporal scale entirely different from that preached by the

Fig. C3.15a,b
Marble samples from Iona and Tiree, associated with the work of Rudolf Erich Raspe for the Duke of Argyll

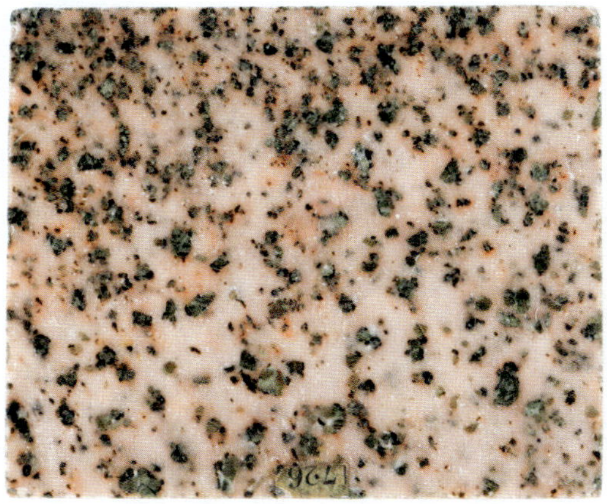

(a)
Pink marble with dark green grains of clinopyroxene, from Ballyphetrish, on Tiree (GLAHM 116217)

This marble was discovered by Rudolf Erich Raspe during his mineral survey for the Duke of Argyll. Two tiny trial quarries were opened around 1790, but the venture swiftly folded. This was the only period that the Tiree marble was worked, so the sawn and polished specimens found widely in geological collections across Europe were probably sent out by Raspe as a marketing exercise.

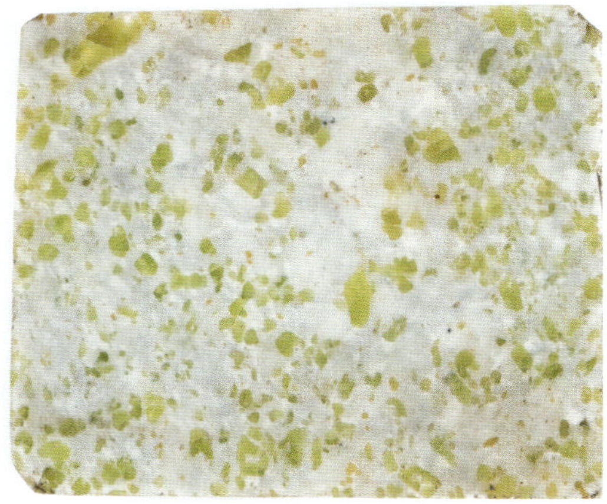

(b)
Serpentine marble from Iona (GLAHM 116263)

Raspe rediscovered the medieval source of marble that had been used on Iona and, with the Duke of Argyll, planned to rework the stone in 1790–2. The venture was unsuccessful, but it paved the way for later nineteenth- and twentieth-century successful working of the Iona marble.

Church. Hutton's theory of eternal cycles was also a political wager. To what degree could humans master and manage the cycles of the geological world? What sort of political regime was best suited to control the economy of nature? A drawing of Glen Tilt by Hutton's travel companion Clerk made at the time of the visit hints at the anthropocentric vision of geology at the heart of this vision (Figs C3.18–C3.20). Clerk was a gentleman farmer, draughtsman and author of a controversial work on naval tactics, whose brother George Clerk-Maxwell had served on the Board for the Annexed Estates; he was also a founding member of the Highland Society of Edinburgh, a private association dedicated to Highland improvement. Clerk's image of Glen Tilt strongly reflected this family legacy (Fig. C3.19). He placed the hunting lodge in a vast landscape of broken rocks. A screen of leafy trees surrounded the tiny white building in the centre. The trees were in turn enveloped on the right by a low wall. On each side of the lodge, steep hillsides rose in eroded terraces towards a sky barely glimpsed. A road meandered up to the lodge between dark boulders, which dominated the foreground. The sinuous line drew the observer into the funnel of the valley. The vertical fall of the sides and the gargantuan boulders at their foot prodded the observer to imagine the sublime horror of recurring landslides. Clerk in fact seems to have exaggerated the angle of the gradient. He also bathed the sides of the valley in a strong and hazy light. The walls of granite and schistus seemed on the verge of melting into the atmosphere, transient like clouds, a passing mirage. The presence of the many mature trees in the enclosure assured the reader that the lodge had stood safe for decades if not centuries. The violent force of erosion so visible on the hillsides acted at a rate too slow to menace the human world below (Hutton 1899, I, 12–16).

Such a nesting of scales was characteristic of Hutton's geology. Towards the end of the survey of Glen Tilt, Hutton

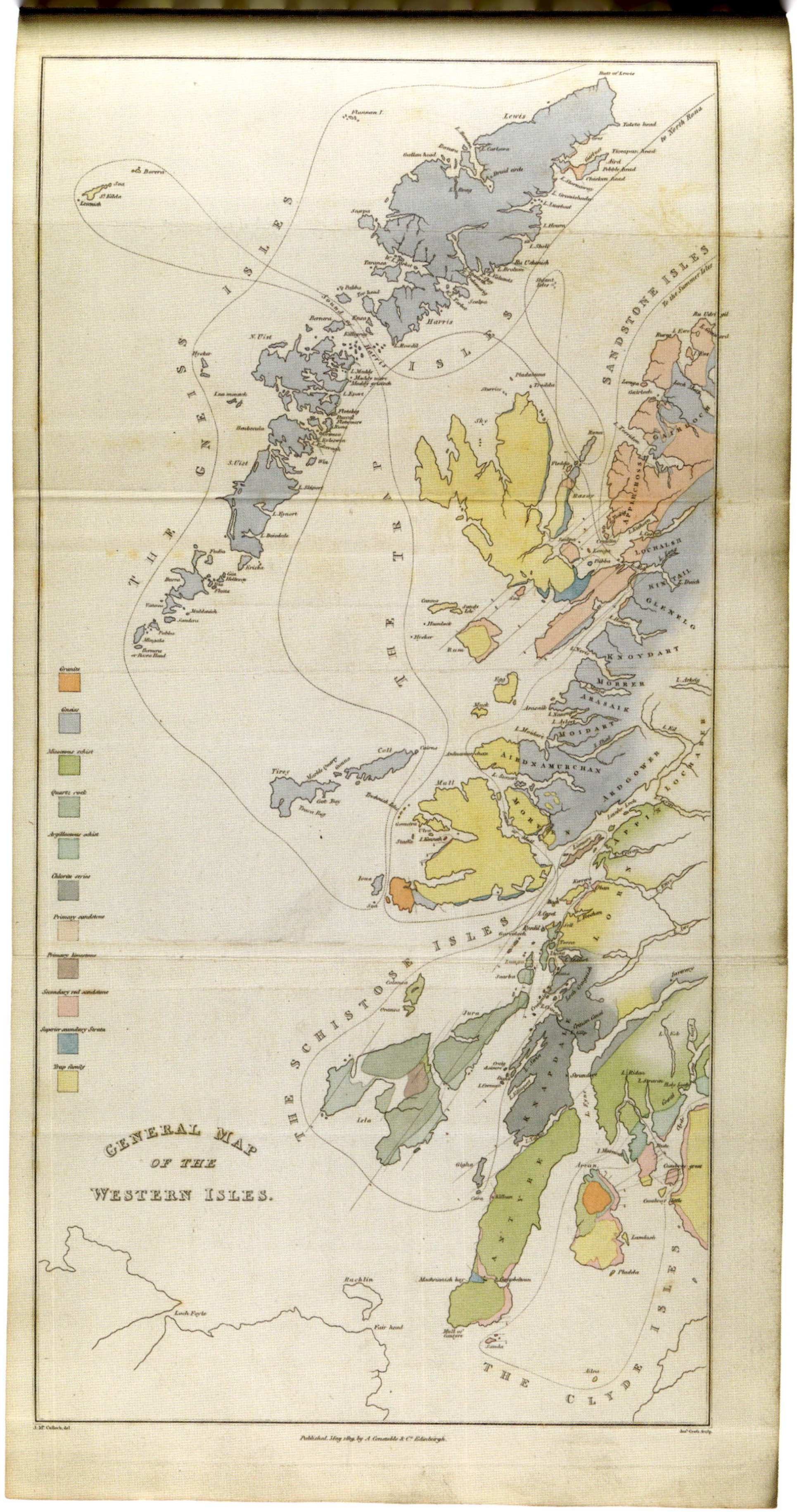

Fig. C3.16
Joseph Cross after John Macculloch, 'Geological Map of the Islands', in John Macculloch, *A Description of the Western Islands of Scotland, Including the Isle of Man: Comprising an Account of their Geological Structure: With Remarks on their Agriculture, Scenery, and Antiquities* (London, 1819), Vol. 3, p. 62 (GLA LRA HA12215)

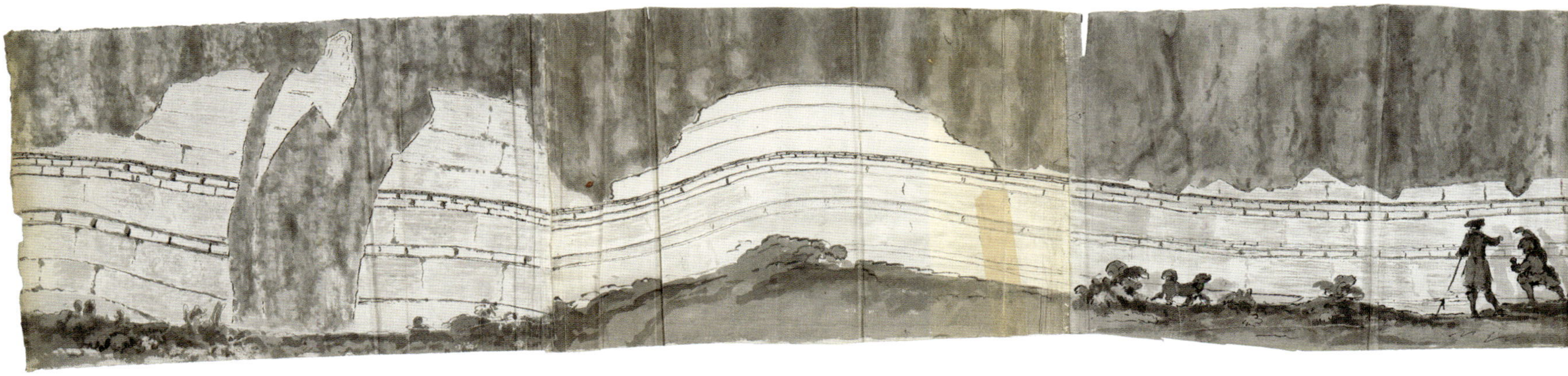

Fig. C3.17
Above. John Clerk of Eldin, geological sketch of Salisbury Crags, Edinburgh, c. 1780s, pen and wash, from album of drawings with illustrations for Hutton (PC)

Fig. C3.18
Right. John Clerk of Eldin, View looking upstream from Dail-an-eas Bridge, Glen Tilt, 1785, pen and wash, from album of drawings with illustrations for Hutton (PC)

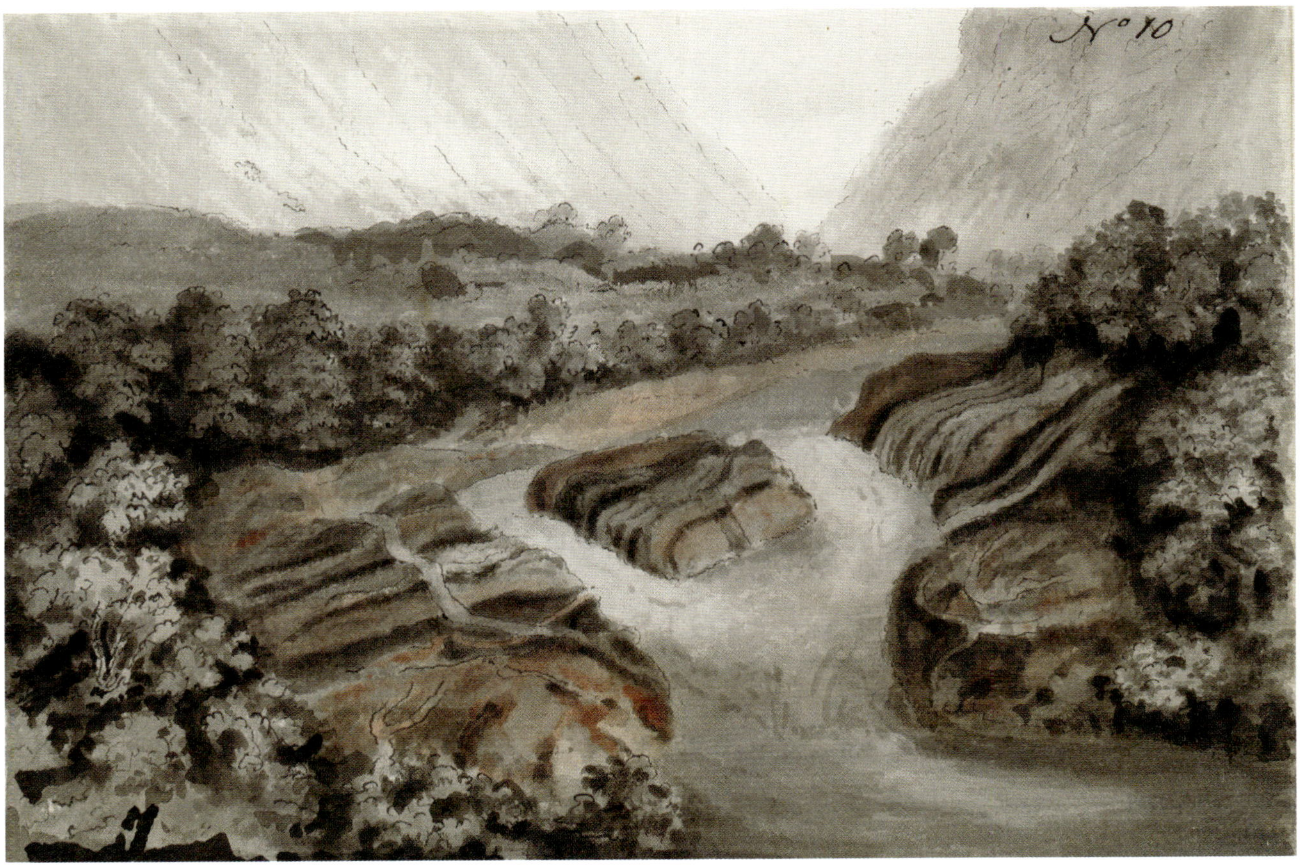

These remarkable drawings were created to illustrate Hutton's *Theory of the Earth*. In his attempts to capture the inner workings of the earth, Clerk of Eldin employed delicate washes of colour and shifted readily between cross-sections, plans and views, at times combining these different perspectives on the same sheet. Figures and narrative incident also played a not entirely incidental role. Like the sketching artist in the foreground of many a landscape, or the titling of a scene as 'done from the life' or 'from nature', the figures scrutinising the sandstone strata of Salisbury Crags signify the importance of actual encounters with places and things out there in the world to any claims to 'accuracy' or 'truth' that might be made. Such elements add a reflective or scenic note too. In Clerk's drawings, the Dail-An-Eas bridge over the Tilt or the Duke of Atholl's hunting lodge are picturesque accents that in their ordinary

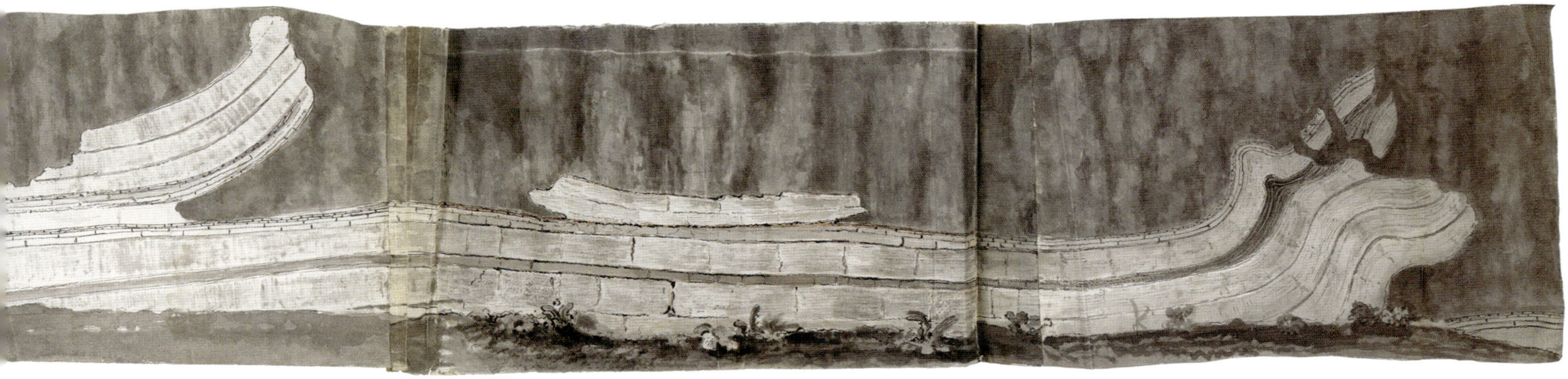

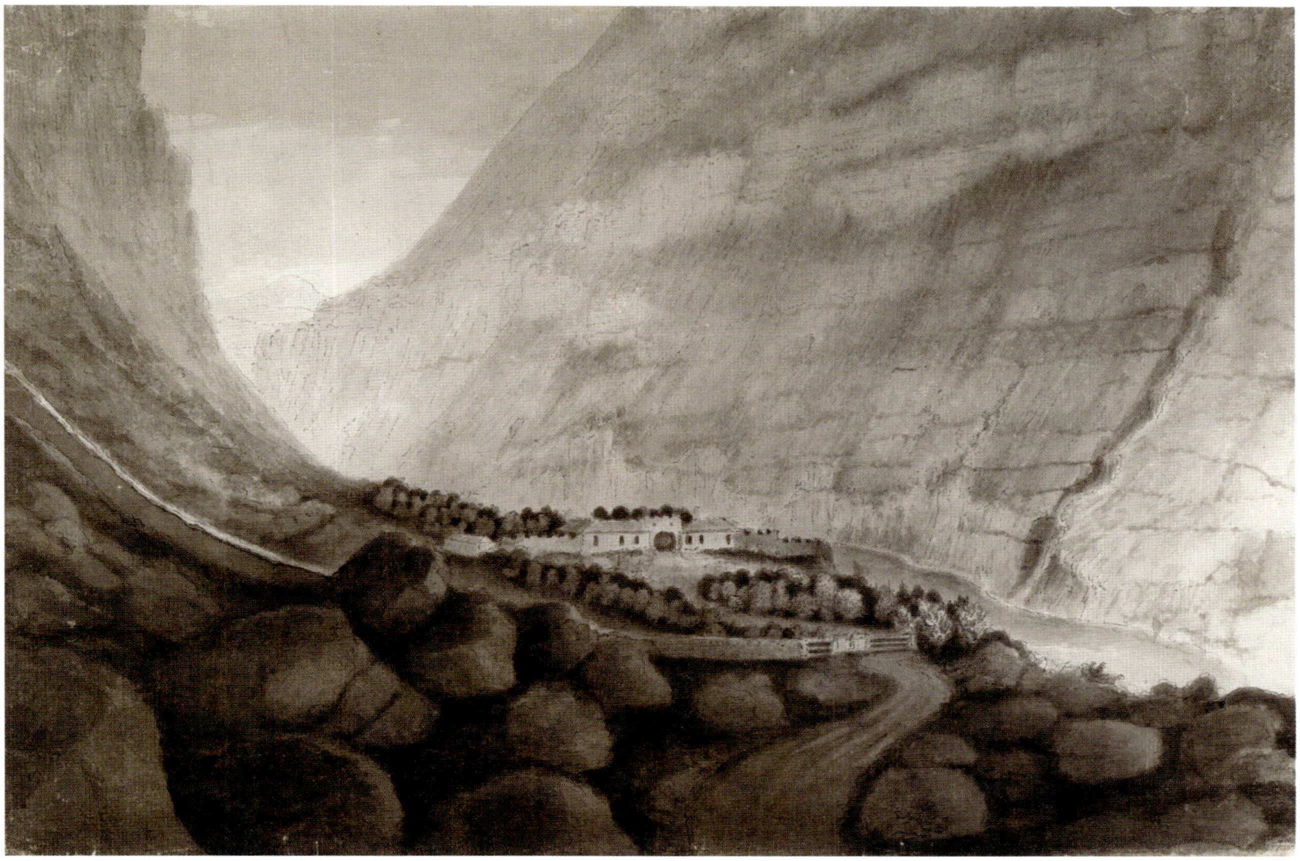

Fig. C3.19
Left. John Clerk of Eldin, Forest Lodge, Glen Tilt (hunting lodge of the Duke of Atholl), 1785, pen and wash, from album of drawings with illustrations for Hutton (PC)

everydayness also make for a series of dramatic and affecting contrasts with the elementary forces laid out below. With fieldwork being carried out at sites such as Glen Tilt, just north of Atholl House, philosophical enquiries of the kind undertaken by Hutton and others were in some ways no less a part of proprietary culture than the grand landscaping schemes being captured by artists such as Charles Steuart and William Tomkins. It made the landed estate a rural counterpart as it were to the learned spaces of Glasgow or Edinburgh. Featured in the plates of works like Pennant's *Tours*, they appeared as sites of philosophical and social experiment as well as places of scenic beauty.

Fig. C3.20a, b
Specimens from Glen Tilt, collected by John Playfair and Lord Webb-Seymour to illustrate the work of their friend James Hutton in developing the ideas of granite as an igneous rock, and igneous intrusion as a geological process. Although these specimens were collected in 1807 after Hutton's death, they were carefully collected to match the features examined by Hutton around 1780 at the same locality.

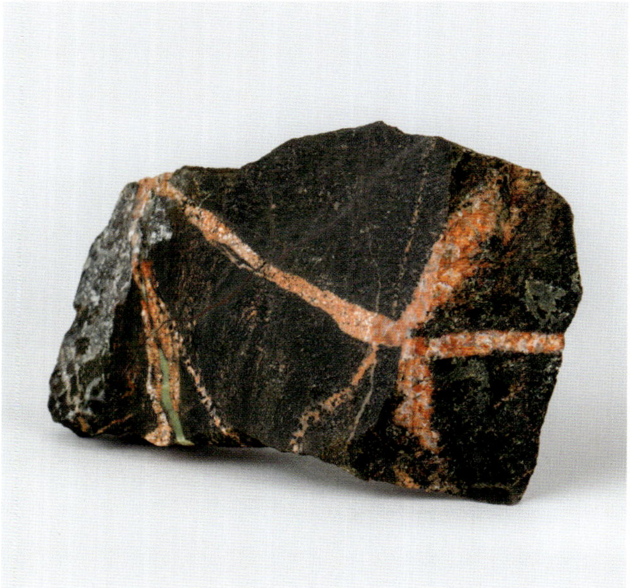

(a)
Pink granite veins cutting metamorphosed sandstone, Glen Tilt (GLAHM: 106965)

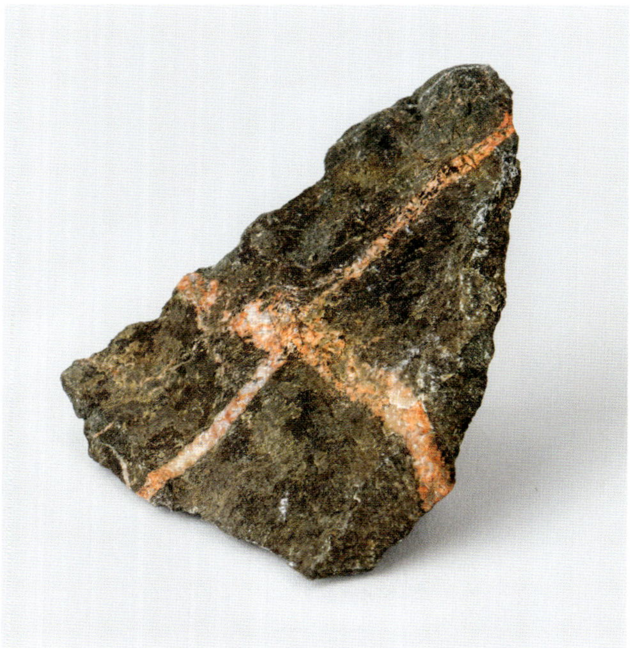

(b)
Intersecting veins of pink granite cutting dark metamorphosed sandstone, Glen Tilt (GLAHM: 106042)

lifted his gaze from the veins of granite and porphyry he had followed so closely across the valley. He now invited the reader to take in the region as a whole: 'This alpine country of Scotland may be considered as a mass of strata elevated in their place and situation, being now, instead of horizontal, almost vertical; and inclined sometimes towards the north-west, sometimes again towards the south-east . . .' The movement upwards was at the same time a movement inwards to the hidden strata of the mountains and backwards into geological time. In this way, Hutton made the earth lurch impossibly, from a 'horizontal' to an 'almost vertical' position, forcing plains to become alpine peaks. Next, he followed the River Tay past Atholl's estate to Dunkeld and the remnant of an 'ancient plain . . . 200 feet above the present level of the water'. In this dried-out riverbed, he discovered a tell-tale 'mixture of . . . broken schistus with . . . white granite', which he had uncovered a few days earlier in the high valley of Glen Tarf far upstream. This was proof of the 'great operation of water, in wasting and wearing the materials of this high land, in forming the valleys between the mountains, and carrying an immense mass of matter from the summit of those mountains into the sea'. Even the most 'consolidated bodies' and 'most indestructible' substances must crumble until 'in the course of time' 'stupendous gaps' are hollowed out of the mountains. A more traditional religious observer might have taken the destructive power of water as an illustration of the evanescence of all material things. Hutton instead argued for a theodicy of erosion, deifying nature. The inexorable attrition of the Highland mountains provided the soil necessary for agriculture in the Lowlands. 'The continual tendency of these operations, natural to the surface of the earth, is to diminish the heights of the mountains, to form plains below and to provide soil for the growth of plants' (Hutton 1899, I, 26–30).

Hutton's eternal economy of nature was in fact steeped in practical farming experience. After a few years spent farming in East Anglia and then Berwickshire, Hutton moved to Edinburgh in 1767 where he acted as an enthusiastic advocate for the mixed husbandry model of the south-east. He also began meteorological observations of the Scottish climate in 1773–1774 to discover what crops were best suited to local weather patterns. His notes on farming were incorporated into a large treatise entitled *Elements of Agriculture*, though the book remained unfinished and unpublished at Hutton's death in 1797. Like his

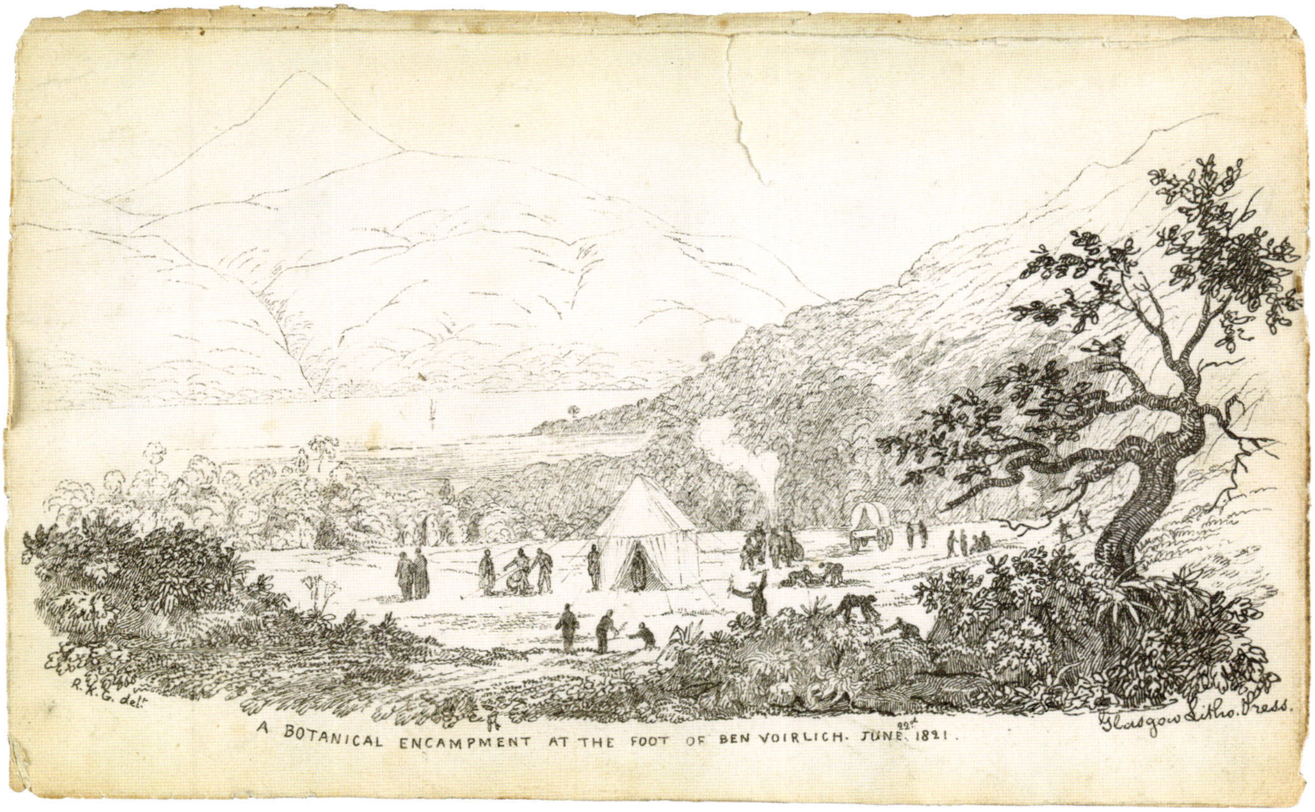

Fig. C3.21
Robert Kaye Greville, *A Botanical Encampment at the Foot of Ben Voirlich*, 22 June 1821, lithograph (GLAHM:150471)

Possibly the earliest British image of organised botanical fieldwork before the advent of photography, this lithograph published in a local newspaper is a reminder of the important role played by Glasgow University in the exploration of Scotland's natural flora.

good friend Adam Smith, Hutton held an abiding fascination with the self-regulating properties of large-scale systems. The natural world was for Hutton a tangle of large and small cycles that all contributed to the perpetual renewal of soil fertility over time. While Hutton's concept of geological time set him apart among the natural historians of the Scottish Enlightenment, he was utterly conventional in his understanding of wealth as a gift of nature improved by agriculture and gardening (Jones 1985; Withers 1994).

ACKNOWLEDGEMENTS

I am deeply grateful to the editors of this volume, Nigel Leask, Anne Dulau Beveridge and John Bonehill, for all their helpful comments and encouragement as well as their assistance in selecting images and objects that represent and explore the natural history of the Scottish Enlightenment. I would also like to express my warm gratitude to Henry Noltie who helped locate Lightfoot's *Fucus* in the herbaria of the Royal Botanic Gardens of Edinburgh. The section 'The Caledonian Forest' includes an excerpt from my essay 'Adam Smith in the Forest' published in *The Social Lives of the Forests: The Past, Present, and Future of Woodland Resurgence*, ed. Susanna Hecht, Kathleen Morrison and Christine Padoch (University of Chicago Press, 2014). The section 'The Time of Soil and Rocks' includes an excerpt from my essay 'Abundance and Scarcity in Geological Time, 1784–1844', published in *Nature, Action and the Future Political Thought and the Environment*, ed. Sophie Smith and Katrina Forrester (Cambridge University Press, 2018). I am grateful to the University of Chicago Press and Cambridge University Press for permitting me to print these previously published passages.

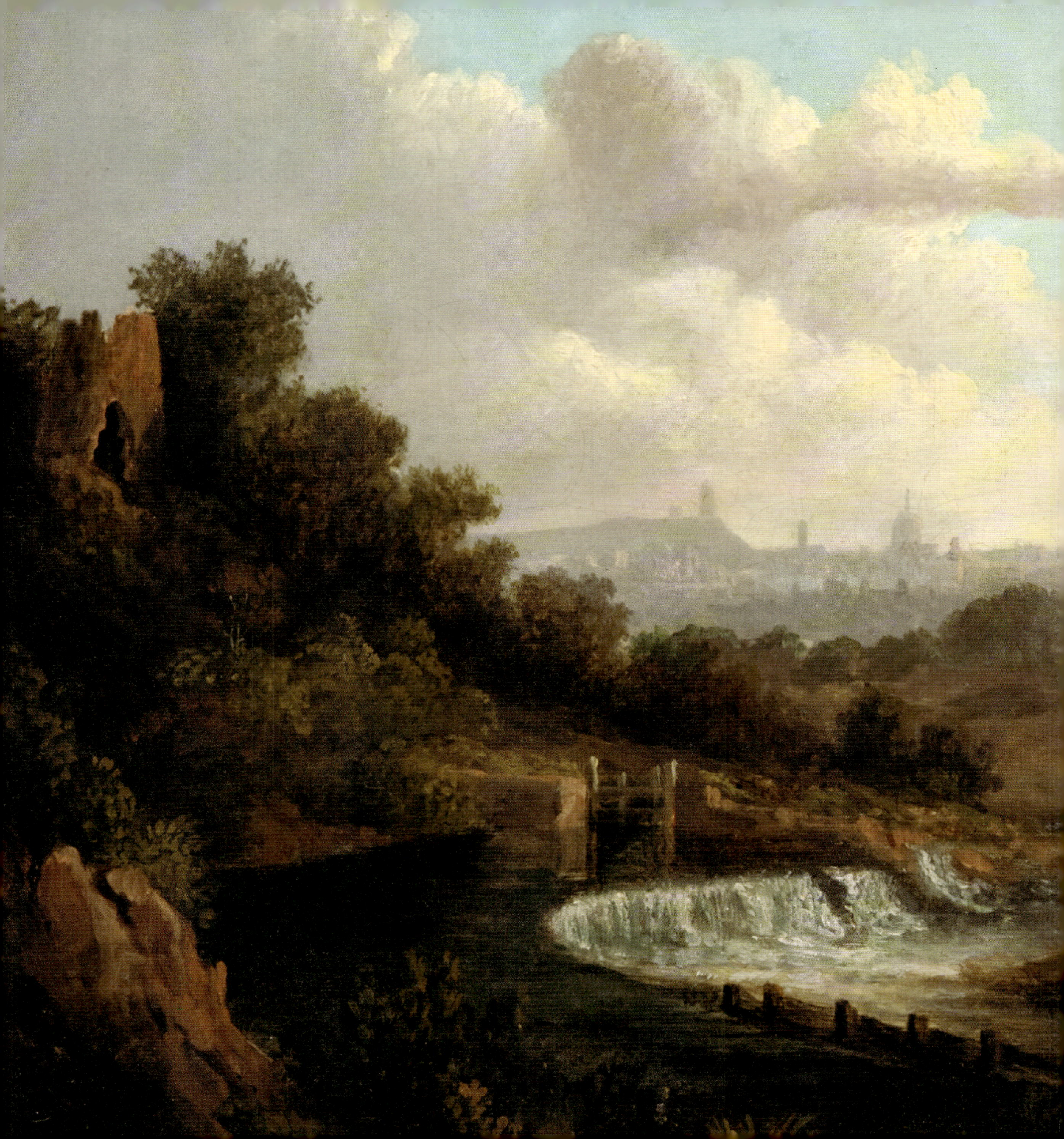

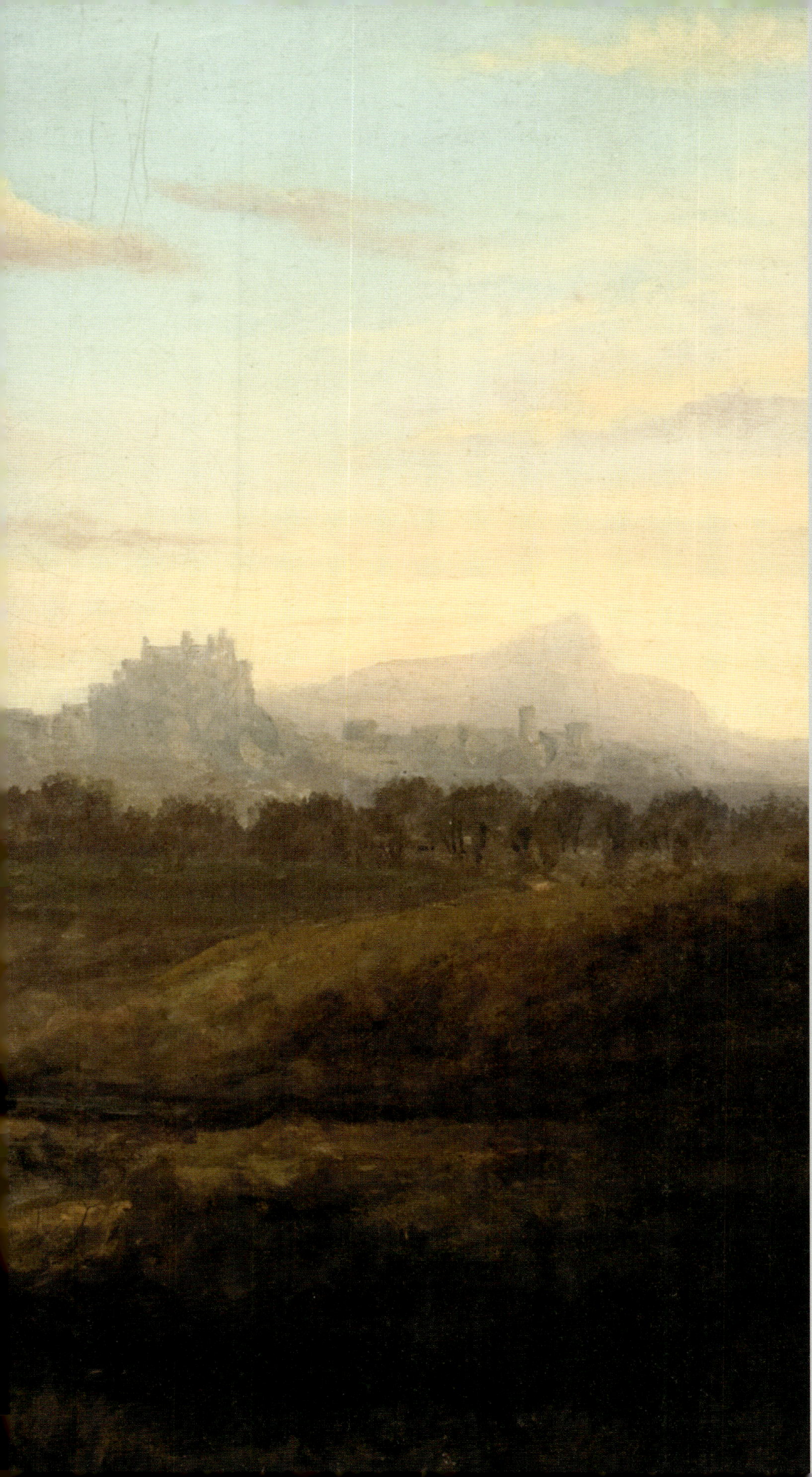

SECTION THREE

Custom and Improvement

John Bonehill

Fig. S3.1
Alexander Nasmyth, *Edinburgh from the West*, 1818–1825, oil on canvas (GLAHA:43981)

Taken from just above the Cramond falls, five miles or so to the west of the capital, Alexander Nasmyth's view of Edinburgh is one of a long series of prospects of the city essayed by the painter from various vantage points. Here, with the landmark buildings and dramatic crags that mark the urban skyline framed by the tower ruins and rural setting of the foreground, the vision is of a harmonious fusion of architectural and natural elements, of city and country. In this, Nasmyth gestures to the growing integration of these realms, including discrete but telling gestures to the improvement of the falls, and to the engineering of the landscape, in the form of the damming of the waters and sluice gates. Indeed, the cascades at the mouth of the River Almond were powering a range of local industries at the time.

'Good roads, canals, and navigable rivers' wrote Adam Smith, 'put the remote parts of the country more nearly upon a level with those in the neighbourhood of the town'. They were thus 'the greatest of all improvements', encouraging 'the cultivation of the remote' while also benefiting urban centres, breaking 'the monopoly of the country in its neighbourhood' (Smith 1776, I, 184). By the time Smith was writing, the wide-ranging effects of such connectedness were already apparent in his native Scotland, with the circulation of people, goods and ideas enabled by the country's still expanding transport system transforming economic, social and cultural life at an accelerated rate. Much of this activity was driven by the profits of Britain's growing maritime empire, as the cities and ports of Scotland's west coast became key co-ordinates in the vast arena of commercial exchange that comprised the circum-Atlantic world. Although Smith's commentary on the benefits of improved travel networks focused on the advantages of local and regional communications, Scotland's sphere of enterprise was now global in scope. Not everywhere was part of this joined-up modern world, however. Some places thrived. Yet, elsewhere, Scotland's progress was faltering, as people and places proved stubbornly resistant to change, or as the country's new transport network privileged the power of some interests over others. Still reliant on ancient drove roads and horse tracks or old coal and salt routes, many of which were unsuited to modern forms of transportation, communities were left by the wayside. In one way or another, all the images and writings featured in this section are connected to the often uneasy relationship between the local and national in eighteenth-century Scotland, between country and town, settlement and movement, custom and improvement.

Attitudes towards custom and improvement were complex: a field of contest in which opposing interests made conflicting claims. Despite the enthusiastic promotion of improvement, by the years around 1800, it was being viewed with wary scepticism by some, as antipathy to the republican modernity of revolutionary France and associated fears of domestic insurrection helped to fuel a distrust of unchecked progress. Thus modernity gave new value to the 'old ways'. Highlighting a slower rhythmed, vernacular sense of existence, at times they might serve as a useful counter to the moral corruption and social break-up that some saw as wrought by the influx of capital. The improving impulse oversaw the building of manufacturing villages and polite townscapes, as well as harbours, canals and roads, establishing new markets and livelihoods; but in other places (especially the Highlands and Islands) modern, profit-orientated improvements caused social dislocation and hardship (Smout 1969; Devine 1994a). Whereas, in the Lowlands, those evicted by the clearances might find alternative employment in new manufactories, in the Highlands and Islands, the plight of displaced cottars and tenants was bleak: they faced the uncertainties of starting anew in a distant land or an economically less secure life if they remained (Devine 2018).

Gazing upon signs of custom and improvement in the Scottish landscape, in their attempts to comprehend its changing face, artists and writers travelling its old ways and new roads exhibited a broad range of responses, from approval to disappointment, fascination to bewilderment. Seen through their eyes, the customary, as it was imaginatively located primarily in labouring and popular culture, was made an object of 'curious' enquiry. Topographical surveys had long sought to record that which was remarkable or wondrous; their authors compiling inventories of local histories, myths and customs. What made a place 'curious' or different from other localities was in a sense what made it meaningful. It was the individuality or idiosyncrasy of a place that was its contribution to the identity of the wider region and by extension the nation. Part philosophical enquiry, part popular entertainment, Thomas Pennant's *Tours* represented a new form of travelogue (Constantine and Leask 2017). Yet they were also firmly located in this tradition of regional surveys, the Welsh traveller's knowledge of Scotland being founded on a well-established combination of observations made 'in the field' and – as we saw in Chapter 1 – the authority of resident 'gentlemen and clergy' for information on matters of dress, language, song or strange observational ritual. With the forces of improvement threatening to erode what made one locale distinct from another, there was a recognition that such 'curiosities' needed to be documented lest they be lost completely.

Skirting the edge of Loch Rannoch, near the eastern end of the annexed estate of the Jacobite Robertson family, the Barony of Struan, Pennant was minded to recount various beliefs and practices particular to the locality, noting:

> The country is perfectly highland; and in spite of the intercourse this and the neighboring parts have of late

> years had with the rest of the world, it still retains some of its antient customs and superstitions: they decline daily, but least their memory should be lost, I shall mention several that are still practised, or but very lately disused in the tract I had passed over. Such a record will have this advantage, when the follies are quite extinct, in teaching the unshackled and enlightened mind the difference between the pure ceremonies of religion, and the wild and anile flights of superstition. (Pennant 1771a, 89)

He went on to detail a clutch of local burial and funeral rites as well as sightings of spectral beings, instances of second sight and magical stones. For Pennant, customary activities and forms of knowledge were 'antiquities' of a kind: curious, residual remnants of a past time, of note largely because memories of them would soon serve only to highlight the progress of the present age.

Looking back on his experiences in the Highlands and performing his own act of Gaelic clairvoyance, Pennant was given 'to imagine the former condition of this part of the Kingdom, and to compare it with the present state', so that 'by a sort of second-sight' you might arrive at 'a probable conjecture of the happy appearance it will assume in a very few years'. Elsewhere, however, he was more equivocal about the country's prospects (Pennant 1771a, 215). At times, the embrace of the rational and useful was disrupted by those very instances of arcane and unruly survivals of a native past he set out to record. In terms of their meanings for resident populations or their place within day-to-day life, the customs of Scotland's localities were ill reconciled with the writer's overarching narrative of patriotic and progressive improvement.

Unlike Samuel Johnson a year or so later, Pennant and other philosophically minded travellers saw rich potential in the Highlands and Islands, even if it was not as yet fully realised. On touring the Western Isles in 1772, Joseph Banks was to lament of Islay that 'cultivation has yet made but a small progress' despite the superior qualities of the island's soil (Banks 1772, 202). By way of example of the backwards, near destitute state he saw as endured by the local population, he asked the artists travelling with him on Islay to draw the stone and turf blackhouses (Gaelic *taigh-dubh*) (Figs S3.2 and S3.3). When engraved

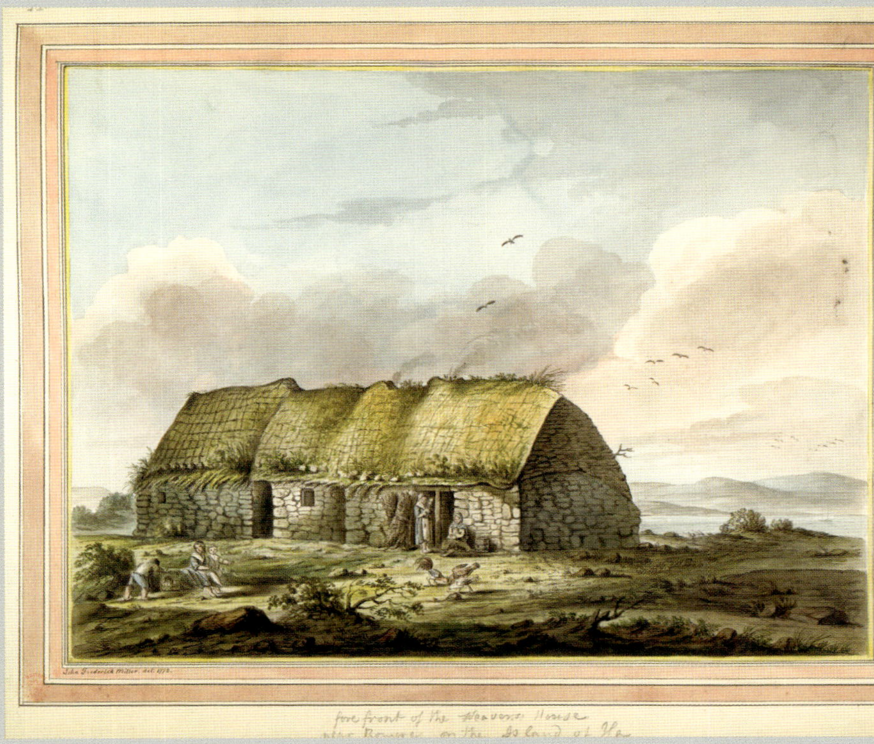

Fig. S3.2
John Frederick Miller, *Forefront of the Weavers House near Bomore on the Island of Ila*, 1772, watercolour
(BL Add MS 15509 f.24)

for Pennant's 1772 *Tour*, John Frederick Miller's remarkable study of the cluttered, fire-lit and smoke-filled interior of the weaver's house – which rather resembles a rustic version of Joseph Wright of Derby's contemporary 'candlelight' pictures – accompanied a few reflections that reinforced this image of a 'set of people worn down with poverty: their habitations scenes of misery' (Pennant 1774b, 261). Yet, although such descriptions of the primitive conditions on the islands conveyed a picture of a Gaelic society alienated from the modern world, that was not quite the case. While the hardship was real enough, economic modernity was making headway. On Islay, Banks took note of Mr Fairbairn's house, where 'a very good air furnace' was used to smelt 'the lead produced by his mines' (Banks 1772, 202) (Fig. S3.4). Islay's proprietor, the rich Glasgow merchant Daniel Campbell, was also making a substantial investment, having already introduced a flax and linen industry at the new village of Bowmore by the time of Banks's visit (see Fig. C2.1). What Miller's view of the exterior of the Weaver's cottage showed was in fact a scene of improvement, in a cottage specially adapted

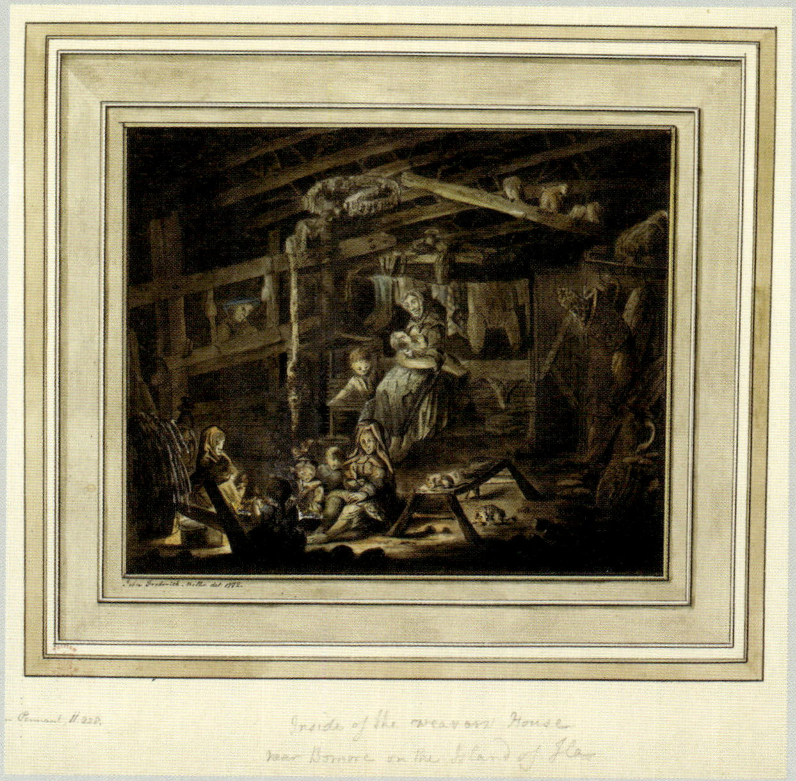

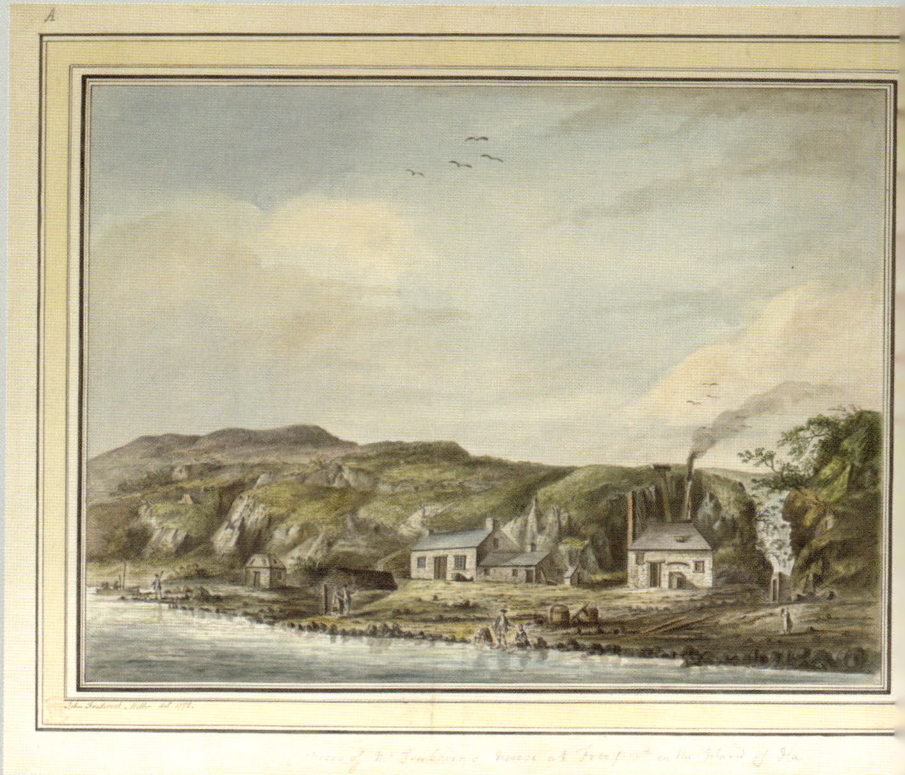

Fig. S3.3
Above left. John Frederick Miller, *Inside of the Weavers House near Bomore on the Island of Ila*, 1772, watercolour (BL Add MS 15509 f.28)

Fig. S3.4
Above right. John Frederick Miller, *View of Mr Freebairns House at Freeport on the Island of Ila*, 1772, watercolour (BL Add MS 15509 f. X)

to accommodate a new loom, even if it is filtered through a notably picturesque sensibility. Such conditions baffled some visitors. 'We came thither too late to see what we expected, a people of peculiar appearance, and a system of antiquated life,' Johnson was famously to lament of the Western Isles, finding them neither wholly one thing nor another (Johnson 1775, 89).

Several commentators laid the blame for the failure to exploit the rich bounty of the land and surrounding waters of the Hebrides on neglectful, absentee landlords. Absenteeism was not necessarily a bar to dutiful estate management, however. Among those patriotic landowners Pennant singled out as model improvers was John, 3rd Earl of Bute, whose meteoric political career (which saw him briefly become first Lord of the Treasury and the first Scotsman to hold the highest office in British politics) prevented him from ever returning to his ancestral seat of Mount Stuart on the Isle of Bute once he left for London shortly after the 'Forty-Five'. Unlike other absentee owners, the earl took a close interest in the improvement of his estate and the welfare of the island's inhabitants, supervising developments at a distance through correspondence and the commission of exhaustive reports. He also kept 'A Journal of the Planting & c. Executed att Mountstewart' which documented an often-experimental approach to silviculture for scenic as well as commercial purposes. Set out in a series of paintings commissioned from Charles Steuart, as well as surveys carried out by leading local authorities, such as John Hope's botanical protégé James Robertson, it was this outlook that informed the earl's plans for improving the island's economy.

Produced in the 1780s, Steuart's paintings reflect on matters of land management and use, location and connection. They include views of one of the garden's temples as well as a cascade that Bute had taken particular care to plant appropriately (Figs S3.5 and S3.6). But the artist also executed a pair of expansive companion views of Mount Stuart: one looking from above the house and out over the Firth of Clyde and another from the sea itself (Fig. S3.7). With the elegant early-eighteenth-century

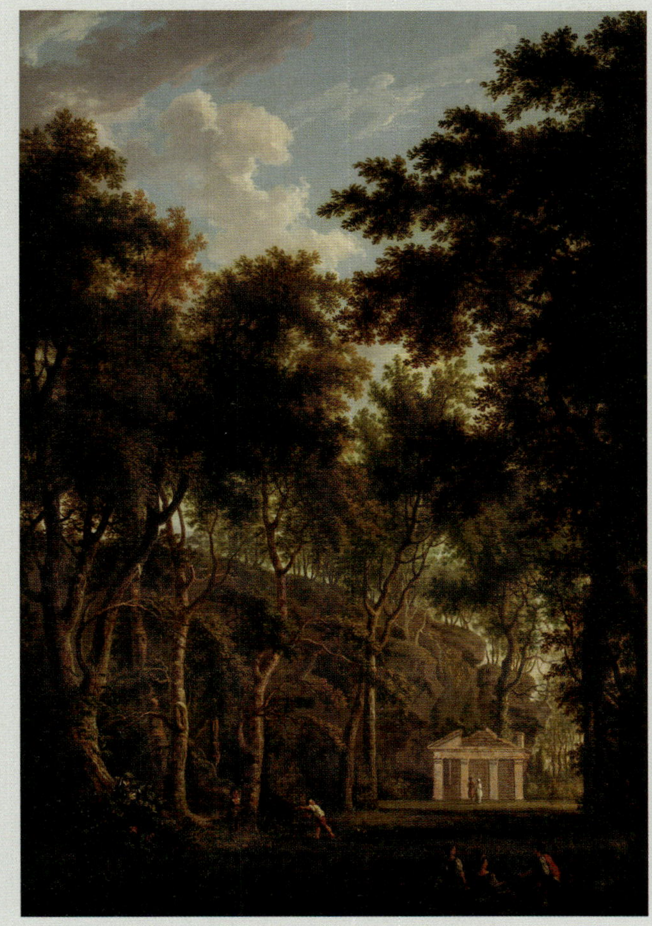

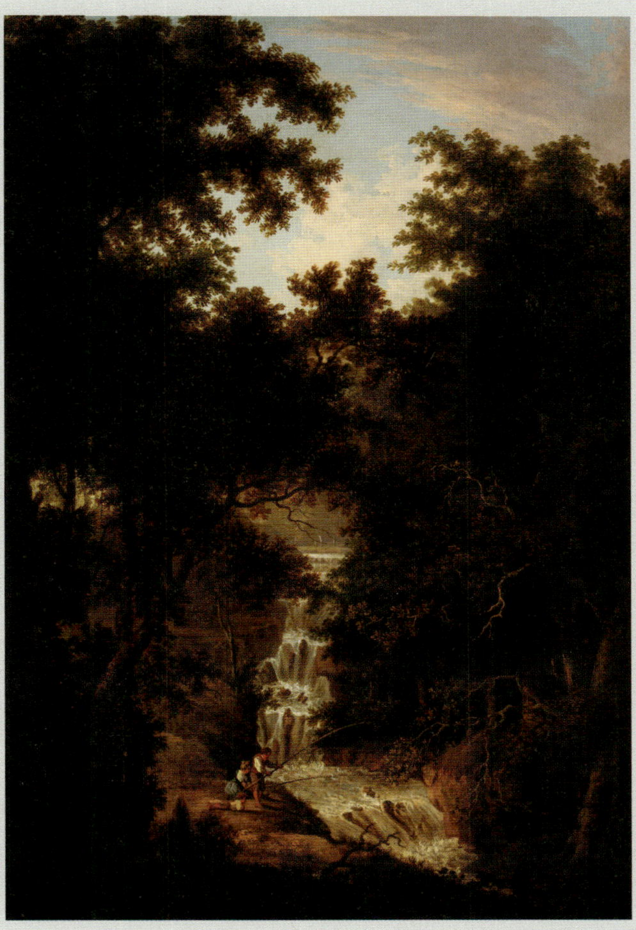

Fig. S3.5
Far left. Charles Steuart, *Beech Walk, Mount Stuart (with Little Temple or Hermitage)*, c. 1780s, oil on canvas (MST)

Fig. S3.6
Left. Charles Steuart, *The Cascade, Mount Stuart*, c. 1780s, oil on canvas (MST)

mansion lost to a fire in the Victorian era and the small coastal hamlet of Scoulag, where visitors to the island like Pennant once made landing, long since swept away, these pictures document a now lost landscape. Indeed, given that the house appears in elevation, as if sampled from a design, pristine and gleaming, despite reports of its ill repair at this time, it may record a landscape that never was or that was only ever envisaged. For Robertson, who spent the best part of three weeks botanising on the island, the estate was notable for its 'large Plantations of Trees, both indigenous and exotick, . . . laid out prettily in Pleasant Walks, and Agreeable Views' (Hope 1768). In Steuart's picture, however, such elements are just part of the highly complex natural and social environment of cultivated, arable land as well as shoreline sand and gravel. Sailing the choppy waters of the foreground, the array of vessels of various sizes make allusion to the island's principal industry, fishing – cod in spring, herring in the autumn – as well as the connections with places elsewhere that for some of those commissioned by its absentee landlord held the promise of bringing Bute into the modern world.

Fishery development had long been recognised as Scotland's main prospect for economic growth (Coull 1996; Harris 2000). Having been prominent in the politics of national regeneration in the lead up to 1707, calls for greater investment in fisheries were revived in the middle decades of the eighteenth century in the interests of shoring up the Union. By the 1780s, the industry was being promoted as morally and socially improving as well as a source of employment and prosperity. Writing around the time of Steuart's paintings, one of the period's principal

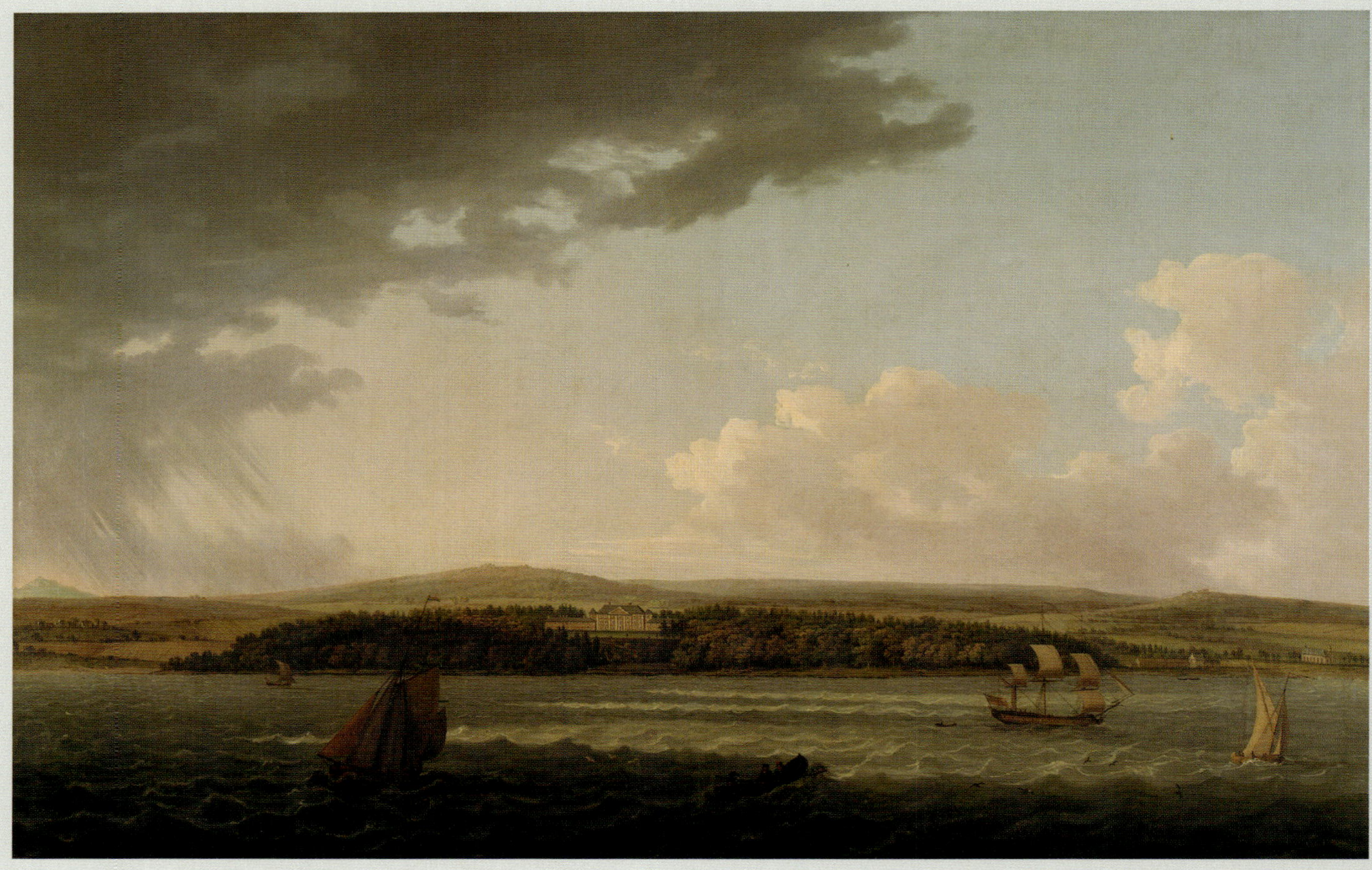

Fig. S3.7
Charles Steuart, *Mount Stuart from the Sea*, c. 1780s, oil on canvas (MST)

piscatorial enthusiasts, the London bookseller and philanthropist John Knox, was to attribute the lack of 'beggars', 'idlers' or 'smugglers' on Bute to the islanders' employment in fisheries (Knox 1785, I, 365). With James Anderson and others, Knox would be one of the chief architects of the British Fisheries Society, which aimed to exploit herring shoals off the west coast through the establishment of planned settlements. Founded in 1786, in the wake of the loss of the American colonies, with Britain's 'empire of the seas' worryingly vulnerable, the society's ambitions were also linked to matters of national security; Knox, for one, argued that since '[t]he strength of the Navy depends chiefly on the extent of our maritime coast', the cause of Scottish fisheries was coterminous with the country's ability to defend its interests (Knox 1786, 9). In one way or another, Scotland's improvement was invariably seen in the context of colonial commerce and maritime power.

In a report on the island, the Edinburgh-based architect George Paterson was to argue that '[t]he Situation of Bute is favourable for Trade and Commerce', not least as 'Navigation to America and the West Indies' was 'more convenient than to the opposite shore where they have of late accumulated great riches by means of their conversation with those parts'. While Bute might hardly hope to 'rival these places in Trade', Paterson was hopeful that it might at least profit from the advantages of its geography, the island being in the 'Vicinity particularly as the Manufacturers' of Glasgow. 'It Circulates industry, and where industry takes root, there wealth is accumulated' he concluded (Paterson 1777). Good transport links, as Smith had it, 'put the

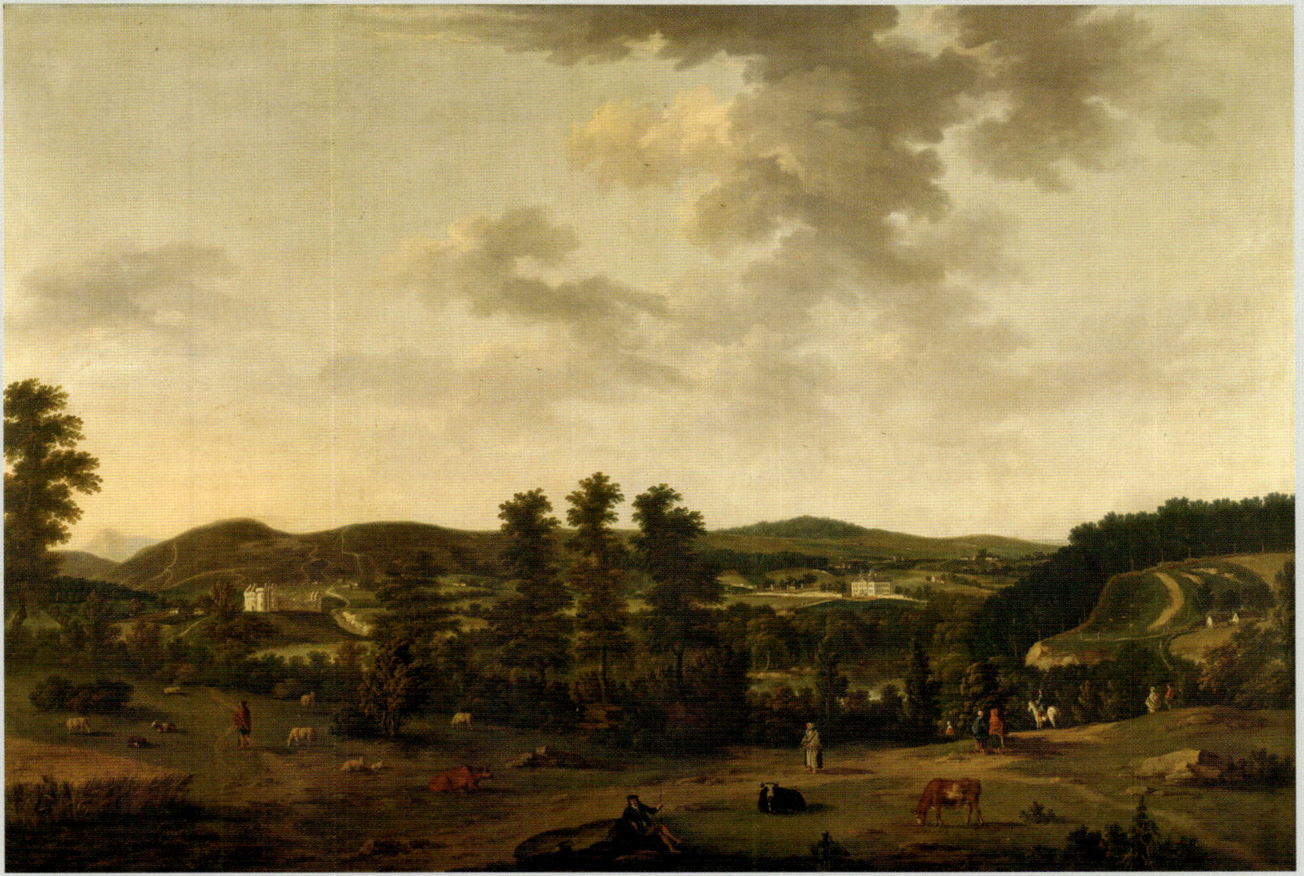

Fig. S3.8
William Tomkins, *View of Balveny Castle*, 1767, oil on canvas (PC)

remote parts of the country more nearly upon a level with those in the neighbourhood of the town' (Smith 1776, I, 184).

While only just finding a foothold in the islands, the mainland was undergoing rapid economic and social transformation in the name of improvement. What had been a Lowland landscape of scattered cot-touns and fermtouns, surrounded by communal runrigs, moorland, scattered trees and grazing lands, was being replaced at an accelerated rate by more productive, neatly fenced, compact farms. In the Highlands, the traditional *baile*, where a number of small tenants had farmed communally under the direction of a tacksman (or *fear-taca*), gave way to single, larger tenancies dedicated to raising black cattle and increasingly sheep. In order to raise their rental income, indebted Highland proprietors were increasingly persuaded to lease out their land to highly capitalised southern sheep farmers, who replaced small, coarse-woolled indigenous animals with improved breeds like the Blackface and Cheviot (see Fig. C3.8). Laying waste to a number of traditional economies and ways of life, these developments often prompted considerable local contention. Such wholesale change was enabled, however, by the wide-ranging authority and power enjoyed by Scottish landowners and the prevalence of short leases. Abandoning the strongly moral customary principle captured by the Gaelic word *dùthchas*, which summoned notions of home, kinship and belonging, but went unrecognised in law, many Highland clan chiefs began to think of themselves as commercial landlords. Obligation and social bonds were traded for rent-racking (Devine 1994b, 23–24, 45–47). In the pursuit of profit, landed estates were enlarged and

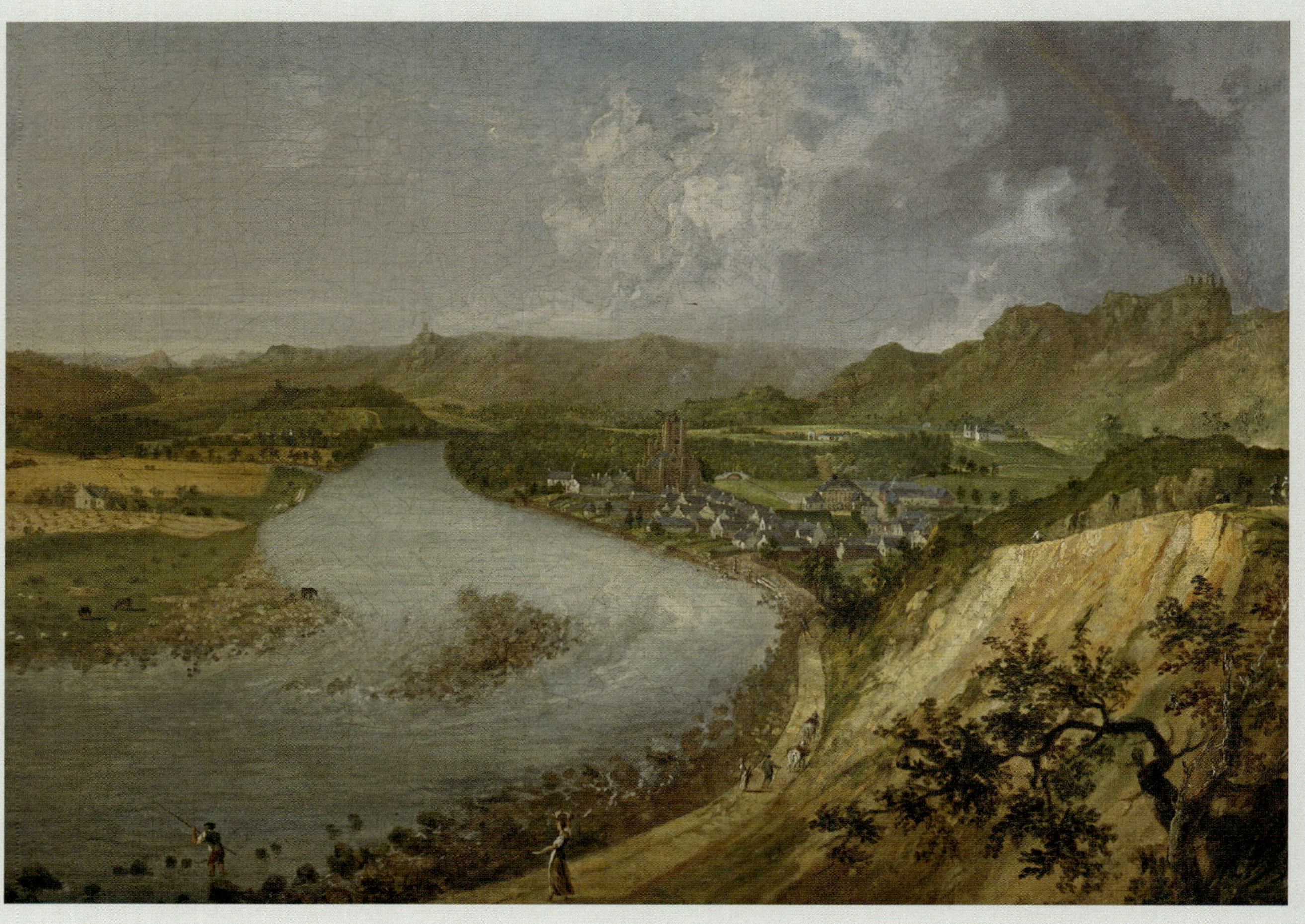

Fig. S3.9
Charles Steuart, *Dunkeld, Perthshire from the East*, 1765, oil on canvas (AE)

remodelled, becoming sites of agricultural, industrial and social experiment and innovation – as Fredrik Jonsson and Christopher Dingwall establish in Chapters 3 and 4 – staging grounds for the practical application of improvement and model showpieces of its virtues. Landowners looked to exploit the mineral wealth of their estates or introduced new crops, livestock, rotations, tools and methods.

No activity spoke more eloquently of a commitment to improvement than the careful cultivation and management of trees and woodland at places like Mount Stuart or on the Perthshire estates of the dukes of Atholl. Supplementing the limited number of native species with exotics that flourished on otherwise economically marginal lands, the great swathes of planting on such properties had a transformative effect on the local landscape. 'Planting ought to be carried on for Beauty, Effect and Profit' wrote John Murray, 4th Duke of Atholl, in his forestry journal (quoted in House and Dingwall 2003, 135). Looking to Virgil's *Georgics*, his words cast the activity in a classical light. Georgic imagery glossed the improved estate as a landscape of beauty and use, pleasure and profit. Trees were a capital resource to be exploited symbolically as well as materially. Together with the establishment of more obviously commercial stands, the planting of policies for scenic as well as practical effect made a potent visual statement about an owner's or a family's connection with, or occupancy and stewardship of, a place. While the large-scale planting of larch on Atholl lands was financially lucrative, its symbolic importance to the navy, building the 'wooden walls' of the nation, also marked it out as a patriotic endeavour. It harnessed the designed landscape to the broader project of the remaking of the Union.

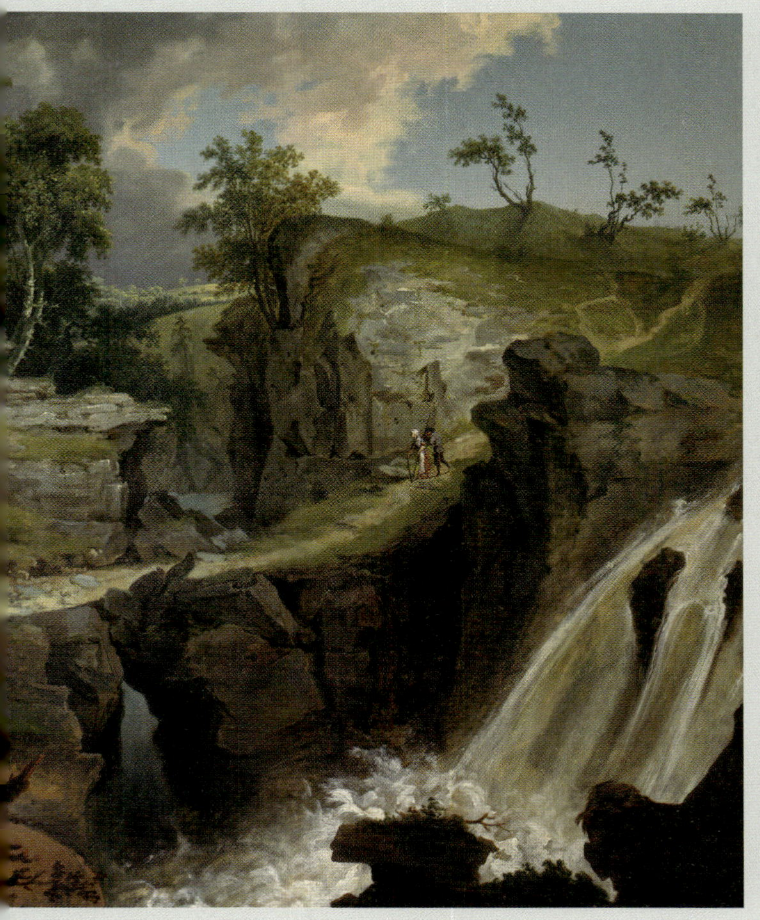

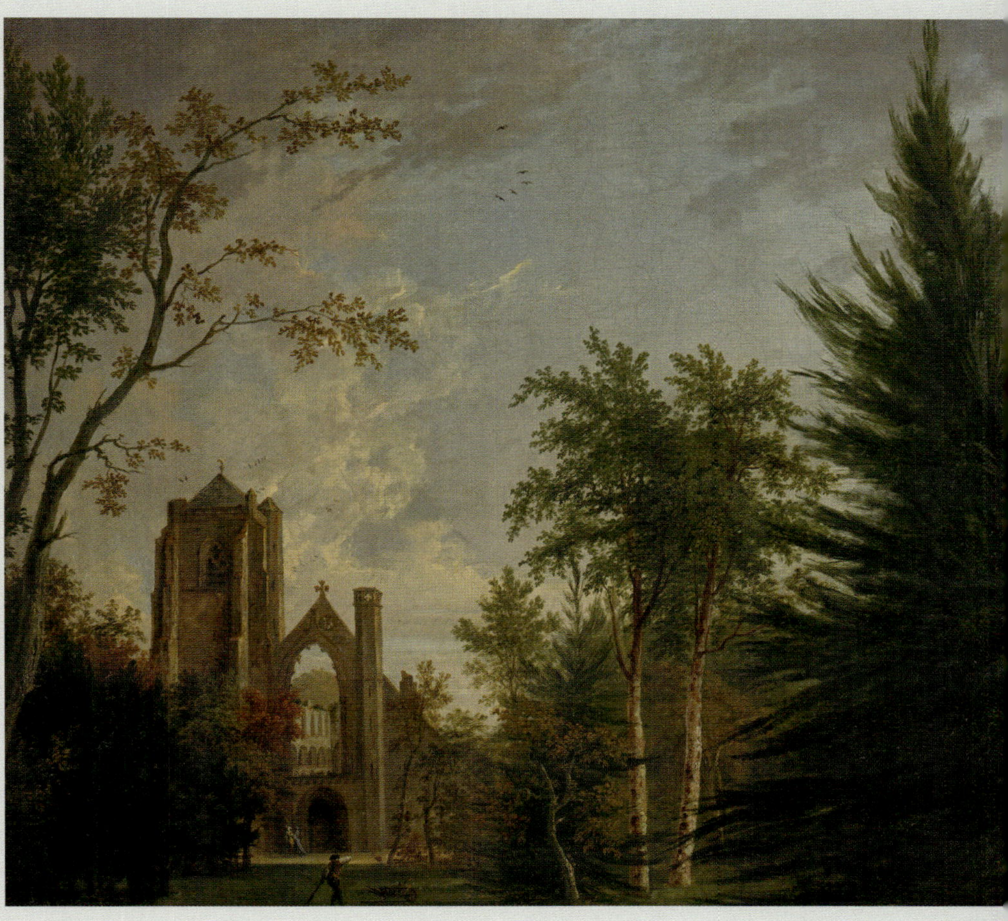

Fig. S3.10
Above left. Charles Steuart, *Falls on the river Bran (Rumbling brig)*, 1765, oil on canvas (AE)

Fig. S3.11
Above right. Charles Steuart, *Dunkeld Cathedral*, 1765, oil on canvas (AE)

Part of a long-lived tradition of prospect-making, the views of estates that Atholl and other local landowners commissioned from the likes of the locally born Steuart (the painter of the view of Mount Stuart discussed above) or the London-based George Barret and William Tomkins displayed the patron's commitment to their lands in paint, invariably celebrating the economic and social benefits wrought by investments in the progressive remodelling of the landscape (Figs S3.8–S3.14 and Figs C5.4–C5.6). There, the cast of characters might take in artists, tourists and estate workers, gardeners, shepherds and field hands, all playing out their roles in the progress of the landscape, in its development and day-to-day use. Such pictures framed the country's landed property as landscapes of beauty and use, of commercial and scenic value, of rich fields and extensive plantations, cataracts and fast-running waters.

Besides their considerable associative power, the waterfalls that obsessed both landowners and tourists in the period also animated the landscape, filling it with movement and noise. But their energy also powered various forms of industry, from fulling to mining. In a striking instance of the alliance of landed and commercial interests, James, 3rd Earl of Hopetoun, in partnership with an English investment group, was notably active in exploiting the outcrops and rich veins of lead that lay on his lands in the Lowther Hills, north of Dumfries, employing the waters of the Glengonnar Valley to drive pumping engines and other machinery. On touring his properties in 1786, the earl commissioned a set of four cabinet-sized pictures from the Scottish artist David Allan of the mining operations at Leadhills to showcase his enlightened brand of landownership, which included the provision of education and housing for the (often English) workforce

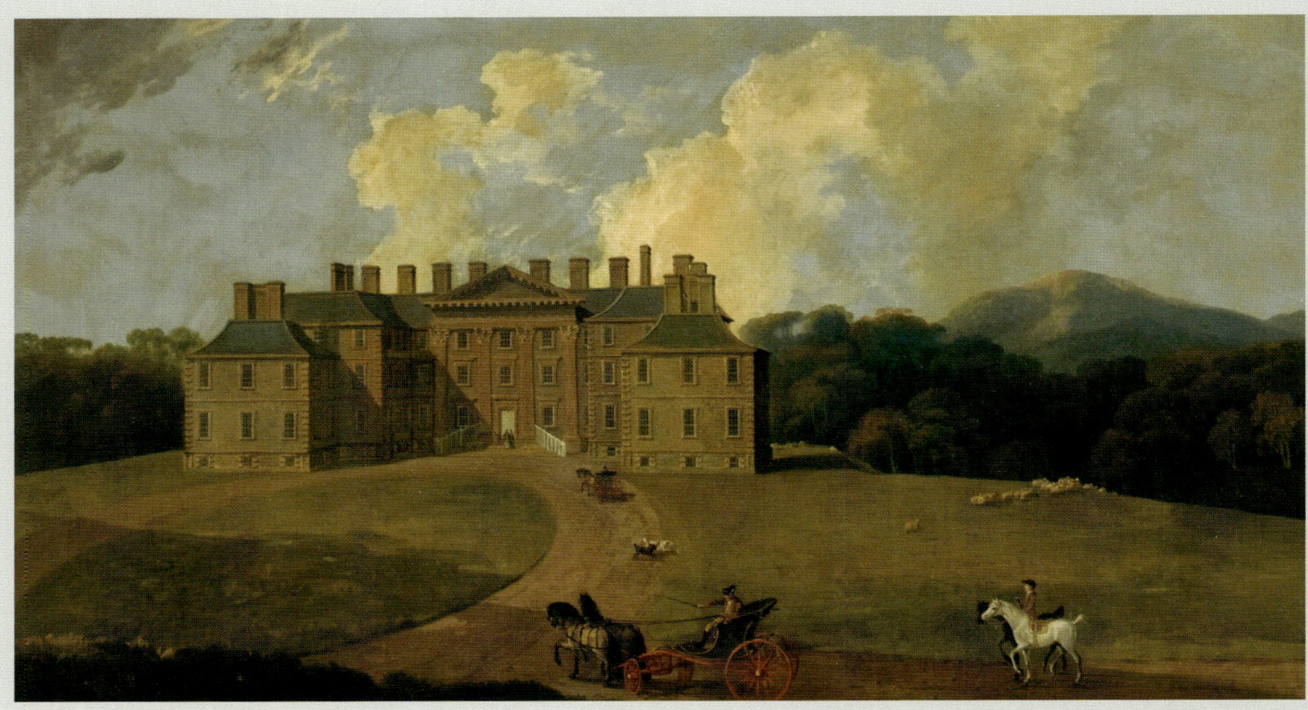

Fig. S3.12
George Barret, *A view of Dalkeith House*, c. 1770, oil on canvas (BC)

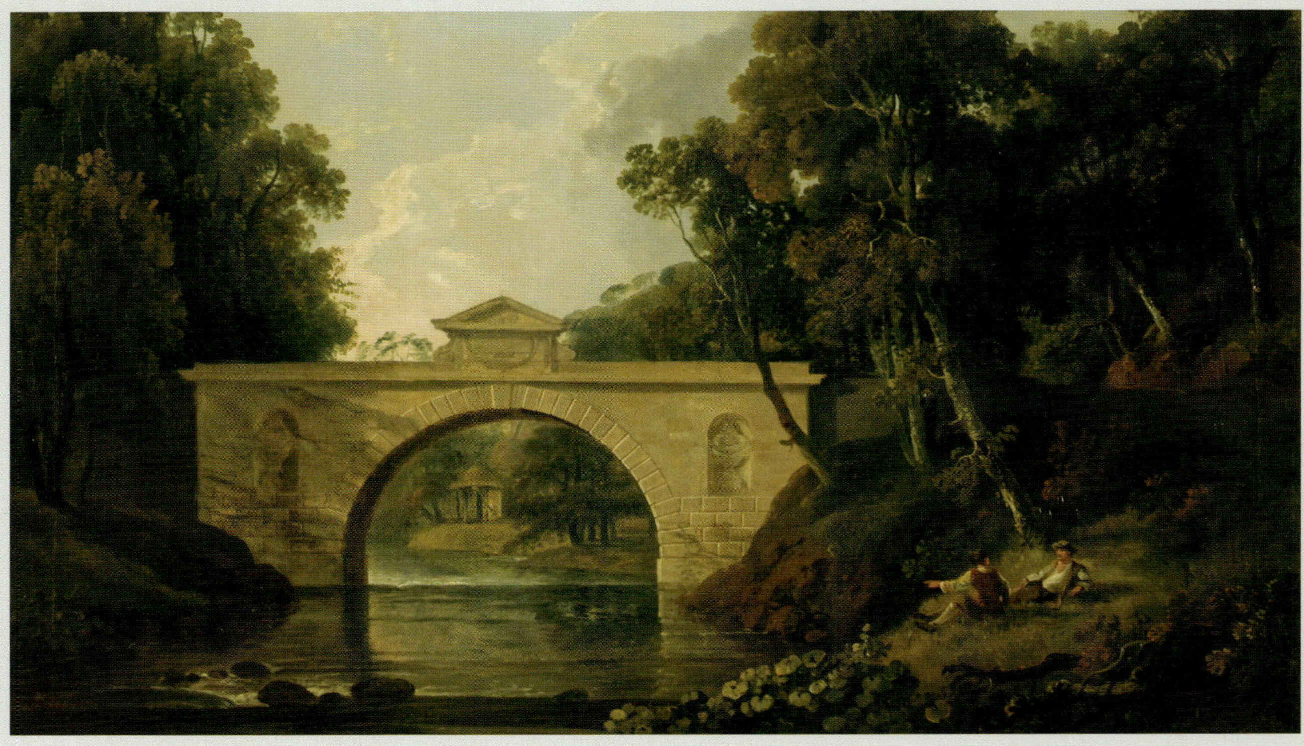

Fig. S3.13
George Barret, *Montagu Bridge, Dalkeith Park*, c. 1770, oil on canvas (BC)

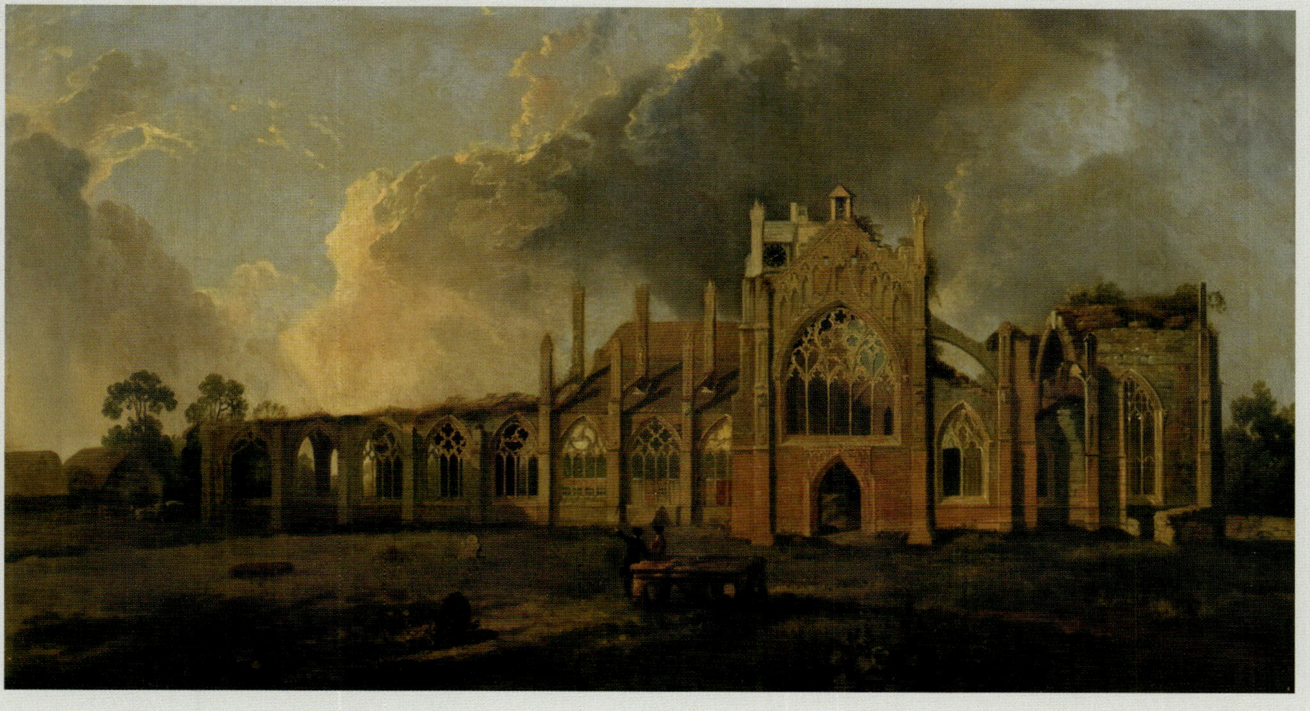

Fig. S3.14
George Barret, *Melrose Abbey*, c. 1770, oil on canvas (BC)

(Fox 2009, 424–426) (Figs S3.15 and S3.16). Although the back-breaking, dirty work of extraction is bypassed in these pictures, the ensemble does take the viewer through the rest of the industrial process, from the dressing of the crude ore by young boys to its sieving and washing, its smelting, to the weighing of finished lead ingots under the beady eye of the head clerk and Hopetoun's bailie. Given that Allan was the son of an Alloa shore-master (who supervised the coal exports of the Mar Erskines), it is not surprising that the artist was closely attentive to the rigours of the work, noting the toxicity of the fumes during the smelting process, for instance, even if its harsher aspects are glossed over. Estate views as much as scenes of 'everyday life', Allan's Leadhills pictures, with their orderly environment and well-fed workers, project an image of good management and paternalism. Much as with the respectable rustics of Paul Sandby's study of an open-air fulling mill (see Fig. S1.11), made the best part of forty years earlier, the figures embody the virtues of industry and productivity. But, in a way only enhanced by the rather theatrical, stage-set-like settings, Allan's tableaux also elicited a degree of sentiment in the viewer that was seldom if ever seen in earlier portrayals of manual labour. Like his study of colliers returning from work, the painted denizens of Leadhills might be seen in the light of a contemporary taste for ordinary scenes and events, often of labour or suffering, as occasions for the polite man or woman of feeling to reflect on (Fig. S3.17).

Scenic prospect hunters in search of dramatic spectacle were as drawn to sites of industry as to natural or designed landscapes, as the presence of those genteel spectators in Allan's scene of children pounding ore indicates. Though he is often thought to be dismissive or at least ambivalent about the landscape of improvement, sites of industry were features of William Gilpin's vision of the picturesque. During his *petit tour* of 1776, he was particularly admiring of 'the great forges of the Carron-works' near Falkirk, finding 'the volumes of smoke, the spiry flames, and the suffocating heat of the glimmering air' of iron manufacture 'wonderfully affecting'. When viewed by night, it was 'inconceivably grand'. Unlike the well-dressed and well-scrubbed workers of Allan's scenes of lead processing in the hillsides of south Lanarkshire, Gilpin was fired by the more 'horrid ideas' prompted by the sight of 'black, sooty figures wheeling about',

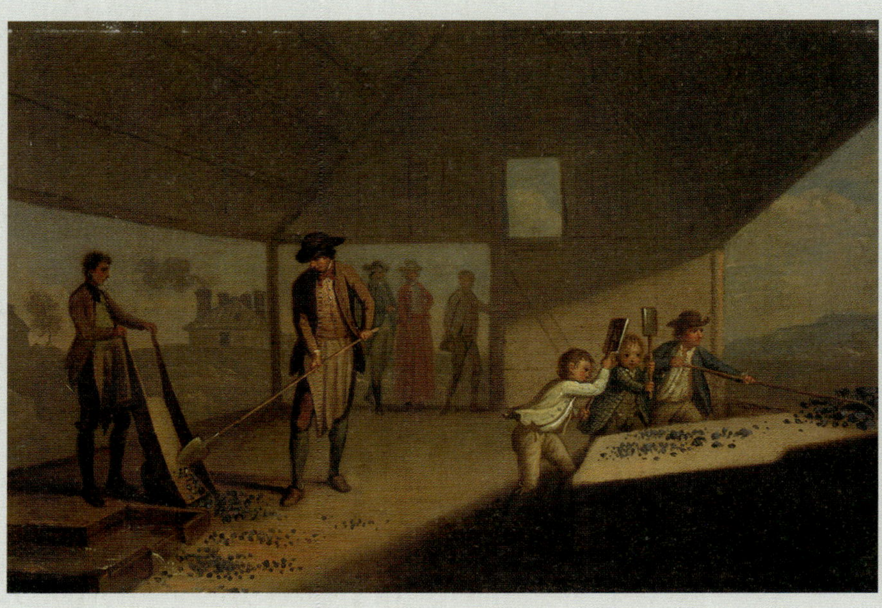

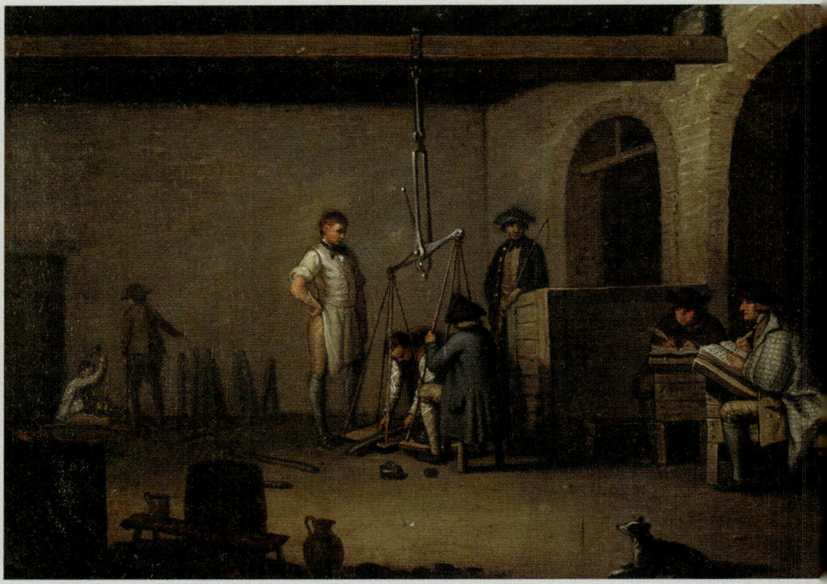

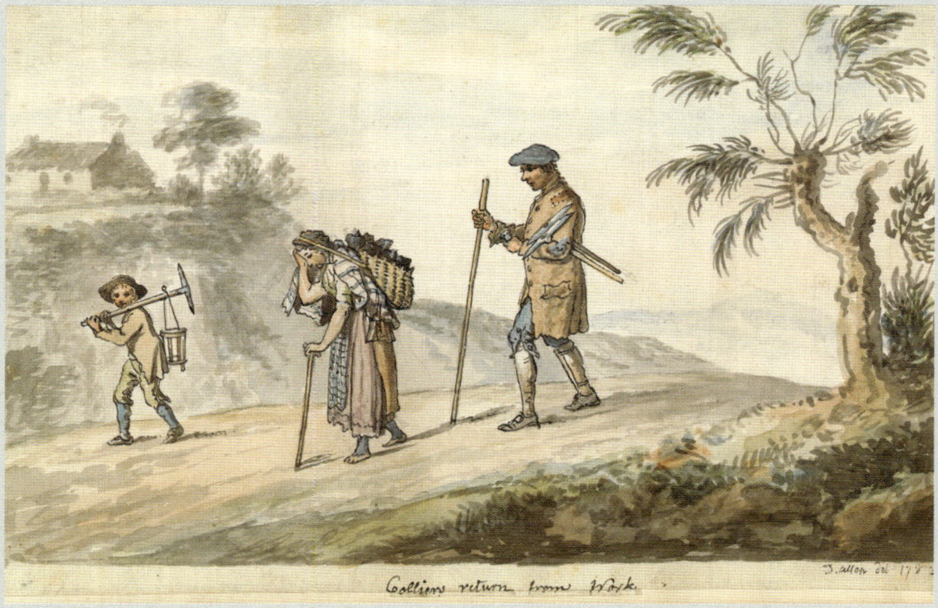

Fig. S3.15
Top left. David Allan, *Lead Processing at Leadhills: Pounding the Ore*, c. 1780s, oil on canvas (NGS NG 2834)

Fig. S3.16
Top right. David Allan, *Lead Processing at Leadhills: Weighing the Lead Bars*, c. 1780s, oil on canvas (NGS NG 2837)

Fig. S3.17
Above. David Allan, *Colliers Returning from Work*, c. 1780s, watercolour pasted in Allan Ramsay, *The Gentle Shepherd, a Pastoral Comedy*, Glasgow, 1796 (GLA ASC Bh14-x.13)

especially as they were illuminated now and again by flickers of 'molten metal glowing hot' (Gilpin 1789b, I, 77–78).

David Allan was among those to latch on to the burgeoning revival of interest in Scottish customs, which was now taking organised form with the recent foundation of Highland Societies in Edinburgh and London. Presided over by a powerful cadre of Scottish peers, and dedicated to ensuring 'remembrance of the Martial Achievements, the Characteristic Dress, or the Language, the Music, or the Customs of their Ancestors', the London body (founded in 1778) had considerable influence, playing an instrumental role in securing the repeal of the statutory proscription of forms of Highland dress in 1782 that had been in place since the 'Forty-Five', and lobbying for the return of forfeited Jacobite estates (Sinclair 1813, 1). Its sponsorship would promote the publication of ballads and vernacular poetry as well as written histories and picturesque prints. Allan was among those quick to capitalise on this high-profile interest in Scottish customs and manners. Having travelled to Italy in the mid 1760s, the artist had made a speciality there of scenes of urban and rural lower-class life of a sentimental character, often focused on open-air amusements and moments of carefree celebration. On relocating to Edinburgh in 1780, Allan struck upon the idea of making similarly themed studies of his native countryside, what he went on to describe as 'Groups of the Manners in Scotland which woud be new & entertaining & good for Engraving' (Allan 1780). Translating the festive imagery of his Italian scenes to the Scottish Highlands and Lowlands, Allan portrayed notably elegant figures striking conventional poses, although a variety of local detail – in matters of costume and 'manners' or a taste for traditional music and dance – help lend some credence to the scenes depicted. Working for John, 4th Duke of Atholl, recent president of the London Highland Society, at the time, Allan pointedly set the first of these scenes on the duke's Perthshire estates.

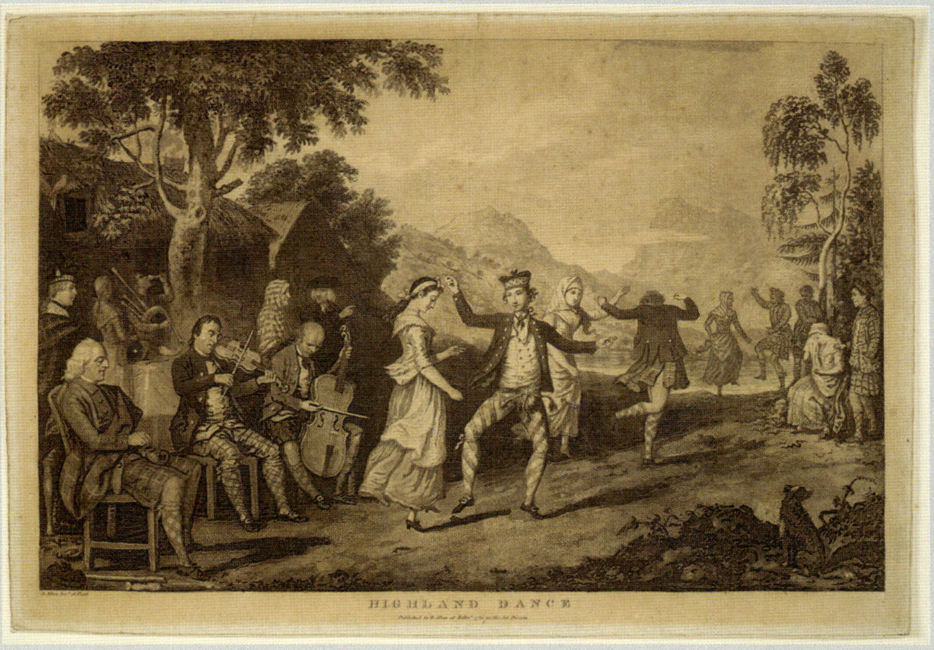

Fig. S3.18
David Allan, *Highland Dance*, published 1783, etching and aquatint (NGS P2765)

Allan's picture of tenant farmers drinking and dancing on the edge of the sweeping parkland of the Atholl policies at Blair is offset by the laborious scenes in the distance: it is as much about the landlord's good stewardship as a display of Highland 'Manners' (Fig. S3.18). By way of encouraging some comparison with his travels on classic ground, in Allan's Highland wedding scene, the folds of plaid wrapping themselves around the protagonists were clearly intended to recall antique drapery (see Fig. S1.21). Yet, however much the artist was concerned to draw such parallels and portray the Highlands as a place which had maintained its connections with ancient tradition, this is no time-locked vision: the modern world has made its presence felt; the women wear fashionable clothes and in Allan's scene of a Highland dance the music is provided by the Duke's fiddler Niel Gow, while the bagpiper takes a break in the background. Such pictures were evidently good sellers: Allan was to go on to produce a series of Highland wedding scenes in this vein. Looking to the work of the modern French master Jean-Baptiste Greuze perhaps, Allan largely eschewed the broad, earthy comedy of Dutch and Flemish scenes of 'common' or 'familiar life' (as they were called) of the previous century in favour of something more refined, where a mix of people from across the social order come together to celebrate this rite of passage, in a dignified image of community, social harmony and moral virtue.

Shortly after his death, Allan was being cast as 'the Scots Hogarth': a painter whose 'characteristic talent' lay 'especially in the ludicrous representation of laughable incidents in low life', his ever 'vigilant eye' falling on the 'eccentric' and 'motley'. Much of this reputation was founded on the sequence of prints the artist had produced for the illustration of a Foulis Press edition of Allan Ramsay's 1725 pastoral comedy *The Gentle Shepherd*, the scenes of Madge and Bauldy's altercations being perhaps the most striking instances of Allan's eye for the droll and 'eccentric' (Brown 1808, II, 629, 630) (Fig. S3.19). The first substantial biography of Allan, attached to an early-nineteenth-century reprint of Ramsay's verse, drew an explicit parallel between the painter and the poet. While they had both drawn on Italian pastoral traditions, the artist and the writer had also been equally concerned to locate their art in a particular, keenly observed place and social milieu. In the words of his biographer, 'with his pencil', the artist had 'kept alive Allan Ramsay's characters, and preserved from change, or decay, their manners, furniture, and accommodations' (Brown 1808, II, 619). This would perhaps imply that the painter was more concerned with cataloguing the quaint or absurd, that which belonged to another time and place, than detailing a disappearing world. If anything, it is an attitude that only becomes more marked in the years after 1800.

Led by David Wilkie, in the generation that followed, a number of artists were to pick up on the narrative and pictorial potential in the imagery of local custom, further transforming what had previously been considered an all-too-lowly, even vulgar, category of pictorial art. Building on Allan's art of feeling, Wilkie in particular treated sociable festivities such as Pitlessie Fair (in a painting of 1804) with an unprecedented degree of

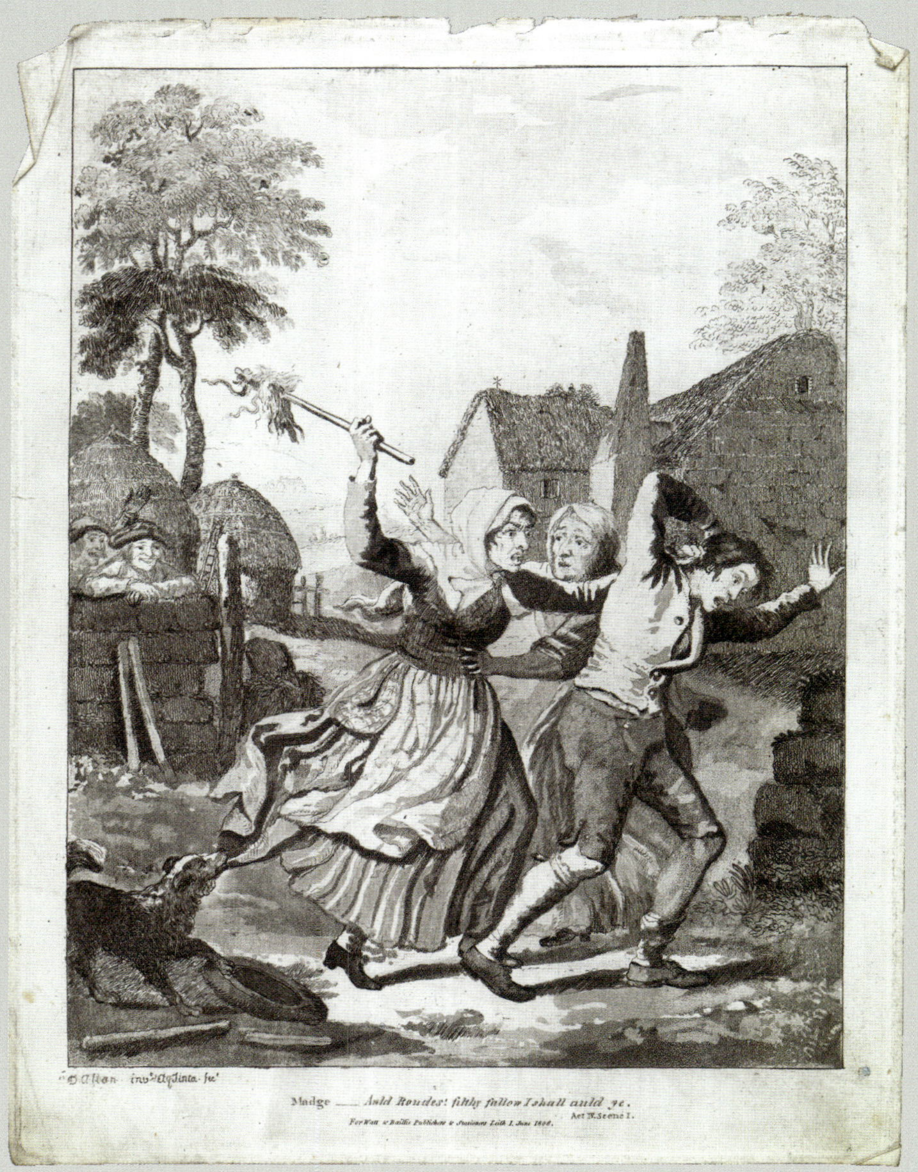

Fig. S3.19
David Allan, 'Madge – Auld Roudes', illustration for Allan Ramsay, *The Gentle Shepherd*, scene 1 act IV, 1788, aquatint (GLAHA:20413)

seriousness, articulating a decidedly ambivalent response to the growing encroachments being made upon customary patterns of the past by improvement (Solkin 2008).

Of course, much as Scotland remained a predominantly rural society, the audiences for Allan's and Wilkie's art were urban ones, cultured, chic and polite. While Wilkie struck out for London, with the exhibition of the showpiece *Pitlessie Fair* at the Royal Academy of Arts leading to a number of prestigious commissions, Allan and other Edinburgh- and Glasgow-based figures by and large looked to appeal to increasingly affluent and culturally aware local audiences. Along the Clyde, for instance, the expansion of Atlantic mercantile activity saw its bankside settlements grow faster than anywhere in the country (see Figs S4.12 and S4.13). Profits from the trade in cotton, sugar and tobacco, as well as other goods and materials, promoted the rise of a local urban élite eager to assert their learning and taste, enlightened credentials and civic pride, investing the proceeds of empire in major public and private building projects that were to transform the physical and social landscape of Scotland's towns and cities. Urban growth and renewal in Scotland, not only in the major centres of Glasgow, Edinburgh and Aberdeen, but in provincial towns like Perth too, dramatised the repudiation of a customary past (Whyte 1999; Harris 2006, 2011a). Sweeping away the cramped and irregular street plans of the past, the modern urban settlement was one of broad, straight thoroughfares, paved and lit, faced with elegant new buildings of brick or stone. In Edinburgh, the contrast between the regular, classicising façades and grid-like planning of the New Town and the densely packed, teetering buildings lining the tangle of narrow closes and streets that made up the Old Town set out the distinction in the starkest terms. Places of genteel assembly, in the form of assembly rooms and theatres, gardens and public walks, were built, not least because any town's claims to civility rested on its capacity to encourage sociability. They were centres of cultural life as much as administrative or economic hubs (Harris 2011b).

Something of this new imagery of politeness underwrites a set of views of Glasgow engraved in and around 1760 by the locally born and trained Robert Paul, a fellow student of Allan at the city's new art academy (Figs S3.20–S3.22). Founded in 1753 by the high-end booksellers and printers Andrew and Robert Foulis, with financial backing from a group of wealthy Glaswegian merchants, the academy was a dedicated 'School for the Art of Design' (Fairfull-Smith 2001). Exemplified by John Gwynn's *Essay of Design*, which had also advocated the foundation of an academy dedicated to the art, the venture embodied a broader fascination with the practical uses of graphic expression and knowledge (Craske 1997). Design was a modern, rational means of organising and planning the world, of ordering and reordering society as well as the environment. With links to the cotton and linen industries, engraving and printing were important to commerce and trade as well as the advancement of the polite arts. For Thomas Pennant, the Foulis brothers were 'good citizens, zealous to promote the welfare and honor of their native place' (Pennant 1771a, 202). Robert Paul's Glasgow prospects gave pictorial expression to these values.

Taken from identifiable stations and co-ordinated by a series of landmarks, Paul's perspectives are all precisely placed. Most adopt a slightly elevated vantage point somewhere on the outskirts of the city, out among the cultivated fields and lush river meadows that fed the growing population. Several of the views pivot around Glasgow Cathedral's lofty spire. In the view of the cathedral from the west, a line of carefully cropped and evenly planted trees denotes 'Fir Park': a detail that adds to the sense of design and management at work in the landscape as a whole. Taken together, Paul's scenes chart the sense of orderly urban expansion and commercial progress. Set against a backdrop that relates the history of the city's development and expansion through its architecture, and populated by gentlemen on horseback and the urbanised polite as well as rural labourers, the series conveys an image of a community united by its past and its modernising present.

Working some half a century later, the locally born artist John Knox created striking views of Glasgow's public buildings and spaces that explored the city's new, further radically transformed modern face and its increasing social complexity (Figs S3.23–S3.25). They convey an image of civic confidence, of a commercially minded city grown affluent through Atlantic trade: Old Glasgow Cross is a bustling thoroughfare, Glasgow Green a place of suburban pastoral. Shown in shooting perspective, Knox's view westwards along Trongate from Glasgow Cross projects a decorous, regularised vision of the city (Fig. S3.23). It grants a certain coherence to the otherwise socially diverse and fragmented panorama of the street. Some are figures drawn from the tradition of urban street Cries that Paul Sandby had turned to in his studies of the denizens of post-Rebellion Edinburgh's coffeehouses, streets and fairs (see Fig. S1.16a–c), but others are clearly observed, characters and personalities Knox might expect a local audience to recognise. Here he was fashioning a distinctly local variation on pictorial tradition.

This is a quality also evident in Knox's scenes of urban leisure

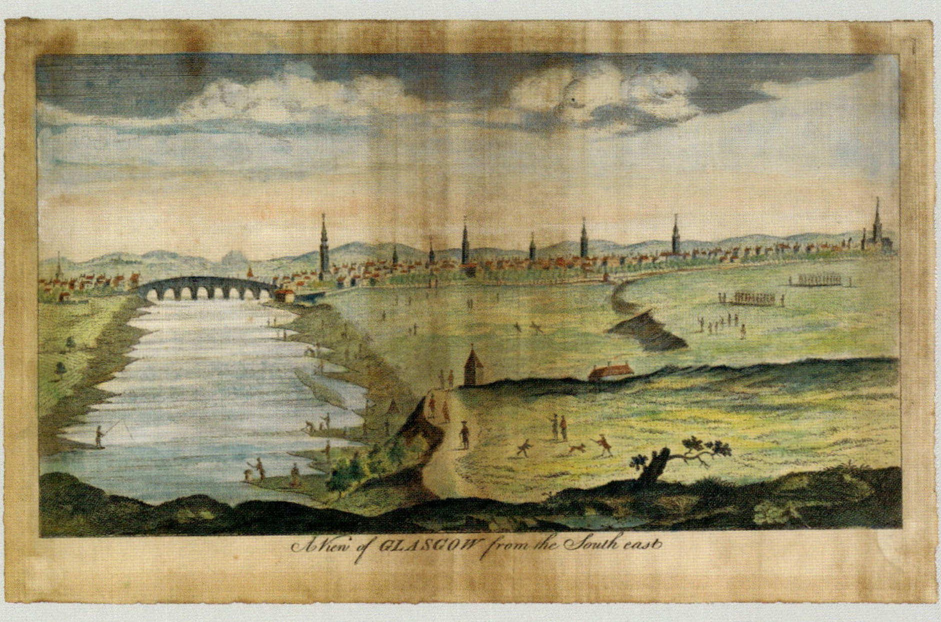

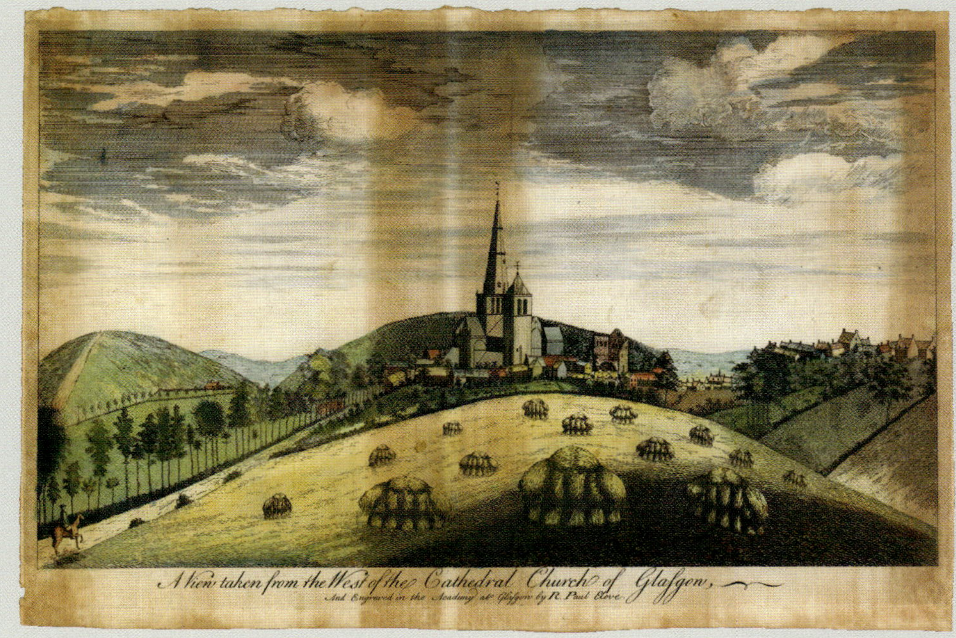

Fig. S3.20
Top. Robert Paul, *A View of Glasgow from the South East*, 1760, hand-coloured engraving (GLAHA:51734)

Fig. S3.21
Above. Robert Paul, *View taken from the West of the Cathedral Church of Glasgow*, c. 1754–1758, hand-coloured engraving (GLAHA:17698)

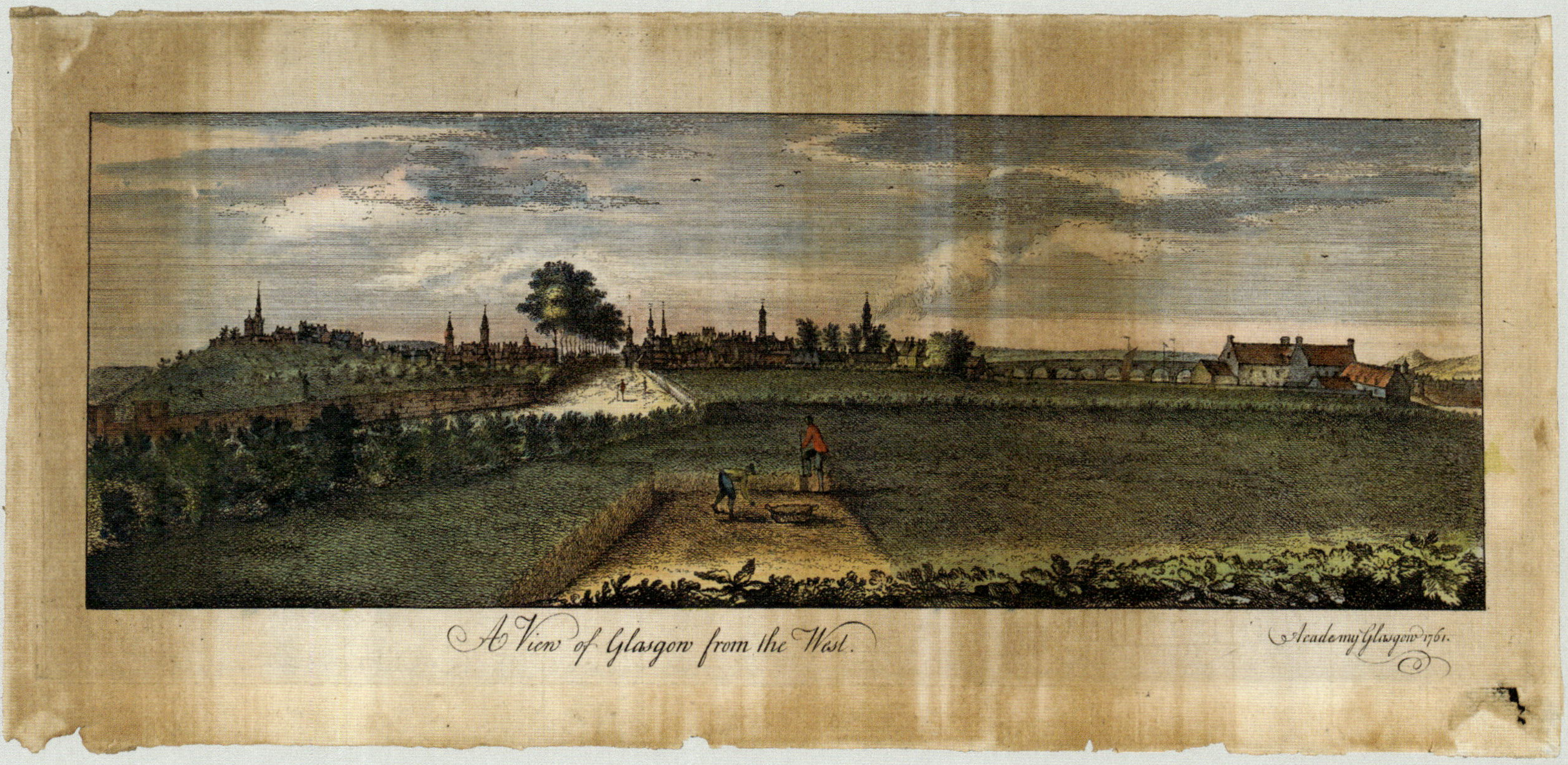

Fig. S3.22
Right. Robert Paul, *A View of Glasgow from the West*, 1761, hand-coloured engraving (GLAHA:17699)

Fig. S3.23
Opposite. John Knox, *Old Glasgow Cross* or *The Trongate*, 1826, oil on canvas (GMC 1352)

Fig. S3.24
Overleaf. John Knox, *Glasgow Fair*, c. 1819–22, oil on canvas (GMC 3718)

and tourism on the northern banks of the Clyde. Glasgow Green was the focus of a major civic improvement scheme at the time Knox was working. Overseen by the local property developer, public official and statistician James Cleland, the fashioning of a modern amenity landscape out of the marshy riverbank involved large-scale earthworks, planting and architectural schemes. '[B]ounded on the south by the beautiful windings of the river' and 'on the west by the Grecian Doric portico of the Public Offices', the Green was unrivalled in its 'picturesque effect and general usefulness', claimed Cleland (1820, 49). Looking out along those 'beautiful windings of the river', and a chain of towering civic landmarks, Knox's view of a regatta connects the progress of the city with that of the Clyde (Fig. S3.25). It is an eminently polite audience that has gathered on the Green to watch the spectacle, socially as much as physically separate from the crowd seated on the opposite bank. Not all of the activities staged on the Green maintained such distinctions, however.

Taking a cue perhaps from Wilkie's innovations, in his view of Glasgow's annual fair, Knox offers up a wry, gently satirical view on the progress of the modern world and its absorption of what had once been distinct or 'eccentric' (Fig. S3.24). In this painting the city's ancient civic 'saturnalia', which had historically been an at times riotous, temporary marketplace for the sale of cattle and horses, is shown colonised by all manner of diversions (King 1987, 157–160). Gaudy billboards advertise the attractions, displays of acrobatics, wild animals and a forthcoming panorama. Booths and sideshows stage various amusements. Stalls sell alcohol and street food. A crowd mills around a cock-fight. Campaigners for abolition compete with hawkers. They all tout for the attention of a vast crowd of fairgoers, some enraptured, others drunk or bored, drawn from across the social spectrum, from peddlers and pickpockets to soldiers in their regimentals, from the down-and-out to the well-to-do, and all every bit part of the spectacle as the entertainments on offer. Looking along the frieze of figures snaking across the foreground, in a gesture to the fair's carnivalesque past perhaps, as well as

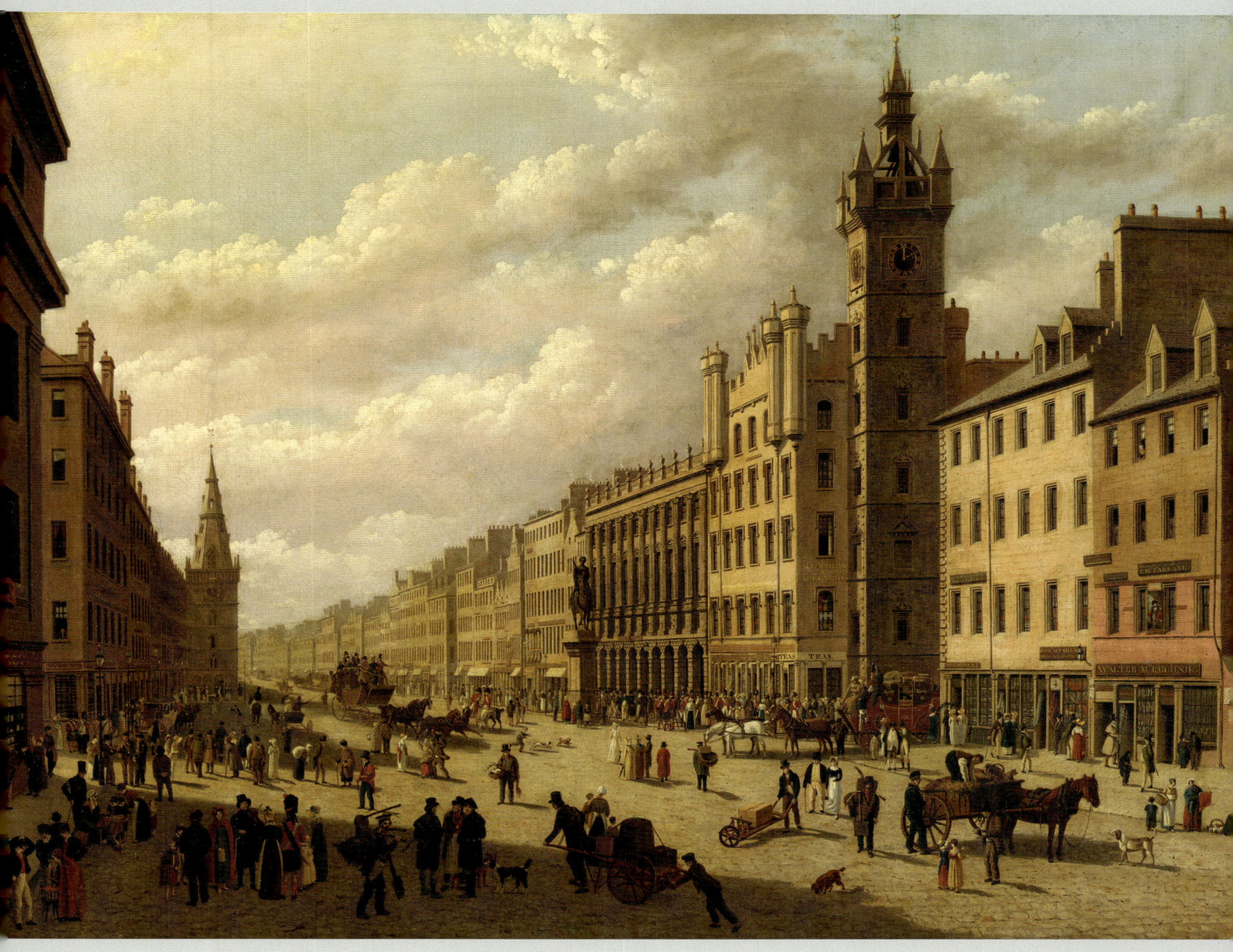

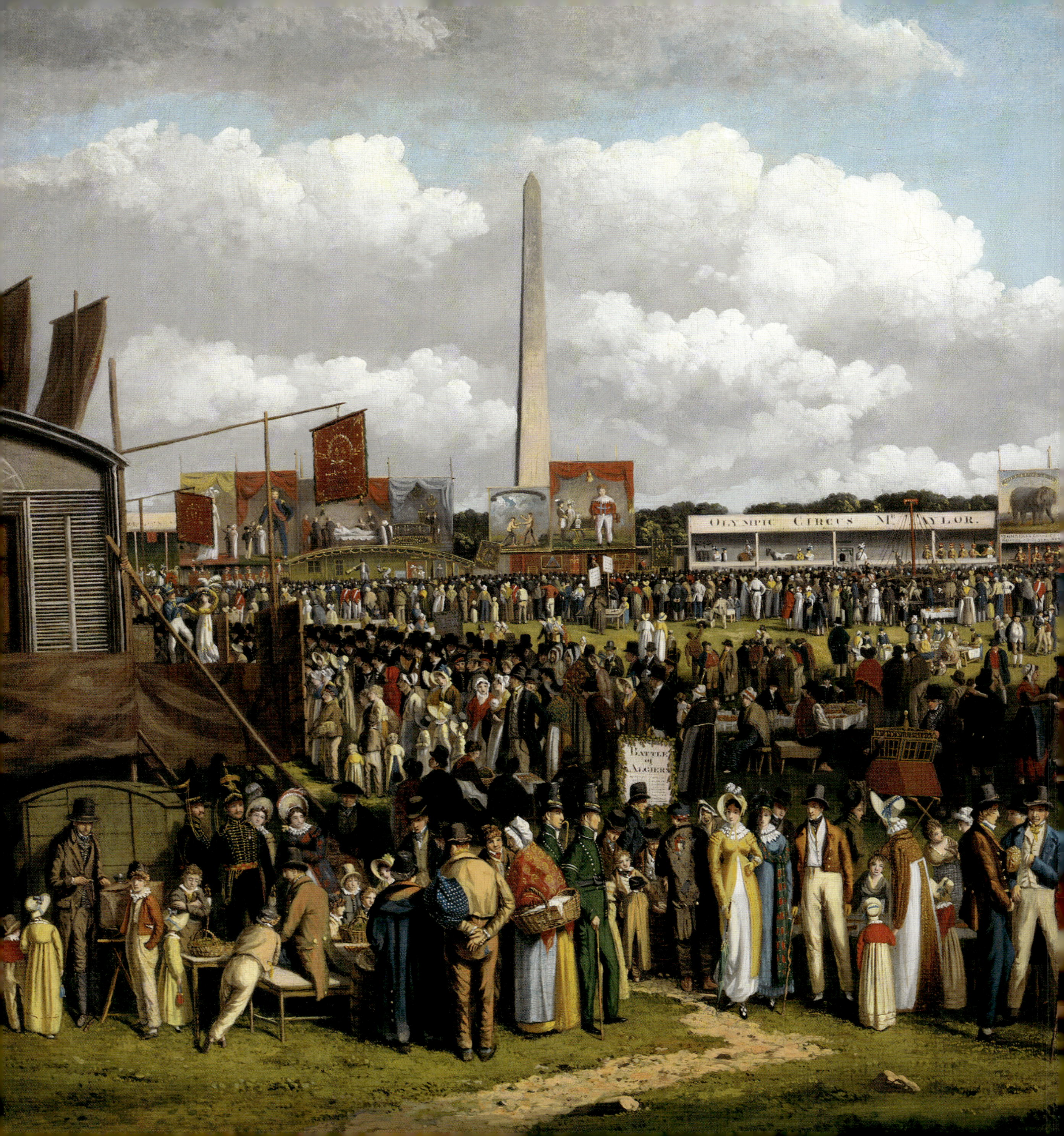
OLYMPIC CIRCUS
BATTLE of ALGIERS

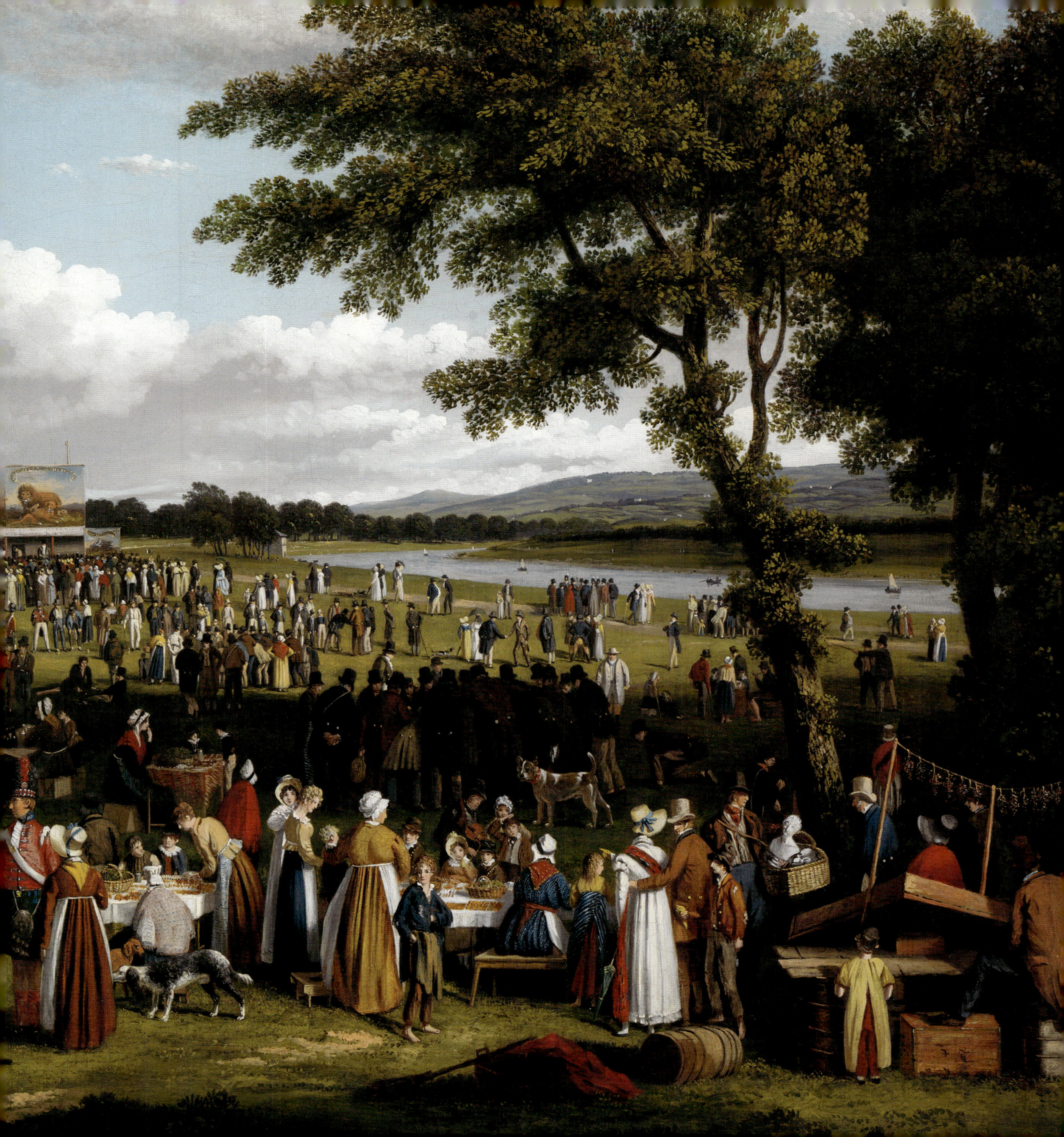

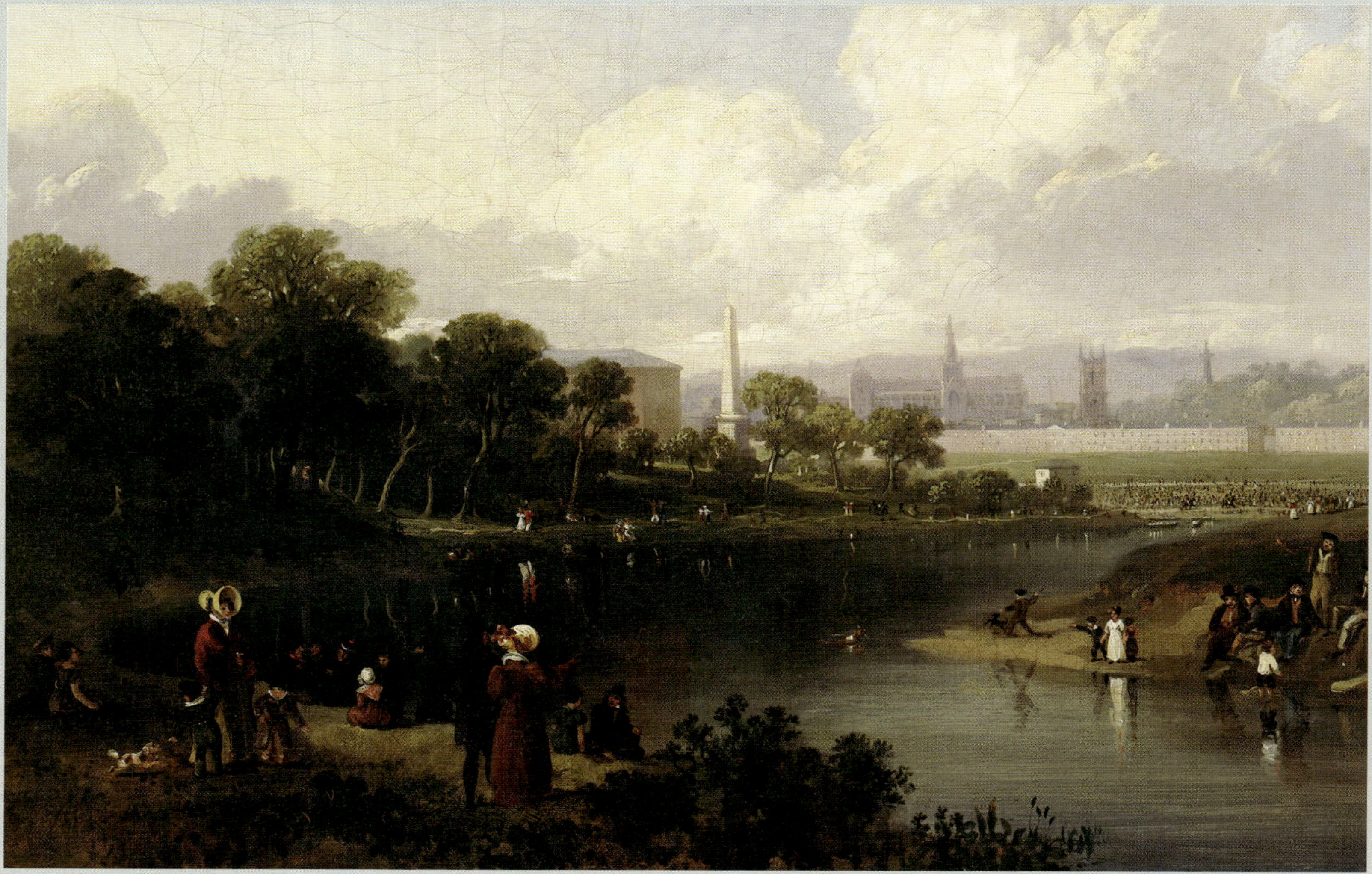

Fig. S3.25
Attributed to John Knox, *Regatta on Glasgow Green*, c. 1820, oil on canvas (PC)

the audiences the artist probably observed, part of the 'fun' is in seeing men and women of careless squalor and ostentatious fashion rubbing shoulders. Unbridled licence of this kind was not necessarily solely comic, however. Taking place in the shadow of the Green's commemorative obelisk to Nelson, the fair makes for a form of patriotic spectacle, the crowd enjoying the historic liberties secured by the nation's military triumphs.

By the time that Knox was painting the ongoing improvement of the modern city, new forms of labour organisation and technology as well as the rise of radical voices were reshaping the world. Thanks to the new canals, roads and other transport links, it was a better connected one, but if anything more not less fragmented, murky and inchoate. Despite (or perhaps because of) their very scale and visibility, quite how things had altered was difficult to pin down. It was trickier still to imagine what they might become in the future. While some trusted in forms of documentary record, as the words and pictures assembled in this section demonstrate, authors and artists turned increasingly to the world of the imagination to try to identify and understand Scotland's role in the new century and ask what was distinct about the people and places met with along both its 'old ways' and its new roads.

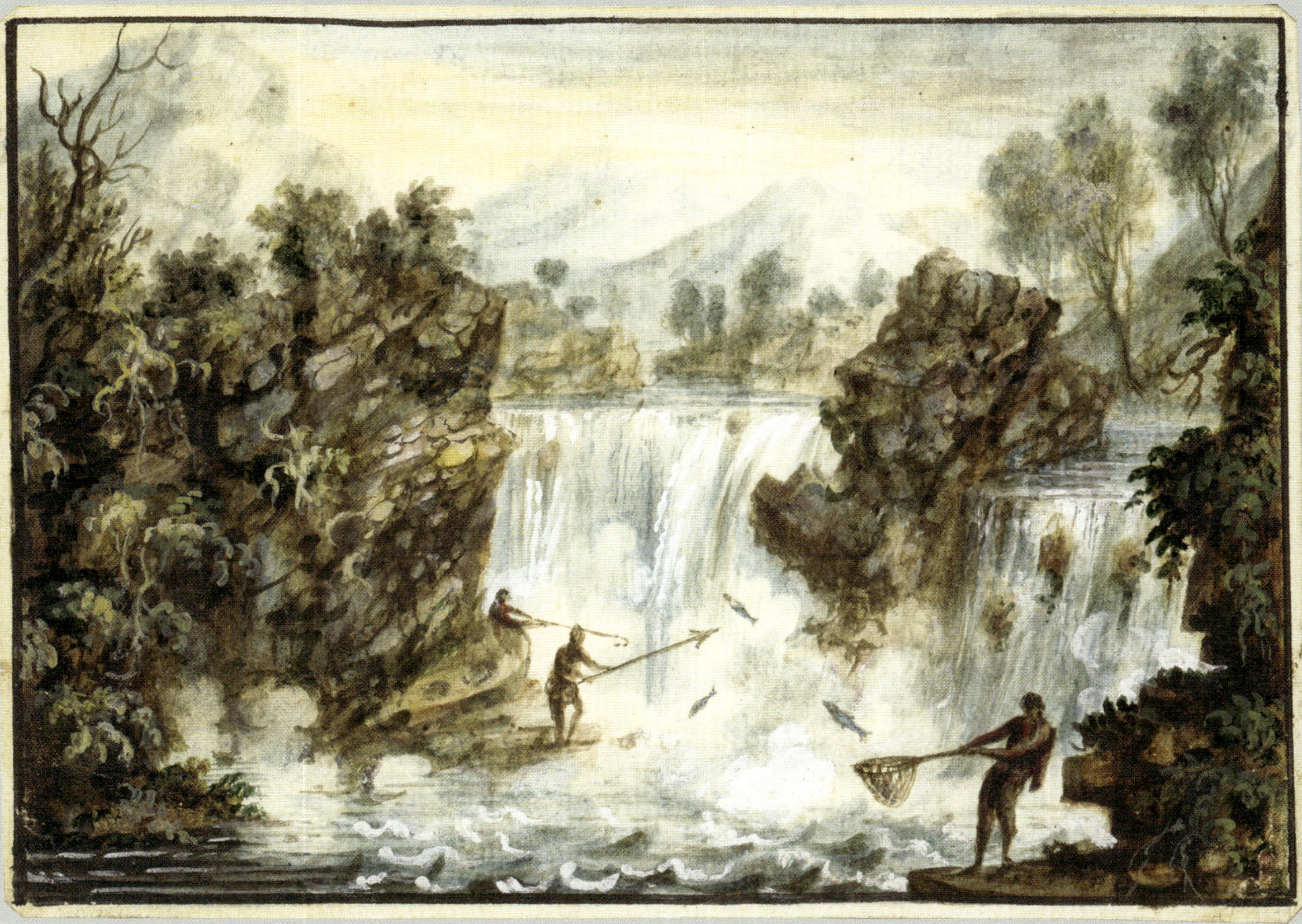

Fig. S3.26
Charles Cordiner, *Salmon Leistering in Glenmoreistoon*, c. 1780s, watercolour in 'Cordiner's drawings' album (BM 1943,0707.1-133)

This striking view of the Falls of the River Moriston, near Loch Ness, was engraved by Peter Mazell for inclusion in Charles Cordiner's *Remarkable Ruins, and Romantic Prospects, of North Britain*, where it accompanied an account of a local custom of 'some amusement', whereby 'young lads, furnished with pikes, and poles with large hooks on them, make an advantageous recreation of catching the salmon which attempt to spring up the Fall: unconscious of its insurmountable height, they repeat these unavailing efforts, until some of those, who have attained dexterity in the art of striking them with the dart, will in a few hours bring ten or a dozen of them to the bank' (Cordiner 1788, unpaginated). Met within the pages of Cordiner's book, such local practices were made part of a distinctly picturesque vision of the country, part of its historic heritage and 'romance'.

CHAPTER FOUR

Roads, Bridges and Designed Landscapes on the Highland Circuit

'There is Much Beauty, Uniting a Secluded Rural Character to the Wildness of Mountain Scenery'

Christopher Dingwall

In 1723 some three hundred members of the nobility and gentry of Scotland gathered together to form 'The Honourable the Society for the Improvement in the Knowledge of Agriculture in Scotland', an initiative described by T.C. Smout as a 'patriotic undertaking' and a 'crusade against ignorance' (Smout 2012). Among its members were several prominent Highland landlords, including James Murray, 2nd Duke of Atholl, and John Campbell, 2nd Earl of Breadalbane, together with Lewis Colquhoun of Luss, Sir William Murray of Ochtertyre and John Farquharson of Invercauld (Maxwell 1743). It was in the following year that General George Wade first came north to supervise the building of the military roads which began the process of making the Highlands accessible for wheeled transport, and which went on to serve as the basis for further road development in the second half of the eighteenth century, opening the way for trade and tourism.

Among the members of the Honourable Society were other pioneering 'improvers', and the enclosure and landscaping of their estates served as an inspiration for others. These men included noteworthy Scottish tree planters such as John Hay, 4th Marquis of Tweeddale, Thomas Hamilton, 6th Earl of Haddington, and Sir Archibald Grant of Monymusk. It is surely noteworthy that Hay had been admitted to the Order of Free Gardeners in 1715, and that the Honourable Society's members also included the Edinburgh nurseryman and garden designer William Boutcher and the influential London-based garden designer and author Stephen Switzer. Switzer, through his book *Ichnographia Rustica*, published in 1718, was a promoter of what he described as 'rural and extensive gardening' in which he saw landscaping extending well beyond the bounds of the formal garden (Switzer 1718; Brogden 2017). Sir John Clerk of Penicuik, another member of the Honourable Society much involved in the enclosure and planting of his estate south of Edinburgh, was the author of a didactic poem entitled *The Country Seat*, written in 1727, though never published.[1] This, too, extolled the beauties of the wider landscape, anticipating the taste for wilder and more natural scenery which developed during the mid eighteenth century, and which had become all the rage for tourists by the end of the century.

Whether or not they were influenced by the likes of Boutcher, Switzer and their successors, many of Scotland's landowners sought to expand their estates in the later eighteenth century, with a view to increasing what Switzer called the 'quiet enjoyment of rural delights', a process of change which sometimes involved remodelling the landscape by diverting roads, building bridges and creating new settlements. In this chapter, evidence from a variety of sources is used to throw light on this process, as it affected the four great designed landscapes that lay on what Thomas Pennant referred to as the *petit tour* of the Scottish Highlands which developed in the late eighteenth century – those of Inveraray Castle, Taymouth Castle, Blair Castle and Dunkeld House (Pennant 1774a [1769], 91).

INVERARAY CASTLE

A traveller following Pennant's *petit tour* clockwise approached Inveraray Castle by way of Loch Lomond and the Rest and Be Thankful, entering the extensive Inveraray designed landscape where the military road crossed the River Fyne. Ian Lindsay and Mary Cosh describe in detail the building of the elegant Garron Bridge in 1749, a quasi-military project which involved General Wade's successor Major William Caulfeild, by then Inspector of Roads and Bridges in North Britain, together with the architect John Adam and the English architect Roger Morris who, with Adam, also designed the so-called Watch-Tower on Dun na Cuaiche, overlooking the castle and its policies. This small building, with its spectacular overview of the castle, its extensive and well-planted designed landscape and Loch Fyne, soon became the principal goal for visitors to Inveraray (Lindsay and Cosh 1973, 125–130). A typical description of the Inveraray landscape is to be found in John Thomson's *Traveller's Guide through Scotland and its Islands*, published in 1818:

> Having seen the castle, the traveller walks through the parks, and crosses the Aray over a very elegant bridge. He now pants for a more enlarged prospect, and the insulated hill of Dunichoich, rising as it were behind the castle, and which has so long stared him in the face, affords him the means . . . On the summit a square tower is erected, from which there is a most extensive prospect. He next visits the Vale of Essachossen, to which he is conducted through a long and dark avenue of aged elms; at the extremity of this vale there is a fine cascade. (Thomson 1818, II, 11–12)

It was in 1744, after inheriting the title from his older brother John, that Archibald Campbell, 3rd Duke of Argyll, began to put into effect plans to remove the Old Town of Inveraray from the shadow of the castle to a new site on the Gallows Foreland Point, a small promontory a short distance to the south, out of sight of the castle. The location of the New Town to the east

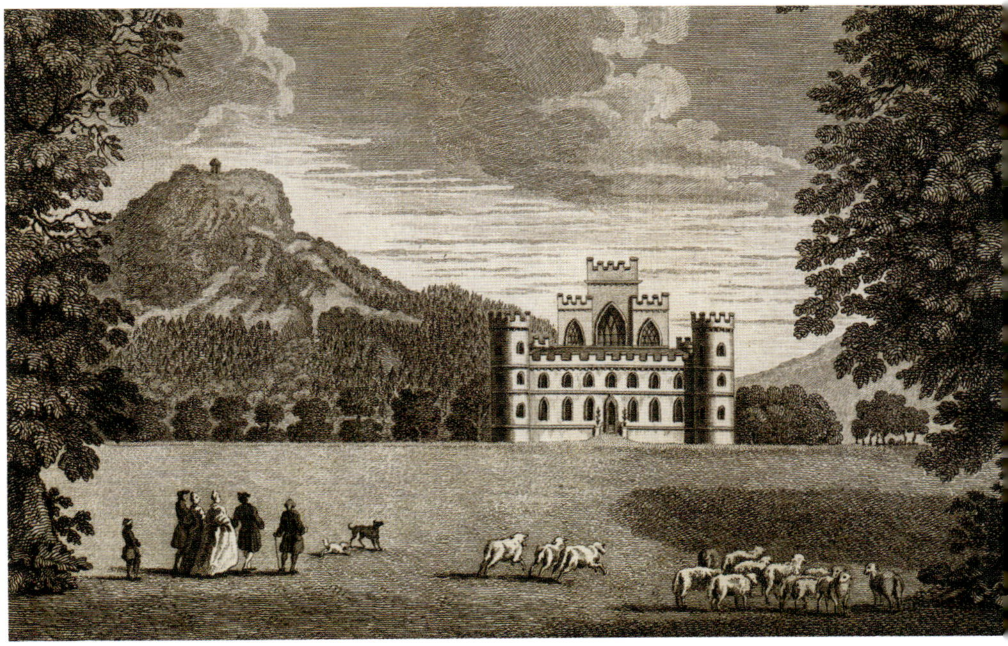

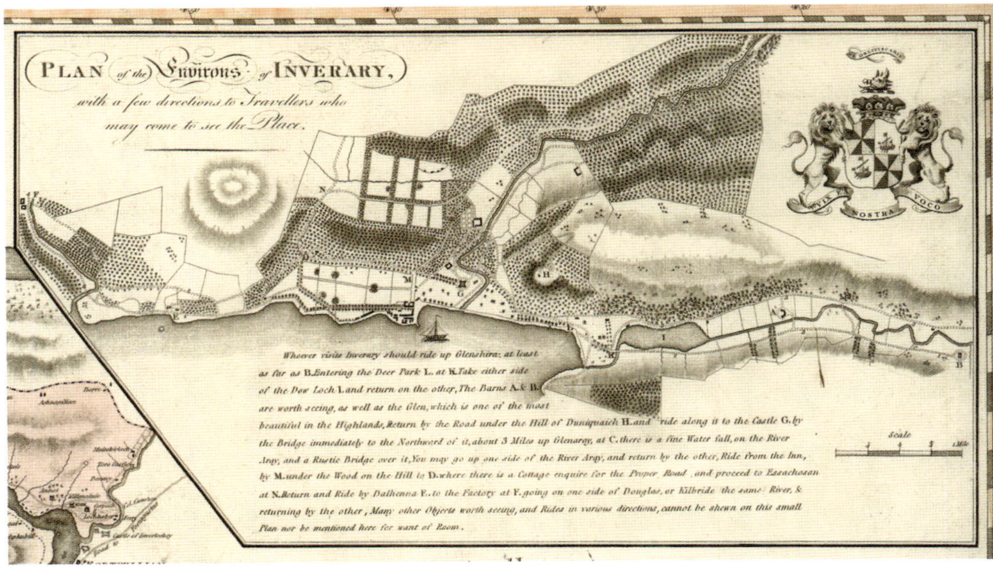

Fig. C4.1
Top. P.C. Canot after Moses Griffith, 'Inverary Castle', engraving in Thomas Pennant, *A Tour in Scotland and Voyage to the Hebrides MDCCLXXII: Part II*, Vol. 2 (London, 1790), plate XVI (GLA ASC Mu6-d.9)

Fig. C4.2
Above. George Langlands, 'Plan of the Environs of Inveraray', inset (detail) on *This Map of Argyllshire*, 1801 (NLS EMS.s.326)

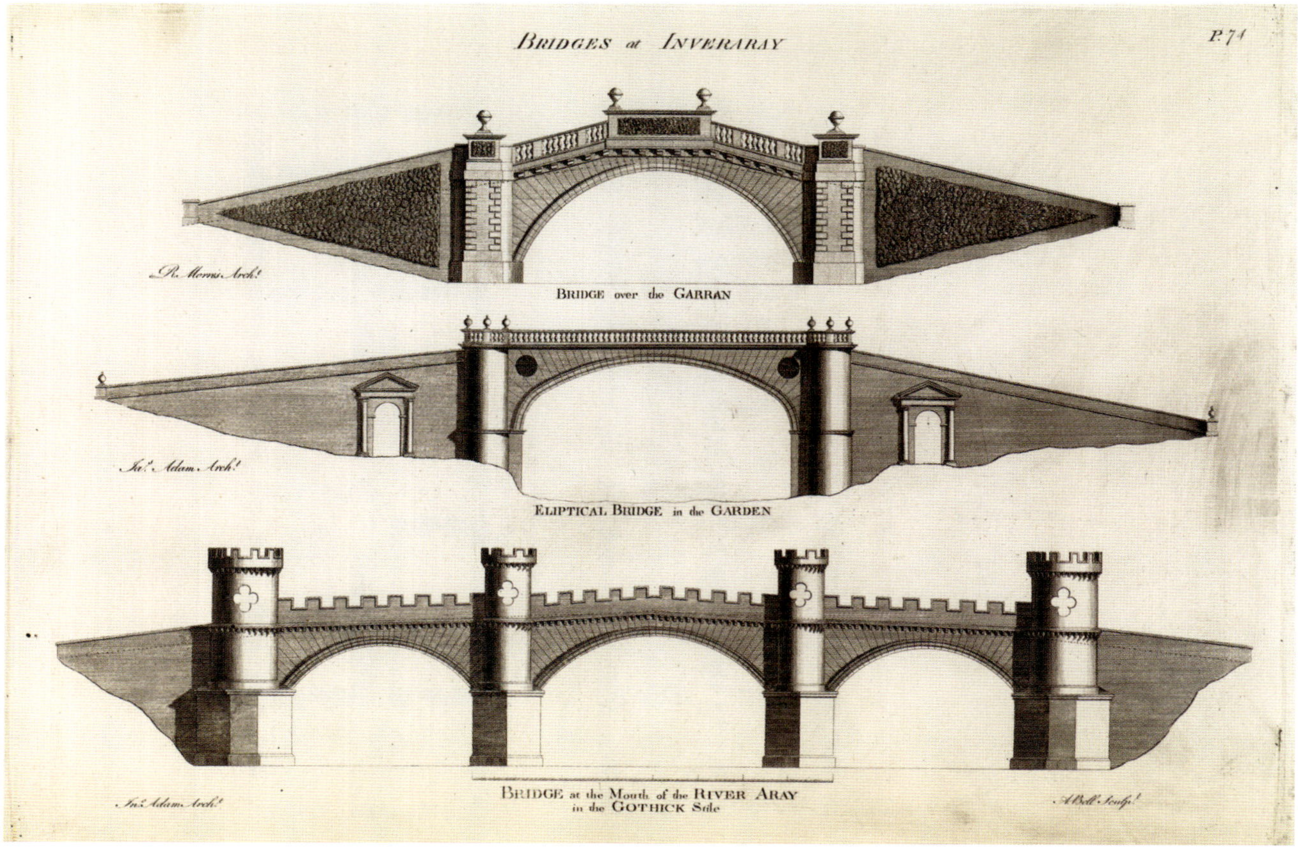

Fig. C4.3
Andrew Bell after William Adam, 'Bridges at Inveraray', engraving in *Vitruvius Scoticus*, first published 1812, pl. 74 (GLA ASC Sp Coll e11)

of the Fisherland Avenue served to emphasise its separation from the expanded policies. To put some distance between travellers and the castle, a westwards diversion of the road approaching the town from the north by way of Glen Aray was also necessary. However, the building of the new roads and bridges did not meet with universal approval: some commentators felt that they were being made for the duke's convenience alone – a complaint dismissed by Lord President of the Court of Session, Duncan Forbes of Culloden, who noted 'how much in the wrong some people were who endeavoured to oppose the new Road, a thing absolutely necessary & usefull both for the Crown & the Subjects' (Lindsay and Cosh 1973, 146–147).

Incorporated into John Adam's design of the New Town of Inveraray was a new inn for the convenience of travellers, intended to replace the cluster of ale houses in the Old Town. While the circuit judge Alexander Lord Auchinleck considered that the inn 'woud in another place be called a palace and have everything good', and J.S. Bailey 'found here not only convenience but elegance' (Lindsay and Cosh 1973, 157 and n.39, 272 and n.68), their view was not shared by Robert Burns during his brief visit in 1787, when he was evidently snubbed by the innkeeper John Frazer, an experience that prompted the poet's celebrated epigram:

> Who'er he be that sojourns here,
> I pity much his case,
> Unless he comes to wait upon
> The Lord their God, his Grace.
> There's naething here but Highland pride,
> And Highland scab and hunger:
> If providence has sent me here,
> 'Twas surely in his anger. (Leask 2014, 136)

After passing picturesque island-studded Loch Awe, the onward journey from Inveraray took the traveller via Dalmally and Tyndrum to Killin, a passage of some 30 miles through scenery lacking in variety, though nonetheless enjoyed by the artist Joseph Farington in 1801 for the interplay of sunlight with the clouds and the surrounding hills 'so as to render the "Landscape of the Desert" sublime' (Farington 1978–84, V, 1655). By the time of Farington's visit, Dalmally, Tyndrum and Killin boasted coaching inns providing accommodation and stabling for travellers, all rated by him in his journal as 'excellent' in spite of the damning account of the inn at Killin given by Sarah Murray five years earlier, a description for which she had to apologise on a later visit (Farington 1978–84, V, 1656; Murray 1799, 80).

Farington reported that from 1791 until 1793 the innkeepers had experimented with provision of chaises for the use of tourists, but were forced to abandon this initiative because of lack of business. While he commented favourably on the mutton that he had at Killin, which he considered to be 'better than I remember ever having tasted, preferable in my opinion to Venison', he also observed that there was no bread to be had, owing to the distance of the inns from suppliers (Farington 1978–84, V, 1656). Things do not appear to have improved much by 1818, when the English poet John Keats passed by Loch Awe in the course of his estimated one-thousand-mile trek on foot and horseback, observing that 'we have lost the sight of white bread entirely', and that he was sickened by having to survive on a diet of 'nothing but eggs all day' (Walker 1992, 187).

East of Killin, there was a choice of two roads running the length of Loch Tay, that on the north side of the loch 'with the habitations of the natives prettily grouped along the sides of the hill . . . the opposite side of the lake is less populous and less fertle, yet from the patches of cornland and frequent woods, exhibits a most beautiful view' (Pennant 1790 [1772], II, 22).

TAYMOUTH CASTLE

The next focus of interest for tourists on the Highland circuit was Taymouth Castle, at the east end of Loch Tay. Here the public road ran along the foot of the Braes of Taymouth to the south of the castle, dividing the parkland from the earl's 'Surprise' terraced walk which afforded northward views over the Taymouth policies. A line drawn on Thomas Winter's *Plan of Taymouth* shows that, as early as 1754, a new alignment had been proposed to divert the public highway to the south, further up the Braes and out of sight of the castle, though it took until 1788 for this to be finalised and adopted. In the 1820s this diversion was still meeting with sustained opposition from a group of Strathtay landowners led by Captain Robertson of Edradynate, who claimed that the new road was too steep for traffic, and who petitioned for the road to be returned to its original line. This matter eventually led to a court case in 1823, which dismissed their complaint.[2]

Although the River Tay had been spanned at Aberfeldy in 1733 by William Adam's Tay Bridge, now commonly referred to as Wade's Bridge, there were evidently problems with the line of the military road that ran north and west from there. Sir Neil Menzies had obstructed a section of the road near Weem, there was a risk of flooding of that section of the road, and the Bridge of Comrie over the Keltneyburn was in a ruinous state. Consequently, beginning in September 1771, a group of the larger landowners in the area supported a subscription established by the Earl of Breadalbane for the building of a new bridge at Kenmore to replace the existing ferry, 'being fully sensible of the great utility a bridge cross the Tay at Kenmore will be to the County in general, and to the adjacent Countries in particular'.[3] With additional subscriptions from smaller landowners and the earl's tenants, work began on the building of the bridge to a design by architect John Baxter, possibly assisted by civil engineer John Smeaton, whose Perth Bridge had been completed in that same year. An inscription on the Kenmore bridge records the gift by the Crown of £1,000 sterling taken from the funds of the Annexed Estates. Consequently, in the course of his second tour of Scotland in 1772, Thomas Pennant was witness to the building of the bridge:

> Cross the Tay on a temporary bridge, just below the discharge from the lake. A most elegant bridge is now constructing in this place under the direction of captain Archibald Campbell, at the expence of Lord Breadalbane, consisting of three large arches; and a smaller one on each side, in case of floods.
> (Pennant 1790 [1772], II, 28)

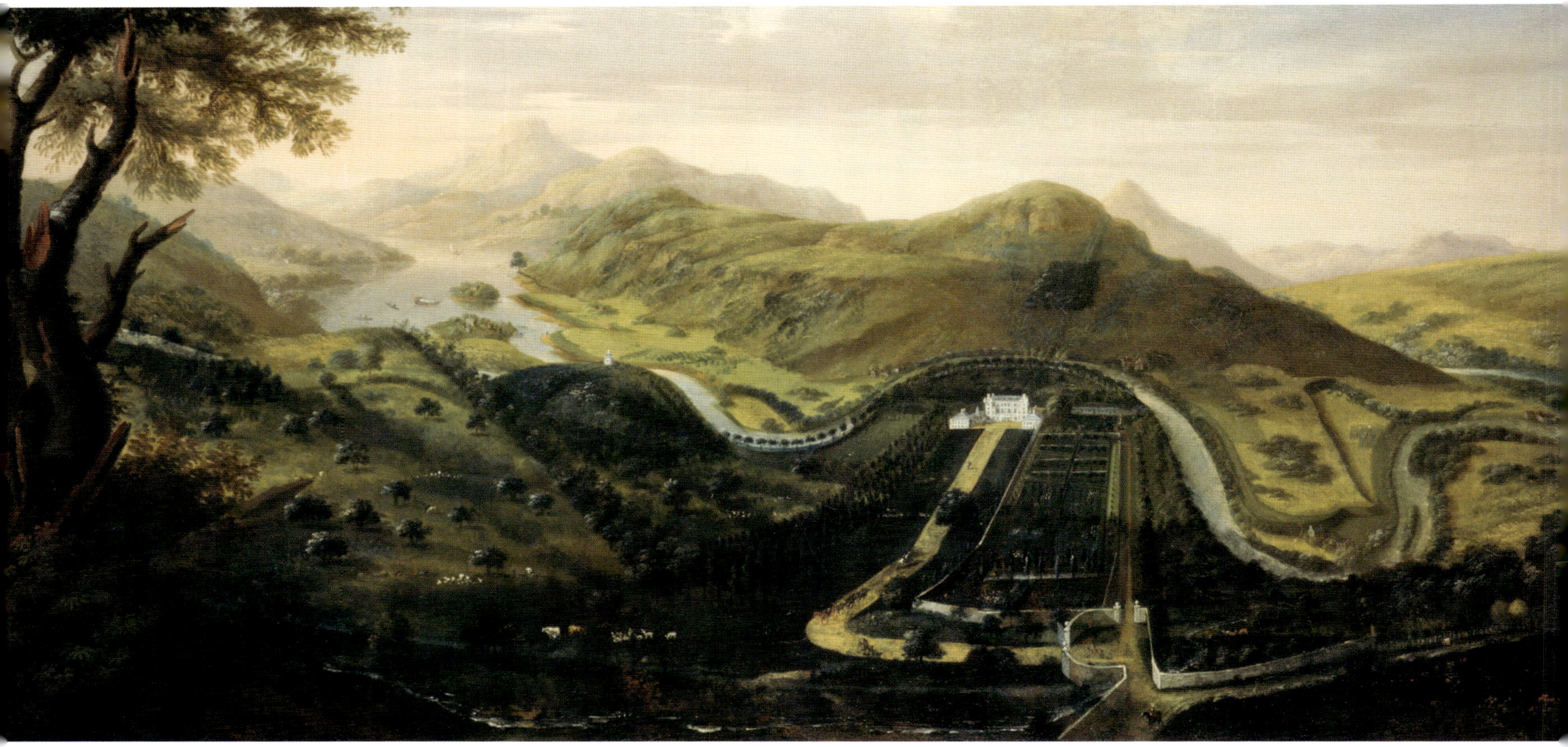

Fig. C4.4
James Norie and Jan Griffier II, *View of Taymouth*, begun 1733 and repainted 1739, oil on canvas (NGS PG2359)

James Norie's view of Taymouth situates the recently improved estate in an extensive regional landscape. Occupying the central ground, the newly laid out policies extend along a north–south axis, straddling the whole glen of the River Tay. Stretching laterally across the width of the canvas, the river's eastward course takes the viewer's eye out to its confluence with the tributary waters of the Lyon at far right. Bringing this vast landscape to scale, Norie's picture greatly compresses the lie of the land. Sheltering the estate and rising over the northern banks of the Tay is the mountainous range dominated by Ben Lawers, which culminates in the hills above the village of Killin at the far western end of the loch. In plotting these co-ordinates, the artist maps out a topographical narrative of the Campbell family's history of occupancy and its often-contested role in shaping life and land around Loch Tay. Just above Killin stood the stronghold of Finlarig, built a century or so earlier, at the same time as Taymouth, by Sir Duncan Campbell, 'Black Duncan', whose seizure of lands and property from rival clans had been formative in the family's local dominance. Building on his acquisitions, by the time John, Lord Glenorchy, commissioned Norie, a series of strategic marriages and opportunistic land grabs had ensured that family interest stretched from Strathtay to the east and the coastal town of Oban to the west.

That said, not everyone seems to have benefited from the new bridge, least of all one Donald McNicol, the ferryman described as a 'fisher at Kenmore', who was obliged to petition in 1775 for compensation for the loss of his three ferry boats, two of which had been commandeered by the bridge builders. Of these, one was sold, one sank in Loch Tay and the third 'was driven by a large speat from the harbour at Kenmore down the river to the Elysian Fields where it sunk and was rendered useless'.[4]

Attention has been drawn elsewhere to the Earl of Breadalbane's complaint to his daughter at the number of visitors whom he had been expected to entertain in 1773, there being a tradition of hospitality by which people of rank armed with letters of introduction might expect to be accommodated by landowners along the way. Other documents among the Breadalbane papers include an anonymous and undated memorandum concerning improvements to be made to the village of Kenmore, including

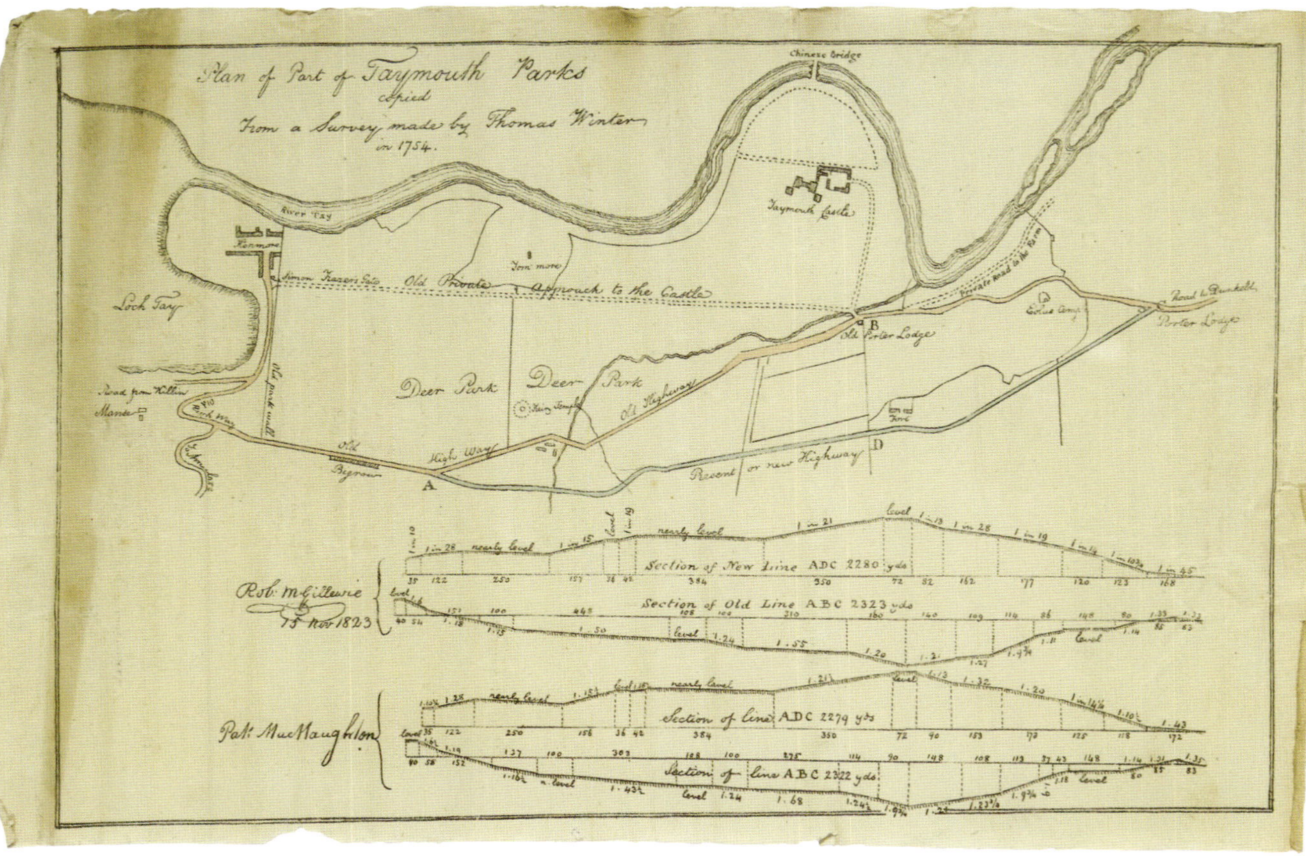

Fig. C4.5
Plan of Part of the Taymouth Parks, dated 1822, based on Thomas Winter's plan of 1754, with old road marked in red and diversion marked in blue, from the Breadalbane Muniments (NRS RHP 92892)

the building of a new inn to accommodate the increasing number of travellers:

> As it is found absolutely necessary in consequence of the improvements and plantations, making and to be made, at the east end of Loch Tay, that the village of Kenmore should be red up, and made (what it was originally intended for) an ornamental village, it is Lord Breadalbane's orders that the tenants of houses in said village do remove all byres, out houses etc. as pointed out by the land surveyor to their lots or acres.[5]

The 'improvements' to the village must already have taken place by the 1760s, as the poet Thomas Gray observed in a letter written to his friend Dr Wharton in 1765 that the Earl had 'built an inn and a town just where his principal walks should have been', as well as describing 'several seats and temples perched on particular rocky eminences'.[6] Among those who stayed at the new inn at Kenmore was Joseph Farington, who described it as 'an excellent house with good accommodation and great civility'. From there he ventured a couple of miles along the south shore of Loch Tay to the hamlet of Acharn where he obtained the services of a guide who conducted him to the series of waterfalls on the Acharn Burn, an extension to the pleasure grounds around Taymouth Castle:

> The lowest and greatest of these is approached through a subterraneous and narrow passage, in some places quite dark, at the end of which is a door which opens into a circular room called the Hermitage, and through a window opposite to the door the fall is seen. (Farington 1978–84, V, 1649)

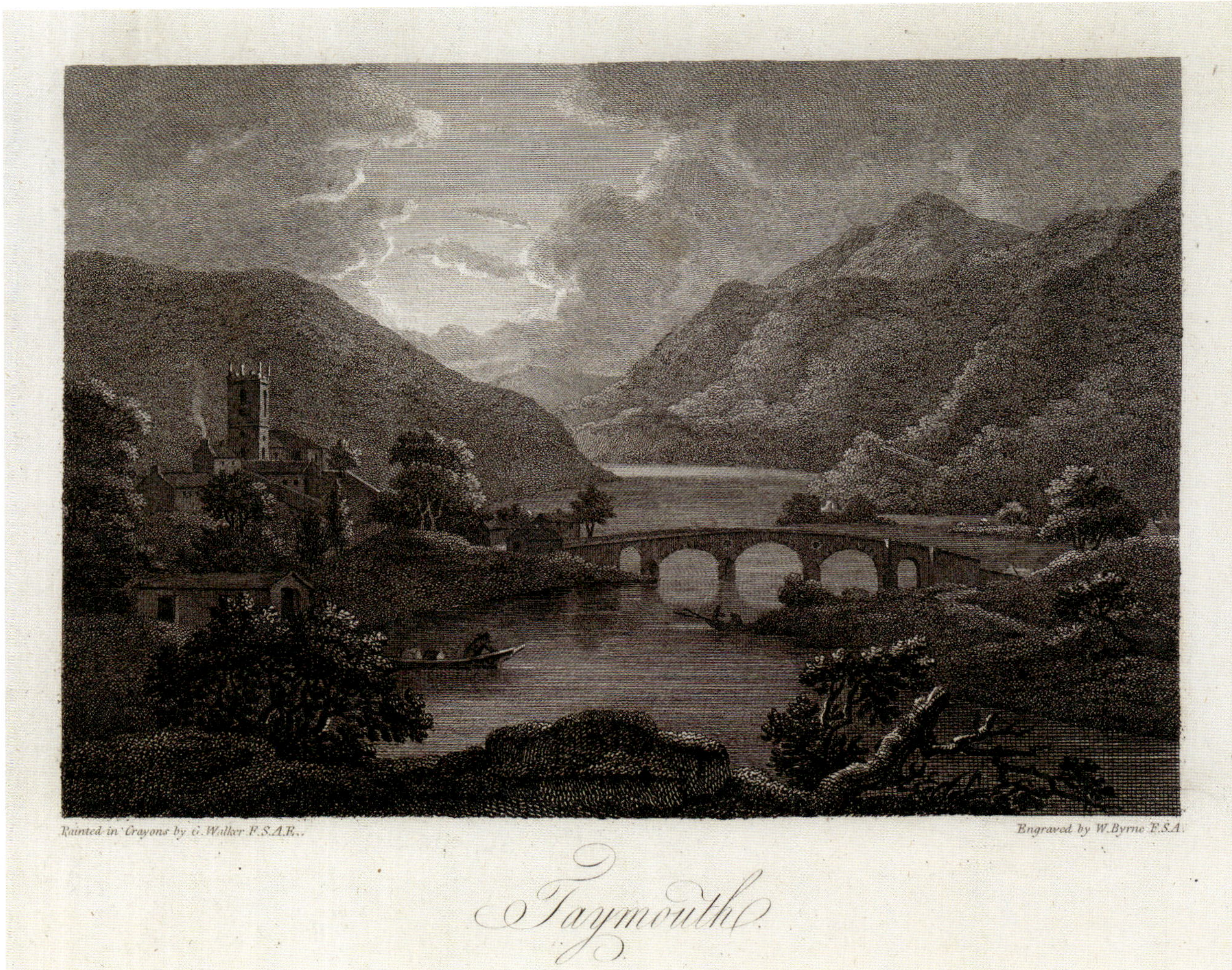

Fig. C4.6
Right. William Byrne after George Walker, 'Taymouth', engraving in James Cririe, *Scottish Scenery: or, Sketches in Verse, Descriptive of Scenes Chiefly in the Highlands of Scotland with Illustrations by George Walker* (London, 1803), opposite p. 59 (GLA ASC Hepburn q35)

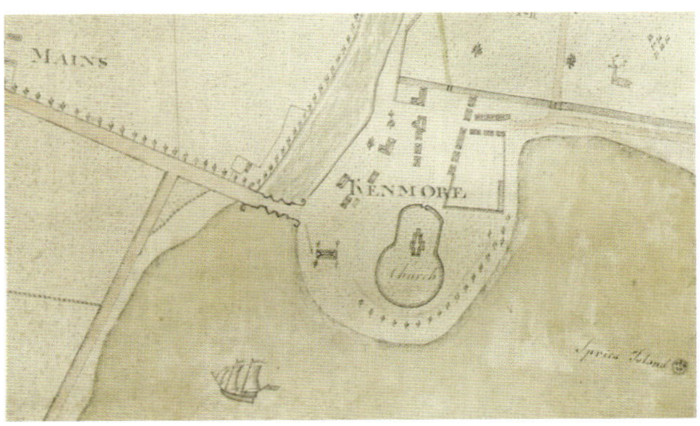

Fig. C4.7
Below. Detail from George Langlands, *Plan of Taymouth Policies*, 1786, showing Baxter's bridge and the village of Kenmore, from the Breadalbane Muniments (NRS RHP 961/2)

Fig. C4.8
Opposite. William Byrne after George Walker, 'Fall of Aharan', engraving in James Cririe, *Scottish Scenery: or, Sketches in Verse, Descriptive of Scenes Chiefly in the Highlands of Scotland with Illustrations by George Walker* (London, 1803), opposite p. 61 (GLA ASC Hepburn q35)

This was the same hermitage that Robert Burns visited in the course of his Highland tour in 1787, which inspired the poem inscribed by him in pencil on the chimney piece in the parlour of the inn, in which he contrasted the richness and beauty of the Taymouth landscape with the wilder landscape of the Sma Glen and Glen Quaich through which he had just passed on his way north (Leask 2014, 147, 358; Lamont Brown 1973, 19, 35–36, nn. 60, 61). By this time there was also an increasing number of foreign visitors following the *petit tour*, among whom was the Polish Princess Izabela Czartoryska, who recorded her visit to Taymouth in 1790 as follows:

> Une tres haute montagne sur la quelle est une plantation immense do toute sortes d'arbres . . . Nous faisons le tour du parc toujours dans le meme gout, planté régulièrement. Il y a un petit chateau crenélé avec de petits cannons d'ou la vue est superbe sur le lac at la rivière. Ensuite nous allons a l'hermitage qui est a deux milles dans un ravin. C'est un petit bois au milieu duquel est un roc sur lequel coule une cascade tres haute.[7]

Although the Earl of Breadalbane, in common with most other landowners at the time, allowed access to the Taymouth Castle policies, the number of visitors had reached such a level by the end of the eighteenth century that he was moved to issue an order that access be controlled, as was already the case at the Duke of Atholl's Hermitage in Dunkeld, where a ticketing system had been introduced as early as 1762, which had succeeded in keeping off the 'lower classt people from making repair to it'.[8] At Taymouth, the move to restrict access is recorded in a brief letter written by the earl to his grounds officer Hugh Cameron in December 1797:

> Hugh. I desire you to proclaim after Church this day that as I find the Terraces and Walks in the Pleasure Ground have been very much hurt of late by the number of people who walk on them, I require all the keys to be delivered up, and if any one is found walking on them without my order or permission, they will be prosecuted as the law directs.[9]

From Kenmore the road led eastwards to Aberfeldy, where the civil engineer Thomas Telford and his young companion the poet Robert Southey paused in 1819 in the course of their journey to inspect Wade's Bridge, built in 1733 to mark the completion of the first phase of military road building. It is clear from Southey's description that the utilitarian Telford saw little merit in William Adam's design:

> Near Aberfeldy is a bridge over the Tay, built by General Wade; but creditable neither to the skill nor taste of the architect . . . At a distance it looks well but makes a wretched appearance upon closer inspection.

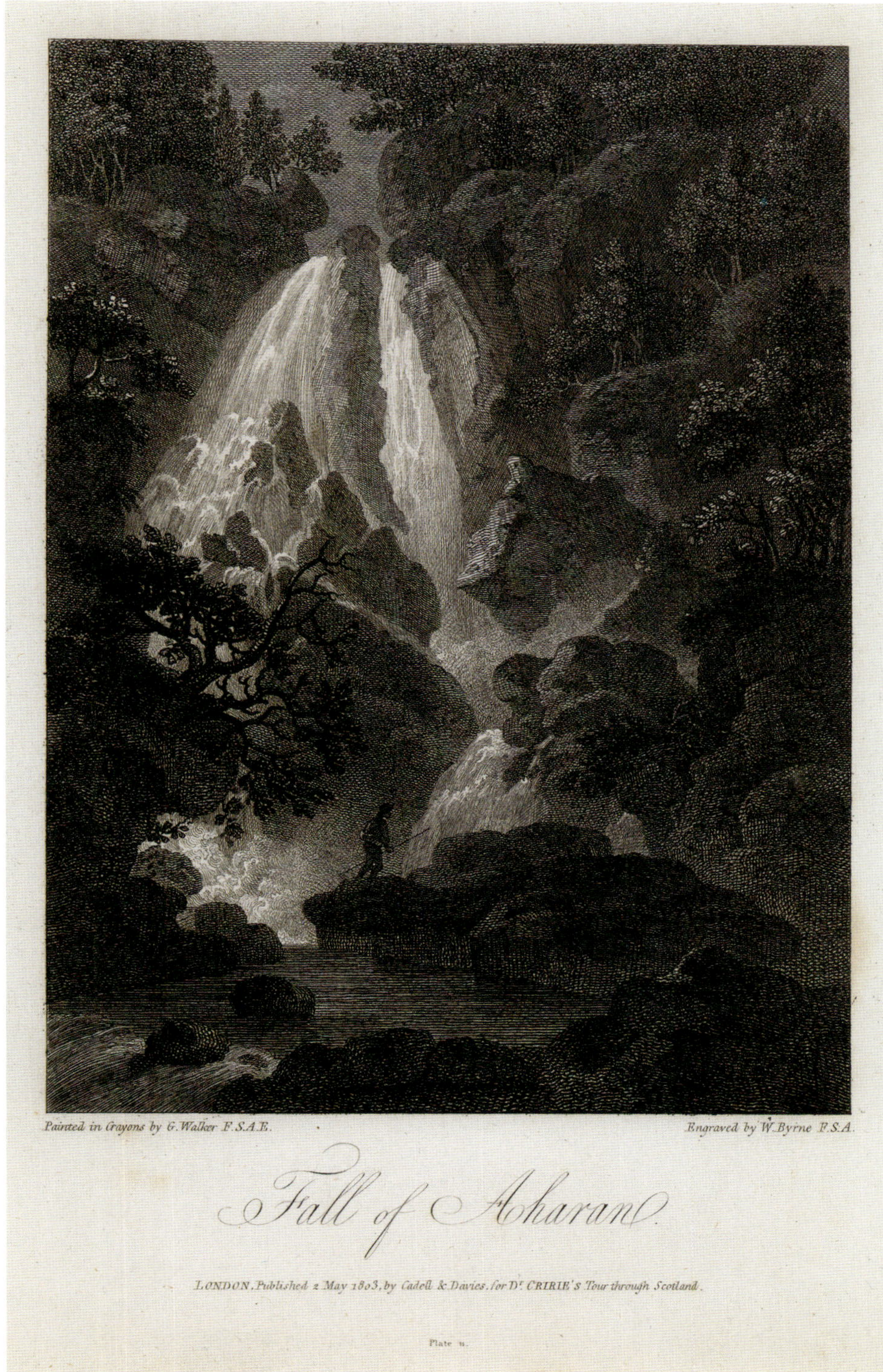

> There are four unmeaning obelisks upon the central arch, and the parapet is so high that you cannot see over it. The foundations are also very insecure, for we went into the bed of the river and examined them.
> (Southey 1972, 44)

Also mentioned by Southey was another popular feature at Aberfeldy to be visited as part of the Highland tour: a series of natural cascades on the Moness Burn above the town, celebrated in verse by Robert Burns in his song 'The Birks of Aberfeldy' following his visit in 1787. Here Joseph Farington engaged a guide to show his party the three principal falls:

> The Third and uppermost fall is very fine . . . the spectator feels himself inclosed in this scene, the passage to which is so narrow that our ladies did not think it prudent to venture over it, and the trees hanging from the rocks cross each other so as to admit only partial lights to fall from above caused an obscurity that much added to the secluded character of the scene.
> (Farington 1978–84, V, 1648)

BLAIR CASTLE

For many travellers in the late eighteenth century and early nineteenth century, the next stop on the Highland circuit was Blair Castle, home of the 4th Duke of Atholl, referred to at this time as Athole House following the removal of its turrets in the wake of the Jacobite risings. Here travellers were obliged to follow the awkward military road that crossed the River Tilt by Old Bridge of Tilt and ran across the parkland immediately to the north of the castle. As well as the road being within sight of the castle, the line of the road meant that 'dry arches' had to be made to allow access from the policies to the picturesque walks on the Banvie Burn and the west bank of the River Tilt without the need for visitors to mix with the common traffic. At Blair, discussion of the possibility of building a bridge further down the Tilt and realigning the road to run south of the castle first took place in 1804 as recorded in a memorandum from the duke's factor Thomas Palliser:

> When I was at Blair, Mr Donaldson, Surveyor of the Military Roads, called on me with a proposal from Col. Anstruther to Your Grace respecting the alteration of the Military Road at Blair, viz., that a bridge should be built over the Tilt as far down the River as a good foundation for a Bridge would permit . . . It appears to me to be a very liberal proposal on the part of the Government; should it meet with your Grace's approbation it will be begun immediately.[10]

As recorded in the *Chronicles of the Atholl and Tullibardine Families*, the project fell through. That discussion of the proposed diversion continued is shown by a letter from Lord Cathcart to the duke, written in 1810, which described the Old Bridge of Tilt as 'narrow defective and ill-placed', and which urged the duke to seek support for the creation of a shorter route 'as an obvious and indisputable utility to the publick'. That said, it took another twelve years for the proposal to be put into effect, as reported in a letter from F. Graham to the Duke of Atholl in 1822 which recorded the laying of the foundation stone for the new bridge, designed by roads engineer John Mitchell:

> During 1822 the Perth and Inverness turnpike road was much altered and improved between Dunkeld and the County march at Drumuachdar at a cost of £10,000. At Blair an entirely new road was formed for upwards of two miles, which struck off from the old highway at Cragan Farm (below Lude), crossed the Tilt by a new bridge near its junction with the Garry, and proceeded parallel with the Garry till it joined the old track a little east of Woodend.[11]

Another letter written to the Duke of Atholl from Inverness in August 1822 by Thomas Telford commented on the 'improved and now excellent state of the road from [Dunkeld] to Blair', describing 'the Bridges at Blair [as] masterly performances of their sort, and suitable to the place':

> Of this line of road, with the exception of a few small hills and quick bends which may yet by degrees be still further improved and protected, the whole may now be declared sufficiently perfect; we did not receive a single jolt.[12]

Although part of the old road leading westwards from Old Bridge of Tilt had to be kept open, allowing access to Glen Tilt and to Blairuachdar via the village of Blair, it was closed further to the west. With a northerly diversion just beyond the small plantation known as Diana's Grove, designed to take it further away from the castle, the old road now forms part of the long carriage drive leading to West Lodge just beyond Woodend. Unlike the situation at Inveraray and Taymouth, there was no plan drawn up for the creation of a new village of Blair Atholl on the Haugh of Blair. Instead, the village developed gradually on the roadside and around the solitary corn mill and a few small cottages that previously stood on the haugh, as seen on James Stobie's county map of 1783. The closure of the old road led to the abandonment and eventual ruination of St Bride's Kirk in Old Blair in favour of a new kirk built in 1825. The long-established coaching inn at Old Blair, where many tourists had stayed around the turn of the nineteenth century, also closed once new hotel accommodation became available in Blair Atholl in 1832. Among those who had lodged at the old inn were Robert Burns's companion William Nicol in 1787, and brother and sister William and Dorothy Wordsworth during their Scottish tour of 1803.

Among the features to be seen at Blair Castle were Diana's Grove and the nine-acre walled Hercules Garden with its ornamental ponds and lead statues, considered by the Rt Rev. Richard Pococke in 1760 to be 'the most beautifull kitchen garden I believe in the World' (Pococke 1887, 230–231). That said, later visitors to Blair were less complimentary about the landscape: the Rev. William Gilpin thought it 'capable of much improvement . . . [being] much injured by vistas, and a kitchen-garden, which tho extraordinary in it's way, is still a nuisance' (Gilpin 1789b, I, 140). The Wordsworths, too, visited the Hercules Garden during their visit in 1803, but were disappointed that the gardener did not offer them some fruit by way of refreshment (Walker 1997).

Contrasting with the formality of the Blair Castle policies were the Falls of Bruar, a couple of miles to the west, the subject of Robert Burns's poem 'The Humble Petition of the Bruar Water to the Noble Duke of Athole', written in 1787, in which he pleaded with the duke to plant trees around the falls. It would seem that it took the poet's untimely death in 1796 for the duke to respond to Burns's plea by planting trees, building bridges and laying out paths so that visitors in search of the sublime could view the falls in safety (Kinsley 1968, I, 335–357; Dingwall 1987).

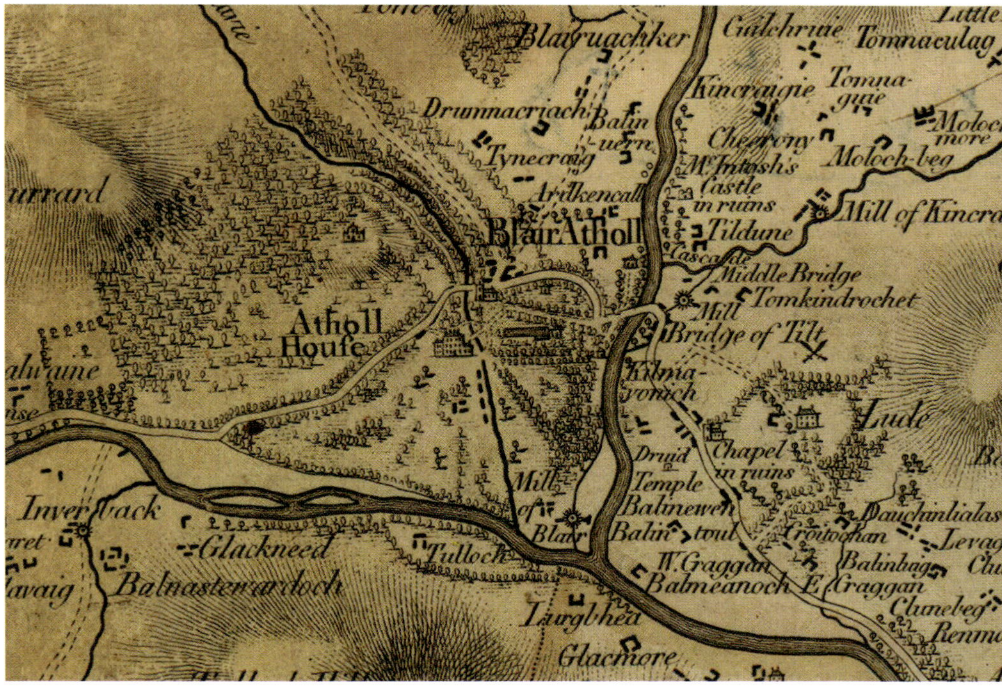

Fig. C4.9
Detail from James Stobie, *Map of the Counties of Perth and Clackmannan*, engraving, 1783, showing Old Bridge of Tilt and Blair Atholl (NLS EMS.b.2.30)

Visiting the falls a few years later in 1803, William and Dorothy Wordsworth were less than complimentary about the Duke's improvements, especially his use of conifers for the planting:

> For [Burns's] sake we wished they had been the natural trees of Scotland, birches, ashes, mountain ashes etc. . . . At present there can be nothing uglier than the whole chasm of the hillside with its formal walks. For aught I know, they are as well managed as they could be; but it is not easy to see the use of a pleasure path leading to nothing in the midst of an unlovely tract of country, though by a tumbling stream of clear water. (Walker 1997, 167–168)

Twelve years on, Elizabeth Grant of Rothiemurchus was equally critical:

> We walked to the Falls of Bruar, first brought into notice by Burns, and then too much made of, as besides planting the banks and conducting a path up the stream, so many summer houses and hermitages

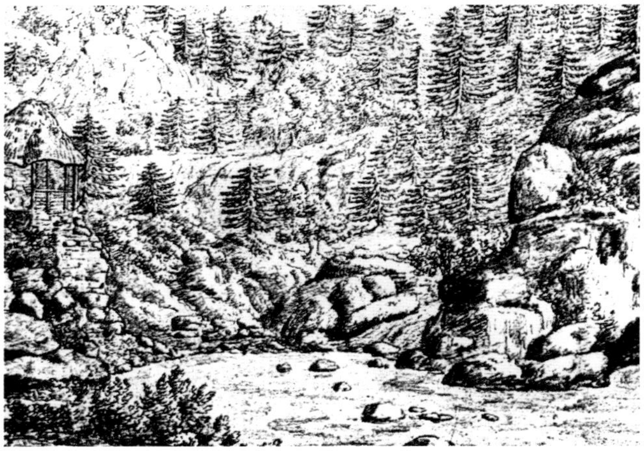

Fig. C4.10
Lady Emily Percy, *Bruar Falls*, 1810, drawing showing coniferous planting and a view of the house overlooking the lower falls (AE)

> and peep-bo places of one sort or another had been planted on favourite situations that the proper character of the wild torrent was completely lost.
> (Grant 1898, 270)

The aforementioned *Chronicles* also record a problem that arose from the realignment of the road – that of creating a new approach to the castle following the abandonment of the military road. Previously there had been an avenue leading down to the castle forecourt from a point on the military road close to [Old] Blair, as marked on Thomas Winter's plan of 1744. Although the avenue trees had been cut down by 1760, the original drive remained in use for a time. Various alternatives were considered, including the building of a third bridge over the Tilt with the idea of creating a new eastern approach to the castle. This proved to be impractical, and resulted in the Miln Road, or cross-axial avenue of the pre-existing formal landscape, being adopted as the main drive, despite the fact that it approached the castle at an awkward angle, passing close by the unattractive service wing (Stewart-Murray 1908, IV, 335).

DUNKELD HOUSE

From Blair, those following Thomas Pennant's *petit tour* route pursued the road south, leading down Strathtay to Dunkeld, often described as the eastern gateway to the Highlands. This stretch of road was traversed by the adventurous 26-year-old antiquary Sir William Burrell in 1758, in the course of a northern tour which took in Inveraray, Taymouth, Blair and Dunkeld, though not in the same order as visited by Pennant a little over ten years later:

> From Blair to Dunkell is 20 miles, the best and pleasantest ride in Scotland, being chiefly through woods of birch on the side of a mountain, at the bottom of which flows the Garry to Killicranky Pass, where it loses itself in the Timmel and a little lower both fall into the Tay. On the opposite side are hills, finely wooded and meadows in the bottom.
> (Burrell 1997, 70)

Had Samuel Johnson and James Boswell taken this road in 1773 on their way to Inverness and the Western Isles, instead of following the east-coast route via Aberdeen, Banff and Elgin, they would surely have come away with a different view than Johnson's well known description of Scotland's hill country as a 'wide extent of hopeless sterility . . . left in its original elemental state, or quickened only with one sullen power of useless vegetation' (Black 2007, 88).

If the Rev. James Robertson, writing in 1799, is to be believed, part of the attractiveness of the road in Strathtay was the result of deliberate landscaping and planting:

> The Dukes of Athol have been at much expence with the road from Dunkeld to Blair. The former direction was frequently changed, to avoid pulls, and where hills were small they have been cut through, and their face covered with green sod, which has a fine effect. Where the appearance of the country was exposed or naked, plantations were made at the Duke's expence, on land which was not his own property.
> (Robertson 1799, 360)

On reaching Dunkeld, eighteenth-century travellers found that they had to cross the River Tay by one of two ferries, there being no bridge over the river between Wade's Tay Bridge in Aberfeldy and John Smeaton's Perth Bridge. Previous attempts to bridge the Tay at Dunkeld had proved unsuccessful, with an earlier structure built in 1617 washed away just four years later. A few travellers on their way north used the East Ferry near Birnam, joining the military road from Coupar Angus which ran between Dunkeld Cathedral and the river, leading onwards through the Duke of Atholl's pleasure grounds to the West Ferry. That said, most travellers chose the West Ferry by Inver as the safer of the two crossings. Having crossed the river at West Ferry travellers followed the military road northwards, hugging the riverbank and passing to the west of the hill of Kings Seat.[13]

The West Ferry was also used by visitors to Dunkeld to cross the Tay and follow the path leading through Inver, where they were obliged to pick up a guide to show them the pleasure ground surrounding the Duke of Atholl's Hermitage and the Falls of Braan. First built in 1757, the Hermitage soon became one of the most visited sites on the Highland tour, its popularity boosted by the 4th Duke's remodelling and renaming of the building as Ossian's Hall (Dingwall and Aldridge 1999). Loved by some visitors for the elaborate and theatrical way in which visitors were made to view the falls through coloured glass or reflected in mirrors, the Hermitage also had its critics, among them William Gilpin, who considered that 'such deceptions are tricks below the dignity of scenes like this' (Gilpin 1789b, I, 123). William Wordsworth was another visitor to voice his dislike of the Hermitage building, finishing his 'Effusion in the Pleasure Ground on the Banks of the Bran' with the lines 'I mused; and thirsting for redress, recoiled into the wilderness' (Walker 1997, 174; Wordsworth 1977, II, 300–301).

The need for a safe river crossing at Dunkeld had long been discussed, as is seen in documents from the period such as a memorandum to be found among the Breadalbane Muniments, addressed to the Right Honourable the Lords Commissioners of his Majesty's Treasury by 'Certain Noblemen and Gentlemen of the County of Perth', signed by the Duke of Atholl, the Earl of Breadalbane and Earl of Kinnoull, along with Thomas Graham of Balgowan and several other landowners:

> Your Memorialists, sensible of how well disposed Government at all times are to assist works of great Public Utility, beg leave to point out to your Lordships the many Advantages which would arise to the Northern parts of Scotland, and to the County in particular from a Bridge being thrown over that large and rapid river, the Tay, in a centrical situation between Perth and Tay Bridge, a space of thirty four miles at present to be crossed in Boats, a mode of Passage which, on the sudden falling of Rain or melting of Snow is often dangerous and sometimes fatal.

Added urgency was given to this matter by a tragic accident that occurred at the East Ferry in November 1766 when a boat carrying thirteen passengers and four horses capsized, resulting in six fatalities, as recorded in a letter from Thomas Bisset to the 3rd Duke of Atholl (Stewart-Murray 1908, 23).

However, it was not until 1802, following a visit to Dunkeld by Thomas Telford, that a move was made by the newly appointed Commissioners of Highland Roads and Bridges to address the problem. Telford, having identified a suitable location halfway between the two ferries, was tasked with designing the new bridge. Rather than raising money for the bridge by public subscription as the Earl of Breadalbane had done some years before, the 4th Duke of Atholl himself undertook to share the expense with the government, provided that he was allowed to charge tolls in order to recoup his investment. In the event, the final cost of the bridge far exceeded the original estimate, so tolls on the bridge continued to be charged by the duke for a number of years after they had been abolished elsewhere, resulting in riots during which the toll gates were thrown into the river. This unhappy situation was only subsequently brought to an end many years later when the bridge was taken over by the County Roads Authority.

Following two years of careful preparation, it took another four and a half years from the laying of the foundation stone in June 1805 for the bridge to be completed and approved by Telford. With the opening of the bridge to traffic in November 1809, and the consequent closure of the two ferries, the opportunity was taken by the 4th Duke of Atholl to close the public road running westwards from the cathedral through the Dunkeld House policies. This was achieved by the creation of Atholl Street and the construction of a new stretch of road looping to the north by Polney Loch and passing between Kings Seat and Craig a Barns to rejoin the military road near Leadpettie Lodge, as indicated on an estate plan drawn by P. Macnaughtan,[14] and as described by the civil engineer Joseph Mitchell in his *Reminiscences of My Life in the Highlands*:

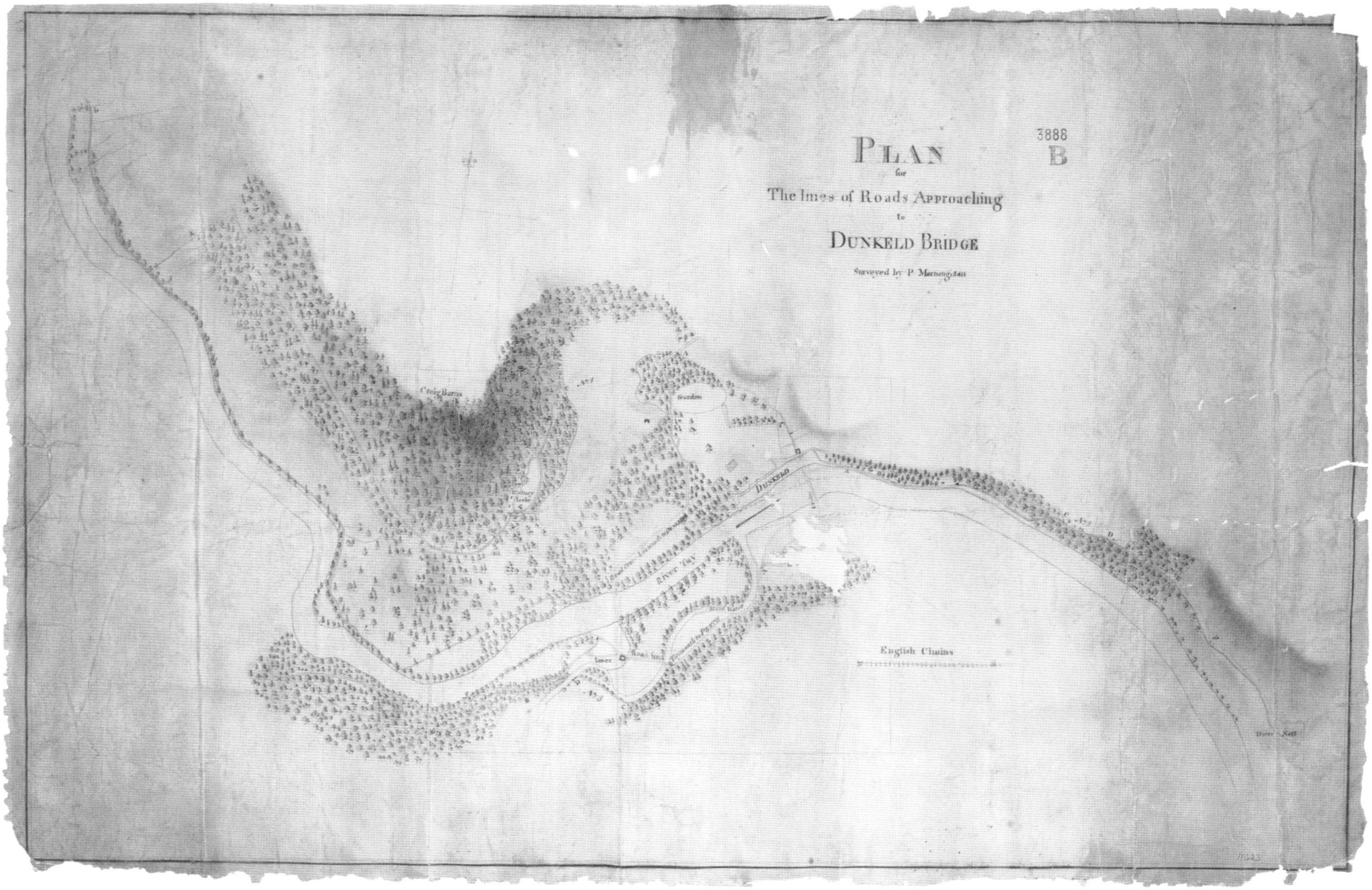

Fig. C4.11
P. Macnaughton, *Plan of Roads Approaching Dunkeld Bridge*, 1802, showing the existing road layout and an indication of possible diversion
(NRS RHP 11623)

> When the Dunkeld Bridge was built in 1809, the Duke constructed a new road in direct line with the bridge, joining the old road three miles north, thus converting the whole wide space between the road and the Tay into the present magnificent demesne. (Mitchell 1971 [1883/1884], 107)

In a letter that Telford wrote to the duke in 1822, referring to the realignment of the road at Blair, he mentions the 'magnificent scenery of Dunkeld (not forgetting The Bridge)', the deliberate underlining of these two words in his letter suggesting that he regarded the new bridge as one of his masterworks.[15] In the archive at Blair Castle there are several hand-drawn plans dating from 1806, showing designs for a regularly planned village to be known as New Dunkeld just to the south of Telford's bridge, incorporating the church of Little Dunkeld.[16] In the event, none of the proposals was acted upon, leaving the nearby village of Birnam to expand westwards towards the bridge in a less ordered way in the decades that followed.

This chapter has sought to demonstrate that, where roads and bridges that were being constructed in the late eighteenth and early nineteenth centuries ran close to existing designed landscapes, landowners often took the opportunity to move roads further away from their mansion houses, and to create new villages for the housing of estate workers and others who had been displaced by the expansion of their policies. The four great houses at Inveraray, Taymouth, Blair and Dunkeld, described here, were not the only examples of this phenomenon.

While the new roads were clearly designed for the benefit of travellers, they were not always appreciated, as Edmund Burt explained in the last of his *Letters from a Gentleman in the North of Scotland* written in the 1730s. Quite apart from those complaining about the wear and tear of the hard new road surfaces on horses' hooves and on their own feet, there were some who feared that the building of bridges would 'render the ordinary people effeminate, and less fit to pass the waters in other places where there are none' (Burt 1998, 298). There is also an amusing anecdote to be found in Robert Southey's account of his Scottish tour made with Thomas Telford in 1819, referring to the road between Dunkeld and Perth:

> Fifteen [miles] to Perth, by a good road. Someone was praising it to the Duke of Athol at whose expense it was made, in presence of Neil Gow, a performer of the violin, of some renown in these parts; Neil, who was a person privileged to say anything, replied 'They may praise your braid roads that gains by 'em: for my part, when I'se gat a wee droppy at Perth, I'se just as lang again in getting hame by the new road as by the auld one'. On such occasions he could manage to keep the road, but it was by a zig-zag course, tacking always from one side of it to the other. (Southey 1972, 49)

NOTES

1 Sir J. Clerk, *The Country Seat: A Poem*, National Records of Scotland (NRS) GD18/4404, 1727. Unpublished manuscript.

2 NRS, Breadalbane Muniments, GD112/47/21, 1823–1824. See also RHP 92892, 1823.

3 NRS, Breadalbane Muniments, GD112/48/3, 1771.

4 NRS, Breadalbane Muniments, GD112/11/1/2/5, 1775.

5 NRS, Breadalbane Muniments, GD112/20/4/1, ND.

6 Thomas Gray, letter to Thomas Wharton, c. 30 September 1765, British Library, Egerton MS 2400, ff. 168–171.

7 Izabela Czartoryska, 'Manuscript Journal of a visit to England and Scotland 1790', Czartoryski Museum, Czart. Ew XVIII/607. See also K. Gmerek, 'Scotland in the Eyes two Polish Lady Travellers', in A. Korzeniowska and I. Szymanska (eds), *Scotland in Europe/Europe in Scotland: Links – Dialogues – Analogies*, Warsaw: Semper, 2013. Translated quotation: 'A very tall mountain covered by an immense plantation with all sorts of trees . . . We made a tour of the park all laid out in the same taste, planted with regularity. There is a small ramparted castle with small canons from which the view over the lake and the river is superb. Next, we go to the hermitage which is situated two miles away in a ravine. There is a small wood in the middle of which is a rock, over which falls a very high waterfall.'

8 NRAS 234, Atholl Estates, Box 49.1.156 records a complaint by gardener James Johnston on 19 June 1762 concerning thefts from the garden by 'goat whey people'; and Box 49.1.210 a subsequent report by Johnston on 2 August 1762 confirming the success of the ticketing system.

9 NRS, Breadalbane Muniments, GD112/20/4/1, ND.

10 NRAS 234, Atholl Estates, Box 48.11.9, 1810.

11 NRAS 234, Atholl Estates, Box 68.12.115, 1822.

12 NRAS 234, Atholl Estates, Box 68.12.283, 1822

13 NRS, RHP 11623, J. Macnaughtan, 'Plan for the Lines of Roads Approaching to Dunkeld Bridge', 1802. This marks the old road, together with a faint indication of the intended line of the new road.

14 NRS, RHP 11623. See previous note.

15 NRAS 234, Atholl Estates, Box 68.12.283, 1822.

16 NRAS 234, Atholl Estates, Estate Plans D27, D28 and D30, 1806.

CHAPTER FIVE

Scotland's Prospects

John Bonehill

Travelling in a coach at speed through Perthshire, William Gilpin was nearly overwhelmed by the endless series of moving pictures framed momentarily by the carriage window:

> The road winding among the hills of this descent, discovers new beauties, as we advance. We had a hasty view of the abbey of Dunkeld – of a picturesque bridge over the Bran – of the mountains, that inviron the whole – and other objects as we passed. The several scenes shifted rapidly . . . There is something very amusing even in a hasty succession of beautiful scenes. The imagination is kept in a pleasing perturbation; while these floating, unconnected ideas become a kind of waking dream; and are often wrought up by fancy into more pleasing pictures; than they in fact appear to be, when they are viewed with deliberate attention. (Gilpin 1789b, I, 112)

For Gilpin, the picturesque was primarily an art of travel. Bringing 'the principles of artificial landscape' to the viewing as well as the depiction of the landscape, the author had advocated taking in 'the *general face of the country*' rather than 'any *particular scene*' (Gilpin 1786, I, xxv). Only touring a region would disclose its characteristic features. But, as Gilpin's remarks on the approach to the eastern gateway to the Highlands illustrate, for him the picturesque was also an art of reverie, of dream-like invention, against which the encounter with the actual landscape often failed to measure up. On taking to Scotland's 'old ways' and new roads, the picturesque eye was as likely to be disappointed as delighted by the passing scenery. Much as his writings had helped foster a taste for craggy, mountainous landscapes, Gilpin struggled to bring the vast, unyielding distances of the Scottish Highlands to scale. Unlike the scenes rushing by the windows of his coach and conjured in the author's mind, they were not readily framed as pictures. The appreciation and depiction of Scotland's varied topographies presented as many challenges as possibilities.

Taking Gilpin's thoughts on these matters as its point of departure, this chapter explores the part played by actual and imaginative forms of travel in making Scottish scenery a subject of landscape art. Going more or less uncharted pictorially until the middle decades of the eighteenth century, the artistic 'discovery' of Scotland was largely enabled in one way or another by the expansion of the country's road and transport network. Whether made along the way or in order to promote such travels, it was closely bound-up with those tours of a variously commercial, militaristic, philosophical or leisurely kind traced by this book. Travel had implications for the perception of the landscape as well as its management and use. Opening up the country imaginatively as much as materially, travel along Scotland's roads, rivers and coasts expanded artists' fields of work and vision, bringing new subjects and ways of seeing it into view. They made Scotland legible, as a picture, as a landscape.

In tracking these developments, this chapter considers travel both as an aspect of artistic practice and as a pictorial motif. Looking across works in various media, it traces the transition from sketch or sketchbook to print or exhibition room, so moving from the field to those places elsewhere in which Scotland's image was variously made, displayed, evaluated and received. It pays attention to matters of landscape aesthetics, to the Old Master traditions that the artists of the period reworked in their depiction of the national territory as well as writers' musings on the picturesque and the Sublime, not just as they framed the views of artists and travellers but as they directed designs on the ground. Historians have long recognised how such models helped shape and reshape the topography of Britain's localities into picture-like conceptions of how they should appear and be appreciated. No less attention falls here, however, on the rich play of interests and more especially those of landed society that 'improved' the Scottish landscape along those lines. Like other forms of enquiry into people and place, the landscape art of the period was as much evaluative as documentary, taking account of the past and present state of things but also the implications of change for the place in question and the country at large. Helping to co-ordinate Scotland as a network of localities, it mapped the country's often uneven and uncertain prospects.

ROAD MAPS AND PICTURES

Roads and bridges, rivers, coastlines or route-ways of some other kind were always prominent features of landscape art. On a formal level, routes of passage guided the viewer's eye through the terrain and connected what were otherwise disparate parts of the pictorial space. They were unifying threads. But, whether stretching left to right or from foreground to background, they often took the spectator on another kind of journey too: an imaginative one, to be aligned with the fictional travels taking place along the route. Sometimes, the narrative was one of day-to-day or seasonal routine, the weary trudge of drovers and livestock or field hands making the short journey to or from work. Other times, it was the countrywide excursions of the philosophical traveller or scenic prospect-hunter that took centre stage. On occasion, the routes taken were where these worlds met, dramatised in pointed or maybe comic contrasts between the polite and the plebeian, the visitor passing through and the local resident.

Beginning with the sharp bend that cuts across the foreground, the road plays a narrative as well as a structural role in Paul Sandby's *South Prospect of Leith* (Fig. C5.1). Workers and pack animals are shown making their way down the historic East Road from Edinburgh to the nearby port. Look closely and entering stage left is a fashionable coach, a swish counterpart to the workaday cart of the adjacent field. Sketched in hesitantly, it has an almost ghostly appearance in the original drawing. But it was firmly part of the design when it was translated into print. Although a timeless scene of harvest and Georgic plenty occupies the centre ground, the coach is one of a number of telling references to the connections of this place with an increasingly dynamic, modern world. Minutely delineated with great delicacy, ships' masts, a mill and a smoking glass-furnace edge the shoreline settlement. They are understated, but these small accents freight this local scene with broader meaning. It becomes a picture about the purposeful fulfilment of the rich potential in the land. 'Prospect' art of this kind encouraged a sense of passage or progress through the landscape, opening up views in time as well as space, of past, present and – as an aim or design – projected futures: usually bright, commercial ones. In this sense, they offered up views of a landscape not so much as it was but as it ought to be.

One of 'numerous sketches from nature' that Sandby was to work up when off-duty from his post with the Board of Ordnance, *South Prospect of Leith* exemplifies the considerable overlaps between his commercial practice and his work for the military (Sandby 1811, 438). Mapmaking and surveying were models for recording the history and economic prospects of a place and establishing its co-ordinates and connections with a wider world. With the primary concern being to facilitate the movement of troops, the focus of the Military Survey had fallen on mapping routes of passage through the landscape. Not surprisingly then, route-ways of various kinds were the subject, as well as the vantage point, for much of Sandby's early art, shaping its scenic and social character (Bonehill and Daniels 2009, 120–151). Views such as that along the East Road to Leith

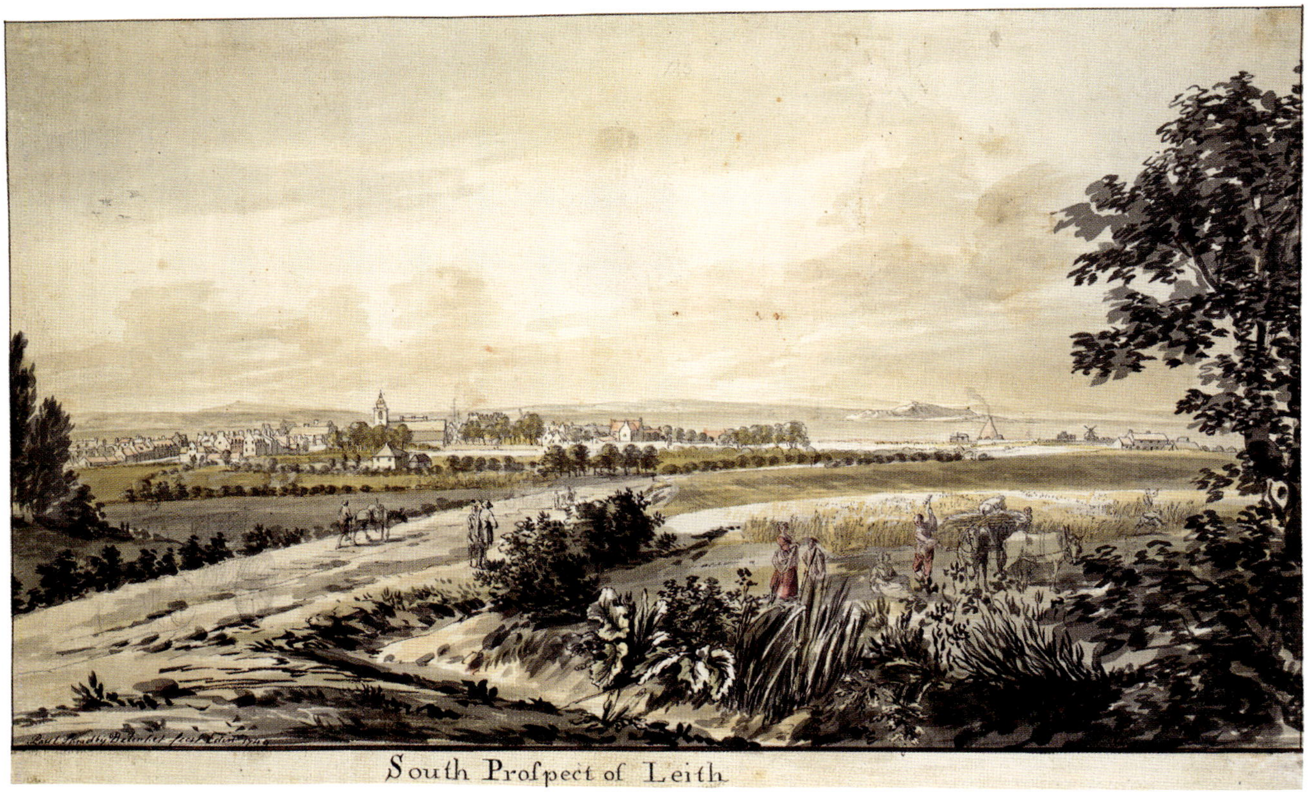

Fig. C5.1
Paul Sandby, *South Prospect of Leith*, 1747, pen, ink and watercolour over pencil (AM WA.C.II.V. 219)

show a concern with their role in articulating the landscape as well as their traffic.

Working for the Ordnance also provided Sandby with introductions to leading cultural and political figures. Offering lucrative building contracts as part of its remit, the Board brokered deals between the Georgian state and a host of civic, commercial, landed and political interests. Through it, Sandby met one of the most prominent beneficiaries of Ordnance appointments, the architectural contractor and designer William Adam (Gifford 1989, 173). He embarked on sketching trips with the architect's sons, James and Robert Adam, and – as we saw in an earlier section – gave lessons to another in their circle, John Clerk of Eldin, who acquired a practised eye for recording the intricacies as well as the broader patterns of the landscape (Fleming 1962a) (see Fig. S1.14). A well-connected member of the Scottish Whig elite and a leading arbiter on matters of artistic taste, his father, Sir John Clerk of Penicuik, was impressed enough by Sandby's talents to recommend him to others in his circle. In what was Sandby's only known private commission of the period, he was to make 'several drawings of the house and policy' at Drumlanrig, the ancestral Nithsdale seat of the dukes of Queensbury (Ferguson 1751) (Fig. C5.2). Showing the hall, set amid gardens, farmland, woods and floodplain, with the mountains of Galloway as backdrop, the only drawing from the set to survive exploits this startling conjunction of raw and improved scenery to dramatic effect. Landed estates and their economies were the ground for much of Sandby's off-duty and official Ordnance work. On the lookout for patrons, Sandby's eye was perhaps caught as much by the power and prestige of places such as Argyll's Inveraray as by their scenic character (see Figs S1.12–S1.13).

When so much else is treated schematically or not at all, the estates of the kingdom's landowners are often picked out with considerable care and great detail in the fair copy of the Military Survey (see Fig. S1.7). Estates such as Inveraray are drawn in a way that attends to the orderly geometry of their design and planting. They appear islands of improvement in an

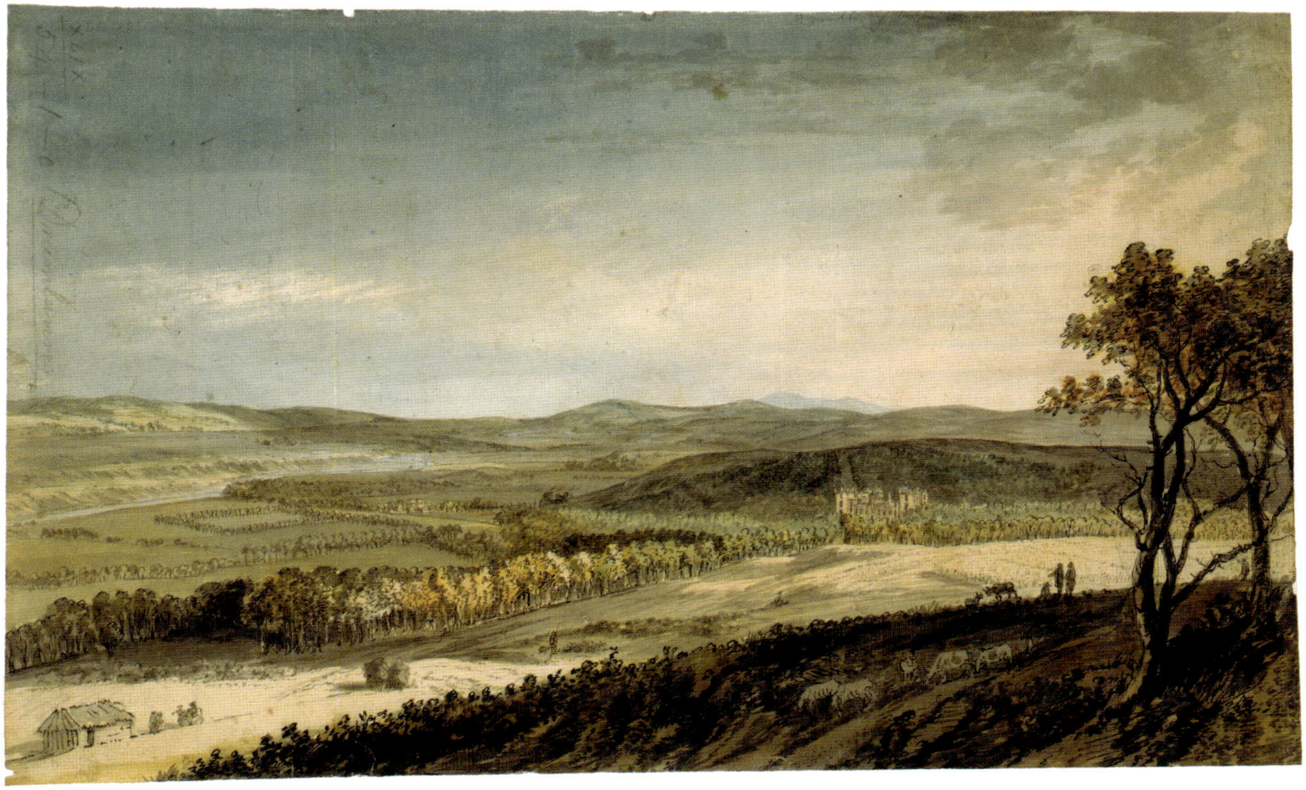

Fig. C5.2
Paul Sandby, *Nithsdale, with Drumlanrig*, c. 1751, pen, wash and watercolour over pencil (BL K.Top.49.54.lc)

otherwise barren, rolling sea of rocky hillsides and treeless plains. A work that makes use of the same hatching technique and palette as the map, even Sandby's famous image of surveying at Loch Rannoch is an estate view, set on lands in Perthshire forfeited by its former Jacobite landowners, the Robertson Barony of Strowan (see Fig. S1.9). Emblematic as much as documentary, the view was a commemorative token, as it were, of the Military Survey, which framed its work as an elegant *fête galante*. Much as it is carefully located, in the shadow of Craig Varr on the far eastern shore of the loch, the drawing is not a straightforward matter of eye-witness record. Like many of Sandby's drawings, it is also a work about viewing and making images, about acts of observation and depiction, often involving instruments, and their role in constructing the landscape. Whether a foreground tree, a fragment of architecture, a sketching artist or gesturing spectator, the framing elements used to guide the eye will often as not work to draw attention to that relationship. It is a picture, a scene, a piece of theatre.

PROSPECTS AND PROPERTY

Surveying the ancestral southern Highland seat of the Campbell earls of Breadalbane, deep in the heart of the Grampians, James Norie's painted prospect of Taymouth is another theatrically framed estate view (see Fig. C4.4). Originally commissioned in 1733, it is a rare example for its time of an important, albeit arguably overlooked, category of landscape art. Other than in a handful of exceptional instances, prior to Sandby's drawings of sites such as Drumlanrig, Scotland's landed property had not received anything like the level of pictorial treatment that had been lavished on estates south of the border (Harris 1979). There, estate portraiture, as it is termed, had been a flourishing genre of modern pictorial art since the Restoration. Demand for such pictures was closely tied to the importance of land and its ownership to social prestige and the exercise of political authority. In Scotland, the taste for estate views emerged only gradually, once the traditional allocation of land as a token of kinship, whereby

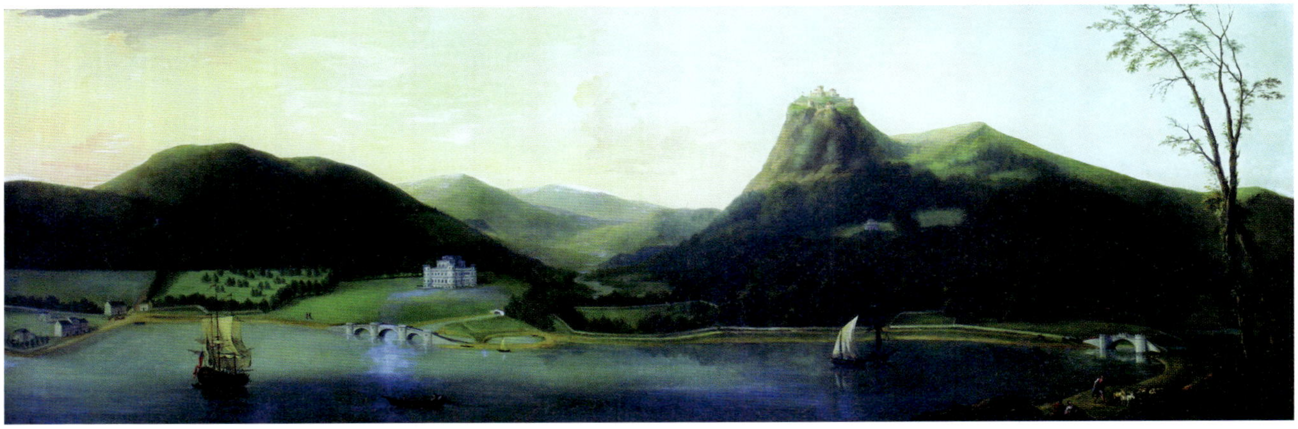

Fig. C5.3
Agostino Brunias, *View of Inveraray*, 1758, oil on canvas (ArE)

territory was held in trust, gave way to a more overtly commercial system of ownership secured by legal title. Looking to the example set by Norie's patron John, Lord Glenorchy, a number of owners were to seize on estate portraiture after mid-century as an expression of their modern standing as both clan laird and propertied gentleman. In one form or another, they would come to largely determine the pictorial image of the Scottish landscape after 1760 or thereabouts, staking it out and packaging it up as a domain of aristocratic grandeur and power.

Taking an elevated, 'bird's-eye' vantage, estate views like Norie's Taymouth prospect are often aligned with mapping (Daniels 1990). Such pictures tabulate land use and property boundaries. Often tied to the improvement of the property, however, like maps, they were as likely to include features not yet built as ones completed, so were as much a matter of design as record. Made in the Italian artist's London studio in 1758, Agostino Brunias's view of Argyll's Inveraray is an almost visionary example of this practice (Fig. C5.3). Setting out his designs on the landscape and presented to the duke as a gift, the picture was commissioned by Robert Adam, not the owner, being intended – as the architect confessed – to lay Argyll 'under obligation to me, on a favourite subject' (Adam 1758). Working from Adam's designs and sketches of Inveraray, Brunias situated the architect's fanciful proposals in an otherworldly setting, staffed with Italianate peasantry, with the modest hill-top look-out of Dun na Cuaiche watch-tower replaced by a fantastical walled citadel and the view-spoiling loch-side town simply imagined away. To Adam's disappointment, while happy enough to accept the picture, Argyll was not willing to go so far as to implement any of the plans set out in this painted blueprint.

With the adjacent hillsides dotted with garden structures, Brunias's outlandish painting illustrates just how closely bound-up estate portraiture as a genre was with changing tastes in landscape design. In formal terms, it is possible to trace this relationship through a gradual lowering and refocusing of the artist's gaze (Daniels 1990). Such developments would see artists abandon the mid-air vantage points of pictures such as Norie's Taymouth, so suited to displaying the geometric alignments typical of garden designs of the early 1700s, for pictorial strategies better attuned to the eccentric open models of landscaping that began to emerge around mid-century. Taking account of the shifting scenes afforded by parkland layouts, with their variously confined, then expansive vistas, the viewpoint on the now often distant house was more likely to be grounded and framed. Narrowing the field of vision still further, artists' views of the picturesque landscapes of the years around 1800, of the kind discussed below, focused on the nooks and crannies of the landscape, a rutted path or the intricate tangle of a tree's root systems. While a little schematic, thinking about the history of the genre in these terms helps draw attention to the complex relationship between the actual lie of the land and its pictorial image.

Just how closely tied the working out of design principles on the ground and the visual image of the estate was at times is exemplified by the almost obsessive documentation in paint of Taymouth's improvement, with its owner marking each new phase with the commission of an artist's view (Holloway and Errington 1978, 13–20; Tait 1980, 33). By 1769, when Thomas Pennant noted 'some views of the fine scenes near his Lordship's

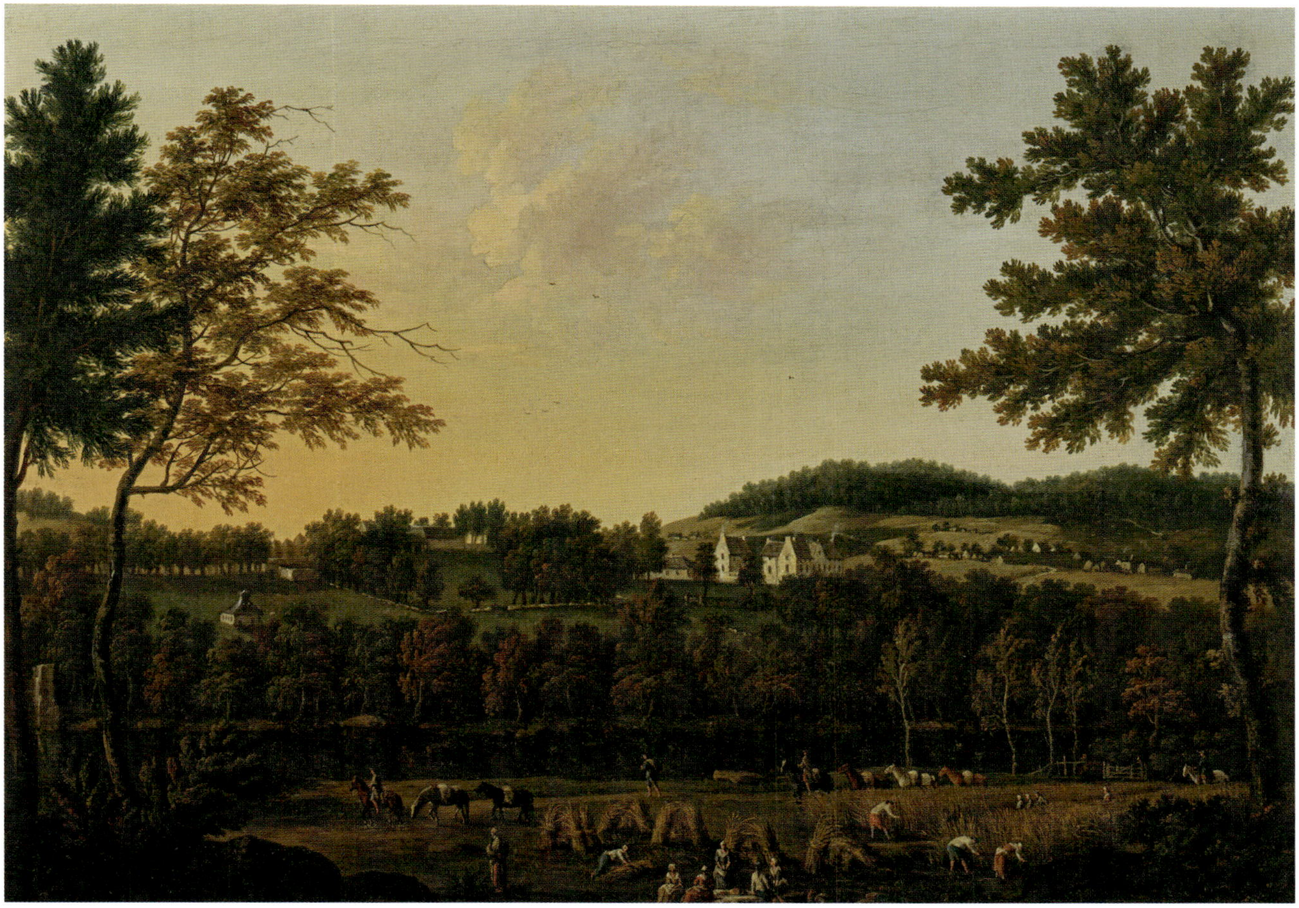

Fig. C5.4
William Tomkins, *View of Rothiemay, upon the Estate of the Earl of Fife, in the County of Bamff*, 1767, oil on canvas (PC)

seat at *Taymouth*' as decorating the Holyrood apartments of the now 3rd Earl of Breadalbane, further views of the Perthshire estate had been ordered from John Sanger and several others (Pennant 1771a, 53). Among them were two artists then cultivating metropolitan profiles with large groups of pictures set on Highland estates: Charles Steuart and William Tomkins.

Widely travelled and extensively patronised, the English artist William Tomkins had a business that rested almost entirely on making estate views. In 1766, he had accepted a commission to paint the Grant family's sprawling estate at Strathspey in the far north-east of Scotland (Seafield Papers 1766). Taking the opportunity to advertise his services to Sir James Grant's neighbours, he also secured the patronage of the earls of Breadalbane, Fife and Findlater. Overtures made by the artist to James Duff, 2nd Earl Fife, proved especially lucrative, leading to an extended ensemble of views that staked out the patron's broad portfolio of regional and national interests, taking in the as yet unfinished Duff House and the sporting seat of Mar Lodge, as well as a newly purchased Thameside London townhouse and other properties (Figs C5.4 and C5.5). Likely as not, the set was meant to commemorate the earl's recent accession to the title and his plans to take forward a series of ambitious improvement schemes at these sites begun by his father. In Tomkins's view of Balvenie House, sitting across from the ruins of the old castle and set well back, surrounded by extensive plantations, ornamental gardens and parkland, rigs and common pasture, his patron's seat is just one element of a dutifully improved, richly varied and fertile valley prospect (see Fig. S3.8). Scattered across the platform-like foreground, a group of assorted rustics act out themes of pastoral ease and Georgic energy. Some take a rest

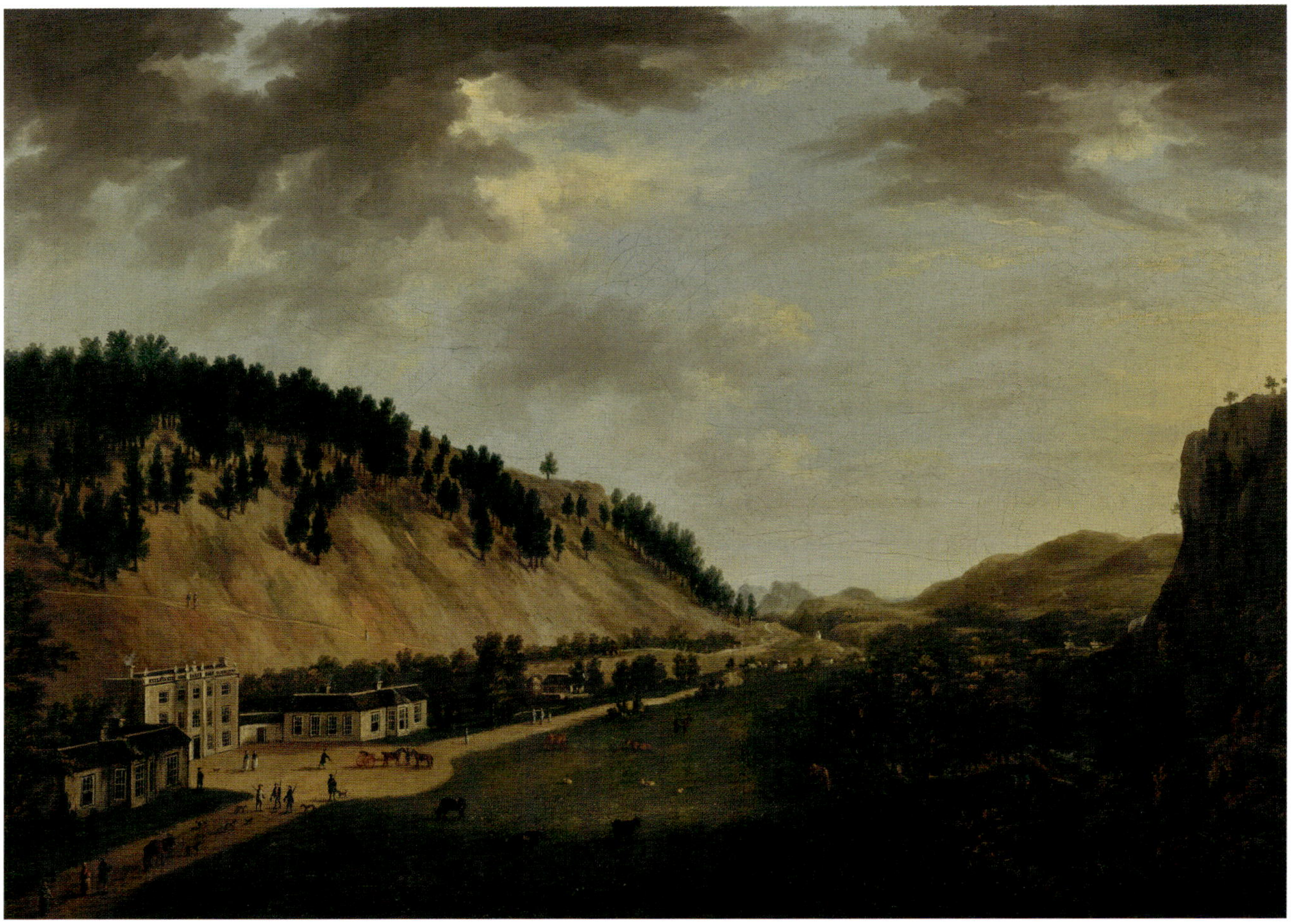

Fig. C5.5
William Tomkins, *View of Mar Lodge, in the Forest of Mar, a Shooting Place in the County of Aberdeen*, 1767, oil on canvas (PC)

from their labours, while others make their way to and from the fields or tend livestock, projecting a vision of the abundance and social well-being of Fife's estate.

In an effort to counter the obstacles to aesthetic appreciation of Highland scenery that writers like Edmund Burt had set out, signs of cultivation and population were being promoted at this time in a widely circulated manuscript authored by a protégé of Argyll's, Sir John Dalrymple. When he set out his 'loose thoughts on gardening' around 1760, the layout of the policies at his patron's Inveraray seat were held up as exemplary of how a 'highland situation' might be improved. Upland terrains were one of four 'capital situations of nature' Dalrymple thought characteristic of the British Isles. He argued that, 'being generally ill inhabited', they had 'too much the appearance of dead life', but added that the man 'fond of great projects, or great exploits; or who has a high regard for the splendour of his ancestors' could not help but be fired by the challenge of such a landscape (Williams 1983, 149). Estate portraiture helped codify such attitudes and articulate them to audiences well beyond the confines of manuscript culture.

Twelve months after his travels in the north-east of Scotland, Tomkins was to showcase the properties of the group of improving landowners that he had successfully petitioned there through the display of a triptych of estate views, including Fife's Rothiemay and Mar Lodge, at one of London's new public art exhibitions. Following an initial exhibition in 1760, these spectacular forms of modern visual display were already established as annual fixtures of the polite social calendar (Solkin 1993, 247–

276). Exposing audiences who had previously had scant opportunity to view contemporary art to their work, Tomkins and his fellow professionals had very quickly understood the importance of exhibitions as forums for the promotion of their abilities and patronage. Shown at the Society of Artists, the capital's most prestigious exhibiting body (until the founding of the Royal Academy of Arts the following year), the paintings that resulted from Tomkins's lucrative tour of Highland estates were among the earliest Scottish scenes to be put on public display in London. Although Paul Sandby had shown a group of five small watercolours of Scottish river scenery and cascades a few years earlier, the scale and subject-matter of Tomkins's oils were of a different order. Yet, for all their novelty, there was also something curiously old-fashioned about Tomkins's pictures. Laying out the terrain as a series of parallel bands, evenly lit and with a mass of painstaking detail creating multiple focal points, his view of Balvenie is a work firmly rooted in the past, in older Dutch and Flemish models of landscape art. In the words of a contemporary critic, 'while finished in a Neat manner', Tomkins's drily descriptive technique meant that his paintings 'want[ed] effect' (*A Critical Examination* 1767, 17). Something more eye-catching was demanded if a picture was going to command attention in the already over-crowded new London showrooms.

In 1767, Tomkins's Scottish scenes were joined at the Society of Artists by a number of other views of named places on noble estates, forming a virtual pictorial survey of aristocratic improvement schemes nationwide. Unlike Tomkins, who was content to align his art with the tried and tested, his fellow exhibitor Charles Steuart showed a keen awareness of the latest developments in his *View of a waterfall, fifty feet high, from the Hermitage in the Duke of Athol's gardens at Dunkeld* (Fig. C5.6). Ordered by John Murray, 3rd Duke of Atholl, on his inheritance of the title, it is a remarkable picture. It was, at least in part, a response to the work of the Dublin-born painter George Barret, who on moving to London a few years earlier had quickly established a reputation at exhibition with a series of dramatic, attention-grabbing oils, which combined unusual subject-matter with a distinctive sense of colour and handling. On being exhibited in the capital, Barret's paintings of the spectacular natural wonders on the boundaries of Edward, Lord Powerscourt's Wicklow demesne on the River Dargle had considerable appeal (O'Kane 2013, 114–119) (Fig. C5.7).

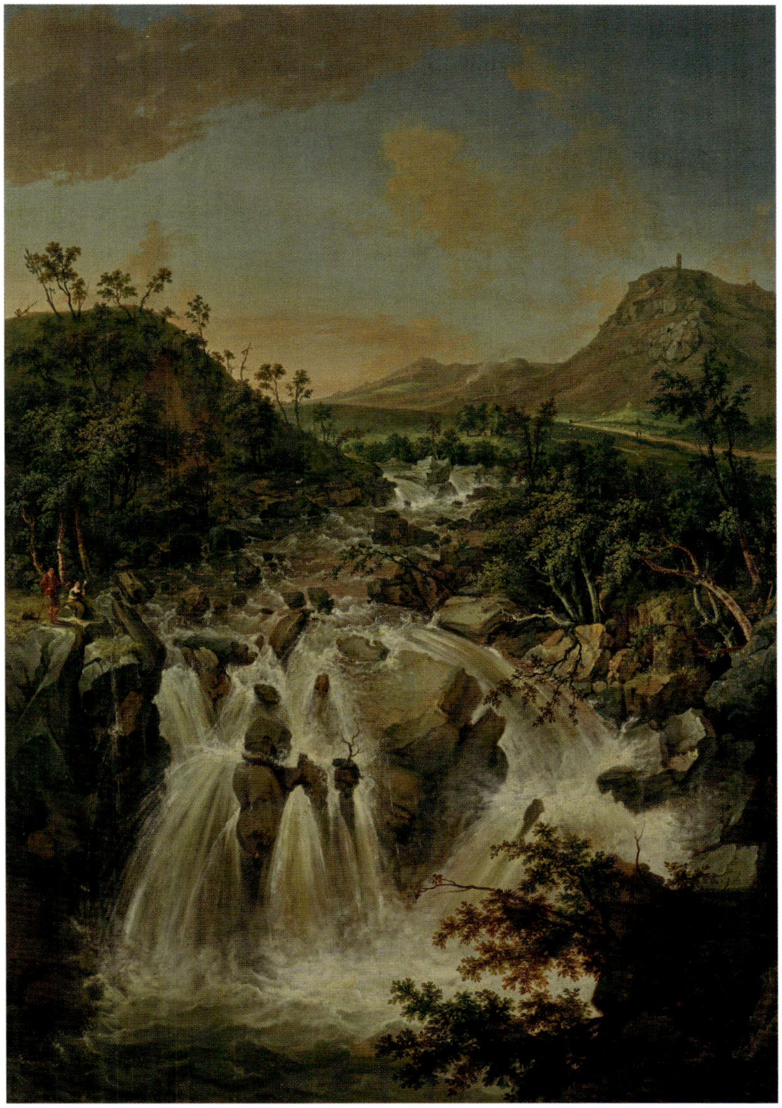

Fig. C5.6
Charles Steuart, *View of a Waterfall, fifty feet high, from the Hermitage in the Duke of Atholl's gardens at Dunkeld*, 1767, oil on canvas (AE)

Estate portraiture was dismissed by an ambitious metropolitan art world, anxious to assert its academic status and professional independence. Written off as a merely mechanical act of copying, of taking a likeness, and largely shaped and restricted by obeisance to a patron's demands, the genre appeared to offer little opportunity for the display of a distinct artistic sensibility. But, by extending the topographical scope of their art and incorporating a range of artistic, historic, literary and philosophical allusions, Barret was just one of a number of painters at the

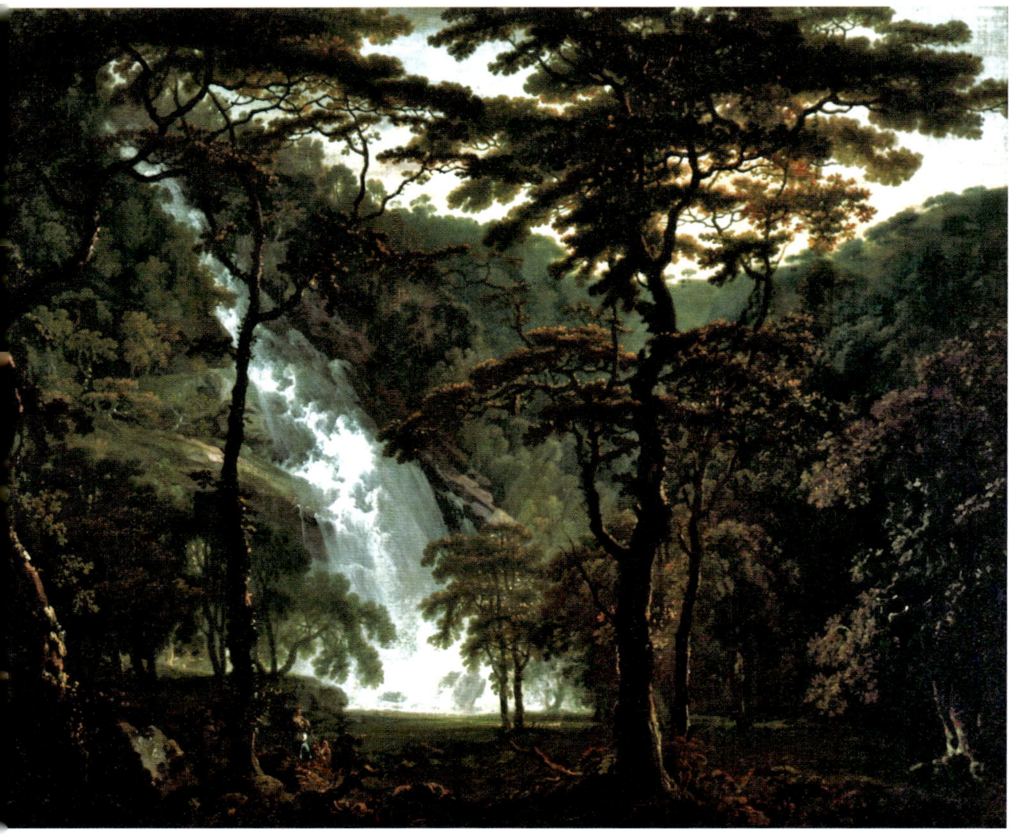

Fig. C5.7
Above. George Barret, *View of the Water-fall at Powerscourt in Ireland*, 1764, oil on canvas (WAG 1758)

Fig. C5.8
Opposite. George Barret, *A View of Dalkeith Park*, c. 1770, oil on canvas (BC)

time looking to shake these associations and raise the genre's cultural register. Besides being the first views of Irish scenery submitted to exhibition in the capital, Barret's observations on what his patron Edmund Burke termed 'the Accidents of Nature', on the fugitive and the transient, also introduced a heightened sense of drama into estate portraiture (Burke 1958–70 [1765], i, 294). His portrayal of cataracts and crags, lakes and mountains, viewed at different times of the day and often illuminated by dramatic lighting effects, has been routinely observed to draw on the aesthetics of the Sublime, as it had been characterised by his sponsor, answering Burke's contention that the quality was to be found in writing but not in painting; Barret took up his patron's advocacy of the 'easy observation of the commonest . . . meanest things in nature' as conveying 'the truest light' (Burke 1757, 38, 129). Having broken new ground in premiering views of the Irish landscape at exhibition, Barret went on to lay claim to being the pre-eminent painter of the wider Celtic fringe by taking on the scenery of Wales and Scotland, the latter in a highly lucrative series of pictures executed for Henry Scott, 3rd Duke of Buccleuch (Fig. C5.8 and Figs S3.12–S3.14). With labourers shown laying new paths and walkways, Barret's scenes depict improvement in action. Recalling some of the views on the River Dargle he had painted for Powerscourt earlier in his career, Barret exploited the dramatic potential of the thickly wooded gorge of the Esk that ran through the policies. Such pictures shifted the focus of the estate portrait away from the house and surrounding parkland to outlying monuments and natural wonders.

With his view of the spectacular Black Linn falls on the River Braan, however, Charles Steuart was to accord such features a far greater visual prominence than in Barret's art or the Old Master models for such craggy scenes. In his 'loose thoughts on gardening', which if not known to Steuart were surely familiar to his patron, Dalrymple had argued that '[t]he two best landscape painters in the world, NICOLAS POUSSIN and SALVATOR ROSA, both delighted in painting the great scenes of nature' that he associated with upland scenery. In Rosa's case, he 'chose terrible and noble natural situations' where there were 'few signs of life', other than perhaps the odd solitary philosopher or small band of brigands (Williams 1983, 151). While Steuart's painting recalls the supposed Sublimity of that artist's 'terrible' scenes, his attempt to render the thunderous progress of the cascading waters and spray thrown up by the deep, foaming pool below had few, if any precedents. Rosa's familiar and clearly inappropriate narratives of travellers set upon by lawless banditti also made way for figures altogether less threatening. Occupying a rocky promontory over the falls, traditionally dressed but classically posed Highlanders, a shepherd and his seated female companion, dressing a distaff, introduce an emblematic note, the formerly unruly native peoples now like those found in Tomkins's pictures also made 'civilised' by the forces of commerce and polite taste.

For all of his concern to align his art with Old Master tradition, and so style the Highlands as 'classic ground', Perthshire-born Steuart, a Gaelic speaker, ran a distinctly local eye over the scenery he was tasked with painting (Irwin 1977). His local connections shaped his art and career. While the itinerant Tomkins worked a series of neighbouring estates and then moved on, Steuart relied on a tightly knit, consistently loyal patronage network, who called on him to paint their lands

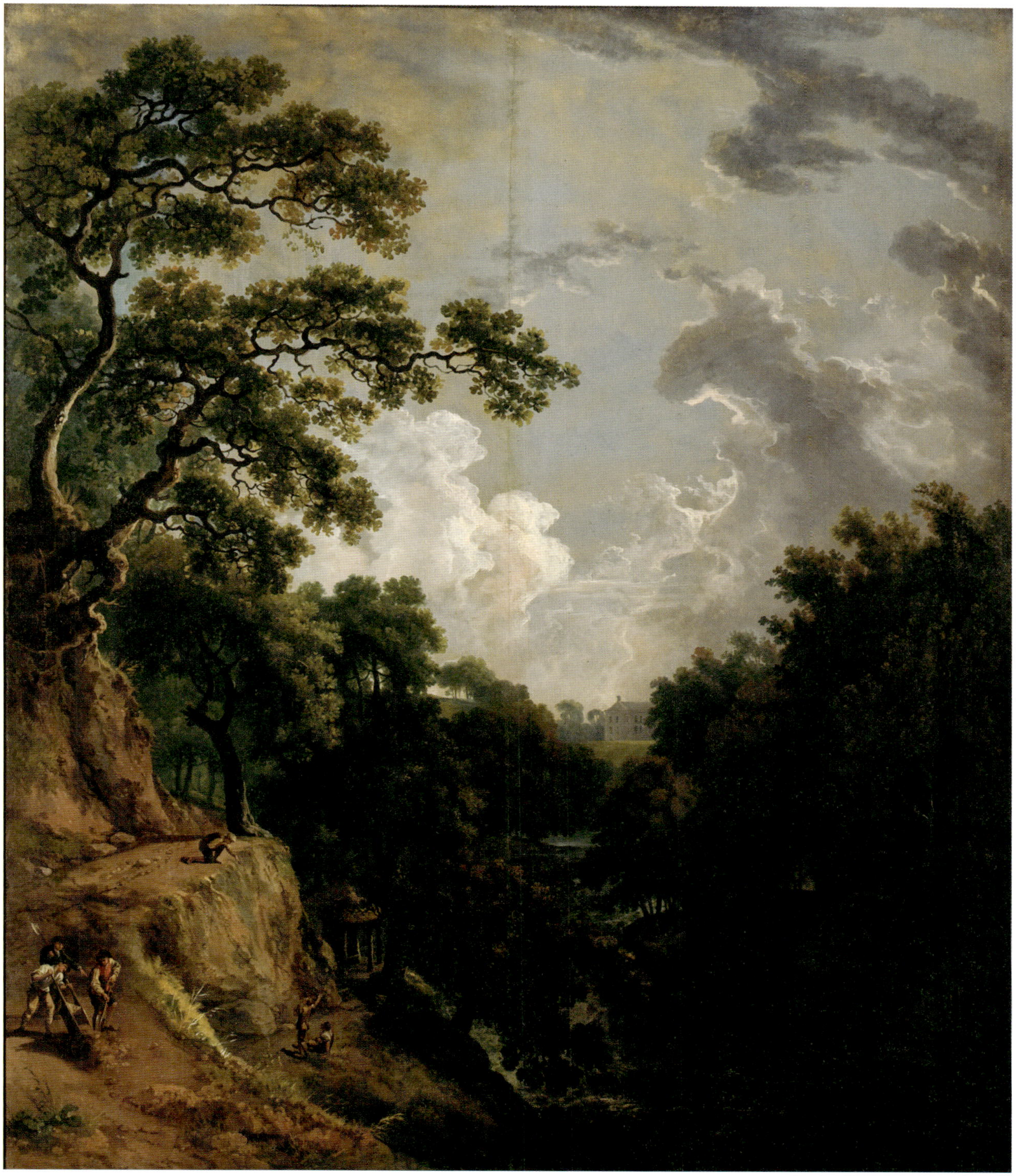

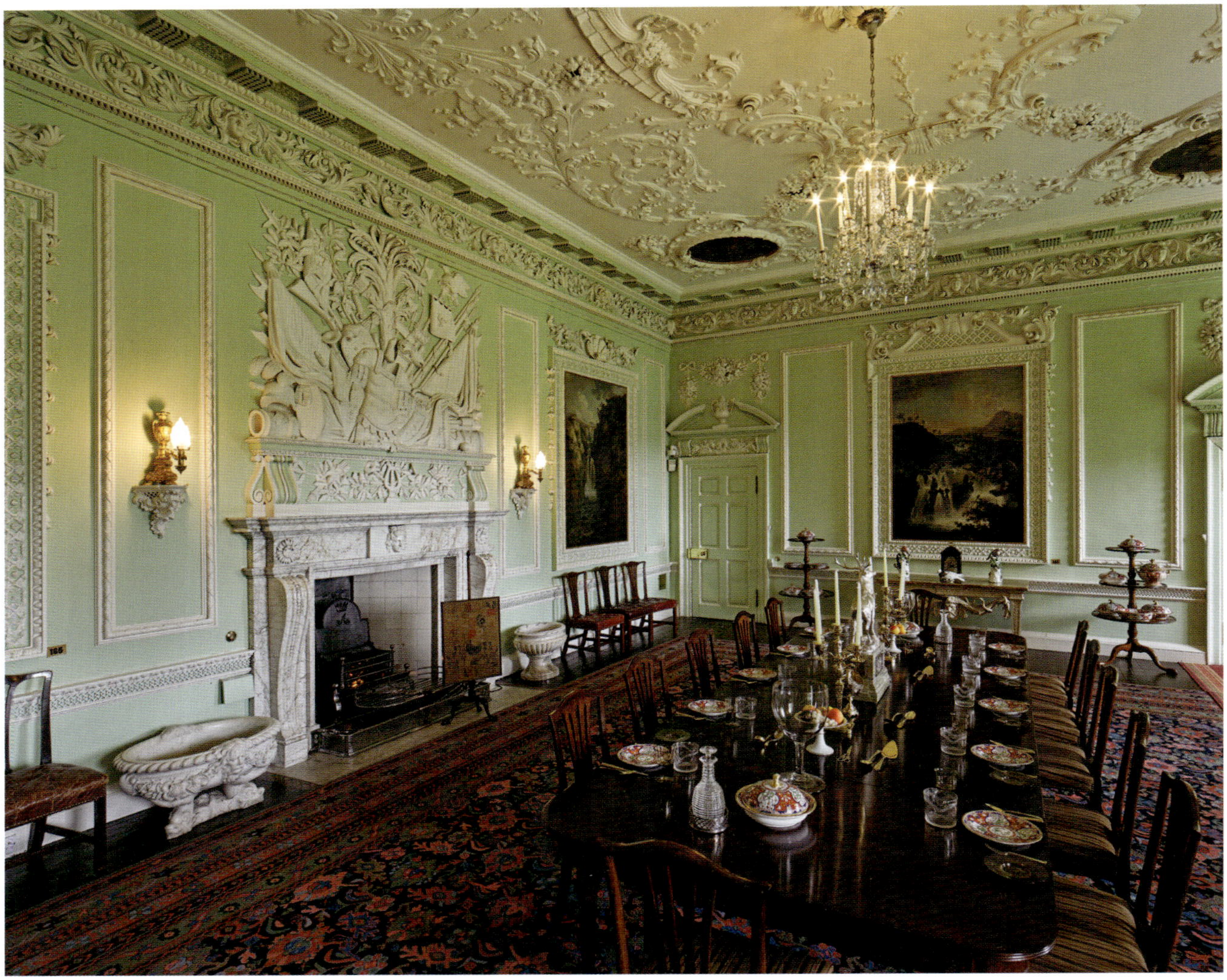

Fig. C5.9
Dining Room, Atholl House (now Blair Castle), photograph (AE)

multiple times over an extended period. Working for successive dukes of Atholl, he also enjoyed favour with Breadalbane as well as John, 3rd Earl of Bute, and his son-in-law Sir James Lowther (see Figs S3.5–S3.7). Together with his architect brother George, Charles Steuart appears to have seldom moved outside of the protection of this restricted, but enormously powerful, set, who owned estates south of the border as well as extensive lands in the north.

Based in London since the early 1760s, Steuart was to send a series of views set on and about Murray family lands to exhibition ahead of their installation at Atholl House (now Blair Castle), where the series was displayed to spectacular effect in the dining room (Coltman 2019, 90–96) (Fig. C5.9). Having spent much of the summer of 1764 at Dunkeld, 'taking Views' and probably giving drawing lessons, he had worked up a series of small oil paintings, as samples of a sort, for the carefully worked-out Atholl scheme (Figs S3.9–S3.11). Beginning with the large, ambitious oil of the Braan Falls that he submitted to the Society of Artists in 1767, Steuart would go on to exhibit a garden-like view of the Tayside ruins of Dunkeld Cathedral and an extensive prospect northwards along the river valley from the fields of the Torrvald farmstead. Ten years or so later, he was to complete the dining-room scheme for John Murray, the new 4th Duke of Atholl. Shifting the focus to the landscaping around Atholl itself, his views of falls on the River Bruar completed a decorative programme decades in the making. When *in situ*, framed by the dining room's window views out over Atholl's designed landscape and the ornate plasterwork of the interior by Timothy Clayton, Steuart's paintings sealed a complex allegory on the arts of war and peace. Borrowing a motif of Roman origin used frequently in funerary sculpture, Clayton's chimney piece took the form of a temporary field monument to a fallen warrior, encircled with trophies of war and heraldic emblems of the Murray family's entitlement. Its imagery celebrated the military past that secured those flanking scenes of present-day pastoral peace and Georgic abundance furnished by Steuart. It looked to the authority of Roman antiquity, but this iconography made allusion to Scotland's own classical past too.

Pointed up by the title in the catalogue, the vantage point for the picture Steuart exhibited at the Society of Artists in 1767 was 'the Hermitage': a decidedly theatrical viewing station set on a rocky outcrop that looked out on the Black Linn Falls. Writing just a few years earlier, Dalrymple had recommended making a feature of 'natural cascades' in Highland settings, as 'by their motion and sound' they might 'rouse and animate the attention from that stupor which the view of great and dreary objects creates' (Williams 1983, 150). Though the Falls of Braan were perhaps the best known, as we saw in the previous chapter, several neighbouring estates established such elemental features as designed set-pieces. Their development at sites such as Blair Moss House and the Acharn Hermitage made them key aspects of the imaginative geography of the region. While their encounter in the landscape or as they were recalled in a picture was understood as summoning the kind of affective charge that Dalrymple had identified, such powerfully emotive scenery also activated the historical imagination. Through their reading of James Macpherson's *Ossian*, London audiences were afforded new ways of appreciating the ruggedness and grandeur of the scenery of Steuart's pictures. Seen through that literary lens, they were comprehensible as views that recalled the topographical combinations of cataracts, caves and crags, haunted by the ghosts of noble warriors, which figured Ossianic space. Once the look-out over the Black Linn Falls was rebuilt in the early 1780s, to a design by George Steuart and renamed Ossian's Hall, they would be made more pronounced. But trails of allusion to Ossian's narratives of battle, exile and loss ran through Steuart's Highland estate scenes from the beginning.

Exhibition of Barret's, Steuart's and Tomkins's views of Scottish estates gave these sites a national profile, over and above reports made in the epistolary and word-of-mouth culture of the period. Indeed, it would be several more years before written accounts of sites such as the Dunkeld Hermitage were to appear in print. Together with several other local landowners, Atholl clearly understood the exhibition as a new means of displaying, portraying and promoting the Highlands and the landowners' place and position in that landscape. The display of such pictures in London was part and parcel of a wider concern led by Atholl to develop Perthshire and the wider region as a touring landscape, worth viewing and writing about, sketching and painting.

VIEWS AND VISIONS

Given the significance of forms of pictorial record to his enterprise, it is hardly surprising that Thomas Pennant made plans for a 'Lanscape [sic] painter' to be among the 'troop' accompanying him on his second Scottish tour (Pennant 1771b, I, 20). His belief in the explanatory power of visual images was borne out by the generous number and ever-changing make-up of illustrative plates interleaved throughout the various editions of his pioneering *Tours of Scotland*. Moreover, as the business-minded Pennant well appreciated, recent advances in the quality of domestic engraving had also made illustrative plates increasingly important to the commercial viability of the travel account. Though he was 'disappointed' by him in the end, and forced to rely on his 'servant' Moses Griffith's artistic skills, the painter that he had hoped to have accompany him on the journey through Scotland in 1772 was William Tomkins (Tomkins 1772; Pennant 1772, I, 23). It seems likely that the Welsh naturalist had approached the painter on the strength of the Scottish scenes he had shown recently in London, since plates of pictures that had appeared at exhibition by Steuart as well as Tomkins were featured in the various editions of Pennant's tours. Other than the designs produced by Griffith, the circumstances in which the images that accompanied Pennant's texts were produced were usually quite detached from the tour itself or the writing

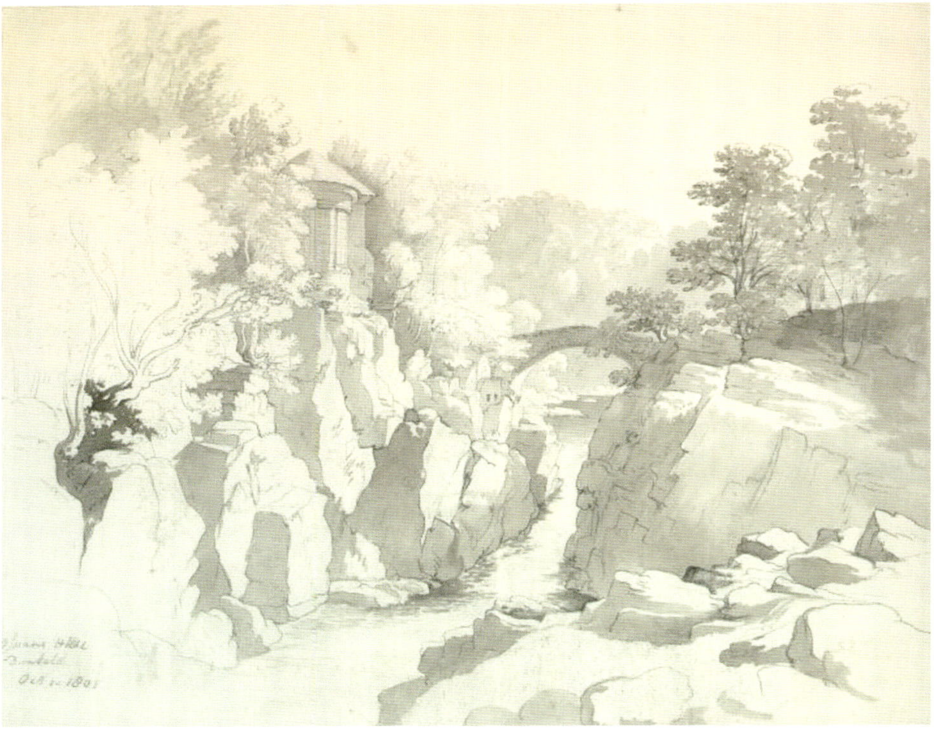

Fig. C5.10
Joseph Farington, *Ossian's Hall, Dunkeld*, 1 October 1801, pencil and wash (BM 1938, 1112.9)

of the account. Still, their selection was always judicious. They were carefully located and sometimes gestured to in the accompanying text. Plates acted as moments of diversion or rest from the journey, or else served as a further level of commentary, offering variously complementary and competing points of view, as it were, on the places encountered along the way. They added further to the chorus of voices, made up of correspondents and earlier authors, which jostled for attention in Pennant's texts. Though pleased to find his Perthshire seat 'finely puff'd' in the first published *Tour of Scotland*, the Earl of Breadalbane was to think the accompanying engraving, after a now untraced painting by Tomkins of Taymouth's Acharn cascade, 'ill represented' (Breadalbane 1771). Yet, with Pennant's *Tours* highlighting the improvement of Taymouth and the adjacent country on the national stage, the earl was happy to allow further works to be included in later editions. It was not just the author who had a stake in the illustration of his work.

In his search for works to accompany the various editions of his *Tours* across the British Isles, Pennant was able to draw on an established but rapidly expanding market for images of the national territory. There had been a lively demand for prints that encouraged admiration of native 'picturesque' and 'romantic' scenes for several decades; the publication of an engraving like that after Sandby's view of Leith was an attempt to profit from their growing popularity (Clayton 1995). Such publications targeted and aimed to promote an as-yet-undeveloped domestic tourist market or appealed to those print collectors who preferred more vicarious forms of travel. It meant that, with the growth of a highly organised, nationwide tourist infrastructure a few decades later, artists and publishers were well placed to exploit the polite vogue for viewing places of wild, untamed nature or sites of historic or industrial interest as well as the houses and parks of the country's elite.

By the turn of the century, looking to capitalise on the taste for Scottish scenery promoted by the likes of Pennant, scores of professionals were taking to the road. Usually commissioned by a print publisher, Joseph Farington, J.M.W. Turner and William Daniell, as well as many now lesser-known names, headed out in search of the picturesque and the Sublime. Following the established itineraries of noteworthy objects and places, they were to find themselves asked to frame up sights that, while novel pictorial subjects in the 1760s, were fast becoming hackneyed. On walking out to the Dunkeld Hermitage, during a tour of 1801, Farington for one could not help but recall the 'many drawings' of it he had seen in London, even if none of them had conveyed any 'adequate idea of the Scenery' as he was to encounter it. When it came to his own on-site sketch, the low vantage-point and framing elements were probably indebted as much to an earlier engraving after John 'Warwick' Smith as the actual view from the banks of the Braan (Fig. C5.10). Brought to mind when standing before such sights, writers' words and artists' pictures acted as points of reference for the tourist to recollect and imaginatively recreate. They conditioned the experience. For example, thinking Ossian's Hall an absurdity, 'ill adapted to the stile of the Landscape' surrounding it, Farington merely echoed the censorious remarks of others, William Gilpin being perhaps the best known of its critics (Farington 1978–84, V, 1641). Not all of Farington's fellow artists were as willing to submit to accepted opinion, however. Some of the more ambitious chafed against established views and viewpoints, exchanging the detached observational procedures of pictorial tradition for more immersive, personal forms of experience and expression.

Despite Gilpin's occasional interest in matters of improvement, such as Argyll's at Inveraray, the perspective of the picturesque tourist was poorly reconciled with signs of progress in the landscape. To adopt this point of view marked a wholesale departure from those who had, from Burt onwards, thought improvement a necessary precondition to making a landscape. It made Scotland's landed estates key sites of conflict. For Gilpin, all that the engineering of 'cascades, and slopes, and other puerilities' at Atholl's Braan-side pleasure grounds had achieved, as Nigel Leask points out in Chapter 1, was to turn a setting otherwise 'calculated to receive all the grandeur of landscape' into a stretch of fashionable, but to him vulgar, parkland. Writing of the viewing station over the Black Linn Falls, soon to be styled Ossian's Hall in honour of the country's bardic past, Gilpin dismissed it as a mere 'summer-house' (Gilpin 1789b, I, 114, 123). It was hardly a fitting tribute to the spirit of liberty and rebellion that Gilpin expressed admiration for when passing through Glencoe.

What may well have troubled Gilpin about Atholl's feature-piece building was its resemblance to forms of popular theatre. In an effort to explain the hall's workings to himself, on his Hermitage pilgrimage, the English tourist the Rev. John Sime assembled a sheet of drawings setting out the location, look and sightlines of the hall in a sketch map, elevation and cutaway profile (Fig. C5.11). Plotting the winding walks and river crossing around the apsidal-ended structure, Sime's ground plan maps the series of arboreal screens and openings around the riverside viewing station that helped create a sense of drama on the approach to Ossian's Hall. As Sime's sectional sketch shows, on entering, visitors found themselves in a small, gothic antechamber, confronted by a large painting of the bard, if not by Charles Steuart then by his brother, the architect of this miniature theatre. Beyond lay 'an interior apartment, spacious, light, airy, and elegant' as one contemporary had it, which led to an open balcony above the Black Linn Falls. By all accounts, the auditory and visual sensation was overwhelming. While 'the stunning din' and sight of the cataract 'co-operated . . . to impress the feelings with a pleasing and solemn awe', for one visitor the reverie was 'disagreeably broken' by the 'glaring gaiety of the room'. Suited more to a '*boudoir* than a hermitage', its fine furnishings were at odds with the elemental power of the falls. It was little more than showmanship. Its striving for effect, whereby mirrors 'inlaid round the walls, and in the ceiling' afforded 'various reflections of the whitened volume of water, as it pours down the cataract; like smoke, like flame, like boiling oil', was of a kind with increasingly commonplace, technology-driven forms of commercial urban spectacle: the beguiling world of wonderous transformation and imaginative transport delivered by dioramas, panoramas and illuminated transparencies (Heron 1793, 170–171; Altick 1978; Hyde 1988; Stafford and Terpak 2001). Like Robert Barker's 'panorama' (the term the entrepreneur coined in 1791 to lend cultural heft to his new 360-degree 'view of any country or situation'), Atholl's temple to the Celtic bard turned the landscape into a room (Barker 1796, 166). One belonged to the realm of the country estate, the other the modern city, but the theatrical set-pieces of the period's designed landscapes and the taste for spectacular landscape entertainments were of a part, eliciting emotive responses through trickery. Both fed the making of landscape as a pictorial art, as they learned from its conventions. Several historians have, for instance, explored the links between the commanding 'all-embracing view' afforded by the panorama and the visual mastery associated with the military prospect and the estate portrait (Bermingham 2001; Charlesworth 1996; Oleksijczuk 2011). But, conversely perhaps, the experience of a landscape like that of the Hermitage might also prompt a more intimate short-focus or altogether unfocused form of viewing and picture-making.

Beginning in 1786, the 4th Duke of Atholl commissioned more than fifty views of his properties from the Gilpin family-sponsored painter John 'Warwick' Smith, mostly set on his ancestral Perthshire estates (Fig. C5.12). Such an extensive pictorial survey was unusual. In the mid 1790s, the artist was to execute a set of perspectives of the picturesque improvement of Thomas Johnes's showpiece Cardiganshire estate of Hafod. But that commission was for only fifteen drawings and intended to illustrate James Edward Smith's *Tour to Hafod* (1810). Other than the self-published aquatint of Ossian's Hall that was the probable reference point for Farington's drawing, Smith's Perthshire scenes would not seem to have been intended for wider circulation. However, much like the views he was to execute for his Welsh patron, they do take the viewer on a 'tour'. Looking across the series as a whole, which was probably originally kept in a library

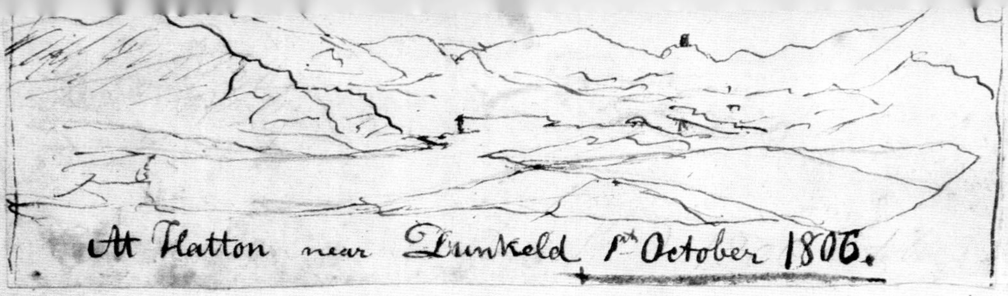

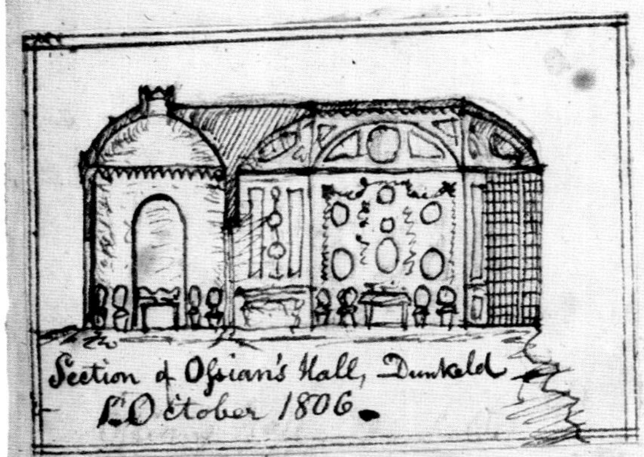

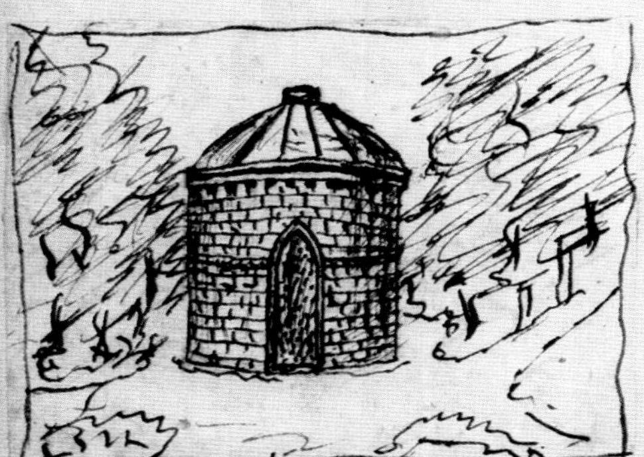

Ossian's Hall - Dunkeld -

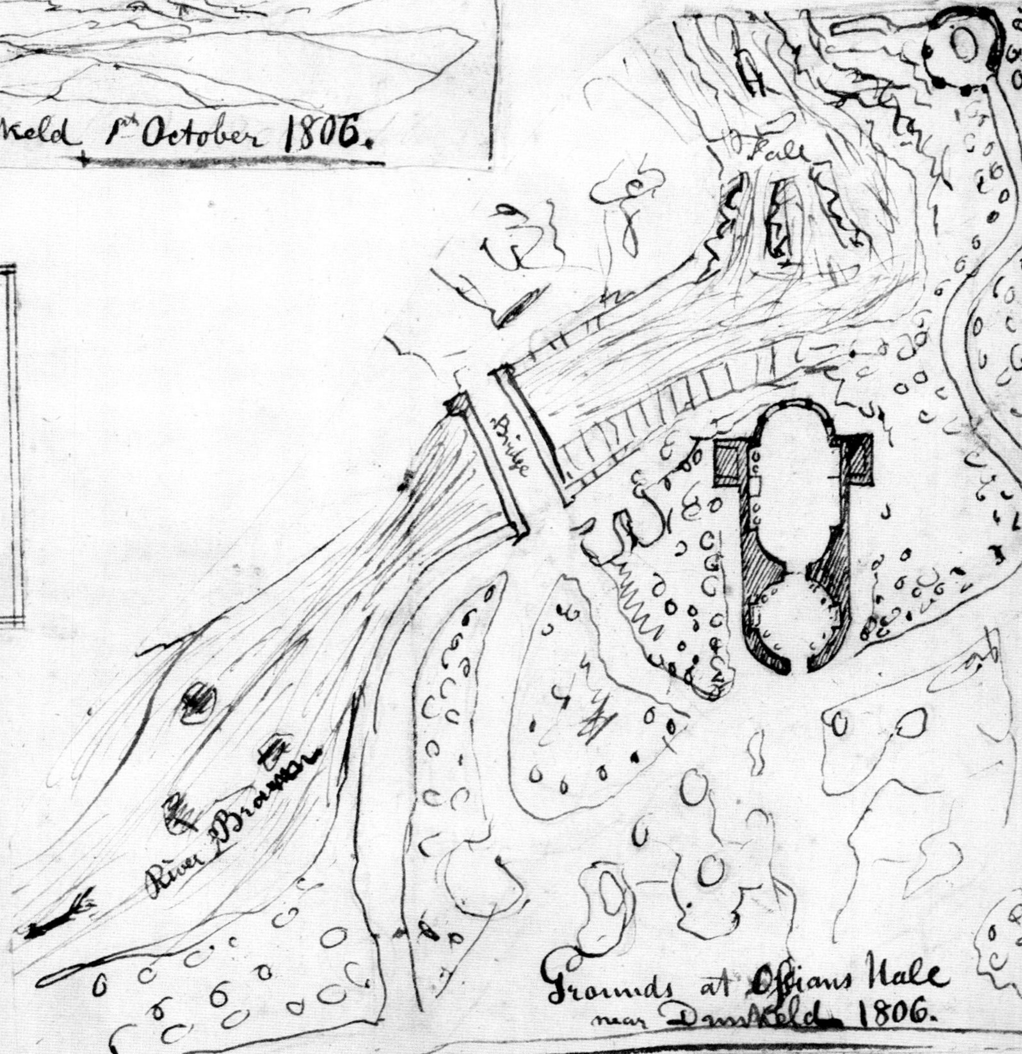

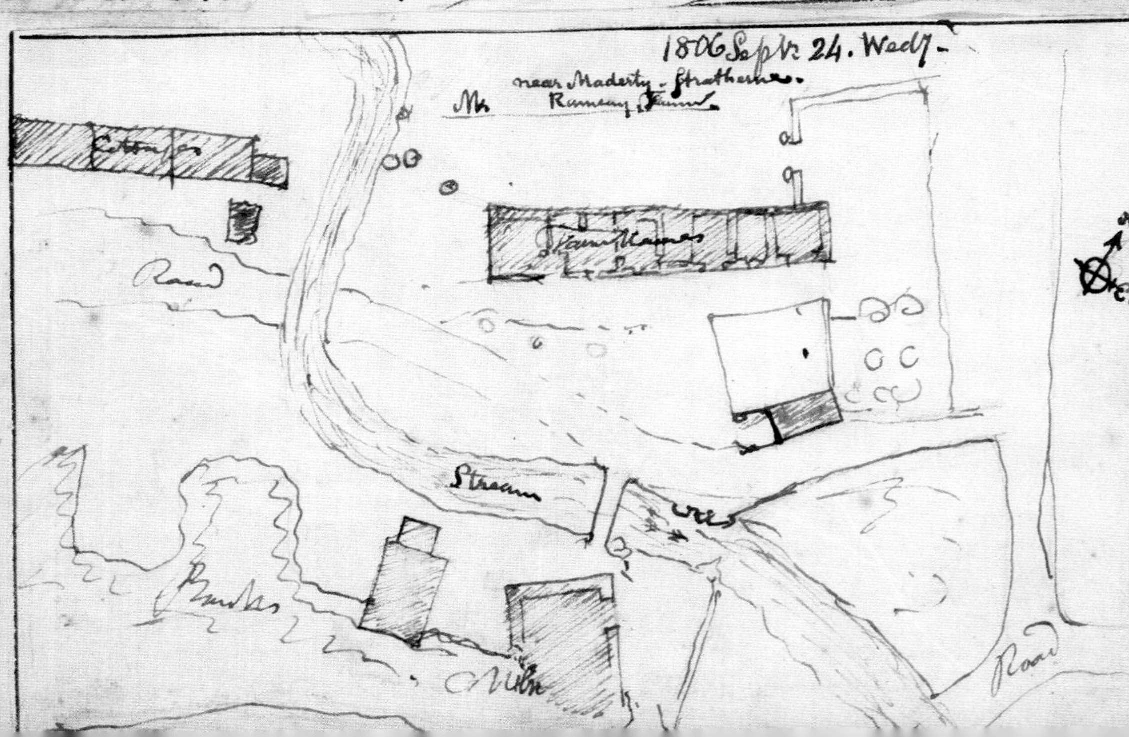

folio for close perusal, there is a sense of constant diversion and faltering, staccato-like progress through the landscape. Sudden bursts of scenery emerge from the shadows of rocky crevices or thick woodland, in ways which mirror the effects of concealment and surprise the landscaping strived for on the ground. In Smith's drawings, the pleasures of the landscape traversed do not reside solely in a series of static confrontations with its sights and wonders. At times, the artist's gaze falls on the ground beneath him rather than up ahead, on the confluence of the waters of the Garry and Tilt or the granite rocks met with on a walk up Craig-y-Bairns.

Technically, Smith's work represented a development of the 'stained drawing', as it was called, with which Sandby had been associated. Less reliant on line and looking to exploit the potential of watercolour, Smith achieved brilliant effects of light and atmosphere through the use of transparent washes. Famously, however, J.M.W. Turner was dismissive of what he saw as 'Warwick' Smith's 'mechanically systematic process of Drawing', telling Farington that he avoided any such rote means in his own work, employing instead an improvised, in-the-moment kind of approach, involving a whole repertory of techniques, of blotting, rubbing, scraping, scratching and stopping out, until an image began to emerge that 'at last expresses in some degree the idea in his mind' (Farington 1978–84, IV, 1255). In 1801, a short journey into Scotland, on the back of a sketching trip to the Lakes, allowed Turner to try out these innovative methods of picture-making on many of the places and sites on Atholl lands that Smith had spent the past decade and a half painting. The differences between their approaches is instructive. Whereas the older artist, when faced with scenes of wild nature, frequently looked to bring them within the compass of the familiar, falling back on the tried-and-trusted planar divisions and framing devices of the landscape art of the past, Turner attempted to find some kind of pictorial equivalent for the messy, overgrown tangle of a woodland scene. Hastily drawn and highly schematic, his sketches of sites along the Braan abandon the static, staged vantage-points of the banks and head off-track, capturing a sense of immersion in the landscape (Fig. C5.13). Turner's pictorial shorthand is such that details can be slow to reveal themselves. He concentrates on the component parts of nature or reduces a wider, more general view to the sketchiest of outlines. The artist was far from alone in looking to capture such contingencies; one writer at the time noted how 'every change of situation in a spectator, changes the point of view relating to an object seen, and may be said to form a new landscape' (*Landscape Magazine* 1793, 14). Nature offered up an endless variety of perspectives as the artist moved in relation to it.

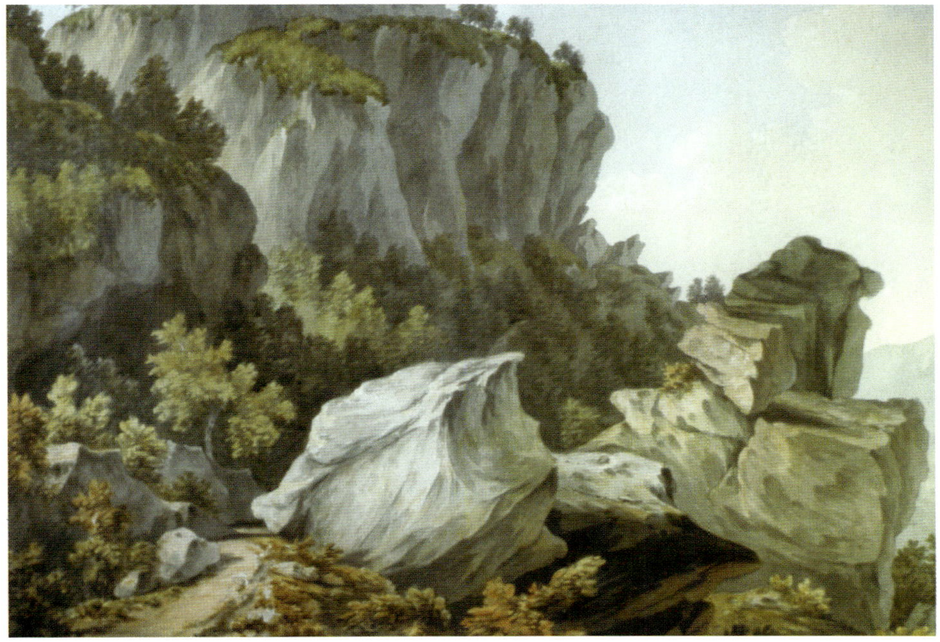

Fig. C5.11
Opposite. Reverend John Sime, *Grounds at Ossian's Hall, near Dunkeld*, 1806, pencil and pen (HES SC 681241)

Fig. C5.12
Above. John 'Warwick' Smith, *View on Craig y Bairns, Perthshire*, c. late 1780s, watercolour (AE)

Turning to the watercolours that Turner was to work up from memory as much as the spare outlines and colour notes of his pocket-sized sketchbooks, there is a similar sense of the artist wrestling with a quality of light or the weather of a particular day (Fig. C5.14). Together with the *virtuoso* mastery of his medium, it is a property that distinguished the work of the modern artist from those reliant on the learnt formulas and optical devices like the *camera obscura* characteristic of the amateur artist–tourist or the less culturally ambitious fellow professional. With that in mind, it may be that Gilpin's significance for the professional artists who followed him on the Scottish tour lay more in the taste for views of the domestic landscape that his writings helped create than in his aesthetic programme, except as that was, if anything, a model and a method to be rejected. Though his writings were sensitive to the qualities of a changeful sky, and encouraged an awareness of the contingencies of light and weather in the appreciation of nature, this

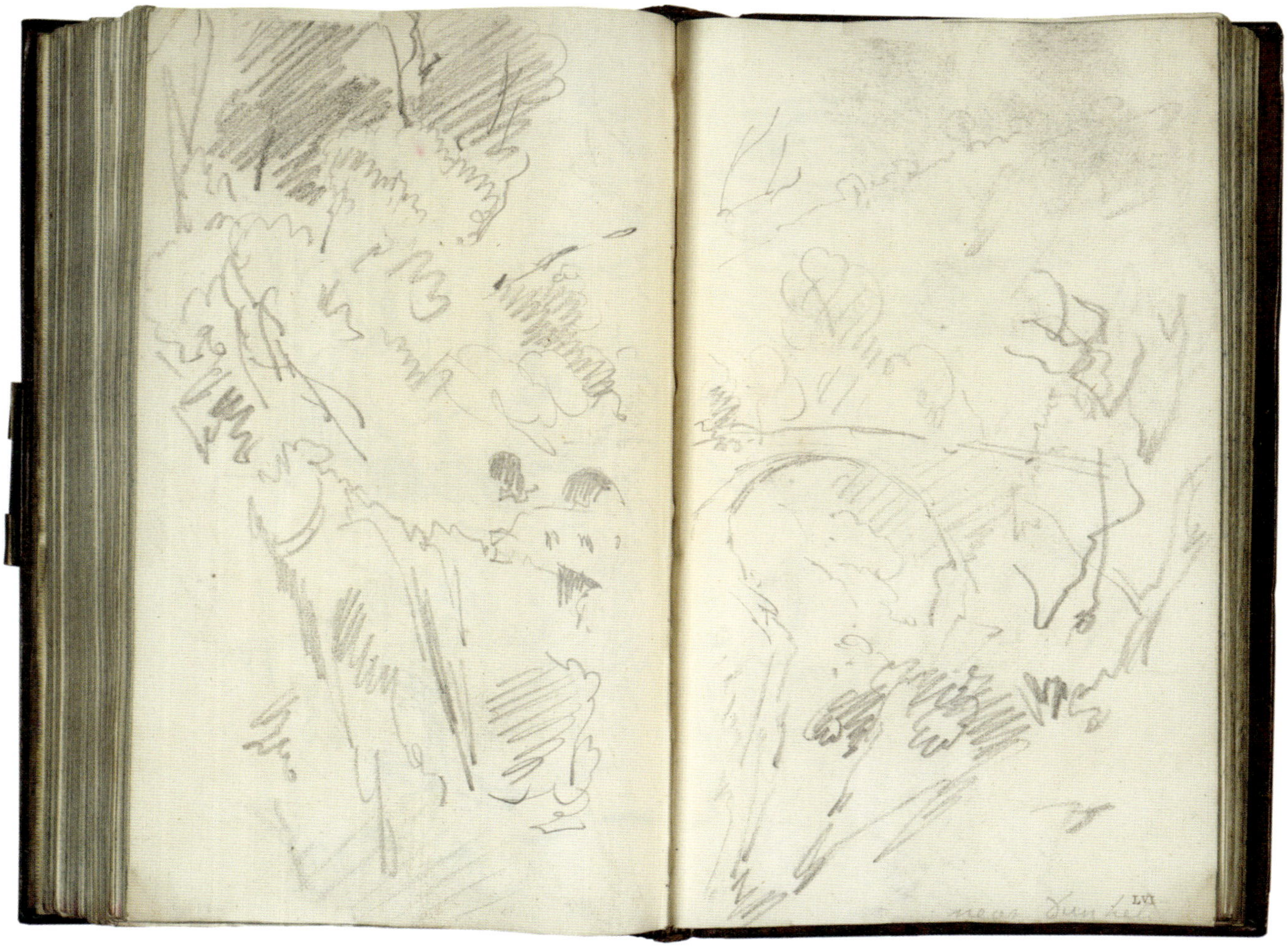

Fig. C5.13
Joseph Mallord William Turner, *Hermitage Bridge, Dunkeld*, 1801, pencil from Scotch Lakes Sketchbook [Finberg LVI] (TG D03177–D03178)

was less apparent in the accompanying aquatints. The rules of art that he adhered to were not flexible enough to capture those fleeting scenes glanced through the carriage window that so delighted him. In this sense, the set of principles he advocated was as out of step with the value increasingly placed on the artist's unique, unconditioned response, as registered in their individual touch or signature style, as it was with the tastes of the aristocratic land owners whose landscapes even the likes of Turner were still obliged to paint.

Though the work of a tourist–amateur, rather than the professional artists that have been the focus of this chapter, by way of a conclusion we might look closely at one further image of the landscape around Atholl's Dunkeld estate (Fig. C5.15). A Lowland Scot, colonial official and ex-military man, trained to sharpen his eye with a sketchbook by his tutor Paul Sandby, the artist George Heriot was taking in the changing face of the country after many years overseas (Finley 1983). Arriving at Dunkeld, he was clearly struck by the dramatic efforts to build Thomas Telford's new bridge over the Tay introduced in Chapter 4. The scarcity alone of images portraying the mechanics of road and bridge building in the Highlands make this little-known watercolour worthy of our attention. But, more than that, in the circumstances of its making as well as its imagery, Heriot's drawing also allows us to review the broad range of social forces and relations that combined to remake Scotland's localities and

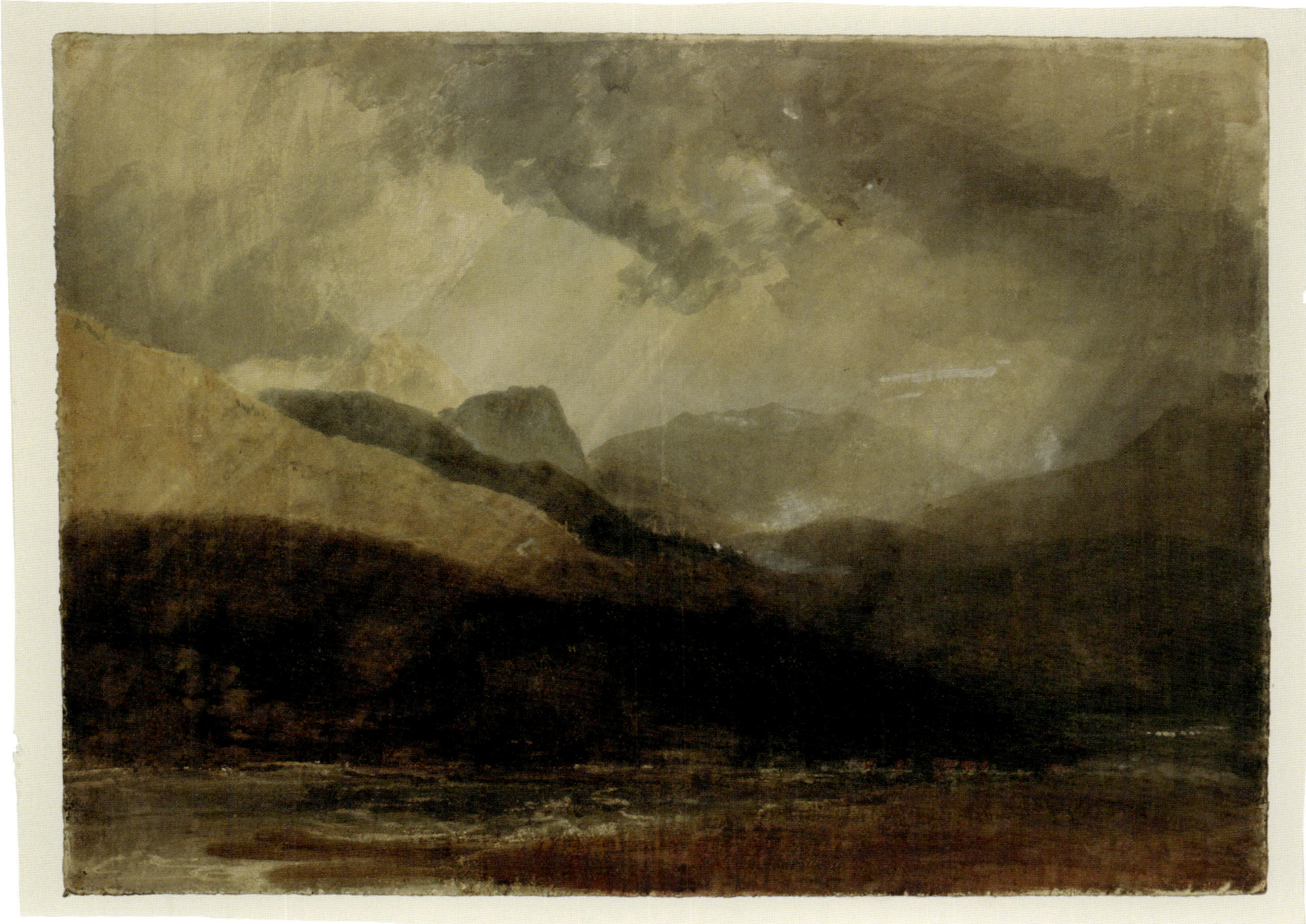

spur the inter-related practices of landscape art and travel traced by this chapter.

Stationed on the river's southern banks, Heriot took care to situate Telford's new technological wonder in relation to several landmark features of what was a now canonical cultural landscape. Stretching out across the swift, hazardous currents of the Tay, the rhythmic framework of the modern bridge arches frames the skeletal remnants of the cathedral on the far shore. Beyond the screen of buildings and woodland that edge the far bank lies the parkland of Atholl's Dunkeld House. With the duke making a hefty financial investment in the scheme, its inclusion is a reminder that the project was in some senses an extension of aristocratic power. Back across the river and framed by the branches of a decorative larch, which allude either to the ducal plantations across the way or to the role the wood had in the building of the bridge, a stretch of gravel deposit is enlivened

Fig. C5.14
Joseph Mallord William Turner, *Blair Atholl, Looking Towards Killiecrankie*, c. 1801, watercolour and gouache with stopping-out from 'Watercolours Derived from the 1801 Scottish Tour', accepted by the nation as part of the Turner Bequest 1856 (TG D04179)

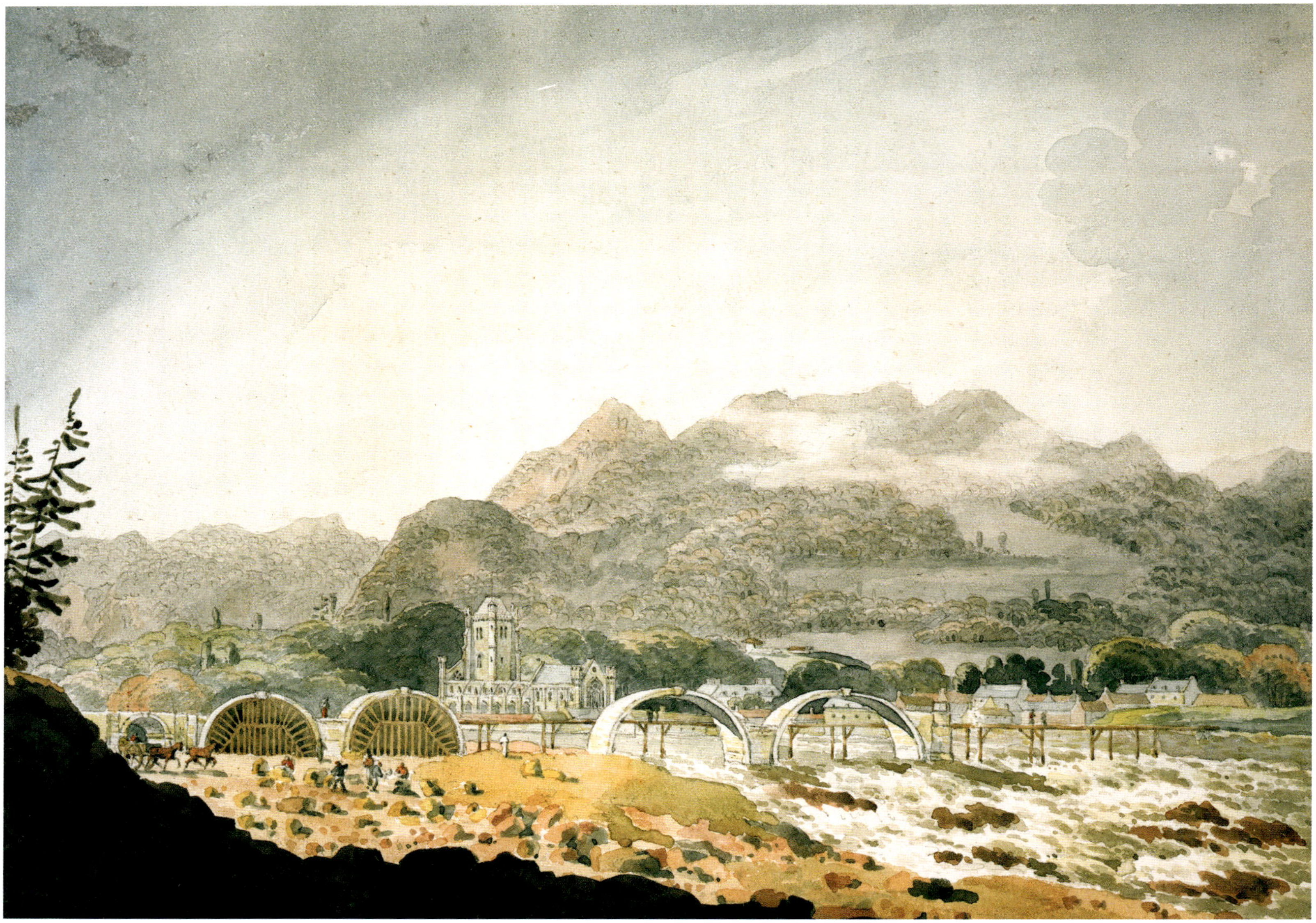

Fig. C5.15
George Heriot, *The Building of Telford's Bridge at Dunkeld, Perthshire*, 1806, watercolour (HES A 33037 CN)

with anecdotal incident, most notably a party of labourers dressing locally quarried sandstone. Cutting back across the picture-plane is a temporary wooden pont that shadows the masonry piers and arches already in place. All of this finely observed detail leads the viewer neatly through the construction process. But the artist's concerns were not so narrowly documentary perhaps. There is something poetic in the contrast of the mundanity of the labourers' toil and the epic grandeur of the situation. Moreover, in the startling conjunction of the cathedral's Gothic arches with those of the bridge taking shape before them, the drawing makes deliberate allusion to the play of past and present in the making of this landscape.

Others were to cast Telford's improvements to the country's infrastructure in a scenic light; William Daniell, for one, took delight in the stark contrast between the slender lattice ironwork structure that carried the Great North Road across the Kyle of

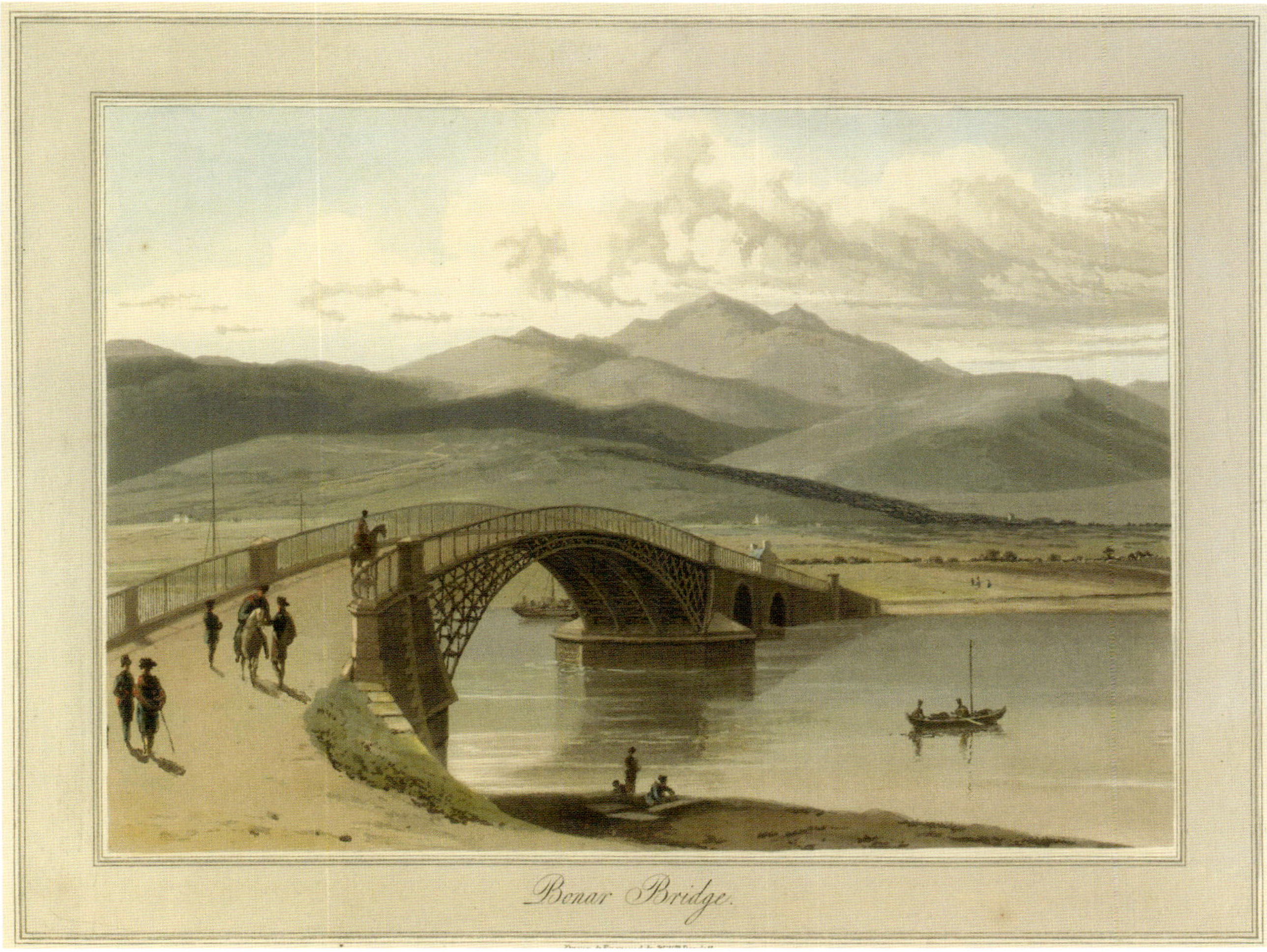

Fig. C5.16
William Daniell, *Bonar Bridge*, c. 1814, aquatint in *A Voyage Round the North and North West Coast of Scotland, and the Adjacent Islands* [1820] (Al R5CDKT)

Sutherland at Bonar Bridge and the bare expanses of the surrounding hillsides (Fig. C5.16). Such images are rarely so poignant as Heriot's drawing, however. On one level, as Telford's plans saw buildings pulled down and roads redirected, Heriot's picture reflects on what was about to be swept away. But, on another, the drawing pays homage to the forces galvanising the landscape, that combination of civic, commercial and landed interests that were driving projects like the Dunkeld bridge development at a local and national level. Moreover, it is an image that, in the artist's biography and in the conditions around its making as much as its subject-matter, brings together several notable tensions in the picturing of land and life in Scotland. The work of a Lowland Scot, training his military-educated eye on the transformation of the Highlands, Heriot's drawing exemplifies just some of the complex exchanges and interactions that went into making Scottish scenery the subject of landscape art. Whether it evolved out of the cultural to and fro between untamed wilds and improved landscape, Highland estates and London exhibitions, the commercialised popularisation of the arts and professional artistic ambition, or the rooted local point of view and the restless touristic eye, the art of travel played an important role in cultivating the taste for the startling scenery brought into view along Scotland's 'old ways' and new roads.

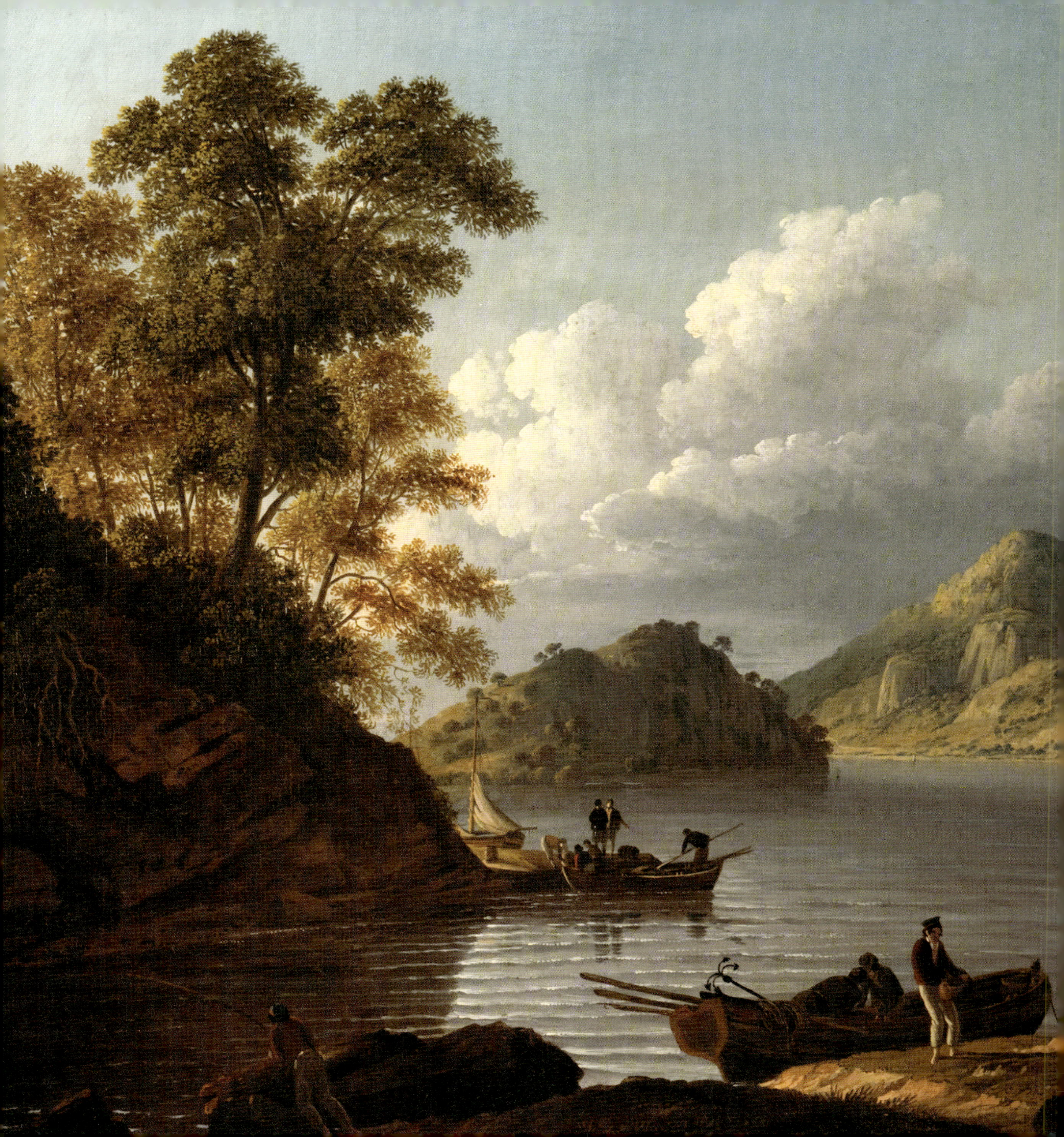

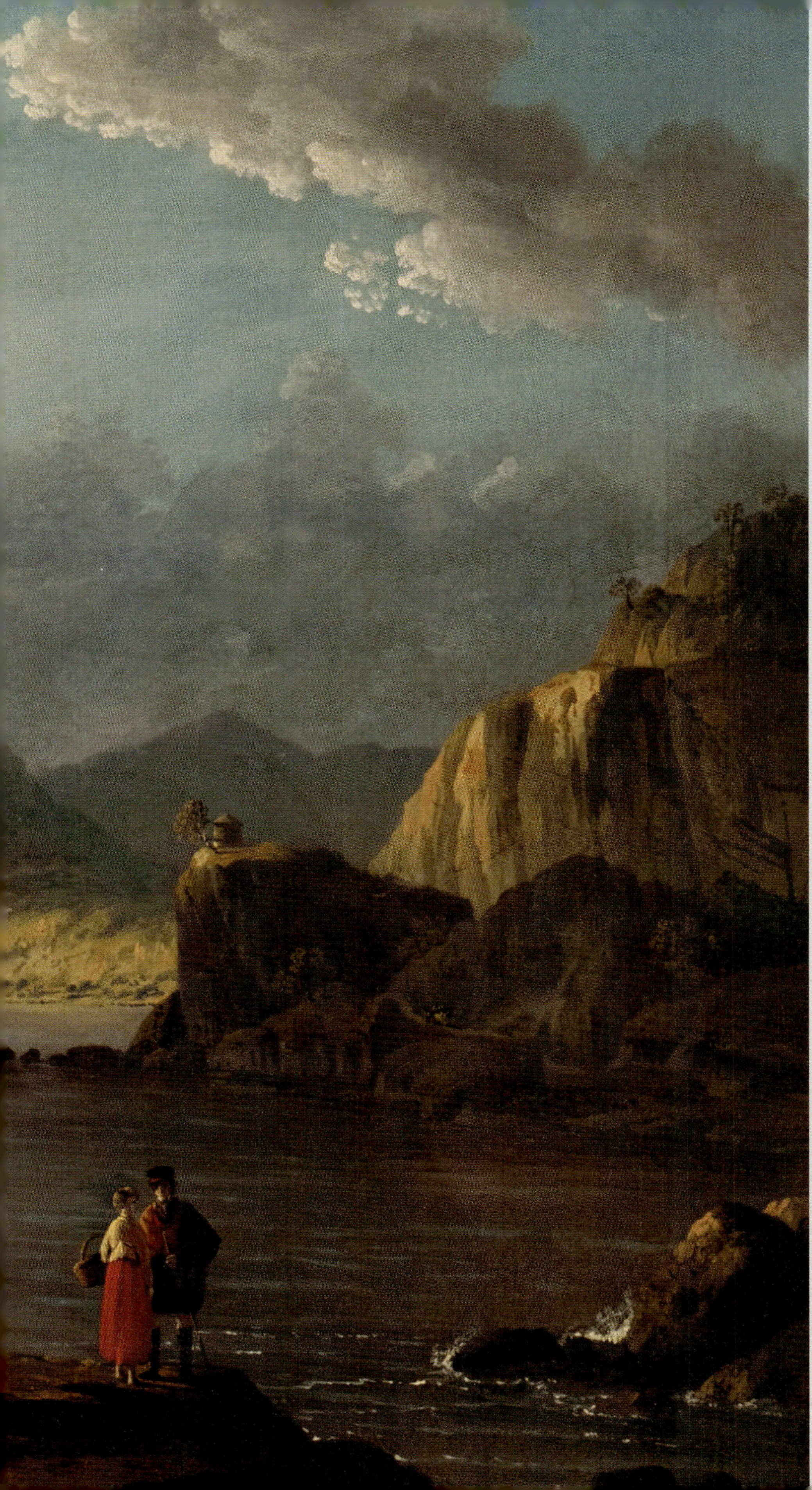

SECTION FOUR

Picturesque Prospects and Literary Landscapes

John Bonehill and Nigel Leask

Fig. S4.1
John Knox, *Highland Loch Scene (Loch Katrine)*, c. 1820s, oil on canvas (GMC PC.131)

The summer dawn's reflected hue
To purple changed Loch Katrine blue;
Mildly and soft the western breeze
Just kiss'd the Lake, just stirred the trees,
And the pleased lake, like maiden coy,
Trembled but dimpled not for joy;
The mountain shadows on her breast
Were neither broken nor at rest;
In bright uncertainty they lie,
Like future joys to Fancy's eye.

(Sir Walter Scott, *The Lady of the Lake*, Canto 3, st. 2, in *Poetical Works of Sir Walter Scott*, ed. J. Logie Robertson (London, 1913), 229–230)

Fig. S4.2
Opposite. John Knox, *Landscape with Tourists at Loch Katrine*, c. 1815–20, oil on canvas (NGS NG 2557)

Painted sometime around 1815 or thereabouts, John Knox's view of Loch Katrine is unusual in placing modern tourists admiring a sublime Highland landscape so explicitly centre-stage (Fig. S4.2).[1] It features two fashionable young gentlemen and their elegant female companion pausing to take the view up the loch from the popular beauty spot known as 'the Trossachs'. Judging by their parasols and picnic basket, they are about to take a boat to the wooded islet towards which one of the men gestures, his words drowned out by the kilted bagpiper beside him. His theatrical flourish enforces the message that this is a landscape of epic scale and spectacle: its drama lies not only in the shaggy woodland of the water's edge or the twin summits of Ben Venue soaring above the rocky backdrop, but in its rich, albeit recent, literary associations. Like hundreds of other tourists, the party have been drawn to this spot by Walter Scott's best-selling poem of 1810, *The Lady of the Lake*, which gave new resonance to the scenic attractions of this relatively accessible but until then not regularly visited area of the Highlands: Isabella Spence estimated that five hundred tourist carriages visited the Trossachs in the first year of publication alone (Spence 1811, I, 200). Knox's tourists are bound for 'Ellen's Isle', the setting of the poem's opening cantos: like Scott's protagonist James Fitz-James, diverted from his stag hunt by the charms of Ellen Douglas (the eponymous 'Lady of the Lake'), and her own beloved Malcolm Graeme, the two young men and their female companion are indulging in their own 'holiday romance' (Watson 2012, 59).

We might imagine that the party, having left their carriage at Ardcheanochrochan Inn (a recently converted farmhouse, serving refreshments to tourists from nearby Callander or Aberfoyle), have just descended the steep path from the wicker hut, visible on the promontory above them, to the loch-side quay where boats were 'kept in readiness to row visitors across to the little island' made famous by Scott (Meissner 1820, 59). According to the minister of Callander, the Rev. James Robertson, writing in the *Statistical Account* in 1794, there were 'two hutts of wicker work . . . for the accomodation of strangers' wishing to admire and sketch 'this wild and picturesque landscape' (Robertson 1794, 579). They had been erected by Lady Clementina Drummond, daughter of the Jacobite 11th Earl of Perth, who later, in 1807, would marry the wealthy English nobleman Peter Burrell, 22nd Baron Willoughby of Eresby. Like those similar viewing pavilions erected on the Atholl and Breadalbane estates discussed in Chapter 4, the wicker huts – made accessible by a new road, blasted out of the rock – had therefore framed visitors' perspectives on the scenery long before the publication of Scott's poem. Their presence also gave the lie to Sarah Murray's claim to have 'discovered' the Trossachs in 1796: she had gone so far indeed as to name the promontory 'Murray Point', though fortunately the name did not stick (Murray 1799, 150; Leyden 1903, 15–16). Seen from the south-west, though now more distant and right of centre, this jutting headland also features prominently in another view of Loch Katrine by Knox, of a different character, but still primarily a study of its literary landmarks (see Fig. S4.1).

In *Recollections of a Tour Made in Scotland in 1803*, Dorothy Wordsworth described the poet Samuel Taylor Coleridge hailing her from one of the huts 'with a shout of triumph . . . exult[ing] in the glory of Scotland'. Ascending with her brother William to join Coleridge, on the 'high and perpendicular rock, that rises from the bed of the lake', she had admired the view of Ben Venue and Loch Katrine, concluding that 'the place was all eye, and completely satisfied the sense and the heart' (Walker 1997, 103–104, 104). The popularity of the Trossachs as a tourist destination in 1803 is demonstrated by the fact that Dorothy obtained a slim guidebook based on Robertson's account, entitled *Sketch of the Most Remarkable Scenery near Callander,* from a waiter in a local inn (Fig. S4.3). In 1806, the minister Patrick Graham published his rival *Sketches Descriptive of Picturesque Scenery, on the Southern Confines of Perthshire, including the Trossachs*, advocating the approach from Aberfoyle, his text originally intended as letterpress for a series of printed views after Joseph Farington. Scott plundered all these tourist sources in creating his romantic vision of the Trossachs, as is evident from the copious notes to *The Lady of the Lake*. How appropriate then that, in 1820, the inn at Callander provided 'copies of all Scott's poems, maps of those districts which the bard has rendered classic ground, and a little description of the scenery about Loch Katrine, prepared by the landlord of the inn, and which consisted of quotations from the "Lady of the Lake"' (Meissner 1820, 59).

In the wake of the poem's success, Lady Perth's huts indicated an onward journey through the literary landscape of Scott's medieval romance. Here in the Trossachs, events 'which had no reality, save in the imagination of the Poet' were 'regarded as historical facts' (Meissner 1820, 59). Alighting on Ellen's Isle, Knox's *tourists à la mode* would have identified with Fitz-James's vision of

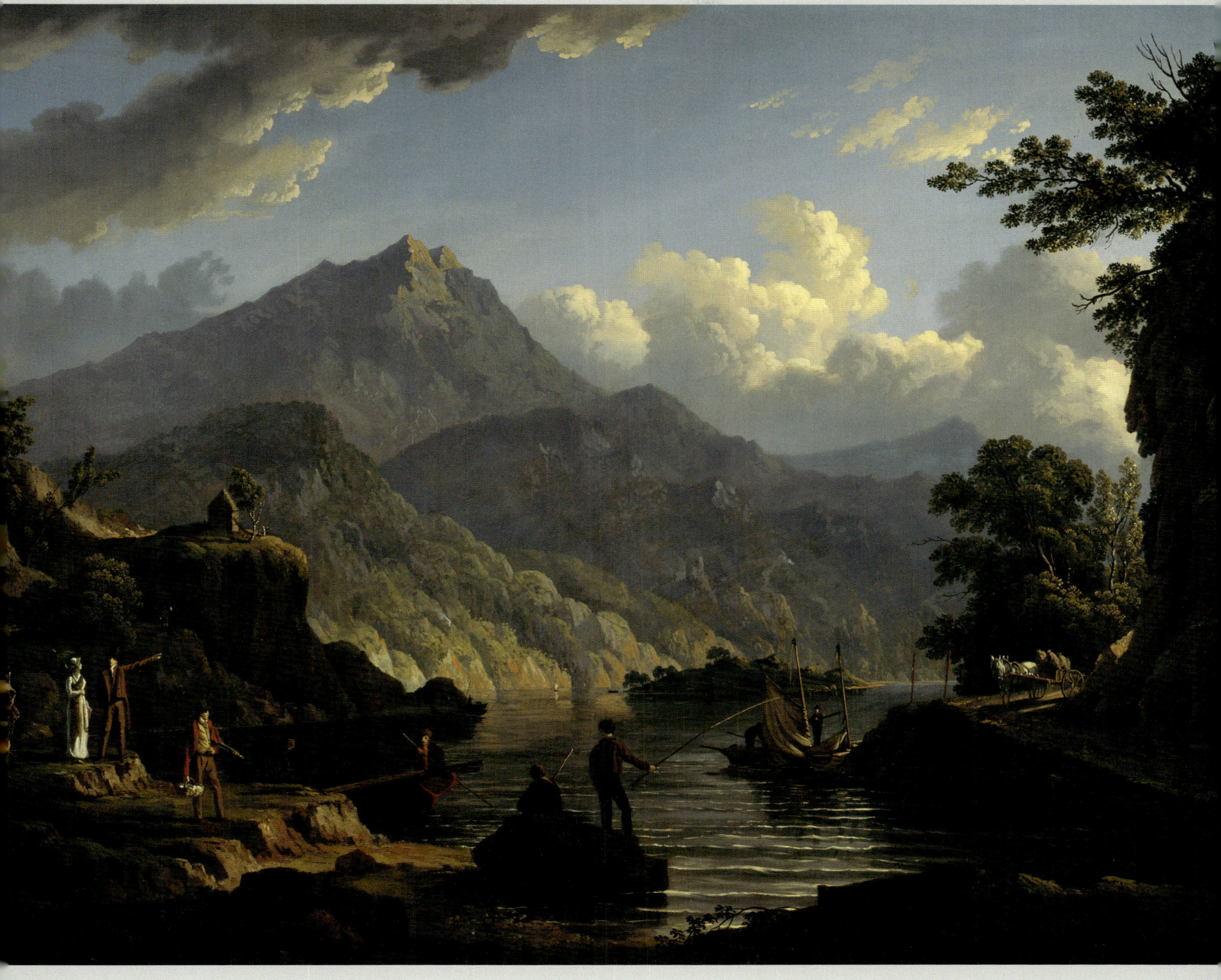

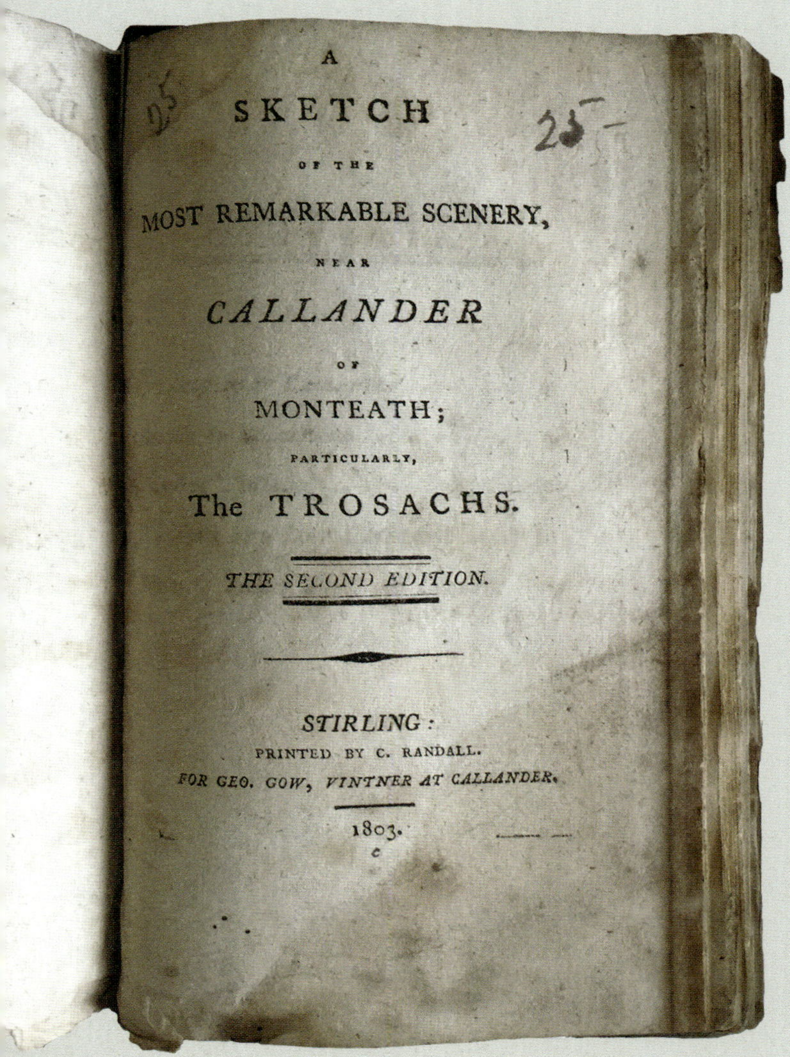

A
SKETCH
OF THE
MOST REMARKABLE SCENERY,
NEAR
CALLANDER
OF
MONTEATH;
PARTICULARLY,
The TROSACHS.
THE SECOND EDITION.
STIRLING:
PRINTED BY C. RANDALL.
FOR GEO. GOW, VINTNER AT CALLANDER.
1803.

Fig. S4.3
Above. [Anon.], *A Sketch of the Most Remarkable Scenery near Callander . . . particularly the Trosachs* 1803
(GLA LRA HA12399)

Fig. S4.4
Opposite. Charles Steuart, *Waterfall*, 1765, oil on canvas
(GLAHA:44054)

Ellen's 'silvan hall': true to the poem, in the 1820s, a hut on the island (which is just visible in the painting) was hung with animal skins, furnished with 'rustic heather-covered chairs' as well as an 'old table with helmets, axes & c. on it', according to the Yorkshire diarist Anne Lister (quoted in McHugh 2018, 425). Meanwhile our tourists' bagpiper (hired for the day) would 'send the bold pibroch from afar', prompting memories of the arrival of the war barges of 'Roderigh Vich Alpine dhu' in the poem's second canto, and the singing of 'Hail to the Chief' by his loyal clansmen (Scott 1913, 222–223; Watson 2012, 65). On taking leave of Ellen's island, the party would return via a cove situated at the base of Ben Venue, its location marked by a rising plume of smoke in Knox's picture, where they might experience the Gothic frisson of the 'Den of the Ghost', redesignated 'the Goblin-cave' by Scott (Murray 1799, 152; Scott 1913, 237).

Surveying a range of images and texts along the way, made both by and for those travelling through Scotland in the latter eighteenth and early nineteenth centuries, this closing section of *Old Ways New Roads* explores how leisure tourists of the kind depicted by Knox distinguished themselves from the antiquaries, naturalists and surveyors of previous generations. Starting with the ways the literary landscapes of Macpherson's *Ossian* and the picturesque prospects of Gilpin and his numerous imitators framed touristic encounters with Scottish scenery, it then examines how Scott's novels and poetry reinvigorated that experience for artists and tour writers by exerting the kind of imaginative pull which Knox's view of Loch Katrine captured so richly and inventively.

Passing through Glencroe on the military road, during a tour of 1766, the celebrated English bluestocking Elizabeth Montagu was one of the first to describe Highland scenery in the manner of Macpherson's *Ossian*, writing: 'The cheeks of the mountains were furrowd by falling streams, & the grey mold of age upon them; here and there a firr tree shatterd by a thousand storms, & huge rocks that had roll'd half way down . . . formd the terrible sublime'. She had come prepared for travelling 'ye classic ground', keeping a copy of *Ossian* close to hand (quoted in Ross 1965, 218, 228). We have seen in earlier chapters how this Ossianic taste for scenes of sublimity began to shape and give meaning to the designed landscape at places like the Dukes of Atholl's Dunkeld pleasure grounds, as they were laid out with the tourist at least partly in mind (see Fig. S2.21), or framed in the painted cataracts of Charles Steuart (Fig. S4.4). *Ossian* was to remain a key reference point in the appreciation of Highland scenery into the early nineteenth century, as the title of a striking oil painting exhibited by J.M.W. Turner at the Royal Academy in 1802 testifies: *Ben Lomond Mountains, Scotland: The Traveller – Vide Ossian's 'War of Caros'* (Fig. S4.5). Other than a tiny shield and sword-bearing figure, who may allude to the tragic character of Lamor from 'The War of Caros', Turner's reference to Macpherson's tale of stormy conflict is an oblique one, absorbed into the sublime mountain landscape.

That viewing and describing Scotland's waterfalls also represented 'classic ground' would seem to be the implication of the vaguely antique costume of the spectators in the painting

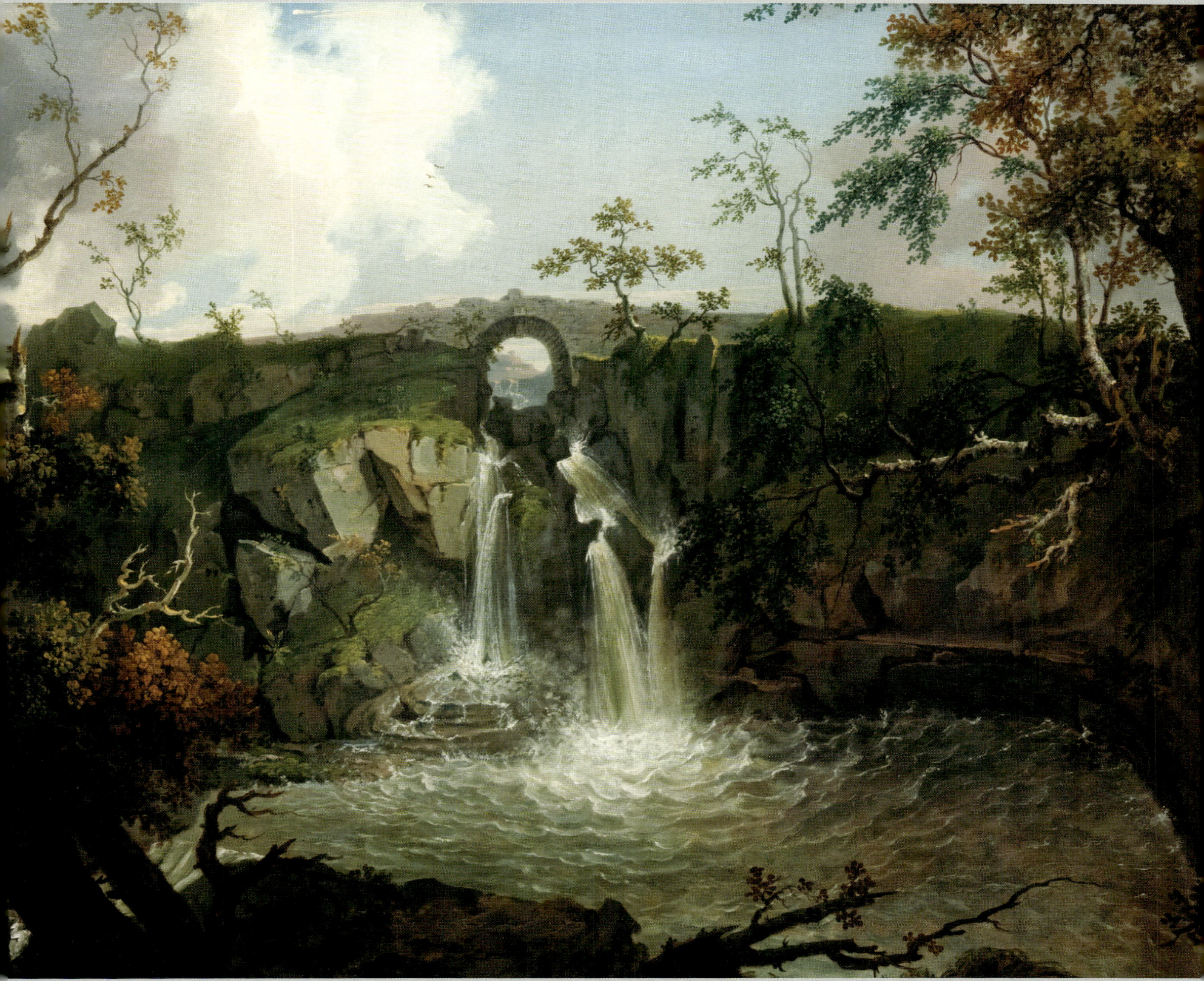

Fig. S4.5
Joseph Mallord William Turner, *Ben Lomond Mountains, Scotland: The Traveller – Vide Ossian's War of Caros*, c. 1803, oil on canvas (FM M. Add.17)

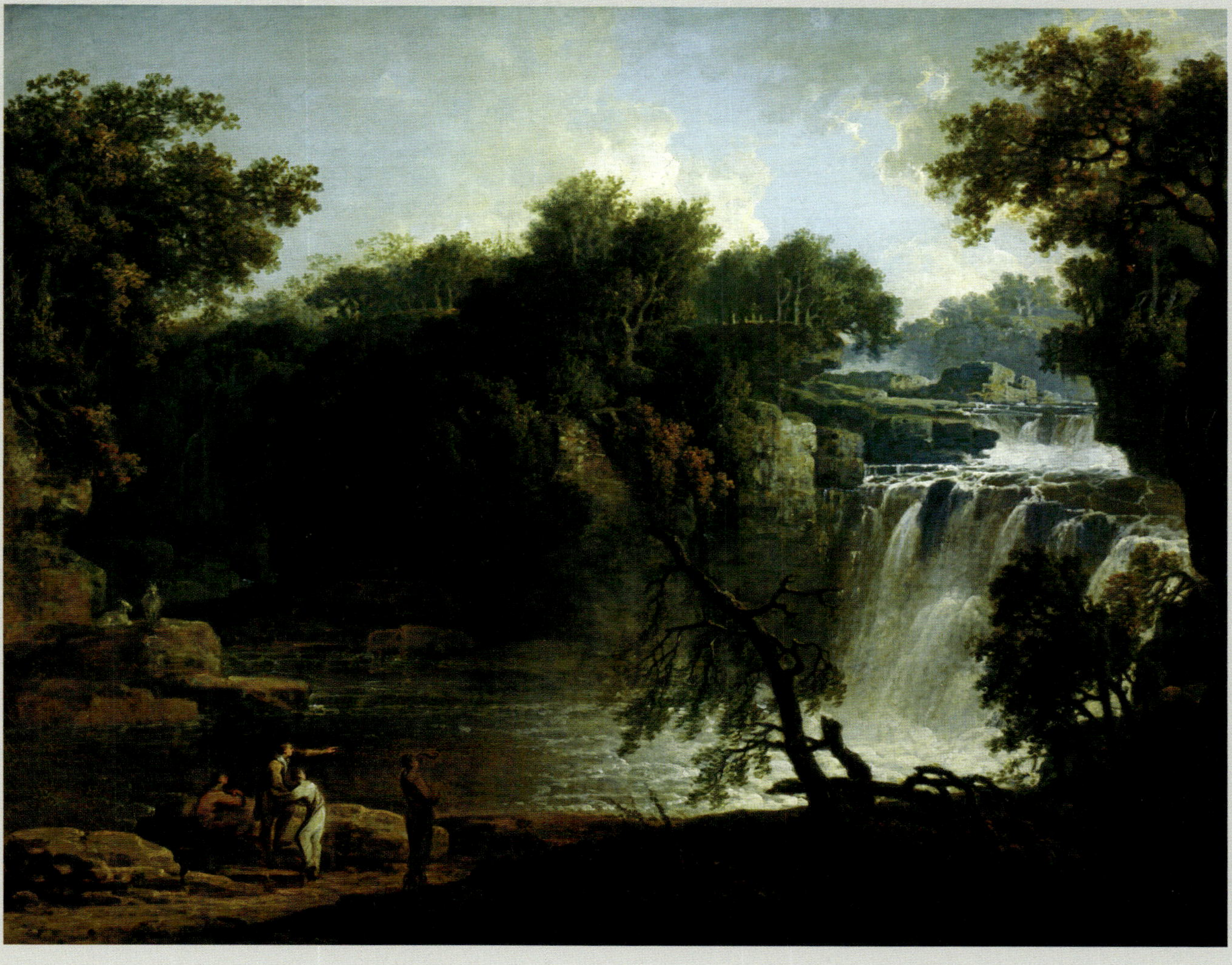

Fig. S4.6
Jacob More, *View of Corehouse Linn, on the River Clyde near Lanark* [The Falls of Clyde, Cora Linn], 1771, oil on canvas (NGS NG 1897)

Jacob More exhibited as *A View of Corehouse Linn, on the River Clyde near Lanark*, at London's Society of Artists in 1771 (Fig. S4.6). In his 1801 *Remarks on Local Scenery and Manners*, John Stoddart praised More's painting of Cora Linn for its 'boldness of . . . design' and 'brilliantly illumined spray': but much as he admired the beauty and variety of the Falls of Clyde, he found the celebrated Falls of Foyers above Loch Ness more sublime. Here, the 'darkness and imprisonment of wild overhanging crags, inexpressibly awful' was heightened by 'the ceaseless toil of the struggling river, by the thundering sounds of a thousand echoes, and . . . by the mighty summit of Meal Fourvouny, rising behind the lake' (Stoddart 1801, II, 76–77). Stoddart alluded not to *Ossian* but to Robert Burns's lines on 'The Falls of Fyers' too, even if he found them wanting in poetical effect: 'As high in air the bursting torrents flow, / As deep recoiling surge foam below' (Kinsley 1968, lines 5–6; Stoddart 1801, II, 76). Another poetic fruit of Burns's 1787 Highland Tour was his 'Lines written at Taymouth', praising the Acharn Falls as viewed from Breadalbane's Hermitage: 'Poetic ardours in my bosom swell, / Lone wandering by the hermit's mossy cell: / The sweeping theatre of hanging woods / Th' incessant roar of headlong tumbling floods' (Kinsley 1968, lines 17–20, n. 174) (Fig. S4.7). As we have seen, the Wordsworths' visit to the Falls of Bruar at Atholl was also made 'for the sake of Burns' (Kinsley 1968, n. 172; Walker 1997, 167).

If footstepping literary sites was one essential motivation for

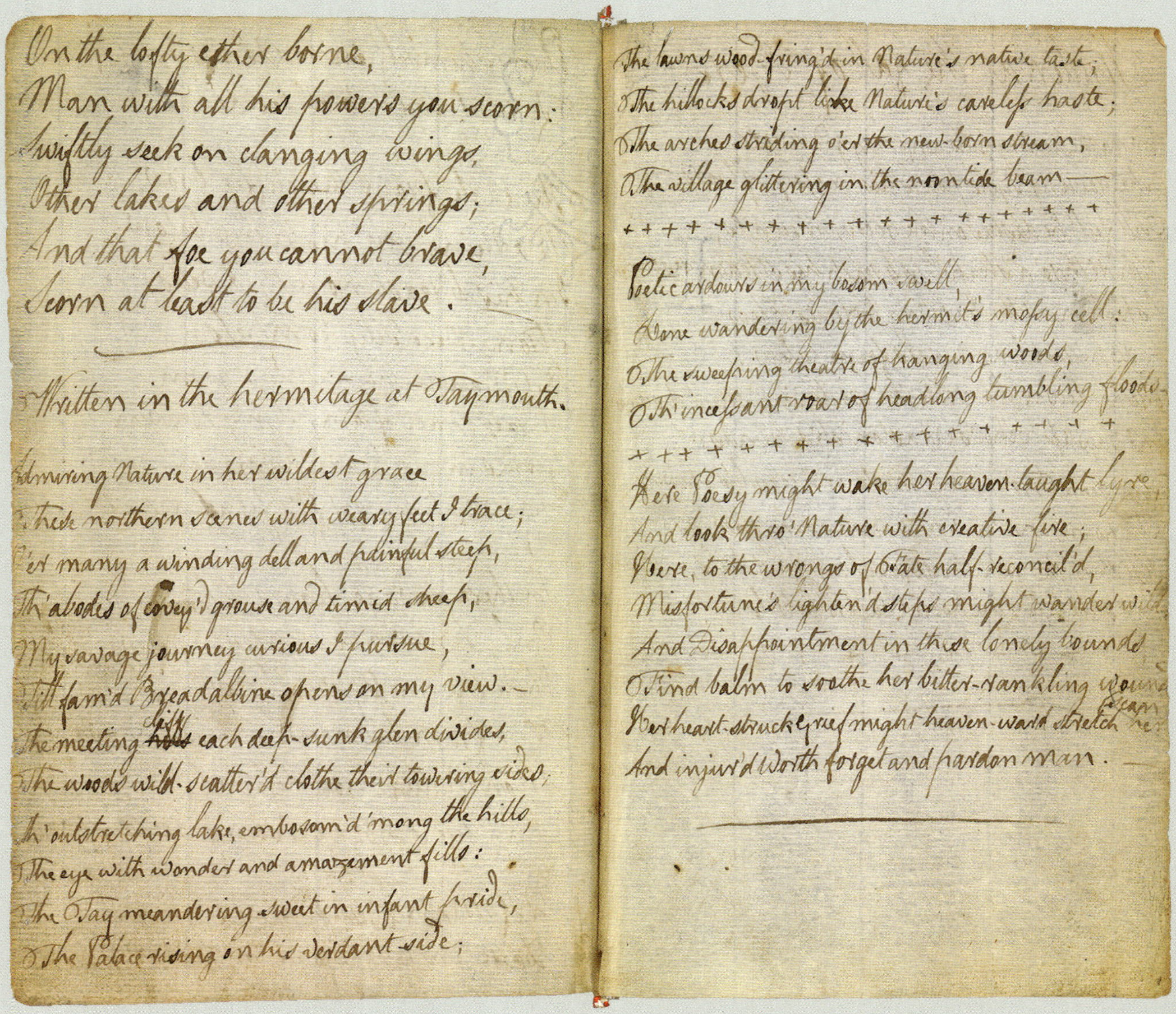
On the lofty ether borne,
Man with all his powers you scorn;
Swiftly seek on clanging wings,
Other lakes and other springs;
And that foe you cannot brave,
Scorn at least to be his slave.

Written in the hermitage at Taymouth.

Admiring Nature in her wildest grace
These northern scenes with weary feet I trace;
O'er many a winding dell and painful steep,
Th' abodes of covey'd grouse and timid sheep,
My savage journey curious I pursue,
Till fam'd Breadalbine opens on my view.—
The meeting cliffs each deep-sunk glen divides,
The woods wild-scatter'd clothe their towering sides;
Th' outstretching lake, embosom'd 'mong the hills,
The eye with wonder and amazement fills:
The Tay meandering sweet in infant pride,
The Palace rising on his verdant side;
The lawns wood-fring'd in Nature's native taste;
The hillocks dropt in Nature's careless haste;
The arches striding o'er the new-born stream,
The village glittering in the noontide beam—
+ + + + + + + + + + + + + + + + + + + +
Poetic ardours in my bosom swell,
Lone wandering by the hermit's mossy cell:
The sweeping theatre of hanging woods,
Th' incessant roar of headlong tumbling floods—
+ + + + + + + + + + + + + + + + + + +
Here Poesy might wake her heaven-taught lyre,
And look thro' Nature with creative fire;
Here, to the wrongs of Fate half-reconcil'd,
Misfortune's lighten'd steps might wander wild;
And Disappointment in these lonely bounds
Find balm to soothe her bitter-rankling wounds:
Here heart-struck Grief might heaven-ward stretch her scan,
And injur'd Worth forget and pardon man.—

Fig. S4.7
Robert Burns, the final lines of 'On Scaring some Waterfowl in Loch Turit', and the full poem 'Written in the Hermitage at Taymouth', in *Poems* (Edinburgh, 1787) (GLA ASC RB 2521)

Both these poems were written during Burns's visits to the Highlands in 1787. The first was composed when he was a guest of Sir William Murray of Ochtertyre in September 1787, the second during his earlier visit to Taymouth. First published in the newspapers in 1787, the second poem was subsequently included in the 1793 Edinburgh edition of *Poems*, with the title 'Written with a Pencil over the Chimney-piece, in the Parlour of the Inn at Kenmore, Taymouth'; it can still be seen on the wall at the Kenmore Hotel today.

Scottish tourism in the Romantic period, another was the search for picturesque scenery. William Gilpin – whose 1776 two-week 'hasty journey' round the *petit tour* bypassed the as-yet 'undiscovered' Trossachs – argued that for those wishing 'to *study landscape*' the Scottish Highlands were especially educational. Scenes of lakes, rivers and mountains found there were 'schools in which *the elements* of landscape [might be] taught'. Such features were all about 'great outlines', not detail. '[T]he art of finishing is frippery', Gilpin warned (Gilpin 1789b, II, 129). His view of the castle-rock of Dumbarton ably illustrates these principles (see Fig. C1.4). With the luminous, enveloping mist flattening and softening its contours, unifying its broken, disparate parts but obscuring its more distinctive features, the fortress is rendered barely distinguishable from the rock and the smoking industry represented by Alexander Nasmyth in his view of Dumbarton discussed below (see Fig. S4.12). Yet, for all that Gilpin dilated at length on the rugged, sublime profiles of Highland scenery, it posed a challenge, in that it often lacked the 'variety' afforded by judicious, 'tasteful' improvement that 'the picturesque eye' craved (Gilpin 1789b, II, 121). Not all tourists applied Gilpin's theories with quite his degree of rigour, but they made ready use of his language. In 1789, Hester Piozzi observed that 'Scotch Prospects do above all others excel in those Qualities justly termed Picturesque, while a rich & fertile Foreground is almost always contrasted by lofty Mountains and a Blue Expanse of Ocean in the Offskip' (Piozzi 1789). Here, a pictorially derived perspective and vocabulary, albeit employed far more broadly and vaguely than Gilpin ever intended, afforded a way of articulating and displaying feeling and sentiment.

Although this lack of precision irritated Uvedale Price and other theorists of the picturesque, if we consider the titles of Scottish tours published around 1800, when the genre peaked in popularity, it is notable that their references to *'Beauties'*, '*Observations*' and '*Scenery*' owed a patent debt to Gilpin. Still, this did not prevent Stoddart, whose 1801 *Remarks* was perhaps the most impressive publication of this kind, from making a number of disparaging mentions of Gilpin, arguing that 'the taste of that gentleman commonly induces him to sketch views, not as they *are*, but as they *should be*'. As we saw in Chapter 1, Stoddart (partly anxious to assert the distinctiveness of his own richly illustrated book) struck a Wordsworthian note in claiming that 'the old mode of composing pictures by certain formulae . . . seems (at least in landscape) to have given way to the study of nature'. Yet the plates illustrating his book – mainly engraved from paintings by his travelling companion John Claud Nattes – were a mixed bag of the adventurous and the conventional. Although they included a view of the Eildon hills by watercolourist Thomas Girtin, 'executed with all the spirit and effect, for which he is so remarkable', most of the plates were rather more orthodox in composition and manner, including work by Stoddart himself (Stoddart 1801, I, 203, 5–6; II, 279) (see Fig. C1.5). Stoddart visited Roslin Glen, and scrambling along the river banks found a viewpoint from which to sketch a scene:

> at once beautifully wild, and awfully sublime. The shattered rocks afford but a narrow passage to the dashing stream below, while their projecting brows, darkened with wood, nearly meet together above, and the ruined turrets are faintly seen between the branches.
> (Stoddart 1801, I, 136)

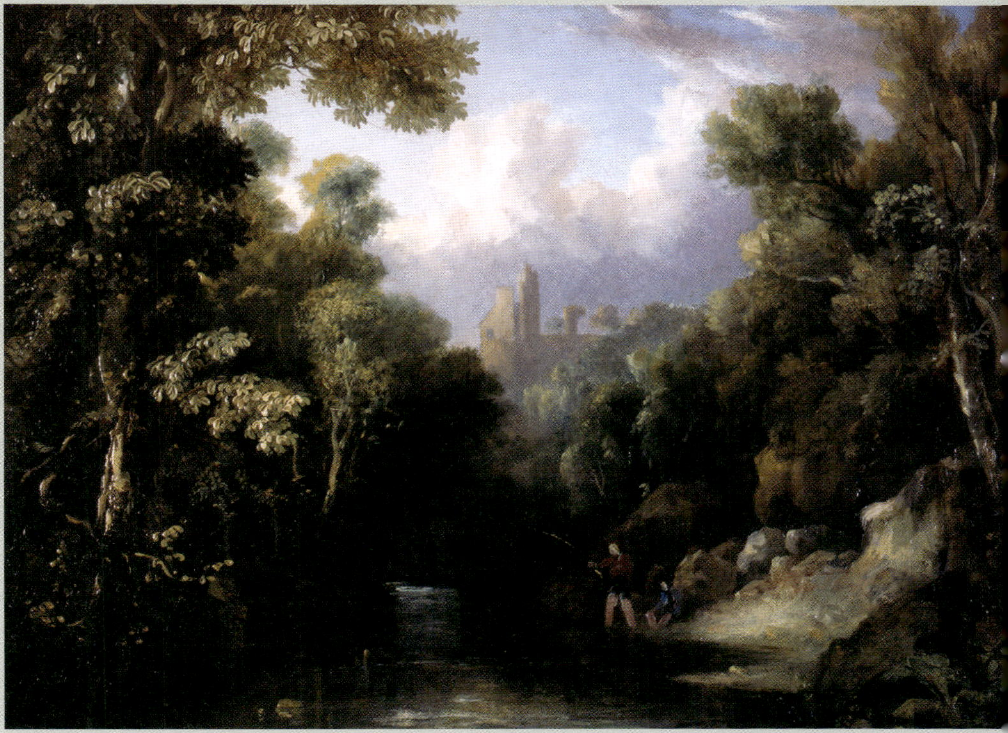

Fig. S4.8
John Thomson of Duddingston, *Rosslyn Castle*, c. 1830, oil on canvas (GLAHA: 44104)

Stoddart's plate provided the basis for John Thomson of Duddingston's 1830 oil painting *Rosslyn Castle*: Thomson (a friend of Sir Walter Scott and minister of Duddingston from 1805 until his death in 1840) had been taught by Alexander Nasmyth, and like Stoddart was a devotee of sketching outdoors (Fig. S4.8). Less conventionally, but following Nasmyth's recommendation, Stoddart also visited a 'singular' lime quarry at Gilmerton 'which would have struck none but a painter's eye', and printed a plate based on a drawing by 'my friend Mr Williams' showing the faint light reflected on the quarry's 'massy pillars' (Stoddart 1801, I, 88–89); perhaps inspired by Stoddart's print, Nasmyth himself drew the quarry in 1809 (Fig. S4.9).

Underpinning Stoddart's eagerness to distinguish his *Remarks* from 'the mushroom productions of every summer' that were pouring from the press around 1800 is a sense that what was once thrillingly novel even ten years earlier was already becoming tired (Stoddart 1801, I, vii). Like his friends the Wordsworths in the Trossachs, Stoddart and his companion Nattes had distinguished themselves from the mass of tourists by travelling as pedestrians, a

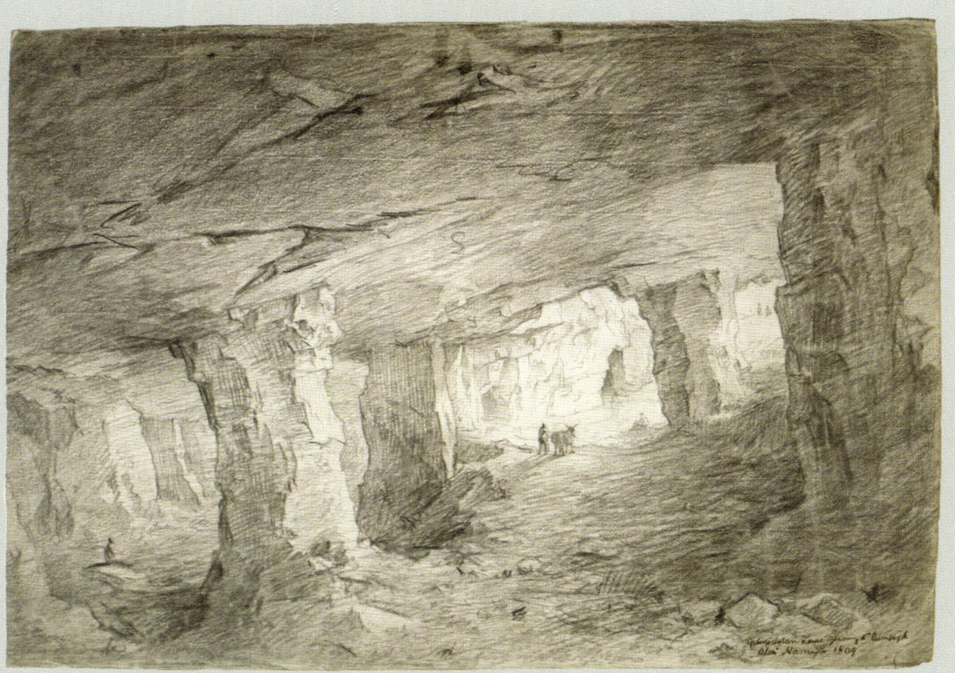

Fig. S4.9
Alexander Nasmyth, *Gilmerton Lane Quarry*, drawing, 1809 (NGS D5600)

mode of travel often favoured by younger radicals who sought better to gauge the condition of the common people by abandoning the privileges of chaises and barouches (Jarvis 1997). Among those taking to the road in this manner were the Englishman John Bristed and his friend William Cowan, medical students at Edinburgh University, who tramped the *petit tour* in 1800 disguised as American sailors, in an attempt to pre-empt national prejudices (Leask 2019) (see Fig. 0.4). By contrast, however, Stoddart warned female tourists to avoid pedestrianism, and to follow the example of Sarah Murray, 'whose persevering admiration of the beauties of Nature, ha[d] enabled her to encounter many fatigues unusal to a female' (Stoddart 1801, I, 118–119). Travelling in a chaise accompanied by two servants and a driver, the 52-year-old widow Sarah Murray claimed erroneously that her *Companion and Useful Guide to the Beauties of Scotland* (1799) was the first tourist guidebook of its kind, the commercial aims of which would seem to contradict her own rather exclusive claims of having 'seen Scotland, and its natural beauties, more completely than any other individual' (Murray 1799, 42–34). Such claims were attempts to counter the repetitiveness and uniformity now creeping into tour writing as well as its illustration, in works like Stoddart's, Thomas Garnett's *Observations on a Tour through the Highlands* (1800), or Alexander Campbell's *Journey from Edinburgh through Parts of North Britain* (1802). These were followed in 1803 by the Edinburgh schoolmaster James Cririe's *Scottish Scenery; or, Sketches in Verse descriptive of Scenes chiefly in the Highlands of Scotland*, the first published poetical account of the *petit tour*, his anodyne blank verse serving mostly as letterpress text for William Byrne's engravings after George Walker's original drawings (see Fig. S2.21). An ex-student of the Foulis Academy and a watercolourist based in Edinburgh, Walker executed twenty views to accompany Cririe's words; Cririe acclaimed them as the first new views of key sites on the *petit tour* to be published since Pennant's pioneering *Tours*. Yet, despite these claims, with a full fifth of them focused on waterfalls, there was an inescapable sense of reiteration, of little new being left to say.

On the face of it, Col. Thomas Thornton's *A Sporting Tour Through the Northern Parts of England and Great Part of the Highlands of Scotland* had some claim to originality, not least as a vivid portrait of eighteenth-century Speyside. Not published until 1804, but based on a lavish tour of the mid 1780s, the book's focus on angling, hawking and shooting anticipated the near mania for Highland field sports that was to become so marked in the middle decades of the nineteenth century (see Fig. S4.22 below). Thornton, an eccentric Yorkshire bon-viveur, was a fanatical sportsman as well as incorrigible self-publicist, employing the Sawrey Gilpin-trained artist George Garrard to document the tour. Garrard treated the commission seriously, introducing a sense of gravity to his views of the Highland landscape that the accompanying text largely lacked. Framed by skeletal remains of horses, Garrard's view of deer on the banks of Loch Enoch (Einich) in the Cairngorms connects the grim material fact of death and decay with the sublime wilderness of the locale (Fig. S4.10). Reviewing the book for the *Edinburgh Review*, Walter Scott commended Garrard's designs but dismissed Thornton's 'long, minute, and prolix account of every grouse or blackcock which had the honour to fall by the gun of our literary sportsman – of every pike which gorged his bait – of every bird which was pounced by his hawks'. Of '[t]he descriptions of the Highland landscapes which the colonel met with on his route', Scott observed that they were 'very similar to what are usually found in books of the kind, abounding in all the slang by which tourists delight to describe what can never be understood from description' (Scott 1805, 404).

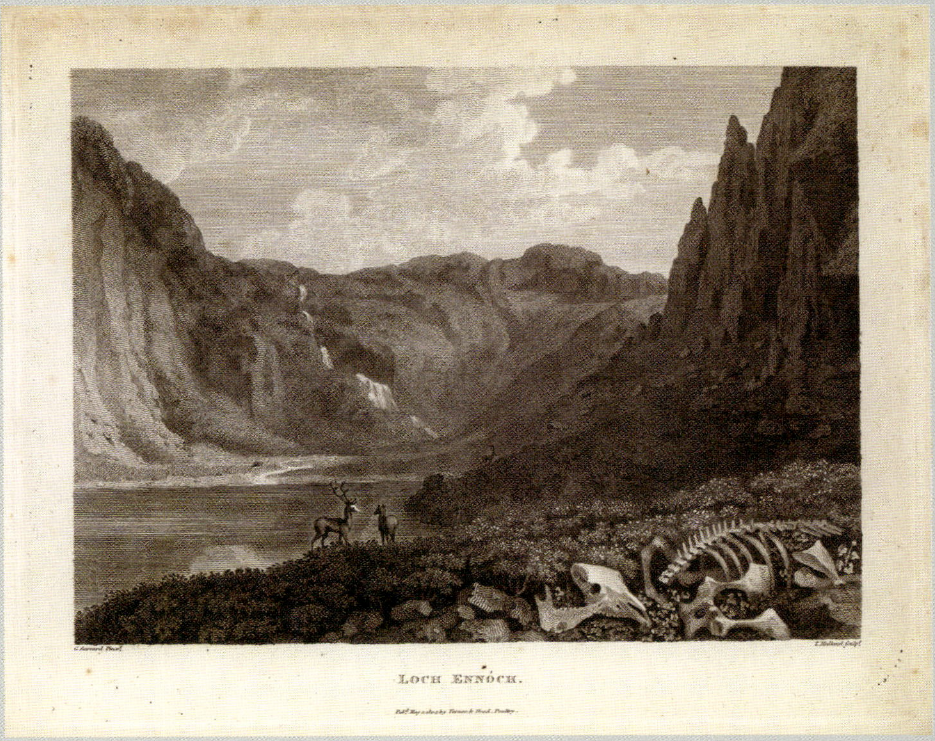

Fig. S4.10
George Garrard, 'Loch Ennoch', engraving in Thomas Thornton, *A Sporting Tour through the Northern Parts of England, and Great Part of the Highlands of Scotland* . . . (London, 1804), pl. 9, p. 105 (GLA ASC Mu5-c.1)

This anticipated Scott's even more disparaging review, four years later in 1809, of Sir John Carr's *Caledonian Sketches* discussed in Chapter 1, with its complaint that 'it would, perhaps, be somewhat difficult to bring us news from Scotland', given the 'hundred volumes' that had already appeared on the subject (Scott 1809, 182). Clearly, the illustrated Scottish tour account associated with Pennant, Gilpin, Stoddart and now Carr had become 'hackneyed': but not for long, as the imaginative resonance of the country's landscapes would be renewed and amplified in Scott's own writings. Building on the success of his narrative poem *The Lay of the Last Minstrel* (1805), with its sixteenth-century Borders setting, Scott now turned his pen to romancing the Highlands in a series of best-selling poems and novels, notably *The Lady of the Lake* (1810), *Waverley* (1814), *The Lord of the Isles* (1815) and *Rob Roy* (1817). Largely inspired by these works, a new wave of tourism powered by steamboat transport, and facilitated by Thomas Telford's roads and bridges, poured into Scotland in the years after Waterloo, at a time of radical unrest in the Lowlands and draconian clearances in the Highlands. On 15 August 1812, the Scottish engineer and entrepreneur Henry Bell launched the first regular steamboat passenger service along the River Clyde (or anywhere in Europe for that matter) between Glasgow, Greenock and Helensburgh. John Knox's painting *First Steamboat on the Clyde* (c. 1820) commemorated the *Comet*'s maiden voyage (Fig. S4.11). He had painted at least one previous version of this view from Dalnottar Hill, which he seems to have updated here by simply adding the steamboat referred to in the painting's title, and the sails of a boat entering the recently completed Caledonian Canal in the foreground. It is an image of passage and progress, of the impact of commerce and industry on the local landscape, which now included steam-powered tourism.

The new vistas opened on the Clyde estuary by steam travel may also have inspired Alexander Nasmyth's companion views of *Dumbarton Castle and Town with Ben Lomond* and *Ardencapel House, from Roseneath* (Figs S4.12 and S4.13). Taken together, they reflect on the shifting topography of the riverbank: the former painting subtly balances Scotland's historic past and sublime landscape with an industrial future hinted at by the smoking glass furnaces beneath Dumbarton Rock; the latter is an estate scene, paying tribute to the patronage of the noble proprietors of Ardencapel, the Dukes of Argyll. Appropriately enough, the pair was purchased by James Watt, born at Greenock on the other side of the Clyde, whose invention of the condensing cylinder steam engine had enabled the new technology. Doubtless Watt relished Nasmyth's painterly vision of the 'old ways and new roads' along the Clyde.

Steam-power fuelled the tourist imagination, although it was not universally favoured. When on a steamboat excursion across Loch Lomond in 1825, the Wrexham banker and Scott-enthusiast John Bowman found himself transported with pleasure, finding 'as the vessel alters her course . . . the grouping of the scenery is perpetually changing giving the idea of enchantment'. With a bagpiper playing Jacobite tunes and 'Gathering pibrochs', his mind was filled with visions of 'hundreds of kilted highlanders' straight out of the pages of *Rob Roy* (Bowman 1986, 38). Yet, by contrast, others found steam-power was hard to square with picturesque repose and romantic reverie. John Keats, making a pedestrian tour in 1818 with his friend Charles Brown, complained that 'Steam boats on Loch Lomond and Barouches on its sides take a little from the Pleasure of such romantic chaps as Brown and I' (Walker

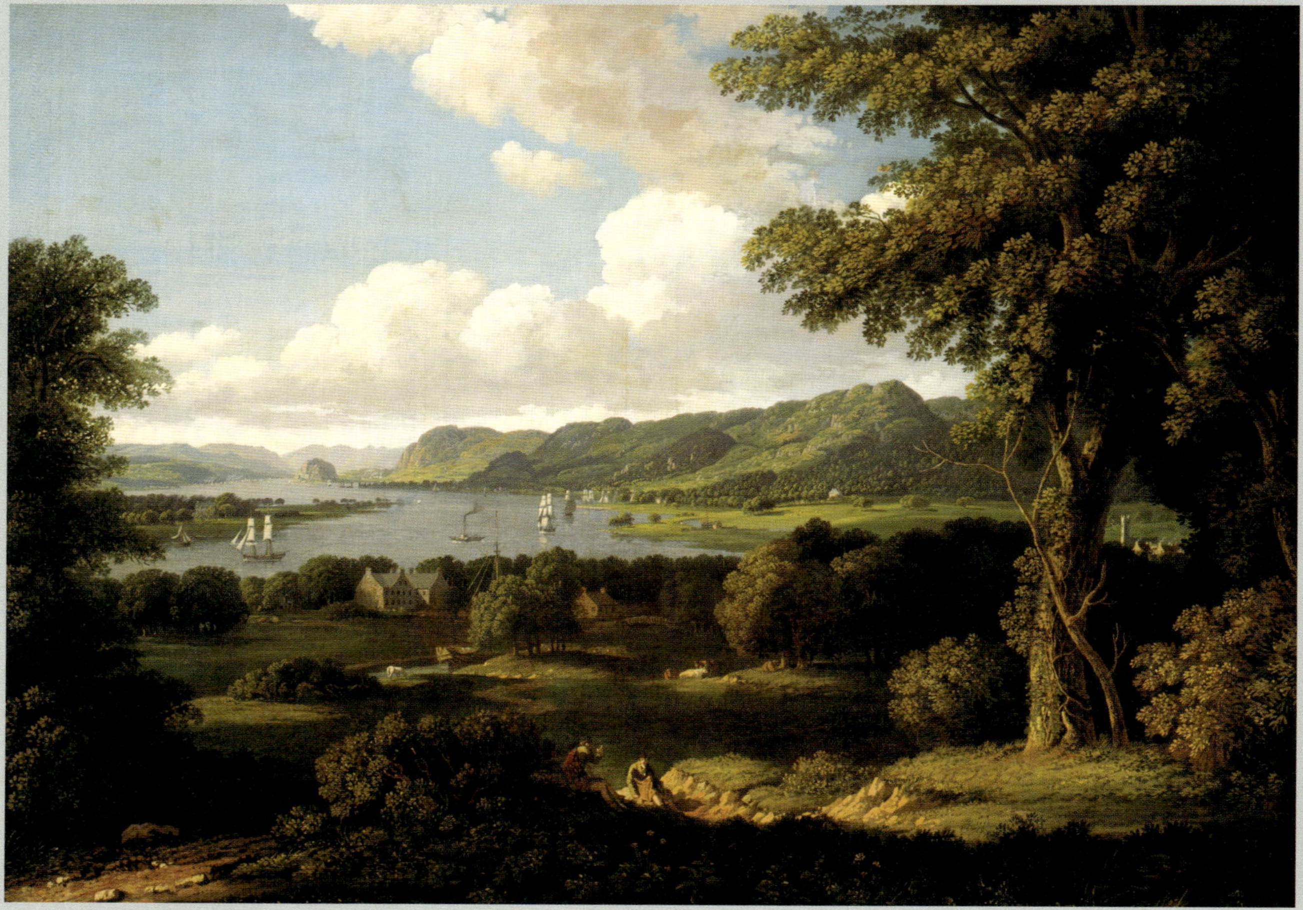

Fig. S4.11
John Knox, *First Steamboat on the Clyde*, c. 1820, oil on canvas (GMC 2342)

1992, 183). Although Keats's tour was in many ways a homage to his literary heroes Wordsworth and Burns, uncharacteristically he showed little enthusiasm for Scott, deliberately giving the Trossachs a wide berth (Leask 2020, 270–275). For others, however, distaste for the new mode of transport was less about the dirt, noise or speed (which bothered many) than about the passengers. Though he considered Loch Lomond 'the paragon of the Scottish lakes', the geologist John Macculloch commented waspishly that 'the steam boat is now to be seen, daily ploughing its fiery way over the tranquil expanse; loaded with freight as intellectual as those of a Margate hoy' (Macculloch 1824 I, 211, 207).

Such snobbish disdain for the changing and increasingly diverse social make-up of tourism was also registered in contemporary graphic and literary satire, a genre in which the follies of affectation and pretension were attacked remorselessly. Scottish tourism was subject to parody and ridicule practically from the beginning, with James Boswell and Johnson's travels prompting a series of satirical squibs of a variously visceral and genial tone. Among the latter were the twenty graphic satires etched by Thomas Rowlandson after designs by Henry Bunbury and Samuel Collings illustrating Boswell's 1785 *Journal of a Tour to the Hebrides*. Brought together the following year by the London publisher Elizabeth Jackson as *Picturesque Beauties of Boswell*, the prints recast the tour in comic terms. Several mocked Boswell's ancestry and titled status as well as his literary pretensions, the frontispiece to the series portraying 'the Laird of Auckinleck' as a childish, deluded buffoon, holding a rattle and mooing, in the

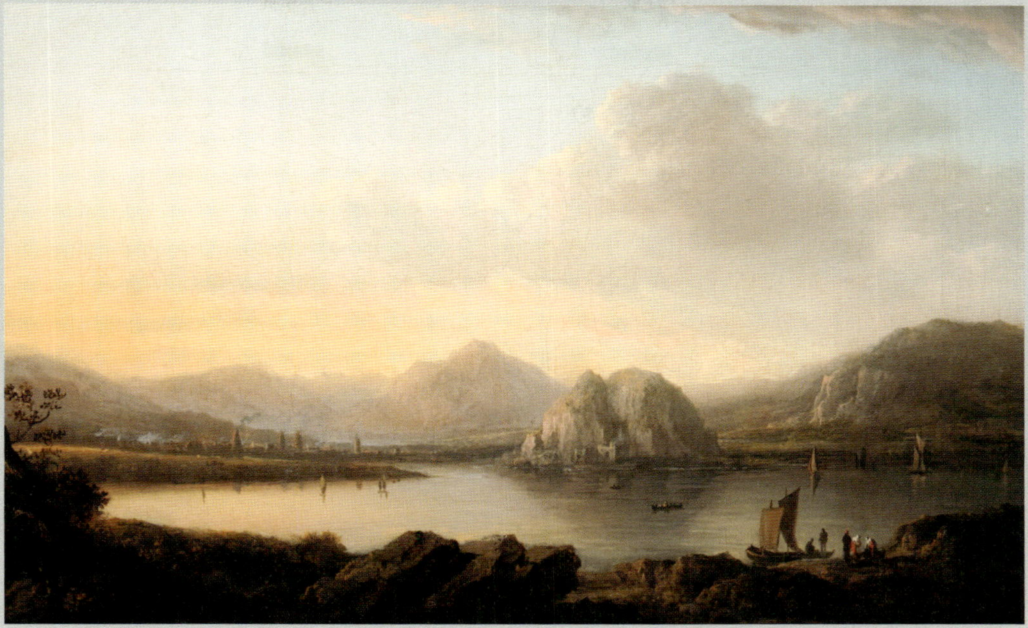

Fig. S4.12
Alexander Nasmyth, *Dumbarton Castle and Town with Ben Lomond*, 1816, oil on canvas (GLAHA:51732)

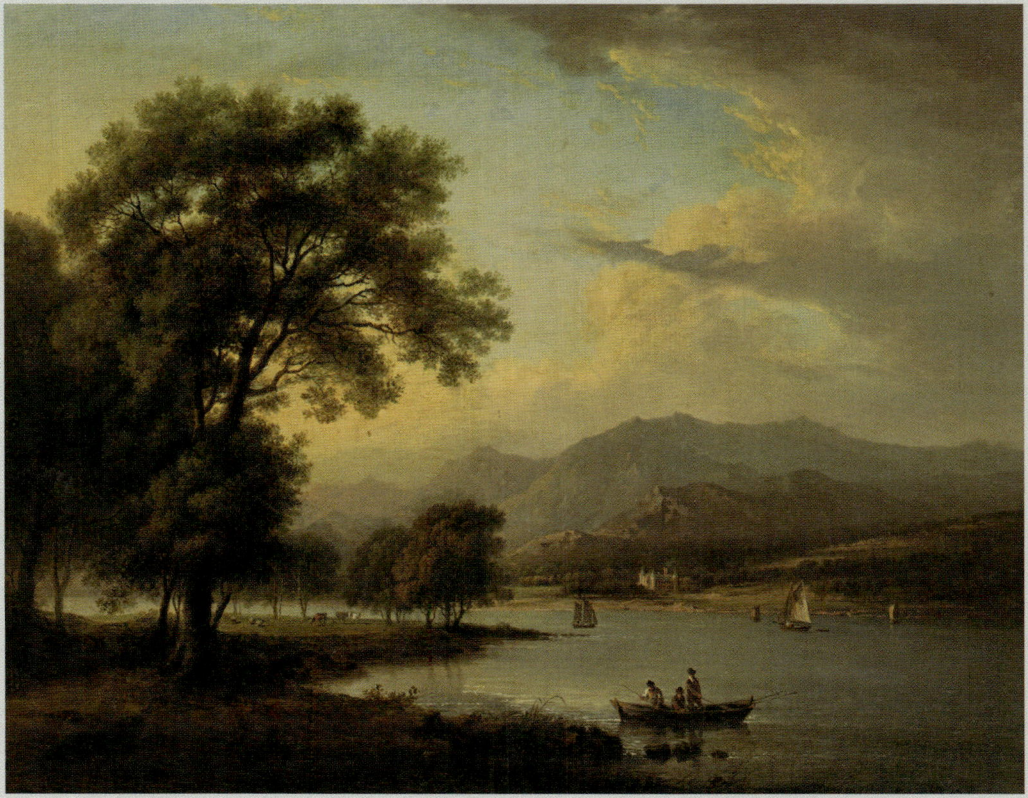

Fig. S4.13
Alexander Nasmyth, *Ardencapel House, from Roseneath*, c. 1818, oil on canvas (PC)

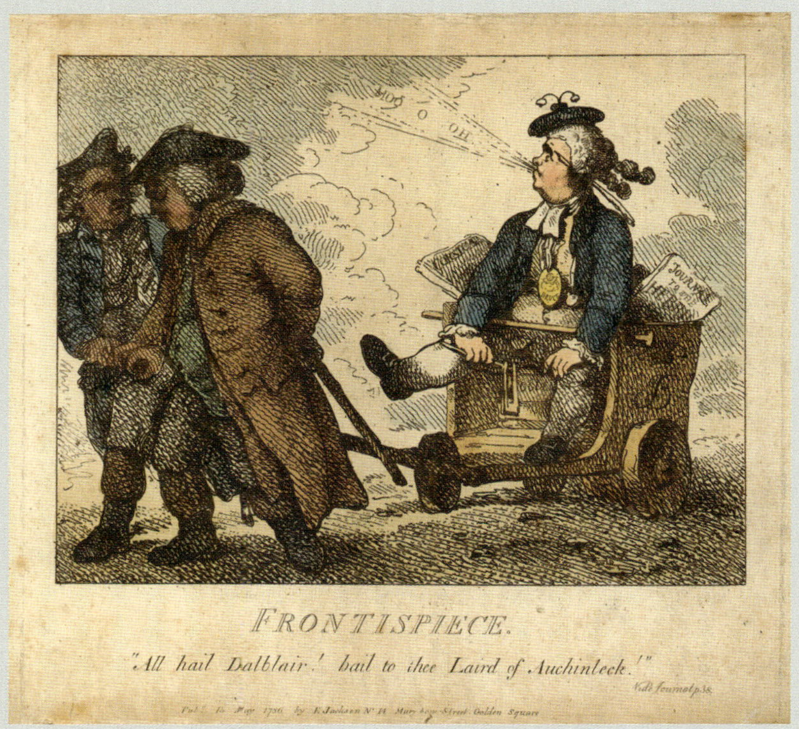

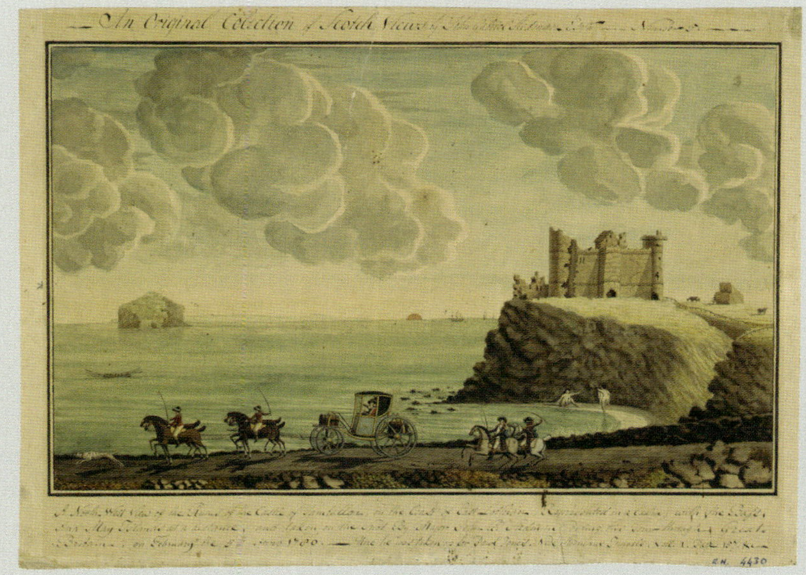

Fig. S4.14
Top. Thomas Rowlandson after Samuel Collins, frontispiece 'All hail Dalblair, hail to the Laird of Auchinleck', from *Picturesque Beauties of Boswell* (London, 1785–6), coloured etching (WZC)

Fig. S4.15
Above. Major John Gabriel Stedman, *A North West View of the Ruins of the Castle of Tantallon*, in *An Original Collection of Scottish Views*, 1780, watercolour (NGS D 4430)

manner of a mock triumph, his carriage drawn by Johnson and Pasquale Paoli, the subject of his Corsican journal (Fig. S4.14).

But the celebrity tourist was not the only focus of satire. Drawn up a few years earlier around the turn of the decade, a series of scenes depicting the touristic encounter with Scotland's antiquities and natural wonders by the Scoto-Dutch soldier and traveller John Gabriel Stedman have a distinctly comic edge. To judge by their careful framing, inscription and journal references, his scenes of tourists exploring the ruins of Tantallon Castle and the volcanic crag of Bass Rock were intended to illustrate a lost (or never realised) tour account of sorts (Figs S4.15 and S4.16). On close inspection, two young local women cast as classical nudes can be seen on the sands below the cliff-top fortress of Tantallon. In the companion scene of boating in the Firth of Forth, the sea-bathing of young local men catches the eye of one of the absurdly over-dressed women of the fashionable party touring the Bass Rock, who trains a spy-glass in their direction rather than any of the surrounding historic and picturesque sites. There is a bawdy, ribald aspect about these modish but far from respectable tourists, quite distinct from the chaste and resolutely masculine world of Pennant's and Johnson's tours.

A book-length poem published in 1821, entitled *The Tour of Dr Prosody in Search of the Antique and Picturesque through Scotland* and richly illustrated with twenty aquatints, looked back wryly on the era of travel writing epitomised by those authors. With his now deeply unfashionable powdered wig, curiosity for antiquities and penchant for picturesque sketching, the character of Dr Prosody recalled the three giants of Scottish tour writing, Johnson, Pennant and Gilpin, and the now exhausted literary genre they had inspired (Leask 2020, 275). Looking to capitalise on the enormous success of William Combe and Thomas Rowlandson's 1812 *Tour of Dr Syntax in Search of the Picturesque*, the book's anonymous author and artists use Prosody's various mishaps to target the affected attitudes of tourists who fancied themselves as antiquaries, naturalists or picturesque artists. Travelling with his Scottish servant 'Archie' and the Edinburgh antiquary 'Dr Factobend', Prosody visits all the major tourist sites celebrated over the previous half century of travel writing about Scotland, from the Western Isles and the Orkneys to the destinations of the *petit tour* and on to the newly fashionable Trossachs. At Cora Linn, Prosody embarks with sketchbook in hand on a perilous, Gilpinesque search for the most picturesque vantage-point at the expense of all caution until he finds himself abruptly 'tumbled from his horrid station' (Anon 1821, 89) (Fig. S4.17).

Another satirical tour published just four years later, Michael Egerton's *Airy Nothings; or, Scraps and Naughts, and Odd-cum-Shorts*, took the form of a rapid comic jaunt or 'Circumbendibus Hop, Step, and Jump' through the tourist hotspots of the British Isles, as undertaken by one 'Olio Rigmaroll'. Egerton's gentle satire poked fun at the activities, dress and manners of locals and tourists alike: his illustrative plates and loosely connected fragments of prose and verse relating to the Scottish leg take in a combination of the familiar and novel, from the urban street commerce that had caught the eye of artists since Paul Sandby to Loch Lomond's new paddle steamer (see Fig. C6.11). In its highly contracted, whistlestop form, with the sense of restless transit created by its successive images of speeding coaches and ferry boats, *Airy Nothings* took aim at the growing commodification of the traveller's experience of Scotland. What had taken travellers like Boswell and Johnson a full three months could now be achieved in a fortnight. The experience of visiting a land once 'as little known to its southern brethren as *Kamtschatka*' (Pennant 1793, 11) was now packaged up, regimented and timetabled. Guides not only pointed visitors in the direction of what to see but what to take from the experience.

Such publications paradoxically fed off the same modern consumer tourism that they satirised. By the time Egerton's burlesque appeared, much to his distaste, Scott's writings had played an instrumental role in greatly expanding the very area of publishing he had taken to task as a critic. Over fifty accounts of tours and travels in Scotland were published in the 1820s alone, with several bestsellers among them (Nenadic 1999, 215). These years were to see a related proliferation of illustrations and paintings depicting Scottish sites and scenes, which if not directly inspired by Scott's numerous writings as often as not recalled them. For all the striking pictorial drama of its contrasts of light and scale, turbulent sea and skies, and narrative of maritime disaster and peril, Nasmyth's magnificent *View of Tantallon Castle and the Bass Rock* (1819), as a site celebrated in the author's early bestselling *Marmion* (1808), is also a picture shot through with the historical resonances of 'Scotland' (Fig. S4.18). Touring Scotland in 1831 to make sketches for the publisher Robert Cadell's lavish new edition of Scott's *Poetical Works*, Turner adopted a

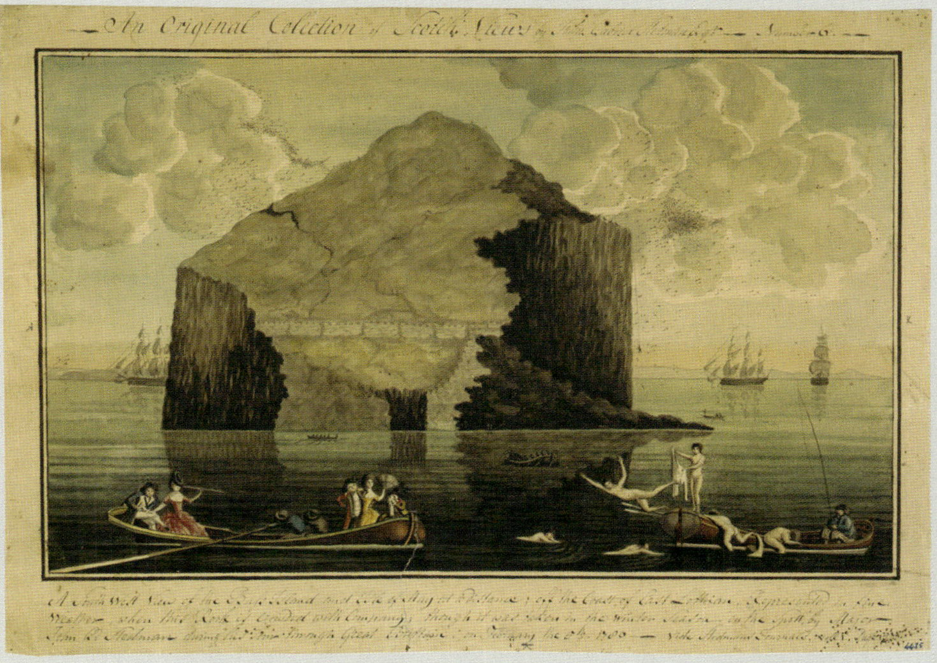

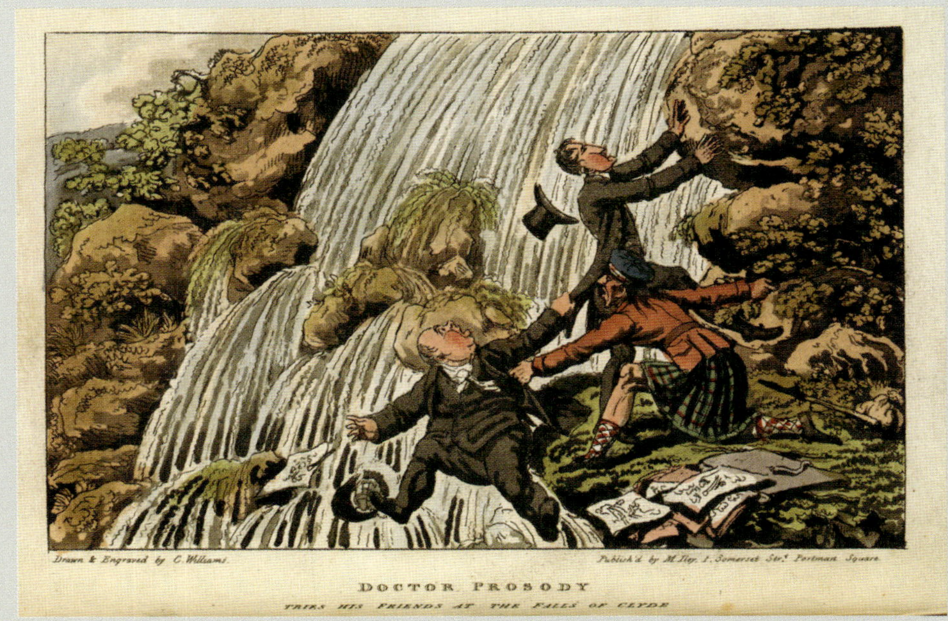

Fig. S4.16
Top. Major John Gabriel Stedman, *The Bass Rock*, in *An Original Collection of Scottish Views*, 1780, watercolour (NGS D 4435)

Fig. S4.17
Above. Charles Williams, 'Dr Prosody Tries his Friends at the Falls of Clyde', coloured aquatint in *The Tour of Doctor Prosody* (London, 1821), after p. 11 (GLA ASC RQ BCGE)

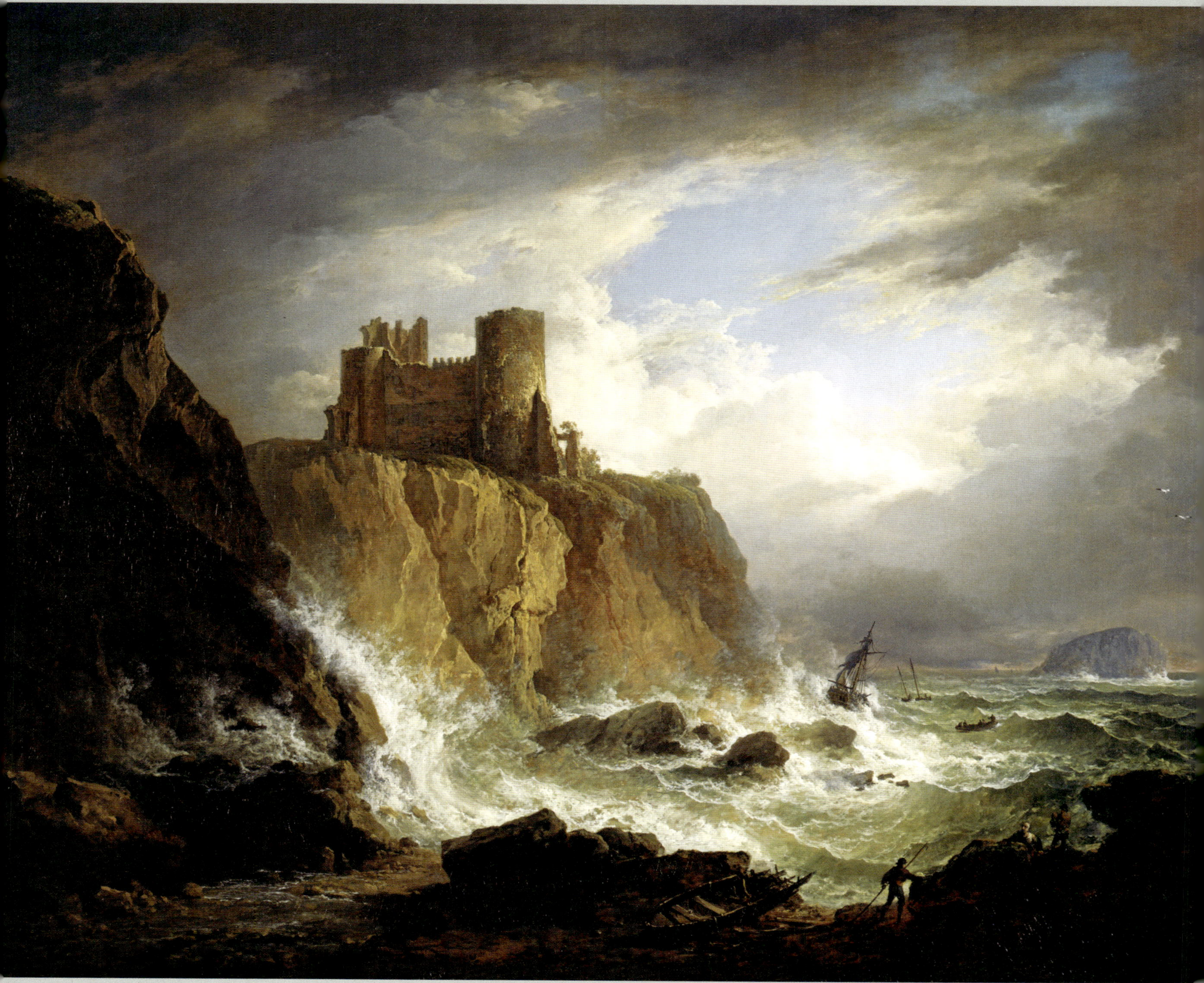

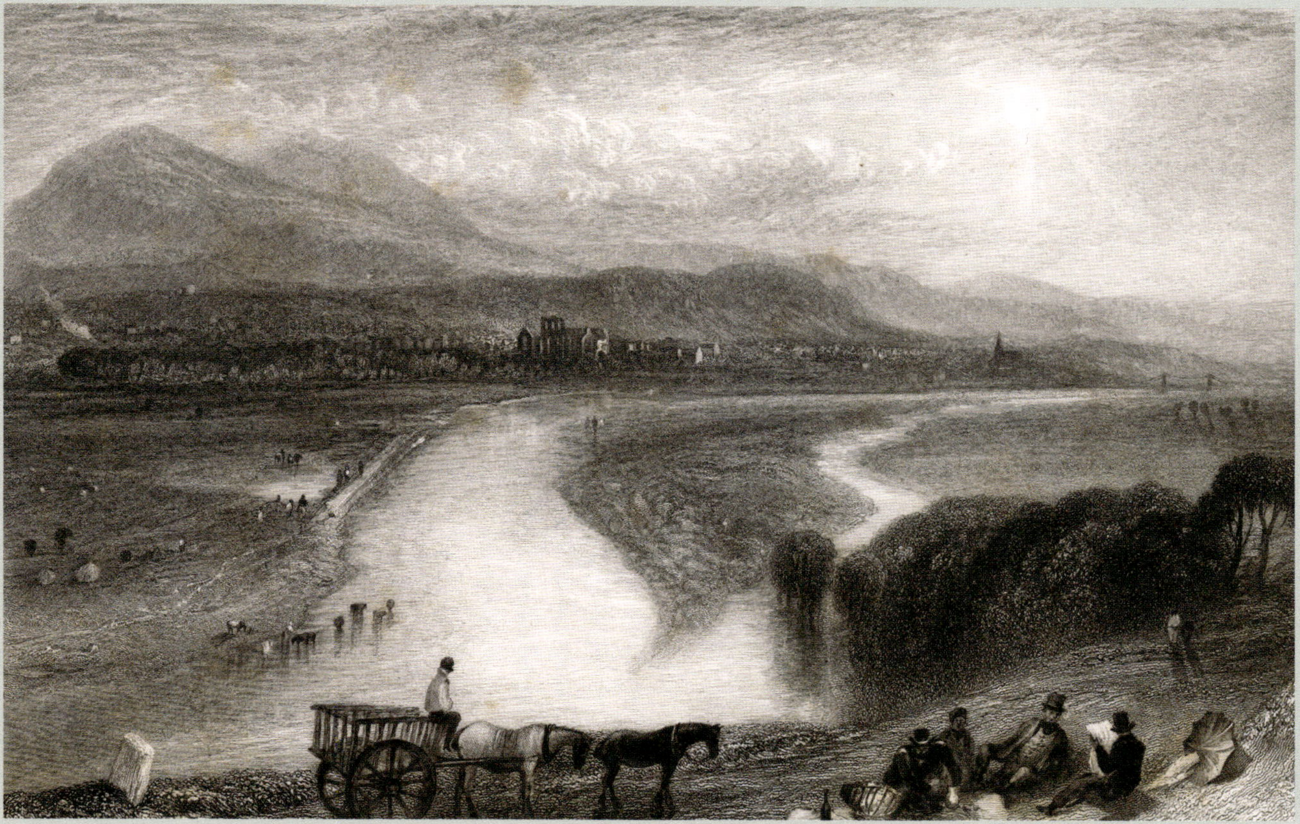

Fig. S4.18
Opposite. Alexander Nasmyth, *A View of Tantallon Castle and the Bass Rock*, 1819, oil on canvas (NGS NG 2627)

Fig. S4.19
Left. William Miller after Joseph Mallord William Turner, 'Melrose', 1834, engraving from *Scott's Poetical Works* (GLAHA: 9897)

more detached, deliberately touristic perspective on its sites and the texts his designs were meant to accompany. He made drawings of the Lowland and Highland settings of Scott's poetry, but none of its characters or incidents put in an appearance (Wood 2001, 174–186). Instead the artist, publisher and writer lounge together on the banks of the Tweed across from a distant Melrose Abbey (Fig. S4.19). Vulnerable and exposed to the elements, Turner and his guide cling to a promontory overlooking Lake Coruisk (Fig. S4.20). A solitary sightseer, presumably drawn there by reading *The Lady of the Lake*, looks out on Loch Katrine (Fig. S4.21). Like the young tourists of Knox's painting with which this section began, acting out their own version of the chivalric plot of Scott's poem, these figures enter and become players in a scene.

David Wilkie was another who saw potential in making Scott-related places and themes the subject of his art. In 1817, the painter – a Fife-born Lowland Scot who had never previously travelled north – embarked on an extended three-month-long Highland tour, following an itinerary drawn up for him by Scott (Marks 1998). *The Death of the Red Deer* is one of several pictures of Highland scenes to derive from the tour that owed a debt to Scott's romantic vision of Scottish life and legend (Fig. S4.22). Set in Glen Tilt on the Blair Atholl estate, and recalling a hunt the artist had witnessed when visiting the 4th Duke of Atholl, Wilkie's small oil is essentially a group portrait of household retainers, including the stalker 'McIntyre' and the duke's piper 'McGregor'. They were named in a print, after the picture, that eventually appeared some twenty or so years later aiming to capitalise on the mania for deer stalking in the Scottish Highlands then rising to its peak. Indeed, the earlier painting anticipates 'the great age of slaughter' as field sports won royal approval in the 1830s and 1840s, and the grouse and stalking seasons dictated the calendar of polite British society. When Queen Victoria and Prince Albert purchased the Balmoral estate on Royal Deeside in 1852,

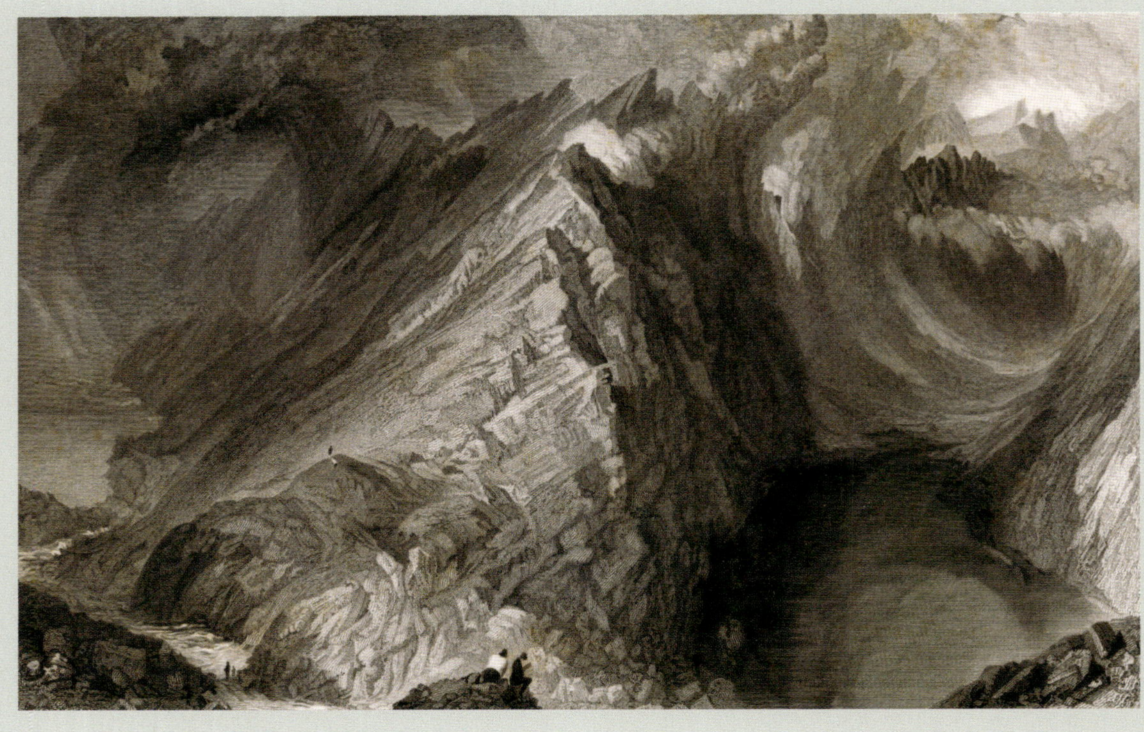

Fig. S4.20
Henry Le Keux after Joseph Mallord William Turner, 'Loch Coriskin' [Loch Coruisk], 1834, engraving in *Scott's Poetical Works* GLAHA: 9903)

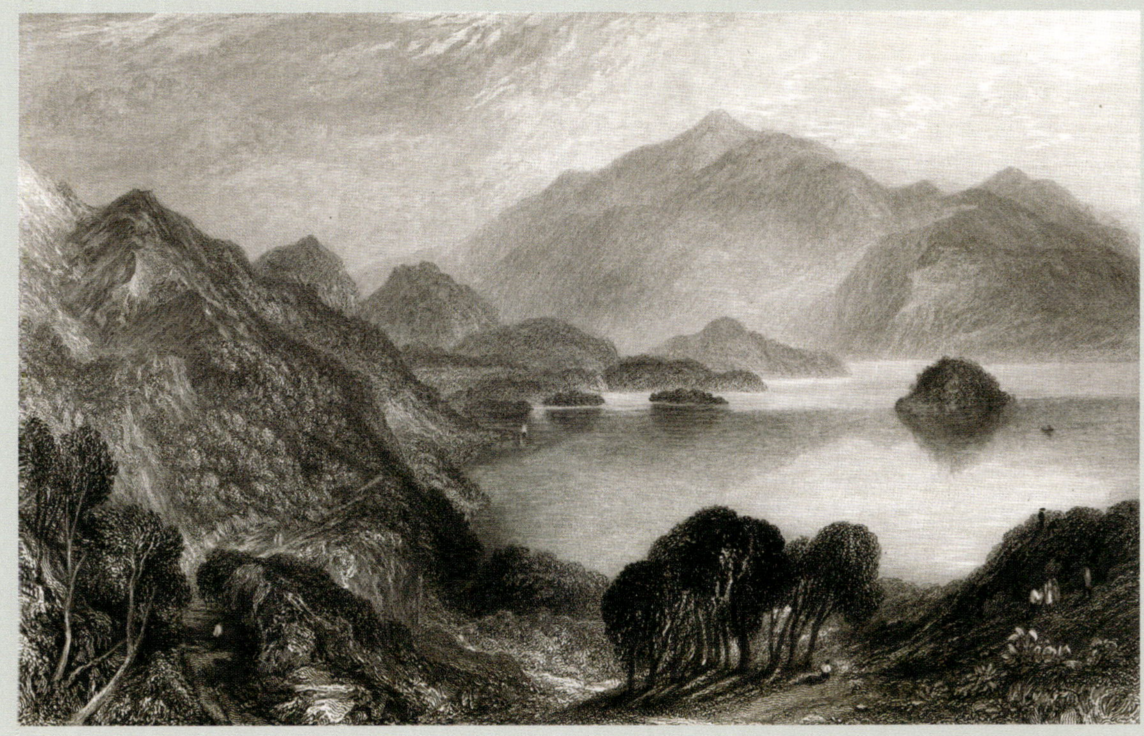

Fig. S4.21
William Miller after Joseph Mallord William Turner, 'Loch Katrine', 1834, engraving in *Scott's Poetical Works* (GLAHA: 1715)

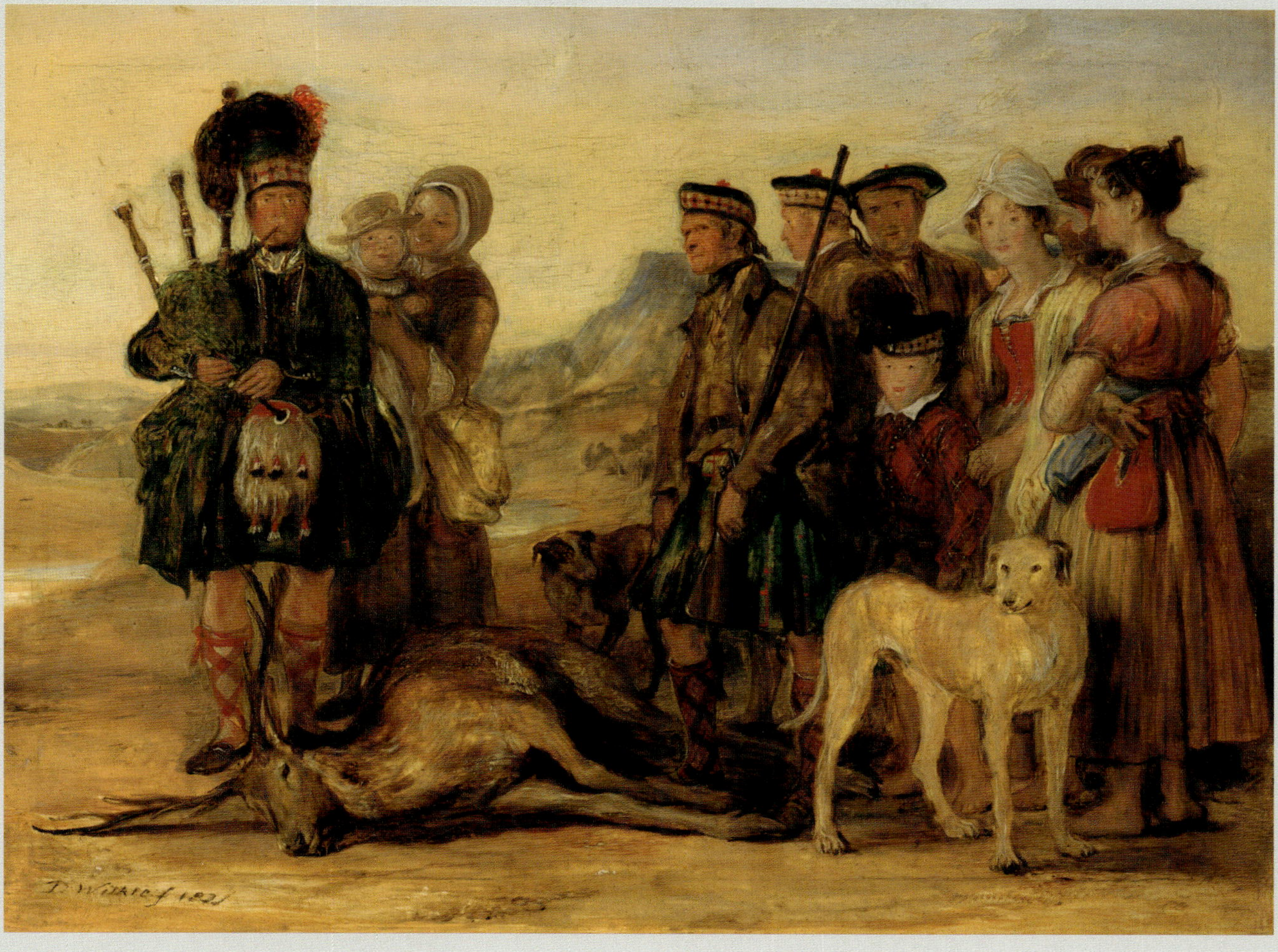

Fig. S4.22
David Wilkie, oil sketch for *The Death of the Red Deer*, c. 1821, oil on canvas (AE)

The Hunter mark'd that mountain high,
The lone lake's western boundary,
And deem'd the stag must turn to bay,
Where that huge rampart barr'd the way;
Already glorying in the prize,
Measured his antlers with his eyes;
For the death-wound and death-halloo,
Muster'd his breath, his whinyard drew . . .

(Sir Walter Scott, *The Lady of the Lake*, Canto 1, st. 8, in *Poetical Works of Sir Walter Scott*, ed. J. Logie Robertson (London, 1913), 209)

the new castle designed by J. & W. Smith retained more of the character of a shooting lodge than a baronial seat like Blair or Taymouth Castle (Miers 2017, 45–67, 107–108). Both the Highland sporting phenomenon and Victorian 'Balmorality' still drew heavily on Scott's mythic Scotland, seizing on the supposed natural wildness of the scenery and fauna of the kingdom's great fiefdoms (Donald 2007, 292–293).

NOTES

1 On the basis of the lady's dress with its high 'empire' waistline, which went out of fashion by 1825, the painting might be speculatively dated c. 1815–1820. Personal communication from Sally Tuckett.

CHAPTER SIX

Portable Knick-knacks or the Material Culture of Travel

'Adieu to Scotland, Oatcake & Naked Feet'

Viccy Coltman

In July 1805, John Elliot made an ink and watercolour sketch of his two-man cabin on board the *William Pitt*, as the ship was preparing to depart for the six-month passage to Madras in the British East Indies (Fig. C6.1).[1] He dispatched the sketch in a letter to his mother, in which he described it as 'an exact plan everything is painted as it really is'. The plan included his reflected self-portrait – note his annotation 'looking glass with me in it' – written clockwise around the frame shown hanging on the left-hand wall. The sketch gives the dimensions of the cabin as a snug 8 foot by 9 foot 10 inches. In addition to the permanent fixtures of the door, beams and a port hole, it reproduces various pieces of furniture for this temporary home, including a door mat, a chair, a 'sopha' which Elliot had fashioned by putting two trunks together, a table, wash-hand stand and a chest of drawers. Through the centre 'there is a curtain goes across here that we can let down when ever we like', Elliot explained. Other objects of material culture are shown hanging from the walls, with, on the right, a towel suspended between two pewter jugs to either side of the door, 'nankeen gaters', a pair of shoes and one of a pair of bookshelves. On the bookshelf, the titles of the volumes lying horizontally read the Bible and 'LAST LAY', the latter an abbreviation for Walter Scott's *Lay of the Last Minstrel* poem, which was published the same year as the 17-year-old Elliot embarked on his career with the East India Company.

Scott's poems and novels were widely read by company servants in India, and by Scots in particular, drawn to the evocations of the landscapes of their native country, from which they were dislocated for years and even decades. A month after his arrival at Madras, John wrote that he found the landscape of the Indian subcontinent 'quite disgusting to my Scotch eyes & I should be quite delighted to have some pictures with very green grass (for there is no verdure here at all) very high hills, and very rapid rivers'.[2] Green grass, high hills and rapid rivers were the characteristic landscape features of Elliot's home, the Scottish Borders. A year later he entreated his mother to 'tell Walter Scott that if it had not been for the Lay of the Last Minstrel I should have been dead of the Blue Devils long ago, but I go on travelling over the ground with William Deloraine till I get right again'.[3] Reading Scott's poem enabled the homesick Elliot to revisit imaginatively his boyhood landscapes of the Scottish Borders via the travels of Deloraine.

In July 1805, however, John was 'full of business in getting his cabin to rights' prior to their embarkation, which meant making it as comfortable as possible. 'His cabin is extremely good', his father Gilbert Elliot, Lord Minto (who later joined John in India when he became Governor-General) reassured his absent wife, 'but he will be a good deal annoyed by having a companion in it, especially one who does not seem bright – a green bay curtain however, will divide them by day, leaving two good berths, of which John's is far the best having the port entirely to himself, that is to say a large light & airy windows'.[4] In addition to people, objects (notably books) acted as travelling companions whose company was placed on a scale from convivial to tedious. Once at sea, John wrote that 'of all the dull books I ever read I think it [the *Asiatic Miscellany*] is the dullest', whereas he 'like[d] . . . uncommonly' James Thomson's *Seasons* poems.[5] We see the results of John's busyness in July 1805 in the plan he produced for his mother (see Fig. C6.1), which demonstrates how his cabin was fitted and furnished with material objects, some generic to an extended maritime passage, others specific to Elliot and his cabin mate. They included the ink, paper and paints that he used to produce the plan. The plan itself is implicated into this repertoire of things as part of the paraphernalia of travel and its pictorial representation since Elliot cut the paper at its four corners so that his mother might assemble the box-like architecture of his cabin from two-dimensions into three – making a doll's house interior, or a temporary household in miniature (Chen 2015).

This essay offers some preliminary observations about the material culture of domestic travel in Scotland during the second half of the eighteenth and early nineteenth centuries. It opens with the plan of Elliot's cabin to introduce the idea of expanding geographical horizons – since travel in this period was an imperial and European phenomenon, as well as a national one: part of the process of nation building and colonial conquest. As mentioned in the introduction, within the genre of domestic travel literature, mediated impressions of distant lands or first-hand memories of Europe served as more familiar reference points for the traveller who was unfamiliar with Scotland. Hence the 'Nakedness and Misery' of a highland hunt at Tyndrum 'could not be exceeded by the wigwam of a Hottentot', exclaimed the anonymous author of a 1794 manuscript tour of Scotland.[6] The 'change of manners, dress, and character [on entering Langholm, the first village in Scotland] . . . is scarce more violent at Dover and Calais; the people of either sex were in general without shoes or stockings', reported an unidentified traveller the previous year while making the journey from London to Elgin.[7] He also thought the Royal Mile at Edinburgh 'not unlike some of the fine streets in the great Cities of Flanders', while the military garrison at Fort George 'somewhat reminded me of Fort St George in the East Indies [at Madras]'.[8] For the poet Thomas Gray, who visited the Highlands in the autumn

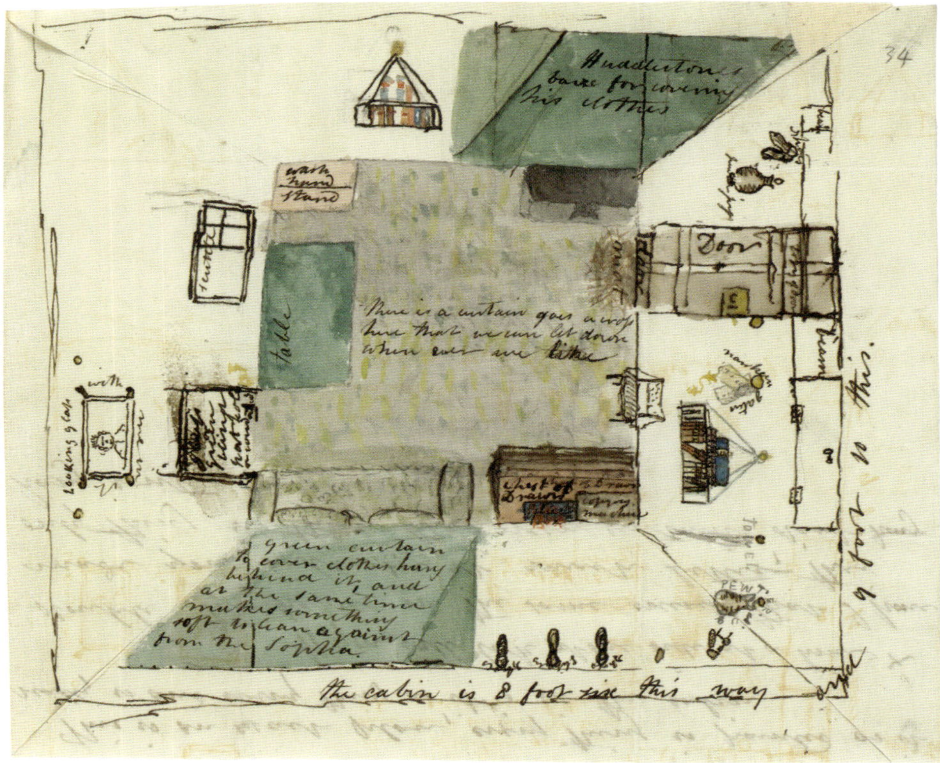

Fig. C6.1
John Elliot, 'every thing is painted as it really is', plan of Elliot's cabin on board the *William Pitt*, July 1805, ink and watercolour (NLS MS. 11094 fo. 34)

of 1765, 'Italy could hardly produce a nobler scene, or a finer season.'[9] The mid to later eighteenth century witnessed the height of the grand tour of Europe, when scores of socially and economically privileged young British men made the ritualised educational pilgrimage to Rome. The material culture of this cosmopolitan rite of passage is better documented than the domestic tour or imperial passage, with Jeremy Black's *The British Abroad: The Grand Tour in the Eighteenth Century* (1992) devoting chapters to transport (by road; by canal, river and sea; by vehicles), accommodation, food and drink (Black 1992). One Alexander Mackinnon wrote a letter to the banker and author Sir William Forbes of Pitsligo on 28 August 1792, offering a series of hints on travelling to the Continent.[10] His advice was as follows: to acquire a strong travelling carriage before the party set off; to obtain bolts and nails for its upkeep on the road; to carry spare sheets for use at inns and a few pounds of tea with four cups and saucers and some small spoons. These objects from distinct histories of transport, textiles, crockery and consumables are united under the rubric of material culture in discussing some of the 'portable knick-knacks' that featured in domestic travel in Scotland.

Existing histories of the fashionable phenomena by scholars including Durie (2003; 2012), Glendening (1997), Gold and Gold (1995) and Grenier (2005) have largely overlooked these aspects of the tour, much as the travellers themselves did, in their published and manuscript accounts. According to the anonymous author of a 1789 tour of Scotland: 'The more I consider the numerous Advantages arising from Travel, the greater Pleasure I receive from reflecting that the love of this species of Education rages with increasing violence in the breasts of my fellow-Countrymen. There certainly is nothing which tends to enlarge the mind as travel . . . It is from this alone that we are to become in after Times a source of pleasure to ourselves, an ornament to our friends, and a desirable companion to all.'[11] The reported 'violence' in the breasts of Britons might be extended to the Continent where war with France led to a massive boost in domestic tourism, although this claim is more often stated than investigated. For later eighteenth-century travellers like this one, the theory behind a tour of Scotland was a pedagogical exercise in self-improvement – where mental and social horizons expanded in tandem with geographical ones. In practice, the reality might be filthy inns, broken carriages, unpassable roads and what one pedestrian traveller, the Rev. James Plumptre, refers to as 'knick-knacks', a term that denotes trifling objects or childish toys. In this chapter, an account of Plumptre's 1799 tour will be followed by analysis of Mrs Sarah Murray's tour, in her *A Companion and Useful Guide to the Beauties of Scotland*, which was published the same year, although I will also refer to writings by other travellers. Murray's title demonstrates the extent to which portable books

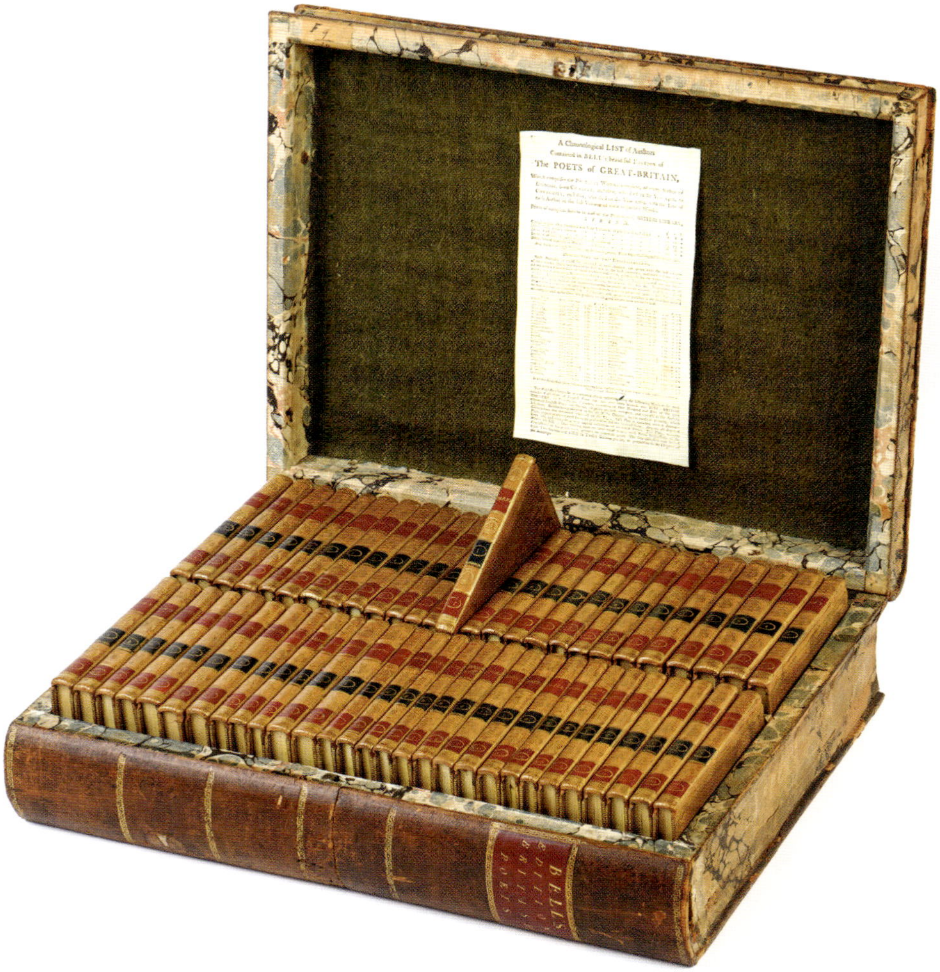

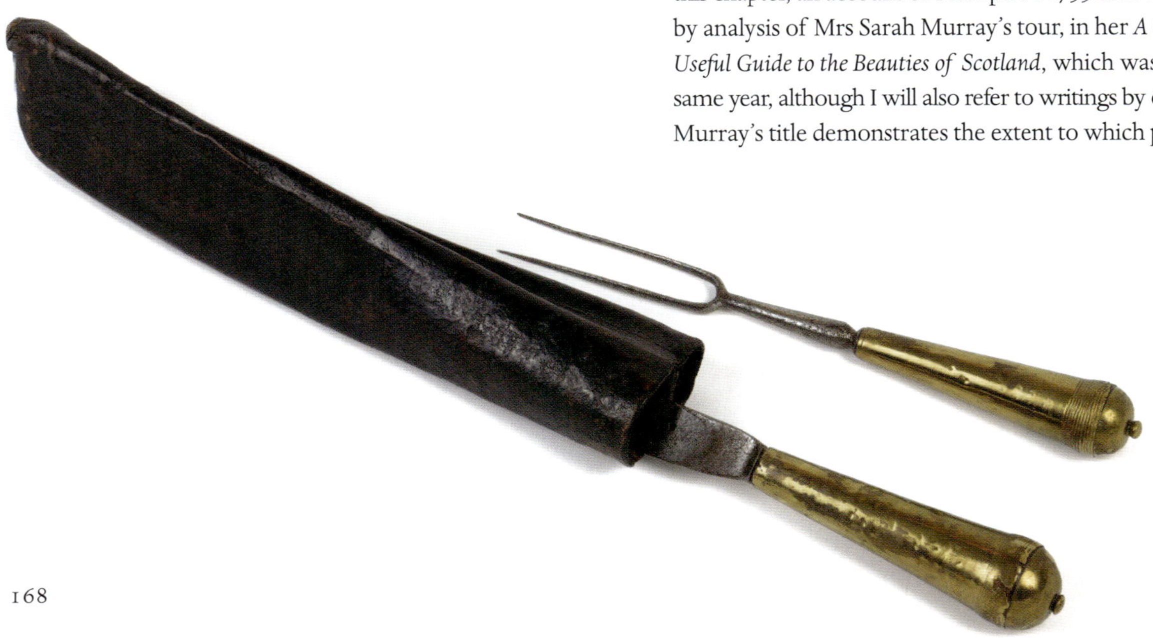

Fig. C6.2
Above. Travelling library, Bell's edition of *The Poets of Great-Britain*, 1770s (WZC)

Fig. C6.3
Right. Travel fork and knife, brass, iron and leather, eighteenth century (WZC)

like her *Guide* could be conceived as themselves forming part of the material appurtenances of travel.

A playwright and Church of England clergyman at the University of Cambridge, James Plumptre was a seasoned traveller who made eight domestic tours between 1790 and 1800, visiting Scotland, Derbyshire, North Wales and the Lake District. His late twentieth-century editor, Ian Ousby, estimates a resulting paper trail of more than 350,000 words, including memoranda taken on the spot and a three-volume narrative of the 1799 journey, which he prepared for publication (Ousby 1992, 18). This tour embraced the north-east coast of England, Scotland, the Lakes and North Wales. During four and a half months on the road, from the end of April, Plumptre records covering a distance of 2,236 miles of which an exacting 1,774¼ – more than three-quarters of the total – were on foot and 461¾ on horseback. Plumptre's preferred mode of travel was by foot and he made detailed notes about pedestrianism or 'minding himself to go afoot' as he put it, citing Acts 20:13. The 1799 tour was Plumptre's third foray into North Britain, aged twenty-eight, with his dog Rover and an occasional servant. We know he made a brief tour of Scotland from 13 August to 3 September 1795 with an unidentified companion. As he left Edinburgh on this

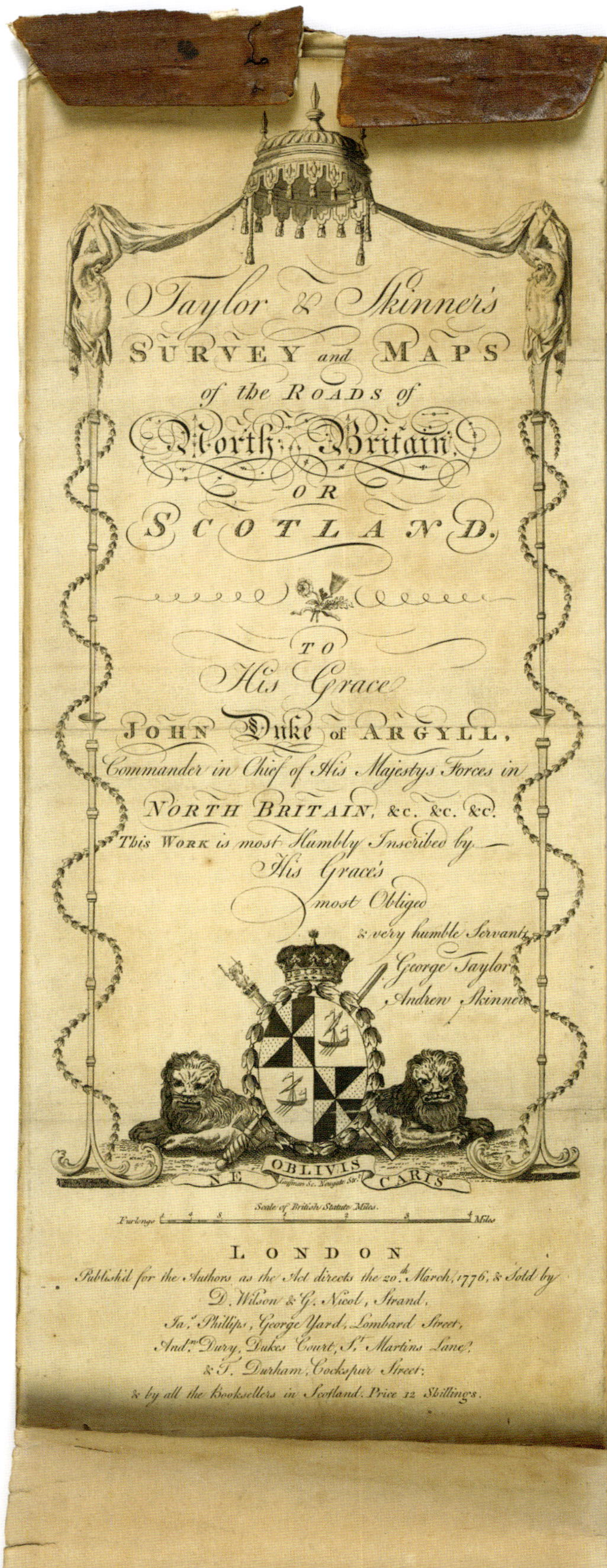
Taylor & Skinner's
SURVEY and MAPS
of the ROADS of
North Britain
OR
SCOTLAND.
TO
His Grace
JOHN Duke of ARGYLL,
Commander in Chief of His Majestys Forces in
NORTH BRITAIN, &c. &c. &c.
This WORK is most Humbly Inscribed by
His Grace's
most Obliged
& very humble Servants,
George Taylor
Andrew Skinner
NE OBLIVISCARIS
Scale of British Statute Miles.
LONDON
Publish'd for the Authors as the Act directs the 20th March, 1776, & Sold by
D. Wilson & G. Nicol, Strand,
Jas. Phillips, George Yard, Lombard Street,
Andw. Dury, Dukes Court, St. Martins Lane,
& T. Durham, Cockspur Street;
& by all the Booksellers in Scotland. Price 12 Shillings.

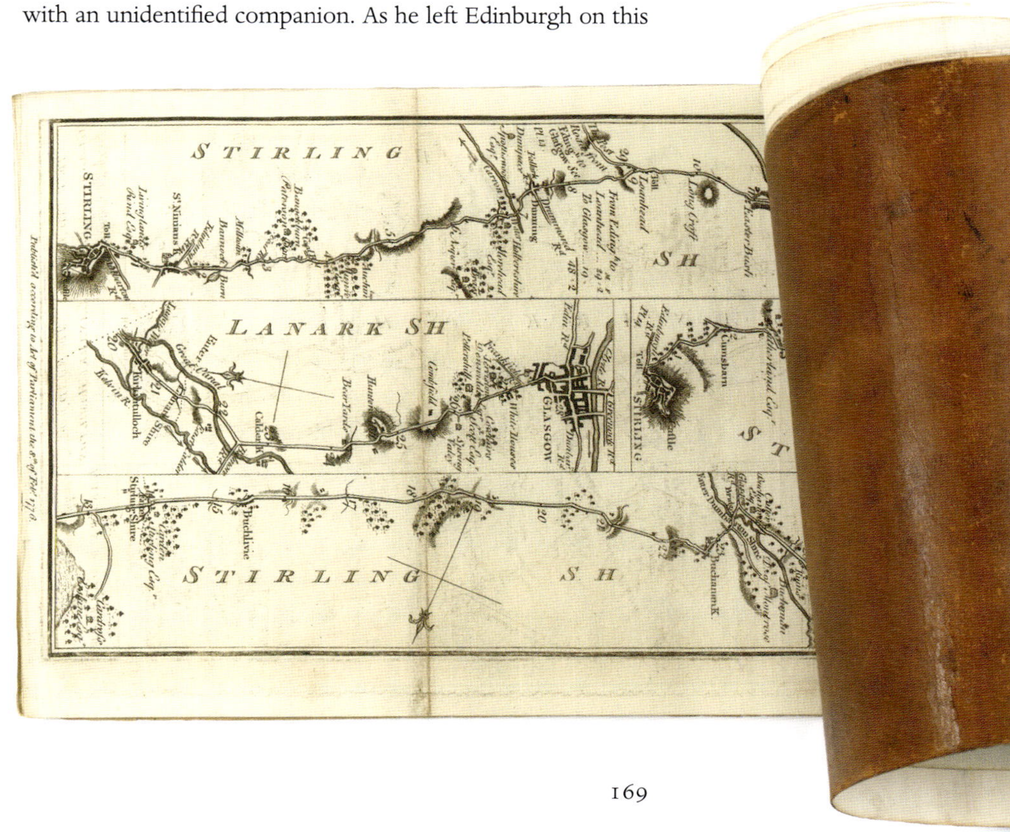

Fig. C6.4
George Taylor and Andrew Skinner, *Survey and Maps of the Roads of North Britain or Scotland* (London, 1776): title page and map in its leather sheaf (WZC)

occasion, he bought a knick-knack in preparation for social interaction further north: 'I equipp'd myself with a snuff box to win the hearts of all Highland lad & laddies and shall in consequence become a snuffer or as they here express themselves I shall snuff.'[12] He also bought a copy of Shakespeare's *Macbeth* in Kinross 'to enjoy properly the enchanted poetic ground we are soon to tread'.[13]

As discussed in Chapter 1, at different periods and various locations across the Highlands, Lowlands and Borders, Scotland's 'poetic ground' was associated with Ossian, Robert Burns and, most notably, Walter Scott's *Lady of the Lake*; Shakespeare's *Macbeth* could be added to the list. Travellers carried portable copies of these published volumes, read from them *in situ,* and quoted from them in their journals and letters. As discussed in Section 4, Scott's *Lady of the Lake* transformed the Trossachs into a quintessential romantic locality, with its protagonist Fitz-James's 'holiday romance' with Ellen Douglas acting as a model for the tourist's first-hand experience of the region with its characteristic mountains and lochs (Watson 2010). After 1810, the tour of Scotland was most noticeably a romance between Scott and his bewitched readers, like the anonymous author of a 'Journal thro' some parts of Scotland' in 1829 whose quotation of extended cantos on successive pages reveals his seduction by the 'powerful pen' of the 'Great Magician of the North'.[14]

Plumptre returned to Scotland and the Lake District the following summer: his name, address and the date are recorded in the visitors' register at New Lanark on 25 July 1796 (Durie 2003, 27). Visitors' books were one of the means by which domestic travel was institutionalised, representing a more formal means of inscribing oneself into the tour than the graffiti scratched on the columns at the entrance to Fingal's cave on Staffa, for instance. Ian Donnachie has studied the three visitors' books to New Lanark and the Falls of Clyde, which cover the years 1795–1799 and 1821–1832, to provide statistical data about the number and occupational profiles of visitors to these industrial and picturesque locations. When Plumptre visited in 1796 he was one of six or seven hundred annual visitors who included lawyers, merchants, clergy, doctors and teachers, most of whom had a professional interest in New Lanark as what Donnachie terms 'a show-piece of philanthropic management' (Donnachie 2005, 153).

Three years after the visit to New Lanark, Plumptre made his third extended tour of Scotland, and early on in his 'narrative of a pedestrian journey', as he entitled it, he recounted his preparations in an extended passage that is worth quoting at length and in full:

> Mr Boswell, in his Tour to the Hebrides [published 1785], has amused his readers with an account of the dress and equipment of his fellow-traveller. It may perhaps be useful to future Tourists to know in what manner I was fitted out. As it was my intention to make many visits among my own friends and at gentlemen's houses in the course of my journey, it was necessary to have a second suit of cloaths and more linen, than if I had intended to stop only at inns. I therefore took a small portmanteau, sending it from place to place as occasion served, and when obliged to separate from it, I carried a change of linen and a few other necessaries in a netted bag, at my back, made like a shooting bag and lined with oilskin. This I preferred to a knapsack, which I had tried on a former occasion. It not only looked better, but was more commodious, as I could change the position of it from side to side, or even make it bear more upon the back. Besides this I intended my servant from Edinburgh should carry a suit of cloaths &c in a knapsack. Every thing I took with me was new; that besides being handsome, it might stand the wear, and not trouble me with perpetual mending. My travelling coat, of a very dark grey colour, was made with lapelles to button over my breast, and up to my throat, to secure me from cold, and was short in the skirts that it might not be in my way in walking. A crab stick, which had formerly belonged to a great man in our family, was to serve at once as a support and a defence. Besides a sufficient quantity of linen (seven shirts and all other articles suiting) and three pair of well-seasoned shoes, I carried the following knick-knacks: A Grays glass and a Claude Lorrain, – magnifiers for botany, – a small telescope, – a pocket compass and pedometer, – a sixteen foot measure of tape, made to roll round a winch in a small leather case, like a lady's pocket yard-measure, – drawing and memorandum books, – a

> small case with colours &c, a silver pen and pencil, – a pocket and pen knives, – a pocket knife and fork, a pocket pistol [a hip flask] and drinking horn. I had moreover Kitchin's and Brown's maps of Scotland, and Mavor's abridgement of Pennant's, Johnson's & Newte's Tours in Scotland . . . To this small library I added the pocket Edition of Cowper's Poems. (Ousby 1992, 88)

Plumptre's is the most detailed account we have of the paraphernalia of the domestic traveller, offering a list that includes items of dress and textiles with an array of portable, compact objects. Although he does not identify James Boswell's travelling companion Samuel Johnson by name, the former's description of Johnson's attire and accessories is represented in a print published on 18 January 1786 with the caption 'from the life and engrav'd' by Thomas Trotter (Fig. C1.3): 'when journeying [explained Boswell], he wore boots [over black worsted socks], and a very wide brown cloth great coat [over his suit of plain brown clothes], with pockets which might have almost held the two volumes of his folio dictionary; and he carried in his hand a large English oak stick. Let me not be censured for mentioning such minute particulars' (Rogers 1993, 6). Trotter depicts Johnson walking with his stick through the mountainous landscape of the Scottish Highlands, wearing top boots and a tricorn hat, a miniature Boswell at a distance in the left foreground. In order to hold his *Dictionary of the English Language* (1755), Johnson's coat pockets would have needed to be voluminous – about 31 cm in length and able to hold two volumes weighing around 20 lb (Hitchings 2005, 192, 195). The text below the title of the print refers to an episode later in the 1773 tour when Johnson lost the oak stick he brought with him from London while visiting the island of Mull. Boswell explains how it functioned as both walking aid and approximate measuring tool – with nails hammered into it at a distance of a yard and a foot. In 'a country so divested, so denuded of trees' as Scotland, Johnson's lost stick became, in his own words, precious 'timber' (Rogers 1993, 254). More than other hardwoods like the beech or elm, oaks were invested with a complex web of 'venerable, patriarchal, stately, guardian and quintessentially English' associations (Daniels 1988, 48). An oak stick was the portable benchmark by which Johnson would critically measure the Scots and all things Scottish.

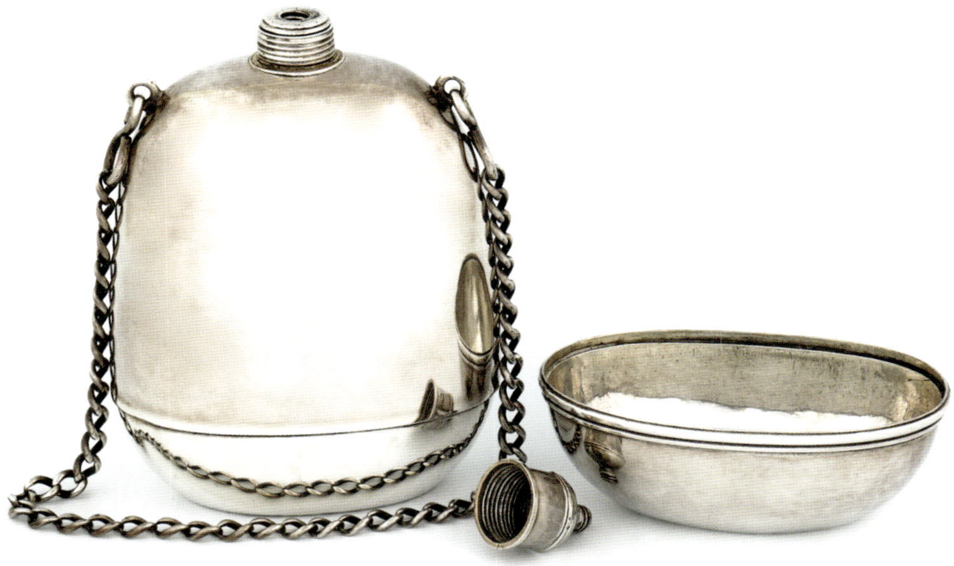

Fig. C6.5
Ebenezer Oliphant, Drinking flask, eighteenth century (WZC)

Among Plumptre's unpublished papers in Cambridge University Library is an inventory of the items that comprised his travelling wardrobe. In the order in which he listed them, it consisted of a black coat, a waistcoat and breeches; a double-breasted travelling coat, a single-breasted waistcoat and breeches with a pocket for his knife, fork, pedometer and garters; 4 shirts [the manuscript journal says 7], 4 cravats, 4 pocket handkerchiefs, 2 silk handkerchiefs, 2 pairs of stockings, 1 pair of black silk stockings, 3 pairs of socks (worsted), 3 pairs of shoes, 2 flannel waistcoats, 2 pairs of drawers and 2 nightcaps.[15] This was Plumptre's sartorial apparel for four and a half months during the spring and summer of 1799 – furnishing him with one set of clothes for socialising and another for travelling; it consisted of items of underwear, outerwear and accessories, in materials including silk, worsted and flannel. With the exception of his three pairs of 'well-seasoned' shoes, all the items in Plumptre's travelling wardrobe were new, including the dark grey coat with its adjustable lapels for warmth and its amenable length for walking.

The vagaries of travelling took its toll on items of dress, reducing them from handsome to shabby in the course of daily wear and tear. When Elizabeth Diggle 'bid adieu to Scotland, oatcake & naked feet' in a letter written at Gretna on 7 July

1788, she noted, 'My hat is faded to pieces, my coat pinched, ink'd & the carriage all faded. Joseph's jacket turned into a brown one & so we make as shabby a figure as need be' (Durie 2012, 36). Diggle's tour from London to the Highlands with her aunt and a servant, Joseph, lasted almost five months, from 19 April to 7 August 1788 and is recorded in a series of letters written to her sister and other family members. These letters were later transcribed into a manuscript journal that is both literary endeavour and material artefact.

The majority of Scottish tours took place, like those of Diggle and Plumptre, between the spring and autumn, with August and September being the most popular months (Durie, 2003, 26). The 'naked feet' that Diggle 'bid adieu' to was the most familiar refrain from travellers, most of whom wrote in horror at this ubiquitous spectacle that they saw as proof of the impoverishment of the Scots. 'Shoes & stockings most superflous [sic] parts of Cloathing [sic] quite the grand Superflu. Witness the numberless dirty human animals I [Lady Grey on her 1755 tour from Berwick to Taymouth] have seen without them from Newcastle hither [Edinburgh].'[16] Scots' unshod feet contrasts with the sturdy shoes of experienced travellers such as Plumptre with his three 'well-seasoned' pairs. The oatcakes that Diggle also bid farewell to in July 1788 will be addressed below with other Scottish foodstuffs, once our rubric for what constitutes the stuff of material culture is extended beyond Plumptre's dress and knick-knacks.

Fig. C6.6
Claude Lorrain mirror, 1737–1767
(SM 1980–1746/2)

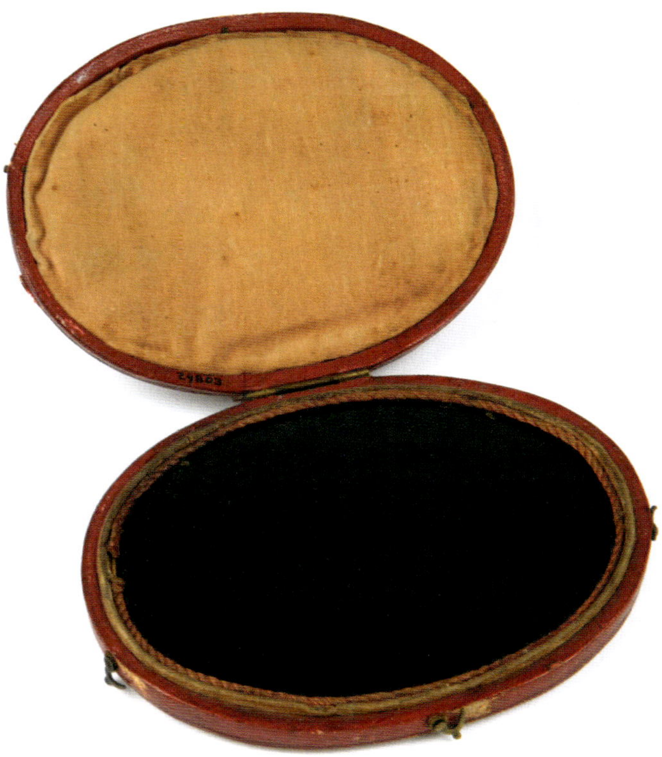

Plumptre uses the term 'knick-knacks' for the portable possessions that he carried in his *sack de nuit*, an oilskin-lined bag (the oilskin an attempt at waterproofing) and in the pockets of his breeches. They included utensils and vessels for eating and drinking. Other objects not listed in the manuscript account of the tour were a snuff box and a tobacco case, a 'case for razor, combs, scizars &c &c' for personal grooming, and a barometer.[17] Among those objects he enumerated in detail was a suite of optical devices for focused viewing: for scrutinising aspects of the landscape at a distance and at close range. There were instruments for navigating, measuring and recording information in the form of written memorandums and painted representations. A Gray's glass, so-called after the poet Thomas Gray, was a flat, convex mirror about 10 centimetres diameter on a black background, whose convex shape reflected in miniature the landscape when the traveller stood with his back to it. The Claude Lorrain was another type of mirrored glass that Plumptre carried (Fig. C6.6); it reflected a painterly landscape that was thought to be similar to the works of the seventeenth-century master. As Malcolm Andrews has noted, in its tinting and distortion it 'helped to superimpose something like a Claudean idiom on British landscape' (Andrews 1989, 69). The camera obscura was a third optical device particularly favoured by travelling artists. Paul Sandby included one in the right foreground of a gouache drawing of c. 1780 of the ruins of Roslin Castle, outside Edinburgh, in which an amateur woman artist, Lady Frances Scott, is shown drawing via the mirrored and projected image of a woman and child on a bridge over the North Esk river (Fig. C6.7). A shepherd gathering his sheep on the hilly pasture behind them completes this pastoral family scene, the picturesque subject of inferred and actual compositions on paper.

While walking to Kenmore and blinded by the reflection of the summer sun bouncing off the road, Plumptre recommended another visual aid in the form of 'a green shade or green spectacles' (Ousby 1992, 115). These proto sunglasses with green glass (Fig. C6.8), known as 'Goldoni glasses' after

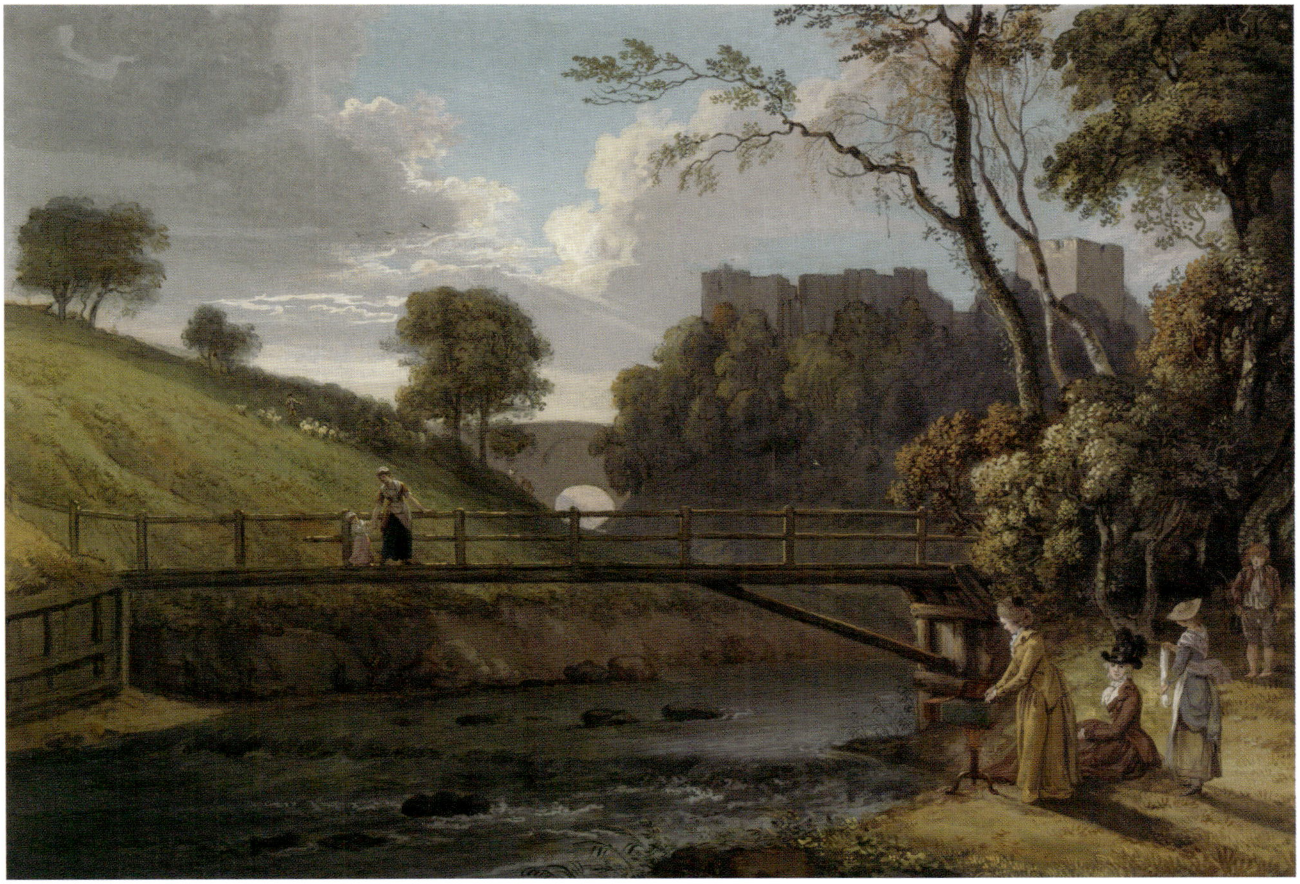

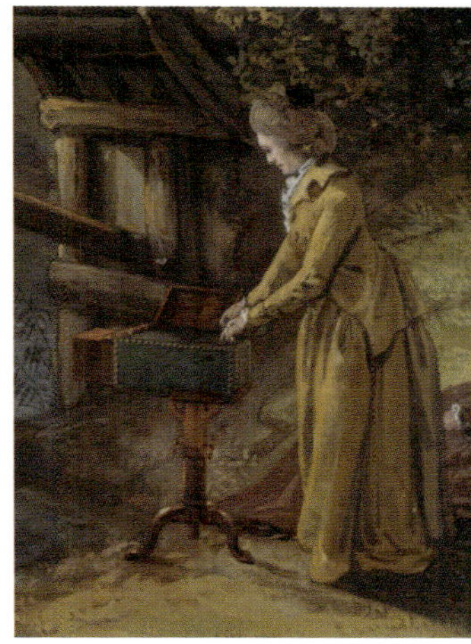

Fig. C6.7
Left. Paul Sandby, *Roslin Castle, Midlothian*, c. 1780, gouache on medium laid paper, mounted on board (YCBA B1975.4.1877)

Above. Detail of camera obscura

the Venetian playwright Carlo Goldoni who popularised them, were missing from Plumptre's roomy luggage, which did however include printed matter in the form of maps and books. He carried two maps: Thomas Kitchin's *Scotland Divided into its Counties from the Latest Surveys* c. 1770, and Thomas Brown's *A New and Accurate Travelling Map of Scotland* c. 1790. While in Edinburgh, a gentleman lent him a third: John Ainslie's *Scotland, Drawn and Engrav'd from a Series of Angles and Astronomical Observations*, which he carried rolled up in a tin case (Ousby 1992, 125, 127). There were also abridged versions of three tours by Thomas Pennant (1769; 1772), Samuel Johnson (1775) and Thomas Newte (1791) published by William Mavor in his multi-volume compendium *The British Tourists; or Traveller's Pocket Companion* (1798–1800). Pennant and Johnson are (by now) familiar travellers to the reader of this volume, as they were to James Plumptre and others of his ilk, the most frequently cited in both published and manuscript accounts of journeys to Scotland in the period. 'Thomas Newte' is perhaps less well known. His *Prospects and Observations; on a Tour in England and Scotland: Natural, Oeconomical and Literary* (London, 1791), which he describes as 'a kind of Geographical Anatomy', includes a fold-out map of Scotland.[18] Newte's subtitle demonstrates how the genre of travel literature devoted to Scotland was becoming increasingly specialist, a phenomenon critiqued to devastating effect in Walter Scott's anonymous review of John Carr's *Caledonian Sketches, or a Tour through Scotland in 1807* in the launch volume of the *Quarterly Review* for 1809, already mentioned in Chapter 1. Among the 'hundred volumes' available in a veritable cavalcade of publications, wrote Scott, 'there is Johnson's Philosophic Tour, Pennant's Descriptive Tour, Gilpin's Picturesque

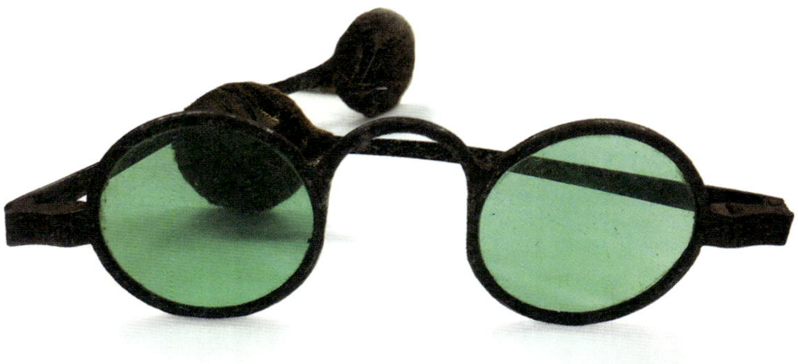

Fig. C6.8
Above. Steel frame sunglasses, mid eighteenth century (NMS T.1968.2)

Tour, Stoddart's Sketching Tour, Garnet's Medical Tour, Mrs. Murray's Familiar Tour, Newte's Nautical Tour, Mawman's Bookselling Tour, Campbell's Crazy Tour, Lithie's Insipid Tour, and Boswell's fantastic Tour, with the Humours of the Bear and the Monkey' (Scott 1809, 182).

Scott's review cites 'Mrs. Murray's Familiar Tour' before it descends into the overt satire of the crazy or insipid tour: the same year that Plumptre made his third extended tour of Scotland, 1799, Mrs Sarah Murray 'of Kensington' (as she is presented on her title page) published her *Companion and Useful Guide to the Beauties of Scotland* (Hagglund 2010, 54–76). Murray was a 52-year-old widow when she left London in May 1796, travelling nearly 2,000 miles by carriage with a maid, a manservant and a driver for five months. Hers is a substantial volume of 396 pages divided into three parts, as indicated by the remainder of its long title: *. . . to the Lakes of Westmoreland, Cumberland, and Lancashire; and to the Curiosities in the District of Craven, in the West Riding of Yorkshire to which is added, a more particular description of Scotland especially to that part of it called the Highlands*. The sections are uneven, with fifteen chapters making the last third the most sizable. The volume opens with a preface in which Murray offers a series of authoritative instructions to the reader, who is addressed directly. 'Provide yourself with a strong roomy carriage', she begins, and proceeds to list the parts required for possible repairs to said carriage along the route – the likes of linch-pins, shackles, a turn-screw, a hammer and some straps. Having dealt with the exterior body of the carriage, Murray

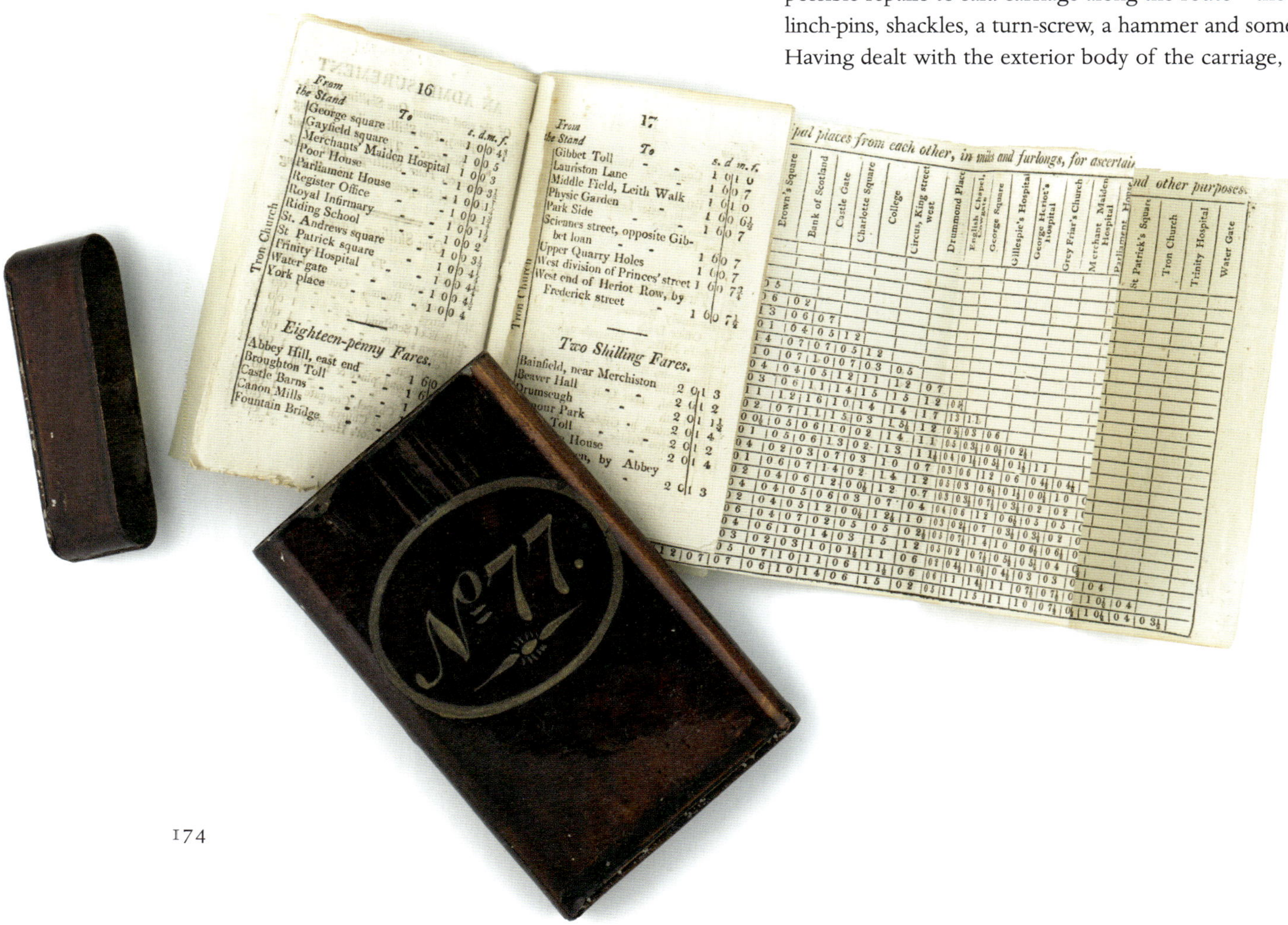

Fig. C6.9
Right. Regulations for Hackney coaches in original tin case labelled 'No 77', 1811, Edinburgh (WZC)

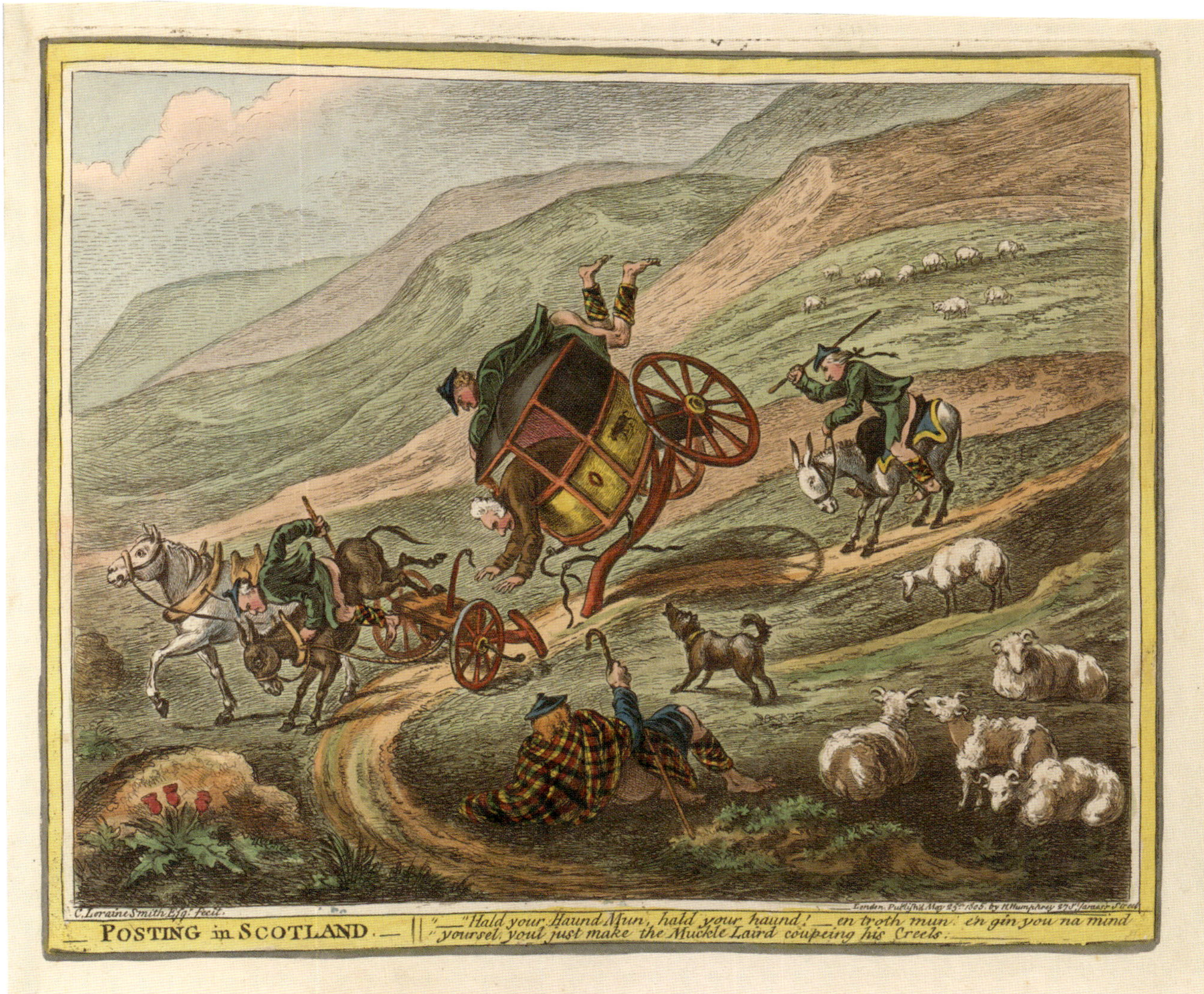

Fig. C6.10
James Gillray, *Posting in Scotland*, 1805, coloured engraving (BRBML)

ventures into its interior for which she prescribes a box that should form a table on the travellers' laps, with a part with holes for wine bottles to be stored upright. 'The part above the bottles, to hold tea, sugar, bread and meat; a tumbler glass, knife and fork and salt cellar, with two or three napkins: the box to have a very good lock.' Having specified basic picnic-like provisions in the form of foodstuffs and utensils for eating, she turns to 'such conveniences' as linen: recommending bed linen, six towels ('at least'), a blanket, quilt and two pillows. Instructions follow for a seat behind the carriage for a manservant.

Murray's description of the carriage exterior, essential provisions for its upkeep and bespoke interior fittings echoes the substance of the letter Mackinnon wrote to Forbes concerning his incipient grand tour of Europe discussed above. It also extends our rubric of 'knick-knacks' beyond Plumptre's travelling dress and portable, hand-held artefacts to embrace a more capacious world of goods, including the modes and means of transport, modifications to landscape views, and food and drink for the road. According to this more elastic definition, James Gillray's graphic satire *Posting in Scotland* from 1805 can be taken to depict the hazards of travelling by carriage on zig-zag roads in the mountainous Highlands (Fig. C6.10).

The road in question might be one of those 'old ways' mentioned by Edmund Burt, in the last of his *Letters from a Gentleman in the North of Scotland* quoted in the introduction of the present volume, or else a 'new road' in bad repair. As a post-chaise drawn by a horse and a mule approaches a hair-pin bend in the road, the springs and perch snap, the front wheels come off, jolting the occupant through the front window. Four Scottish Highlanders are shown in front of, behind, on top of and reclining next to the ruptured carriage. All of them are barefoot and bare-buttocked in this similarly exposed landscape. They wear pointed blue bonnets and what resemble tartan legwarmers. A reclining shepherd with a staff looks on impassively, accompanied by his dog who barks at the chaise, and five sheep with bare rumps and shorn necks. Without rising to offer assistance, the shepherd enjoins the coachmen to 'hald your Haund Mun' lest the 'Muckle Laird' should 'coup his Creels' ('tumble head over heels'), referring to the unfortunate occupant of the chaise who has presumably been posted to Scotland in a professional capacity, but now finds himself 'posted' through its window. Both the Scots idiom uttered here by the Highland shepherd in Gillray's image, as well as the Gaelic still universally spoken throughout much of Scotland across the Highland line, presented a language barrier to southern tourists: Philothea Perronet Thompson, a 54-year-old woman from Hull who made an eight-week tour, included a list of fifteen 'Scotch terms which were new to us' in her manuscript 'Observations in Scotland in the Summer of 1807' (Robinson 2006, 78). 'The hire's paid' (meaning the fare is paid) was a particularly useful phrase for non-Scottish travellers to master as they explored Scotland by road in a range of vehicles. Thompson and her party hired post-chaises; Dorothy Wordsworth travelled with her brother William and Samuel Taylor Coleridge for six weeks in August and September 1803 in an Irish jaunting car – an open-air two-wheeled cart drawn by a single horse in which the occupants were exposed to the elements. A young unnamed Scottish woman made a tour from Edinburgh into the Highlands with her mother and two sisters from 28 August to 8 September 1820 by 'landaulette', a horse-drawn carriage with a retractable roof. She noted the daily distances, which added up to a total of 310 miles: from Edinburgh to Hamilton was 48 miles, 'rather an exertion for the horses' she thought, whose daily average was between 20 and 25 miles.[19] The 'sketch of a short tour' by Thomas, 2nd Earl of Longford, opens with a list of the distances travelled in his short tour of June 1793 with laconic descriptions of the road, ranging from 'tolerably good', to 'dreary' to 'very rough'.[20]

The 'colossus of roads' was how the poet laureate Robert Southey described Thomas Telford, the great Scottish-born engineer responsible for realising the Act of 1803 'for making Roads and building Bridges in the Highlands of Scotland' (Haldane 1962, 45). Southey met Telford for the first time when they travelled in Scotland in 1819, with Telford's close friend the statistician John Rickman, his wife, two children and a nursemaid for part of the route. Southey's journal of their tour was published over a century later in 1929 and it valorises Telford's built structures at the same time as it denigrates those of General George Wade constructed in the 1720s and 1730s: 'Telford's is a happy life: everywhere making roads, building bridges, forming canals, and creating harbours – works of sure, solid, permanent utility' (Southey 1929, 54). For the road to Fort Augustus, Wade 'followed the old horse track, instead of surveying the country like an engineer' (in other words like the professional engineer Telford) (Southey 1929, 178). While Telford's bridge at Dunkeld was 'one of the finest in Scotland', Wade's over the River Tay near Aberfeldy (constructed in 1733 at enormous expense) was 'creditable neither to the skill nor taste of the architect' opined Southey, who judged all the latter's bridges 'miserably constructed' (Southey 1929, 46, 44, 98). For Telford's most recent biographer, Southey's 1819 journal of Scotland 'kept up the chatter of a dissatisfied tourist' (Glover 2017, 234). For the historian of material culture, however, the pages of Southey's journal are richly interspersed with objects, dress and textiles, some of which, like his reference to 'the filthy bare-foot fashion of the country', are by now familiar (Southey 1929, 79). On two occasions, at Old Meldrum and Luip, Southey found the rooms in the inns where the party stayed 'as small as a ship's cabin' (Southey 1929, 151). He noted that in poorer inns the sheets were calico and the towels calico too – 'hardly larger than doylies' (Southey 1929, 218). In Glasgow, sheets were coarse cotton (Southey 1929, 248). His journal records the food he ate as well as the wine, beer, port and claret he drank. At Loch Fyne, he dubbed 1819 'the great Herring year – I who have eaten them with proper constancy, at breakfast, at dinner, and at supper also' (Southey 1929, 242–243).

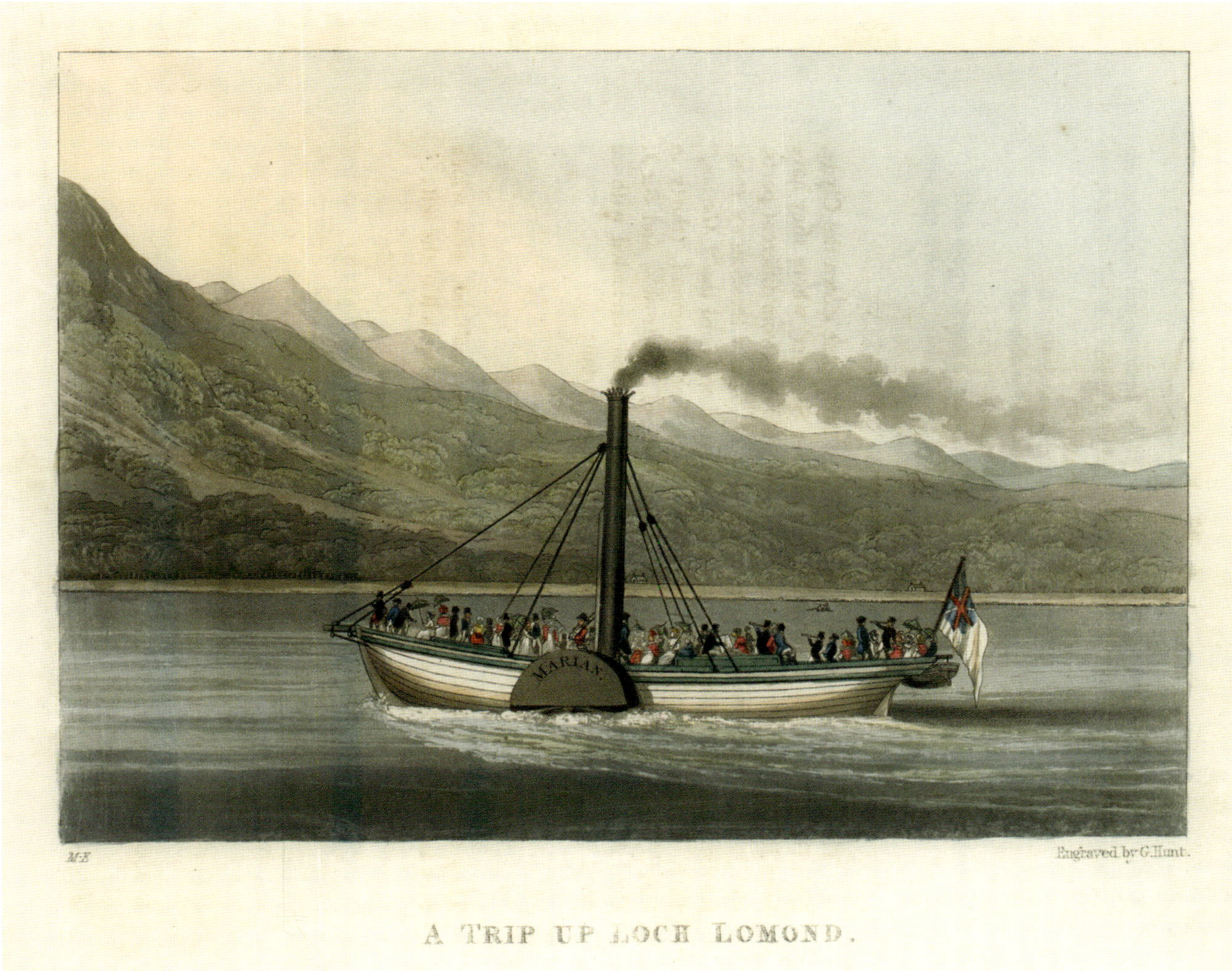

Fig. C6.11
George Hunt after Michael Egerton, 'A Trip up Loch Lomond', coloured engraving in Michael Egerton, *Airy Nothings; or Scraps, and Naughts, and Odd-cum-shorts: in a Circumbendicus Hop, Step, and Jump, by Olio Rigmaroll* (London, 1825) (NLS FB.m.150)

A 'pilgrimage to Scotland by our modern gastronomes is essential' to sample the native salmon trout, wrote Johanna Schopenhauer in the diary she kept while travelling in Britain between 1803 and 1805 (Schopenhauer 1988, 74). As the preparation and display of food is an important aspect of material culture, 'since there are many ways to dress an animal', the essay concludes with a tasting menu of some of the dishes that travellers sampled while on their tours (Deetz 1977, 24). The French aristocrat and student of agriculture Alexandre de La Rochefoucauld travelled with his Polish mentor for five weeks in Scotland in 1786: 'you always seem to be able to find tea, sugar, rum and wine [he wrote to his father]; and to eat, as we did here [Portnacroish, north of Appin] fresh eggs, calf's head, ragout, boiled chicken, and an excellent bullock's tongue, with a potato cake. You may find these details trivial, but I give them with good reason' (Scarfe 2001, 184). Were foodstuffs knick-knacks that were edible – or, in some cases, inedible? Several decades earlier, Sir William Burrell had recorded being 'forced to taste Scotch chicken broth bad enough to poison a Hottentot' during his twelve-week travels in 1758 (Dunbar 1997, 49). Burrell covered 2,535½ miles, making his one of the most prolonged, as well as one of the earliest, northern tours of the period; perhaps the

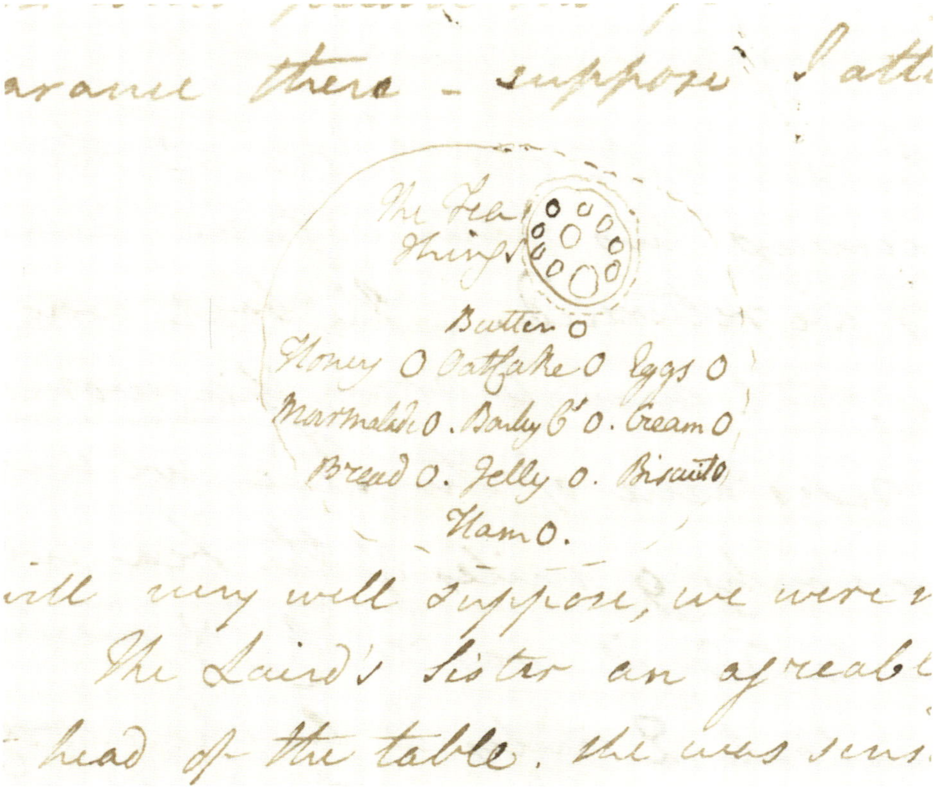

Fig. C6.12
Sketch by Dr Jacob Pattison of the breakfast table at Donollie Castle, August 1780, ink (NLS MS. 6322 folio 32/18)

shortest tour to be written down was *One Day's Journey to the Highlands of Scotland* (Perth, 1784), in which the anonymous traveller rode nearly 40 miles between 7am and 10pm, mainly in search of sites of Ossianic interest.

'This land of oats', is how Dr Jacob Pattison characterised Scotland in his tour of the Highlands in 1780, a culinary trope endorsed by many travellers before and after him who tasted the grain which according to Johnson's *Dictionary* definition 'in England is generally given to horses, but in Scotland supports the people'.[21] One William Dean Ryland of St John's College, Cambridge, was not impressed with the oat bannocks he was served at an inn at Callander: they 'resembl[ed] almost in every particular a flake of mortar from a wall', he wrote in his 1823 'Account of 3 days voyage from London to Edinburgh in the steam packet tourist'.[22]

'A Trip up Loch Lomond' (Fig. C6.11) recognises the emergence of this industrial form of mass transportation powered by steam rather than sail with an image of the *Marian* on Loch Lomond. It is one of a series of twenty-three coloured plates reproduced in a volume entitled *Airy Nothings; or, scraps and naughts, and odd-cum-shorts; in a circumbendibus hop, step, and jump by Olio Rigmaroll*, the pseudonym of Michael Egerton (London, 1825). 'Airy Nothings' seem a close relation of knick-knacks, while the *circumbendibus* follows a satirical journey from London to Scotland, the Lake District, Wales and Ireland. The vessel in Fig. C6.11 is shown steaming up the loch, the tapering view from the boat that of 'a fine skreen of hills, exhibiting from the water a most lovely scene', which the male tourists survey with telescopes, the whole serenaded by a piper to the left of the funnel.[23] Note the women travellers on board the *Marian* holding unfolded umbrellas as alternative screens from the rain: 'It rains almost constantly in the Highlands' observed Elizabeth Selwyn in her 'Northern Tour' of 1822 (Selwyn 1824, 141). Umbrellas must have been indispensable objects of material culture for visitors and locals alike. Look again at the well-dressed figures on the left in Knox's *Landscape with Tourists at Loch Katrine* (see Fig. S4.2) where a woman is shown clutching a small umbrella; one of her male companions on the rocky step below holds a closed umbrella and a basket as the group prepare to be rowed to Ellen's Isle for a picnic lunch.

Of all the meals consumed by travellers, 'Scotch breakfasts are proverbially good', stated Thermuthis Collinson, who made 'A Tour Through Some of the Southern and Western Counties of Scotland' in 1812.[24] Jacob Pattison quoted Samuel Johnson: 'Sup where you will, breakfast in the Highlands' (Rogers 1993, 113), and noted 'the justness of the remark' in relation to a breakfast he and his travelling companion Lister enjoyed in August 1780 at Donollie Castle near Oban.[25] 'A large breakfast table, sometime in getting ready, at length shone in full luxuriance', Pattison described in one of thirty-four numbered letters, many addressed to a Miss P., which were later transcribed into a manuscript journal of his travels. Pattison sketched the table with its 'tea things' arranged at the top accompanying assorted dishes of butter, honey, oat cake, eggs, marmalade, barley cakes, cream, bread, jelly, biscuits and ham (Fig. C6.12). 'Every thing that could please the eye or tempt the palate made its appearance there', he proclaimed, making the Highland breakfast table a material culture feast for the eye and the palate; in Johnson's memorable phrase, a 'quest of sensual gratifications', satiated.

In the preceding discussion (with its abundant quotations from a variety of published and manuscript sources), items of material culture tend to be relegated to the realm of the frivolous – the accompaniments of an insipid rather than an improving tour. We saw Boswell having to apologise to his reader for discussing the 'minute particulars' of Johnson's travelling dress and accessories, while Plumptre listed his knick-knacks, using a term that suggests their lowly status as trifles, and de La Rochefoucauld was likewise apologetic for providing 'trivial' details about his rich and diverse diet. Yet this chapter has demonstrated that the material paraphernalia of travel facilitated the tour and the traveller in a number of fundamental ways: providing the means and modes of passage as well as items of dress and subsistence, such material objects enhanced the experience and were duly recorded in tourists' letters and journals. Although they provided the footing and the furnishings for travellers to concentrate on the sights that captured their attention, sights that have continued to captivate historians of domestic tourism, portable knick-knacks have been too often excluded from studies of travel in this period.

ACKNOWLEDGEMENTS

I am indebted to John Bonehill, Anne Dulau Beveridge and Nigel Leask for inviting me to contribute to this publication. I would like to thank them and the other contributors for their generosity in sharing materials with me for this essay. Thanks also to Freya Gowrley, Hannah Lund, Neil Handley, Curator at the College of Optometrists, Kirsty McHugh and Catriona Murray for their insights. Kirsty's PhD in progress at the University of Wales Centre for Advanced Welsh & Celtic Studies is 'Northern English Travellers to Wales and Scotland 1760–1840: A Study of Manuscript Accounts from Yorkshire and Lancashire'.

NOTES

1 National Library of Scotland (hereafter NLS), MS. 11094, folio 34.
2 11 May 1806: NLS, MS. 11094, folio 94.
3 6 May 1807: NLS, MS. 11094, folio 126.
4 17 July 1805: NLS, MS. 11058, folio 48.
5 NLS, MS. 11094, folio 71.
6 Hottentot was the name used by Europeans to denote the Khoikhoi people of Southern Africa. NLS, Acc. 8272: https://editions.curioustravellers.ac.uk/pages/show.html?document=0051.xml
7 NLS, MS. 29492, folio 28.
8 NLS, MS. 29492, folios 31, 50.
9 Thomas Gray to William Mason [8 November 1765], Thomas Gray Archive: https://www.thomasgray.org/cgi-bin/display.cgi?text=tgal0469. Kinsley (2008, 156 and 160–168) notes the analogies in travel writing between sites in Britain with those of Europe and further afield, the latter of which she discusses within a 'discourse of savagery'.
10 NLS, Acc. 4796/115. See also William Patoun, 'Advice on Travel in Italy', c. 1766. Patoun was a Scotsman and tutor to the 9th Earl of Exeter (Ford 1997, xxxix–lii). While making long journeys through unremarkable places he recommends that 'a Cold tongue, or a Piece of roast beef in the Chaise will prove an Excellent Companion' (xli).
11 NLS, MS. 1080.
12 Cambridge University Library (hereafter CUL), Department of Manuscripts and University Archives, James Plumptre: Papers, MS. Add. 5808, folio 10. All Scots (not just Highlanders) were thought to be habitual snuff-takers.
13 CUL, MS. Add. 5808, folio 11.
14 NLS, MS. 3529, folio 100.
15 CUL, MS. Add. 5817.
16 National Records of Scotland (hereafter NRS), RH1/2/507.
17 CUL, MS. Add. 5817.
18 Newte was the pseudonym of William Thomson, a Scottish minister whose *A Tour in England and Scotland in 1785 by an English Gentleman* was first published anonymously in 1788.
19 NRS, RH1/2/819.
20 NRS, RH2/8/49.
21 NLS, MS. 6322, folio 76.
22 NLS, Acc. 8801, folio 54.
23 NLS, Acc. 8272: https://editions.curioustravellers.ac.uk/pages/show.html?document=0051.xml
24 Thermuthis Collinson, 'A Tour Through Some of the Southern and Western Counties of Scotland', British Library, Add. MS. 36454, folio 34.
25 NLS, MS. 6322, folio 18

CHAPTER SEVEN

Panoramas and Landscape

Christina Young

This chapter addresses the contribution made by an influential group of Scottish artists to the development of large-scale painted scenery during the eighteenth and early nineteenth centuries, both as theatre painting, in the form of theatrical painted cloths, but also via the panorama, patented in 1787 by the Irish artist and entrepreneur Robert Barker (1739–1806).[1] Barker stated in his patent that the panorama (allegedly inspired by the view of Edinburgh from Calton Hill) 'is intended, by drawing and painting, and a proper disposition of the whole, to perfect an entire view of any country or situation, as it appears to an observer turning quite around': the panorama visitor could thus 'see the same as those who travel'.[2] In an age before frequent public exhibitions outside Edinburgh, the vast painted cloths on display as panoramas and theatrical sets were likely to have been the only substantial paintings of landscape that most Scottish people would have seen. In Britain, full-scale panoramas have not survived, and there are only approximately sixty extant stage cloths in collections, not including live productions; it is perhaps hard for us therefore to imagine their scale and evocative visual power. Nevertheless, the significant contribution made by the artists who painted them to landscape painting, tourism, popular culture and fine art can be reconstructed through surviving sketches, set designs, newspaper illustrations, prints, reviews, memoirs, playbills, panorama leaflets and easel paintings.

Britain's new transport infrastructure made travelling shows feasible on a scale that allowed for the movement of theatrical sets and panoramas across Scotland, and the rest of Britain and Ireland. Depicting the romantic landscape but also the rising industry and trade of the cities, such shows travelled to entertain the public in Glasgow, Edinburgh, Dublin, Newcastle, London and around the provinces. Panoramas, discussed in the main body of this essay, were large-scale paintings typically on linen (2,500–5,000 square feet) depicting real cityscapes, landscapes or battles. Usually they were hung to form a part or a complete cylinder housed in a circular building (rotunda), illuminated from above by natural light. The space had some form of interior enclosure to prevent the viewer from getting too close to the painting, which would spoil the illusion of being actually at the scene. The skills of the panorama painter could be developed and honed by the experience of scene painting on theatrical cloths (which, like panoramas, were usually executed in glue tempera on a linen canvas), or by apprentice work in decorative house painting. Ever pragmatic, many painters moved between these genres with ease. Panoramas varied in scale from Robert Barker's original view of Edinburgh from Calton Hill, displayed as a half circle (180°) with a diameter of 25 ft when first opened to the public in Edinburgh in 1788, to Barker and Henry Burford's view of Edinburgh in 1806 exhibited in the Leicester Square Rotunda (84 ft in diameter and 35 ft high). Its canvas formed a complete 360°, naturally illuminated from above, and was 'open every lawful day, from nine o'clock till dusk. Admittance One Shilling' (Fig. C7.1). A reviewer of the panorama exhibited at 28 Haymarket in London observed that it 'must prove particularly interesting to their Majesties, the Heir Apparent, and several of the Royal Family, who rarely go abroad. To them views of distant countries will be brought, not like descriptions from the pen of the traveller, geographer, or poet, which, while they inform, leave an anxious wish, a natural desire to behold the scene ungratified.'[3] The visual experience had not diminished for the 1825 version of Barker's 'Edinburgh', as the *Morning Post* declared:

> The whole is admirably painted; and he who has never seen Edinburgh, may, by visiting the Panorama, gain a knowledge of it in an hour, which all the maps and descriptions that have been published would never give; while the sons of Caledonia in the town may renew their acquaintance with 'Auld Reikee,' without the aid of a stage-coach or steam-boat.[4]

Now Loch Lomond could be experienced in a rotunda on Queen Street in Glasgow or the Mound in Edinburgh, at the Theatres Royal in Glasgow, Edinburgh and London; the metropolitan public became immersed in the hills and romantic myths of Scotland. The most celebrated painters of Scottish panoramas, decorative and theatrical scenes of the period established their fine art credentials, and hence the sale of their work, by displaying landscape easel paintings at various new exhibition spaces in Edinburgh and London. This essay will describe how Jacob More, Alexander Nasmyth, John Knox, David Roberts and William Grieve brought spectacular Scottish landscapes to an urban public.

Visual depictions of the Scottish landscape and culture within the public domain had been limited in the early eighteenth century. The foundations for an eventual change in the early nineteenth century were laid in the burgeoning theatres and academies of Edinburgh and Glasgow, and especially through the Nories, a family of decorative house painters who were instrumental in developing a home-grown dynasty of decorative and landscape painters.[5] Many of these painters, including Jacob More, William Delacour, Alexander Runciman and Alexander Nasmyth, were commissioned for decorative schemes of refined

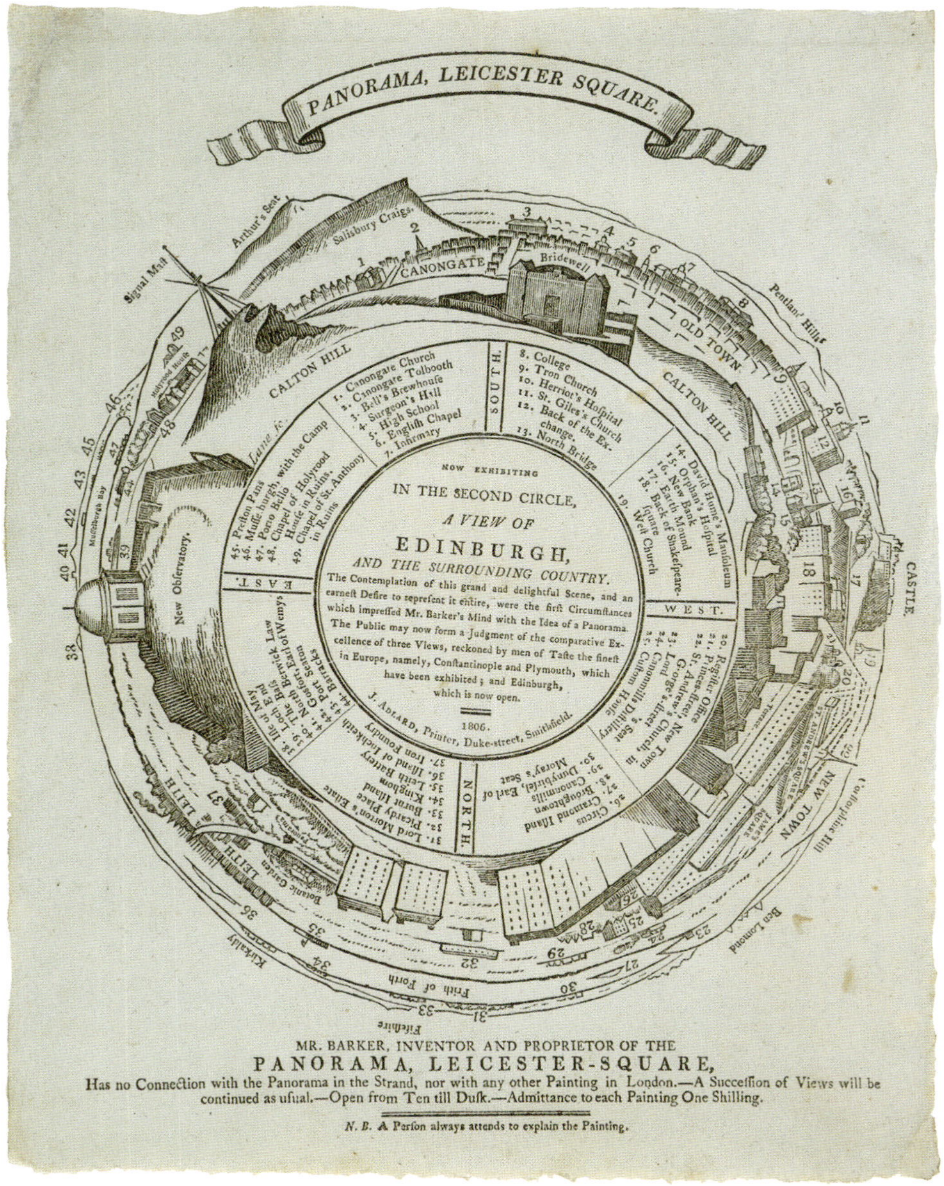

Fig. C7.1
Henry Aston Barker, 'A View of Edinburgh', an advertisement for Robert Barker's Panorama exhibited at Leicester Square, 1806, engraving on paper (NGS P7892)

wilderness, and in Nasmyth's case commissioned to tame physical nature out of doors through landscape design.[6]

The 1788 Theatre Act allowed performances in the provinces for licensed travelling companies and, as the eighteenth century progressed, audiences and critics desired better representations of place and period. Scene painters drew upon descriptions written by travellers, historians and antiquarians, as well as travelling the country themselves with sketchbooks in hand. For example, Thomas Greenwood the Elder used descriptions from Pennant, Dr Johnson and Joseph Banks to paint *Fingal's Cave* for the 1788 Sadlers' Wells production of *Witch of the Lakes* (Rosenfeld 1981, 36). Scenery taken from 'sketches' had by this time become a feature on the playbill.

Evidence of the Nories' involvement in the theatre is quite elusive, although it is known that James Norie Snr had sent his sons James and Robert to apprentice under George Lambert at Covent Garden in 1732.[7] Jacob More's (1740–1797) apprenticeship under Robert Norie, although mainly in decorative house painting (Holloway 1987), would have certainly enabled the *Royal Shepherd* to be performed at the Theatre Royal, Edinburgh, with 'the Scenes and Dresses to be entirely new, and suitable to the characters of Opera. The Scenes invented and painted by Mr Moore.'[8] In 1771, More exhibited paintings of the Falls of Clyde at the Society of Artists in London, including *View of Cora Linn* (see Fig S4.6), one of his most famous works in his own lifetime (Irwin 1972, 776). Alexander Runciman (1736–1785), also an apprentice with Robert Norie, was among the first Scottish artists to tour the country sketching its scenery, historical monuments and literary heroes. He also worked as a decorative painter on the interiors of Edinburgh's Theatre Royal, where the 'ornaments and decorations of the other parts of the theatre over the stage boxes' included 'landscapes done in the same form, by Runciman, the Sir Joshua Reynolds of this country'.[9] The extent of Runciman's direct involvement with scenery painting remains unclear, although he associated with many theatre professionals as a member of Edinburgh's convivial Cape Club.[10]

Within the next generation of Scottish artists, the young Alexander Nasmyth (1758–1840) would follow a similar path; apprenticing at R. Norie & Co, he studied under Runciman at the Trustees Academy in Edinburgh. In a letter to his widow written in 1840, David Wilkie wrote that '[Nasmyth] was the founder of the Landscape Painting school of Scotland, and by his taste and talent has for many years taken a lead in the patriotic aim of enriching his native land with the representation of her romantic scenery' (Cooksey 1991, 7). Nasmyth assimilated a style for which he naturally found an outlet and sense of ownership in Scotland, in which theatrical scenery, panoramas, landscaping and landscape painting played a major role.

His first known scene painting commission was at the Dumfries Theatre in 1792, delivered by his friend the poet Robert Burns, at that time resident at Ellisland, near Dumfries (Cooksey 1991, 62); his most celebrated was in 1805, when he painted the stock scenery (i.e. generic scenery used for multiple productions) for Glasgow's Theatre Royal. This included one scene, the 'magnificent view on the Clyde looking towards Dumbarton Rock . . . [which] was much admired, and was held in great esteem' ([J.] Nasmyth 1885). This composition was to be revisited in at least one oil painting later in his career, as represented on the cover of the present book (see also Fig. S4.12).

As a very competent draughtsman Nasmyth was a master of two-point perspective, which he would have used to create the illusion of three-dimensional space. Of his stock scenery it was said 'The Scenery is executed in the first style of excellence and adds greatly to the well-earned fame of Mr Nasmith. Though generally correct and beautiful, we take liberty to point out the drop-curtain in particular, as being a noble, rich and elegant landscape.'[11] Fig. C7.2 represents an extant preparatory design for a side wing at the Theatre Royal, Glasgow, which gives a good impression of Nasmyth's naturalistic handling of foliage, of which it was commented: 'you could pull aside the branch of a tree and find another beneath it' (MacGeorge 1884, 30). Nasmyth returned to the new Theatre Royal Edinburgh on Leith Walk in 1809 (Jackson 1793). By then he was a celebrity whose work was afforded a prominent place on the playbill: 'Winter's Tale. Not acted in Edinburgh these Twenty Years, – which getting up with New and Splendid Scenery, Dresses and Decorations – The New Scenery and Machinery by Mr Nasmyth of the City'. Nasmyth's fame followed him to London, where he enthralled audiences at the Theatre Royal, Drury lane, like later Scots scene painters David Roberts and Clarkson Stanfield (Ballentine 1866; Merwe 1979, 68).

Sir Walter Scott's verse romances and novels gave a new resonance to Scottish landscapes, as discussed in Chapter 1 and Section 4. The dramatisations of *Lady of the Lake*, *Heart of Mid-Lothian* and especially *Rob Roy* were to become regular favourites (Cameron 1988). Scott's descriptions of place, and dramatisations of his works, provided a legitimate visual language for Scottish scene painters to explore and to make their own. In 1820, Edinburgh's Theatre Royal produced *Heart of Mid-Lothian*, the playbill announcing 'The views of Edinburgh and its Vicinity painted by Mr Nasmyth. The other Scenery designed by Mr Pyett, and by Mr Roberts of the Theatre Royal, Glasgow.'[12] The 1819 Covent Garden production had scenery by William Grieve 'painted from sketches made by Alexander Nasmyth Esq.'. It has been suggested that Nasmyth adapted the set designs for a London production and audience (Bell 2019). However, given that Grieve's family was from Perth, and he had already succeeded with the earlier production of *Rob Roy* at the Theatre Royal, Edinburgh,[13] he probably felt perfectly comfortable with reimaging his own native land for a London audience; he evidently succeeded in making it 'beautiful beyond description . . . we have seen nothing so rich, graphic and masterly as the first scene of Salisbury Crags and Arthur Seat, Dean's Cottage' (Rosenfeld 1981). Fig. C7.3 shows Grieve's watercolour for this first scene, from which he would have squared up the full-scale stage cloth.

As in Edinburgh, the establishment of permanent theatres in Glasgow, including the Dunlop Street Theatre in 1782 and the New Theatre, Queen Street, in 1805, coincided with the rise of the new phenomenon of the travelling panorama. The latest panorama would be on show for a few weeks to months before moving to another city, usually exhibited in temporary buildings. Alexander Nasmyth's only known panorama, a view of London, was painted with Richard Cooper (Jnr) and exhibited in Glasgow in 1801, followed by Edinburgh, before travelling to Dublin in August 1803 (Rockett and Rockett 2011, 114). It was advertised to the public – in a 'building erected on purpose in Ingram Street . . . on three thousand five hundred square feet of canvas . . . Grand New Panorama of London . . . London as seen from the Ruins of Albion Mills'.[14] Nasmyth's panorama coincided with the expiry of Barker's patent, after which he scaled up his panoramas and displayed them in a new brick rotunda at Leicester Square, London.[15] Other artists then also started to exploit the genre, seeing the commercial potential of this public spectacle, often exhibited in smaller wooden rotundas: in Glasgow, known locations were in Ingram Street, Queen Street and later Buchanan Street.

It was, however, the Glasgow painter John Knox (1776–1845) who, at least in the early part of his career, was to become arguably the most influential painter of panoramas that were renowned for their accuracy, spectacular vistas and wealth of local detail, and which consciously catered to the growing public appetite for landscapes from the Clyde, and beyond Glasgow to the Trossachs, the setting of Scott's poem *The Lady of the*

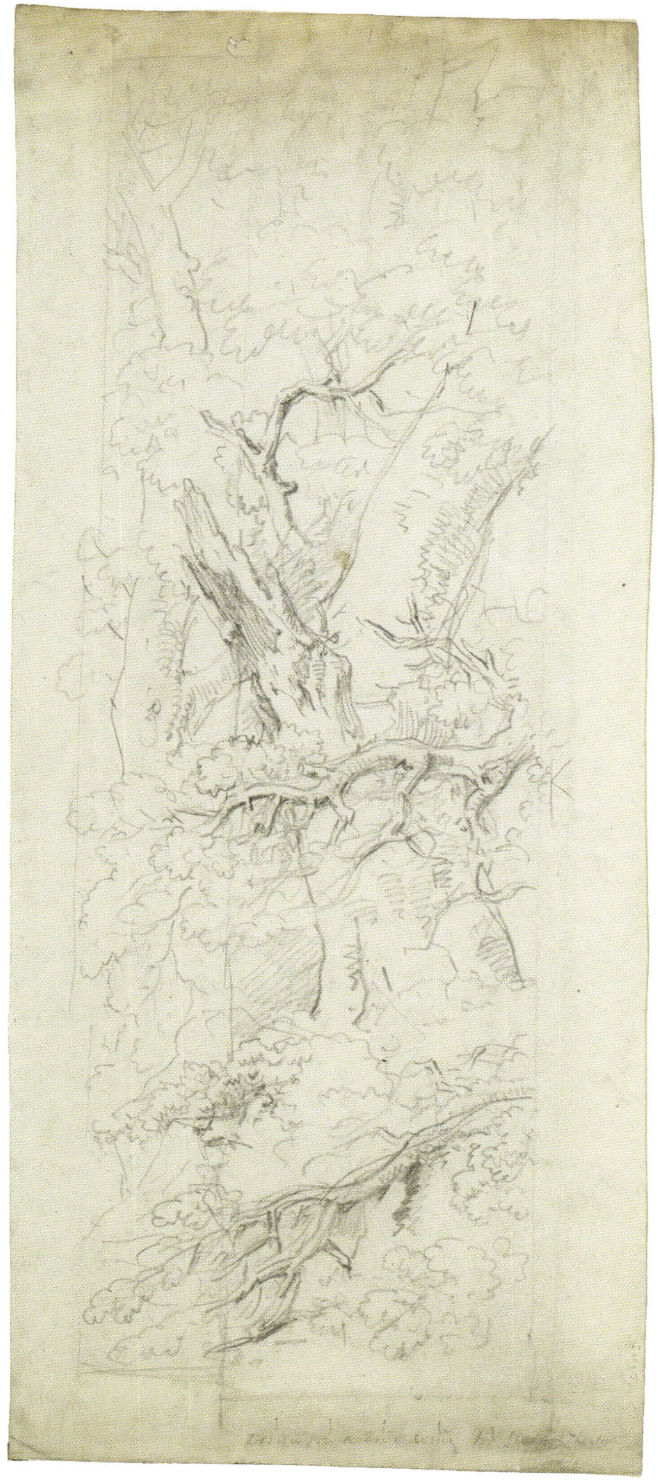

Fig. C7.2
Alexander Nasmyth, 'A Tree', design for a stage flat [verso: View of Dumbarton], drawing (NGS D5060)

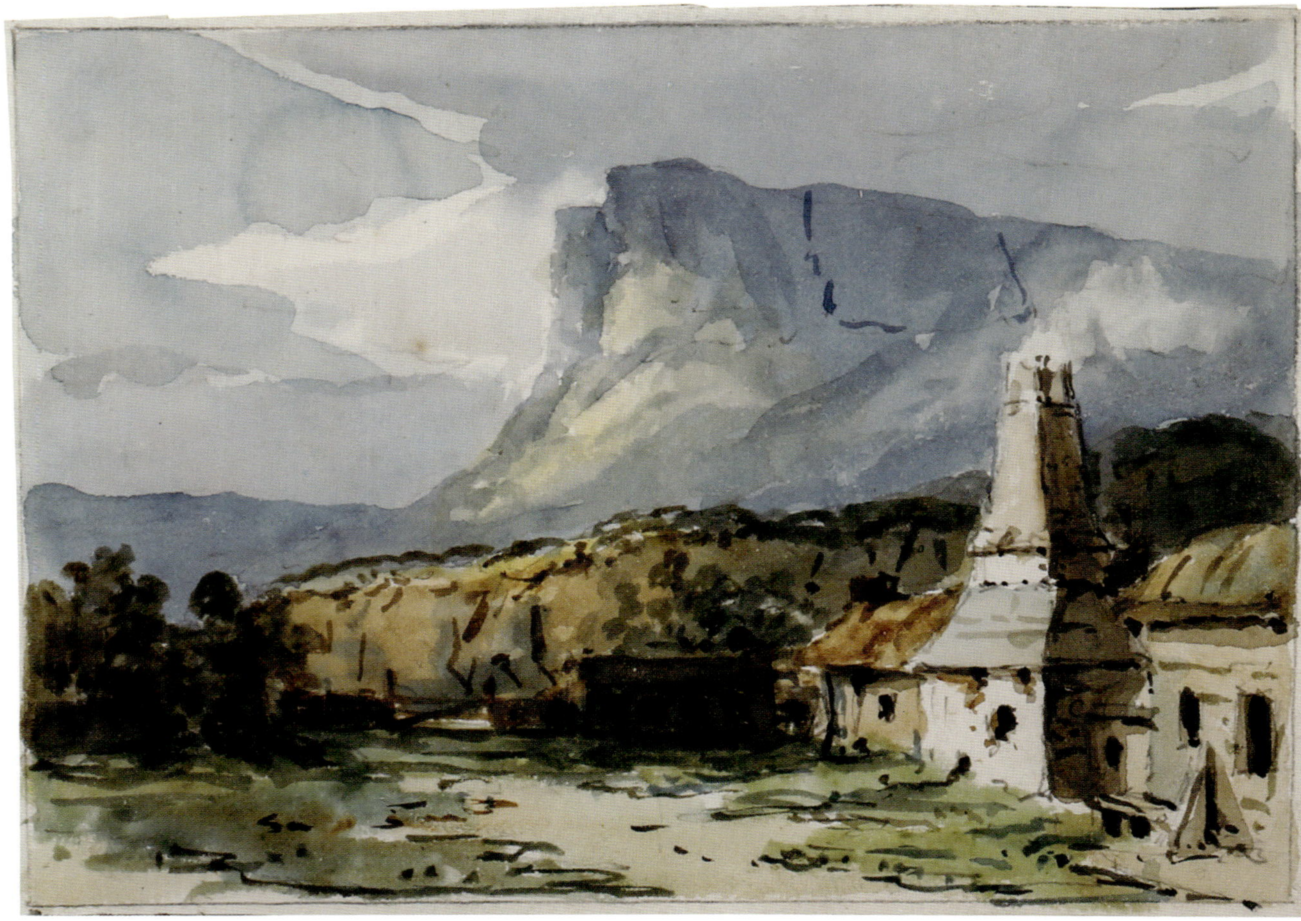

Fig. C7.3
The Grieve family, set design for *Heart of Mid-Lothian*, watercolour, Grieve Family Collection of Theatre Designs (SHL MS 1007/549)

Lake (1810). Knox is an enigma in many ways, information about his early years and training apparently as ephemeral as the large-scale panoramas he painted. Born in 1776, the son of a Paisley yarn merchant, he moved aged twelve to Glasgow, and must have had opportunities to see Barker's panorama of Edinburgh, as well as Nasmyth's scene painting or his panorama of London.[16] He may have worked under Alexander Nasmyth, although no evidence survives to associate Knox with an apprenticeship either in painting or house painting. Despite the many contrasts between Nasmyth's Italianate landscapes and Knox's later landscapes in oil, Knox may well have picked up his fundamental skills from Nasmyth, skills that equipped him to paint on a vast scale, and to enthral the public with romantic landscapes and topical scenes closer to home.

In 1809, although registered as 'John Knox (portrait painter), 34 Miller Street, Glasgow' (Stuart 1988), he was already expanding beyond portraiture and developing his own style through depicting his adopted city. On 19 February 1808, the *Glasgow Herald* announced: 'we have pleasure in informing the public, that Mr Knox's Panoramic View of the City is now finished', displayed 'at the large wooden building, south side of the New Theatre, Queen-street, Glasgow', before moving to other venues.[17] Knox's *Glasgow Old Bridge* panorama moved to the D'Olier Street rotunda in Dublin in 1811, before returning to Glasgow in 1813 with 'the New Jail' and 'All the New Additions, with a great number of fine Figures'.[18] The smaller oil painting version that Knox produced later (Fig. C7.4) lives up to the *Glasgow Herald*'s praise of its numerous 'fine figures' and its vivid representation of a

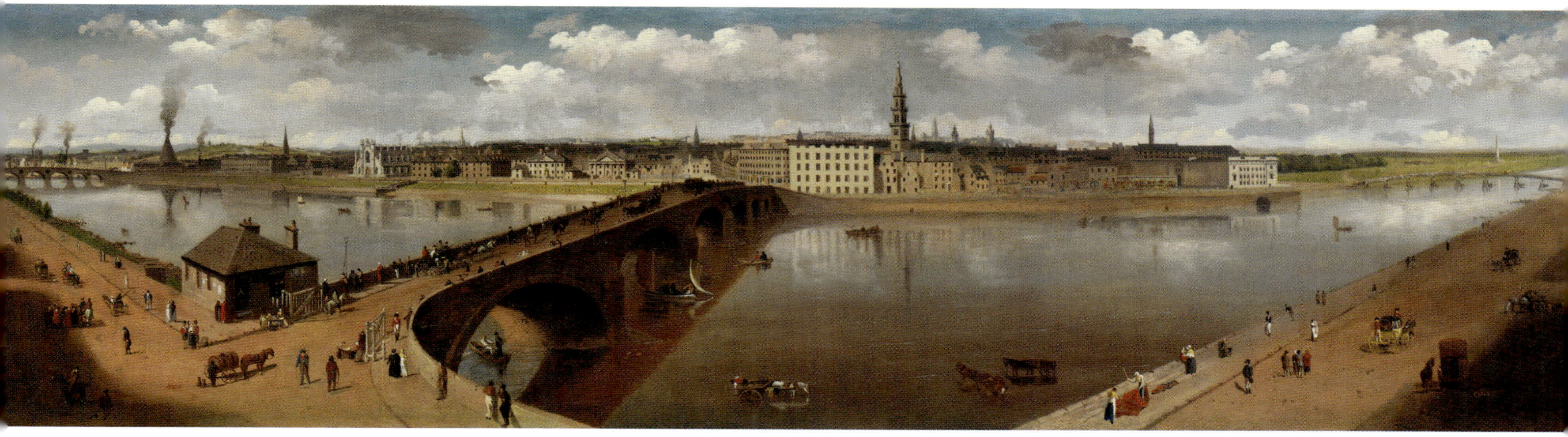

city in transition, from the fields of Glasgow Green to the developing industries in Anderston with their smoking chimneys. Knox maintained the perspective that he used for the original panorama canvas, so that, when curved around to form 270°, the bridges take up the correct orientations. But the fact that the Roman Catholic Cathedral of St Andrews shown in the oil painting was not built until 1816 confirms that this is a scaled-down adaptation of the original panorama, showing all the changes to the fast-developing urban landscape over three years. The perspective 'taken from an elevation situation at the South End of the Old Bridge', as described in the advert, is also preserved, suggesting that a visitor to the panorama would be virtually transported to the scene, standing high on the viewing platform.

Knox employed a similarly elevated perspective again for his next panorama, where 'The View is taken within one hundred feet of the top of the mountain', 'encouraged by the reception of his last Painting, viz. the View of the City'; Knox's *Grand Panoramic Painting of the View from Ben Lomond* was first exhibited on 2 January 1810 (Fig. C7.5). Like his Glasgow panorama, it was displayed again in May with 'many considerable improvements and additional figures',[19] moving to London, Edinburgh,[20] and then Dublin in 1812, where Knox simultaneously displayed the painting *City of Glasgow*. This time Knox produced two smaller oil painting versions of the complete 270° panorama, making up a pair (Figs C7.6 and C7.7). One version includes 'additional figures' (Figs C7.8 and C7.9), suggesting that he

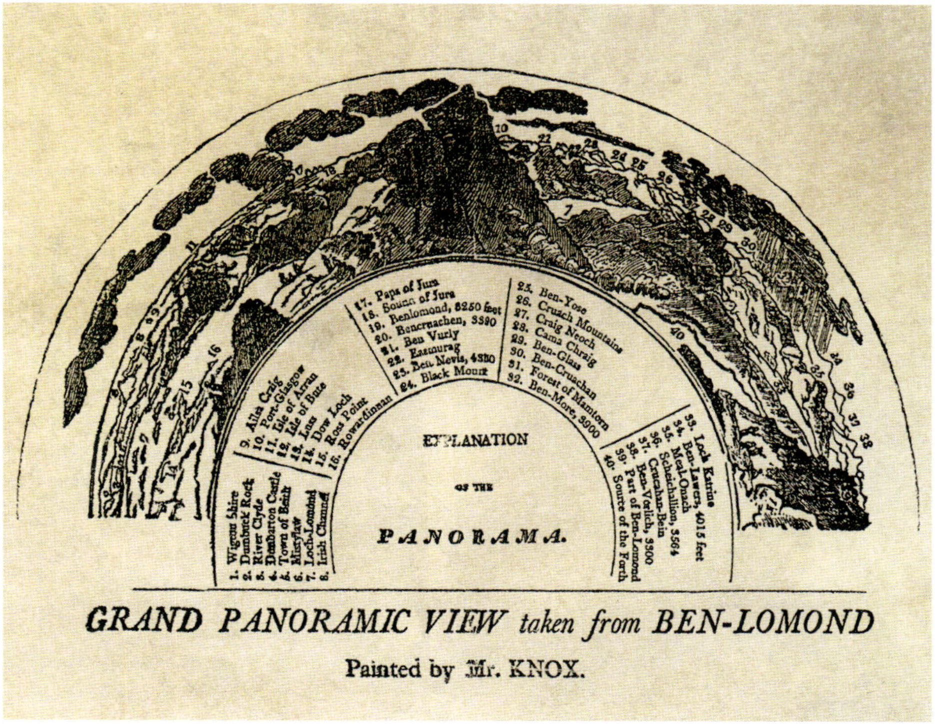

Fig. C7.4
Top. John Knox, *Old Glasgow Bridge*, c. 1817, oil on canvas (GMC OG.1955.119)

Fig. C7.5
Above. 'Orientation Plan of the Panorama' reproduced in George Fairfull-Smith, *The Wealth of a City*, Glasgow Art Index, 2010 (PC)

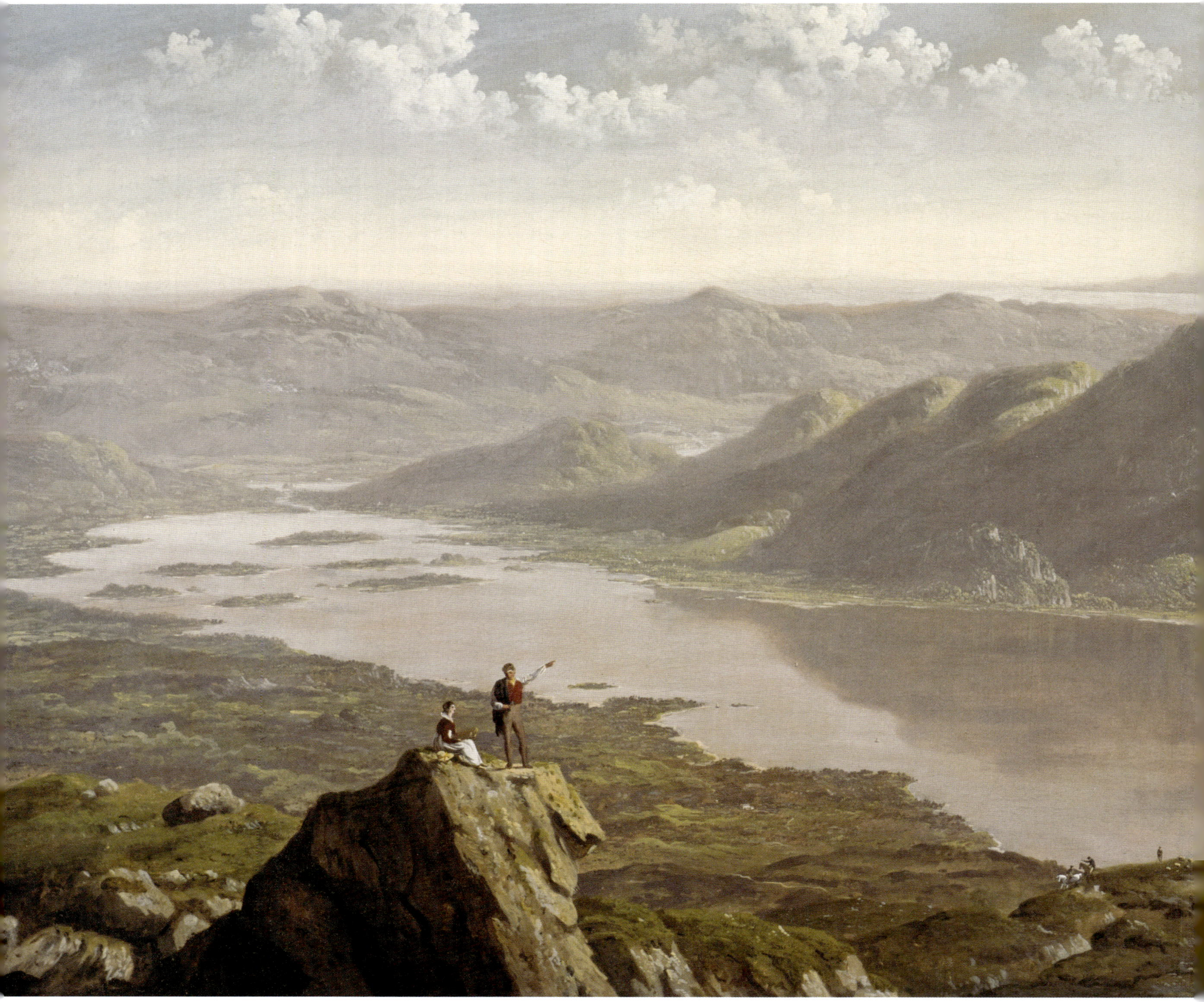

Fig. C7.6
John Knox, *South Western Views from Loch Lomond*, oil on canvas (NGS 002.97)

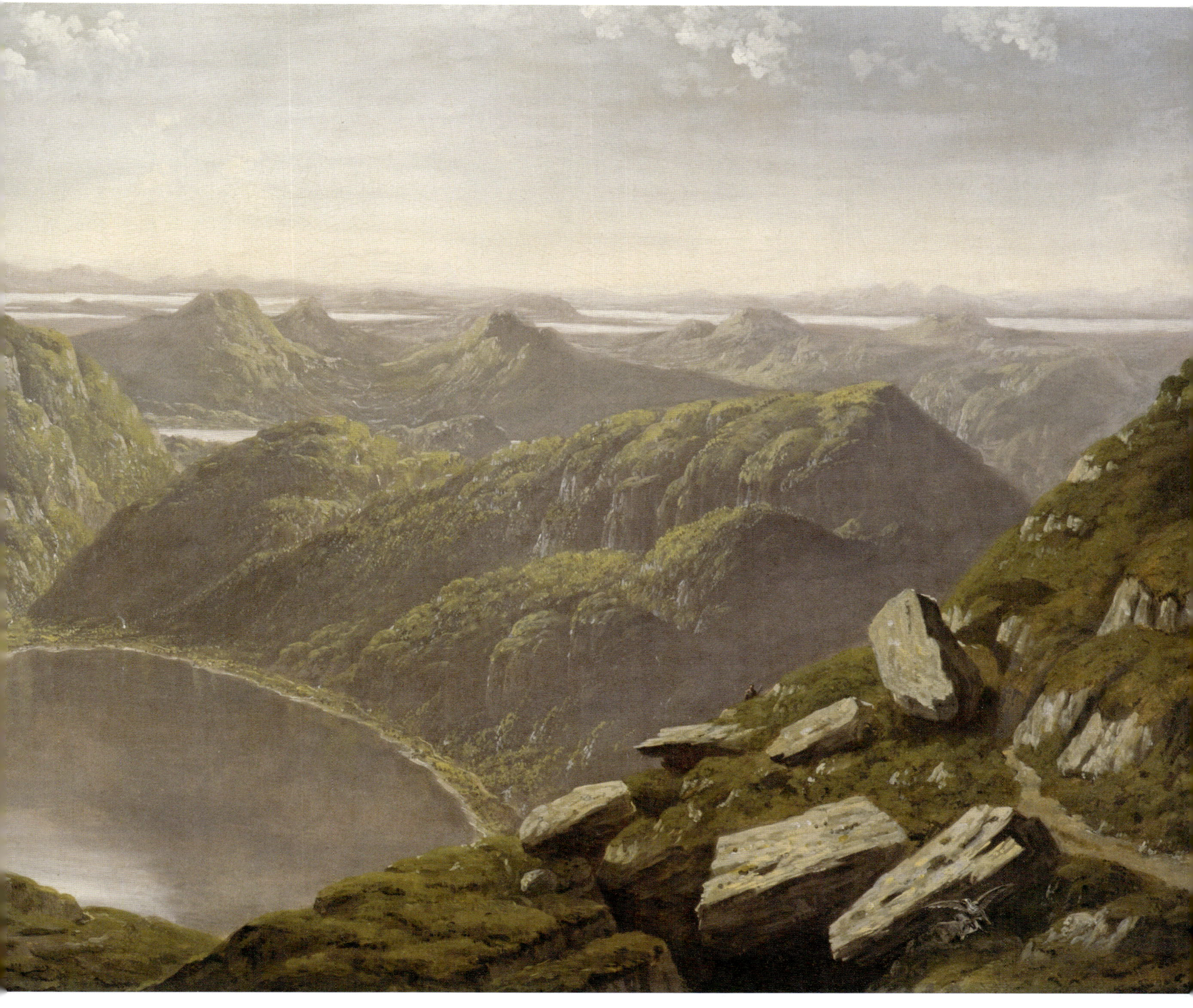

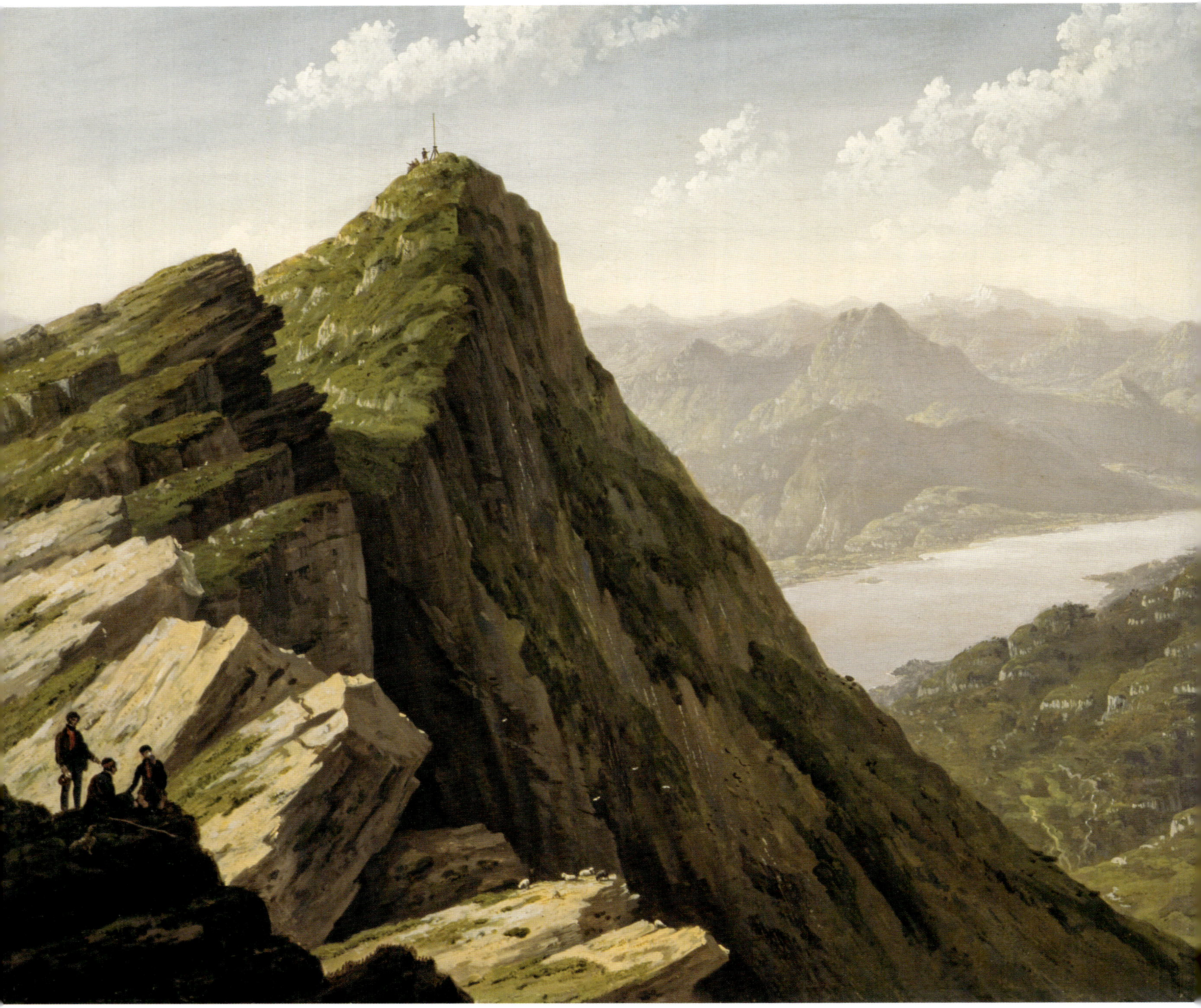

Fig. C7.7
John Knox, *North Western Views from Loch Lomond*, oil on canvas (NGS 001.97)

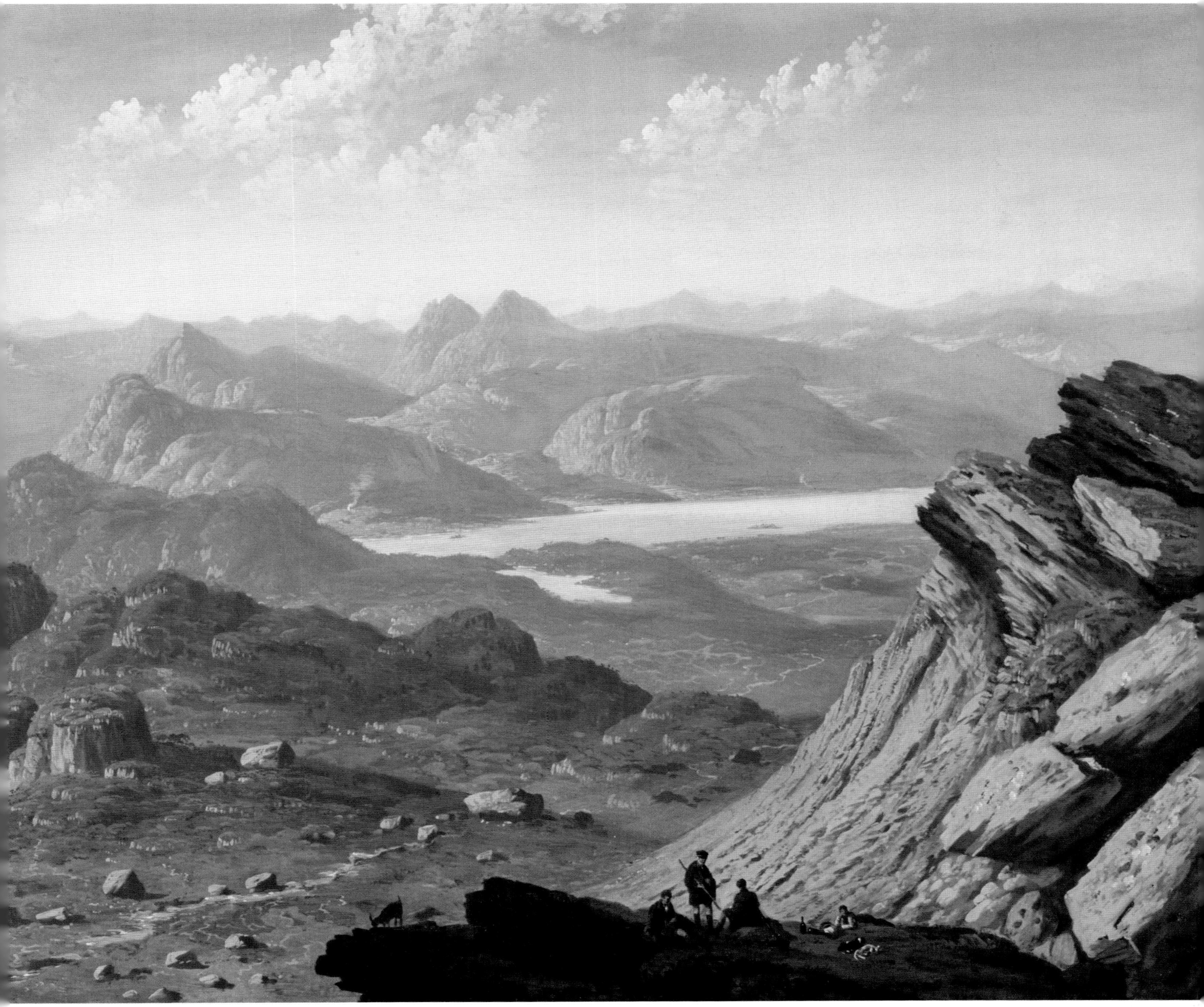

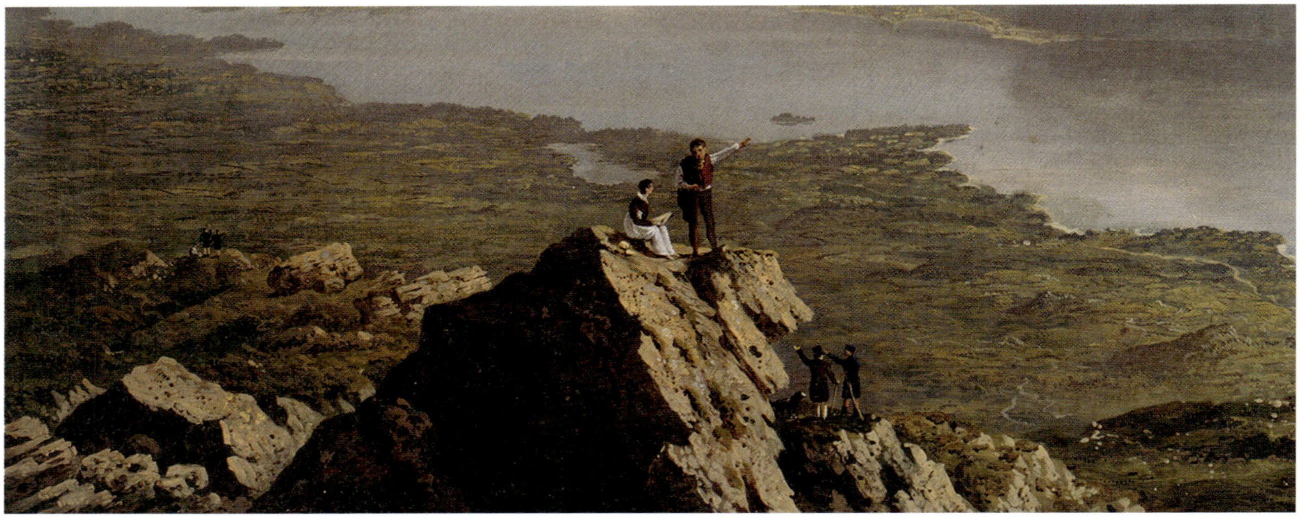

Fig. C7.8
Right. John Knox, Detail in *South Western Views from Loch Lomond*, c. 1834 (GMC 448)

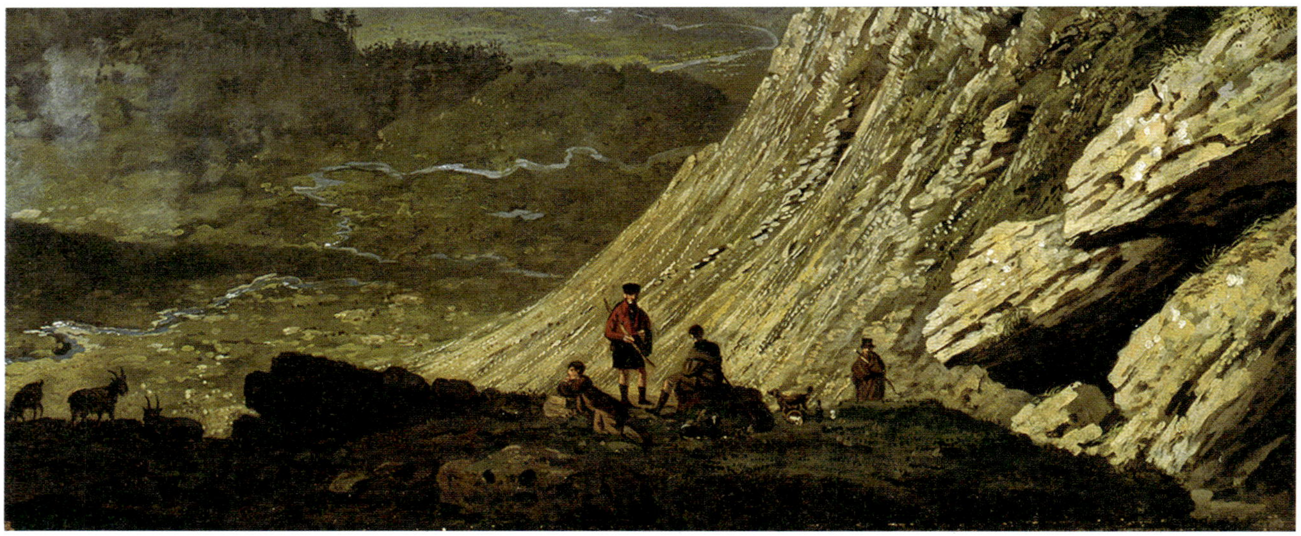

Fig. C7.9
Below. John Knox Detail in *North Western Views from Loch Lomond*, c. 1834 (GMC 460)

painted his smaller copies soon after, or perhaps in preparation for, the large panorama, with 'many considerable improvements'. The paintings convey the grandeur of the Highland landscape; Ben Lomond's peak is central in the overall composition, while the loch extends into the distance with hills below; Loch Arklet is on the right. The wildness of the landscape is hinted at by the bird of prey feasting on a deer carcass on the lower right-hand side (Fig. C7.6). But this is also a landscape that is accessible to tourists: in the foreground of the peak, gillies eat their picnic, and sheep and goats graze on a precipitous edge, while towards the loch two figures on horseback move along the path; on the far left on an outcrop a gentleman in fine dress points to the landscape, as his female companion sits with a large sketchbook on her lap. Both the south-western and north-western views of Loch Lomond work equally well as separate paintings, each embodying similar elements of composition; in the distance are mountains and lochs, while the foreground is populated by tourists and their guides, conveying a subtle emotion which draws the viewer into the painting.

Knox's panoramas captured the spirit of emotional and

philosophical engagement with mountainous landscape characteristic of the romantic sublime. The high vantage-point from which the viewer is drawn into the painting serves two aims: it provides a sense of sublime awe and wonder; and, in the context of the rotunda version, it enhances a sense of immersion in the landscape. As Barker had written in his patent for the invention of the panorama 'the inner enclosure may be elevated, at the will of the artist, so as to make observers, on whatever situation he may wish they should imagine themselves, feel as if really on the very spot'.[21] Paramount to both panoramas and theatrical painting was the ability to create an illusion achieved through compositional devices of 270° or 360° view and two-point perspective. Like Alexander Nasmyth's theatrical painting, the surviving paintings of John Knox's panoramas show that he clearly mastered the techniques necessary to create both illusion and the romantic sublime.

Knox was to repeat this visual device with his third panorama, *A View of Dublin*, which was displayed in Glasgow in 1812. It employed the same visual references that made for public acclaim: a view of the city out to the lighthouse and the distant Wicklow hills, and importantly a 'number of excellent representations of persons of notoriety', picking up on some of the themes of the visual culture of the Irish tour discussed by Mary-Ann Constantine and Finola O'Kane in Chapter 8.[22] In 1813, all three of Knox's panoramas were on exhibition, to which he added 'The Grand Historical Transparent Painting of the Taking and the Burning of Moscow . . . from the most authentic accounts of this most awful and tremendous event'. The effects described of 'Buildings on Fire . . . Rockets, and Red Hot Balls' were to be seen by artificial light.[23] This painting was a departure from Knox's earlier panoramas: transparency painting required a different technique as it was usually lit with artificial light from behind, rather than natural light from above.[24] Knox's final panorama returned to his more familiar compositional style in a 'Grand Panoramic Painting', *Gibraltar*. Stretched finances resulting from the expense of heating the rotunda in winter for a snowbound public may suggest why *Gibraltar* was to be the last panorama that Knox ever displayed (Young 2020). By March 1814, the *Glasgow Herald* announced that 'any person neglecting this opportunity certainly will lose a sight of the Grandest Subject ever exhibited in this Country'.

By 1814, Knox was conducting both a private and a public drawing school in Glasgow, one operated from Dunlop Street, the other from Brownfield (Capon 2019, 65).[25] It is here that Daniel Macnee (1806–1882) and Horatio McCulloch (1805–1867) were apprentices, although there is no evidence that either artist executed theatrical or scene painting.[26] One of the few descriptions of the activities of an apprentice under Knox is given by William Leitch (1804–1883), who was originally a scene painter at the Theatre Royal, Queen Street, in 1824, and later a drawing master at Balmoral (MacGeorge 1884, 63). Leitch describes 'the simple beauty' of David Roberts's outline for scenery at the Theatre Royal, Glasgow, and describes meetings with his friends Macnee, McCulloch and Nasmyth. He also recalls:

> Macnee and I were not at school together, but I often saw him. I spent much of my spare time with him in his mother's house, and we were always drawing. Macnee was at that time an articled pupil to an artist then very popular in Glasgow – Mr. John Knox. On one occasion he showed me two little paintings in oil, copies from Mr Knox – Views of Dumbarton Castle – and as I expressed a desire to try something in oil, he offered to let me have one of them to copy at home. (MacGeorge 1884, 23)

From this period on, the 'very popular' John Knox focused on his drawing schools, lithography and oil painting, exhibiting five works at his first exhibition in 1821 at the Glasgow Institution for Promoting and Encouraging the Fine Arts in the West of Scotland.[27] In 1828 he published two volumes of lithographs entitled *Scottish Scenery Drawn upon a Stone*, while continuing to paint landscapes around Glasgow, as well as significant episodes in the city's civic and commercial life. In the two oil paintings of Loch Katrine, discussed in more detail in Section 4, Knox has painted a tranquil foreground of shore and loch bathed in light in which the intimate closeness of the figures of tourists are set, accompanied in the second painting by a kilted bagpiper. With the twin peaks of Ben Venue towering in the background, *Tourists at Loch Katrine* employs similar compositional devices as the Loch Lomond panorama, and was probably painted around the same period (see Figs S4.1 and S4.2).[28]

In contrast, Knox's paintings *Glasgow Fair* (c. 1819) and *Old Glasgow Cross* (c. 1826) (see Figs S3.23 and S3.24) are urban

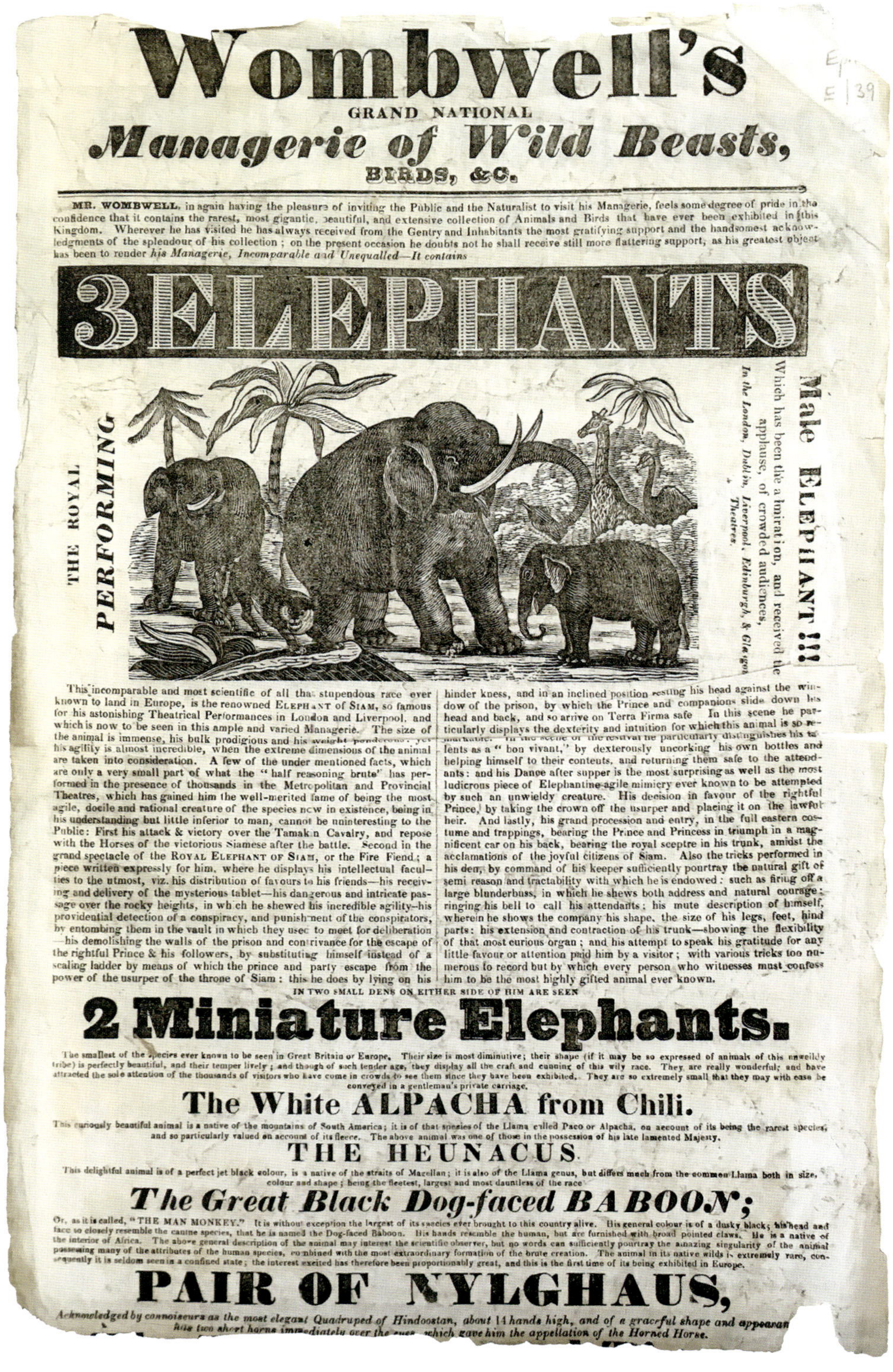

subjects with specific local interest, in which bigger groups and individuals (some of whom are thought to be identifiable) go about their business and pleasure (Meacock 2019). *Glasgow Fair* also depicts the travelling shows of the day: Wombwell's 'Managerie of Wild Beasts' (Fig. C7.10), the Olympic Circus and a billboard advertisement for a 'Battle of Algiers' panorama. In *Glasgow Cross* Knox depicted the city's commercial heart: as the city expanded, the road network became ever more important, leading to the construction of Thomas Telford's road linking Carlyle to Glasgow in 1806. Both of Knox's city paintings attest to their importance in extending trade, tourism and entertainment between the towns of Scotland, to the Highlands and from the South.

Although Barker's first panorama was eschewed by the fine artists of the Royal Academy, panoramas became a popular way of bringing exotic scenes and landscapes, as well as significant historical events, closer to home. Touring panoramas across Britain also took the Scottish landscape to those who had never experienced it first-hand. Increasingly artists and theatre companies toured the provinces, finding new patrons and audiences. In the theatres, the Scottish vernacular and National Drama were flourishing, with the dramatisations of Sir Walter Scott's novels and scenery painted by Nasmyth, Roberts and Grieve. As John Macculloch wrote in 1824, highlighting the links between theatrical performances and Scott tourism, 'as Rob Roy now blusters at Convent-garden and the Lyceum, and as Aberfoyle is gone to Wapping, so Wapping and the Strand must also come to Aberfoyle' (Macculloch 1824, I, 195). As this suggests, such vicarious urban spectacles often created a taste for experiencing the real thing. But ultimately, even within ten years of their creation, ephemeral scenery and panoramas, and the views they depicted, could only be imagined through the watercolours, lithographs and smaller-scale oil paintings that brought the reimagined Scottish landscape into the galleries and drawing rooms of Britain. These extant works are the legacy of a period in which Scottish landscape painters played a major role in popular culture and fine art, as well as in the development of travel and tourism.

Fig. C7.10
Left. Poster for Wombwell's 'Managerie of Wild Beasts' (GLA ASC Eph. E/38)

NOTES

1 This essay is an output from a major research project entitled 'The Power to Transform: The History of Painted Stage Cloths and the Scenic Art Profession in Britain', conducted by the author as part of a Leverhulme Fellowship (https://powertotransform.gla.ac.uk/) in which the history and significance of Scottish scene painters is covered in detail.

2 BL General Reference Collection 258.d.13–27, Vols 1–15 (1794–1801).

3 Cited in Ellis 2008.

4 *Morning Post*, 5 April 1825.

5 James Norie (1684–1757) was followed by his sons James, George and Robert, becoming 'Robert Norie & Co' (Holloway 1987; Einberg 2001).

6 Nasmyth was commissioned for a wide range of landscape projects, notably, for the 5th Duke of Argyll's estates of Inverarary and Rosneath (Cooksey 1991; Nasmyth 1885).There were also commissions for Runcimen and Delacour (Fleming 1962b).

7 Evidence for the Nories apprenticing under Lambert is based on a letter, Paton to Gough, 23 Feb. 1784, held at the National Libraries of Scotland MS29.5.7.f230 NLS MS29.5.7. Cited in Holloway 1994.

8 *Edinburgh Evening Courant*, 21 January 1769. Cited in Andrew 1981.

9 Letter XXX on the Ridotto, 6 April 1775, p. 249 (Topham 1776).

10 National Libraries of Scotland MS 2002. 'Alphabetical List, undated, of members of the Knights Champions of the Most Sovereign and Social Order of the Cape'. Cited in Macmillan 1973.

11 *Glasgow Theatrical Register*, 'Containing Cursory Remarks on the Performances at The Theatre Royal, Crawford and McKenzie, Glasgow'. Part VI, No. 1, 1 May 1805. Glasgow University Sp Coll GB 247 Bh12–h.35.

12 NLS R283C971.

13 NLS R283C918a.

14 *Glasgow Courier*, 1 July 1801. The original *Panorama of London . . . as seen from Albion Mills* was painted and exhibited by Barker in 1791.

15 Barker's original timber building for his panoramas on Leith Walk, Edinburgh, was advertised for sale in 1806, with a seven-year lease still to run, having 'a clear space of fifty feet diameter within the room'. The commercial bias is evident, as the advert continues 'Any person wishing to purchase it with a view to exhibit Panoramas, may be supplied occasionally with these, by Mr Henry Ashton Barker of Leicester Square, London' (19 July 1806, *Caledonian Mercury*).

16 By then 'John Knox & Sons' were trading from Glassford Street, Glasgow. It is possible that John Knox Jnr was working for his father at this point, with his elder brother Henry and younger brother William (Stuart 1988).

17 It ran from February until July 1809 then moved to the Mound, Edinburgh (*Caledonian Mercury*, 17 June 1809), before moving to Mr Wigley's large exhibition room at Spring Gardens, London (*Morning Post*, 10 July 1810). The large room was 52 feet wide and 62 feet long and had been used to display panoramas since 1796 (Hyde 1988).

18 *Glasgow Herald*, 3 May 1813.

19 *Glasgow Courier*, 2 January 1810; *Glasgow Herald*, 28 May 1810.

20 The panorama remained until 22 August 1811, moving again to Dublin on 22 January 1812 to Sackville Street (Ref FJ 22/01/1812, cited by Rockett 2011, 116).

21 BL General Reference Collection 258.d.13–27, Vols 1–15 (1794–1801).

22 Knox is not known to have exhibited a smaller oil painting version of *A View of Dublin*, unlike *View from Old Glasgow Bridge* and *View from Ben Lomond*.

23 *Glasgow Herald*, 16 July 1813.

24 The technique of transparency painting allowed the illumination of the canvas from the front and the reverse and was usually executed on linen or muslin which was stretched then sized with animal skin glue. The colours were applied thinly without a preparatory ground layer, as this would have prevented the transmission of the light through the canvas. The techniques could be executed in water colours or pigments in oil diluted with varnish. There is no evidence to establish which method Knox employed, as he would have been proficient in both. The City Halls used for entertainment, exhibitions and music were in Candleriggs Street, the painting may have been displayed in its 'large room'.

25 *Glasgow Courier*, 21 February 1814.

26 It is not clear whether any of Knox's students or his brothers assisted in the painting of his panoramas. John Knox's son Thomas was eventually to exhibit at the Royal Academy in 1848. He died in 1850 aged 41 (Stuart 1988) and would therefore have been too young to be more than a colour-boy fetching materials and mixing pigments between 1809 and 1814.

27 Including 'A View of the Clyde from Dalnottar Hill, two views of Loch Lomond, one of Loach Ard and Inveraray from Dunoquoich' (McClure 1974). Knox exhibited in ten exhibitions between 1821 and 1835. The first exhibition in which the smaller oil painting versions of 'View From Loch Lomond' were shown was at the Dilettante Society in 1829 (marked 'not for sale') and again in 1834. In 1831, he exhibited at the Glasgow Dilettante Society and later that year left for the Continent, at which point his collection of Dutch and Flemish paintings were sold by his brother Robert (Stuart, 1988). We can assume that some of these paintings were used in Knox's drawing school for copying. Knox went to live in London and exhibited at the Royal Academy, living at 130 Jermyn Street in 1829 (two entries) and again after his trip abroad at 1 Upper Gloucester Place in 1832 and 1834 (three entries) (A. Graves, *The Royal Academy of Arts: A Complete Dictionary of Contributors and their Work from its Foundation in 1769 to 1904*, Graves and Co., 1905–6).

28 The date of the painting is unconfirmed. Its first recorded exhibition was in 1829.

CHAPTER EIGHT

Picturesque Tours of Wales and Ireland

'A New Object of Pursuit'

Mary-Ann Constantine and Finola O'Kane

In his *Observations on the River Wye and Several Parts of South Wales, etc. Relative chiefly to Picturesque Beauty: Made in the Summer of the Year 1770* (1789a [1782]), William Gilpin placed the origins of the picturesque in Wales – or at least in the fluid, 'mazy' borderlands of the River Wye, whose many prospects had inspired 'a new object of pursuit; that of examining the face of a country *by the rules of picturesque beauty*: opening up the sources of pleasure which are derived from the comparison' (Gilpin 1789a [1782], 1). Exploring Scotland in 1776, Gilpin paired it conceptually with Ireland (which he does not seem to have visited), concluding that these were the only countries that were 'picturesque in a state of nature . . . consisting of variety both of soil, and ground'. Although 'the face of England' was 'varied', he felt that it had been 'more beautiful in a state of nature' than in its 'current state of cultivation' (Gilpin 1789b, II, 113–114). Gilpin's comments help to illuminate the significance of the Scottish tour in relation to the picturesque attractions of the English Lakes, Wales and Ireland, with the latter two perhaps providing closer parallels, on account of their cultural and linguistic differences from England. In surveying the rise of domestic tourism in both Wales and Ireland, the present essay aims to offer some useful points of triangulation with Scotland which is the focus of *Old Ways New Roads*.

Another key comparative exercise in what might be called 'four nations' picturesque was Paul Sandby's *The Virtuosi's Museum, Containing Select Views of England, Scotland and Ireland* (1778–1781), which presented the constituent countries of Britain, in no discernible geographical order, in over 100 plates with brief written descriptions; the captions to the Scottish views often quote directly from Thomas Pennant's *Tours* in Scotland of 1769 and 1772. Despite its tripartite title, eighteen of these images were actually from Wales, many reused (like their Scottish counterparts) from Sandby's earlier tours of the country; a later expanded edition of the work made reparation in its title for that silent, and rather disconcerting, elision. The views of Ireland (a place which Sandby, like Gilpin, had never actually visited) were all achieved by a form of artistic remote control – engraved from drawings taken on the spot by other people. Sandby's images were reassuringly 'calculated to improve the taste and polish of the manners of her subjects without corrupting their hearts' (Sandby 1778, Preface), and the effect of this visual sampling was a gradual conceptual homogenisation of the British Isles, seemingly united in a taste for the picturesque. Yet the surge in 'home' touring which underpinned the production of these views and thousands like them also produced written accounts. These often actively sought to stress cultural distinctiveness, and could not avoid commenting on such difficult and contentious subjects as politics, religion and relative poverty. In teasing counterpoint to the visual concordance that developed between the peripheral countries of the British Isles, there

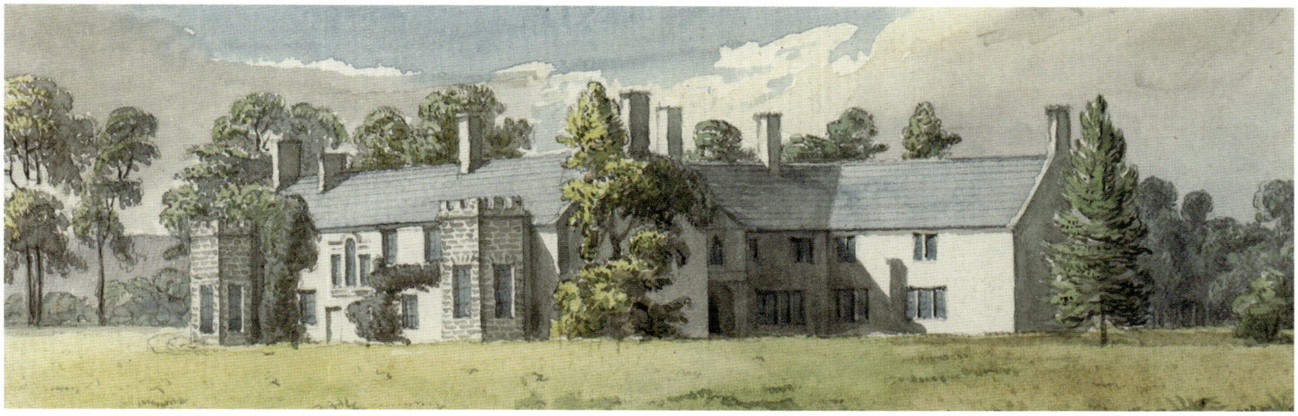

Fig. C8.1
Moses Griffith, 'Gwaenynog, Denbigh', in Thomas Pennant's *Extra-Illustrated Tours in Wales* (1770s or 1780s), Vol. 6, p. 7 (NLW W6)

emerged a kaleidoscopic impression of native *difference,* and although many tour guides and tourists sought to 'confine the sight to the view of many objects of the beautiful scenery' (Barton 1751, 6), the locality (and the locals) continued to edge around the picture frame. If Wales and Ireland shared the picturesque family likeness, they nonetheless had distinctive characters of their own (Andrews 1989; O'Kane 2013).

THE WELSH TOURS

> Wales has nothing that can much excite or gratify curiosity. The mode of life is entirely English. I am glad that I have seen it, though I have seen nothing, because now I know that there is nothing to be seen. (Redford 1992, 151)

Writing to his friend John Taylor in October 1774, Samuel Johnson gave a decidedly downbeat assessment of his recent journey into north Wales. Although travelling in the company of his close friends Hester and Henry Thrale, who were visiting Hester's newly inherited property at Bachegraig, he had not found it an especially uplifting experience. As his journal testifies, he felt unwell for much of the time and could muster little enthusiasm for walks to waterfalls or visits to ruins; he refers frequently to a variety of ailments and remedies, and to nights of broken sleep. Only the imposing Edwardian castles of the north-west coast roused him to anything approaching admiration: having risen to the challenge of climbing up to the Eagle Tower in Caernarfon Castle, he admitted, 'I did not think there had been such buildings. It surpassed my Ideas' (Bristow 1995, 47).

Perhaps the main, if unspoken, problem with Wales was that it was not Scotland. Johnson had sent the manuscript of his *Journey to the Western Isles* to his publisher the day before leaving on his trip with the Thrales, and his thoughts were clearly still with the more arduous, and more deeply felt, experiences of the previous year. Little in the Welsh landscapes he encountered, or the people he met, matched those of the Scottish tour. It felt 'entirely English'; it was not foreign enough. There was, nonetheless, some grudging praise for the hospitality he received at Gwaenynog Hall near Denbigh, the residence of Colonel John Middleton. 'Middleton is the only man, who, in Wales, has talked to me of literature', noted Johnson, and added (belying his comments on cultural sameness and revealing his long-standing interest in this particular *non*-anglophone culture): 'After dinner, the talk was of preserving the Welsh language. I offered them a scheme' (Bristow 1995, 42). The Middletons, for their part, felt sufficiently honoured by the visit to commission a monument to him by the banks of the River Ystrad: it reads 'This Spot was often dignified by the presence of Samuel Johnson LLD, whose moral Writings, exactly conformable to the Precepts of Christianity, give Ardour to Virtue and Confidence to Truth.'

The same spot was also dignified, at much the same time, by the presence of another traveller recently returned from a tour to the Hebrides. Thomas Pennant, encouraged by the reception given to his two published accounts of Scottish tours, had begun in the early 1770s to gather material for his *Tours in Wales* (Evans 1987; Constantine and Leask 2017). These would be

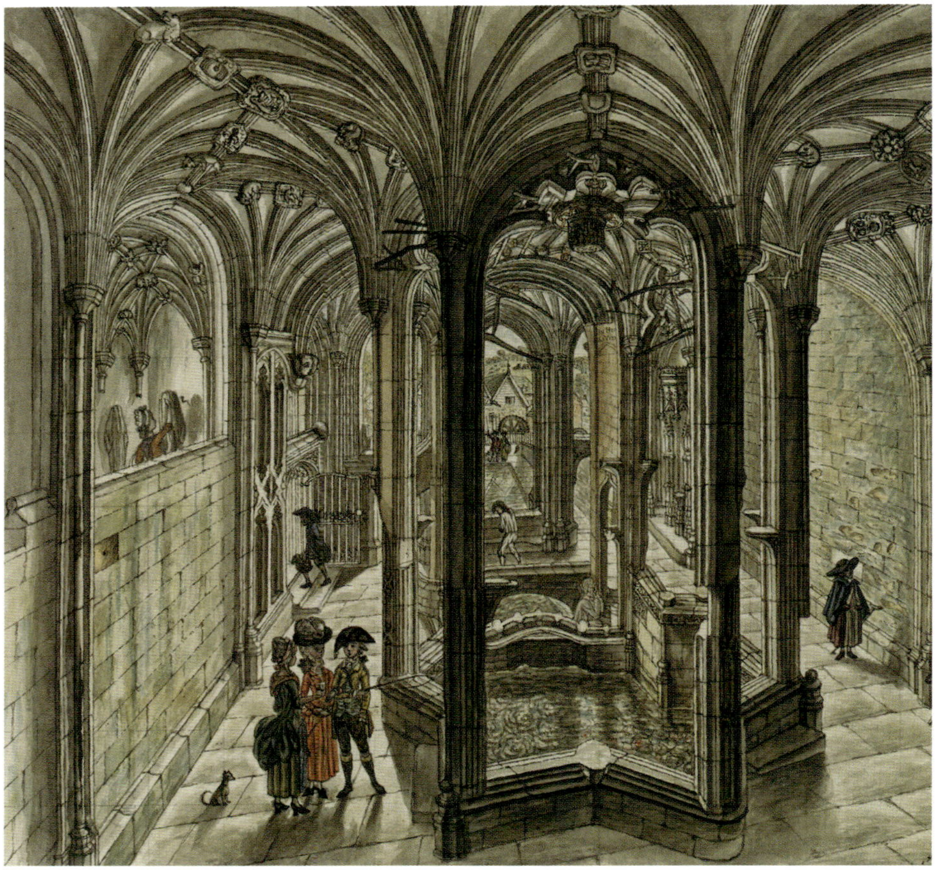

Fig. C8.2
Above. John Ingleby, 'St Winifred's Well, Holywell', in Thomas Pennant's *Extra-Illustrated Tours in Wales* (1770s–1780s), p. 278 (NLW)

Fig. C8.3
Opposite. Joseph Mallord William Turner, *Dolbadarn Castle*, c. 1798–99, oil on canvas (NLW 99401497302419)

published in three parts between 1778 and 1783, profoundly shaping perceptions of Welsh landscapes, sites and sights for decades to come. Had Johnson been in a position to read Pennant on Wales, as he had on Scotland, it is unlikely that he would have found 'nothing' to see. Unlike the linear itineraries of his Scottish travels, Pennant's Welsh *Tours* are woven together from a series of excursions made, usually on horseback, from various bases at gentry houses across north Wales. Gwaenynog was a typical example: here, enjoying the famous Middleton hospitality, he was able to combine 'rummaging among the family papers' with a thorough exploration of the area, to produce a characteristic blend of local history and antiquarian enquiry with descriptions of houses and fine views (Pennant 1784, 50). His 'servant–artist' Moses Griffith, who had accompanied him on the second Scottish tour, also painted watercolours of Gwaenynog Hall and other local sites, to be included in a lavish extra-illustrated volume of the *Tours* (Fig. C8.1).[1] Pennant's interest in the visual record, which stemmed in part from his publications in natural history, had been encouraged by his correspondence with Richard Gough at the Society of Antiquaries; as with the Scottish tours, his publications on Wales included engravings of picturesque scenes and antiquities by various artists, including Paul Sandby, John Ingleby and Richard Wilson, as well as those by Griffith.

THE NORTH WALES TOUR

It was, however, the written content of the *Tours in Wales* which did most to shape the itineraries and the perceptions of subsequent travellers in north Wales. As innumerable textual echoes, acknowledgements and footnotes attest, places like Holywell (where the miraculous spring of St Winifred remained an important stopping-off point for those on their way to Ireland – see Fig. C8.2) or the dramatic castles at Caernarfon and Conwy, the druid circles on Anglesey and even the view from the top of Snowdon, were often experienced and described through the authoritative lens of Pennant's volumes (Constantine 2014; Constantine forthcoming).

Sites that were easily reached by coach developed a tourist infrastructure of inns and guides; and by the turn of the century some of the more inaccessible parts of Snowdonia were opening up through the building of roads, like the one from Caernarfon to Capel Curig, that served both the slate industry and the burgeoning tourist market. The Birmingham-based novelist Catherine Hutton, travelling in 1800, noted acerbically how rapid and superficial many of these journeys had become: 'no tourist, except Pennant, has seen Wales. To travel post in Wales is to fly' (Hutton 1800, 137). The rise in popularity of the walking tour, however, opened up places off the main coach routes, and pedestrian tourists (derided by one Welsh reverend for their 'silly and ridiculous whim of converting pleasure into toil') pursued botanical, antiquarian and geological interests in more challenging territory. Many artists, inspired by the work of Richard Wilson and Paul Sandby in the mountains of north Wales, also travelled on foot: they included Edward Pugh, John and Cornelius Varley and (five separate times in the 1790s) the young J.M.W. Turner (Fig. C8.3), all hunting – as many of them

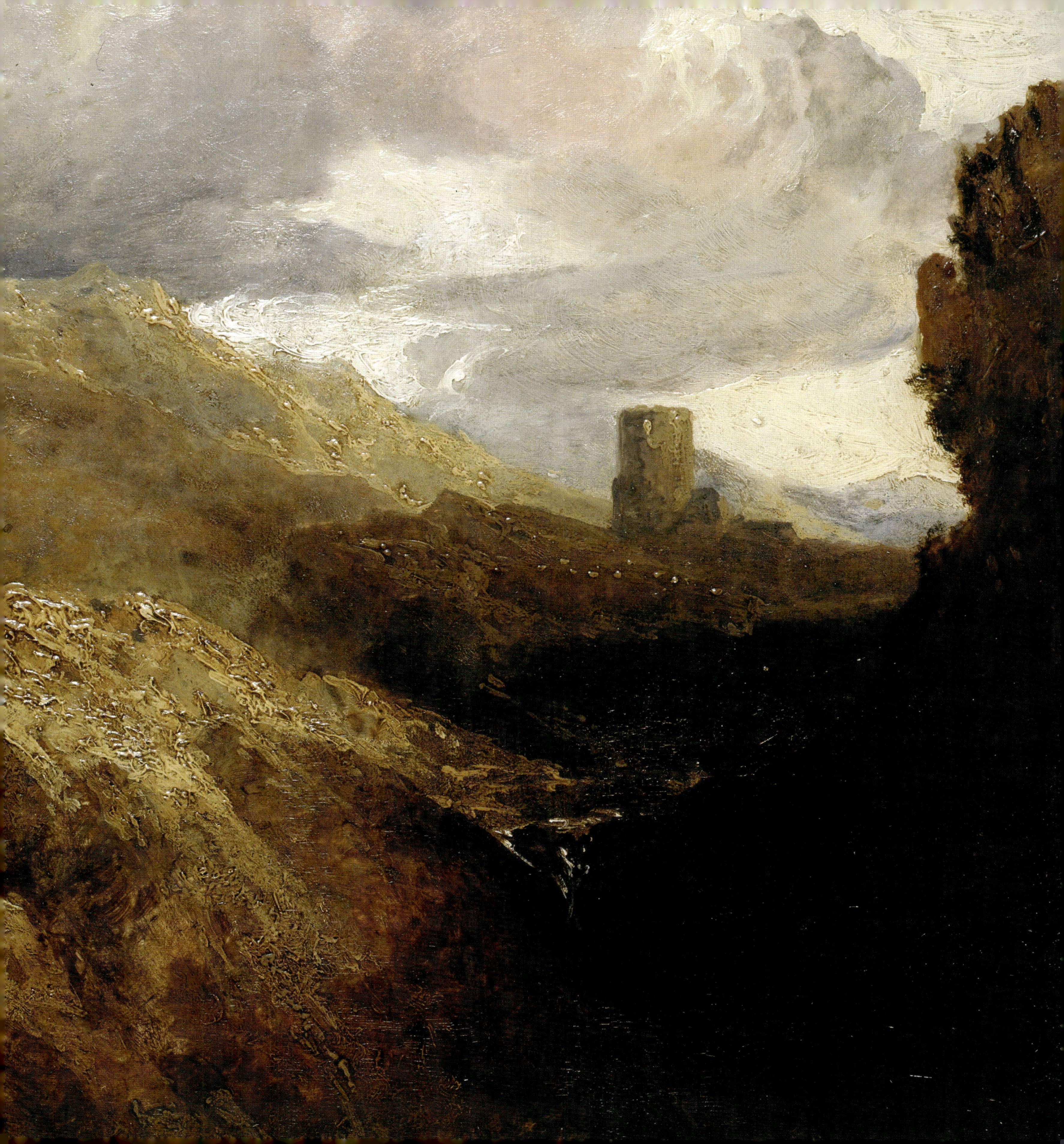

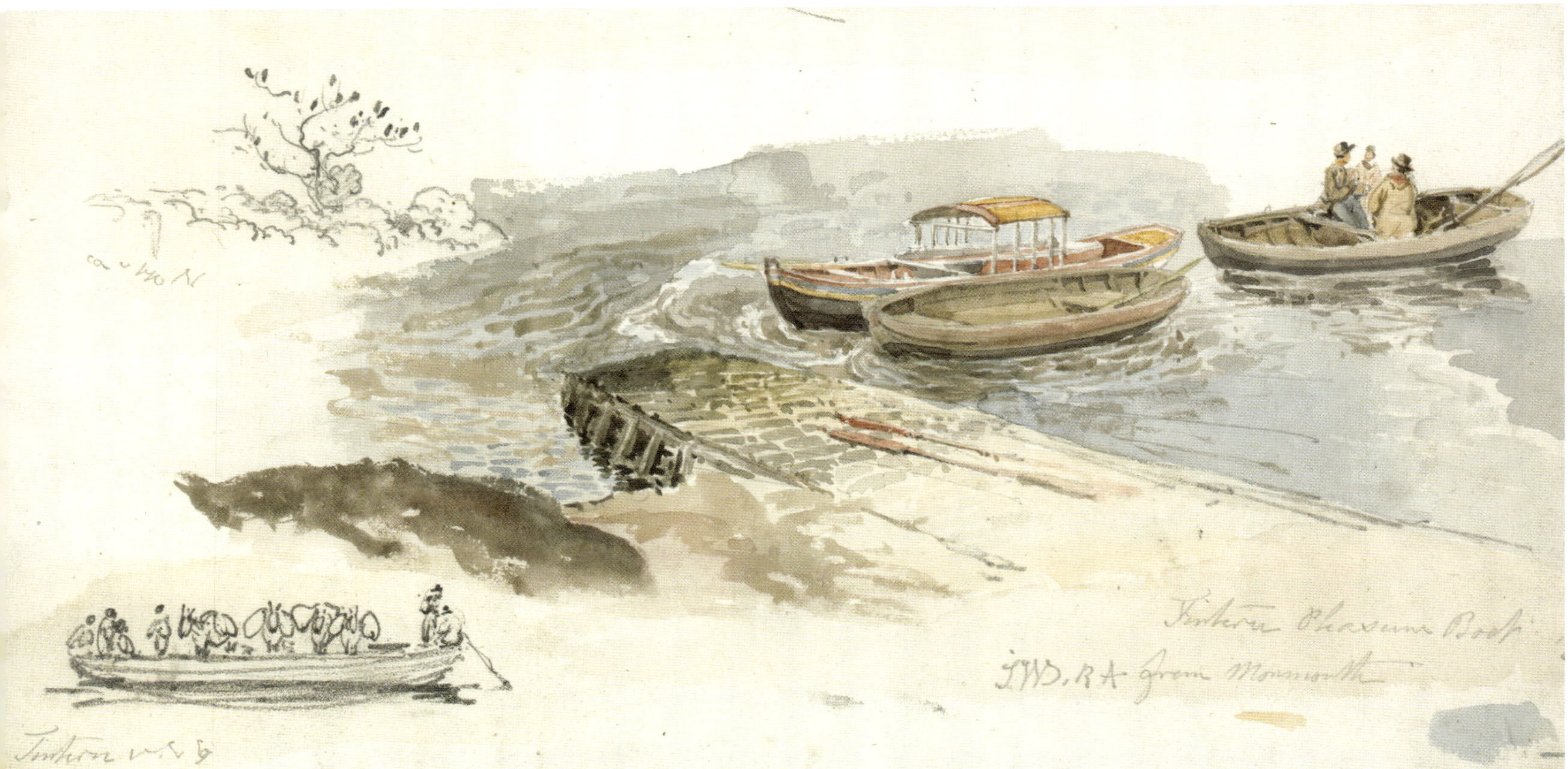

Fig. C8.4
James Ward, 'A Canopied Boat and Two Rowing Boats at a Jetty; inset left, a Pencil Study of the Tintern Livestock Ferry-boat', probably c. 1802, watercolour (YCBA B2001.2.1336)

would in Scotland – for new painterly prospects (Bishop 2015; Barrell 2013). And there was interest, too, in local 'customs and manners' – if surprisingly little curiosity about the Welsh language, in what was still largely a monoglot society.

TOURS OF THE WYE AND SOUTH WALES

> A Book only of Picturesque Beauty is to me as palling as a Dinner made up of Plumb-cake, Trifle, and Carraway Comfits. But, mark me, I had rather have Gilpin's Plumb-cake than Pennant's hard Dumplings. (Michael Tyson to Richard Gough, 1779, in Nichols 1814, 657–658)

Pennant claimed quite candidly to have no interest in south Wales, and visitors to the southern counties had other writers to guide them. William Gilpin's *Observations on the River Wye, and Several Parts of South Wales* (1789a [1782]), based on a journey made in 1770, became a founding text of the picturesque movement and brought large numbers of visitors into Wales. Some crossed the Severn by ferry from Bristol, but many followed Gilpin's example and began their tours at Ross, catching pleasure boats, especially designed for writing and sketching, down the sinuous River Wye to Monmouth and Chepstow, and discovering in that fluid borderland views of Welsh hills and English forests alternating in quick succession (Fig. C8.4). Thanks to Gilpin's writings, and the relative accessibility from London of south Wales, Wye Valley tourism developed early, and by the 1800s was largely choreographed by the energetic printer and publisher Charles Heath of Monmouth, whose cheap, portable guidebooks extracted the 'beauties' of writers such as Gilpin and William Mason, and included potted histories of the castles and ruins to be visited en route (Matheson 2013).

Within the space of a generation, Tintern Abbey went from being a little-known ruin to an exceptionally well-visited tourist site, captured, described and remediated in myriad words and images (Fig. C8.5). In 1761, Richard Gough had written admiringly of 'this beautifull Structure of which I find yet no account in any author' (Gough 1761, 12); half a century later the French visitor Louis Simond despaired of finding his own voice in a site overrun by other tourists: 'each with his Gilpin or his Cambrian Guide in his hand, and each, no doubt, writing a journal. This is rather ridiculous and discouraging' (cited in Matheson 2013, 140). As Suzanne Matheson observes, post-1800 tourist accounts are often highly self-conscious, displaying a 'greater sense of being written within an existing and familiar narrative' (Matheson 2007, n.p.).

Gilpin's account of south Wales, determinedly focused on matters of shape and form, 'the rules of picturesque beauty' (1789a [1782], 1–2), smoothly elides any sense of a cultural or linguistic border and makes nothing at all of a landscape's potential 'Welshness', in stark contrast to his remarks on Scotland, as discussed in Section 4. This was not, however, the case with all who followed him, and many writers did take the time to discover the histories of Welsh–Norman conflict embodied in a string of castles along the south coast (and the subject of prints by Sandby and Thomas Jones from as early as the mid 1770s), or to compare the zeal of the pious incumbents of ruined medieval monasteries with the increasingly visible 'enthusiasm' of Welsh Methodist preachers. Antiquity and modernity formed striking visual contrasts at places like Neath, where the medieval abbey and modern ironworks stood side by side. As in Scotland, where visits to the Carron ironworks became increasingly popular, the south Wales tour frequently incorporated visits to the factories and furnaces that fed the rapidly growing coal and iron industries. The chemist Michael Faraday, travelling through Wales in 1819, had professional reasons to examine the ironworks at Merthyr Tydfil (Tomos 1972), but many tourists were intrigued by the complex processes at work, and found the sights and sounds of the forges both alarming and aesthetically impressive. A young Breton aristocrat visiting Dowlais in 1839 described the scene from his bedroom window: 'At night all these furnaces lit up in a circle create the most magnificent effect; like fourteen houses all ablaze' (Constantine and Postic 2019, 114). Improvement, both agricultural and industrial, is a key theme in tours to all parts of Wales, as it is in Scotland.

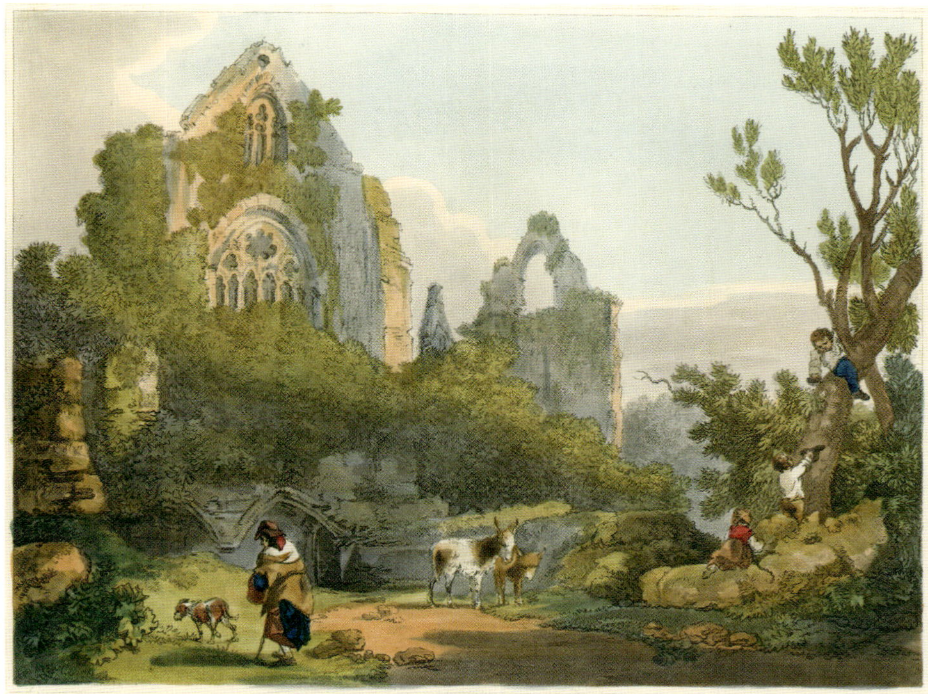

Fig. C8.5
William Pickett and John Clarke after Philippe-Jacques de Loutherbourg, 'Tintern Abbey', hand-coloured etching and aquatint in Philippe-Jacques de Loutherbourg, *The Romantic and Picturesque Scenery of England and Wales* . . . (London, 1805) (RAA 06/1322)

HAFOD AND MID WALES

Unless travellers were prospecting for silver or lead, boggy, inaccessible mid Wales had little to tempt them, until the late 1780s when a few hardy souls did venture to the coast at Aberystwyth, a kind of Brighton-on-a-budget. Over the following decade, another reason to explore this *terra incognita* emerged: Hafod Uchtryd, the estate of Thomas Johnes, hidden in the Ystwyth Valley about 15 miles from the coast and 4 miles from the spectacular waterfalls at Devil's Bridge (Macve 2004). Johnes was born in Herefordshire in 1748; his mother was a cousin of the landscape artist Richard Payne Knight, owner of the remodelled estate at Downton on the Rock. Uvedale Price of Foxley was another influential landscaping neighbour, and it is also very likely that Johnes, who attended lectures on logic and moral philosophy in Edinburgh in 1767, was inspired by a visit to the

Duke of Atholl's great picturesquing project at Dunkeld, discussed in Chapter 4 (see also Dingwall 1996).

When his father died in 1780, leaving estates in mid Wales, Johnes settled in Hafod. He married his Welsh first cousin, Jane, and they began a programme of rebuilding, planting, and agricultural, social and aesthetic improvement. The house, completed by 1788, was a mixed classical/gothic fantasy, designed by Thomas Baldwin of Bath and later developed by Nash; a catastrophic fire in 1807 destroyed much of the building, including the famous octagonal library, which housed beautiful medieval books, prints and manuscripts. Over three decades, Johnes planted somewhere in the region of 4 million trees, created walks and gardens, and diverted and enhanced waterfalls. He also built a church and a school, and was closely involved in the agricultural improvement of this intrinsically unforgiving environment.

By the 1790s and early 1800s a steady flow of written tours, prints and engravings testify to the area's growing importance as a tourist magnet: visitors included J.M.W. Turner, the Welsh poet Iolo Morganwg, and possibly Samuel Taylor Coleridge and his walking companion Joseph Hucks, who passed close by in 1794. By 1796 Johnes had also developed the Hafod Arms at neighbouring Devil's Bridge, where, as J.E. Smith delicately put it, 'travellers who are strangers to him' (as opposed to invited guests) could buy tickets for the estate (Smith 1810, 21). Over the next decade one can see Johnes paradoxically encouraging, and recoiling from, the whole notion of the 'tourist', with its attendant anxieties of invasion by members of a different class shot through with flickers of a more national resentment. 'Saxon' visitors to Wales, complained Johnes, regarded the place as 'un pays conquis . . . and think everything may be had and done here with impunity' (Moore-Colyer 1992, 159).

The second edition of Gilpin's influential *Observations on the River Wye* (1789a [1782]) contains four pages on the Hafod estate, with succinct descriptions of the house and grounds.

> It's [sic] banks consist of great variety of wooded recesses – hills – sides of mountains – and contracted vallies – thwarting, and opposing each other in various forms: and adorned with little cascades running every where among them, in guttered chasms. Of the grandeur and beauty of these scenes I can speak as an eye-witness: for though I was never on the spot, I have seen a large collection of drawings, and sketches (not fewer than between twenty or thirty) which were taken from them. (Gilpin 1789a [1782], 79)

One of the earliest and most-read descriptions of the place, then (like Sandby and Gilpin's comments on Irish landscapes) is not an eye-witness account, and is already filtered through the medium of art (in this instance, probably a series of sketches by Thomas Jones). As with the Wye Valley, Hafod becomes a self-consciously mediated site, with visual and written depictions interacting with and sometimes influencing the landscape itself. George Cumberland's *An Attempt to Describe Hafod* (1796), a valuable early record of the various walks and sights on the estate, brings to the fore the dynamics between the walking viewer and the artfully shifting scenes. After reading it Johnes wrote to tell the author:

> I am beginning this day on a new walk . . . and shall probably set about in the summer the walk up the river above the stone bridge, which so pleased you. I must also change the walk over the Millbrook, to make it correspond with your description. (Moore-Colyer 1992, 119)

Where Cumberland's sentences followed the twists and turns of the paths above the River Ystwyth, now the walks must follow the sentences. Art and landscape are also consciously intertwined in a work by the botanist James Edward Smith, founder of the Linnaean Society and a close friend of the Johnes family (Smith 1810). The text of this work was illustrated by J.C. Stadler's engravings of a series of watercolours by John Warwick Smith, which had been painted much earlier, possibly in 1792, and Smith's account engages in dialogue with them, sometimes critically ('the artist has, for some reasons of his own, drawn the house of a much larger proportion'), and sometimes providing updates where earlier views have been obscured by the growing trees, or new walks added (Fig. C8.6). (Warwick Smith also painted a series of picturesque views of the Duke of Atholl's estate at Dunkeld, discussed by John Bonehill in Chapter 5). Hafod was thus both a developing entity and a place continually assessed and perceived *through* the medium of art, underlining

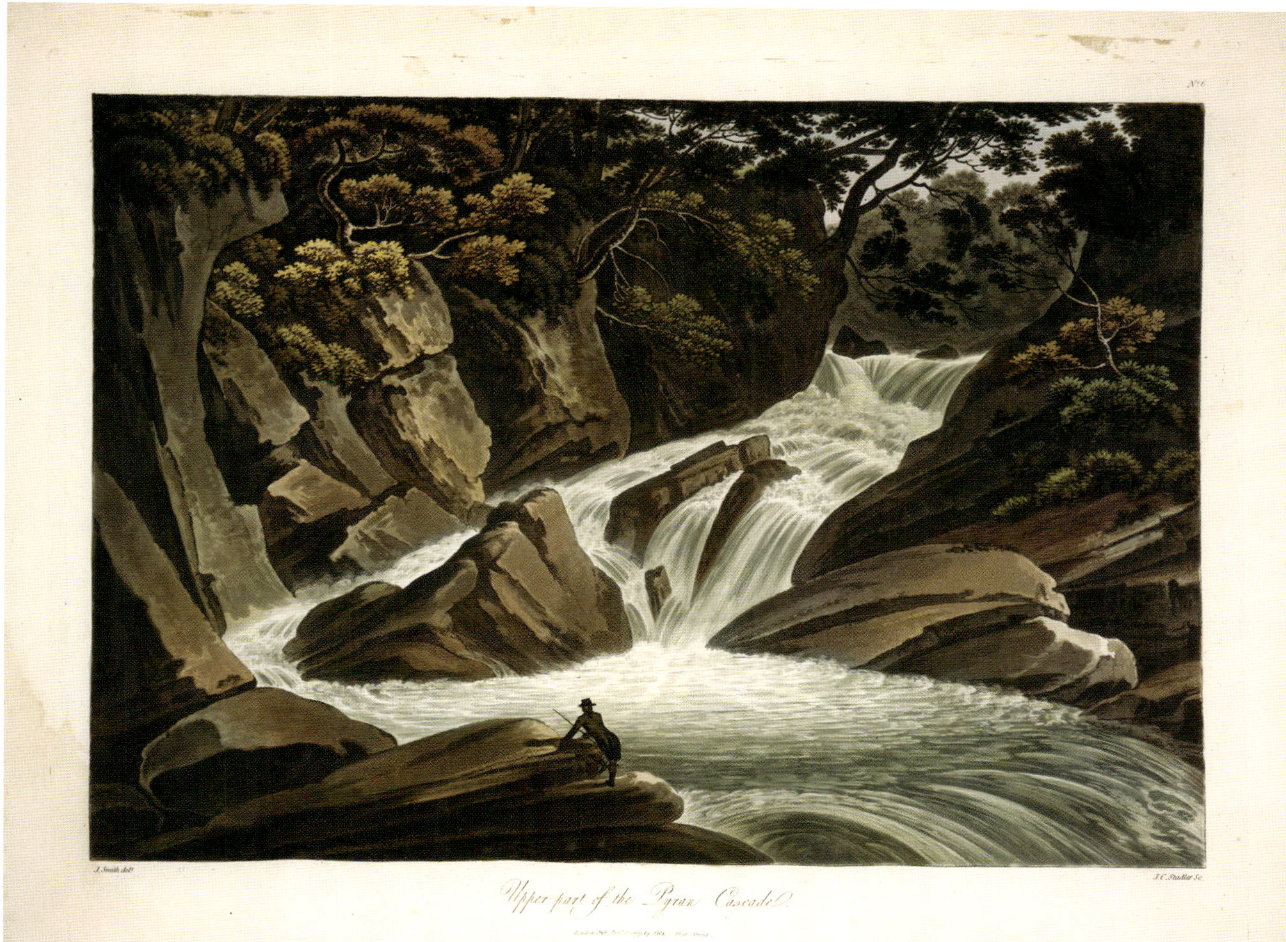

Fig. C8.6
Joseph Constantine Stadler after John Warwick Smith, 'Upper part of Piran Cascade', aquatint in James Edward Smith, *Fifteen Views Illustrative of a Tour to Hafod in Cardiganshire* (London, 1810), pl. 6 (NLW BV2202F)

the observation made by Stephen Daniels and Dennis Cosgrove (1988, 1): 'A landscape park is more palpable but no more real, no less imaginary, than a landscape painting or poem.'

FROM WALES TO IRELAND

The main route from London to Dublin went from Chester to Holyhead, and many of those travelling to Ireland became, if not always willingly, visitors to Wales. In 1727 Jonathan Swift spent a miserable week waiting for the Irish packet to sail, penning a diary and some angry verses about the 'muddy ale and mouldy bread' of his smoky lodgings (Rogers 1983, 329–333; Connolly 2019). After the Irish uprising in 1798, Beaumaris and the towns of the north-west coast of Wales received considerable numbers of refugees from across the Irish Sea. During her stay in a boarding house in Caernarfon, Catherine Hutton befriended a traumatised woman whose brother's home had been 'plundered by rebels'; she had fled from home with no friends or servants, 'and I am told, that here she sleeps in her cloaths' (Hutton 1799, 84). A striking sequence of watercolours by Turner from 1798 show British warships manoeuvring against bloody sunsets around Caernarfon Castle, collapsing images of past and present conflict on that vulnerable west coast (Fig. C8.7). Tourist itineraries cut disconcertingly across the enforced movements of lives disrupted and destroyed by war, and the

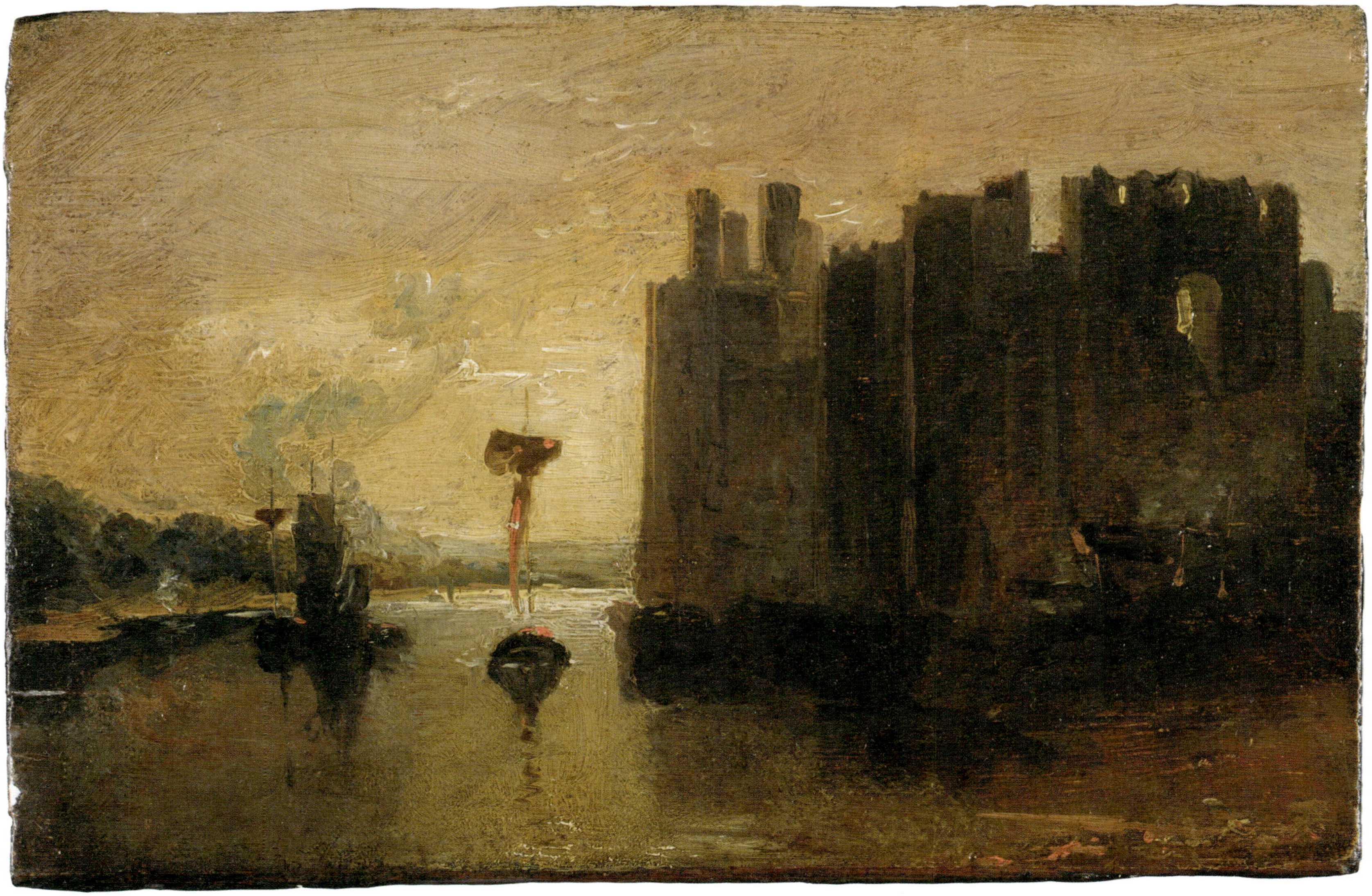

Fig. C8.7
Joseph Mallord William Turner, *Caernarvon Castle*, c. 1798, oil on panel (TG N01867)

new roads enabling business and leisure in north Wales were also busy with British soldiers. As Hywel Davies (2013, 261) has noted, of 'the thirteen militia regiments in Ireland raised in England and Wales, six of them were Welsh', among them the 'Ancient Britons' under Sir Watkin Williams-Wynn, long remembered in Ireland for their brutal treatment of the rebel forces. As with the presence of Highland forces in Ireland discussed below, the genteel 'picturesquing' of the four nations also masked a bloody 'theatre of war'.

THE IRISH TOURS

For English, Welsh, Scottish and European travellers, Ireland lay across the Irish Sea, and this interstitial maritime space affected its perception from within and without. In 1751, Richard Barton encouraged the 'Gentlemen of fancy' of Trinity College, Dublin (whose estate included parts of the Killarney environs), to 'return after a summer's recreation, with descriptions of beautiful rural Scenes' so that 'then might Ireland soon be painted,

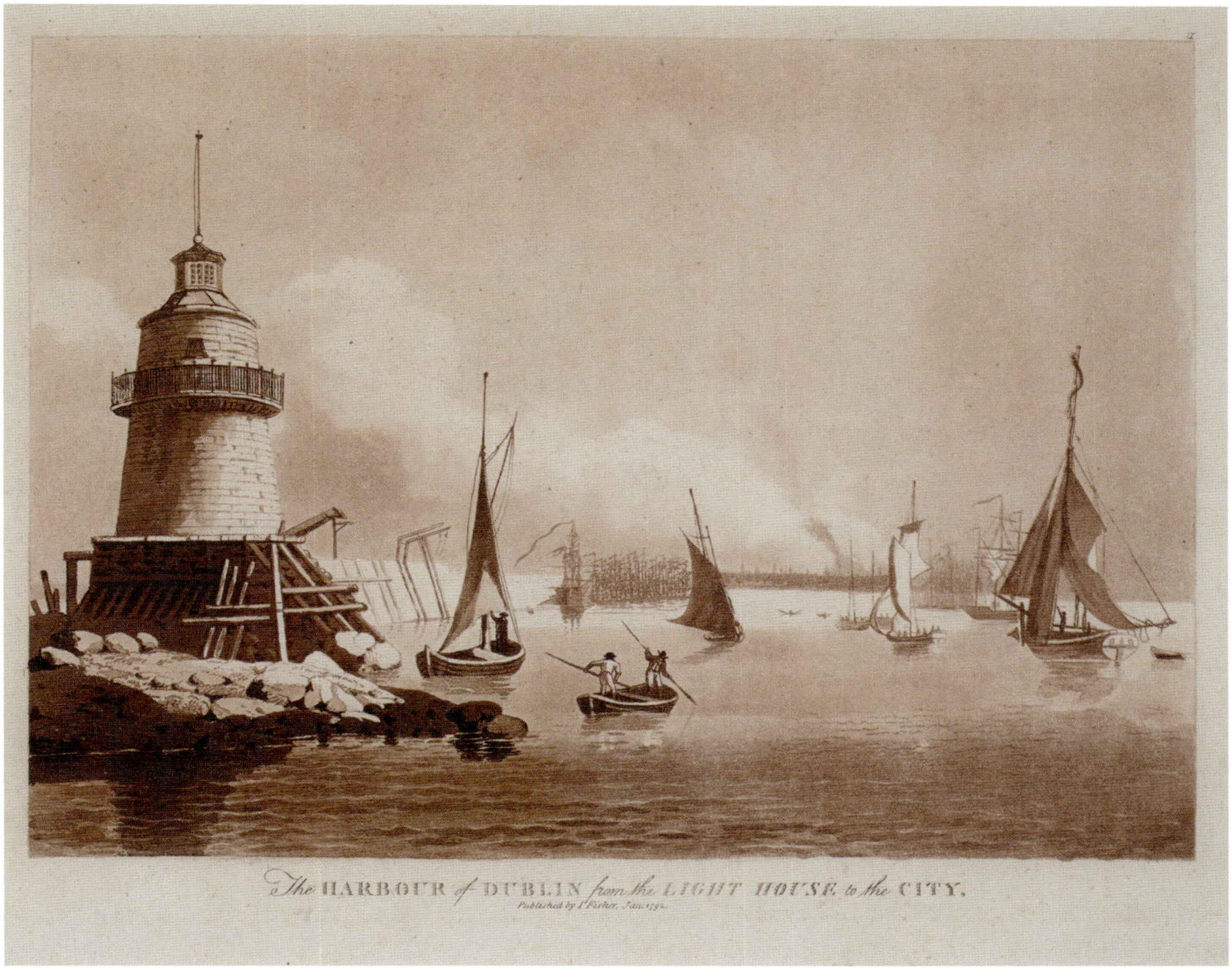

Fig. C8.8
Jonathan Fisher, 'Harbour of Dublin from the Lighthouse to the City', coloured aquatint in *Scenery of Ireland* (Dublin, 1795), pl. 1 (NLI ILB 9141)

and foreigners charmed', suggesting that tourism was clearly not intended as a native past-time (Barton 1751, A2). Initially Ireland's many gentlemen improvers encouraged the Irish to promote tourism principally for its economic benefits rather than for individual gratification alone (perhaps in contrast to the Dukes of Atholl or Argyll in Scotland, who were more patriotically motivated to enhance their ancestral estates, as discussed in Chapter 4). Some forty years later, this focus on tourism as a form of landscape improvement was evident in Jonathan Fisher's choice of a leading image for his 1791 publication *Scenery of Ireland*, with its viewpoint that of a traveller arriving into Dublin Bay by boat, implicitly from Wales (Fig. C8.8). Ireland's tours continued to start and end at sea, and this nautical distance from the mainland of Great Britain and the rest of Europe was made part of Ireland's attraction. Charles Smith introduced the country as 'a kind of terra incognita to the greater part of Europe' to readers of *The Ancient and Present State of the County of Kerry*, claiming that it bore comparison with 'the ultima Thule of the ancients' by remaining 'in obscurity to the rest of the learned world, who are still amused with fables, and very false and scandalous accounts of it' (Smith 1979 [1756], 5). This otherness was emphasised in accounts that stressed the differences of nationality,

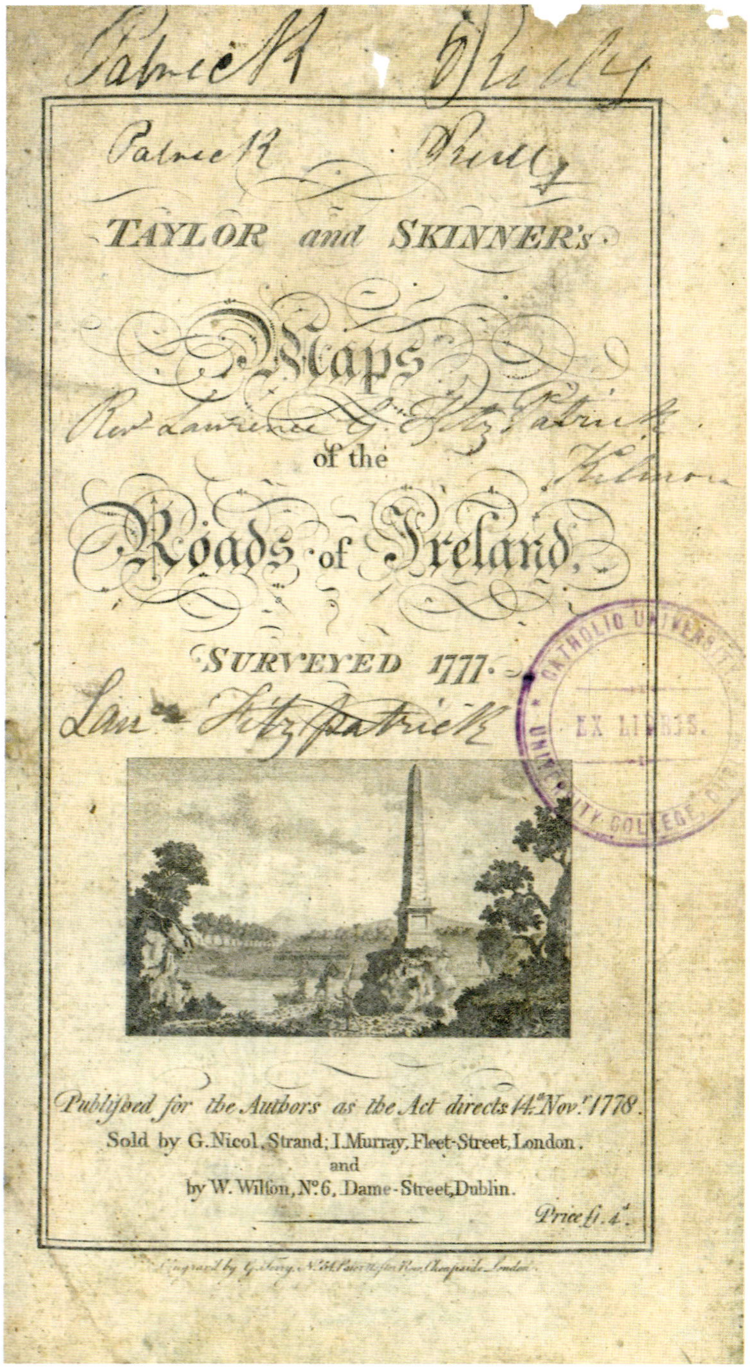

Fig. C8.9
Title page to George Taylor and Andrew Skinner, *Maps of the Roads of Ireland, Surveyed 1777* (London, 1778) (GLA ASC q396)

religion, language, dress, custom and tradition that separated the natives from those touring the country, also often the case in contemporary accounts of the Scottish Highlands.

If many Scots viewed their 1707 Union with Great Britain as 'a negotiated partnership between two independent states', Ireland, in contrast, 'had been annexed to England by conquest and its military subordination to London was reinforced by the Williamite victories of the 1690s, the presence of an army of occupation of around 12,000 regular soldiers, the appointment of Englishmen to high political and ecclesiastical office, and the control of Irish legislative decisions' (cited in Devine 2006, 36). (In Scotland, the 1715 and 1745 uprisings had also created a 'theatre of war' and a landscape transformed by the Hanoverian military infrastructure, as discussed in Section 1 'The Theatre of War', although the military occupation was never on the scale of Ireland.) The occupation of Ireland led mapmakers to provide interpretative frameworks for travellers, so that they would arrive at the correct perception of the landscapes that they viewed. Nowhere is this clearer than in the frontispiece for *Taylor and Skinner's Maps of the Roads of Ireland* by George Taylor and Andrew Skinner: the image depicted the 1691 Williamite victory at the Battle of the Boyne (Fig. C8.9), in case the battle's significance for the history of Ireland had escaped anyone travelling the Irish roads. (Although Culloden, the nearest Scottish equivalent, did become a tourist site, its rhetorical and visual invocation was somewhat less triumphalist, perhaps because of the stigma cast over the Hanoverian victory by the atrocities committed by Cumberland's troops.) In contrast, *Taylor and Skinner's Survey and Maps of the Roads of North Britain or Scotland* featured a predictable text-only dedication to 'John, Duke of Argyll, Commander in Chief of his Majesty's Forces in North Britain' (Taylor, 1776, Frontispiece). Though texts like Pennant's *Tours* and William Warrington's *History of Wales* (1786) made tourists well aware of past Welsh–English conflicts, mapmakers did not need such interpretative framing devices for those crossing the border into Wales.

DEVELOPING TOURIST LANDSCAPES

Once safely landed in Ireland the development of tourism moved from east to west, with the line between 'acceptable' and 'unacceptable' tourist environments also moving westward and into more rugged territories over time. The Earl of Orrery, when visiting the Dingle peninsula in 1735, had not seen 'a more dismal Country since [he] came into the World'; it seemed 'as if nature had brought forth a Monster', the roads were 'shocking & dangerous; not a Tree, nor a House, to be seen' and 'nothing but hideous Rocks and black Boggs to be view'd on every Side' (FitzGerald 1972, 48). Yet by 1756, when Charles Smith produced *The Ancient and Present State of the County of Kerry*, an image of the barren rock Skellig Michael off the coast of Kerry was acceptable. Landscape artists were pressed into service very early on in the Irish tours, and landscapes that did not have a powerfully proficient artist to represent them could languish in the evolving native and foreign tourist markets. Places had to be successfully 'disseminated' in books of views, with Dublin's publishing houses ensuring the growing popularity of Ireland's landscapes by reducing the reach and choice of London. If Thomas Roberts's oil paintings of Croagh Patrick, Nephin and other Connacht landscapes (which are now lost) had been more widely disseminated as prints, the landscapes of Galway and Mayo might have reached an audience before the nineteenth century. The modern popularity of Connemara arguably stems from the success of paintings by James Arthur O'Connor and nineteenth-century tour guides such as the husband and wife team of Mr. & Mrs. S. C. Hall's *Ireland, its Scenery, Character* (Hall and Hall 1841): as in Wales and Scotland, the heavily mediated nature of such landscapes produced an intensely choreographed tourist experience.

The most successful Irish tourist landscapes were those that mixed lake, mountain and improved farmland, preferably dotted with a few ruins. The Wicklow tour remained perennially popular for its adjacency to Dublin (like the Trossachs, discussed in Chaper 1 and Section 4, which although a much later discovery than Wicklow, shared its accessibity, in this case from Stirling and Glasgow), while Killarney's principal attraction continued to lie partly in its distance away from the capital city (O'Kane 2013, 34–35). Killarney especially was thought to be 'one of the Beauties of nature, exclusive of Art; of which She may justly be very proud' (FitzGerald 1972, 56). Killarney's upper lake (which had deeply impressed Pennant as young man in 1754) made a sublime rear ground to the middle ground of the lower lake and a foreground of Kenmare demesne in Jonathan Fisher's leading view of Killarney in 1776 (Fig. C8.10). Wicklow's Glendalough shared the same structure of an upper and a lower lake, the home of a powerful landlord set centrally in a demesne landscape, with a circuit walk and some monastic or castle ruins. Yet ecclesiastical ruins in Ireland, where the Dissolution of the Monasteries was not a positive history for the largely Catholic population, could prove highly problematic, in contrast to Presbyterian Scotland. This ambivalence towards the making of a picturesque landscape, which implicitly accommodated ruined buildings for interest and scale, tended to give the Irish tours a pronounced improving and forward-looking cast, perhaps most effectively demonstrated by Charles Smith in his topographical histories of Cork and Kerry (1815 [1750]; 1979 [1756]).

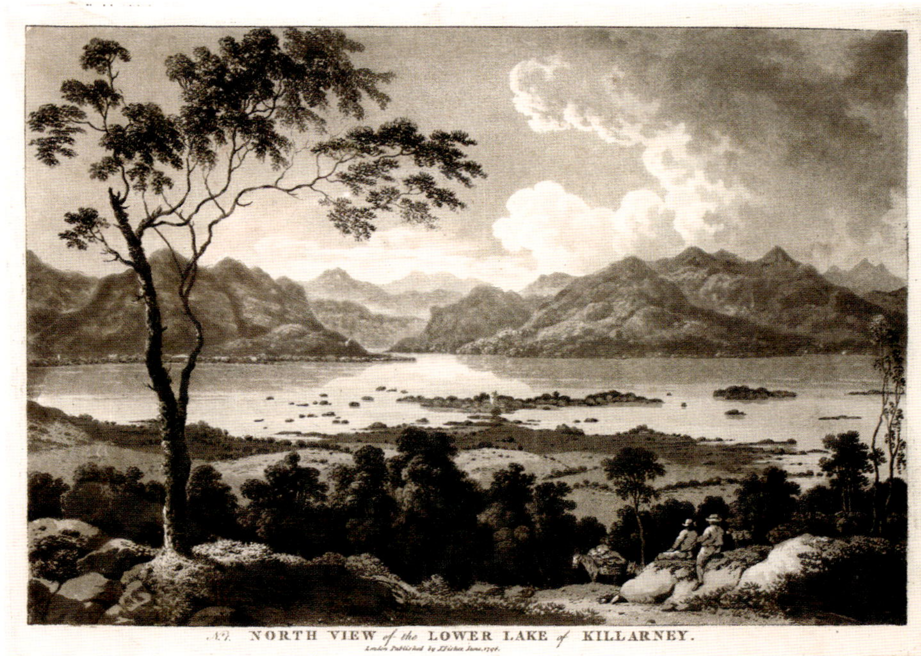

Fig. C8.10
Jonathan Fisher, 'North View of the Lower Lake of Killarney', aquatint in *Scenery of Ireland, Illustrated in a Series of Prints of Select Views, Castles, and Abbies. . . being an Appendix to his Scenery of Ireland* (Dublin, 1795–96), no. 1 (NLI)

Just as Thomas Pennant published the canonical tour narratives of Scotland and Wales in the 1770s and 1780s, so Arthur Young dominated Irish travel writing from the 1770s onwards, and his *Tour in Ireland 1776–1779* (Young 1780) set the itinerary and reinforced much of the existing tourist hierarchy of Wicklow, the Causeway and Killarney; his attempt to promote the tour of the two Lough Ernes, also depicted powerfully by Thomas Roberts, did not leap the various demesne walls to become a larger tourist circuit. Young, unlike Francis Grose and Thomas

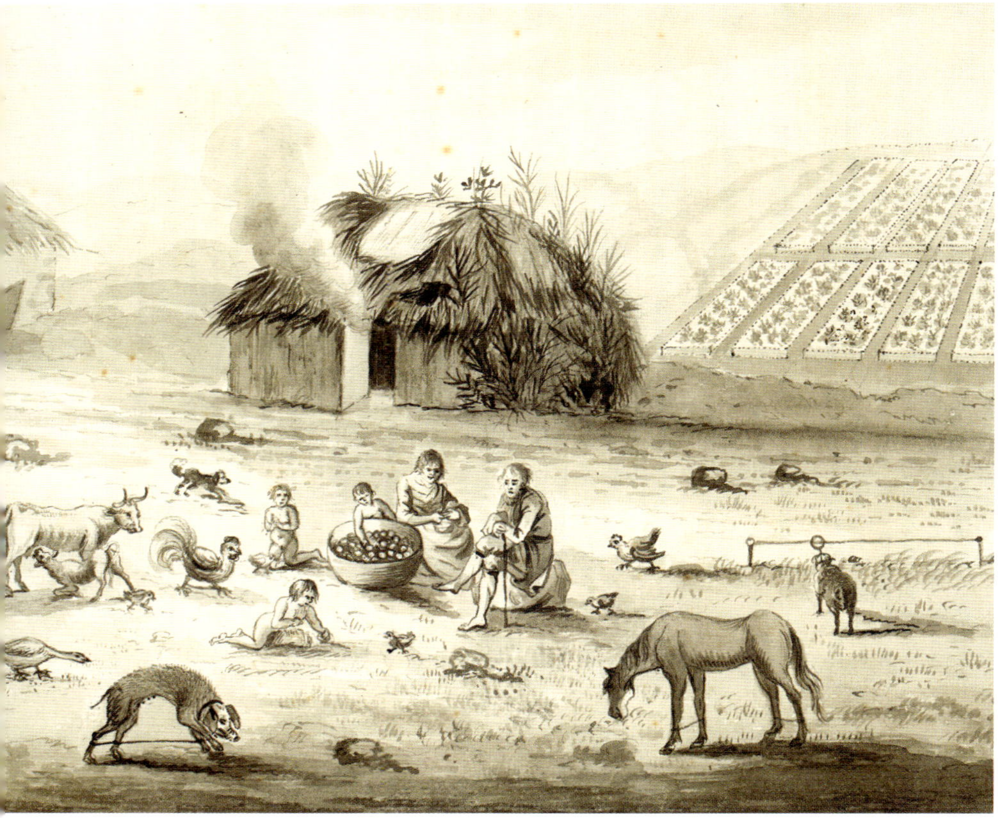

Fig. C8.11
Arthur Young, 'An Irish Cabbin', pen and wash drawing, inserted after page 24 of extra-illustrated edition of Arthur Young, *A Tour in Ireland . . .*, vol. 1/1, London, 1780 (NLI LO10203)

Wright who preceded him (or for that matter Pennant in Scotland), did not have much interest in antiquarianism. His interests were more economic and anthropological, and this led him to acutely observe Ireland's poverty and related social, sectarian and landscape structures. As the eighteenth century progressed, compounding already severe problems with a demographic boom, many tourists felt that 'too much of Ireland approximated to the Highlands: [but] what was in Scotland the minority problem was in Ireland quite simply the majority problem' (Cullen, Smout and Gibson 1988, 114). Young's powerful image of a poverty-stricken family outside their 'Irish cabin' was much redacted in its final printed form (Fig. C8.11). It contrasts sharply with the almost genteel figure that greets a kneeling women and small child outside the door of their sheelin in Thomas Pennant's view of the western isles of Jura from 1772 (see Fig. C2.3). Scotland and Wales continued to be conjured at particular locations on the Irish tours, most notably in county Antrim, where the coast of Scotland is visible at only 16 miles away. Scotland was also present physically in the design of some Irish landscapes. Downhill, the seat of Lord Bristol in County Derry, was 'an extraordinary Mansion, upon a high cliff near the Sea, without Trees, open to the Atlantick, but with Distant Views, of the Giants Causeway, some parts of Scotland & the Islands of Isla & Jura, part of the Hebrides' (Conolly 1786). When the Italian artist Antonio de Bittio (1722–1797) painted the island of Staffa and Fingal's cave he carefully recorded on the grisaille drawing that while it lay 'west of Mull in Scotland 7 miles' it was but 60 miles 'N. of Giant's Causeway in Ireland' (Fig. C8.12). De Bittio completed a pendant view of the Causeway to make the sibling relationship apparent (Fig. C8.13).[2]

TOURS AND CONFLICT: IRISH LANDSCAPES OF WAR

In Scotland by the 1780s even some of the more recalcitrant Gaels had been slowly, and often successfully, transformed from Jacobite rebels into British military heroes. In Ireland such a transformation remained elusive, as the key ideological hurdles of religion and monarchy remained, particularly in the many locations where the landscape retained a pronounced sectarian structure. Ireland continued to be 'in a much more dependent relationship with England than Scotland had ever been, even after the apparent loss of independence in 1707' (Devine 2006, 36) and this was emphasised in the aftermath of the failed United Irishmen's rebellion of 1798. Highland Gaels, like the Welsh 'Ancient Britons', played a key role in suppressing the uprising: indeed the incorporation of the Highland fencible regiments into the British army had proved so successful that the British military were widely caricatured in Ireland wearing the kilt (Fig. C8.14). The graphic series of caricatures produced to depict the story of 'The Newry Lass' saw the Highland regiments positioned as ardent and vitriolic imperialists, a strange inversion of both countries' shared Gaelic heritage.

The tropes and practices of tourism could, on the other hand, be deployed in the revolutionary cause, sometimes in quite unexpected ways. In June 1795 Theobald Wolfe Tone, in the company of the other United Irishmen, had sworn the move-

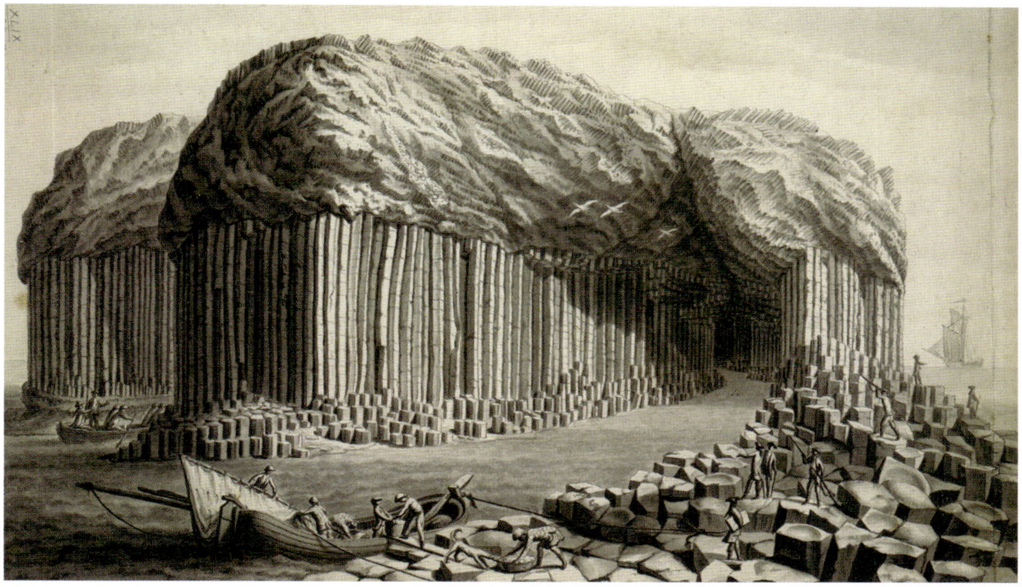

Fig. C8.12
Antonio de Bittio, *View of the Basaltic Columns of the Island of Staffa*, ink drawing, 1775 (BL K.Top.49.39.a)

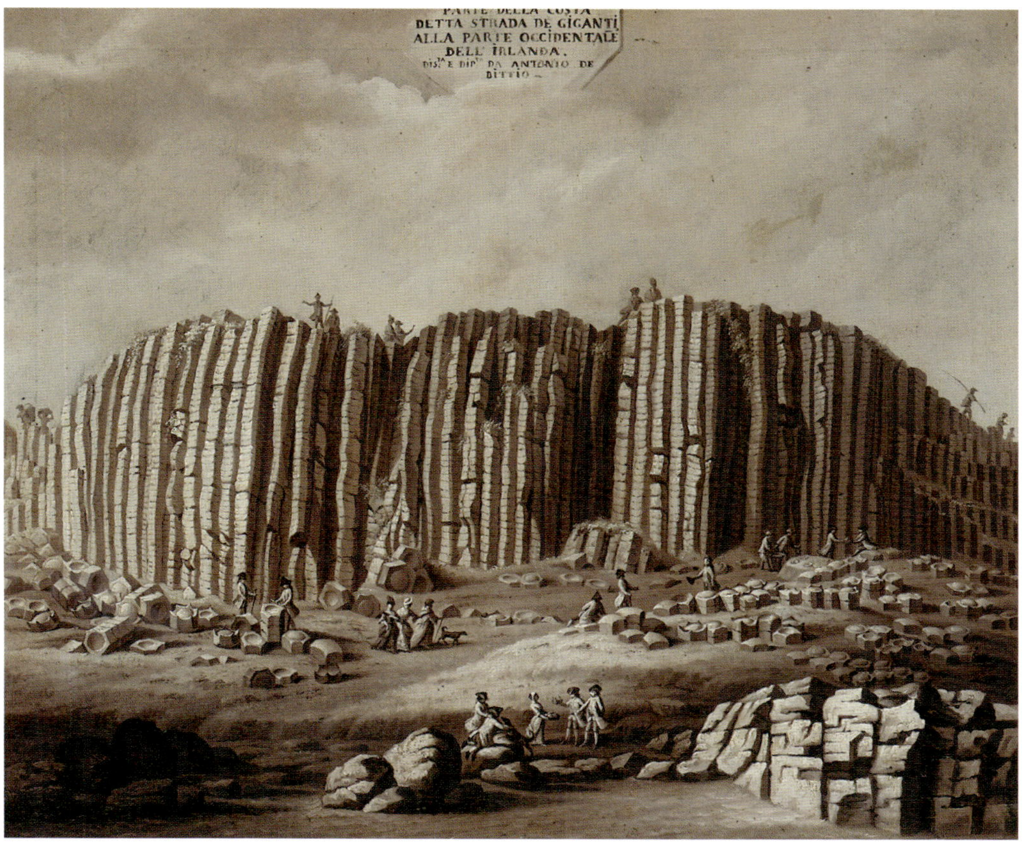

Fig. C8.13
Antonio de Bittio, *The Giant's Causeway, Ireland*, c. 1775, oil on canvas (PC)

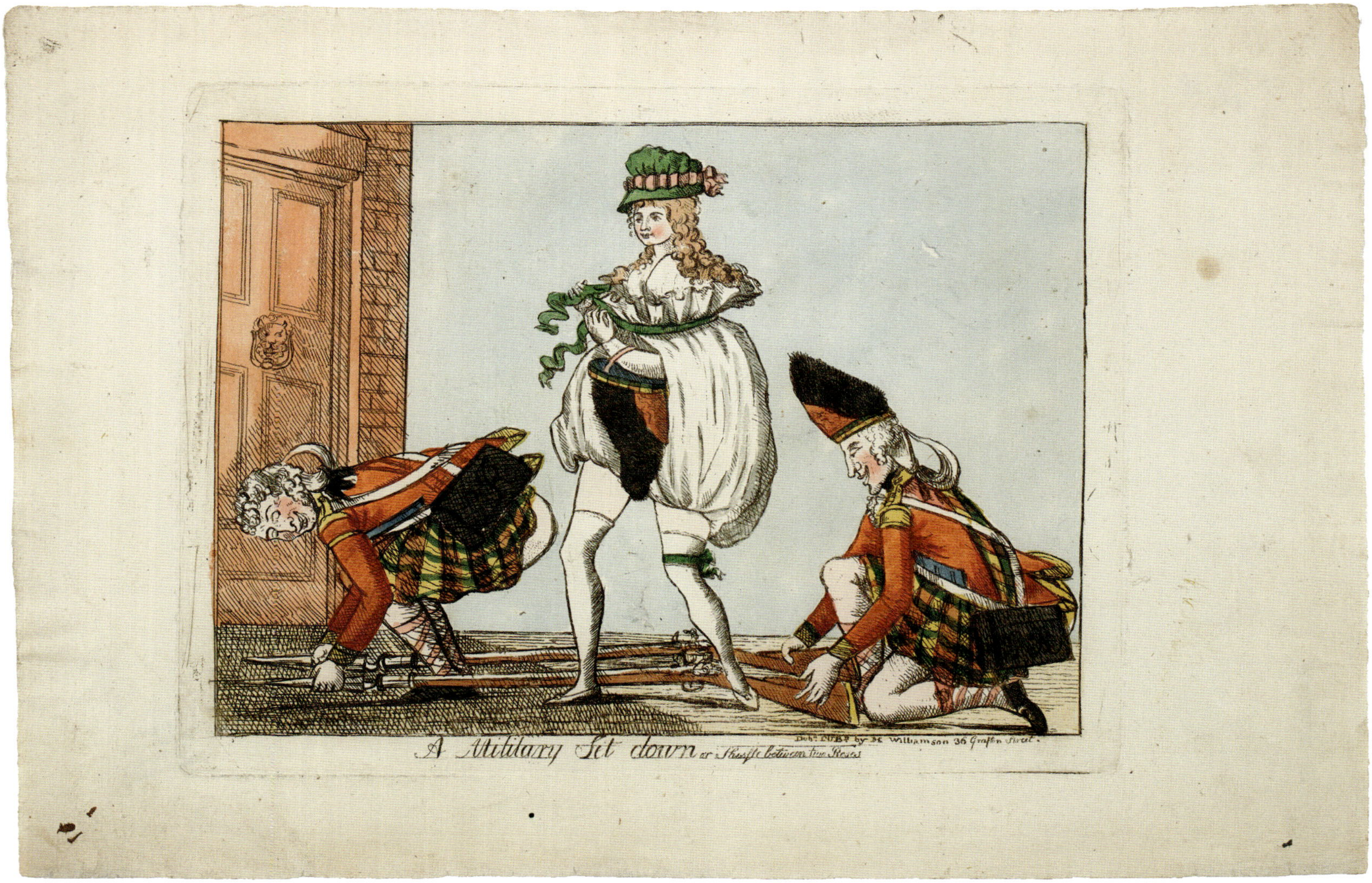

Fig. C8.14
Anon., *A Military Set Down or Thistle between Two Roses*, c. 1797–98, coloured etching (NLI PD 2121 TX 1 (58))

ment's formation oath in its founding landscape, McArt's Fort on the mountain of Cave Hill outside Belfast in Northern Ireland. The day after the oath-swearing ceremony the revolutionaries pitched a tent in Belfast Castle's deer park, where they 'dined and spent the day together deliciously'; touring the wider countryside, the next day was 'one of the most agreeable in their lives', comprising 'an excursion to Ram's Island, a beautiful and romantic spot in Lough Neagh' (Tone 1826, 128). With this leisurely tour of the Belfast region somewhat contradicting any sense of imminent danger, Wolfe Tone and his comrades finally embarked on board the ship *Cincinnatus* for Philadelphia on 13 June. In 1796, Lord Edward Fitzgerald and Arthur O'Connor made a European tour to Hamburg and thence to Switzerland, its revolutionary purpose partially concealed behind a veil of landscape tourism. Their walking tour 'to Berne, Freibourg, Lausanne and Lake Geneva, returning by Lake Neuchatel' was not the innocent appreciation of views and scenes that it appeared. Describing to his mother how they had undertaken the tour 'with true Rousseau enthusiasm', Fitzgerald forbore to mention that O'Connor had continued into France to make plans with General Lazare Hoche for a French military landing at Bantry Bay (Campbell 1904, 107–108). Returning to England, O'Connor's promise to Hoche not to lose a minute with preparations was overwhelmed by the duties of a returning tourist. Only 'after visiting all my beloved friends and giving some little presents to some of them' did he return to Ireland in time for the rebellion (O'Connor n.d., V, 247).

In Wicklow the eye of the roving tourist, concerned with finding the most picturesque prospects, neatly coincided with that of the military road surveyor and strategist. As discussed in other essays in this book, military roads were serviceable for the purposes of tourists, notably in Scotland, where Wade and Caulfeild's 'new roads' accommodated later tours of the Highlands. Yet it was rare for military and tourism projects to proceed blatantly in tandem. That such overlap should occur during the ongoing Irish insurrections of 1798–1809 suggests the power of images and of the landscape itself to both supply and concurrently undermine revolutionary discourse (O'Kane 2017). Irish images of military survey and construction diverge powerfully from Paul Sandby's well-known depictions of surveying parties along Scottish military roads in the 1760s (Bonehill and Daniels 2017; see Fig. S1.9). In those images the kilted highlanders stand tall and equal to the English surveyors and genteel noblemen and women. Together they form polite groupings within successfully negotiated British landscapes of improvement. In contrast Thomas Sautelle Roberts's Wicklow images depict Scottish Highlanders as the hierarchical instructors of a native workforce – mercenaries brought in to tame a foreign landscape and its people (Fig. C8.15). Using Scottish Highlanders to tame the Irish drew the eye away from London, where the origins of centralised and calculated military strategy invariably lay.

Incongruous images of displaced Scottish Highlanders in an Irish 'highland' setting served to highlight the diverging identities of the two countries in the early 1800s. When Wicklow's road was complete, local gentry suggested that the government buy 'the waste mountain land on either side of the military road, and settle a colony there of Highland soldiers': hoping to divert Scottish Gaels seeking to emigrate to America, the proprietors believed that they 'should soon behold a sturdy race of loyal mountaineers, who would not only greatly improve the appearance of the country, but would strengthen the hands of government by rendering what has lately been considered the shelter for lawless rebels, the residence of a population, grateful to those who had rescued them from a transatlantic emigration' (O'Keeffe 1996, 61). The unrealistic aspects of the proposal (most would-be Highland emigrants around 1800 had no desire to be 'rescued' from their planned settlement in North America) must have been evident to even the most inexperienced and naive officials in Dublin Castle.

Amalgamating and overlaying the military and tourist itineraries encouraged improvements that served both agendas. Surveyors such as Robert Fraser, charged with producing a *General View of the Agriculture and Mineralogy, Present State and Circumstances of the County of Wicklow* for the Royal Dublin Society, converted his findings into one of Wicklow's first tour guides. The 'Statistical Survey' he made of the area around Lugnaquilla, Wicklow's highest mountain, saw his host Mr Hume 'pitch a marquee' for the party 'on the top of Knocknamunion, a very high mountain, at the head of the glen of Imale' to provide Fraser with 'a convenient opportunity of choosing a clear atmosphere for exploring the extensive mountain of Lugnaquilla, from the summit of which you obtain by far the most expanded view of the whole range of mountains and adjacent country' (Fraser 1801, 29). Such viewpoints were then perpetuated in other tour guides, and this particular episode was revisited by the Rev. G.N. Wright in order to introduce a frisson of past dangers, now tamed and averted, into his narrative. Fraser's party had 'spent some time beneath a marquee upon the mountains, during which a party of armed rebels lay concealed in a cave amongst the precipices, fortunately both parties were then ignorant of each other's presence' (Wright 1822, 96). Like many Jacobite sites in Scotland, here a 'theatre of war' was reinvented as a tourist attraction, although in the Irish case with an extraordinary simultaneity.

Many of the subsequent narratives of Scottish painting – the connection of laird and people, the melding of Gaelic, Jacobite and British identity and the gradual 'royalisation' of Scotland were not possible in Ireland.[3] As Lord Shelburne had observed in a letter of 1772, the most serious problem continued to be 'the People', who were 'Highlanders in manner and character, without the only virtue in Highlanders – attachment to a chief' (Petty-Fitzmaurice 1837, 65). The apex of chiefdom was royalty and while Ireland might be 'wild', it was emphatically not 'majestic'. Queen Victoria could not live quietly in an Irish Balmoral,

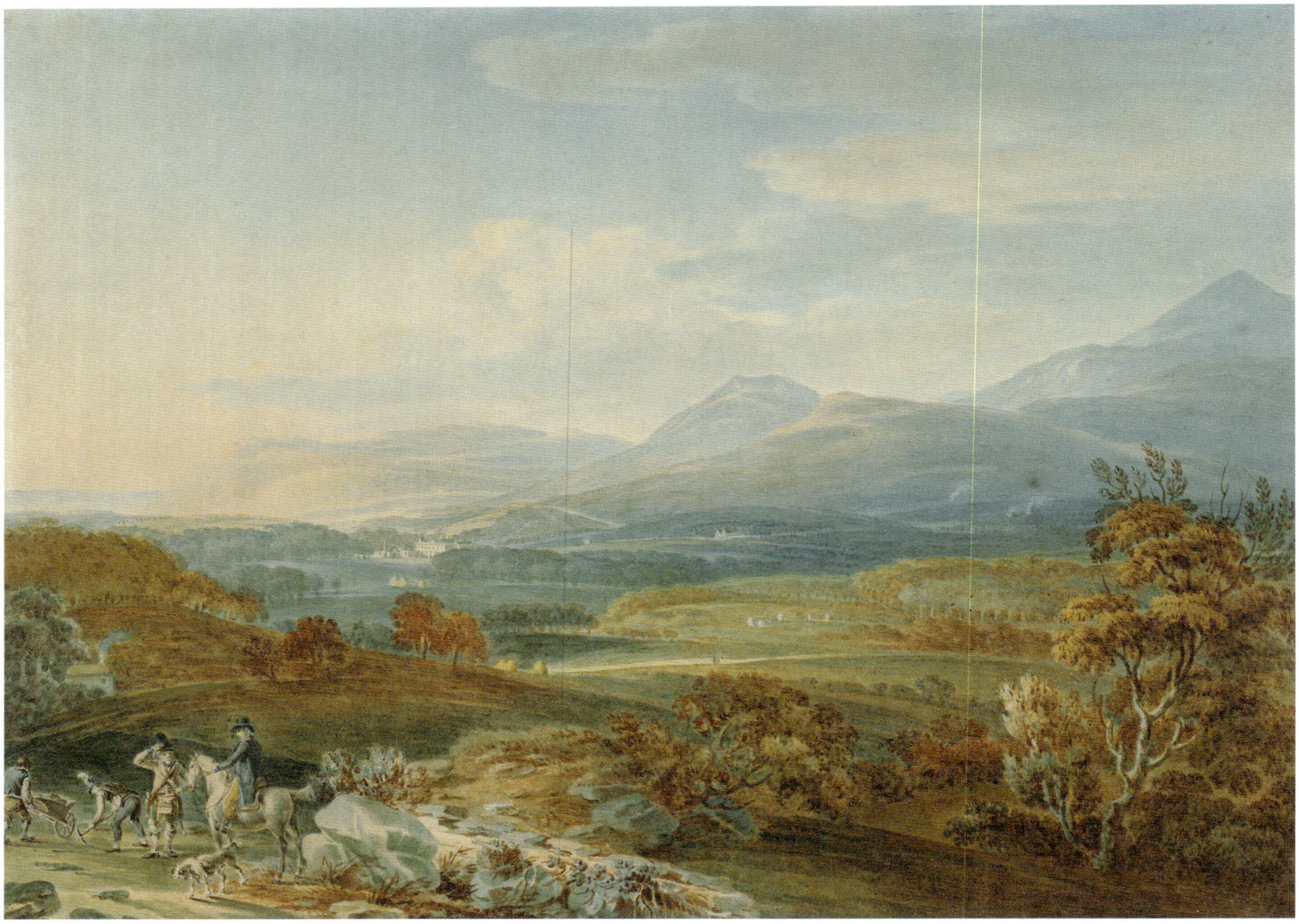

Fig. C8.15
Thomas Sautelle Roberts, *A View of Powerscourt with the Golden Spears to the Right (the Small and Big Sugar Loaves) and Bray Head beyond, in County Wicklow*, 1798, watercolour (PC)

and few Irish landed families could play convincingly at dressing-up in kilts or, like the equally loyal cultural revivalists at Llanover, in Welsh peasant costumes evoking homespun *brethyn* in silk and taffeta. Irish native customs remained ring-fenced by religious and political identities, and while some Irish families could bridge both, they rarely thought it wise to do so. The seventy landscape paintings of Scotland in the Royal Collection are countered by a miserable three of Ireland, two of the three depicting Queen Victoria arriving or leaving Ireland in the royal yacht (Fig. C8.16). The Royal Collection's eight landscape paintings of Wales include such uncomplicated views as Sir Augustus Wall Callcott's *A Scene near Capel-Curig, North Wales* of 1811, an eminently picturesque prospect.[4]

CONCLUSION: WALES, IRELAND, SCOTLAND

'The picturesque' is a highly unstable concept, as shifting and various as the landscapes it describes; yet its use during the Romantic period as a lens through which to perceive and describe Ireland, Wales and Scotland cannot be ignored. As this brief account suggests, picturesque strategies of depicting the peripheries could result in the elision of cultural difference, and a ruthlessly Gilpinian approach to viewing landscape (an approach that happily not even Gilpin always managed to sustain) displays little curiosity about the histories and lived experiences of its aesthetically placed figures. A more capacious form of picturesque, such as that of Paul Sandby, can, however, include

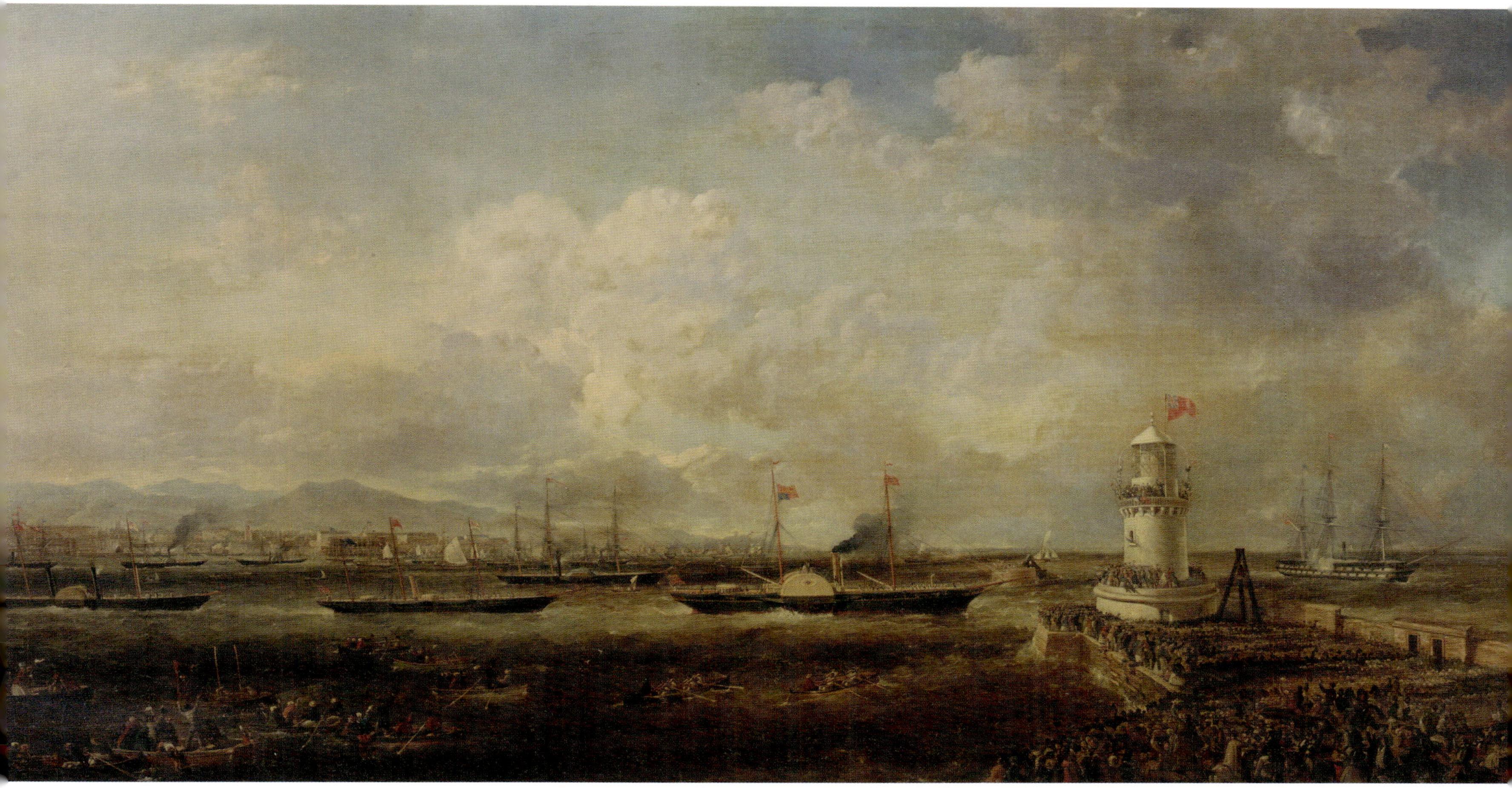

figures whose presence indicates a wealth of potential stories, and written tours are rich in encounters which (although they frequently reveal more about the writer than the subject) at least gesture towards an interest in the lives of others: at their best, as in a writer like Catherine Hutton, they offer an intelligent sympathy. Moreover, the notion of the picturesque, like that of Britishness, is inevitably a collaborative affair; even if mediated by a metropolitan aesthetic, it is not solely imposed from above or outside but developed, as in Johnes's grand project at Hafod, through various kinds of 'transperipheral' relations, borrowings and emulation, which are themselves often the result of the experience of travel around these islands.

NOTES

1 Held at the National Library of Wales, Pennant's extra-illustrated Welsh *Tours* can be viewed online at https://www.library.wales/discover/digital-gallery/pictures/a-tour-in-wales/. For Pennant's involvement with the art of extra-illustration or grangerization see Jones 2018.

2 The pendant pair were sold in SALE 7524, 'Turin London Corfu The Collection of Giorgio Marsan and Umberta Nasi', London, 12–13 December 2007, Lot 310.

3 As witnessed, for example, in the *Wild and Majestic* exhibition and catalogue at the National Museum of Scotland, 26 June–10 November 2019 (Watt and Waine 2019).

4 See https://www.rct.uk/collection, accessed 4.12.2019.

Fig. C8.16
Matthew Kendrick, *Queen Victoria's Departure from Queenstown, Ireland*, 1849, oil on canvas
(RCT RCIN 405384)

BIBLIOGRAPHY

Adam 1758: Robert Adam, letter to James Adam, 17 June 1758, Papers of Clerk family of Penicuik, Midlothian, National Records of Scotland, Edinburgh, GD18/4848.

Adamson 2014: Donald Beck Adamson, 'Commercialisation, Change and Continuity: An Archaeological Study of Rural Commercial Practice in the Scottish Highlands', PhD thesis, University of Glasgow, 2014.

Addison 1726: Joseph Addison, *Dialogues Upon the Usefulness of Ancient Medals*, London, 1726.

Allan 1780: David Allan, letter to Sir William Hamilton, 6 November 1780, Hopetoun archive, Edinburgh, bundle 3482.

Allardyce 1896: James Allardyce, *Historical Papers Relating to the Jacobite Period, 1699–1750*, Vol. II, Aberdeen: Spalding Club, 1896.

Altick 1978: Richard Altick, *The Shows of London*, Cambridge, MA: University of Harvard Press, 1978.

Andrew 1981: P. Andrew, 'Jacob More 1740–1793', PhD thesis, University of Edinburgh, 1981.

Andrews 1989: Malcolm Andrews, *The Search for the Picturesque: Landscape Aesthetics and Tourism in Britain, 1760–1800*, Aldershot: Scholar Press, 1989.

Anon 1821: *The Tour of Doctor Prosody: in Search of the Antique and Picturesque, through Scotland, the Hebrides, the Orkney and Shetland Isles*, London, 1821.

Arrowsmith 1809: Aaron Arrowsmith, *Memoir Relative to the Construction of the Map of Scotland*, London and Edinburgh: Aaron Arrowsmith; Constable and Company, 1809.

Baines 1997: Paul Baines, 'Ossianic Geographies: Fingalian Figures on the Scottish Tour', *Scotlands*, 4:1 (1997), 44–61.

Ballentine 1866: J. Ballentine, *The Life of David Roberts, RA: Compiled from his Journal and Other Sources*, Edinburgh: Adam and Charles Black, 1866.

Banks 1772: Joseph Banks, 'The Journals of Joseph Banks' Voyage up Great Britain's West Coast to Iceland and to the Orkney Isles July to October 1772', *Proceedings of the American Philosophical Society*, 117 (1772), 186–226.

Barker 1796: Robert Barker, 'Specification of the Patent Granted to Mr. Robert Barker . . . Called by Him "La Nature à Coup d'Oeil"', *Repertory of Arts and Manufactures*, 4 (1796), 165–167.

Barrell 2013: John Barrell, *Edward Pugh of Ruthin 1763–1813: 'A Native Artist'*, Cardiff: University of Wales Press, 2013.

Barton 1751: Richard Barton, *Some Remarks, Towards a Full Description of Upper and Lower Lough Lene*, Dublin: S. Powell, 1751.

Bell 2015: Barbara Bell, 'The Scottish Theatrical Landscape leading into the Emergence of the National Drama', *International Journal of Scottish Theatre and Screen*, 8:1 (2015), 27–53.

Bell 2019: Barbara Bell, '. . . Arranged in a Fanciful Manner and in an Ancient Style: The First Scenic Realisations of Scott's Work and the Desire for a New "Realism" on Scottish Stages', *Studies in Scottish Literature* 44:2 (2019), 23–38.

Bermingham 2000: Ann Bermingham, *Learning to Draw: Studies in the Cultural History of a Polite and Useful Art*, New Haven and London: Yale University Press, 2001.

Bermingham 2001: Ann Bermingham, 'Landscape-o-Rama: The Exhibition Landscape and the Rise of Popular Landscape Entertainments', in David H. Solkin (ed.), *Art on the Line: The Royal Academy Exhibitions at Somerset House, 1780–1836*, New Haven and London: Yale University Press, 2001, 127–143.

Bishop 2015: Peter Bishop, *The Mountains of Snowdonia in Art: The Visualisation of Mountain Scenery from the mid-Eighteenth Century to the Present Day,* Gwasg Carreg Gwalch: Llanrwst, 2015.

Black 1992: Jeremy Black, *The British Abroad: The Grand Tour in the Eighteenth Century*, Stroud: Sutton, 1992.

Black 2007: Samuel Johnson, *'To the Hebrides': Samuel Johnson's Journey to the Western Islands of Scotland, and James Boswell's Journal of a Tour to the Hebrides,* ed. Ronald Black, Edinburgh: Birlinn, 2007.

Bonehill 2014: John Bonehill, '"New Scenes drawn by the pencil of Truth": Joseph Banks' Northern Voyage', *Journal of Historical Geography*, 43 (2014), 9–27.

Bonehill and Daniels 2009: John Bonehill and Stephen Daniels (eds), *Paul Sandby: Picturing Britain*, exhibition catalogue, London, 2009.

Bonehill and Daniels 2017: John Bonehill and Stephen Daniels, 'Designs on the Landscape: Paul and Thomas Sandby in North Britain', *Oxford Art Journal*, 40:2 (2017), 223–248.

Boutcher 1775: William Boutcher, *A Treatise on Forest-Trees*, Edinburgh: J. Murray, 1775.

Bowman 1986 [1825]: John Eddowes Bowman, *The Highlands and Islands: A Nineteenth Century Tour*, ed. Celia Miller, Gloucester: Alan Sutton, 1986.

Breadalbane 1771: John Campbell, 3rd Earl of Breadalbane, letter to Jemima Yorke, December 1771, Bedfordshire Archives and Records Service, Bedford, L30/9/17/167.

Bristed 1803: John Bristed, *Anthroplanomenos; or, a Pedestrian Tour through Parts of the Highlands of Scotland, in 1801*, 2 vols, London: J. Wallis, 1803.

Bristow 1995, *Dr Johnson and Mrs Thrale's Tour in North Wales 1774*, edited with an introduction and notes by Adrian Bristow, Wrexham: Bridge Books, 1995.

Brogden 2017: W.A. Brogden, *Ichnographia Rustica: Steven Switzer and the Designed Landscape*, Abingdon and New York: Routledge, 2017.

Brown 1808: Robert Brown, 'Memoir of David Allan, the Scots' Hogarth', in Allan Ramsay, *The Gentle Shepherd*, 2 vols, Edinburgh: W. Martin et al., 1808, Vol. II, 619–631.

Brown 1973 [1891]: Hume Brown, *Early Travellers in Scotland*, Edinburgh: Mercat Press, 1973.

Brown 1980: Iain Gordon Brown, *The Hobby-Horsical Antiquary: A Scottish Character 1640–1830*, Edinburgh: National Library of Scotland, 1980.

Brown 1987: Iain Gordon Brown, 'Modern Rome and Ancient Caledonia: the Union and the Politics of Scottish Culture', in Andrew Hook (ed.), *The History of Scottish Literature, Vol. 2, 1660–1800*, Aberdeen: Aberdeen University Press, 1987.

Brown and Cheape 2010: Capt. John Maclean of Kingairloch, *Witness to Rebellion: John Maclean's Journal of the 'Forty-Five and the Penicuik Drawings*, ed. Iain Gordon Brown and Hugh Cheape (Tuckwell Press, 1996), 2nd edn, Edinburgh: John Donald in association with the National Library of Scotland, 2010.

Browne 1825: [James Browne], *A Critical Examination of Dr Macculloch's Work on the Highlands and Western Islands of Scotland,* Edinburgh and London: D. Lizars, 1825.

Burke 1757: Edmund Burke, *A Philosophical Enquiry into the Origin of our Ideas of the Sublime and Beautiful,* London: R. and J. Dodsley, 1757.

Burke 1958–70 [1765]: Edmund Burke, letter to James Barry [after 19 February 1765], in *The Correspondence of Edmund Burke*, 10 vols, ed. T.W. Copeland *et al.*, Cambridge: Cambridge University Press, 1958–70.

Burrell 1997: *Sir William Burrell's Northern Tour* 1758, ed. John G. Dunbar, East Linton: Tuckwell Press, in association with the European Ethnological Research Centre, and the National Museum of Scotland, 1997.

Burt 1998 [1754]: [Edmund Burt], *Letters from a Gentleman in the North of Scotland to his Friend in London*, introduction by Charles Withers, Edinburgh: Birlinn, 1998.

Byam Shaw 1989: Christina Byam Shaw (ed.), *Pigeon-Holes of Memory: The life and times of Dr John Mackenzie (1803–1886)*, 2nd edn, London: Constable, 1989.

Caimbeul 1785: Aonghas Caimbeul, *Òran Nuadh Ghàidhealach*, Edinburgh: R. Fleming, 1785.

Cameron 1988: A. Cameron, 'Scottish Drama in the Nineteenth Century', in Douglas Gifford (ed.), *The History of Scottish Literature: Vol. 3, Nineteenth Century*, Aberdeen: Aberdeen University Press, 1988.

Campbell 1904: Gerard Campbell, *Edward & Pamela Fitzgerald*, London: Edward Arnold, 1904.

Cant 1981: Ronald G. Cant, 'David Steuart Erskine, 11th Earl of Buchan', in A.S. Bell (ed.), *The Scottish Antiquarian Tradition: Essays to Mark the Bicentenary of the Society of Antiquarians of Scotland and its Museum, 1780–1980*, Edinburgh: John Donald, 1981.

Capon 2019: M. Capon, 'The Structure of Seeing: The Panaoramic Paintings of John Knox and Digital Space', Technical Art History MLitt thesis, Glasgow University, 2019.

Chalmers 1807: George Chalmers, *Caledonia: Or, An Account Historical and Topographic, of North Britain*, 4 vols, London: Cadell and Davies, 1807.

Chambers 1934: Robert Chambers, *History of the Rebellion of 1745–6*, 7th edn, Edinburgh: W & R Chambers, 1934.

Chapman, 1939: R.W. Chapman (ed.), *Johnson's Journey to the Western Islands of Scotland and Boswell's Journal of a Tour to the Hebrides with Samuel Johnson LLD*, London: Oxford University Press, 1939.

Charlesworth 1996: Michael Charlesworth, 'Thomas Sandby Climbs the Hoober Stand: The Politics of Panoramic Drawing in Eighteenth-Century Britain', *Art History*, 19:2 (1996), 247–266.

Cheape 1995: Hugh Cheape, 'Song on the Lowland Shepherds: Popular Reaction to the Highland Clearances', *Scottish Economic and Social History*, 15 (1995), 85–100.

Cheape 2011: Hugh Cheape, 'Song on the Good Points of a Highland Cow', *Review of Scottish Culture*, 23 (2011), 141–144.

Chen 2015: Nancy Wei-Ning Chen, 'Playing with Size and Reality: The Fascination of a Dolls' House World', *Children's Literature in Education*, 46 (2015), 278–295.

Christian 1990: Jessica Christian, 'Paul Sandby and the Military Survey of Scotland', in Nicholas Alfrey and Stephen Daniels (eds), *Mapping the Landscape: Essays on Art and Cartography*, exhibition catalogue, Nottingham, 1990, 18–22.

Christian and Stiller 2000: Jessica Christian and Charles Stiller, *Iona Portrayed: The Island through Artists' Eyes, 1760–1960*, New Iona Press, 2000.

Clan Donald Lands Trust: Typescript 'Report of John Blackadder, Surveyor, on Lord Macdonald's Estates of Sky and North Uist, 1799', University of Hull Archives, Bosville Macdonald Papers GB 50 U DDBM/27/3.

Clayton 1995: Timothy Clayton, 'The Print and the Spread of the Picturesque Ideal', in Dana Arnold (ed.), *The Picturesque in Late Georgian England*, London: Georgian Group, 1995, 11–19.

Cleland 1820: James Cleland, *The Rise and Progress of the City of Glasgow; Comprising an Account of its Ancient and Modern History, Its Trade, Manufactures, Commerce, and Other Concerns*, Glasgow: Young, Gallie & Co., 1820.

Clyde 1998: Robert Clyde, *From Rebel to Hero: The Image of the Highlander, 1745–1830*, East Linton: Tuckwell Press, 1998.

Colbert 2012: Benjamin Colbert, ed., *Travel Writing and Tourism in Britain and Ireland*, Basingstoke: Palgrave Macmillan, 2012.

Coltman 2019: Viccy Coltman, *Art and Identity in Scotland: A Cultural History from the Jacobite Rising of 1745 to Walter Scott*, Cambridge: Cambridge University Press, 2019.

Companion 1820: *Steam Boat Companion, and Stranger's Guide to the Western Islands and Highlands of Scotland*, Glasgow: J. Lumsden & Son, 1820.

Connolly 2019: Claire Connolly, 'Too Rough for Verse? Sea Crossings in Irish Culture', unpublished Parnell Lecture, Cambridge, 2019.

Conolly 1786: Thomas Conolly, letter to his uncle, 19 Nov. 1786, Trinity College Dublin, Mss 3974–3984a, no. 912.

Constantine 2014: Mary-Ann Constantine, '"To Trace Thy Country's Glories to their Source": Dangerous History in Thomas Pennant's *Tour in Wales*', in Porscha Fermanis and John Regan (eds), *Rethinking British Romantic History 1770–1845*, Oxford: Oxford University Press, 2015, 121–143.

Constantine forthcoming: Mary-Ann Constantine, *Curious Travellers: The Welsh Tour 1720–1820*, Oxford: Oxford University Press, forthcoming.

Constantine and Leask 2017: Mary-Ann Constantine and Nigel Leask (eds), *Enlightenment Travel and British Identities: Thomas Pennant's Tours in Scotland and Wales*, London: Anthem Press, 2017.

Constantine and Postic 2019: Mary-Ann Constantine and Fañch Postic (eds & trans) *Letters Written and Received by Théodore Hersart de la Villemarqué During his Visit to Wales and England (1838–1839)*: https://hal.univ-brest.fr/hal-02350747/document

Cooksey 1991: J. Cooksey, *Alexander Nasmyth, A Man of the Scottish Renaissance*, Haddington: Whittingehame House Publishing, 1991.

Cordiner 1788: Charles Cordiner, *Remarkable Ruins, and Romantic Prospects, of North Britain; with Ancient Monuments and Singular Subjects of Natural History*, London: Peter Mazell, 1788.

Coull 1996: James Coull, *The Sea Fisheries of Scotland: A Historical Geography*, Edinburgh: John Donald, 1996.

Craske 1997: Matthew Craske, 'Plan and Control: Design and the Competitive Spirit in Early and Mid-Eighteenth-Century England', *Journal of Design History*, 12:3 (1997), 187–216.

A Critical Examination 1767: *A Critical Examination of the Pictures, Sculptures, Designs in Architecture, Models, Drawings, Prints, &c. Exhibited at the Great Room in Spring-Gardens, Charing-Cross*, London, 1767.

Cullen, Smout and Gibson 1988: L.M. Cullen, T.C. Smout and A. Gibson, 'Wages and Comparative Development in Ireland and Scotland, 1565–1780', in R. Mitchison and P. Roebuck (eds), *Economy and Society in Scotland and Ireland 1500–1939*, Edinburgh: John Donald, 105–116.

Daniell 2006: [William Daniell], *Daniell's Scotland: William Daniell's A Voyage Round the Coast of Scotland and the Adjacent Isles, 1815–22*, 2 vols, Edinburgh: Birlinn in association with the National Library of Scotland, 2006.

Daniels 1988: Stephen Daniels, 'The Political Iconography of Woodland in Later Georgian England', in Denis Cosgrove and Stephen Daniels (eds), *The Iconography of Landscape: Essays on the Symbolic Representation, Design and Use of Past Environments*, Cambridge: Cambridge University Press, 1988, 43–82.

Daniels 1990: Stephen Daniels, 'Goodly Prospects: English Estate Portraiture, 1670–1730', in Nicholas Alfrey and Stephen Daniels (eds), *Mapping the Landscape: Essays on Art and Cartography*, exhibition catalogue, Nottingham, 1990, 9–12.

Daniels and Cosgrove 1988: Stephen Daniels and Dennis Cosgrove, 'Introduction: Iconography and Landscape' in Stephen Daniels and Denis Cosgrove (eds), *The Iconography of Landscape: Essays on the Symbolic Representation, Design and Use of Past Environments*, Cambridge: Cambridge University Press, 1988, 1–10.

Davies 2013: Hywel M. Davies, 'Terror, Treason and Tourism: the French in Pembrokeshire 1797', in Mary-Ann Constantine and Dafydd Johnston (eds), *"Footsteps of Liberty and Revolt": Essays on Wales and the French Revolution* Cardiff: University of Wales Press, 2013, 247–720.

Dean 1992: Dennis Dean, *James Hutton and the History of Geology*, Ithaca, NY: Cornell University Press, 1992.

Deetz 1977: James Deetz, *In Small Things Forgotten: The Archaeology of Early American Life*, New York: Anchor Press, 1977.

Defoe 1724–27: Daniel Defoe, *A Tour Thro' the Whole Island of Great Britain*, 3 vols, London: G. Strahan, 1724–27.

Devine 1994a: T.M. Devine, *Clanship to Crofters' War: The Social Transformation of the Scottish Highlands*, Manchester: Manchester University Press, 1994.

Devine 1994b: T.M. Devine, 'The Making of a Farming Elite? Lowland Scotland, 1750–1850', in T.M. Devine (ed.) *Scottish Elites*, Edinburgh: John Donald, 1994, 62–76.

Devine 2006: T.M. Devine, 'Irish and Scottish Development Revisited', in T.M. Devine (ed.), *Clearance and Improvement: Land, Power and People in Scotland, 1700–1900*, Edinburgh: John Donald, 2006.

Devine 2018: T.M. Devine, *The Scottish Clearances: A History of the Dispossessed*, London: Allen Lane, 2018.

Dingwall 1987: Christopher Dingwall, *The Falls of Bruar: A Garden in the Wild*, privately printed, Dundee: Stevenson Ltd, 1987.

Dingwall 1994: Christopher Dingwall, 'Gardens in the Wild', *Garden History*, 22:2 (1994), 133–156.

Dingwall 1996: Christopher Dingwall, 'Descriptions of Walks in Picturesque and Sublime Landscapes in Scotland which might have been Visited by Thomas Johnes in the Course of a Tour of Scotland [and] Some Additional Notes', Ceredigion County Archives FOH.A/07/03, 1996.

Dingwall 1997: Christopher Dingwall, 'Ossian and Dunkeld: A Hall of Mirrors', *Scotlands*, 4:1 (1997), 62–70.

Dingwall and Aldridge 1999: C.H. Dingwall and Don Aldridge, *The Hall of Mirrors: Reflections on the Sublime and on the Iconography of Ossian at the Hermitage, Dunkeld*, New Arcadian Journal, 47/48, 1999.

Donald 2007: Diana Donald, *Picturing Animals in Britain*, New Haven, CT, and London: Yale University Press, 2007.

Donnachie 2005: Ian Donnachie, 'Historic Tourism to New Lanark and the Falls of Clyde, 1795–1830: The Evidence of Contemporary Visiting Books and Related Sources', *Journal of Tourism and Cultural Change*, 2:3 (2005), 145–163.

Dunbar 1997: John G. Dunbar (ed.), *Sir William Burrell's Northern Tour, 1758*, East Linton: Tuckwell Press, 1997.

Durie 2003: Alastair J. Durie, *Scotland for the Holidays: Tourism in Scotland, c. 1780–1939*, East Linton: Tuckwell, 2003.

Durie 2012: Alastair J. Durie (ed.), *Travels in Scotland, 1788–1881: A Selection from Contemporary Tourist Journals*, Woodbridge: Boydell Press, 2012.

Dwelly 1967: Edward Dwelly, *The Illustrated Gaelic–English Dictionary*, 6th edn, Glasgow: Alex MacLaren and Sons, 1967.

Einberg 2001: E. Einberg, 'Catalogue Raisonne of the Works of George Lambert', *Journal of the Warburg and Courtauld Institutes*, 63 (2001), 111–126.

Ellis 2008: M. Ellis, '"Spectacles within Doors": Panoramas of London in the 1790s', *Romanticism*, 14:2 (2008), 133–148.

Evans 1987: R. Paul Evans, 'Thomas Pennant (1726–1798): The Father of Cambrian Tourists', *Welsh History Review* 13:4 (1987), 395–417.

Evans 2017: R. Paul Evans, '"A Round Jump from Ornithology to Antiquity": the Development of Pennant's Tours', in Mary-Ann Constantine and Nigel Leask (eds), *Enlightenment Travel and British Identities: Thomas Pennant's Tours in Scotland and Wales*, London: Anthem, 2017, 14–37.

Fairfull-Smith 2001: George Fairfull-Smith, *The Foulis Press and the Foulis Academy: Glasgow's Eighteenth-Century School of Art and Design*, Glasgow: Glasgow Art Index, 2001.

Farington 1978–84: Joseph Farington, *The Diary of Joseph Farington*, 17 vols, ed. Kenneth Garlick, Angus Macintyre and Kathryn Cave, New Haven and London: Yale University Press, 1978–84.

Ferguson 1751: James Ferguson, letter to Sir John Clerk of Penicuik, 22 March 1751, National Archives of Scotland, Edinburgh, GD18/4676.

Finley 1983: Gerald Finley, *George Heriot: Postmaster-Painter of the Canadas*, Toronto: University of Toronto Press, 1983.

FitzGerald 1972: Desmond FitzGerald, the Knight of Glin, 'Lord Orrery's travels in Kerry, 1735', *Journal of the Kerry Archaeological and Historical Society*, 5 (1972), 46–59.

Fleet, Wilkes and Withers 2012: Christopher Fleet, Margaret Wilkes and Charles W.J. Withers, *Scotland: Mapping the Nation*, Edinburgh: Birlinn, 2012.

Fleming 1962a: John Fleming, *Robert Adam and His Circle: In Edinburgh and Rome*, London: J. Murray, 1962.

Fleming 1962b: J. Fleming, 'Enigma of a Rococo Artist', *Country Life*, 131 (1962), 1224–1226.

Ford 1997: Brinsley Ford, *A Dictionary of British and Irish Travellers in Italy, 1701–1800*, New Haven and London: Yale University Press, 1997.

Forsyth 1900: William Forsyth, *In the Shadow of Cairngorm: Chronicles of the United Parishes of Abernethy and Kincardine*, Inverness: Northern Counties Publishing Company, 1900.

Fox 2009: Celina Fox, *The Arts of Industry in the Age of Enlightenment*, New Haven, CT, and London: Yale University Press, 2009.

Fraser 1801: *General View of the Agriculture and Mineralogy, Present State and Circumstances of the County of Wicklow*, Dublin: Royal Dublin Society, 1801.

Furniss 2018: Tom Furniss, *Discovering the Footsteps of Time: Geological Travel Writing about Scotland, 1700–1820*, Edinburgh: Edinburgh University Press, 2018.

Gascoigne 2003: John Gascoigne, *Joseph Banks and the English Enlightenment: Useful Knowledge and Polite Culture*, Cambridge: Cambridge University Press, 2003.

Gidal 2015: Eric Gidal, *Ossianic Unconformities: Bardic Poetry in the Industrial Age*, Charlottesville, VA and London: University of Virigina Press, 2015.

Gifford 1989: John Gifford, *William Adam, 1689–1748: A Life and Times of Scotland's Universal Architect*, Edinburgh: Mainstream, 1989.

Gilpin 1786: William Gilpin, *Observations, Relative Chiefly to Picturesque Beauty, Made in the Year 1772, on Several Parts of England; Particularly the Mountains, and Lakes of Cumberland, and Westmoreland*, 2 vols, London: R. Blamire, 1786.

Gilpin 1789a [1782]: William Gilpin, *Observations on the River Wye and Several Parts of South Wales, &c. Relative chiefly to Picturesque Beauty: Made in the Summer of the Year 1770*, 2nd edn, London: R. Blamire, 1789.

Gilpin 1789b: William Gilpin, *Observations, Relative Chiefly to Picturesque Beauty, Made in the Year 1776, on Several Parts of Great Britain, Particularly the High-Lands of Scotland*, 2 vols, London: R. Blamire, 1789.

Glacken, 1967: Clarence J. Glacken, *Traces on the Rhodian Shore: Nature and Culture in Western Thought from Ancient Times to the End of the Eighteenth Century*, Berkeley, CA: University of California Press, 1967.

Glasgow Theatrical Register 1805: Glasgow Theatrical Register, Containing Cursory Remarks on the Performances at The Theatre Royal, Crawford and McKenzie, Glasgow. Part VI, No. 1, 1 May 1805. Glasgow University Sp Coll Bh12-h.35.

Glendening 1997: John Glendening, *The High Road: Romantic Tourism, Scotland and Literature, 1720–1820*, Basingstoke: Macmillan, 1997.

Glover 2017: Julian Glover, *Man of Iron: Thomas Telford and the Building of Britain*, London and New Haven: Yale University Press, 2017.

Gold and Gold 1995: J.R. Gold and M.M. Gold, *Imagining Scotland: Tradition, Representation and Promotion in Scottish Tourism since 1750*, Aldershot: Scolar Press, 1995.

Golinski, 2007: Jan Golinski, *British Weather and the Climate of Enlightenment*, Chicago, IL: University of Chicago Press, 2007.

Gough 1761: Richard Gough, 'Tour of South Wales 1761', Bodleian MS Top Gen e.27.

Graham 1818: Elizabeth Susannah Graham, 'Tour in Scotland', unpublished MS, 1818: https://editions.curioustravellers.ac.uk/doc/0062

Grant 1898: *Memoirs of A Highland Lady: The Autobiography of Elizabeth Grant of Rothiemurchus 1797–1830*, ed. Lady J.M. Strachey, London: John Murray.

Grant 1931: I.F. Grant, *In the Tracks of Montrose*, London: Alexander Maclehose, 1931.

Grant 1941: William Grant (ed.), *The Scottish National Dictionary*, Vol. II, Edinburgh: Scottish National Dictionary Association, 1941.

Grenier 2005: Katherine Haldane Grenier, *Tourism and Identity in Scotland, 1770–1914: Creating Caledonia*, Abingdon: Ashgate, 2005.

Grose 1791: Francis Grose, *The Grumbler*, London, 1791.

Guldi 2012: Jo Guldi, *Roads to Power: Britain Invents the Infrastructure State*, Cambridge, MA: Harvard University Press, 2012.

Hagglund 2010: Betty Hagglund, *Tourists and Travellers: Women's Non-fictional Writing about Scotland, 1770–1830*, Bristol: Channel View Publications, 2010.

Haldane 1952: A.R.B. Haldane, *The Drove Roads of Scotland*, Edinburgh: Nelson, 1952.

Haldane 1962: A.R.B. Haldane, *New Ways through the Glens: Highland Road, Bridge and Canal Makers in the Early Nineteenth Century*, Newton Abbot: David & Charles, 1962.

Haldane 1997: A.R.B. Haldane, *The Drove Roads of Scotland*, Edinburgh: Birlinn, 1997.

Hall and Hall 1841: Samuel Carter Hall and Anna Maria Hall, *Ireland: Its Scenery, Character* etc., London, 1841.

Harris 1979: John Harris, *The Artist and the Country House*, London: Sotheby's, 1979.

Harris 2000: Bob Harris, 'Scotland's Herring Fisheries and the Prosperity of the Nation, c. 1660–1760', *Scottish Historical Review*, 79: 207 (2000), 39–60.

Harris 2006: Bob Harris, 'Towns, Improvement and Cultural Change in Georgian Scotland: the Evidence of the Angus Burghs, c. 1760–1820', *Urban History*, 33:2 (2006), 195–212.

Harris 2011a: Bob Harris, 'Cultural Change in Provincial Scottish Towns, c. 1700–1 820', *The Historical Journal*, Vol. 54, No. 1 (2011), pp. 105–41

Harris 2011b: Bob Harris, 'The Enlightenment, Towns and Urban Society in Scotland, *c.* 1760–1820', *English Historical Review*, 126:522 (2011), 1097–1136.

Henderson and Dickson 1994: D.M. Henderson and J.H. Dickson (eds), *A Naturalist in the Highlands: James Robertson, His Life and Travels in Scotland, 1767–1771*, Edinburgh: Scottish Academic Press, 1994.

Heron 1793: Robert Heron, *Observations Made in a Journey through the Western Counties of Scotland; in the Autumn of MDCCXCII*, 2 vols, Perth: R. Morison, 1793.

Hitchings 2005: Henry Hitchings, *Dr. Johnson's Dictionary: The Extraordinary Story of the Book that Defined the World*, London: John Murray, 2005.

Hodson 2011: Yolande Hodson, '"The Lucubrations of his Leisure Hours": William Roy's *Military Antiquities of the Romans in Britain 1793*', *Scottish Geographical Journal*, 127:2 (2011), 117–132.

Holloway 1987: J. Holloway, *Jacob More*, Edinburgh: National Galleries of Scotland, 1987.

Holloway 1994: J. Holloway, *The Norie Family*, Edinburgh: National Galleries of Scotland, 1994.

Holloway and Errington 1978: James Holloway and Lindsay Errington, *The Discovery of Scotland: The Appreciation of Scottish Scenery through Two Centuries of Painting*, Edinburgh: National Gallery of Scotland, 1978.

Hope 1768: John Hope, letter to John Stuart, 3rd Earl of Bute, 12 August 1768, Mount Stuart archive, Isle of Bute, BU 164 (1768).

House and Dingwall 2003: Syd House and Christopher Dingwall, '"A Nation of Planters": Introducing the New Trees, 1650–1900', in T.C. Smout (ed.), *People and Woods in Scotland: A History*, Edinburgh: Edinburgh University Press, 2003, 128–157.

Hunter 2016: James Hunter, *Set Adrift Upon the World: The Sutherland Clearances*, Edinburgh: Birlinn, 2016.

Hutchinson 2006: Roger Hutchinson, *Calum's Road*, Edinburgh: Birlinn, 2006.

Hutton 1799: Catherine Hutton, letter to Thomas Hutton (Caernarvon, 30 August 1799), National Library of Wales MS 19079C.

Hutton 1800: Catherine Hutton, letter to Thomas Hutton (Shrewsbury, 21 September 1800), National Library of Wales MS 19079C. Editions of Catherine Hutton's tours are now available at: https://editions.curioustravellers.ac.uk/tours

Hutton 1899: James Hutton, *Theory of the Earth*, ed. A. Geike, 3 vols, London, 1899.

Hutton and Leask 2017: Ailsa Hutton and Nigel Leask, '"The First Antiquary of His Country": Robert Riddell's Extra-Illustrated and Annotated Volumes of Thomas Pennant's Tours in Scotland', in Mary-Ann Constantine and Nigel Leask (eds), *Enlightenment Travel and British Identities: Thomas Pennant's Tours in Scotland and Wales*, London: Anthem, 2017, 123–140.

Hyde 1988: Ralph Hyde, *Panoramania! The Art and Entertainment of the 'All-embracing' View*, exhibition catalogue, London: Guildhall, 1988.

Irwin 1972: David Irwin, 'Jacob More, Neo-Classical Landscape Painter', *Burlington Magazine*, 114:836 (1972), 774–779.

Irwin 1977: David Irwin, 'Charles Steuart, Landscape-Painter', *Apollo* (October 1977), 300–303.

Jackson 1793: John Jackson, *History of the Scottish Stage*, Edinburgh, 1793.

Jamieson 1818: [Edmund Burt], *Letters from the North of Scotland*, ed. Robert Jamieson, 5th edn, 2 vols, London: Rest Fenner, 1818.

Jarvis 1997: Robin Jarvis, *Romantic Writing and Pedestrian Travel*, Basingstoke: Macmillan, 1997.

Jenkins 1972: Ralph Jenkins, '"And I travelled after him": Johnson and Pennant in Scotland', *Texas Studies in Literature and Language*, 14:3 (1972), 445–462.

Johnson 1775: Samuel Johnson, *A Journey to the Western Islands of Scotland*, London: W. Strahan and T. Cadell, 1775.

Johnson and Boswell 1984: Samuel Johnson and James Boswell, *A Journey to the Western Islands of Scotland and The Journal of a Tour to the Hebrides*, ed. with intro. by Peter Levi, London: Penguin, 1984.

Jones 1851: William D. Jones, *Records of the Royal Military Academy*, London: Parker, Furnival and Parker, 1851.

Jones 1985: Jean Jones, 'James Hutton's Agricultural Research and Life as a Farmer', *Annals of Science*, 42 (1985), 573–601.

Jones 2018: Ffion Mair Jones, 'A New Look at the Correspondence of Thomas Pennant and Richard Bull (1773–1798)': https://editions.curioustravellers.ac.uk/pages/new_look_Pennant_Bull.html

Jonsson 2013: Fredrik Albritton Jonsson, *Enlightenment's Frontier: The Scottish Highlands and the Origins of Environmentalism*, New Haven, CT: Yale University Press, 2013.

Jonsson 2016: Fredrik Albritton Jonsson, 'Scottish Tobacco and Rhubarb: The Natural Order of Civil Cameralism in the Scottish Enlightenment', *Eighteenth-Century Studies*, 49:2 (2016), 129–147.

Keay 1984: John Keay, *Highland Drove*, London: John Murray, 1984.

Kennedy 1898: Rev. John Kennedy, 'Poems from the MacLagan MSS', *Transactions of the Gaelic Society of Inverness*, 22 (1897–1898), 168–172.

Kennedy 2003: Andrew Kennedy, 'Representing the Three Kingdoms: Hanoverianism and the Virtuosi's Museum', in Mark Dorrian and Gillian Rose (eds), *Deterritorialisations: Revisioning Landscape and Politics*, London and New York: Black Dog, 2003, 272–283.

Kennedy-Fraser and MacLeod 1917: Marjory Kennedy-Fraser and Kenneth MacLeod, *Songs of the Hebrides*, Volume II, London: Boosey & Co.

King 1987: Elspeth King, 'Popular Culture in Glasgow', in R.A. Cage (ed.), *The Working Class in Glasgow 1750–1914*, Beckenham: Croom Helm, 1987, 142–188.

Kinsley 1968: *Poems and Songs of Robert Burns*, ed. James Kinsley, 3 vols, Oxford: Clarendon Press, 1968.

Kinsley 2008: Zoë Kinsley, *Women Writing the Home Tour, 1682–1812*, Aldershot: Ashgate, 2008.

Knox 1785: John Knox, *A View of the British Empire, More Especially Scotland: With Some Proposals for the Improvement of that Country, the Extension of Its Fisheries, and the Relief of the People*, 2 vols, London: J. Walter, 1785.

Knox 1786: John Knox, *A Discourse on the Expediency of Establishing Fishing Stations, or Small Towns, in the Highlands of Scotland and the Hebride Islands*, London: J. Walter, 1786.

Koerner 1999: Lisbet Koerner, *Linnaeus: Nature and Nation*, Cambridge, MA: Harvard University Press, 1999.

Lamont Brown 1973: Raymond Lamont Brown, *Robert Burns's Tours of the Highlands and Stirlingshire*, 1787, Ipswich: Boydell, 1973.

Landscape Magazine 1793: *The Landscape Magazine: Containing Preceptive Principles of Landscape*, London: C. Taylor, 1793.

Leask 2010: Nigel Leask, *Robert Burns and Pastoral: Poetry and Improvement in Late Eighteenth Century Scotland*, Oxford: Oxford University Press.

Leask 2014: Robert Burns, 'Tours of the Highlands and Lowlands in 1787', newly transcribed from MS and fully annotated, ed. Nigel Leask, *Commonplace Books, Tour Journals and Miscellaneous Prose, Oxford Edition of the Works of Robert Burns*, Vol. 1, Oxford: Oxford University Press, 2014, Ch. 7.

Leask 2016: Nigel Leask, 'Fingalian Topographies: *Ossian* and the Highland Tour, 1760–1805', *Journal for Eighteenth-Century Studies*, 39:2 (2016), 183–196.

Leask 2019: Nigel Leask, 'Philosophical Vagabonds: Pedestrianism, Politics and Improvement on the Scottish Tour', *Studies in Scottish Literature*, 45:1 (2019), 3–22.

Leask 2020: Nigel Leask, *Stepping Westward: Writing the Highland Tour, c. 1720–1830*, Oxford: Oxford University Press, 2020.

Leneman 1986: Leah Leneman, *Living in Atholl; A Social History of the Estates 1685–1785*, Edinburgh: Edinburgh University Press, 1986.

Leyden 1903: John Leyden, *Journal of a Tour in the Highlands and Western Isles of Scotland in 1800*, Edinburgh: Blackwood, 1903.

Lightfoot 1789: John Lightfoot, *Flora Scotica: Or A Systematic Arrangement, in the Linnaean Method, of the Native Plants of Scotland and the Hebrides*, 2nd edn, 2 vols, London, BHJC, 1789.

Lindsay and Cosh 1973: I.G. Lindsay and Mary Cosh, *Inveraray and the Dukes of Argyll*, Edinburgh: Edinburgh University Press, 1973.

McClure 1974: Ian McClure, *An Exhibition of the Work of the Artist John Knox 1778–1845 and the Glasgow of his Day*, exhibition catalogue, Glasgow, 1974.

Macculloch 1824: John Macculloch, *The Highlands and Western Isles of Scotland . . . in Letters to Sir Walter Scott, Bart*, 4 vols, London: Longman, 1824.

Macfarlane 2012: Robert Macfarlane, *The Old Ways: A Journey on Foot*, London: Penguin, 2012.

MacGeorge 1884: A. MacGeorge, *William Leighton Leitch: A Memoir*, London: Blackie, 1884.

MacGregor 1878: Rev. Alexander MacGregor, 'John MacDonald – An Adherent of Prince Charles', *Celtic Magazine*, 3 (1877–1878), 462–466.

McHugh 2018: Kirsty McHugh, 'Sightseeing, Social Climbing, Steamboats and Sex: Anne Lister's 1828 Tour of Scotland', *Studies in Travel Writing*, 22:4 (2018), 420–435.

Macinnes 1996: Allan I. Macinnes, *Clanship, Commerce and the House of Stuart, 1603–1788*, East Lothian: Tuckwell Press, 1996.

Macinnes 2015: Allan I. Macinnes, 'Contrasts and Tensions: Highlands and Lowlands in the 19th Century', in Christopher Maclachlan and Ronald Renton (eds), *Gael and Lowlander in Scottish Literature: Cross-Currents in Scottish Writing in the 19th Century*, Glasgow: ASLS, 2015, 1–21.

MacInnes 1894: Rev. Duncan MacInnes, 'Notes of Gaelic Technical Terms', *Transactions of the Gaelic Society of Inverness*, 19 (1893–1894), 214–216.

Maciver 1795: Rev. Colin Maciver, 'The Parish of Glenelg', *The Statistical Account of Scotland*, Vol. 16, Edinburgh, 1795, 265–274.

Mackay 1919: J.G. Mackay, 'Social Life in Skye from Legend and Story – Part I', *Transactions of the Gaelic Society of Inverness*, 29 (1914–1919), 260–290.

MacKay 1980: Margaret M. MacKay, ed., *The Rev Dr John Walker's Report on the Hebrides of 1764 and 1771*, Edinburgh: John Donald, 1980.

Mackenzie 1922: Osgood Hanbury Mackenzie, *A Hundred Years in the Highlands*, London: Edward Arnold, 1922.

Macleod 2012: Anne Macleod, *'From an Antique Land': Visual Representations of the Highlands and Islands, 1700–1880*, Edinburgh: John Donald, 2012.

MacLeòid 2019: Seonachan MacLeòid, 'Breacais, An t-Eilean Sgitheanach', fiosrachadh pearsanta, 12 March 2019.

Macmillan 1973: J.D. Macmillan, 'The Earlier Career of Alexander Runciman and the Influences that Shaped His Style', PhD Thesis, University of Edinburgh 1973.

McNeil 2007: Kenneth McNeil, *Scotland, Britain, Empire: Writing the Highlands, 1760–1860*, Columbus: Ohio State University Press, 2007.

Macpherson 1762: James Macpherson, *Fingal: An Ancient Epic Poem, in Six Books*, London: T. Becket, 1762.

Macpherson 1996: James Macpherson, *The Poems of Ossian and Related Works*, ed. Howard Gaskill, introduction by Fiona Stafford, Edinburgh: Edinburgh University Press, 1996.

Macve 2004: Jennifer Macve, *The Hafod Landscape: An Illustrated History and Guide*, Hafod Trust, 2004.

Marks 1998: Arthur Marks, 'Testaments to a Friendship: David Wilkie's Portraits of Walter Scott', *Studies in Romanticism*, 37:3 (1998), 351–393.

Matheson 2007: C.S. Matheson, 'Vagrant Dwellers: Tours and Tourism', Tintern Abbey and Romantic Tourism in Wales, 2007: https:/deep blue.lib.umich.edu/ bitstream/handle/2027.42/144575/ tours.html

Matheson 2013: C.S. Matheson, '"I Wanted Some Intelligent Guide": Charles Heath and the *Historical and Descriptive Accounts of the Ancient and Present State of Tintern Abbey*', *Romanticism* 19:2 (2013), 138–152.

Maxwell 1743: R. Maxwell (ed.), *Select Transactions of the Honourable the Society of Improvers in the Knowledge of Agriculture in Scotland*, Edinburgh, 1743.

Meacock 2019: Jo Meacock, Unpublished transcript of Friends of Glasgow Museum Lecture, Glasgow, 2019

Meek 1995: Donald E. Meek (ed.), *Tuath is Tighearna: Tenants and Landlords*, Scottish Gaelic Texts Society, Edinburgh: Scottish Academic Press, 1995.

Meissner 1820: 'A Pedestrian Tour through the Highlands, by Dr Meissner', *New Monthly Magazine*, 14 (1820), 57–63.

Merwe 1979: Pieter Van der Merwe, 'The Life and Theatrical Career of Clarkson Stansfield', PhD thesis, University of Bristol, 1979.

Michasiw 1992: Kim Ian Michasiw, 'Nine Revisionist Theses on the Picturesque', *Representations*, 38 (1992), 76–100.

Miers 2017: Mary Miers, *Highland Retreats: The Architecture and Interiors of Scotland's Romantic North*, New York: Rizzoli, 2017.

Mitchell 1880: Arthur Mitchell, *The Past in the Present: What is Civilisation?*, Edinburgh: David Douglas, 1880.

Mitchell 1901: Sir Arthur Mitchell, 'A List of Travels, Tours, Journeys, Voyages, Cruises, Excursions, Wanderings, Rambles, Visits, Etc., Relating to Scotland', *Proceedings of the Society of Antiquaries of Scotland*, 35 (1901), 431–638. Supplements in 36 (1905), 500–527, and 44 (1910), 390–405.

Mitchell 1971 [1883/1884]: Joseph Mitchell, *Reminiscences of my Life in the Highlands*, 2 vols, Newton Abbot: David & Charles, 1971.

Monthly Review 1775: *The Monthly Review, or Literary Journal*, 51 (January 1775)

Moore-Colyer 1992: Richard Moore Colyer (ed.), *A Land of Pure Delight: Selections from the Letters of Thomas Johnes of Hafod*, Llandysul: Gomer, 1992.

Morison 1793: Rev. Roderick Morison, 'The Parish of Kintail', *The Statistical Account of Scotland*, Vol. 6, Edinburgh, 1793, 242–254.

Munro 1994: Neil Munro, *The New Road*, introduction by Brian Osborne, Edinburgh: B&W, 1994.

Murchison 1988: Thomas Moffat Murchison (ed.), *Sgriobhaidhean Choinnich MhicLeoid. The Gaelic Prose of Kenneth MacLeod*, Edinburgh: Scottish Gaelic Texts Society, 1988.

Murray 1799: Hon. Mrs Sarah Murray of Kensington, *A Companion and Useful Guide to the Beauties of Scotland*, London, printed for the author, 1799.

Myrone 2009: Felicity Myrone, '"The Monarch of the Plain": Paul Sandby and topography', in John Bonehill and Stephen Daniels (eds), *Paul Sandby: Picturing Britain*, exhibition catalogue, London, 2009, 56–63.

Nasmyth 1885: *James Nasmyth: Engineer, An Autobiography*, ed. Samuel Smiles, 2002 Blackmask Online: www.blackmask.com [accessed 27 June 2019]

Nenadic 1999: Stana Nenadic, 'Romanticism and the Urge to Consume in the First Half of the Nineteenth Century', in Maxine Berg and Helen Clifford (eds), *Consumers and Luxury: Consumer Culture in Europe 1650–1850*, Manchester: Manchester University Press, 1999, 208–227.

Newton 2006: Michael Newton (ed.), *Dùthchas nan Gàidheal: Selected Essays of John MacInnes*, Edinburgh: Birlinn, 2006.

Nic a' Phearsoin 1891: Mairi Nic a' Phearsoin, *Dain agus Orain Ghaidhlig*. Inbhirnis: A agus U MacCoinnich, 1891.

Nichols 1814: John Nichols, *Literary Anecdotes of the Eighteenth Century*, Vol. 8, London, published for the author, 1814.

Nickelsen 2018: Kärin Nickelsen, 'Image and Nature', in H.A. Curry, N. Jardine, J. Andrew and E.C. Spary (eds), *Worlds of Natural History*, Cambridge: Cambridge University Press, 2018.

Nicolson 1881: Alexander Nicolson (ed.), *A Collection of Gaelic Proverbs*, Edinburgh: MacLachlan and Stewart, 1881.

O'Connor [n.d.]: Arthur O'Connor's Mss, Le Chateau de Bignon, Loiret, France, n.d.

O'Kane 2013: Finola O'Kane, *Ireland and the Picturesque: Design, Landscape Painting and Tourism in Ireland, 1700–1840*, New Haven and London: Yale University Press, 2013.

O'Kane 2017: Finola O'Kane, 'The Military Roads of Country Wicklow', British Library 'Picturing Places' website: https://www.bl.uk/picturing-places/articles/ the-military-roads-of-county-wicklow

O'Kane 2019: Finola O'Kane, 'A Picturesque Tour of Killarney', British Library 'Picturing Places' website: https://www.bl.uk/picturing-places/articles/a-picturesque-tour-of-killarney

O'Keeffe 1996: Peter J. O'Keeffe, *Alexander Taylor's Roadworks in Ireland 1780–1827*, Institute of Asphalt Technology, Irish Branch, 1996.

Oleksijczuk 2011: Denise Oleksijczuk, *The First Panoramas: Visions of British Imperialism*, Minneapolis, MN: University of Minnesota Press, 2011.

Ousby 1992: Ian Ousby (ed.), *James Plumptre's Britain: The journals of a tourist in the 1790s*, London: Hutchinson, 1992.

Parry 1995: Graham Parry, *The Trophies of Time: English Antiquarians of the Seventeenth Century*, Oxford: Oxford University Press, 1995.

Paterson 1777: George Paterson, 'Notes Mark't Down for the Perusal of the Earl of Butes Commissioners Respecting the Management of the Island of Bute', June 1777, Mount Stuart archive, Isle of Bute, BU/162/6 (1754–1777).

Pennant 1771a: Thomas Pennant, *A Tour in Scotland, MDCCLXIX*, Chester: J. Monk, 1771.

Pennant 1771b: Thomas Pennant, letter to George Paton, 24 April 1771, National Library of Scotland, ADV. MSS. 29.5.5, 2 vols.

Pennant 1772: Thomas Pennant, letter to George Paton, 13 May 1772, NLS ADV. MSS. 29.5.5, 2 vols.

Pennant 1774a [1772]: Thomas Pennant, *A Tour in Scotland, 1769*, 3rd edn, Warrington: W. Eyres, 1774.

Pennant 1774b: Thomas Pennant, *A Tour in Scotland, and Voyage to the Hebrides, 1772*, Chester: J. Monk, 1774.

Pennant 1784: Thomas Pennant, *A Tour in Wales*, 2 vols, London: Henry Hughes, 1784.

Pennant 1790 [1774]: Thomas Pennant, *A Tour in Scotland and Voyage to the Hebrides, 1772*, 2 vols, London, 1790.

Pennant 1793: Thomas Pennant, *The Literary Life*, London, 1793.

Pennant 1979: Thomas Pennant, *A Tour in Scotland, 1769*, 3rd edn, facsimile with intro by Barry Knight, Perth: Melven Press, 1979.

Pennant 1998: Thomas Pennant, *A Tour in Scotland and Voyage to the Hebrides, 1772*, introduction by Charles W.J. Withers, Edinburgh: Birlinn, 1998.

Petty-Fitzmaurice 1837: Henry Petty-Fitzmaurice (Marquis of Lansdowne), *Glanerought and the Petty-Fitzmaurices*, Oxford, 1837.

Piozzi 1789: Hester Piozzi, 'Journey through the North of England & Part of Scotland Wales &c', John Rylands Library, University of Manchester, 133 Eng MS, 623: https://editions.curioustravellers.ac.uk/ doc/0005

Pittock 2016: Murray Pittock, *Culloden*, Oxford: Oxford University Press, 2016.

Pochin Mould 1950: D.D.C. Pochin Mould, *The Roads from the Isles: A Study of the North-West Highland Tracks*, Edinburgh: Oliver and Boyd, 1950.

Pococke 1887: Rev. Richard Pococke, *Tours in Scotland 1747, 1750, 1760*, ed. Daniel William Kemp, Scottish History Society, 1st series, Vol. 1, Edinburgh, 1887.

Prebble 2000: John Prebble, *The King's Jaunt: George IV in Edinburgh*, Edinburgh: Birlinn.

Quarterly Review 1810: *Quarterly Review*, 3 (May 1810), 6.

Rackwitz 2007: Martin Rackwitz, *Travels to Terra Incognita: The Scottish Highlands and Hebrides in Early Modern Travellers Accounts c. 1600–1800*, Berlin and New York: Munchen and Waxman Munster, 2007.

Rauschenberg 1973: Roy A. Rauschenberg (ed.), 'The Journal of Joseph Banks's Voyage Up Great Britain's West Coast to Iceland and to the Orkney Isles July to October 1772', *Proceedings of the American Philosophical Society*, 117:3 (1973), 186–226.

Redford 1992: Bruce Redford (ed.), *Letters of Samuel Johnson, Volume II, 1773–76*, Oxford: Clarendon Press, 1992.

Richards 2002: Eric Richards, *The Highland Clearances: People, Landlords and Rural Turmoil*, Edinburgh: Birlinn, 2002.

Robertson 1794: Rev. James Robertson, 'Parish of Callander', in *Statistical Account of Scotland*, vol. 11, Edinburgh, 574–627.

Robertson 1799: Rev. James Robertson, *General View of the Agriculture in the County of Perth*, Perth, 1799.

Robertson 1941: Rev. A.E. Robertson, *Old Tracks, Cross-country Routes and 'Coffin Roads' in the North-west Highlands*. Edinburgh: Darien Press, 1941.

Robinson 2006: A.R.B. Robinson, *Seeking the Scots: An English Woman's Journey in 1807*, Skelton: A.R.B. Robinson, 2006.

Rockett and Rockett 2011: K. Rockett and E. Rockett, *Magic Lantern, Panorama and Moving Picture Shows in Ireland 1786–1909*, Dublin: Four Courts Press, 2011.

Rogers 1983: Pat Rogers (ed.), *Jonathan Swift, Complete Poems*, London: Penguin, 1983.

Rogers 1993: Pat Rogers (ed.), *Johnson and Boswell in Scotland: A Journey to the Hebrides*, New Haven and London: Yale University Press, 1993.

Rosenfeld 1981: S. Rosenfeld, *Georgian Scene Painter and Scene Painting*, Cambridge: Cambridge University Press, 1981.

Ross 1888: Alexander Ross, 'Old Highland Roads', *Transactions of the Gaelic Society of Inverness* 14 (1887–1888), 172–193.

Ross 1965: Ian Ross, 'A Bluestocking over the Border: Mrs Elizabeth Montagu's Aesthetic Adventures, 1766', *Huntingdon Library Quarterly*, 28:3 (1965), 213–233.

Roy 1785: William Roy, 'An Account of the Measurement of a Base on Hounslow-Heath', *Philosophical Transactions of the Royal Society of London*, 75 (1785), 385–480.

Roy 1793: [William Roy], *The Military Antiquities of the Romans in Britain, by the Late William Roy, FRS, FSA*, London: Society of Antiquities of London, 1793.

Roy 2007 [1747–55]: William Roy, *The Great Map: The Military Survey of Scotland, 1747–55*, Edinburgh: Birlinn, 2007.

Sandby 1778: Paul Sandby, *The Virtuosi's Museum Containing Select Views of England, Scotland and Ireland*, London: G. Kearsly, 1778.

Sandby 1811: [Thomas Paul Sandby], 'Memoirs of the Late Paul Sandby, Esq. R.A.', *Monthly Magazine; or, British Register*, 31 (1811), 437–441.

Scarfe 2001: Norman Scarfe (ed.), *To the Highlands in 1786: The Inquisitive Journey of a Young French Aristocrat*, Woodbridge: Boydell Press, 2001.

Schopenhauer 1988: Johanna Schopenhauer, *A Lady Travels: Journeys in England and Scotland*, London: Routledge, 1988.

Scott 1805 : [Walter Scott], 'On Thornton's Sporting Tour', *Edinburgh Review*, 5:10 (1805), 398–405.

Scott 1809: [Walter Scott], 'Carr's *Caledonian Sketches*', *Quarterly Review*, 1:1 (1809), 182.

Scott 1816: [Walter Scott], 'Culloden Papers', *Quarterly Review*, 14:28 (1816), 283–333

Scott 1829–33: Sir Walter Scott, 'Magnum Opus', Introduction to *The Fortunes of Nigel*, *Waverley Novels*, 48 vols, Edinburgh.

Scott 1913: *Poetical Works of Sir Walter Scott*, ed. J. Logie Robertson, London: Frowde.

Scott 1999: Walter Scott, *The Antiquary*, ed. David Hewitt, introduction by David Punter, London: Penguin, 1999.

Seafield Papers 1766: Receipt, 28 October 1766, National Records of Scotland, Edinburgh, Seafield Papers, GD 248/530/1.

Selwyn 1824: Elizabeth Selwyn, *Journals of Excursions Through the Most Interesting Parts of England, Wales and Scotland, During the Summers and Autumns of 1819, 1820, 1821, 1822 & 1823*, London: Plummer and Brewis, 1824.

Sinclair 1807: Sir John Sinclair, *The Poems of Ossian, in the original Gaelic*, 3 vols., Edinburgh, 1807.

Sinclair 1813: Sir John Sinclair, *An Account of the Highland Society of London*, London: B. McMillan, 1813.

Skelton 1967: R.A. Skelton, *The Military Survey of Scotland, 1747–1755*, Edinburgh: Edinburgh University Press, 1967.

Smethurst 2012: Paul Smethurst, 'Peripheral Vision, Landscape, and Nation-Building in Thomas Pennant's Tours in Scotland, 1769–72', in Benjamin Colbert, ed., *Travel Writing and Tourism in Britain and Ireland*, Basingstoke: Palgrave Macmillan, 2012, 13–30.

Smiles 2000: Sam Smiles, *Eyewitness: Artists and Visual Documentation in Britain, 1770–1830*, Aldershot: Ashgate, 2000.

Smith 1776: Adam Smith, *An Inquiry into the Nature and Causes of the Wealth of Nations*, 2 vols, London: W. Strahan, 1776.

Smith 1815 [1750]: Charles Smith, *The Antient and Present State of the County and City of Cork*, 2 vols, Cork, 1815.

Smith 1979 [1756]: Charles Smith, *The Ancient and Present State of the County of Kerry*, Dublin & Cork: Mercier, 1979.

Smith 1810: J.E. Smith, *Fifteen Views Illustrative of a Tour to Havod in Cardiganshire, 1810*, London: White & Co., 1810: https://www.library.wales/discover/digital-gallery/pictures/tour-of-hafod/

Smith 1982: Annette M. Smith, *Jacobite Estates of the Forty-Five*, Edinburgh: John Donald, 1982.

Smout 1969: T.C. Smout, *A History of the Scottish People, 1560–1830*, London: Collins, 1969.

Smout 2000: T.C. Smout, *Nature Contested: Environmental History in Scotland and Northern England Since 1600*, Edinburgh: Edinburgh University Press, 2000.

Smout 2012: T.C. Smout, 'A New Look at the Scottish Improvers', *Scottish Historical Review*, 91(1), 25–149.

Smout, MacDonald and Watson 2005: T.C. Smout, Alan R. MacDonald and Fiona J. Watson, *A History of the Native Woodlands of Scotland, 1500–1920*, Edinburgh: Edinburgh University Press, 2005.

Solkin 1993: David H. Solkin, *Painting for Money: The Visual Arts and the Public Sphere in Eighteenth-Century England*, New Haven and London: Yale University Press, 1993.

Solkin 2008: David H. Solkin, *Painting Out of the Ordinary: Modernity and the Art of Everday Life in Early Nineteenth-Century England*, New Haven, CT, and London: Yale University Press, 2008.

Southey 1929: Robert Southey, *Journal of a Tour in Scotland in 1819*, London: John Murray, 1929.

Southey 1972 [1929]: Robert Southey, *Journal of a Tour in Scotland in 1819*, Memoirs of a Tour in Scotland in 1819, Edinburgh: Mercat Press, 1972.

Spalding Miscellany I 1842: *Miscellany of the Spalding Club I*, Aberdeen: Spalding Club, 1842.

Spence 1811: Elizabeth Isabella Spence, *Sketches of the Present Manners, Customs, and Scenery of Scotland*, 2 vols, 2nd edn, London: Longmans & Co., 1811.

Stafford and Terpak 2001: Barbara Maria Stafford and Frances Terpak, *Devices of Wonder: From the World in a Box to Images on a Screen*, Los Angeles, CA: Getty Publications, 2001.

Stewart 1822: David Stewart, *Sketches of the Character, Manners and Present State of the Highlanders of Scotland*, 2nd edn, 2 vols, Edinburgh: Archibald Constable & Co, 1822.

Stewart-Murray 1908: J.J.H.H. Stewart-Murray, Seventh Duke of Atholl (ed.), *Chronicles of the Atholl and Tullibardine Families*, Vol. 4, privately printed, Edinburgh: Ballantyne Press, 1908.

Stoddart 1801: Thomas Stoddart, *Remarks on Local Scenery and Manners in Scotland during the Years 1799–1800*, 2 vols, London, 1801.

Stone 1989: Jeffrey C. Stone, *The Pont Manuscript Maps of Scotland*, Tring: Map Collector Publications, 1989.

Stone 1991: Jeffrey Stone, *Illustrated Maps of Scotland from Blaeu's Atlas Novus of the 17th Century*, London: Studio Editions, 1991.

Stuart 1988: M. Stuart, Notes on Glasgow Fair by John Knox, Glasgow Museums Curatorial File, 1988.

Sweet 2004: Rosemary Sweet, *Antiquaries: The Discovery of the Past in Eighteenth-Century Britain*, London: Hambledon, 2004.

Switzer 1718: Stephen Switzer, *Ichnographia Rustica, or the Nobleman, Gentleman or Gardener's Recreation*, London, 1718.

Tait 1980: Alan Tait, *The Landscape Garden in Scotland, 1735–1835*, Edinburgh: Edinburgh University Press, 1980.

Taylor 1776: George Taylor and Andrew Skinner, *Taylor and Skinner's Survey and Maps of the Roads of North Britain or Scotland*, London, 1776.

Taylor 1778: George Taylor and Andrew Skinner, *Taylor and Skinner's Maps of the Roads of Ireland*, London, 1778.

Taylor 1976: William Taylor, *The Military Roads in Scotland*, Newton Abbot: David & Charles, 1976.

Thomson 1818: John Thomson (ed.), 2 vols, *The Traveller's Guide through Scotland and its Islands*, Edinburgh: J. Thomson & Co., 1818.

Tomkins 1772: William Tomkins, letters to Sir James Grant, 25 and 29 May 1772, National Records of Scotland, Edinburgh, Seafield Papers, D248/179/1, GD248/678/5.

Tomos 1972: Dafydd Tomos (ed.), *Michael Faraday in Wales, Including Faraday's Journal of his Tour through Wales in 1819*, Denbigh: Gwasg Gee, 1972.

Tone 1826: Theobald Wolfe Tone, *Life of Theobald Wolfe Tone,* Washington: Gales & Seaton, 1826.

Topham 1776: E. Topham, 'Letter XXX on the Ridotto to Miss Lucinda B – Edinburgh, April 6, 1775', *Letters from Edinburgh; written in the years 1774 and 1775, containing some observations on the Diversions, Manners, and Laws, of the Scotch Nation, during a six-month residence in Edinburgh.* https://archive.org/details/bub_gb_1HZbAAAAQAAJ/page/n269 [accessed 12 July 2019]

Trumpener 1997: Katie Trumpener, *Bardic Nationalism: The Romantic Novel and the British Empire*, Princeton, NJ: Princeton University Press, 1997.

Van der Merwe 1979: Pieter der Van Merwe, 'The Life and Theatrical Career of Clarkson Stansfield', PhD thesis, University of Bristol, 1979.

Walker 1992: Carol Kyros Walker, *Walking North with Keats*, New Haven, CT, and London: Yale University Press, 1992.

Walker 1997: Dorothy Wordsworth, *Recollections of a Tour Made in Scotland*, introduction, notes and photographs by Carol Kyros Walker, New Haven, CT, and London: Yale University Press, 1997.

Walker 2002: *'Breaking Away': Coleridge in Scotland*, ed. with introduction by Carol Kyros Walker, New Haven and London: Yale University Press, 2002.

Watson 1747: [David Watson], 'Some Observations concerning the Highlands of Scotland' [September 1747], British Library, London, Add MS 35890, ff. 158–159.

Watson 1904: W.J. Watson, *Place-Names of Ross and Cromarty*, Inverness: Northern Counties Printing Co., 1904.

Watson 1959: William J. Watson, *Bardachd Ghàidhlig: Specimens of Gaelic Poetry 1550–1900*, 3rd edn, An Comunn Gàidhealach, 1959.

Watson 2010: Nicola J. Watson, 'Readers of Romantic Locality: Tourists, Loch Katrine and *The Lady of the Lake*', in Christoph Bode and Jacqueline Labbe (eds), *Romantic Localities: Europe Writes Place*, London: Pickering and Chatto, 2010, 67–79.

Watson 2012: Nicola J. Watson, 'Holiday Romance; or, Loch Katrine and the Literary Tourist', in Ian Brown (ed.), *Literary Tourism, the Trossachs, and Sir Walter Scott*, Glasgow: ASLS, 29–44.

Watt and Waine 2019: Patrick Watt and Rose Waine, *Wild and Majestic: Romantic Visions of Scotland,* exhibition and catalogue, National Museum of Scotland, Edinburgh, 2019.

Whyte 1999: Ian D. Whyte, 'Urbanization', in T.M. Devine and J.R. Young (eds), *Eighteenth-Century Scotland: New Perspectives*, East Linton: Tuckwell Press, 1999, 176–194.

Williams 1983: Robert Williams, 'Sir John Dalrymple's "An Essay on Landscape Gardening"', *Journal of Garden History*, 3:2 (1983), 144–156.

Withers 1982: Charles Withers, 'The Historical Creation of the Scottish Highlands', in Ian Donnachie and Christopher Whatley (eds), *The Manufacture of Scottish History*, Edinburgh: Polygon, 1982, 143–156.

Withers 1995: Charles W.J. Withers, 'Geography, Natural History and the Eighteenth-Century Enlightenment: Putting the World in Place', *History Workshop Journal*, 39 (1995), 136–163.

Withers 1994: Charles W.J. Withers, 'On Georgics and Geology: James Hutton's "Elements of Agriculture" and Agricultural Science in Eighteenth-Century Scotland', *Agricultural History Review* 42 (1994), 38–48.

Womack 1989: Peter Womack, *Improvement and Romance: Constructing the Myth of the Highlands,* Basingstoke: Macmillan, 1989.

Wood 2001: Gillen D'Arcy Wood, *The Schock of the Real: Romanticism and Visual Culture, 1760–1860*, Houndsmills: Palgrave, 2001.

Wordsworth 1952: Dorothy Wordsworth, 'My Second Tour in Scotland' (1822), in E. De Selincourt, *Journals of Dorothy Wordsworth*, 2 vols, London: Macmillan, Vol. II, 1952, 337–398.

Wordsworth 1977: *William Wordsworth: The Poems*, ed. John O. Hayden, 2 vols, Harmondsworth: Penguin, 1977.

Wright 1822: Rev. George N. Wright, *Tours in Ireland or, Guides to the lakes of Killarney; the County of Wicklow; and the Giants Causeway, illustrated by Maps; and Engravings, after Drawings by George Petrie*, London: Baldwin, Cradock and Joy, 1822.

Young 1780: Arthur Young, *A Tour in Ireland with General Observations on the Present State of that Kingdom made in the Years 1776, 1777, and 1778 and Brought Down to the End of 1779,* London: T. Cadell and J. Dodsley, 1780.

Young 2020: C. Young, 'The Panoramic World of John Knox', 2020: https://powertotransform.gla.ac.uk/

Youngson 1973: A.J. Youngson, *After the Forty-Five: The Economic Impact on the Scottish Highlands*, Edinburgh: Edinburgh University Press, 1973.

PHOTOGRAPH CREDITS

For permission to reproduce works from their collections, we would like to thank the following institutions and individuals:

Alamy (Al)
Photography: British Library
Figs. C3.10, C5.16

Argyle Estate (ArE)
Reproduced with permission of His Grace the Duke of Argyll
Fig. C5.3

Ashmolean, University of Oxford (AM)
Photo © Ashmolean Museum, University of Oxford
Fig. C5.1

Atholl Estate (AE)
Reproduced with permission of His Grace the Duke of Atholl
Photos © Atholl Estate
Figs S3.9, S3.10, S3.11, C4.10, S4.22, C5.6, C5.9, C5.12

Beinecke Rare Book and Manuscript Library, Yale University (BRBML)
Fig. C6.10

Bowhill House, Scottish Borders (BC)
Photos © The Buccleuch Collections / Bridgeman Images
Figs S3.12, S3.13, S3.14, C5.8

The British Library (BL)
Photo © The British Library Board
Figs C1.2, S1.4, S1.7, S1.9, S1.13, C2.1, S2.1, S2.5, S2.8, S2.9, S2.20, S3.2, S3.3, S3.4, C5.2, C8.12

The British Museum (BM)
Photos © The Trustees of the British Museum
Figs S1.16a–c, S2.29, S3.26, C5.10

The Fife Collection (FC)
Reproduced with permission of His Grace the Duke of Fife
Photos © The Fife Collection
Figs S3.8, C5.4, C5.5

Fitzwilliam Museum, Cambridge (FM)
Photo © Fitzwilliam Museum, Cambridge
Fig. S4.5

Glasgow Museums (GMC)
Photos © CSG CIC Glasgow Museums Collection
Figs C1.7, S2.27, S3.23, S3.24, S4.1, S4.11, C7.4, C7.8, C7.9

Historic Environment Scotland (HES)
Photos © Courtesy of HES
Figs C5.11, C5.15

The Hunterian, University of Glasgow (GLAHA/GLAHM)
Photos © The Hunterian, University of Glasgow 2020
Figs S1.10, S1.21, S1.22, S2.3, S2.4, S2.6, S2.13, S2.17, S2.19, S2.22, S2.28, C3.13, C3.14a–c, C3.15a, b, C3.20a, b, C3.21, S3.1, S3.19, S3.20, S3.21, S3.22, S4.4, S4.8, S4.12, S4.19, S4.20, S4.21

Inverness Museum & Art Gallery (IMAG)
MEM Donaldson Collection, Inverness Museum & Art Gallery, High Life Highland
Fig. C2.5

The Lewis Walpole Library, Yale University (LWL)
Courtesy of the Lewis Walpole Library, Yale University
Fig. S2.26

Mount Stuart Trust (MST)
Figs S3.5, S3.6, S3.7

National Galleries of Scotland (NGS)
Figs 0.1, S1.1, S1.11, S1.12, S1.14a–b, S1.15a, b, S1.17, S1.21, C2.9, C2.11, S2.7, S2.18, S3.15, S3.16, S3.18, C4.4, S4.2, S4.6, S4.9, S4.15, S4.16, S4.18, C7.1, C7.2, C7.6, C7.7

National Library of Ireland (NLI)
Courtesy of the National Library of Ireland
Figs C8.8, C8.10, C8.11, C8.14

National Library of Scotland (NLS)
Creative Commons Attribution 4.0 (CC BY)
Figs S1.2, C2.2, C4.2, C4.9, C6.1, C6.11, C6.13

National Library of Wales – Llyfrgell Genedlaethol Cymru (NLW)
Creative Commons Attribution 4.0 (CC BY)
Figs S1.19, C2.4, C8.1, C8.2, C8.3, C8.6

National Museums Scotland (NMS)
Images © National Museums Scotland
Figs C2.10, C6.8

National Records of Scotland (NRS)
Photos © National Records of Scotland
Figs C4.5, C4.7, C4.11

Nigel Leask (NL)
Figs S2.12, C3.5

Nottingham City Museums & Galleries (NCM)
By permission of Nottingham City Museums & Galleries
NCM 1987-1032
Fig. S1.20

Penicuik House (PH)
Figs S1.14, S1.18, C3.17, C3.18, C3.19

Private Collections (PC)
Figs C1.5, C2.6, S2.2, S3.25 (Image courtesy of Lyon & Turnbull), S4.13, C7.5, C8.13 (Photo © Christie's Images/Bridgeman Images), C8.15

Royal Academy of Arts (RAA)
Photo © Royal Academy of Arts, London.
Fig. C8.5

Royal Botanic Garden Edinburgh (RBGE)
Figs C3.1, C3.2, C3.3, C3.8, C3.9, C3.11

Royal Collection Trust (RCT)
Photos © Her Majesty Queen Elizabeth II 2020
Figs S1.5, S1.6, C8.16

Science Museum (SM)
Photos © Science Museum/Science & Society Picture Library
Fig. C6.6

Senate House Library, University of London (SHL)
Fig. C7.3

Tate (TG)
Photos © Tate
Figs C5.13, C5.14, C8.7

University of Glasgow Library, Archives and Special Collections (GLA ASC)
Photos © University of Glasgow Library GLA ASC
Figs 0.3, 0.4, C1.1, C1.4, C1.6 (GLA LRA), C1.9, C2.3, C2.7, C2.8, S2.10, S2.11, S2.15, S2.16, S2.21, S2.23, S2.24, S2.25, C3.4, C3.6, C3.7, C3.16 (GLA LRA), S3.17, C4.1, C4.3, C4.6, C4.8, S4.3 (GLA LRA), S4.7, S4.10, S4.17, C7.10, C8.9

Walker Art Gallery, Liverpool (WAG)
Courtesy of National Museums Liverpool, Walker Art Gallery
Fig. C5.7

William Zachs Collection (WZC)
Photos © William Zachs
Figs C3.12, S4.14, C6.2, C6.3, C6.4, C6.5, C6.9

Yale Center for British Art, Paul Mellon Collection (YCBA)
Figs C1.3, C1.8, C6.7, C8.4

The following photographs were commissioned from Antonia Reeve:
Figs C3.12, S2.2, S3.8, S3.9, S3.10, S3.11, S4.13, S4.14, S4.22, C4.10, C5.4, C5.5, C5.6, C5.9, C5.12, C6.2, C6.3, C6.4, C6.5, C6.9

INDEX